WEAKENING PHILOSOPHY

Weakening Philosophy

Essays in Honour of
Gianni Vattimo

Edited by
SANTIAGO ZABALA

McGill-Queen's University Press
Montreal & Kingston · London · Ithaca

© McGill-Queen's University Press 2007
ISBN: 978-0-7735-3142-0 (cloth)
ISBN: 978-0-7735-3143-7 (paper)

Legal deposit first quarter 2007
Bibliothèque nationale du Québec

Printed in Canada on acid-free paper.

McGill-Queen's University Press acknowledges the support of the Canada
Council for the Arts for our publishing program. We also acknowledge the
financial support of the Government of Canada through the Book Publishing Industry Development Program (BPIDP) for our publishing activities.

Library and Archives Canada Cataloguing in Publication

Weakening philosophy : essays in honour of Gianni Vattimo / edited by
Santiago Zabala.

Includes bibliographical references and index.

ISBN 978-0-7735-3142-0 (bnd)
ISBN 978-0-7735-3143-7 (pbk)

1. Vattimo, Gianni, 1936–. I. Zabala, Santiago, 1975–.

B3654.V384W43 2007   195   C2006–905065-1

Typeset in 10½/13 Sabon by True to Type

Frontispiece: photograph by Marco Montanari, www.marcomontanari.com

Contents

Acknowledgments

My primary debt of gratitude in the making of this volume goes to Philip Cercone, Michael Haskell, Ron Curtis, and Olga Stein. For offering valuable suggestions along the way, many thanks to Barry Allen, William McCuaig, Aden Bar-Tura, Ugo Ugazio, Jeff W. Robbins, Giovanni Giorgio, Lucio Saviani, and Philip Larrey. Once again, the encouragement of Marta Moretti, Ana Messuti, and Pablo Cardoso was essential. Finally, thanks to the contributors and translators for their willingness to participate and for their fine essays and translations. This book is dedicated to Gianni Vattimo on the occasion of his seventieth birthday. His publications, teaching, and political activism have inspired several generations of nondogmatic philosophers, among whom I am proud to include myself.

Reiner Schürmann's essay previously appeared in the *Graduate Faculty Philosophy Journal* 10, no. 1 (spring 1984). Santiago Zabala's essay previously appeared in a slightly different form under the title "Deconstruction, Semantics, and Interpretation," in *Aquinas* 48, no. 3 (2005), published by Lateran University Press. Teresa Oñate's essay was partially based on another essay published under the title "Gianni Vattimo's Contribution to Twentieth-Century Hermeneutics," in *Azafea* 5 (2003). I am grateful to the editors of the *Graduate Faculty Philosophy Journal*, *Aquinas*, and *Azafea* for permission to reprint these essays.

WEAKENING PHILOSOPHY

1

Introduction:
Gianni Vattimo and Weak Philosophy

SANTIAGO ZABALA

His temperament, his elegance, his sense of humour and his wit – behind which a restrained seriousness lies concealed – have diffused his philosophical thought throughout America, France, Eastern Europe and, in general, throughout the whole realm of the world's philosophical culture, along with the key concept of hermeneutics. Vattimo has specifically called hermeneutics a koiné: the common language in which philosophical thought after Heidegger and Wittgenstein, after Quine, Derrida and Ricoeur, has spread everywhere; virtually a universal philosophical language.

Hans-Georg Gadamer

THE END OF THE WAR, CATHOLICISM, AND UMBERTO ECO

Gianni Vattimo is a world-renowned Italian philosopher. He has received the Max Planck Award for Humanities Sciences in 1992, the Order of Merit of the Italian Republic in 1996, the Hannah Arendt Prize for Political Thinking in 2002, and the President's Medal from Georgetown University in 2006, and he has honorary doctorates from many universities. His best-known books are *The End of Modernity*; *The Adventure of Difference*; *The Transparent Society*; *Beyond Interpretation*; *Belief*; *Vocazione e responsabilità del filosofo* (*The vocation and responsibility of the philosopher*); *After Christianity*; *Nihilism and Emancipation*; *Dialogue with Nietzsche*; *Religion*, coedited with Jacques Derrida; and *The Future of Religion*, recently co-authored with Richard Rorty. Vattimo's philosophy, called *weak thought*, has helped not only to modify the role of philosophy within the boundaries of the academic community, but also to reaffirm the political and religious responsibility of the philosopher in the social life that surrounds him or her. As one of the first philosophers to become a member of the European Parliament and shape its constitution, he was able to practise his theories as a politician and to experience the operations of the European Union from within. The views that have made him famous as an internationally acclaimed intellectual arise out of his strictly philosophical reflections: his weakening of the metaphysical nature of intellectual power, scientific methods and religious beliefs, and our dogmatic interpretation of them.

This volume contains critical essays by twenty-one distinguished philosophers and theologians – including some of the most interesting philosophers and theologians writing today – from different nations and cultural backgrounds, in honour of Vattimo's seventieth birthday. It also contains a response by Vattimo. Each contributor was invited either to confront his ideas or to comment on Vattimo's philosophy in one of the three parts that constitute the book. The first part, entitled "Weakening Metaphysical Power," contains essays by Umberto Eco, Charles Taylor, Giacomo Marramao, Wolfgang Welsch, Hugh J. Silverman, Reiner Schürmann, and Pier Aldo Rovatti. The second part, entitled "Weakening Metaphysical Methods," contains essays by Richard Rorty, Manfred Frank, James Risser, Jean Grondin, Rüdiger Bubner, Santiago Zabala, and Paolo Flores d'Arcais. And, finally, the third part, entitled "Weakening Metaphysical Beliefs," contains essays by Nancy K. Frankenberry, Fernando Savater, Jack Miles, Jeffrey Perl, Carmelo Dotolo, Teresa Oñate, and Jean-Luc Nancy. I will not summarize all these essays here, because it would be impossible to capture the rich detail, rigour, and depth of the analyses you will find in them. Instead, since little has been written about Vattimo's intellectual and biographical life, I intend this introduction to serve as a road map for all those who want to know who Gianni Vattimo is and what his weak philosophy consists of.

Vattimo was born on 4 January 1936 in Turin, where he experienced directly not only the fascist regime and the destruction of his home by bombardments during the Second World War but also his father's death from pneumonia when he was only a year old. In 1942, his family moved back to his father's home town, Cetraro, in the region of Calabria, where he spent his youth with peasant relatives to avoid the war. In September 1945, he, his mother, and his sister moved back to Turin, where he continued school and was often teased by his schoolmates because of his Southern Italian accent. Although the Vattimos mostly lived on the pension from his father's service as a policeman, his mother worked at home as a tailor, and Vattimo recalls helping her on various occasions. Young Vattimo was supposed to be the educated member of the family, so his sister was obliged by their mother to speak to him in proper Italian and not in the dialect of Piemonte. During his secondary-school years, Vattimo read many of Jack London's novels and also wrote his own, but the main experience of his youth was certainly his Catholic education and practice. Although his mother and sister were not particularly religious and although Vattimo never thought about becoming a priest, from the age of twelve he went to mass every morning to receive communion. He became a leader of the Catholic Action Group, and by the end of high school, he had even became the diocesan representative of the Student Movement's Catholic Action Group.

It was during these years that his long friendship with Umberto Eco began. Eco at the time was in his early twenties and a national Catholic leader. Vattimo recalls that although Eco was widely admired (since he was studying with Luigi Pareyson (1918–91), who is now considered the greatest Italian philosopher since Giovanni Gentile and Benedetto Croce, and who later also became Vattimo's main tutor), many had doubts about the strength of his religious beliefs, since he rarely attended mass. When Vattimo started university, Eco had just finished his thesis, entitled *"The Aesthetics of Thomas Aquinas"* (which Vattimo reviewed in 1956, in his first publication), under the supervision of Pareyson (Eco subsequently became Pareyson's assistant). Eco not only introduced Pareyson to Vattimo but also became "a kind of old comrade or vice-maestro in the school of Pareyson," as Vattimo often remembers.

Vattimo began his study of philosophy in order to further his activities as a delegate of the Student Movement's Catholic Action Group in the 1950s. He became involved in the group mostly for sociopolitical reasons: in other words, in order to combine religion and politics, he chose philosophy. Although his priest, Pietro Caramello, introduced him to the study of Thomas Aquinas when he was only a teenager, Vattimo always felt that there was something too rigid and dogmatic in the Church's educational system. He now remembers that he began to distrust the Church mostly because of its rigid anticommunist ideology, which stood more and more in opposition to his progressive, left-wing attitudes. In 1948, as the Soviet Union was invading Czechoslovakia

and building the Iron Curtain, Vattimo participated in Italy's general
elections, helping his older friends distribute the Christian Democrats'
electoral manifesto throughout Turin. That year, the fear of communism, the possibility of a Red Revolution (Yugoslavia was just around
the corner), and the attempted assassination of Palmiro Togliatti were
real threats for most Italians. Although the Christian Democratic Party
had the majority in the government, the political battle was not only
between the Catholics and atheists but also (for young Catholics such
as Vattimo) between "anticommunists" and "catto-communists," and
therefore between the Vatican's fear of communist dictators and a
Christian socialist ideology that was mainly interested in social justice
(supported in part by some religious communists). During the 1950s
Vattimo and his young friends felt much closer to this second position:
although they did not want Italy to become a communist state, they did
want Italian politics to make a democratic shift toward the left, toward
social justice, and the labour unions. The unions, during this anticommunist era, had to cope with Fiat's interest (with the support of the
Vatican) in keeping communist workers away from their military fac-
tories, which at the time were building arms for NATO.

A UNIVERSITY DEGREE, TELEVISION, AND THE TEACHINGS OF LUIGI PAREYSON

Although Vattimo was still a member of the Catholic youth groups
when he started university in 1954, he, along with some other
members, was asked to leave the group because of his progressive political positions, which had become too radical for the Church. It was
then that Vattimo and some friends founded an intercultural centre
called the Mounier Group, after Emmanuel Mounier. Many progressive
Italian intellectuals from all over Italy, such as Lelio Basso, joined the
group's debates. During this period Vattimo, Eco, and Furio Colombo
were hired by a secular, liberal director (Filiberto Guala) of the public
Italian TV network (RAI) and were asked to take a three-month TV
course in Milan. Since Vattimo was starting university at the time, he
asked to be transferred to Turin after the course.

The RAI asked Vattimo to come up with new television programs and
documentaries, and in the spring of 1955, with Colombo, he started a
successful youth program called *Horizon*, which also strove to communicate some information that the news services had censored. He also
participated in and hosted another successful program, *The Machine in*

Order to Live, which concerned human physiology. In the spring of 1957, the central directors of the RAI decided to replace Mr Guala with a director more ideologically friendly to the Christian Democratic Party. Since he was unable to work with the new Christian Democrat director, who censored the news, and since he also had to deal with Caramello and Pareyson, who wanted him to concentrate on teaching, Vattimo ended his television career. It was then that he started to teach a course called Religion and Common Knowledge in a professional school, in order to pay for his university studies. In 1959 he was fired from this position after taking some of his students to a demonstration against South African apartheid. This and other events (such as being arrested for demonstrating for the freedom to strike in private industrial zones) characterized Vattimo's "communist Catholicism" during his university years. He continued to teach until 1962 at the Rosmini high school of Turin.

Vattimo's friendly relationship with Pareyson characterized all his university years. Thanks to Pareyson he became part of another Catholic group, formed around Professor Giovanni Getto and the future bishop of Turin, Michele Pellegrino, who used to teach Christian literature in the university. Although Vattimo had not yet graduated in 1959, Pareyson, who was supervising Vattimo's thesis on the concept of "doing" in Aristotle, had already given him the keys to the distinguished Aesthetic Institute of the university, which he had founded. Vattimo was to assist him by writing on modern and contemporary philosophy for the *Philosophical Encyclopedia* of the Center for Christian Philosophical studies at Gallarate. Pareyson was one of the first and most important interpreters of existentialism, German idealism, hermeneutics, and aesthetic philosophy in Italy, to the point that after the publication of his *Aesthetics: Theory of Formativity* in 1954, Hans Georg Gadamer (1900–2002), specified in *Truth and Method* that the "aesthetic object is not constituted in the aesthetic experience of grasping it, but the work of art itself is experienced in its aesthetic quality through the process of its concretization and creation. In this I agree fully with Luigi Pareyson's aesthetics of '*formatività*.'"

Once Vattimo had received his degree at the end of 1959 (it should be stressed that his degree, the Laurea, was the highest degree one could receive in Italian universities at the time and that Pareyson had Vattimo's thesis published in 1961), he became Pareyson's assistant, not only helping him edit his publications but also substituting for him sometimes in his courses on aesthetics. Pareyson influenced Vattimo politically also. Even before sending him to Heidelberg to study with Gadamer and Karl Löwith (1897–1973), he told Vattimo about his years as a partisan during the war and about his anticapitalist attitude (which was mostly determined by his Pascalian anti-illuminist conception of the world). During the next two years, Vattimo, thanks to a scholarship from the Fondazione Pietro Martinetti of the University of Turin and from the Alexander von Humboldt-Stiftung of Bad Godesberg (for which he was recommended by Gadamer himself), was able to start translating *Truth and Method* and to finish his PHD thesis on Heidegger's thought. The thesis, which became his second book, *Essere, storia e linguaggio in Heidegger* (Being, history, and language in Heidegger), was published in 1963. These degrees and publications qualified Vattimo to teach aesthetics as an adjunct professor in the University of Turin, where he has been since 1964.

THE HEIDELBERG YEARS,
WITH LÖWITH AND GADAMER

In Heidelberg Vattimo experienced a political shift from his former "Catto-communist" position to what he then called a "Catto-Heideggerian" mentality. In other words, Vattimo did not stop believing in God, but he did start to interpret and transform the God of the Bible into the "Heideggerian Being." This Heideggerian Being is much more relaxed, not only because it excludes the discipline of the Church (which, we must stress, Vattimo always despised, particularly when it dictated a "natural" sexual behaviour for all believers) but also because it acknowledges that it is not only through ethics that one may be blessed.

Although today Vattimo does not think he really inherited much from Löwith, he does remember that during his period in Heidelberg they became good friends, not only because Löwith spoke Italian well but also because he was very friendly with foreign students. Vattimo does not think he really understood much of Löwith's *From Hegel to Nietzsche*, but he does find his *Meaning in History*, wherein Löwith developed his theory of secularization, to be essential. The idea that the history of Western thought is nothing more than the history of the secularization of the Bible is certainly Löwith's greatest achievement, but Vattimo does not accept the way he concluded this argument. Löwith's conclusion that Nietzsche should become pagan again but cannot because there is always a moment of "decision" outside one's history (the eternal recurrence instituted with an act that is not part of the eternal recurrence) is a still too ambiguous a conclusion for Vattimo.

Vattimo and Gadamer also had a very friendly relationship, but since Vattimo was translating his major book, on occasion they had to discuss various terminological and grammatical issues, which became real philosophical discussions. Vattimo recalls that the translation into Italian of Gadamer's best-known dictum – "Sein, das verstanden werden kann, ist Sprache" (Being that can be understood is language)" – was tricky because if the commas are omitted, as they are in the English and French translations, then the dictum could be interpreted as identifying too easily the sphere of beings offering themselves to comprehension within language. Instead, Vattimo opted for the second alternative, with the commas, as in German, because it emphasized that Being is language and its characteristic is the possibility of being comprehended. Gadamer never wanted to express his preference for Vattimo's choice of the second alternative, because he always wanted translators to translate with freedom and self-determination. In 1995, Gadamer remembered Vattimo as "certainly a little younger than my earliest Italian students: but it was he who accomplished the particular task of making my universe of thought known in Italy, by translating my main work, *Truth and Method* ... A certain taste for games – and a certain taste for risk, which is peculiar to every player – has constantly shielded him from any infelicitous dogmatism: these same characteristics have made him an excellent translator."

Vattimo remembers that after this translation, his relationship with Gadamer really started to grow, but he always thought that Gadamer continued to be too platonic and metaphysical, protecting the human sciences against modern scientism at all cost, mainly because he was not "Heideggerian" enough. Gadamer, according to Vattimo, never really approved of Heidegger's critique and destruction of the history of ontology, because he never actually understood, by his famous dictum, that all "Being is language," as he should have. What Vattimo always approved of in Gadamer instead was his version of Hegelian idealism, which had many affinities with Benedetto Croce's philosophical interpretation of the history of the Spirit. When Vattimo now affirms that "emancipation" is "weakening" and that weakening is nothing else than transferring everything to the realm of symbolism and simulacrum, he intends that "emancipation" as a Hegelian spiritualization without the absolute Spirit. Since Pareyson was much closer to a theologian and Gadamer to a historicist, Vattimo was able to inherit,

through Löwith and Croce, a "never-ending philosophy" that transferred everything into the objective and historical spiritual world we all
belong to.

During the 1960s Vattimo published many books, and he finished his
translation of *Truth and Method* in 1969. Pareyson at the time called
him on the phone every afternoon to discuss his readings and writings.
In 1964 Vattimo was invited to participate at Royamount in one of the
conferences of the so-called Nietzsche renaissance organized by Gilles
Deleuze and Pierre Klossowski. He published his first university course,
entitled *Arte e verità nel pensiero di M. Heidegger* (Art and truth in
Martin Heidegger's thought), in 1966 and two years later became full
professor of aesthetics at the University of Turin. At the same time,
Vattimo, while convalescing from ulcer surgery, read the work of
Herbert Marcuse so carefully that he became a "Maoist." To Pareyson
this was a catastrophe, but Vattimo explained to him not only that his
own observations against Soviet communism were the same as Marcuse's in *Soviet Marxism* but also that the argument of Lukács against
bourgeois science was very close to what Heidegger said against positivism. It was then that Vattimo also taught his first course on Ernst
Bloch and realized that the "wholly other God" of Karl Barth was the
"future God" of Bloch. However, Vattimo was supposed to be the brilliant new young Catholic professor of aesthetics in the eyes of the
Catholic Church, which was beginning to fit more closely with his philosophy, as we will see.

Although Vattimo knew many students who participated in the
revolts of 1968, he always felt, together with Pareyson, much more
radical than the students because he was "Heideggerian." The revolutionary students in Italy wanted to reinvigorate the "department" with
a more democratic structure, but "department" was a term they had
inherited from the United States. Vattimo and Pareyson were particularly anticapitalist at the time, since they believed that Heidegger's arguments against modernity were the same as those of Lukács but that
Lukács was not radical enough, since he did not think in terms of Being
but only in terms of "power" (as did the students).

Until the end of the 1970s, Vattimo published a book almost every
year: *Poesia e ontologia* (Poetry and ontology, 1967), *Schleiermacher:*

Filosofo dell'interpretazione (Schleiermacher: Philosopher of interpretation, 1968), *Introduzione all'estetica di Hegel* (Introduction to Hegel's aesthetics, 1970), *Introduzione a Heidegger* (Introduction to Heidegger, 1971), *Arte e utopia* (Art and utopia, 1972), *Il soggetto e la maschera: Nietzsche e il problema della liberazione* (The subject and its mask: Nietzsche and the problem of liberation, 1974), and *Estetica moderna* (Modern aesthetics, 1977), edited by Vattimo. *Il soggetto e la maschera*, which was written as a politico-philosophical manifesto for the new democratic left, is certainly Vattimo's favourite book. From 1974 to 1978, Vattimo's professional and political career began to be of national interest, as he not only succeeded Pareyson as the chair of aesthetics but also become the dean of the faculty, holding that position until 1983. In 1978, while still dean of the faculty, he and other distinguished philosophers, such as Norberto Bobbio, were threatened by an anarchist group called the Red Brigades, which accused the philosophers of not being radical enough. Although from 1972 onward everybody in Turin knew that Vattimo lived with his companion, Gianpiero Cavaglià, his real public "outing" occurred in 1976, when the Italian Radical Party designated Vattimo as the candidate on their Homosexual List (FUORI), spreading the news in the national newspapers, without his consent, for the elections of that year. Although he was not elected, during these years he did help the Radical Party win the referendum regarding divorce.

"PENSIERO DEBOLE," TERRORISM, AND POSTMODERNITY

In 1983, Vattimo and Pier Aldo Rovatti edited *Il Pensiero debole* (Weak thought) for Feltrinelli publishers, with the participation of Umberto Eco, Diego Marconi, Gianni Carchia, Leonardo Amoroso, Giampiero Comolli, Filippo Costa, Franco Crespi, Alessandro Dal Lago, and Maurizio Ferraris. In Italy and abroad this book created a vast cultural and political debate, which marked most of Vattimo's research and publications of the 1980s. During these years he also published *The Adventure of Difference: Philosophy after Nietzsche and Heidegger* (1980), *Al di là del soggetto* (Beyond the Subject, 1981), *Nietzsche: An Introduction* (1984), *The End of Modernity: Nihilism and Hermeneutics in Postmodern Culture* (1985), and *The Transparent Society* (1989), and in 1986 he hosted a TV program for the RAI called *La clessidra*, where in eight episodes he discussed philosophical problems with the most famous Italian philosophers of the time: Emanuele Severino, Carlo Sini, Pier Aldo Rovatti, Italo Mancini, Francesco Barone, Remo Bodei, Vittorio Mathieu, and Mario Perniola. The dialogues from this program were published by Garzanti in 1990. In 1988, *La Stampa*, the Turin newspaper, published *Le mezze verità* (Half truths), a book including all the essays Vattimo had written for them since 1977. For over a decade Vattimo participated in many UNESCO Philosophical Forums organized by Jérôme Bindé in Paris (together with Jean Baudrillard, Paul Ricoeur, Jacques Derrida, and others) and also organized and participated in the Phenomenological Seminars of Perugia (with Thomas Sheehan, Emanuele Severino, Reiner Schürmann, Gadamer, Valerio Verra, Franco Crespi, and others), where hermeneutics and weak thought were intensely discussed.

Vattimo has explained on several occasions that the expression "weak thought" was drawn from an essay by Carlo Augusto Viano ("Reason, Abundance, and Belief," in *Crisi delle regione* [The Crisis of Reason], a famous book edited by Aldo Giorgio Gargani in 1979) and that he used the concept for the first time in the essay "Toward an Ontology of Decline," written in 1979 (and included in *Al di là del soggetto*), where he specifically announces that no one has ever interpreted Heidegger's ontology as "an ontology of the decline," as a weak ontology, because interpreters continue to think of Heidegger's meditation on Being in foundational, or metaphysical, terms.

Weak thought has a political and ideological justification: when Vattimo published *Il soggetto e la maschera* (1974), in his mind the book was supposed to be the political-philosophical manifesto for the new democratic left, for the people who not only wanted to change the relationships of power but also the structure of the subject. But the left did not pay much attention to it. Many of the activist students were, instead, radical young revolutionary Leninists. It was during the late 1970s that terrorism started to develop in Italy, and some of Vattimo's students were arrested and accused of having connections with terrorists. The conceptual problem started for Vattimo when some of these arrested students wrote letters from prison (read to Vattimo by other students) that were, to Vattimo, full of a "metaphysical and violent rhetorical subjectivity" that he could not accept either morally or philosophically. Vattimo realized at the time that his "Nietzschean superman revolutionary subject" (described in *The Subject and Its Mask*) had been misinterpreted and could not be identified with the students' "Leninist revolutionary subject." Mostly, reading these "metaphysical" letters made Vattimo realize that the ethical interpretation of nihilism and of Heidegger's ontological difference created and justified weak thought. Weak thought came to life not out of fear of terrorism but as a response to the terrorist interpretation of the Italian democratic left during the 1970s, as a recognition of the unacceptability of the Red Brigades' violence.

Pareyson's, Löwith's, and Gadamer's teaching and his own reading of Croce, Marcuse, Benjamin, Barth, Bloch, Nietzsche, Heidegger, and Lukács allowed Vattimo to understand that philosophy in the nineteenth and twentieth centuries involved the negation of stable structures of Being, to which thought must adapt itself in order to "found" itself upon solid certainties. Every age has its own metaphysics, its own descriptive theory of objects, and although nineteenth-century metaphysical historicism had started partly to dissolve the "stability of Being," Vattimo has always been persuaded that it was Nietzsche and Heidegger who did more than any other philosophers to radically transform the idea of "modern thinking," which had been dominated by the belief in a progressive enlightenment toward foundational truth. He has emphasized mainly this thesis in his three most successful books of the 1980s: *The Adventure of Difference*, *The End of Modernity*, and *The Transparent Society* (which Jean-François Lyotard cited as "of major importance to the debate of the postmodern condition").

In these three books Vattimo explained that philosophy, after Nietzsche and Heidegger's deconstruction of Western values, must be an "adventure of difference," thought liberated from Platonic ideological condemnation, so that it will not err by reducing everything to a single ideological principle. Vattimo believes that the end of modernity, in other words, "postmodernity," acquires philosophical credibility only when it is seen in relation to the Nietzschean problematic of the "eternal return" and the Heideggerian problematic of the "overcoming of metaphysics." Although Nietzsche and Heidegger criticized and deconstructed the heritage of European thought, they did not propose a means for a critical solution, dissolution, or overcoming of it. And this is what makes them so important to Vattimo. In fact, Nietzsche and Heidegger are the only philosophers who have not outlined a "new" philosophy, a new intellectual program, as Schopenhauer and Sartre did. According to Vattimo's investigations, Nietzsche and Heidegger have indirectly suggested that in order to be able to speak of Being, we must remember, as many philosophers have forgotten, that "ontology" is nothing more than the interpretation of our condition; therefore

Being is its "event," and hermeneutics is needed in order to learn to interpret the event of Being.

If the ancients' ways of thinking were governed by a cyclical vision of the course of events, moderns by secularizing the Judeo-Christian heritage, and postmoderns by "the end of history," or the "end of unitary and privileged history," then what is the specific philosophy that corresponds to this epoch of Being? According to Vattimo, if this dissolution marks the end of historiography as an image of a unitary process of narration of events, the answer must rest in the recognition that at the end of modernity the "adventure of the differences" begins for philosophy. In other words, in order to cope with these "journeys of differences," philosophy must not only recognize Being as an event, the interpretative nature of the concept of truth, but also recognize its own intellectual status as "weak thought." According to Vattimo, during the waning of modernity our experience of unlimited interpretability has led to the weakening of the cogent force of reality; what used to be considered facts are now taken as interpretations. After Marx's critique of ideology, after the Nietzschean critique of the notion of *Das Ding an Sich* (the Thing in Itself), after Freud's explanation of the unconscious, and after Heidegger's radical deconstruction of onto-theology, we can no longer believe that we can understand Being once and for all as a kind of incontrovertible evidence. Thanks to Marx, Nietzsche, Freud, and Heidegger, we are led to doubt exactly about all that appears as the most obvious. If religious institutions like the Vatican, political empires such as United States, and televisions networks such as NBC and CNN define "objective" truths through artificial preaching, capitalist propaganda, and selected news, philosophy has to show that truth is a "game of interpretations," always marked by the interests that inspire them.

It is important to emphasize that Vattimo does not regard postmodernity as a radical "rupture" with modernity, because for him postmodernism is a new attitude to the modern; in particular, it is an attitude that understands the objectivist conditions of the philosophies of the Enlightenment. In order to explain philosophically this new attitude to the modern, Vattimo uses Heidegger's most characteristic philosophical terminology: the German concepts *Verwindung* and *Überwindung*. The latter suggests a sort of attitude that consists in overcoming modernity by a Hegelian *Aufhebung*, an overcoming that goes beyond and leaves behind, falling unconsciously again to modern foundations. Instead, using the German term *Verwindung*, we should think of "turning to new purposes" "surpassing," "twisting," "resigning," and "accepting ironically" modernity. It is in this second sense that Vattimo offers us the idea of weak thought as an aspect of the postmodern attitude and approach not only toward modernity but also toward traditional metaphysical onto-theology. Richard Rorty has explained that "the relationship between predecessor and successor would be conceived, as Vattimo has emphasized, not as the power-laden relation of 'overcoming' (*Überwindung*) but as the gentler relation of turning to new 'purposes' (*Verwindung*)."

HERMENEUTICS AS THE *KOINÉ* OF POSTMODERNITY

It is only within this hermeneutical framework that preferences can be delineated for political or religious projects. The strong theory of weakness consists of a philosophy that does not derive from the world "as it is," but from the world viewed as the production of interpretations throughout the history of human cultures. This philosophy today is hermeneutics, and Vattimo has individuated in it a "*koiné*: the common language," explained Gadamer, "in which philosophical thought after Heidegger and Wittgenstein, after Quine, Derrida and Ricoeur, has spread everywhere; virtually a universal philosophical language." Although hermeneutics is at the origin of weak thought, Vattimo always recalls that the Saussurean linguistic structuralism of the 1960s and the development of Wittgensteinian language games in some analytical philosophy also played a great part in developing the idea that although there are no facts, just interpretations, these interpretations are always inside language – as the dicta of Heidegger and Gadamer emphasized: "Language is the house of Being" and "Being that can be understood is language."

The term "hermeneutics" derives from a Greek word connected with the name of the god Hermes, the reputed messenger and interpreter of the gods, and originally hermeneutics was concerned more narrowly with interpreting sacred texts. It evolved in response not only to the "religious" need to determine correct rules for the valid interpretation of the Bible but also to the "scientific" empiricist foundationalism of logical positivism, thereby creating serious political and cultural changes, just as Martin Luther's Protestant Reformation and Thomas Kuhn's explanation of the structure of scientific revolutions did.

Luther and Kuhn, in very different ages, showed that religious faith and scientific knowledge change not through the confrontation of the official interpretation with hard facts but by a social struggle between contending interpretations of intrinsically ambiguous evidence.

Although hermeneutics had its origins in problems of biblical exegesis and in the development of a theoretical framework to govern such exegetical practice, beginning in the eighteenth and early nineteenth centuries, theorists such as Johann Martin Chladenius, Georg Friedrich Meier, Friedrich Ast, and Friedrich Schleiermacher developed hermeneutics into a more encompassing theory of textual interpretation in general: they developed rules that provided the basis for good interpretive practice regardless of the subject matter. Through Dilthey and Heidegger hermeneutics became a complete and recognized philosophical position in twentieth-century German philosophy. Dilthey saw interpretation as a method for the social and human sciences, and Heidegger saw it as an "ontological event," an interaction between interpreter and text that is part of the history of what we understand.

One of the greatest results of the analysis of interpretation in the nineteenth century was the recognition of "the hermeneutical circle," first developed by Schleiermacher. Vattimo several times explained in his courses that understanding the "circularity" of interpretation is essential to understanding our postmodern approach, not only toward modernity but also toward traditional metaphysical onto-theology, because if every interpretation is itself based on another interpretation, then the circle of interpretation cannot be escaped or overcome completely, as is expressed by the German term *Verwindung*. Vattimo went further in considering interpretation as a process of weakening, a process in which the weight of objective structures must be infinitely weakened. Philosophy is not scientific knowledge of the external, universal structures of being; nor is it knowledge from the external and universal form of God. It is, rather, the "weak interpretation of an epoch." This helps to show, for example, that when Nietzsche says that "God is dead," he is making an "announcement" and not a "claim." Hermeneutics does not teach that God does not exist; it teaches that our experience has been transformed in such a way that we no longer conceive ultimate objective truths. We have learned to respond only to appeals and announcements.

WEAK THOUGHT, CHRISTIANITY, AND DERRIDA

It is important to point out that Vattimo's formulation of weak thought was mostly motivated by ethical and religious reasons prompted by both the violent metaphysical rhetoric of subjectivity that characterized the letters of the arrested students of the late 1960s and by Heidegger's concept of "ontological difference," which shows the impossibility of an absolute philosophical foundation that could produce an absolute principle. Vattimo always prefers a nihilist (left-wing) rather than a negative theological (right-wing) interpretation of Heidegger. (With "left" and "right" Vattimo does not allude to politics but to their meaning in the Hegelian school). The right-wing interpretation "demands" the return of Being by overcoming (*Überwindung*) metaphysics as an effort, and the left-wing a "resigning" (*Verwindung*) to the reading of the history of Being as an interminable weakening of Being. Vattimo justifies this interpretation by pointing out that the ontological difference serves to put an end to identifying Being with beings, and therefore "existence" (human beings) with "objectivity" (objects), which gives birth to totalitarian societies, since it identifies man's Being with the machine, as shown in Charlie Chaplin's *Modern Times*.

Weak thought becomes strong thought, on the one hand, because we realize through it that our life is conditioned by history and, on the other hand, because it is a responsible ethical project, since we must live our lives in an authentic form (in Heidegger's terms, opposing it to an inauthentic *Dasein*). Vattimo has always understood Pareyson's main dictum, "of truth there is nothing but interpretation and ... there is nothing but interpretation of truth," as insisting upon the passage from "truth as objectivity" to "truth as charity, or *pietas*," from "philosophy as the mirror of nature" (as Rorty titled his classic text) to "philosophy as the ability to listen to the other." The history of political power in the West is nothing but a weakening of strong structures of power: from absolute monarchy to the constitutional and democratic state, from the authoritarian biblical interpretation of the Church to the Bible of the people as translated by Luther. If "interpreting" is nothing but a form of weakening the strong structures of the presence of an object "out there" (the "real"), then the postmodern age is not only the age when the ethical dangers of this identification are recognized but also the age that marks the religious comeback of Christianity.

The Christian doctrine concerning the incarnation of the Son of God could be also considered as an example of Vattimo's ontology of weakening. Reading Girard's thesis in *Things Hidden since the Foundation of the World* and *Violence and the Sacred*, Vattimo discovered in the Bible a rejection of victimization: what before had been an ethical weakening became a Christian weakening. The "desacralizing work of the Paraclete," together with its notion of secularization as a weakening of Being, enabled Vattimo to recognize that Heidegger, through nihilism, was already responding to these postmetaphysical problems. But whereas Heidegger intuitively felt Christianity to be part of the problem and thus sought different answers, Vattimo not only sees in the secularizing work of the Christian gospel something to be embraced but also proposes a philosophy of weakening based especially in the Christian concept of kenotic (self-emptying) love as found in Philippians 2:5–11. The history of human emancipation as a progressive dissolution of violence and dogmas is the widest definition we can give of weak thought. Girard recently observed that Vattimo is very different from Heidegger, and he clearly understands the importance and the centrality of Christian belief in defining the destiny of Western culture and civilization, and in fact at the end he dwells on the notion of *agape* as the result of the anti-metaphysical revolution of Christianity.

Weak thought is not simply a philosophy that abandons claims to global and metaphysical visions, since it is more aware of its own limits. It is above all a theory of weakening as the character of the event of Being in the epoch of the end of metaphysics. If Nietzsche's, Heidegger's, and Derrida's deconstruction of objective knowledge cannot be replaced with a more "adequate" or "correct" conception of Reality, then the history of metaphysics cannot be conceived of merely as a history of errors. Is weak thought then the philosophy of the plurality of philosophies? Weak thought is a valid theory only on the basis of hermeneutical justifications. Vattimo has responded to this criticism by pointing out several times the conceptual problem of "liberalism": liberalism is supposed to be the theory of liberty, but once liberalism is instituted in a society, what do liberalists do? Instituting liberalism is never something that can come to an end, because claiming that there is a plurality of philosophies involves taking an enormous number of critical positions on all absolute principles. Plurality then becomes a philosophy in itself. Since there are always going to be absolute principles to deconstruct, consume, reject, and weaken, the "thought of plurality" is also a specific thought that fights to affirm a never-ending position as nihilism. This is why weak thought no longer tries to answer the classical ontological question, Why should Being *be*, and why is there not rather nothing? Instead, weak thought asks a new, postmetaphysical question: What does Being mean in our actual life today? Or, What is left of Being today? Vattimo also recognizes that when one formulates this question as "what is left" of something, it is also a weak hermeneutical question, because it does not request a description of objects but a cultural, political, and philosophical project for the future – as we will see.

Since the early 1980s Vattimo has been known as the main proponent of weak thought as a philosophy, but he is not alone. Prominent contemporary philosophers such as Pier Aldo Rovatti, Richard Rorty, Fernando Savater, and others have described themselves as "weak thinkers" on many occasions. Vattimo has always recognized in Eco's main novels, *The Name of the Rose* and *Foucault's Pendulum*, a certain spirit of weak thinking. The former develops around something particularly marginal, something that is concerned with humour, and the other develops around a quest for the Holy Grail – a quest that develops only because a superficial note is found. This is the spirit of weak thinking, which can also be found marvelously expressed in Nietzsche's aphorism from *Origin and Meaning*, where he writes that "the progressive knowledge of the origin increases the insignificance of the origin," because the notion of "history" is a process of weakening: a process by which the peremptory nature of reality is weakened and in which reality becomes a set of shared discourses. According to Vattimo, weak thought has helped philosophy to become an edifying discourse rather than a demonstrative one, a discourse more oriented toward the edification of humanity than toward the development of knowledge and progress. The duty of the philosopher no longer corresponds to the Platonic agenda of guiding humanity to understanding the Eternal; rather, the philosopher redirects humanity toward history, in order to form an "ontology of weakness" or, as we will see further, an "ontology of actuality." Weak thought is by no means a weakness of thinking as such, but since thinking is no longer demonstrative but rather edifying, it has become weaker.

Vattimo spoke several times with Pareyson about weak thought and wrote an essay entitled *Ermeneutica e secolorizzazione* (Hermeneutics and Secularization, 1986), included in *Etica dell'interpretazione*, where he objects to Pareyson that he is not a weak enough thinker, as he should be on the basis of his own "ontology of freedom." Pareyson, on the other hand, observed that in order not to lose the distinction between good and bad, truth and falsehood, or the criteria for interpretation, there should always be an "original principle of the inexhaustibleness with which one establishes some sort of relation" (which was one of Pareyson's main theses).

Vattimo recalls now that before weak thought became a specific philosophy of weakening or a philosophy of history as weakening, it developed as he confronted French philosophy, mainly in the work of Michael Foucault, Gilles Deleuze, Jean Francois Lyotard, Jacques Derrida, and

René Girard. He became acquainted with all of them and not only often invited Lyotard and Derrida to give conferences in Turin, but also edited several books with Derrida. After becoming a full professor of aesthetics in 1968, he travelled often to Paris and wrote several forewords to the books of these French philosophers in Italian translation. But Vattimo realized that although Derrida's position came closest to weak thought, it could not be identified with Derrida's deconstructive philosophy (it could be identified instead with Rorty's neopragmatism), because weak thought is also in part a consequence of deconstruction.

Derrida is still too metaphysical for Vattimo, since he sees the "difference" as something that is in some sense beyond us, in a sort of negative theology. In a conference in Paris in 2000 entitled Jewishnesses: Questions for Jacques Derrida, organized by Joseph Cohen and Raphael Zagury-Orly, Vattimo, in his lecture ("Historicité et différence"), showed that Derrida has remained an existentialist philosopher because he does not have a philosophical "philosophy of history." During the debate, in the morning with Vattimo and in the afternoon with Habermas, Derrida recognized that Vattimo's observations were quite right, and they both agreed that for Derrida there is always a vertical relationship with God but not a horizontal one, since he is Jewish and not Christian. The Messiah for Derrida has not only still to come but has also to be something completely "different," radically "different." Vattimo's main objection during the debate with Derrida was the fact that without a philosophy of history it is not possible to know whether something is completely different when it appears.

BEYOND INTERPRETATION
AND THE PHILOSOPHICAL YEARBOOKS

In 1993 Umberto Eco invited Vattimo to give some lectures at the University of Bologna, the tenth distinguished Lezioni Italiane (Paul C.W. Davies, Wolf Lepenies, Hilary Putnam, André Green, and other intellectuals have also given these lectures, organized by the Sigma-Tau Foundation and the Laterza Publishing House). The lectures were published as *Beyond Interpretation: The Meaning of Hermeneutics for Philosophy* (1994), which analyzed the too narrow and literal sense the notion of weakness had taken since its formulation in 1979. In this book Vattimo specifically emphasizes one of his major theses: philosophers used to think they were able to describe the world, but now the moment has arrived to interpret it, because culture has experienced a compartmentalization of language, a division of labour, and the many forms of discontinuity to which we are exposed by the rapidity of the transformations of our world (including the transformation by the Internet, above all). If, as Nietzsche lucidly recognized in his classic proposition, "there are no facts, but only interpretations, and this is an interpretation too," then "interpretations" (and especially this second one) can be argued only as an interested response to a particular historical situation; they can be described not as objective findings based on external facts but as facts that enter into the same historical situation to which they correspond.

Arguing in favour of the "nihilistic vocation of hermeneutics," Vattimo explains why for some radical continuators of Heidegger, such as Derrida, it is not possible to speak of Being: they believe that to do so would involve a sort of lapse back into the metaphysics of foundations. Instead, Vattimo truly believes it is still possible to elaborate ontology, and this should not be seen as a risky foundational choice, because weak thought is a conscious philosophy of the interpretative nature of truth. For this reason we must replace, as mentioned above, the classical metaphysical questions – Why *is* Being, and why *is* there not, rather, nothing? And, why is it such as it is? – with the new postmetaphysical question concerning how our "objective" knowledge is subject to conditions rooted in the character of Being as it is given to us today. This new weak formulation of the classical metaphysical question helps philosophy respond (after the end of modernity, or metaphysics) to the event of Being in its "adventure of differences." The difference, though, lies in the "interpretation": philosophy is not the expression of the age; it is interpretation. And although it does strive to be persuasive, it also acknowledges its own contingency, liberty, and perilousness. It is not just Hegel who seems to be returning; empiricism is playing a part as well. Vattimo's main point is that when defined as the "ontology of actuality" (an expresion first used by Foucault), philosophy can be practised as an interpretation of the epoch, a giving-form to widely felt sentiments about the meaning of being alive in a certain society and in a certain historical world.

From 1986 to 1995 Vattimo edited the Italian Philosophical Yearbooks, an annual series from Giuseppe Laterza publishers on the most dominant and relevant themes of the international philosophical debates. The titles chosen by Vattimo were *Secolarizzazione* (Secularization, 1986), *Storia e teoria* (History and theory, 1987), *Evidenza e fondamento* (Evidence and foundation, 1988), *Lebensphilosophie* (Life Philosophy, 1989), *Oltre la svolta linguistica* (Beyond the Linguistic Turn, 1990), *La razionalità dell'ermeneutica* (The rationality of hermeneutics, 1991),

Alleggerimento come responsibilità (Lightening as responsibility, 1992), *La filosofia tra pubblicità e segreto* (Philosophy between publicity and secrets, 1993), *Esemplarità e argomentazione* (Exemplarity and argumentation, 1994), and *Filosofia e poesia* (Philosophy and poetry, 1995). Jean-François Lyotard, Hans-Georg Gadamer, Jacques Rolland, Richard Rorty, Odo Marquard, François Wahl, Stanley Rosen, Karl-Otto Apel, Alain Badiou, Rüdiger Bubner, Fernando Gil, Dominique Janicaud, Marc Richir, Fernando Savater, Eugenio Trias, Daniel Charles, Manfred Frank, and Jacques Derrida, along with Italian philosophers such as Umberto Eco, Vincenzo Vitiello, Giacomo Marramao, Maurizio Ferraris, and Emanuele Severino, contributed to these books.

In 1992 Giuseppe Laterza decided to expand these volumes by creating a European Yearbook series edited by Derrida and Vattimo, with the editorial participation of Éditions du Seuil of France. Together with Thierry Marchaisse, Giuseppe Laterza, and Maurizio Ferraris, Derrida and Vattimo decided that the first theme should be religion, and they organized a seminar (sponsored by the Instituto Italiano per gli studi filosofici) that took place from 28 February through 1 March 1994 at Capri, with the participation of Gadamer, Derrida, Vattimo, Trias, and others. The second (and last) European Yearbook edited by Derrida and Vattimo was entitled *Law, Justice, and Interpretation*, and it came from a seminar that took place on 26 and 27 May 1995, in Trento. For this volume Derrida and Vattimo invited jurists such as Duncan Kennedy, Oliver Gerstenberg, Mario Barcellona, Mauro Bussani, and others to reflect on whether law and justice are complementary or alternative fields of study.

Vattimo developed both themes from the European Yearbooks in his philosophical research from 1996 onward with the publication of four books: *Belief* (1996), *After Christianity* (2002), *Nihilism and Emancipation* (2004), and *The Future of Religion* (2005), which he coauthored with Richard Rorty. In *Belief* and *After Christianity*, Vattimo explains that now that metaphysics has finally been deconstructed, we must recognize the illusionary aspect of worldviews as philosophical foundations. He posited "conversational charity" instead of "objective truth" and showed that the reasons to believe that Being is weakened may be found also in the Bible's Incarnation doctrine. Since the Incarnation was an act of *kenosis*, by which God turned *everything* over to human beings, weak thought reflects the most faithful philosophical position of the Christian religious experience. Vattimo also responded to the main question that the end of metaphysics has raised in the philosophy of religion: Is a Christian philosophy possible? Vattimo thinks that "it is not possible to have a non-Christian philosophy" because philosophy is a historical product of our Western culture and civilization. Philosophy came to us in this moment from Greek culture, which has been transmitted to us throughout the Middle Ages and modernity; Vattimo, therefore, is persuaded that there is no philosophy in the West that has nothing to do with this Christian transmission. A philosophy that would neglect this Christian transmission would simply qualify not as a philosophy but as a pretentious natural science.

Vattimo has on many occasions quoted two archetypical expressions of the philosophical and religious tradition of the West in order to point out that the plurality of meanings of Being in classical philosophy are given in a framework akin to that marked by Christianity: "to on léghetai pollachôs" (Being is said in many ways), from Aristotle, and "multifariam, multisque, modis olim loquens, Deus patribus in prophetis: novissime diebus istis locutus est nobis Filio" (at many moments in the past and by many means, God spoke to our ancestors through the prophets; but in our time, the final days, he has spoken to us in the person of his Son, whom he appointed heir of all things and through whom he made the ages), from St Paul. It seems impossible to Vattimo to philosophize outside this horizon of the West, because its own terminology and culture have been influenced by it. Vattimo always recalls a paradoxical Italian expression, "grazie a Dio sono ateo" (Thank God, I am an atheist), in order to explain that it is mainly thanks to Christianity that we are atheists, because our philosophy is a secularized (no longer metaphysical) version of Greek philosophy passed through Christian culture. Although there may be someone who does not want to recognize himself as a Christian philosopher (hence Bertrand Russell's *Why I Am Not a Christian*) or does not want to recognize that modern Europe is essentially Christian, he would still have to acknowledge the Christian and biblical historical condition of philosophy in modern Europe.

THE CONSEQUENCES OF *BELIEF* IN THE CHURCH AND WORKING WITH RORTY

Since the publication of *Belief*, Vattimo has received hundreds of letters of support from many theologians, nuns, and priests around the world. Private seminars organized to study the text took place between students and professors in distinguished pontifical universities throughout the world. Although Vattimo's religious texts have only recently been adopted by some pontifical universities' liberal arts courses, because of his criticism of the dogmatic political positions of the Church, the largest and most complete investigation of Vattimo's philosophy ever written came surprisingly from a PHD candidate in theology (now a professor) in the Pontifical Gregorian University of Rome: Carmelo Dotolo, who worked under the supervision of distinguished Bishop Rino Fisichella. Dotolo's five-hundred page book, entitled *Fundamental Theology: Facing the Challenges of Gianni Vattimo's Weak Thought*, was published in 1999 with a foreword by Bishop Fisichella.

In 1996 Vattimo, together with Edward Said, Umberto Eco, and others, was awarded the annual Italian Academy Lectureship by the Italian Academy for Advanced Studies in America at Columbia University in New York City. His lectures there gave birth to *After Christianity*, which involved a specific philosophical request to recognize the possibility of and need for a "nonreligious Christianity." This phrase refers to the cultural nature of being a Christian today: according to Vattimo, one can be a Christian only culturally and not metaphysically, because it seems quite unlikely that we should think that God is a transcendent entity that sent us someone who appeared as a man and talked about God and asked us to declare ourselves Christians. No true Christian, thinks Vattimo, could explicitly believe in this objective and metaphysical description.

Vattimo's religious and political investigations continued in the two books I edited for him during the first years of the new millennium, while he was still a European Union deputy: *Nihilism and Emancipation* (2004) and *The Future of Religion* (2005), coauthored with Richard Rorty. *Nihilism and Emancipation* contains fourteen essays divided into three parts: "Ethics," "Politics," and "Law." As Vattimo explains in the introduction, these areas are all unified in the two words of the title: "nihilism," which refers to the dissolution of any ultimate foundation, and "emancipation," the process in which constraints are shed. Ethics, politics, and the law become "nihilist" because we now know, after the end of metaphysics, that we can comprehend universal principles and ideals only by recognizing that "truth" can be constructed only by an edifying consensus reached through dialogue – without claiming any right in the name of these universal principles or ideals.

Vattimo shows in these essays that weak thought relies fundamentally on the principle of the plurality of interpretations, therefore on the inescapable idea that we should gradually set our norms and rules independently of the limits of what were supposedly "natural" or "foundational" ideals, in order to create a positive political project for the future. In the collegial foreword, which he wrote for us, Rorty specifically points out that

Vattimo calls this Heideggerian outlook "nihilism" because it is not a positive doctrine, but rather a series of negations – denials that any proposed principle or jargon or insight enjoys a privileged reality to the nature of man or of the universe. For the idea that either of these *has* a nature is no longer credible. Vattimo wants to show how leftist political and social initiatives can not only survive, but can profit from, jettisoning traditional philosophical attempts to reveal such things as The Ultimate Nature of Reality or The Ultimate Meaning of Human Life.

Rorty goes on to say that one of Vattimo's

most distinctive contributions to philosophical thinking is the suggestion that the Internet provides a model for things in general – that thinking about the World Wide Web helps us to get away from Platonic essentialism, the quest for underlying natures, by helping us see everything as a constantly changing network of relations. The result of adopting this model is what Vattimo calls "a weak ontology, or better, an ontology of the weakening of being." Such an ontology, he argues, "supplies philosophical reasons for preferring a liberal, tolerant, and democratic society rather than an authoritarian and totalitarian one."

On 11 and 12 February 2000, Erwin Teufel, Rüdiger Bubner, Michael Theunissen, Gianni Vattimo, and Richard Rorty were invited to speak at the University of Heidelberg to celebrate the one hundredth anniversary of Gadamer's birth. Since the early 1980s, Vattimo and Rorty had written several essays and forewords for their respective English and Italian editions, and Rorty also wrote in his *Essays on Heidegger and Others* that his own work "should be read as examples of what a group of contemporary Italian philosophers have called 'weak thought' – philosophical reflection which does not attempt a radical criticism of contemporary culture, does not attempt to refound or remotivate it, but simply assembles reminders and suggests some interesting possibilities." Although Vattimo and Rorty have always recognized that their philosophical positions are very close, the distinguished German philosopher Michael Theunissen confirmed this when he stated in his lecture at the Gadamer celebration that "the reception of philosophical Hermeneutics has for several decades shown two dominant tendencies: one is expansive, opening it up to other currents of thought, while the other is reflexive, orienting it toward the tradition. Rorty and Vattimo well exemplify these two trends."

In 2002 Vattimo was invited to Berlin to attend the celebrations of
the Meister Eckhart prize awarded to Rorty, who was to lead a conference on Vattimo's *Belief*. It was then that I asked Gianni to write an
essay responding to Rorty's comments, in order to put together a book.
This essay became "The Age of Interpretation," and after Rorty agreed
to put together a book with both texts, the three of us met in Paris on
16 December 2002 to discuss the future of religion after metaphysics,
which became the dialogue of the book. The discussion lasted more
than two hours and was then revised by both Rorty and Vattimo. One
of the main points of the discussion was the similarity between John
Dewey's American pragmatism and Benedetto Croce's Italian idealism.
Rorty and Vattimo pointed out that not only do both schools of
thought take a philosophical position that combines Hegel without
eschatology and Heidegger without metaphysics (as Robert Brandom's
latest work, *Tales of the Mighty Dead*, shows), but they also take a
postmetaphysical position without the idea that we could ever reach a
point of culmination. Rorty and Vattimo agreed that the future of religion will depend on a position that is "beyond atheism and theism," a
hermeneutical guide without the unreasonable disciplinary constraints
the Catholic Church continues to impose.

MEMBERSHIP IN THE EUROPEAN PARLIAMENT AND
SHAPING THE CONVENTION ON THE FUTURE OF EUROPE

Although Vattimo had been quite involved in leftist politics since 1976,
when he published *The Subject and Its Mask*, his book on Nietzsche, it
was not until the early 1990s that he began again to be engaged as he
was during the 1950s. Before winning a seat as a deputy in the European Parliament in 1999, Vattimo was very involved, as were many
Italians, in the political enthusiasm surrounding Tangentopoli (Italian
for "bribe city"), which was like a revolution for Italian politics. In
1992, a nationwide Italian police investigation into political corruption
led to the demise of the so-called First Republic (and to the disappearance of the party of Vattimo's youth, the Christian Democrats).

After this revolution began to quietly die (many intellectuals stopped
taking any interest), Vattimo instead increased his comments on the
political debate in two major Italians newspapers, *La Stampa* and
L'Unità, in order to criticise not only the end of the political enthusiasm
for Tangentopoli but also the beginning of Silvio Berlusconi's regime
(whose House of Liberty coalition includes the neofascist National
Alliance of Gianfranco Fini and the xenophobic Northern League of

Umberto Bossi). Vattimo's articles in the national newspapers started to involve him in political debates in Turin, to the point that the democratic party of the left wanted him to run for mayor of that city. Instead, Vattimo decided to run and was elected as a deputy for the European Community and participated for five years as a member of the Commission of Freedom and Citizens' Rights, Justice, and Internal Affairs; the Commission for Culture, Youth, Education, Communication, and Sport; and the interparliamentary delegation EU-China.

Vattimo's political work as a deputy for the Party of European Socialists (from 1999 to 2004) was mainly influenced by his philosophical and political convictions. In November 2000, in order to denounce an initiative of the neofascist National Alliance governor of Lazio, Francesco Storace, an initiative that called for a "review" of school textbooks (Storace believed the textbooks were not critical enough of the antifascist rebels of World War II and too critical of those who sided with Mussolini), Vattimo not only organized a conference at the European Parliament of Brussels but also had distinguished intellectual figures such as Jürgen Habermas, Oliver Duhamel, and Norberto Bobbio sign a petition against this initiative. Enrique Baron Crespo, Umberto Eco, Fernando Savater, Nicola Tranfaglia, among others, participated in the conference, which took place on 29 March 2001 and gave birth to a book entitled *Linguaggi e temi della destra in Europa* (Language and themes in right wing Europe).

Vattimo took another serious action against Berlusconi on 2 July 2003, the day before Berlusconi began his six-month term in the rotating European Union presidency, by distributing to all European parliaments a small brochure outlining Berlusconi's life and the charges that had been made against him, including alleged bribery of judges, money laundering, tax evasion, and false accounting, charges prepared by two distinguished Italian journalists, Marco Travaglio and Peter Gomez. The next day, as Berlusconi began setting out his program for Italy's presidency of the EU, protesters led by a dozen Green Party members of the European Parliament started waving placards bearing the word "Justice." A few days later Vattimo and other member of the parliament signed a letter expressing solidarity with Martin Schulz, whom Berlusconi had insulted on the same day (Berlusconi had suggested him for the part of a Nazi guard in an Italian movie about concentration camps) simply because Schulz had asked Berlusconi to justify comments by Umberto Bossi, a member of Berlusconi's coalition government, who suggested that "boats carrying immigrants to Italian shores should be shot at by the navy." These and other actions were taken by Vattimo in order to denounce Berlusconi's regime to the EU.

Although Italy was one of the major promoters at the Convention on the Future of Europe, led by Giscard d'Estaing, of the idea that Christian values appear somewhere in the European constitution, Vattimo instead felt much closer to countries such as France, which have a clear sense of their secularist tradition. Some of the Italian political leaders mentioned above felt that a reference to Christian values would make it more difficult to expand the EU in the future to include Muslim countries such as Turkey, but they were forgetting that pluralist, modern Europe is beyond the need to refer to a single religion in the EU constitution. Vattimo thought it would be a mistake to add the specific words "Christian values" to the constitution because it is precisely in order to uphold these same Christian values that Europe is secular: the force of the Gospels and of Jesus' teaching provides the foundation of the secularity of any democratic state today.

The final draft of the constitution spoke of "drawing inspiration from the cultural, religious, and humanist inheritance of Europe," and referred to "the values which, still present in its heritage, have embedded within the life of society the central role of the human person and his or her inviolable and inalienable rights, and respect for law." Vattimo was very happy with this draft because it made clear that although Europe is mainly Christian, it does not need to demand and constantly recall it. The Vatican's insistence on inserting the concept of Christianity in the constitution seemed to Vattimo part of a dogmatically metaphysical philosophy strange to the plurality of Europe. Although Vattimo valued France's traditional state secularism, he found it a scandal that President Chirac decided not to allow Muslim pupils to wear veils in school a few months later, since he saw in this act "ostentatious signs of religious proselytism" and "something aggressive." On 4 March 2004, the French newspaper *Libération* published an interview with Vattimo by Robert Maggiori where Vattimo clearly explained "that secularity means liberating, not prohibiting" and that "a state is secular to the extent that it does not adopt a philosophy that excludes religions and their manifestations, but on the contrary, enables and permits many religious symbols to manifest themselves without limits." Although Vattimo felt happy to have helped shape the European Constitution, he always reminded his students that constitutions are read only when they are violated by someone, that they are nothing but "negative limits to violations."

Hardly anyone invokes constitutions in order to say that something should or should not be done.

FROM DEMOCRACY TO SOCIALISM
THROUGH WEAK THOUGHT

Vattimo, together with Jürgen Habermas, Peter Singer, Otfried Höffe, Seyla Benhabib, Iris Young, and many others were invited to the twenty-first World Philosophy Congress in August 2003 organized by the Turkish Philosophy Board Association and the International Philosophy Organizations Federation and supported by the Turkish Ministry of Foreign Affairs. Postmodern thought, technology, globalization, cultural identity, human rights, and the new international order were discussed extensively in the week-long congress, entitled Philosophy Facing World Problems. Vattimo and Habermas opened the congress and gave the most relevant lectures of the week. Vattimo analyzed Karl Popper's "open society" and Martin Heidegger's "end of metaphysics" in his talk, "Heidegger: Philosopher of Democracy."

Where he not only identified the "end of philosophy as metaphysics" with the "end of totalitarian governments" but also suggested that our democratic states may function correctly only in a globalized world where power (or truth) is not in the hands of only one central political system (an allusion to Plato's philosopher-kings). Popper's objections to Plato are the same as Heidegger's objections to metaphysics, which he always regarded as Platonic. In this conference Vattimo declared that proposing an "ontology of actuality" (and therefore suggesting the need for a new postmetaphysical question, namely, How much is our objective knowledge subject to conditions rooted in the meaning of Being as it is given to us today?) is not very different from the project of positing a different political situation. While Heidegger continued to search for Being in what he thought were privileged places, such as Anaximander's sayings or the poems of Parmenides or Hölderlin, Being could also be found (as he also suggested but without developing the suggestion) in the "act which founds a state" or, as Vattimo now suggests, in the votes of citizens: there is no justification for Being's speaking mainly through a hermetic poetical language rather than in collective events. Vattimo concluded his lecture by recognizing that perhaps in our "age of democracies" the way in which Being is given to us is something much more spacious and less definable – democratic political elections.

In 2004 Vattimo published *Il socialismo ossia L'europa* (Socialism, hence Europe), which was part of his own political program for the European elections of 2004. Although Berlusconi's regime lost the elections, Vattimo himself was not reelected and decided to stop his political career in order to dedicate his time exclusively to philosophy. Although Vattimo had been involved in politics since his youth, it was only at this time that he clearly realized how his books, articles, and conferences of the preceding decades showed that it was "weak thought" that directed him toward a political position demanding a reduction of violence, an intensification of social dialogue, respect for minorities, and a plurality of information, which he found in the liberal-left rather than in the conservative-right parties and in the European Union rather than in Italian national politics.

Hermeneutics, according to Vattimo, is probably the philosophical stance that most faithfully reflects the pluralism of modern Western democratic societies (as he shows in *Nihilism and Emancipation*). But how is all this translated into a political project? Philosophically, rather than theorizing that "Being is language," in his political career Vattimo has practised a politics that increasingly allows the "collective language" to be the "event" of Being. Since hermeneutics is not a descriptive philosophy but rather a projected one, its project continually needs a vast teleological horizon in order to emancipate thought from ideological foundations. Vattimo's "hermeneutical political project" is interested only in the development of liberty, therefore in promoting a society capable of allowing all citizens to decide for themselves which life they prefer to live. This postmetaphysical project does not want to impose a "natural law" on everybody: the sole meaning of natural law for Vattimo is the law of the struggle for life ("the strongest win, the weakest lose"); the ones who claim to be the defenders of a "natural right" are generally the dominating classes.

One of the main reasons Vattimo wanted to become a European deputy in 1999 and again in 2004 was that he found this "hermeneutical political project" could be more easily developed in the European Union than in Italian national politics. In Italy, social issues such as embryonic cloning, euthanasia, drug legalization, civil rights, artificial fertilization, and gay marriage continue to be blocked because politicians are afraid of the judgments of the Vatican, which still exerts a tremendous power over Italian voters. Vattimo knew that such issues could be discussed freely in the European Union not only because it had a wider, transnational platform but most of all because it was not conditioned by local authorities such as the Vatican. So those social issues have a greater possibility of being resolved in Europe than in Italy, or in other individual nations).

Europe, for Vattimo, is not an institution in which some countries reach the "level" of the others, but, on the contrary, it is one in which members become involved in the joint construction of a "superior" level of civil freedom for resolving these social issues. Realizing the Kantian dream of cosmopolitism, that is, the march toward world unity, was another possibility Vattimo saw in Europe, because the union represented the first time a transnational state had been constituted freely, not by occupation, invasion, or war, as most of the individual European nations had been. To Vattimo the European Union should be considered as representing serious progress in political civility, because it does not have a "natural base" but rather a "volunteered and deliberated base of diversities." Since the European Union is not constituted by only one language, religion, or race but by a great number of them, it must allow its boundaries to continually expand. Vattimo was once prompted in a meeting with Romano Prodi to declare (with caution), therefore, that "the European Union does not have real limits" because as a community it positively recognizes itself as embracing a system of values that could be recognized by other nations outside Europe. Since theoretically it does not have rigid borders but rather borders that depend only on the goodwill of its citizens, the union can build a wider community around certain values as long as all members accept new member-nations as they arise.

When Vattimo was awarded the Hannah Arendt Prize for Political Thinking in 2002, in Bremen, he gave a lecture entitled "Globalization and the Relevance of Socialism," where he not only showed how the new entity of secularized nations in Europe was taking shape but also the failure of what Michael Hardt and Antonio Negri called "empire." Being a European politician made Vattimo realize that the Kantian dream of cosmopolitism is threatened when power is concentrated in only one centre, as the United States of America is trying to ensure today. In this lecture he showed that we need at least three or four more centres of power in order to maintain a certain balance for peace in the world, because "an order" is supposed to be a system where no weaker force is controlled by a stronger one. Vattimo sees the European Union not as a model for a new universal United Nations but as an example for the constitution of a world dialogue. Being a politician in the European Union did not mean for Vattimo being part of a race or language; rather, it meant being part of a political system that recognized its own pluralistic unity not as a natural foundation but as a harmony of diversities. It is in this harmony of diversities, as Vattimo points out, that the future citizen, who will have two or three mother tongues, will start to appear and function (as Canada has wonderfully shown).

Marx, according to Vattimo, was right when he argued that the logic of capitalism – as a system that increases the number of the poor by decreasing the number of the rich – would end up stimulating a revolt of the poor. Vattimo regards the antiglobalization movements as fundamental voices of our present time and defines them as "our political hope for the future." If they are going to be able to give themselves a political voice, these movements must announce their hopes in an electoral and democratic voice in order to be institutionalized in some way. If they do not find this political institution, their members risk being marginalized as an anarchic group distributing only narcotics and video games, ending up as the poor, revolutionary consumers of the rich capitalized nations of the world.

Vattimo does not believe that the terrorist attacks of 11 September 2001 in New York, of 11 March 2004 in Madrid, and of 7 July 2005 in London, and the illegitimate wars in Afghanistan and Iraq, were caused by Samuel P. Huntington's "clash of civilizations" and problems of class conflict; if this had been the case, we would have to presume an identification of the cultures of the Third World with the new proletariat whose development Marx predicted. Although the Islamic fundamentalists are attacking the Western way of life in response to our invasions and attempts to control their oil resources, they cannot legitimately claim to represent the Third World, since, for example, the extremely oppressive Taliban social order that used to host bin Laden never claimed to represent the Third World in general. How could a regime that constantly violated fundamental human rights be considered the representative of a global revolt against the exploitation of Western capitalism and the oppression of economic freedom? Not only do poor Islamic citizens not have the religious motivation that would be necessary to accept the kind of discipline that bin Laden demands, neither do the opponents of globalization in the West have any faith in bin Laden's anti-Western propaganda.

After the attacks of 2001, 2004, and 2005, most politicians were concerned only with explaining why a war on terrorism is different from conventional war, but in his newspaper editorials Vattimo showed that they should concentrate on the fundamental consequences of this "war on terrorism" for individual freedom: the unsatisfactory restrictions on democratic freedom and the inequitable invasions of privacy. Intensifying privacy controls on individuals would be fine if by "individuals" we meant all people, regardless of the colour of their skin, their social status, their religion, and their nationality. If we were all meticulously checked at all times and if everyone had access to all the information about any citizen's bank account, job, or taxes, this would, Vattimo thinks, set in motion all the consequences of what he calls a "transparent society" in his 1989 book *The Transparent Society*. If our lives became completely transparent, if all information was made available online and for everyone, we would certainly reduce today's inadequate restrictions of democratic freedom and, at the same time, reduce the economic power of the terrorist. Today terrorists surely benefit from the secrets that still exist between banks and their clients. The problem of international finance is that its capitalist mechanism works through a combination of intuition, gambling, and, especially, privileged information. Since banking secrecy is necessary not only for terrorist groups but also for our capitalist economy, ending terrorism depends on ending a capitalist economic system that is based on defending client secrecy at all costs. Vattimo thinks that if the West wants to prevail over terrorism, it should start by not only making bank accounts public but also by respecting human rights. But it can do so only by transforming the relationship between citizens and the state through a federation of open societies that cannot fall into authoritarianism.

Vattimo's "hermeneutical political project" for a transparent society is based on the idea that socialism is the destiny of humanity – socialism as intense state control of our collective lives accompanied by an absolute democratization of all institutional and governmental powers. This is possible only in a truly transparent democratic society that leaves an open space even for those who do not want to take part in the social conversation and do not share the common binding principles. In such a society, violence would be defined as "the silencing of questions," because the greatest moments of violence in history have always been justified by metaphysical structures and ultimate truths. Vattimo's weak thought can help the world political culture understand that true respect for human dignity is respect for individual freedom, not respect for some preexisting natural or religious metaphysical essence.

This introduction has provided only a modest glimpse into the exciting life and work of one of today's major philosophers, but I hope it will give the reader an indication of who Vattimo is and what his weakened philosophy is all about. The essays, and Vattimo's conclusion, that constitute this volume will be a continuation of this process.

I would like to remember Jacques Derrida's willingness to participate in this festschrift. Vattimo and Derrida were very close friends who not only collaborated on many projects but who, according to Vattimo, best understood the need for philosophy to overcome metaphysics. Derrida was one of the first philosophers I asked to participate when I was organizing this book in 2003, and on 20 June 2003, he wrote me a letter saying, "Cher Santiago Zabala, Comme je vous l'avais déjà dit, bien sûr, si je peux participer au livre projeté sur mon ami Vattimo, je le ferai avec joie. Mais, connaissant aujourd'hui les limites de mon temps et de mes forces, je ne peux vous faire pour l'instant aucune promesse ferme. J'espère simplement pouvoir en reparler l'an prochain avec vous. Avec mes vœux les plus cordiaux." (Dear Santiago Zabala, as I have already told you that I will participate in this future book on my friend Vattimo, I will do so with joy. But knowing today the limitations on my time and my strength, I cannot at this time make you a firm promise. I hope merely to be able to talk to you next year. With my most cordial best wishes.)" Then on 28 January 2004, he wrote again, explaining, "Je ne peux malheureusement, pour de sérieuses raisons de santé, que reporter encore ma décision. Bien entendu si avant la fin de 2004 je pouvais écrire un texte pour mon ami Gianni je le ferais de grand cœur. Mais je ne peux pas m'y engager aujourd'hui." (I cannot, unfortunately, due to serious matters of my health. But know that if before the end of 2004 I can write an essay for my friend Gianni, I will do so with great joy. But I cannot commit myself at this time.) The last time Vattimo saw Derrida was during the summer of 2004 at a conference in Avignon, where Derrida told Vattimo that he would do his best to try to participate in the festschrift, but on Saturday, 9 October 2004, Derrida died in Paris. Vattimo considered Derrida not only one of the most important philosophers of his generation but also the one who best understood and encouraged weak thought's development as a possible variation and confirmation of his philosophy.

NOTE

The epigraph to this chapter is drawn from an appreciation of Vattimo that Gadamer contributed to a festschrift for Vattimo's sixtieth birthday: *Interpretazione ed emancipazione: Studi in onore di Gianni Vattimo*, eds. Gianni Carchia and Maurizio Ferraris (Turin: Cortina editore 1996), 7.

PART ONE
Weakening Metaphysical Power

2

Weak Thought
and the Limits of Interpretation

UMBERTO ECO
Translated by Antonio Calcagno

To elaborate my position regarding the "weak thought" of Gianni Vattimo I am obliged to speak first about myself.

In 1986, I wrote an essay for a collection edited by Georges Duby on Latin thought, where I tried to identify the notion of *limit* as the fundamental idea of latinity.[1] I realized that perhaps because of this essay, I had some years later entitled one of my books *The Limits of Interpretation*.[2]

According to Greek rationalism – from Plato to Aristotle and beyond – to know is to know by a cause. Even to define God is to define a cause such that there can exist no other cause. To explain the world by causes is to elaborate a notion of a unidirectional chain: if a movement goes from Alpha to Omega, no force can make it go from Omega towards Alpha (in the fable of Phaedrus the wolf is an abuser exactly because it claims to reverse this principle). To found such a unidirectional chain one must assume some principles beforehand: the principle of identity (A = B), the principle of noncontradiction, and the principle of the excluded middle. The typical mode of reasoning of Western rationalism derives from this, namely, *modus ponens*: if *a* then *b*; but *a*; thus *b*.

Latin rationalism accepts the principles of Greek rationalism, but it transforms them and enriches them in a juridical and contractual sense. The basic principle thus becomes the notion of *limes*, that is, of the border and thus of the limit.

The Latin obsession with the spatial border was born with the myth of foundation. Romulus drew a line of demarcation and killed his brother because he did not respect it. Without the recognition of a border there can be no *civitas*. Bridges (*pontes*) are sacrilegious because they cross the *sulcus*, this circle of water that defines the limits of the city. This is why their construction can be made only under the strict ritual control of the *pontifex*. The ideology of the *pax romana* was based on the precision of borders. The force of the Empire lay in the fact of knowing on which *vallum*, inside which *limen*, it was necessary to set up the defence. When there was no longer a clear notion of borders and when the Barbarians (nomads who abandoned their territory of origin and crossed any land as if it was theirs, always ready to abandon it) imposed their nomadic vision, the capital of the Empire could be everywhere and little by little it collapsed.

In crossing the Rubicon, Julius Caesar was perfectly conscious of committing a sacrilege, but this is not all. In addition, he knew that later it would be impossible for him to return. *Alea jacta est*. For time also has its borders: it is not reversible. We cannot erase what was done. It was this principle that would guide Latin syntax. The direction and order of time, which form a cosmological linearity, become a system of logical subordinations in the *consecutio temporum*. Thought can recognize, align, and look at the facts only if it first finds an order that connects them. Consider the masterpiece of factual realism that is the ablative absolute. It establishes that something, once done or presupposed, can no longer be put into question.

Saint Thomas, in a *quaestio quodlibetalis* (5.2.3) asks, "utrum Deus possit virginem reparare." Can God make virginal once again a woman who has lost her virginity? His answer is firm. God has the power to forgive, to return to the virgin her state of grace, and by a miracle to restore her with her corporeal integrity. But even God cannot make that which once was into something that never happened, because this violation of the temporal laws would be against God's nature. Once a given fact has happened, even for God, *alea jacta est*.

Still today, it is this model of rationalism that dominates mathematics, logic, science, and computer programming. However, what we call the Greek heritage does not amount to all this. Aristotle is Greek, but so are the mysteries of Eleusis. The Greek world is eternally attracted by the *apeiron* (the infinite, which has neither limit nor direction). Fascinated by infinity, Greek civilization elaborates, at the same time that it elaborates the concepts of identity and noncontradiction, the idea of continual metamorphosis, symbolized by Hermes, an evanescent, ambiguous being, father of all the arts but god of thieves, *juvenis* and *senex* at the same time. In the myth of Hermes, the principles of identity, noncontradiction, and the excluded middle are denied; the causal chains fold into themselves in a spiral, the after precedes the before, the god knows no more spatial borders and can be, under different forms, in different places at the same moment.

Now, if I reconsider the course of my research, I notice that it always places itself under the sign of a limit to be identified. All the fascination that I could bring out regarding hermetic thought was the subject of my novels – understood as the grotesque representation of a mental perversion.

Certainly, we could say that although I began my philosophical research with a study of the aesthetics of Thomas Aquinas, I became immediately fascinated afterwards by the opening of an infinite number of possible interpretations such that I even wrote a book entitled *The Open Work* – which celebrates the activity of the interpreter as fundamental for the life of a work of art and whose final chapter was dedicated to the most unlimited work, Joyce's *Finnegans Wake*.[3] Moreover, this book opened with a citation from Apollinaire: "Pity pity for us – we who fight on the borders of the unlimited and the future."

And indeed, when twenty years later I wrote *The Limits of Interpretation*, somebody wondered if I had not withdrawn my praise for this opening, which serves as the point of departure for any work of art as a series of possible interpretations – if not an infinite series, then at least an indefinite one. However, such an objection did not take into account that my title, *The Open Work*, was an oxymoron. That which opened itself was nevertheless a work and thus a form, something that was already there before one began to interpret it. In this way, I developed the aesthetics of my master, Luigi Pareyson, which was based on a continual dialectic between the legality of a form and the initiative of its interpretations, between freedom and fidelity.

My theory of interpretive cooperation of narrative texts, developed in *The Role of the Reader*,[4] took the same direction. The Italian title of that book was *Lector in fabula*,[5] and even that formula was an oxymoron. My book celebrated the cooperation of the reader insofar as every text tries to provide every "empirical" reader with instructions for becoming the Model Reader of *that* text.

If these were my premises, it was inevitable that I had to discuss deconstruction, at least insofar as my premises related to an old polemical assertion of Valéry according to which there is no true sense of a text. I have often repeated that my antideconstructive critique did not aim directly at Derrida – for whom deconstruction was a method of interrogation of philosophical texts. He has never denied that there are limits, or textual *guardrails* that control an interpretation, which is not the case for his American followers. In any case, I countered any celebration of interpretation as misinterpretation.

I established a sort of Popperian principle according to which if one cannot legitimate good interpretations, it is always possible to invalidate the bad ones. A text must be taken as the parameter of its own interpretations (even if each new interpretation enriches our comprehension of this text, that is, even if every text is always the sum of its proper linear manifestation and its given interpretations). But to take a text as a parameter of its own interpretations, one must admit, at least for the moment, that there exists a critical language acting as a meta-language authorising the comparison of the text with all of its history and with the new interpretation.

I understand that this position seems offensively neopositivist. Indeed, it is against the notion of interpretative meta-language that the Derridean idea of deconstruction and drift arises. But I did not say that there is a metalanguage different from ordinary language. I said that the notion of interpretation requires that a part of our ordinary language may be used in order to interpret another part of the same language. Its root lies in the Peircian principle of interpretance and unlimited semiosis.

A critical metalanguage is not a language different from the object language. It is a portion of the same object language, and in this way, it is the function that any language fulfils when it speaks about itself.

The autocontradictory character of the alternative position is proof of the validity of the thesis I maintain.

Let us suppose that a theory asserts that any interpretation of a text is a misinterpretation. Let us suppose that there are two texts, Alfa and Beta. Alfa is given to a reader, and this reader obviously cannot but misunderstand it. Let suppose that his misreading is expressed by a text Sigma. Let us now give the texts Alfa, Beta, and Sigma to a second subject, telling him/her that every interpretation is a misinterpretation and then asking him/her to decide whether Sigma is a misinterpretation of Alfa or a misinterpretation of Beta.

Let us suppose now that the second subject says that Sigma is a misinterpretation of Alfa. Shall we say that he/she is right? Let us suppose, on the contrary, that the subject says that Sigma is a misinterpretation of Beta. Shall we say that he/she is wrong? In both cases, if we approve or disapprove of the subject's answer, we are supposed to believe that a text controls and selects not only its own interpretations but also its own misinterpretations. By approving or disapproving of the answers of the second subject, we would behave as somebody who does not absolutely consider that any interpretation is a misinterpretation, because we use the original text as a parameter for distinguishing between right and wrong interpretations. Any sign of approval or disapproval of the second subject's answer would presuppose on our part both a previous interpretation of Alfa (to be considered as the only correct one) and our confidence in a critical metalanguage to be used in order to say why Sigma is a misinterpretation of Alfa and not of Beta.

The only means to escape this contradiction would be to assume that whatever the subject's answer, it is good. Sigma could be a misinterpretation just as Alfa and Beta could. In this case, it could also be the misinterpretation of any other possible text. This being said, Sigma would indubitably be, then, a text, and a perfectly autonomous one; but why thus define it as a misinterpretation of another text? If it is the misinterpretation of any other text, it is nobody's interpretation: Sigma would exist for itself and would demand no other text as its own parameter.

But such a solution, even though philosophically "elegant," implies a major inconvenience, namely, the collapse of any theory of textual interpretation: texts exist, but no other text can speak about them. This amounts to saying that somebody speaks but that nobody can venture to say what that person says. At most, we could say that we used a first text to produce a new one, but that after the appearance of the new text, we should consider the previous one only as a vague stimulus that influenced in some ungraspable way the production of the new text.

In order to escape such a predicament, in my *The Role of the Reader* I outlined a dialectic between *intentio operis* and *intentio lectoris* that represented a semiotic way of reproposing the dialectic between Work and Opening.

Such had been my position about the interpretation of texts. But these convictions could only bring me to widen this vision of the interpretation of texts to the world in general. And, moreover, I could not do otherwise because I was becoming closer (at least from the beginning of the seventies) to Peirce's theory of interpretation.

At that time I had to reconcile my ideas regarding the limits of interpretation with the notion of *encyclopaedia*, as opposed to the hierarchical and tree-like structure of the dictionary. At the beginning of the eighties, in *Semiotics and the Philosophy of Language*,[6] I had structured my criticism of the dictionary as a Porphyrian Tree by opposing as an alternative the encyclopaedia as a rhizomatic and labyrinthine structure. Now, one could say that in a labyrinth there are no privileged directions, and thus there is no limit. But if we want to remain faithful to the metaphor of the labyrinth, we must remember that a labyrinth is always something preconstructed, where the freedom of the guest is in a sense limited by possible routes, and, in the second place, that the labyrinth of the encyclopaedia is not a natural fact but a social product and thus the result of a series of negotiations, rules put forth by a Community.

Let us now turn to Gianni Vattimo. In 1983, I contributed a piece for the collection *Il pensiero debole*, edited by Gianni Vattimo and Pier Aldo Rovatti (Milan: Feltrinelli). This collection was designed to be, in the mind of its creators, a discussion between authors of various positions around this proposition of "weak thought," the copyright of which belonged for a long time to Vattimo. Indeed, in my contribution ("L'antiporfirio") I opposed the positions of (let us say) *strong weak thought* (i.e., the hermeneutic line of Nietzsche-Heidegger) to the Peircean philosophy of conjecture and fallibilism. Certain readers, however (in general, those who do not read the books but only their titles), took the Vattimo-Rovatti's anthology as a manifesto, and I realized later that they definitely enlisted me among the theorists of the weak thought.

What are the differences between my positions and the theory of weak thought? I tried to trace them in my book *Kant and the Platypus*, which begins with a chapter on Being, where I elaborated models of our interpretation of the world.

Let us build an elementary model that contains a World and a Mind that knows it. The World is a set consisting of elements (let me call them *atoms*, in the sense of *elements*, or *stoikheîa*) structured according to a reciprocal relationship. As for the Mind, it is not necessary to conceive it as a human mind, as a brain, as a *res cogitans*, or whatever: the Mind is only a simple device capable of organizing propositions, offering us a description of the world. This device consists, in its turn, of elements (which we could call neurons, bytes, or *stoikheîa*, again, but let me call them, for the sake of convenience, *symbols*).

By World, we understand the universe in its "maximum" version,

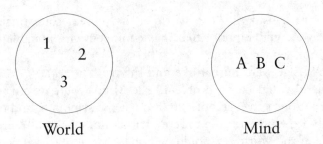

Figure 1
First possibility: 123 = ABC.
Second possibility: 123 = ABC, BCA, CAB, ACB, BAC, CBA.

that is, the universe that includes what we consider as the actual universe as well as the infinity of possible universes. This universe includes real objects as well as abstract, ideal, or fictional entities, from God and the Pythagorean theorem to Odin or Tom Thumb.

To oppose a Mind to the World could make one think of a form of Cartesian dualism, of *res cogitans* and *res extensa*. Indeed, we should conceive of a World capable of interpreting itself, which delegates a part of itself for this purpose such that some of its infinite or indefinite atoms take the role of symbols that could represent all other atoms. This is exactly what we human beings do, for example, when we use certain sounds (that we utter as words of our ordinary language) to define phonological phenomena. In other words, the World as the totality of being is something that secretes in its periphery (or in its centre, or here and there in its interstices) a part of itself as a means to interpret itself.

Thus the Mind could be represented not as if put *before* the World but as if *contained* by the World, and it could have a structure that enabled it not only to talk of the world (which is opposed to it) but also of itself as a part of the world and of the same process whereby it, a part of the interpreted, may serve as interpreter. At this point, however, we would no longer have a model but precisely what the model was clumsily trying to describe. Let us therefore accept all the limitations, and the apparently dualistic nature of the model, and continue.

First hypothesis. Let us imagine that the World is composed of three atoms (1, 2, 3) and that the Mind has three symbols (A, B, C). The three worldly atoms could combine in six different ways, but if we limited ourselves to considering the World in its present state (including its history), we could suppose that it is equipped with a stable structure given by the sequence 123.

If knowledge were mirror-like and the truth *adaequatio rei et intellectus* there would be no problem. The Mind would assign (not arbitrarily) to atom 1 the symbol A, to atom 2 the symbol B, and to atom 3 the symbol C, and with the ordered triplet ABC it would represent the structure of the World. It should be noted that in this case there would be no need to say that the mind "interprets" the World: it *would represent it in a mirror-like way*.

A problem arises if the assignation of the symbols to atoms is arbitrary: for example, the Mind could also assign A to 3, B to 1, and C to 2, and by combinatorial analysis it would have six possibilities of faithfully representing the same 123 structure. It would be as if the Mind disposed of six different languages to describe a World that was always the same one and to describe it in such a way that different triplets of symbols always stated the same proposition. If we admit the possibility of total synonymy, the six descriptions would still be six mirror-like representations. But the metaphor of six different mirror images of the same object allows us to think that either the object or the mirror have moved every time, providing six different aspects. At this point it would be better to go back to talking about six interpretations.

Second hypothesis. The symbols used by the Mind are less numerous than the atoms of the World. The symbols used by the Mind are still three, but the atoms of the World are ten (1, 2, 3 ... 10). If the World were always structured by triplets of atoms, by factorial calculation it could group its ten atoms into 720 different ternary structures. The Mind would then have six triplets of symbols (ABC, BCA, CAB, ACB, BAC, CBA) to account for 720 triplets of atoms. Different worldly events, from different perspectives, could be interpreted by the same symbols themselves, which amounts to saying, for example, that we would always be obliged to use the ABC triplet of symbols to represent 123, or 345, or 547. We would have a bewildering superabundance of homonyms.

The problem would not change – except for ulterior complications – if the World were organized not in a stable manner but chaotically (and if it were capricious, evolutionary, bent on restructuring itself in time). By continually changing the structure of the triplets, the language of the Mind would have to adapt itself continually, always because of an excess of homonyms, to the different situations.

Figure 2
First possibility: the World groups its ten atoms into 720 different ternary structures. The Mind would then have six triplets of symbols (ABC, BCA, CAB, ACB,
BAC, CBA) to account for 720 triplets of atoms, which amounts to saying, for
example, that we would always be obliged to use the triplet of symbols to represent ABC 123, now 345, now 547.
Second possibility: the World is hyperstructured; that is to say, it is organized in
accordance with a sole structure given by a particular sequence of ten atoms. By
combinatorial analysis, the World could organize itself into 3,628,800 different
decuples, or combinations. The Mind would still have only six triplets of symbols
with which to describe it. It could try to describe the World only a piece at a time,
as if it were looking at it through a keyhole, and it would never be able to
describe it in its entirety.

But it would be worse if the World were hyperstructured, that is to
say, if it were organized in accordance with a single structure given by
a particular sequence of ten atoms. By combinatorial analysis, the
World could organize itself into 3,628,800 different decuplets or combinations (let us not even think of a world that readjusts itself through
successive hyperstructuring, that is, one that changed the arrangement
of sequences at every moment or every ten thousand years). Even in the
event of the World's having a fixed structure (that is, if it were organized in a single decuplet) the Mind would still have only six triplets of
symbols with which to describe it. It could try to describe it only a piece
at a time, as if it were looking at it through a keyhole, and it would
never be able to describe it in its entirety. Which seems very like what
happens to us now and what has been happening to us in the course of
the millennia.

Third hypothesis. The Mind has more elements than the World. The
mind possesses ten symbols (A, B, C, D, E, F, G, H, I, J) and the World has

Figure 3

Example: The Mind could represent the world structure 123 through 3,628,800 decuples.

only three atoms (1, 2, and 3). And that is not all, the Mind can combine these ten symbols in duplets, triplets, quadruplets, and so on; as if to say that the cerebral structure had more neurones and more possible combinations among them than the number of the atoms and their combinations identifiable in the World. It is clear that this hypothesis should be immediately abandoned, because it clashes with the initial assumption that the Mind is also part of the World. However, we could also think of a World that in some way secretes more *res cogitans* than *res extensa,* that is, one that has produced an extremely small number of material structures, using few atoms, and that keeps others in reserve for use only as symbols of the Mind.

It would follow from this that the Mind would have an astronomical number of combinations of symbols to represent the worldly structure 123 (or at most its six possible combinations), always from a different point of view. The Mind could, for example, represent 123 through 3,628,800 decuplets, each of which not only accounts for 123 but also for the hour and the day on which it is represented, the internal state of the Mind itself in that moment, and the ends and intentions according to which the Mind represents it (granted that a Mind as rich as this one also has ends and intentions). There would be an excess of thought in relation to the simplicity of the world; we would have an abundance of *synonyms,* or else the stock of possible representations would exceed the number of the possible existing structures. And perhaps this is the way it happens, given that we can lie and construct fantastic worlds, imagine and foresee alternative states of things. In this case the Mind could very well represent even the various ways in which it is in the world. Such a Mind could write the *Divine Comedy* even if the

Figure 4
The Mind has an astronomical number of propositions at its disposal to describe
an astronomical number of worldly structures.

infundibular structure of the inferno did not exist in the World, or it
could construct geometries with no counterpart in the material order of
the World. It could even set itself the problem of the definition of being,
duplicate entities and being, formulate the question why there is something rather than nothing – given that it could talk in many ways of this
something – without ever being sure it was saying it the right way.

Fourth hypothesis. The Mind has ten symbols, as many as there are
atoms in the world, and both Mind and World can combine their elements, as in the third hypothesis, into duplets, triplets, quadruplets ...
decuplets. The Mind would then have an astronomical number of
propositions at its disposal to describe an astronomical number of
worldly structures, with all the possible synonymies that derive from
them. Moreover, the Mind could also (given the abundance of worldly
combinations not yet realized) design modifications of the World.

There would be not an excess of thought with respect to the simplicity of the World, as in the third hypothesis, but a sort of continuous
challenge among contenders fighting each other on a potentially equal
footing but in reality changing weapons for every attack and thus
putting their adversaries in difficulty. The Mind would confront the
World with an excess of perspectives; the World would avoid the
Mind's traps by continuously changing the rules (including those of the
Mind itself).

Yet again, all this seems very similar to something that has happened
and is happening to us.

Indeed, we are not obliged to decide which of our four hypotheses it
is necessary to retain. I think that they are quite valid in the sense that
they verify themselves in different moments of our interaction with

what surrounds us, but in any case each of the four hypotheses confirms that we cannot conceive facts except through interpretations.

But we cannot avoid a final question – a question that has become central in the postmodern world: if the perspectives on being are infinite, or at least astronomically indefinite, does this mean that one equals the other, that all are equally good, that every statement that says something is true, or that – as Feyerabend has said about scientific theories – anything goes?

This would mean to say that the final truth lies beyond the limits of the Western logocentric model, that it eludes the principles of identity, of noncontradiction, and of the law of excluded middle, that being coincides precisely with the kaleidoscope of truth that we formulate by attempting to name it, that there is no transcendental meaning, that being is the same process of continuous deconstruction in which our speaking of it makes it ever more fluid, malleable, elusive or – as Gianni Vattimo once said – moth-eaten and friable; in other words, rhyzomatic, a network of jumping-off points that can be travelled along according to an infinity of different options, a labyrinth.

Such an idea was born with Nietzsche, who was still not yet thirty, in *Ueber Wahrheit und Lüge im aussermoralischen Sinne*. Since nature has thrown away the key, the intellect plays on fictions that it calls truth, or systems of concepts, based on the legislation of language. Nietzsche's first reaction owes, I would say, a debt to Hume; the second is more decidedly sceptical (why do we designate things on the basis of an arbitrary selection of properties?); the third is a prelude to the Sapir-Whorf hypothesis (different languages organize experience in different ways); the fourth is Kantian (the thing in itself may not be grasped by the constructor of the language): we think we talk about (and know) trees, colours, snow, and flowers, but they are metaphors that do not correspond to the original essences. Every word becomes concept by its pallid universality taking the colour out of the differences between fundamentally unequal things: thus we think that in correspondence with the multiplicity of individual leaves there exists a primordial "leaf" on "the model of which all leaves have supposedly been woven, drawn, circumscribed, coloured, wrinkled, and painted – but by a clumsy hand – in such a way that no exemplar would seem to be correct and reliable as a faithful copy of the original shape." It costs us an effort to admit that birds or insects perceive the world differently from us, nor is there any sense in saying which of the perceptions is more correct, because we would need that criterion of "exact perception" that does not exist (ibid., 365), because "nature instead knows no form and no concept, and therefore no genus either but only an *x*, for us unattainable and indefinable."

Truth becomes then "a mobile army of metaphors, metonymies, and anthropomorphisms" that subsequently gel into knowledge, "illusions whose illusory nature has been forgotten," coins whose images have been worn away and are taken into consideration only as metal, so we become accustomed to lying according to convention, in a style that is binding for everyone, placing our actions under the control of abstractions, and having reduced the metaphors to *schemata* and *concepts*. Thence a pyramidal order of castes and ranks, laws and delimitations, constructed entirely by language, an immense "Roman columbarium," the graveyard of intuition.

That this is an excellent portrait of how the edifice of language regiments the landscape of the entities, or perhaps of a being that refuses to become set within categorial systems, is undeniable. But two questions are missing: whether by adapting to the constrictions of this columbarium we can manage to reckon with the world in some way (which would be no insignificant observation), and whether it doesn't happen that every so often the world obliges us to restructure the columbarium, or even to choose an alternative form to the columbarium (which is at the end of the day the problem of the revolution of cognitive paradigms). Nietzsche, who after all supplies us with the image of *one* of the ways of explaining the world that I outlined in the preceding paragraph, does not seem to ask himself whether or not the world has many possible forms. His is a portrait of a holistic system where no new factual judgment can intervene to throw the system into confusion.

In other words, to tell the (textual) truth, he recognizes the existence of natural constrictions and knows a way of change. The constrictions appear to him as "terrible forces" that put continuous pressure on us, opposing "scientific" truths with other truths of a different nature; but evidently he refuses to recognize them by conceptualizing them in their turn, since it was to escape from them that we forged ourselves, by way of defence, a conceptual suit of armour. The change is possible, not as a restructuring, but as a permanent poetic revolution: "If each of us, for himself, had a different sensation, if we ourselves could perceive now as birds, now as worms, now as plants, or if one of us saw the same stimulus as red and another saw it as blue, and if a third were even to hear this stimulus as a sound, then no one could talk of such regularity in nature."

And thus in Nietzsche's view art (and with it myth) "continuously muddles the rubrics and the compartments of concepts, presenting new transcriptions, metaphors, and metonymies; it continuously reveals the desire to give the subsisting world of waking man a figure so multi-coloured, irregular, devoid of consequences, incoherent, exciting and eternally new, which is that provided by the world of dreams" – a dream of trees that conceal nymphs and of gods in the form of bulls dragging along virgins.

But here the final decision is missing. Either we accept that what surrounds us, and the way in which we have tried to order it, cannot be lived in, and so we deny it and opt for dreams as an escape from reality (which is reminiscent of Pascal, for whom dreaming of being king really *every night* was sufficient grounds for happiness) – but Nietzsche himself admits that this would be a deception, and the dominion of art over life. Or, and this is what Nietzsche's followers have taken as the real lesson, art can say what it says because it is being itself, in its languid weakness and generosity, that accepts this definition too and takes pleasure from seeing itself seen as changeable, a dreamer, extenuatingly vigorous and victoriously weak. However, at the same time, in Vattimo's words, it must be seen no longer as "fullness, presence or foundation, but rather as fracture, absence of foundation, work and pain."[7] Being can therefore be said only insofar as it is in decline, it does not impose itself but absconds. This brings us to an "ontology organized in 'weak' categories."[8] Nietzsche's announcement of the death of God is nothing more than the proclamation of the end of the stable structure of being.[9] Being exists only "as suspension and withdrawal."[10]

But once the principle is accepted that being can be spoken of only in many ways, what is it that prevents us from believing that all perspectives are good and that therefore not only being strikes us as an effect of language but that it is radically the effect of language and nothing else but the effect of language, and precisely of that form of language that can permit itself the greatest unruliness: the language of myth and of poetry? Being would therefore be, as well as moth-eaten, malleable, and weak, pure *flatus vocis*. At this point it really would be the work of the Poets, understood as dreamers, liars, imitators of nothing, capable of irresponsibly putting an equine head on a human body and turning every entity into a Chimaera.

Not at all a comforting decision, given that once we have reckoned with being, we would find ourselves having to reckon with the subject that emits this *flatus vocis* (which is, moreover, the limit of every magic idealism). And that is not all. While it is a principle of hermeneutics that there are no facts but only interpretations, this does not prevent us from asking if there might not perchance be "bad" interpretations. Because to say that there are no facts but only interpretations certainly means saying that those that appear to us as facts are the effect of interpretation, but not that every possible interpretation produces something that, in the light of subsequent interpretations, we are obliged to consider as if it were a fact. In other words, the fact that every winning poker hand is constructed by a choice (maybe encouraged by chance) on the part of the player does not mean that every hand the player lays down is a winning one. It would be sufficient if my opponent played a royal flush to my three of a kind for my bet would be shown to be fallacious. Does our game with being begin as soon as Something replies with a royal flush to our three aces?

The real problem with every "deconstructive" argumentation about the classic concept of truth is not to demonstrate that the paradigm on the basis of which we reason could be fallacious. It looks as if everybody is in agreement about this, by now. The world as we represent it to ourselves is an effect of interpretation. The problem has more to do with the nature of the guarantees that authorize us to attempt a new paradigm that others must not recognize as delirium, pure imagination of the impossible. What is the criterion that allows us to distinguish between dream, poetic invention, and an "acid trip" (because there are people who after having taken the drug throw themselves out of windows convinced they can fly, only to wind up splattered all over the ground; an end, mark you, in net contrast with their hopes and intentions) and acceptable statements about the things of the physical or historical world around us?

We can even posit, as Vattimo does,[11] a difference between epistemology, which is "the construction of a body of rigorous knowledge and the solution of problems in the light of paradigms that lay down the rules for the verification of propositions" (and which seems to correspond to Nietzsche's portrait of the conceptual universe of a given culture) and hermeneutics as "the activity that takes place during the encounter with different paradigmatic horizons, which do not allow themselves to be assessed on the basis of some kind of conformity (to rules or, in the final analysis, to the thing), but exist as 'poetic' proposals of other worlds, of the establishment of new rules." What new rule should the Community prefer and what others condemn as folly? There are and will always be those who wish to demonstrate that the world is square, or that we do not live on the exterior but on the interior of its crust, that statues weep, that you can bend forks by television, or that apes descend from men – and to be flexibly honest and not dogmatic, we likewise need to find a public criterion with which to judge if their ideas are in some way acceptable.

In a debate held in 1990 with regard to the existence or otherwise of textual criteria of interpretation, Richard Rorty – broadening the discourse to include criteria of interpretation of things that are in the world – denied that the use made of a screwdriver to tighten screws is imposed by the object itself, while the use made of it to open a package is imposed by our subjectivity (he was discussing my distinction between the interpretation and the use of a text, as outlined in *The Role of the Reader*).[12]

In the oral debate Rorty also alluded to the right we would have to interpret a screwdriver as something useful to scratch our ears with. This explains my reply, which also remained in the printed version of the debate, without my knowing that in the speech sent by Rorty to the publisher the allusion to ear scratching had disappeared. Evidently Rorty had interpreted it as a simple *boutade*, an off-the-cuff remark made in the course of the conversation, and therefore I abstain from attributing this no longer documented example to him. But if Rorty does not use it, someone else might and therefore my counterobjection is still valid. A screwdriver can serve also to open a package (given that it is an instrument with a cutting point and one that is easy to use in order to exert force on something resistant); but it is inadvisable to use it for rummaging about in your ear, precisely because it is sharp and too long to allow the hand to control the action required for such a delicate operation. And so it would be better to use a light stick with a wad of cotton wool at its tip.

It suffices to imagine a possible world in which there is only a hand, a screwdriver, and an ear (and at most a package and a screw) for the argument to acquire all its ontological value: there is something in the conformation both of my body and the screwdriver that prevents me from interpreting the latter at my whim.

So now we might get out of this tangle: does there exist *a hard core of being* of such a nature that some things we say about it and for it cannot and must not be taken as holding good (and if they are said by the Poets, let them be held good only insofar as they refer to a possible world but not to a world of real facts)?

As usual, metaphors are efficacious but risky. By talking of a "hard core" I do not think of something tangible and solid, as if it were a "kernel" that, by biting into being, we might one day reveal. What I am talking about is not the Law of laws. Let us try rather to identify some *lines of resistance*, perhaps mobile, vagabond, which cause the discourse to seize up, so that even in the absence of any previous rule there arises, within the discourse, a phantasm, the hint of an anacoluthon, or the block of an aphasia.

That being places limits on the discourse through which we establish ourselves in its horizon is not the negation of hermeneutic activity: instead it is the condition for it. If we were to assume that everything can be said of being, the adventure of continuously questioning it would no longer have any sense. It would suffice to talk about it randomly. Continuous questioning appears reasonable and human precisely because it is assumed that there is a Limit.

For want of anything better, we have the fundamental experience of a Limit, of which language can say but beyond which it fades away into silence; it is the experience of Death.

Because we speak about being, knowing that there is at least one limit ("all people are mortal"), we can continue to wonder if there are no others. We learn by experience that nature seems to manifest stable tendencies. It is not necessary to think of obscure and complex laws, like that of universal gravitation, but of simpler, more immediate experiences, such as the rising and setting of the sun, gravity, the objective existence of the species. The universals may well be a figment and infirmity of thought, but once dog and cat have been identified as species, we learn immediately that if we unite a dog and a dog, another dog is born of it, but if we unite a dog with a cat, nothing is born of it – and even if something were born, it would not be able to reproduce itself. This still does not mean that there is a certain (I would like to say "Darwinian") reality of the genera and species. It is only intended to suggest that *something* resistant has driven us to invent general terms (whose extension we can always review and correct). The objection that one day some biotechnology might make this grain obsolete is invalid: the fact that any breach of it would require a technology (which by definition alters natural limits) means that natural limits exist.

There is nothing to exclude that there might be a world in which these confines between the species might not exist, where the confines are other or even absent – that is, a world in which there are no natural genera and in which the crossing of a camel with a locomotive might produce a square root. Nevertheless, if I can think of a possible world in which only non-Euclidean geometries are valid, the only way I can think of a non-Euclidean geometry is to establish its rules and therefore its limits.

My idea of a series of resistance of being arises from semiotics, the semiotics of Hjelmslev. We use signs to express a content, and this content is carved out and organized in different forms by different cultures (and languages). What is it made from? From an amorphous stuff, amorphous before language has carried out its vivisection of it, which we will call the *continuum* of the content, all that may be experienced, said, and thought: the infinite horizon, if you will, of that which is, has been, and will be, both out of necessity and out of contingency. It would seem that before a culture has organized it linguistically in the form of content, this *continuum* is everything and nothing, and therefore eludes all determination. Nevertheless, scholars and translators have always been perplexed by the fact that Hjelmslev called it *mening*. In the English translation (which the author co-signed with his translator),[13] *mening* is translated by "purport," but it is evident that this *mening* also means "sense."

Hjelmslev says that different expressions such as *jeg véd det ikke*, I do not know, *je ne sais pas, naluvara* (as well as expressions such as *piove, il pleut*, it is raining) "have a factor in common, namely the purport, the thought itself," even though this purport still exists as an amorphous mass and receives a particular form only in and through a particular language.

What does it mean to say there is "purport" before any sensate articulation effected by language? If we translate Hjelmslev's *mening* as "sense," we have to understand it as *direction* or *tendency* (in many languages a one-way street is a street with a *single sense*). This would mean that in the magma of the *continuum* there are lines of resistance and possibilities of flow, as in the grain of wood or marble, which make it easier to cut in one direction rather than another.

If the *continuum* has a grain, unexpected and mysterious as it may be, then we cannot say all we want to say. Being may not be comparable to a one-way street but to a network of multilane freeways along which one can travel in *more than one direction*; but despite this, some roads will nonetheless remain deadends. There are things that cannot be done (or said).

To say that there are lines of resistance does not yet mean, as Peirce would have said, that there are universal laws at work in nature. The hypothesis of universal laws (or the hypothesis of a specific law) is only one of the ways in which we react to the onset of a resistance. To state that there are lines of resistance merely means that our language does not construct being *ex novo*: it questions it, in some way always finding something *already given* (even though being already given does not mean being already finished and completed). Even if being were moth-eaten, there would always be a fabric whose warp and web, confused by the infinite holes that have eaten into it, still subsist in some stubborn way.

This *already given* is in fact what we have called the lines of resistance. The appearance of these Resistances is the nearest thing that can be found, before any First Philosophy or Theology, to the idea of God or Law. Certainly it is a God who manifests himself (if and when he manifests himself) as pure Negativity, pure Limit, pure "No," that of which language cannot or must not talk. In this sense it is something very different from the God of the revealed religions, or it assumes only His severest traits, those of the exclusive Lord of Interdiction, incapable of saying so much as "go forth and multiply," but only intent on repeating "thou shalt not eat from this tree."

Obviously to state that being says no is another metaphor. In fact Being says no in the same way a tortoise would say no if we asked it to fly. It is not that the tortoise realizes it *cannot* fly. It is the bird that flies, in its own way it knows it can fly, and it does not conceive of not being able to fly. The tortoise proceeds on its earthbound path, positively, and does not know the condition of not being a tortoise. It is we, given that the Mind can also provide imaginary representations of impossible worlds, who ask things to be what they are not, and when they carry on being what they are, we think they are telling us no and setting limits for us. We are the ones who think that our leg (in articulating at the knee) can describe some angles, from one hundred and eighty to forty-five degrees, but it *cannot* trace an angle of three hundred and sixty degrees. The leg – for what little a leg can be said to "know" – is unaware of any limits and is aware only of possibilities. To us, who capriciously would like to live on, death itself appears as a limit, but for the organism it arrives when things go exactly as they must.

Being never tells us no. Simply, faced with a demanding question on our part, it does not give the answer we would have wished. But the limit is in our desire, in our reaching out for absolute freedom.

What I have just said about the world or about being generally can be said for bigger reasons of the texts we produce or that we interpret after others produced them. And so, the open multiplicity of our interpretations is always confronted with the solidity of the *already given* and of the *already said*. Our freedom plays on this limit.

We are opposing to the limit of the *already given* the force of a *conjectural thought*. If Vattimo said that his "weakness" is a metaphor for the assumption that every knowledge cannot be but conjectural, then (at least on this point) we can agree.

NOTES

1 "La ligne et le labyrinthe: Les structures de la pensée latine," in Georges Duby, ed., *Civilisation latine* (Paris: Orban 1986).

2 Bloomington: Indiana University Press 1990

3 *Opera aperta* (Milan: Bompiani 1962; English tr. Cambridge: Harvard University Press 1989).

4 Bloomington: Indiana University Press 1981.

5 Milano: Bompiani 1979.

6 Bloomington: Indiana University Press 1984.

7 G. Vattimo, *The Adventures of Difference: Philosophy after Nietzsche and Heidegger* (1980), trans. Cyprian Blamires with the assistance of Thomas Harrison (Baltimore: Johns Hopkins University Press 1993), 73.

8 Ibid., 5

9 G. Vattimo, "Dialectics, Difference, and Weak Thought," trans. Thomas Harrison, *Graduate Faculty Philosophy Journal* 10, no. 1 (spring 1984): 158. (Editor's note: this essay was originally presented in Vattimo and Rovatti's edited collection *Il pensiero debole*).

10 G. Vattimo, *Beyond Interpretation* (1994), trans. David Webb (Cambridge: Polity Press 1997), 13.

11 Ibid., 79.

12 See Umberto Eco, *Interpretation and Overinterpretation* (Cambridge: Cambridge University Press 1992).

13 Prolegomena to a Theory of Language (Madison: Wisconsin University Press 1943).

3

Modern Moral Rationalism

CHARLES TAYLOR

There is a mode of thinking in modern moral philosophy that is perhaps most evident in analytical philosophy in the Anglo-Saxon world, but also influential elsewhere. Analytic philosophy has lots of good qualities. But one of its drawbacks is a tendency to narrowness on certain questions. And one of the most marked sites of this narrowness is in moral philosophy.

The narrowness concerns more than just the range of doctrines considered, though it also consists in that. But more fundamentally, it has restricted the range of questions that it seems sensible to ask. In the end it has restricted our understanding of what morality is.

I have tried to sum this latter point up by saying that Anglo-Saxon moral philosophy has tended to see morality as concerned with questions of what we ought to do and to occlude or exclude questions about what it is good to be or what it is good to love. The focus is on obligatory action, which means that it turns away from questions in which obligation is not really the issue, as well as those where not just actions but ways of life or ways of being is what we have to weigh.

Another shorthand way of putting this point is that this philosophy tended to restrict itself to the right, at the expense of the good. If issues of the good life were allowed, independently of the issue of what is right, they were seen as a second zone of practical consideration, lacking the urgency and high priority of the moral. (Habermas has formulated this priority, which shows that this philosophical temper has gone beyond the Anglo-Saxon world.)

From within this narrow perspective, it could seem that moral philosophy had two main intellectual tasks: 1 try to work out exactly what the considerations are that tell us which action is right; 2 try to show that these are the right considerations, against other rival candidates.

Task 1 has a place because our sense of what is right starts off fuzzy and powerful, with strong but unclear intuitions; it stands in need of clarification. Task 2 is the exercise of founding.

It is not surprising that within this philosophical climate, the two main contenders were utilitarianism and Kant. For some writers, the main philosophical debate seems to be between these two outlooks. Rawls, in some sense inspired by Kant, seemed to assume in his original *Theory of Justice* that the rival he had to defeat was utilitarianism. The rest of the philosophical universe was given much shorter shrift.

I believe that this whole style of thinking offers a paradigm example of the kind of overreach of rationalism that Gianni Vattimo has been so effectively criticising as a feature of our world. First of all, it represents an astonishing narrowing of the scope of ethics in the light even of the Western tradition. This point has been made by a number of critics in recent years. Bernard Williams, for instance, points out the striking contrast between the ancients, whose starting point was the issue of the good life for a human being and who derived what we are to do in any given situation from their definition of such a worthwhile life, and many of our contemporaries who jump right in to the question of what we ought to do, as though this was a self-sufficient area.[1]

One could go beyond this and say that the ancients made the issue of moral motivation central. Plato, in *The Republic* for instance, answers the question of justice (which includes how we ought to act) by bringing us back to the issue of the right desire or motivation. The crucial question is what we love, in the sense of *philein*, whether reason, the Ideas, the true order of things, on one hand; or our desires and the appearances on the other (or indeed, as a third possibility, whether we are moved primarily to affirm ourselves, to be the "winners," the leaders, those who earn glory and honour: the so-called *philonikoi*).[2] From out of the right kind of *philein*, we can identify what the right thing to do is, and not otherwise. But the whole procedure of modern moral rationalism assumes the contrary: we can establish the "principles" by which we can select the right action without reference to the kind of motivation that might be sufficient to carry it out. We can enquire how to create the adequate motivation for our previously identified moral standards, as for instance Jonathan Glover does in a very interesting and often moving way in his *Humanity*, without any hint that the argument might have to proceed in the other direction.[3]

One could argue that the kind of understanding that emerges from the New Testament resembles in this respect Plato's rather than that of modern rationalism. How the Samaritan comes to see that he should rescue the wounded man is that he is moved in a certain way. "He had compassion on him" (Luke 10:33). It is a kind of being moved that the New Testament identifies very un-Platonically as a bodily feeling: the word *splangnizesthai* tells us that you feel it in your gut. The Samaritan follows his gut rather than an abstractable principle, something like "help people regardless of their ethnic or religious belonging."[4]

This shows the pertinence of a remark that Vattimo has frequently made. When we hear Aristotle say that he prefers the truth above his friends and so will criticize what the Platonists say,[5] we tend to nod in approval: surely he has his priorities right, even if we may not agree in this case. But Vattimo insists that a question is being begged here. We assume that the ethical truth ought to trump our *philia* for our friends. But what if what best deserves to be called moral truth emerges only in a certain kind of *philein*? In this case, the talk of trumping would be absurd and misguided. The fact that we all nod our heads when reading this passage of the *Ethics* shows only that we are so deeply into a rationalist model that this contrary possibility doesn't even occur to us.

Now a countermovement has got going in analytical philosophy in recent years. To some extent, it is the revenge of Nietzsche (Bernard Williams is important here). In another way, it reflects a return of Aristotle. In either case, it wants to restore the wider focus. One way of stating this is to introduce the stipulative distinction whereby "morality" is used for the narrower domain that is concerned with obligatory action and "ethics" for the wider domain, including issues of what is a good or worthwhile life. The influence of Nietzsche is at work here, but using the vocabulary does not mean we have to reject "morality"; it can be seen as a legitimate part of the larger domain of ethics. What it cannot be any more for the users of this vocabulary is the whole, or the one ultimately serious domain of the practical, trumping all others.

I would like to carry the debate a bit farther here. To start with, I want to articulate some of the reasons for the success of modern moral rationalism. I will be confronting them with some of the objections that have been made. There will be two main lines of argument here (in the section that follows). Then I will turn (in the next section) to a third, which concerns the inability of this rationalism to make sense of moral dilemmas. Finally, I will try to sum up the full weakness of contemporary rationalist moralities (in the last section).

First, we have to understand what was going for the narrow focus on morality. Two important orders of reason converged to encourage it: one was moral, one epistemological.

One can still sense the force of the moral reasons in the rhetoric of contemporary philosophers. Object to a utilitarian that one might legitimately put, say, one's own integrity before the obligation to do the act with the highest utility consequences, and one might invite the retort that one is self-indulgent, not really single-mindedly committed to human happiness, as one ought to be. We can see here in secularized form the traces of the Christian origins of this philosophy. If Aristotelian ethics starts with the question of what constitutes a good and worthwhile life and then raises the issue of what I owe to others within this frame, it has seemed to a certain Christian temper, present in all ages but particularly strong during the Reformation and early modern period, that the demands of charity are unconditional, that they override those of fulfilment. Concentrate not on your own condition but on practical benevolence.

This temper was strengthened by the cultural revolution that I have called the affirmation of ordinary life, which dethroned the supposedly higher activities of contemplation and the citizen life and put the centre of gravity of goodness in ordinary living, production and the family. It belongs to this spiritual outlook that our first concern ought to be to increase life, relieve suffering, foster prosperity. Concern above all for the fulness of life smacked of pride, of self-absorption. And beyond that, it was inherently inegalitarian, since the alleged "higher" activities could be carried out only by an élite minority, whereas leading rightly one's ordinary life was open to everyone.

There is a moral temper to which it seems obvious that our major concern must be our dealings with others, in justice and benevolence; and these dealings must be on a level of equality. One can emphasize more justice (Kantians) or benevolence (utilitarians), but there is a shared perspective that is inimical to the ancient primacy of ethics and that draws us powerfully to the narrower definition of the moral.

The second motive is epistemological. It concerns the demands of disengaged reason. I mean here self-monitoring reason, reasoning that can turn on its own proceedings and examine them for accuracy and reliability. We can scrutinize these proceedings to any degree of clarity, even up to the undeniably binding. This is the great contribution of Descartes, which he expressed in terms of *les idées claires et distinctes*.

This is opposed to uses of reason that try to get a good purchase on some domain: analogues of perception, but also discerning the qualities of a piece of music, being able to tell what people are about, how they stand to the matter and to you, and so on. We don't tend to call these "reason," but they have analogies to 'to logistikon' of Plato.

Disengaged reason means that we cease to rely on our engaged sense, our familiarity with some domain, and take a reflexive turn, deriving a method, because methods concern procedure. The sense of freedom and power that goes with this is part of the motivation. This move connects with the primacy of instrumental reason.

In this outlook, the prospect of a single criterion is very exciting. At last the fuzzy intuitions of common sense can be reduced to clarity. What is more, all incommensurabilities and, hence, difficult decisions can be ironed out. Utilitarianism both satisfies this demand for rigour and homogeneity and also fits well with the disengaged stance of instrumental reason. Think of the rhetorical self-portrayal of disengaged reason, daring to withdraw from the hold of sacred hierarchies, to stand back from them and assess them coldly in the light of how much *good* they do. And this good can be clearly measured. Here clarity-rigour, disengagement, and also philanthropy come together.

But Kantianism also gets a charge from being rigorous and homogeneous. Consider this facet of the Rawls phenomenon: people rendered almost drunk by the idea that they can use such rigorous reasoning – even rational choice theory – in ethics. (We should remember how much of the early discussion of *A Theory of Justice* concentrated on the deduction of the maximin principle that would supposedly guide the contractors in deciding the principles of justice behind the veil of ignorance.)

So we have this complex of motivations standing behind morality: the primacy of justice-benevolence with equality, on one hand, and disengaged reason, rigour, clarity, on the other.

Aristotle has offered the most telling criticism of this idea of rigour in his account of practical reason (*phronêsis*).[6] We can reconstruct the point this way: We perceive or intuit that something is right. This is not different in a crucial respect from our perceiving something to be the case. The perception is possible only against a whole background. The background is a grasp we have on things, which can be in some degree articulated, but which remains largely inarticulated, and whose articulation would be an endless task. We can't give an exhaustive list of criteria in either case, because of this role of the background.[7]

This is not to say that articulation doesn't help. We can see that it often does. So someone makes us aware of part of what makes us say that the cat is on the mat; more seriously, what we're doing when we're following signs; more seriously again, how we recognize that this is the beginning of the recapitulation in a movement of sonata form. But relying on the articulated factors itself leans on our background understanding, so that in certain cases, we can see that they are not relevant, or are relevant in a different way.

Somebody makes me aware of the rhetorical tricks my colleagues are using: "Everyone agrees that ... " "It has become clearer and clearer that ..." But I musn't run away and assume that every time these words are pronounced just this kind of trick is being tried, just as a computer program might print out "RT" as it's processing the transcript. What if people begin to build in this sophistication and pronounce these words semi-ironically? What if a culture arises in which everyone really does agree about x?

Similarly with seeing that something is the right thing to do. We may be helped by some articulation, but it could never replace judgment by some algorithmic method. It may help a great deal to know that what is right with this action is, for instance, that it shows real generosity to someone who needs it. But what are the boundaries of need, and what in each case amounts to real generosity?

What is moral understanding? To a large degree, it is a kind of know-how, like tact; for example, knowing how to treat someone with sympathy and consideration.[8] A lot of moral understanding exists at the level of Bourdieu's *habitus*.[9] And if you don't possess some capacities in one or other of these modes of know-how, you won't be able to do the right thing in certain circumstances: for instance, if you lack the tact of sympathy I just mentioned.

But it involves more than know-how, the analogue of smooth, unarticulated expert performance. The moral life is also the object of articulations everywhere. These take various forms. Some of the moral life is laid out in explicit norms, which of course in turn suppose know-how if they are to be obeyed. But there are also other forms of articulation in a broad sense of this term. Our moral consciousness is fed by models and paradigms: certain exemplary people or stories (like the parable of the good Samaritan). These inspire us as well as helping us define what is good. And then there are the various attempts to define the good that philosophy sometimes offers. But these suppose and couldn't replace *habitus* and moral tact.

This seems to condemn the project of devising a single explicit criterion (or indeed, a plurality of such) from which one could derive all and only right actions – the utilitarian calculus or the different formulations of the Categorical Imperative. Because in the light of the above it would seem that knowing the right (or the best) thing to do can rarely if ever be a matter just of applying an explicit criterion.

"Phronetic" judgements often involve assessments of importance. What is need? in the case above. Taking this into account renders highly implausible the kind of clear hierarchy supposed by single-term moralities, where justice-benevolence is on a different plane from the fulfilments of the good life. Suppose I agree that in some sense there is something uniquely weighty about helping others; suppose I think that I ought to be ready to sacrifice myself. Still, I can't just assume that where there is an issue of helping and also one of self-fulfilment and the two considerations pull in opposite directions, I ought to give the priority to helping. Suppose the need of the other is relatively trivial, and the fulfilment in question is central. I don't throw away my career as a concert pianist to raise an extra ten dollars for Oxfam.

Single-term moralities offer us a homogeneous, calculable domain of moral considerations. This seems right to their protagonists *a* because the exaltation of justice-benevolence over issues of fulfilment and the good life simplifies the domain of the moral and *b* because the calculability fits with the dominant models of disengaged reason.

Now there is reason to think that *b* is not a cogent *argument* but rather a good cultural *explanation* for the popularity of single-term theories. Principle *a* is questionable, although one might find it convincing in some form; but even so, this is not a good ground for holding to single-criterion moralities, because even if you grant it, you still can't simply put *all* questions to do with justice-benevolence in a single category, to be decided without reference to any external considerations. You can't just say, this set of considerations *always* has priority, as Kant does with his categorical imperative, because this would be to exclude all questions of importance and put the most trivial demands of justice-benevolence over the most weighty of fulfilment.

Principle **a** is *one* sense that can be given to the slogan "the right has priority over the good." And analogies and close relations emerge in political theory. So, for instance, we entrench rights, and we say, protecting these rights takes precedence over all other considerations, for example, of the public good, happiness, and so forth. A project is being pursued in this entrenchment that we would all agree with. That is, with really essential rights, there shouldn't be any derogation for mere advantage. No one should condemn an innocent person or torture someone or deprive people of the right to speak their minds just because the GNP will go up or most people will have more satisfying lives or be in greater security. But these provisions have to be applied with a sense of how to distinguish the important from the trivial. One of the cases fought under the Canadian Charter of 1982, which won in first instance, was by a man who objected, on grounds of the Charter-protected right to freedom, to the Alberta law requiring the wearing of a seat belt.

But there are also other reasons for adopting single-term moralities. Or rather, the two big domains, epistemic and moral, are refracted in a multiplicity of ways. Here are some of them.

Principle *c*: These moralities deal with questions of fairness and justice between people. And these questions seem to many people more clear-cut, more capable of satisfying and unchallengeable solution than issues about fulfilment and the good life. These latter issues seem to allow of an indefinite proliferation of possible solutions, whereas issues of justice seem to call for clear-cut resolution. Anybody can fantasize about possible fulfilments: I can decide that I ought to spend my life like Simon Stylites atop a pillar. Are you sure you can tell me I'm wrong? But I can't just decide that I need your car, so that makes it all right.

Whether there is anything at all to this, plainly it's what people think. No one thought Rawls was out of his mind to try to decide between different principles of justice with the aid of rational choice theory. (Or perhaps, more correctly, some of us did think he was out of his mind, but we were a distinct minority, as the Rawls boom showed.) But people would have been stunned if he'd proposed to settle in this way questions of the good life.

Modern Western culture has made issues of epistemology central, and this has generated some skepticism about morality. But the skeptical sense falls unequally on the different kinds of consideration. Questions of the good life are more easily declared insoluble than those of justice.

Principle *d*: Another reason for distinguishing justice from the good life lies in our respect for people's freedom, which is also a central good of modern Western culture. Determining what constitutes the good life involves being able to tell people that they're mistaken when they propose another model to themselves. This is part of the suspicion of Aristotle among moderns. He's telling us that a certain form of life is the truly human one. That means that people who live other forms are declared wrong. It is thought that a real respect for their autonomy requires being agnostic on that, allowing them the space to design their own lives without forfeiting the respect and even support of their fellows.

But plainly this courtesy can't be extended to issues of justice, as the point above about my needing your car shows. Moral restrictions intervene where we have to direct the traffic between people seeking to fulfil life plans and giving everybody a chance but they oughtn't to intervene within the itinerary of any one agent, or so we tend to think. So a morality showing respect for freedom (itself an issue of justice) will make a sharp distinction between questions of justice and those of the good life and will moralize the first and leave the second unregulated. And so we generate the single-term moralities concerned with justice-benevolence.

Clearly d is in a relation of mutual support with c.

Principle e: There is a variant of d that returns as a principle of political theory. Someone may deny c as a principle of ethics, think that there are universal truths about the good life, that some people are wrong and are living tawdry and contemptible lives, and that we are perfectly at liberty to tell them so, but nevertheless hold that political society must give everyone the space to develop on their own and that this society should not espouse one or other view of the good life. Dworkin holds something like this.[10] This is a political transposition of a single-term morality. It is a basic definition of liberal society for some, but it doesn't require that these people hold to a single-term morality.

Staying with moral theory (hence leaving aside e), it doesn't seem to me that c or d do anything to make single-term moralities more plausible. Indeed, d may be thought to be incoherent. If there is a real issue of what is the good life for x – and why would there be a reason to take seriously his decisions on it if there weren't? – then why can't he be wrong?

But these reasons help explain something else about these theories: their thinness. They have a narrow view of what morality is as a dimension of human life.

Let's try to get at this issue by taking up the question, what's involved in being a moral agent? Everyone would probably agree: a moral agent is sensitive to, responding to certain considerations, the ones we think of as moral, or a moral agent is capable of responding to these considerations. To speak a dialect of Heideggerese: the agent has moral meanings in his/her world.

So what is it to have these meanings? Much contemporary Anglo-Saxon moral philosophy concentrates on the agent's having a sense that s/he ought to do certain things. The focus is on what we are obliged to do. The intellectual interest concentrates on getting clear what the things we're obliged to do have in common. One theory says that they all involve maximizing human happiness; another that they all involve our not acting on maxims that are not universalizable. Another way of putting this goal: philosophy is seeking here a way of deriving our obligations, a test by which we can see what we're morally obliged to do.

But ethics involves more than what we're obligated to do. It also involves what it is good to be. This is clear when we think of other considerations than those arising from our obligations to others, questions of the good life and human fulfilment. But this other dimension is there even when we are talking about our obligations to others.

The sense that such and such is an action we're obligated to by justice cannot be separated from a sense that being just is a good way to be. If we had the first without any hint of the second, we would be dealing with a compulsion, like the neurotic necessity to wash one's hands or remove the stone from the road. A moral obligation comes across as moral because it's part of a broader sense that includes the goodness, perhaps the nobility or admirability, of being someone who lives up to it.

The obligation to do and the goodness in being are two facets, as it were, of the same sense. Each totally without the other would be something very different from our moral sense: a mere compulsion, on one hand, a detached sense of the superiority of one way over another, on the other hand, comparable to my aesthetic appreciation of cumulus over nimbus clouds, not making any demands on me as an agent.

Contemporary philosophy has explored one facet at length but said almost nothing about the other. But this too can be articulated; something more can be said about the goodness of different ways of being. Traditionally philosophical theory has explored this in the language of virtue. But even more important for our moral consciousness has been the portrayal of good and bad lives in exemplary figures and stories. Our moral understanding would be crippled if we had to do without this. Christian moral theology without the Gospel would be an even stranger affair than it is. Nevertheless, this whole domain of the articulation of the good, whether philosophical or narrative, has been relatively neglected in Anglo-Saxon moral philosophy. Why?

One answer could be the hard-headed reason that we don't need to explore this in order to know what to do. Philosophy should help us clarify obligation. So finding out that what really makes an action obligatory is its furthering the general happiness is really useful stuff. Just being more articulate about the kind of good person you are when you do this adds nothing. It's a form of self-indulgence.

But this won't really stand up. We often need to be clearer on the goods involved in order to deliberate well. Take the domain favoured by single term morality itself: justice-benevolence. There is an internal tension that can arise here between the two terms. The following issue can arise: When should we override justice in the name of benevolence? Should we ever override it at all? Traditionally put, this is the issue of justice versus mercy. To answer these questions, we may find ourselves looking at what kind of good it is to be a just person and what it is to be benevolent. We will be thinking of how to place these two virtues in our lives. A fortiori when it is a matter of thinking how to combine justice-benevolence and the virtues of fulfilment or of the good life. The belief that all the moral deliberation we need can be effected with a calculus of obligated action is another illusion of the erroneous single-term moralities and only makes sense on condition that their homogeneous domain exhausts the moral. Ethical thinking, to use this term for the broader domain, sometimes also requires deliberation about what it is good to be, in order to determine what to do in certain circumstances.

An example derived from Bernard Williams: The course of action with the highest utility consequences clashes with what my integrity would demand. I am minister of forests in the Red-Green coalition government. I am also head of the Green Party. I am reluctantly persuaded that the least bad really available course of action in the situation is to chain-saw a section of rain forest. But I ask the prime minister to relieve me of my portfolio. Let someone else do the deed. Deciding this involves weighing not just actions and their consequences but also qualities of being, that is, assessing the action also by how it fits into a whole life, constituted not only of other actions but also feelings, commitments, solidarities, and so on. The same order of considerations is in play if you think that I am just indulging my image here and ought to take responsibility for what has to be done. In either case, I need to get clear on what it is good to be and how important this is relative to the other considerations in play.

This brings us to the issue of moral dilemmas. Single-term moralities by their very nature have trouble doing justice to these dilemmas. The single criterion is supposed by its very nature to sort them out: you do the act with the greatest utility consequences, or you avoid acting on a non-universalizable maxim. That should end the matter and cut short the angst of what has been called "moral remorse."

But in our reality, things are different. We pursue a plurality of goods.

These goods can conflict in certain circumstances: liberty and equality, justice and mercy, commutative justice and comity, efficient success and compassionate understanding, getting things done bureaucratically (requiring categories, rules) and treating everyone as a unique person, and so on.

Not only does this create dilemmas, but dilemmatic situations differ in nonpredictable ways. This intensifies the need for *phronêsis*. We need a sense of the two goods in conflict in any situation and of the weight of each of the rival demands in relation to its own kind. If one is really weighty and the other relatively trivial, we know which way to lean.

So different examples of the "same" dilemma call for different resolutions. But there is more. It is in the nature of dilemmas that even in a concrete case, they may admit of more than one solution. That is, the "same" dilemma, defined by the goods in conflict, and in this concrete case, may admit of more than one solution, like quadratic equations with two unknowns. Why?

Because we are dealing not only with goods (justice and mercy, liberty and equality) but with the claims of certain people, certain agents. How they choose or can be induced to treat their own claims can have a fateful effect on the outcome. Someone has suffered a historical wrong; commutative justice demands redress. But there are other considerations. What might be considered full redress if we just look at the nature of the wrong will have other effects that may be damaging to parties who are either innocent or whose guilt is not all that total. This is obviously what arises in cases of historical redress: for example, with reparations payments to historical victims or in cases of transition from a despotic exploitative régime to a more open, democratic, egalitarian one. In this latter case, we have also to consider the effects of full reparations on the future coexistence of the descendants of exploiters and exploited in the new régime.

Now one "right" solution might be an all-things-considered award to the victims in a context where the two parties remain locked in conflict, at arm's length. But if they can be brought together, can talk, become motivated to try to find some good future basis for their common existence, then one may emerge with quite a different "award," or solution. Cases of contemporary transitional justice come to mind, like the Truth and Reconciliation Commission in South Africa. Of course, big questions arise about this: did the victims really agree? Who exactly were the victims? Were they rushed, pushed, forced into conceding too much? And so on. But the basic idea behind this kind of procedure was to get the former victims to accept that they could have a maximum of one kind of closure (the truth about what happened) at the cost of renouncing a lot that they could quite legitimately claim of another kind: punishment of the perpetrators, an eye for an eye. The aim was to find an "award" that allowed also for a reconciliation and therefore for living together on a new footing.

The important point here is this: one reason dilemmas admit of more than one solution is that they are frequently also conflicts between claimants, and these conflicts can be differently seen or interpreted by those involved. But further, by moving the interpretations in a certain direction, the same dilemma can be resolved in a less costly way to the two goods. That is, one resolution may be the only right one here, because the parties remain rigidly hostile and opposed to each other, insisting on their full "rights". As a result, the "award" to the victim is in one sense higher, therefore hurting the perpetrator more, but the resulting hostility also deprives the victims and their successors of the goods of comity and collaboration. As against this, the operation of a TRC can lift us to a new point where the issue is not so totally zero-sum. It can bring about, in relation to the first situation of total hostility, a win-win move.

Generalizing this, we can see that dilemmas have to be understood in a kind of two-dimensional space. The horizontal space gives you the dimension in which you have to find the point of resolution, the fair "award," between two parties. The vertical space opens the possibility that by rising higher, you'll accede to a new horizontal space where the resolution will be less painful/damaging for both parties.

Examples of this abound in modern politics. A "fair" resolution for Bosnia after the terrible mutual killing is perhaps this strange tripartite state with separate cantons and a triune presidency, and a great deal of uncertainty and instability. But imagine that, over time, some trust can be reestablished between the parties; then one can see the possibility of moving towards a more normal federal system.

That is why the great benefactors in politics are those whose charismatic interventions help a society to move up in this space; for instance, Mandela, Tutu.

Put another way, we can say that dilemmas of this kind are also trilemmas, or double dilemmas. First, we have to judge between claims A and B; but then we also have to decide whether we will go for the best "award" between A and B on the level we're now on or try to induce people to rise to another level. Great leaders here have a mixture of shrewd judgment of where people can be induced to go, as well as great charismatic power to lead them there. Mandela again.

The vertical dimension I've been talking about here is one of reconciliation and trust. And this whole discussion shows how inadequate it is to define morality in terms of a fixed code. This becomes all the more the case if we introduce a religious perspective, because this can place our actions in two dimensions: one concerns right action, but the other opens an eschatological dimension. This is also a dimension of reconciliation and trust, but it points beyond any merely intrahistorical perspective of possible reconciliation. It can, however, inspire vertical moves in history, like those of Mandela and Tutu. (Tutu's faith commitment is well known; I don't know what Nelson Mandela actually believes, but his whole move was obviously deeply inspired by Christianity, if only historically; forgiveness is a key category, however downplayed as a term here.)

The New Testament is full of indications of this. Take the owner of the vineyard who invited workers in at the beginning of the day, then successively at later hours until the end. His proposal to pay everyone one denarius is obviously outrageous as a suggestion for the basis of wages policy in a stable society; hence the protests of those who came at the beginning of the day. But the parable opens the eschatological dimension of the Kingdom of God: at the height of that vertical space, that's the only appropriate distribution. The Christian perspective has to contain a fundamental tension: God operates in that vertical dimension, as well as being with us horizontally in the person of Christ.[11] No fixed code based on a univocal rational procedure can be adequate to this predicament.

But something like this double-dimensionality is present in the secular world, even for those without faith, so long as they can envisage some transformation in history. Single-factor theories cannot cope with this.

So single-term morality perpetrates a drastic foreshortening of our moral world by concentrating only on what we are obligated to do. But the reduction is even more drastic than I have described hitherto.

I spoke of the things it is good to be, of virtues as "life goods" in *Sources of the Self* (1989). I also distinguished there what I called "constitutive goods." By that I mean features of ourselves or the world or God such that their being what they are is essential to the life goods being good. Examples in well-known traditional views: God having created us and calling us is a constitutive good for Judaeo-Christian-

Islamic theism; the Idea of the Good is one such for Plato; for Aristotle, our being animals having logos is one.

In these well-understood traditional ethics, articulating the life goods quite naturally leads to spelling out the constitutive goods. And moreover, getting clear on these helps to define more clearly and vividly the life goods. This is obvious in the theistic case, where among the most important life goods are the love and worship of God. But we can also see it in Plato, where a deeper understanding of the life dominated by reason has to pass through attaining a vision of the Idea of the Good. The truly good person is inspired to model him/herself on the order shaped by the Good. Similarly for Aristotle, we come to see better how to order the goods in our lives when we understand that we are animals possessing logos.

Now it might be thought that constitutive goods figure only in theistic or "metaphysical" ethics, that they have no place in a modern humanistic outlook. But this would be a mistake. In a modern humanistic ethic, the locus of the constitutive good is displaced onto the human being itself. In Kant, the sense of the dignity of human life as rational agency soaring above everything else in the universe is an example of the identification of a constitutive good in a humanist ethic. My claim is that something like this sense of the dignity and value of human life, of the nobility of rational freedom, underpins the ethical consciousness of our contemporaries and plays the two roles we can see it occupying in Kant's philosophy: it defines what it is about the human being that commands our respect when s/he is the object of our action, and it sets us an ideal for our own action.

And just as defining the virtues helps us to deliberate, understanding better as we do what it is good to be; so this understanding can be further aided by clarifying the constitutive goods. We help to clarify what it is good to be by getting clearer on just what is noble or admirable about the human potential.

Here again, we have two facets of the same exploration. On one face, we are defining the virtues, the qualities of life we want to have; on the other face, we are looking at what is: the human being endowed with its potential in its world. And we are taking inspiration from what we find worthy in this. There is, indeed, an important difference from the earlier theological or "metaphysical" ethics, insofar as on this second face these incorporated elements go beyond human potential: for example, God or the Good. But there is also a substantial overlap, and thinking on these two faces remains part of our moral understanding.

We are in some way *moved* by human powers (just as the theist is moved by the love of God); this forms part of the ethical meanings in our world, along with our sense of what it is good to be and what we ought to do.

The foreshortened single-term morality misses not only life goods but constitutive goods. It neglects not just the unarticulated know-how but misses a lot of what we need to articulate in order to know what to do. But there is an even more serious omission. I have been mainly talking in the previous section as though the point of articulation were to help one see what to do. But some of our articulations not only help us to define better what we want to be and do, they also move us, as I have just indicated. Articulating a constitutive good not only helps us fine-tune what we want to be/do, it also inspires and moves us to want to be/do it. And articulating the virtues can have a similar effect. This is nowhere more evident than in the recounting of the models and paradigms, exemplary people and actions, in real life or in story, that both inspire and guide us. Both functions frequently come together in these narrations, which also involve articulating goods of both kinds. Exemplary figures body forth life goods, but in some cases – the Gospels, the life of the Buddha – part of what is being conveyed is a constitutive good.

Moreover, these two functions are in part interdependent. Seeing better what a certain good involves can change your stance towards it – in either direction, of course: it can increase or decrease your attachment to it. Even more important, appreciating what's good about a good can be an essential condition of making finer discriminations about what it means to realize it. This is the point made by Aristotle where he holds that the *phronimos* has to have the right dispositions in order to discern the good. Bad moral dispositions don't destroy our understanding of mathematics, he says, but they do weaken our grasp of the *archai*, or starting points of moral deliberation.[12] To put it in more Plato-resonant language, in many situations really to know what to do, you have to love the good, and there is thus something self-defeating in confining ethics to the issue of what to do.

We return here to the primacy of a kind of *philein*, which I discussed at the beginning of this chapter.

If we give their due to the full range of ethical meanings, we can see that the fulness of ethical life involves not just doing but also being, and not just these two but also loving (which is shorthand here for being moved by, being inspired by) what is constitutively good. It is a drastic reduction to think that we can capture the moral by focussing only on obligated action, as though it were of no ethical moment what you are and what you love. These are of the essence of ethical life.

One of the reasons for shying away from all this, besides the many enumerated above, is the confused inarticulacy of modern naturalism. This comes from a deep reticence to talk about foundations and an inability to determine how to talk about them (which obviously strengthens the reticence).

After clarifying what we ought to do, utilitarians and contemporary neo-Kantians are left uncertain how to talk about the basis for accepting the whole range of obligations. Sometimes they just shift into another register, like John Mackie, and give a sociobiological account of how it's understandable that we have the norms we do. But that isn't articulating the good, because it in no way makes clearer what is good or admirable about what we seek; it just tries to explain in a quasi-scientific way why we seek it. (Although sometimes it is confusedly taken in the latter manner and then becomes part of the support for a reductive instrumentalist ethic.) Or else, some writers just terminate with the brute fact that our intuitions are what they are.

This is partly because of a confusion about what arguing "foundations" could be. This word is bad, because it implies something to the philosophical ear that is impossible. It implies that you could argue someone who shared absolutely no moral sense at all into morality. "Foundations" means you would have to take him from point zero of moral commitment to the full sweep of obligations you generate by your calculus.

This can't be done, but there is no reason to think that it ought to be or that something terrible is missing because it can't be.[13] The point of articulating our moral sense cannot be to provide foundations in this sense, though it can be a very powerful tool in real moral argument.

The famous line from Dostoyevsky, "If God does not exist, then everything is permitted," is often taken as an assertion that foundations have to be given. If I think God doesn't exist, I feel I can do anything; then you convince me he does, and I suddenly see that there are moral limits. But I think the sentence can be taken as a statement of the constitutive good that someone (Dostoyevsky?) recognizes without supporting a foundationalist view. What's the difference?

Articulating the good is in a way providing reasons, but not in either of the senses that are generally recognized by much contemporary moral philosophy. Let me outline the two senses. The first is giving a basic reason. I want to speak of a basic reason where we argue for doing A on the grounds that it amounts to doing B and where this justification is asymmetrical.

Basic reasons parallel the structure of purposive action. I am phoning George. You ask why? Because he's going to give me a job. Why do I want a job? Because I need the income to live. The action has several descriptions: *a* phoning George, *b* getting a job, *c* finding the means to live. But these are not on the same footing: *c* is basic; I go for *b* only because it amounts in this situation to *c*, and similarly with *a*. If I could live on the dole or find a job some other way, I wouldn't be phoning.

It is one of the self-given tasks of much modern moral theory to identify a basic reason in this sense. Pursuing the greatest happiness of the greatest number is one such. The minister of finance is *a* balancing the budget. She is (quite properly in this context) operating under utilitarian principles, so she is doing it, *b* in order to reduce inflation because **c** she believes that reduced inflation will increase economic well-being. The basic reason is *c*. If you convince her that the conjuncture requires a return to Keynesian policies, she'll run a deficit.

So one way of arguing for something is giving a basic reason. But when you've identified the basic reason and your interlocutor isn't moved by it, where do you go from there? It seems you have to set yourself another task: giving him that basic reason, that is, bringing it about that he takes on that basic reason as his own. Now you need to give reasons of the foundationalist sort.

But the articulation of life and constitutive goods is reason-giving in neither of the above senses. It doesn't give a basic reason for a policy described in less than basic terms, as increasing economic welfare does for balancing the budget. The two descriptions, pre- and post-articulation, of some life or constitutive good aren't related in this way. One gives a fuller, more vivid, or clearer, better-defined understanding of what the good is.

On a theistic view, God's will doesn't stand to loving my neighbour as *c* does to *b* and *a* in the examples above. Or rather, it does so only in the rather warped Occamite theologies that (Alasdair MacIntyre will, I believe, agree with me here)[14] have caused such havoc in early modern thought. On this view, the various actions open to us don't have moral value in themselves, but this is imparted to them only by the command of God. On a less strained and alien view (for instance, Thomist, but not only Thomist), invoking God's will is further expanding what is good about this, which I initially grasp as good by natural reason.

So you don't articulate a basic reason here. But nor can you cause another person to acquire a basic reason from a standing start. You have to draw on the interlocutor's moral understanding. Here's where articulating a constitutive good can awaken a dormant sense in the other person and in this way bring the basic reason to the fore. But there can also be arguments in this domain that can bring the interlocutor over to you. How these function, I have tried to explain at greater length elsewhere.[15]

The distorted understanding of practical reason is one of the grounds that have moved moral philosophy of a naturalist temper to make both kinds of goods an intellectual no-go area. But there also are confusions about what is entailed in the "antimetaphysical" stance of naturalism itself.

Drawing this together, we can see a link between two main lines of criticism offered here of single-term moralities: their attempt to develop high-definition decision procedures, denying the need for *phronêsis*; and their foreshortening of the moral domain.

We see what is wrong with the first when we note that our judgments of what to do take place in the context of a grasp of the good that is largely unarticulated. It consists largely of background understanding. Or else it is presented to us in paradigm persons or actions, or in internalised habitus. It can be articulated to some degree in descriptions of the good, and this can be very important, both for our knowing what to do or be and because it can move us to do or be it. But these descriptions are understood only in the context of background understanding, acquired habits, and paradigms, which can never be transcended or escaped.

When we see what the domain is that permits this articulation, we are induced to burst the boundaries of the foreshortened moral world and recognize the relevance for this world of what we are and love, as well as what we do. We thus conceive the place of articulacy in ethical life very differently. We not only see, *i*, its restricted scope but also, *ii*, its plurality of function: not only helping us to know what to do but also to know what we want to be, and even more crucially making us love the good; and, *iii*, we similarly see that the forms of articulacy are more widely varied, that philosophical definition is one mode, but that our understanding (including philosophical understanding) would be badly impoverished without moral narrative and admiring attention to exemplars.

Once we see this, we can break the spell of the narrow moral rationalism whose supposed strength and rigour merely hides a fundamental weakness. Thinking straight requires that we admit the full *debollezza* of our thought.

NOTES

1 Bernard Williams, *Ethics and the Limits of Philosophy* (Cambridge: Harvard University Press 1986).

2 Plato, *Republic* 9.581c.

3 Jonathan Glover, *Humanity* (New York: Yale University Press 1999).

4 See Ivan Ilich, *The Corruption of Christianity* (Toronto: Anansi 2005).

5 Aristotle, *Nicomachean Ethics* 1.6.

6 Ibid., book 6.

7 John Searle, "Literal Meaning"; Ludwig Wittgenstein, *Philosophical Investigations* (Oxford: Blackwell 1953) and *On Certainty* (Oxford: Blackwell 1977).

8 Cf. Patricia Benner, *From Novice to Expert* (Addison-Wesley 1984), and Hubert Dreyfus and Stuart Dreyfus, *Mind over Machine* (New York: Free Press 1986).

9 Pierre Bourdieu, *Le sens pratique*. I have developed this point further in "To Follow a Rule."

10 Ronald Dworkin, *Taking Rights Seriously* (Cambridge: Harvard University Press 1978).

11 In a profound discussion of the parable of the Good Samaritan, Paul Thibaud remarks that the Samaritan's response should not be seen simply as a one-off act. It inaugurates a new relation. "Cette relation s'étend dans le temps, elle peut connaître des étapes comme le montre l'évocation de la convalescence à l'auberge, elle inaugure un temps meilleur, unissant les protagonistes dans la perspective d'un avenir commun. L'horizon qui s'offre n'est pas un horizon apocalyptique, comme dans nombre d'autres paraboles évangéliques, c'est un horizon historique, d'amélioration du monde" ("L'autre et le prochain," *Esprit* (June 2004). I might add, and Thibaud might well agree here, that this historical horizon makes sense for Christians in relation to the deeper, apocalyptic one.

12 See *Nicomachean Ethics* 6.1140c.10–20.

13 I argue this further in "Explanation and Practical Reason," in *Philosophical Arguments*, (Cambridge: Harvard University Press 1995).

14 See *Three Rival Versions of Moral Enquiry* (Notre Dame: University of Notre Dame Press 1990).

15 In "Explanation and Practical Reason." I owe a great deal to the work of Alasdair MacIntyre in this area. See especially his *Whose Justice? Which Rationality?* (Notre Dame: University of Notre Dame Press 1989).

4

Which Ontology after Metaphysics? Conversations with Gianni Vattimo and Richard Rorty

GIACOMO MARRAMAO

Translated by Robert T. Valgenti

One of Gianni Vattimo's indisputable accomplishments over the past three decades has been to carry forward the "urbanizing of Heidegger" (to use the famous expression of Jürgen Habermas) initiated by the hermeneutics of Hans-Georg Gadamer in his truly *epochemachend* work of 1960 – *Truth and Method*. To that end, Vattimo's philosophical program – expressed by the very successful formula "weak thought," but in my view more adequately summed up in the expression "ontology of decline" – has made crucial contributions to the international scene, thanks to the initial convergence and to the subsequent uninterrupted confrontation with the neopragmatism of Richard Rorty. Based on the unconditional recognition of the importance of their work as authentic points of no-return for contemporary reflection, this essay will approach them with two ends in mind: 1 to bring forth, alongside their similarities and their zones of *overlapping*, some sensible differences between the problematics of these postmetaphysical "Dioscuri"; 2 to explicate some points of divergence between my perspective and theirs, specifically regarding how we understand and engage the postmetaphysical dimension (where I would also place myself). First of all, I must warn that given the otherwise synthetic nature of this text, the two ends that it pursues will give rise not to successive treatments but rather to a reciprocal exchange of counterpoints in a sort of "double movement."

It is well known that both Rorty and Vattimo accept that Western nihilism is historically and culturally situated. Vattimo claims in the introduction to *Nihilism and Emancipation* that "the very idea of a universal truth and a transcultural humanism (examples would be the doctrine of natural law and ultimate foundations) has arisen precisely within this particular culture."[1] From this idea follows the defining trait of our epoch: the "declension" of philosophy into sociology, and therefore the "sociologism" (mainly implicit and unwitting) that permeates contemporary philosophy. Under this rubric, Rorty's diagnosis of the present situation – according to which we currently live in a postphilosophical cultural climate – is undeniably pertinent.[2] Vattimo, however, does not seem satisfied with this claim. Rather, Vattimo wants to bring into question the reasons – not only the philosophical reasons but also the ontological reasons *strictu sensu* – that provide the basis for the present trend of sociologization and culturalization. In this way, the trend in question, which is visible in the realm of techno-science and in the disarticulation of the unity of experience in the multiple social roles that all of us discover and play, is related to the idea of the "epochality" of Being, an idea that was introduced by Heidegger after the *Kehre* through the category of *Ge-Schick* – of a destinal History intended as a mass of "sendings" from which the structure of our postmodern globality, at once uniform and differentiated, homogeneous and specialized, springs forth. It is worthwhile to insist yet again on this acute ontological narrative of the passage of Being from foundational metaphysics grounded upon the doctrine of the categories to the opening towards the *actuality* of the historical-cultural world: that is, to the moment when Vattimo's truly hazardous philosophical project seems tied to this narrative. The "thrownness" [*Geworfenheit*] of existence, which in *Being and Time* still risked being understood as Kantian transcendentalism, "becomes explicitly historical; Heidegger characterizes it repeatedly as a historical-natural language."[3] As a result, from the moment that Being is no longer an objective given that precedes the application of "conceptual schema" or a "pre-categorical" dimension but the very opening of the eventing, it is only within this "event" that the present identification of philosophy with sociology has any meaning.

But at this point, a series of questions presents itself to whomever – like me – does not identify with the Heideggerian reconstruction of the "history of nihilism and metaphysics" in terms of a unilinear trajectory that proceeds from the forgetting of Being to its final "unconcealment" in the *Ereignis*. I will limit myself to two questions that, from my perspective, have particular philosophical relevance: a question about the judgment of "epochality" and a question about the definition of "nihilism."

Regarding the judgment of "epochality,": according to which criteria and/or experiences can we affirm that historicity and contingency belong to our epoch and not to preceding epochs? Does not the definition of the present as the epoch of the opening to sociocultural actuality perhaps carry with it a criterion based on subjective perception of the "actors"? And finally, are not the "narratives" that delineate the occurrence of Western philosophy as an interweaving (or an alternating) of "organic" thought and "critical" thought, foundational strategies and antifoundational tendencies, perhaps more appropriate?

As for the definition of "nihilism," leaving aside the distance – underlined by me on several occasions in some of my works[4] – between the Heideggerian and Nietzschean meanings of nihilism, the question arises, Is antifoundationalism in the absolute sense even possible? Might not a philosophical modality of the logical-linguistic, discursive, or (thinking of political philosophy) contractual-conventional sort represent a (diverse) strategy of foundation? If one reduces the notion of nihilism to that of antiessentialism by making it coincide *sic et simpliciter* with the dissolution of the Subject-substance, must we also not conclude *a fortiori* that a rather large part of modern philosophy must be included in this category (not only Hume but also Hobbes, Kant, and Hegel)? On the other hand, if we accept nihilism in terms of the ontology of decline or even in terms of the erosion (however potential) of *every* foundation, then in what sense does the "constructivity" (to take up a programmatic definition of Vattimo) of hermeneutics distinguish itself from the various forms of absolute skepticism or relativism?

Let us work through this theme of ontology in order to project our insight towards the future of today's postmetaphysical *disputatio*. It is well known that some meaningful expressions of contemporary thought tend towards overcoming the traditional anitheses of ontology and history, on the one hand, or of ontology and epistemology, on the other, symbolizing a sort of *ontologie éclatée*. It is an antisubstantialistic ontology that is affirmed along gnoseo-critico lines (with a return to problems connected to the theory of the objects of knowledge and judgment, *à la* Meinong), as well as along historical-pragmatic lines.

One sees, furthermore, how Vattimo, in respect to Rorty, positively assumes the term "ontology" by taking up in his own way the Foucaultian expression "ontology of actuality." In "Postmodernity, Technology, Ontology" – the opening essay in the collection already cited (excellently edited by his disciple Santiago Zabala) – the specific difference between the perspectives of Rorty and Vattimo is explicated with great clarity and efficacy. Vattimo advances some doubts regarding the ability of pragmatism and neopragmatism to provide "strong" criteria for the justification of a political choice. This is so for the simple but decisive reason that Rorty never expects valid reasons from philosophy regarding the choice of democracy but, rather, expects that just the fact that we prefer to live in a democratic and tolerant society – for a series of reasons connected to the occurrence of the historical-cultural contest in which we find ourselves inserted – constitutes a good reason for abandoning metaphysics and even philosophy. Such a position – which, as we will see in a moment, finds its *pendant* in the thesis of the irrelevancy of history and political experience for the claims of truth in philosophy – refutes the indispensability of the return to ontology, even if in the historicized and open form of the decline and weakening of Being: "It might, however, be objected against Rorty that the kind of self-psychoanalysis of philosophy that he offers in *Philosophy and the Mirror of Nature*, with the aim of ridding current philosophy of its metaphysical heritage, is never fully accomplished; it is an interminabile analysis. *We still require an ontology, if for no other purpose than to demonstrate that ontology is headed toward disintegration.*"[5] A bit later, in the essay dedicated to the relation between philosophy, metaphysics, and democracy, an analogous objection is directed at a "radical interpreter and continuator" of Heidegger, like Jacques Derrida, for whom speaking of Being would be equivalent to a relapse into foundational metaphysics: "Yet to continue to speak of Being and ontology is not an excessive claim; it is rather an expression of modesty on the part of this philosophy, which knows that it is not obliged to respond to truth but only to the need to recompose the experience of a historical phase of humanity that is living trough the fragmentation of the division of labor, the compartmentalization of language, the many forms of discontinuity to which we are exposed by the rapidity of the transformation (technological above all) of our world."[6]

Out of these valuable and precise clarifications emerges the conclusion that – as Santiago Zabala acutely notes in his introduction to the most recent encounter between Rorty and Vattimo in *The Future of Religion* – "this is indeed the fundamental problem of philosophy today: taking leave of the foundational illusion, can philosophy really continue without ontological prejudices?"[7] And yet, two questions remain.

In the first place, does Vattimo's insistence on the necessary recomposition of the *disjecta membra* of languages and of experience not perhaps require a theoretical reconsideration of the problem of power that Rorty – in his important and stimulating collection of essays entitled *Truth and Progress*[8] – seems to consider an inheritance of a metaphysical past, a sort of Phantom of the Opera, clumsily recalling Foucault, that he relegates to the backroom of the West's *Theatrum Philosophicum*. Does the diagnosis of "compartmentalization" and of the reticulated dispersion of the forms of disciplinary ordering, with its logic at once de-territorialized (without a peak and without a centre) and self-referential, propose a new concept of power according to the order of the day: no longer modelled on the *distributive* paradigm but (as recent postfeminist and poststructuralist thought of difference has emphasized) on a *productive* and *generative* paradigm? It is difficult for me to shake the impression that in the final analysis Vattimo leads the discussion back to the persistence (at its base, residual) of strictly metaphysical forms, a place where I, on the other hand, am inclined to discern a new and more pervasive form of power in the operations (that are "weak" only in appearance) of the conventionalization of order and the "disciplinary" sectoring of labour-related functions and the divisions of knowledge.

In the second place, do we not possess the materials sufficient for concluding that ontology does not necessarily imply a restorative operation by *Platus redivivus*? Incidentally, it is helpful not to forget that the "Platonism" of modern science is in every case the unavoidable consequence of a gnoseo-critical acquisition connected to the deception of the senses – and the unavoidable consequence, therefore, of the necessary indispensability of the mathematical method as the *conditio sine qua non* for deciphering the language of nature, at this point clearly forbidden by common sense and its traditional link to sensory perception. All of us have taken to heart the lesson of Edward Said and of his postcolonial followers (from Chakrabarty to Spivak), with their warning to be suspicious of "false universals." But can we really be certain that all scientific practices – which are certainly not reducible to the performative operations of global techno-science – will reforge the connection between the obfuscation and reification of those false universals? Or is it not instead true that the praxis of scientific research attests already with Galileo – with all due respect to Heidegger and the Husserl of the *Krisis* – to the creative and innovative function exercised by dissent in the face of the system of beliefs transmitted by the community of interpreters.

It goes without saying that if the first scientific revolution did not involve any realism free from reflection and correspondence to something that one finds securely grasped "out there," then it was even more the case with the scientific revolutions that followed it. The extension of the semiotic metaphor of the code and the cryptogram – of decodification and of decryption – that took place during the middle of the last century through the transference of evidence from physics to the science of life no longer makes reference to the theme of the "mirror of nature" but rather to that of the isomorphism between the "subject" and "object" of knowing, both implicated in the structure of DNA, in the "strange ring of eternal garland" (an *Eternal Golden Braid*, according to the suggestive expression of Douglas R. Hofstadter)[9] made from the Great Code. This is an entirely new theme, postmodern if you will. But it is also an ancient theme: someone like Umberto Eco, who has long been familiar with the foundations of the great hermetic and cabalistic tradition, knows it well. I do not believe that I am suffering from a fascination with the "myth of the Given" (definitively desacralized by the critique of Sellars and, following his example, McDowell), much less developing a secret nostalgia for "full Being," if I affirm that it is out of this horizon, at once "familiar" and "uncanny" – in the Freudian sense of *das Unheimliche* – that it is necessary in my view to place it in the care of an *ontology of the contingent* that is capable of leaving behind both the hypostasis of metaphysics and also the providential frameworks (more or less secularized) of the history of philosophy. After all, don't Rorty and Vattimo refer us to the modernity of Hume rather than to that of Rousseau or Hegel?

And nevertheless, taking leave precisely from this point, I would like to conclude with a final question by referring to the Rortian thesis of the irrelevancy of history for philosophy, along with the *querelle*, already implied by it, of relativism.

In a recent interview for the Italian magazine *Reset*,[10] Richard Rorty raises several questions that I would like to reflect upon briefly. I have a great appreciation for the acumen and clarity of the arguments put forth in that interview. And yet, some points still remain open to discussion. First of all, there is the relation between philosophy and public life or – if one wishes – between philosophy and politics. In contrast to Rorty, I am convinced that philosophy and politics share a common origin: they have dwelt together from the very beginning in the public space of the polis. From Socrates onward, in fact, philosophizing is characterized by a relation of ambivalence, of proximity-distance, regarding common sense and the languages of the everyday. The "Silenus" pursues the truth with passionate determination, but at the same time looks with contempt upon the contempt the wise show for the beliefs of *common sense* [English in the original]. The new practice that takes on the name of philosophy distinguishes itself rather clearly from prior forms of wisdom (precisely of the *sophoi*, not of the *philosophoi*), as well as from the diverse paths of wisdom (belonging to "other" cultures).

And yet there is more. Politics and philosophy not only share a common origin, but they also belong to each other in their essence. We have everything present from the wonderful beginning of Plato's *Phaedrus*, where Socrates reveals to Phaedrus that in their search for shade outside the walls of Athens he notices his own lack of interest in nature. Socrates points out that what are important for him, what are able to tell him something truly interesting and "perplexing," are certainly not the trees but the men who move about the streets of the city and cross paths in their daily discourse. Here we find ourselves in the presence of a crucial transition, extremely illuminating as to the most basic relation instituted between philosophical questioning and the purely political dimension of the public space.

If we consider the shared origin and shared belonging of philosophy and politics, the thesis proposed by Rorty, according to which there would not be any relation between philosophy and the great historical events, appears to be provocative and in some ways scandalous: I think we should beware of what the French philosopher Vincent Descombes has called "'the philosophy of current events' – the temptation to say that Christianity is impossible after the Borgia papacies, or that poetry is impossible after Auschwitz, or that the existence of the gulag makes it impossible to be a socialist, or that a certain philosophical view cannot be held after 9/11."[11] Once, in the German debate of the last century, there was a person who had at first affirmed that *Weimar ist kein Argument*, just in order to maintain with contemptible shamelessness that *Auschwitz ist kein Argument* – Auschwitz is not a philosophical argument. But how is an idea supported? Is it possible to think that

Auschwitz has not affected the destiny of philosophy? Our way of understanding and perceiving fundamental philosophical questions? And furthermore, is it not a contradiction to deny – as Rorty does – the link between the great events and philosophy in order to affirm that our Western history, comprised of our ideas of freedom, equality, and fraternity, and – why not? – even of public justice, would be nothing other than the product of the secularization of Christianity? And could Christianity – one wonders – be the event par excellence? And if Christianity is an unavoidable event for the succeeding developments of modernity – something on which I believe we all can agree, believers and nonbelievers – for what obscure reason can we legitimately affirm that for philosophy the events have no meaning?

I could be wrong. But I have the feeling that the ethico-political pathos of Gianni Vattimo's most recent works bears a diverse perspective *in nuce*: either according to the relation between historical events and philosophical conceptuality or according to the shared origin of philosophy and politics. Or even better, according to the relation between philosophical integration and – to adopt an Arendtian expression – "the life of the polis." But before I close, I would like to offer a brief conclusion regarding the problem of relativism.

A final point I would like to deal with here regards the risk that, in my view, runs through the relativist and multicultural strain of liberalism today. I fear that in the contemporary world, characterized by a rebirth of fundamentalisms, the "tolerant" version of relativism, postliberal and multicultural, is in danger of being a party to such fundamentalisms. There is a simple and clear reason for this: the multicultural "recognition" of differences translates the idea (a correct one) of the incommensurability of the various visions of the world into a system (an erroneous one) of contiguous ghettos, each one sharing in the common practice of believing itself to be the one that is better than the others. And it is for this reason that the indifference inherent in multicultural tolerance can become objectively (or, in some cases, even subjectively) complicit with fundamentalisms. How, then, can we get to the bottom of the paradox inherent in the relativistic axiom of the incommensurability between the "worlds-of-life" and the constellations of value from diverse cultures? In this regard Richard Rorty exonerates himself by denying – as Hilary Putnam has correctly observed[12] – that there is a problem of truth (a problem of "representation"), and he limits himself to distinguishing pragmatically between the ideas that "succeed in doing it" and those that do not.

While I have developed a sincere admiration for Rorty's skills of argumentation, I nonetheless remain convinced that applying Ockham's razor between philosophy and politics, rationality and history, poses more problems than it is able to resolve. On this ground, the solution I propose is radically diverse. It is a matter, in few words, of beginning to comprehend (as I have tried to show in my most recent work)[13] that *incommensurability* does not in fact mean *incomparability*. It means, rather, that there does not exist, certainly, a predefined hierarchy of the good; but it also means that the way to the good depends on practices, on comparison and on dialogue (which, furthermore, in its Greek meaning does not in fact exclude trauma and discord, fractures and conflicts). The dialogical encounter comes to fruition, however, only if it operates in two directions. On the one side, it deconstructs the essentialistic and utilitarian-proprietarian statute of identity: by reaching the awareness that the identity of any one of us will never find a definite anchor in a *proprium*, in a series of "qualities" (in line with Robert Musil) or authentic attributes, nor will it realize itself in a relation to the world and to others along the lines of appropriation, being itself the result of a web of encounters and of intersections "contaminated" by alterity. On the other side, it de-contextualizes the horizon of the meaning of ethics and politics: if the practices and the contests of value from which one begins can only ever be "localized," the goals of the "politician" (of a "politician" worthy of the name) must be able to transcend the local into a delocalized and universalizing dimension. Yet, the "glo-calized" worldliness in which we find ourselves immersed today appears, on the contrary, to be counter-signed by the proliferation of armour-plated differences, of strategically constructed identities armed as one against the other, and by ethno-cultural contests incapable of delocalizing themselves. If I had to conclude with a slogan that defines my position, I would put it as follows: deconstruct identity, decontextualize politics. I know that it might seem like little more than a slogan. I hold, nevertheless, that this is the task that is required in order to develop philosophy in the current climate of world conflict: in the global Kakania or Babel in which it happens to live.

NOTES

1 Gianni Vattimo, *Nihilism and Emancipation: Ethics, Politics, and Law*, ed. Santiago Zabala (New York: Columbia University Press 2004), xxv.

2 Cf. primarily Richard Rorty, *Contingency, Irony and Solidarity* (Cambridge, Cambridge University Press 1989).

3 Ibid., 6.

4 Cf., for example, G. Marramao, *Kairós: Apologia del tempo debito* (Laterza, Roma-Bari 1992; English translation forthcoming for the Davies Publishing House in 2006).

5 Vattimo, *Nihilism and Emancipation*, 19 (my italics).

6 Ibid., 87.

7 Santiago Zabala, "Introduction: A Religion without Theist or Atheist," in Richard Rorty and Gianni Vattimo, *The Future of Religion*, ed. Santiago Zabala (New York: Columbia University Press 2005), 20.

8 Richard Rorty, *Truth and Progress* (Cambridge: Cambridge University Press 1998).

9 D.R. Hofstadter, *Gödel, Escher, Bach* (New York: Basic Books 1979).

10 "Ma quale capitolazione? Intervista a Richard Rorty," by Giancarlo Bosetti, *Reset*, no. 85 (2004): 55–7.

11 Ibid., 55.

12 Cf. Hilary Putnam, *Realism with a Human Face* (Cambridge: Harvard University Press 1990), chap. 7.

13 Cf. G. Marramao, *Passaggio a Occidente: Filosofia e globalizzazione* (Turin: Bollati Boringhieri 2003; English translation forthcoming by Verso, London–New York).

5

The Human – Over and Over Again

WOLFGANG WELSCH

Translated by Jim Scott

The following remarks seek to relate Gianni Vattimo's thought to modernist thinking. Did the author of *The End of Modernity* depart from the modernist way of thinking, or does he remain its partisan? What boundaries are involved? How might they be crossed?

THE ANTHROPIC MINDSET OF MODERNISM, FOR OVER TWO HUNDRED AND FIFTY YEARS

Diderot 1755

Diderot formulated the fundamental axiom of modernist thinking in 1755: "Man is the unique concept from which one must start and to which one must refer everything back."[1] Diderot states this axiom when considering what the fundamental principle for the organization of the Encyclopedia should be. He is convinced that an approach based on the structure of the world not only is impossible but would above all fail to address the essential fact that all worldly things achieve meaning only through their relationship with the human. "Absent the human ... the sublime and moving drama of nature is nothing but a miserable dumb show. The cosmos falls mute, silence and darkness overwhelm it, all is transformed into a vast wasteland in which phenomena ... appear murky and dull. Only the presence of the human makes the existence of things at all interesting."[2]

The formulaic statement quoted at the beginning of the previous paragraph constitutes the bedrock axiom of modernist thought, which began taking shape in the second half of the eighteenth century. I will refer to it henceforth as "the anthropic principle." We continue to meet up with it right down to the present day.

Diderot's justification of the anthropic principle did not yet wholly satisfy. His motivation was chiefly pragmatic and affected only the semantic dimension of reality. The principle would be completely incontrovertible only if it could be shown that reality itself was *at its core* a human construct.

Kant 1781:
Epistemological Recentring: The World Is Humanworld

Kant provided the perfect justification of the anthropic principle in 1781 with his *Critique of Pure Reason*. His trailblazing insight stated that, contrary to previous thinking, our knowledge does not have to conform to objects but that first and foremost "objects ... conform to our knowledge."[3] Crucial for this view is the notion that all the objects to which we might ever refer are initially determined by the a priori forms of human cognition (forms of intuition plus categories). They have *constitutive* significance for the objects. It follows that the objects of experience are all minted by the "formal conditions of an experience in general"[4] and that we can imagine things that transcend our experience (things-in-themselves, God, and so on) only according to the features of our cognitive structure, that is, in human terms.[5]

This new, Kantian view of our cognition and our relationship to objects and the world means that the human does, in fact, constitute the measure of the world.[6] The fundamental structure of all things is determined by our forms of cognition.[7] The human figuration is the law of the world. The world is humanworld. Everything is determined by the *conditio humana epistemica*.[8]

Thus, Diderot was right in his proclamation of the anthropic principle. He was, in fact, even more profoundly right than he knew. The human is not just the semantic but indeed already the object-constituting principle of the world. Kant gave the anthropic principle its perfect epistemological legitimation.

The Persistence of the Anthropic Principle
into the Present

Following its justification by Kant, the anthropic view dominated modernist thinking. Despite the great variety otherwise present, it remained the common and generally accepted denominator of modernist thought. In the following I will demonstrate this by brief reference, first, to historicism and the new form of hermeneutics, then to Nietzsche, and finally to contemporary scholarship in the humanities and cultural studies. as well as in analytic philosophy.

The Diversification of the Transcendental in Historicism. With the advent of historical thinking toward the end of the eighteenth century and the subsequent rise of historicism, an important change occurs. People realize that human perception is not, as Kant had thought, everywhere and at all times the same but rather that it varies both culturally and historically. Human experience and understanding depend not on an unvarying and universal structure but rather on historically and culturally specific features. But this diversification does not affect the essential fundamental principle of modernity, that we humans can experience and comprehend only by following particular templates and that the objects that we deal with are fundamentally determined by these, our own, templates. The historical diversification even provides for a more extended and radical application of this fundamental principle: reference to an anthropic principle in general is insufficient; instead, it is necessary to recognize and respect various historically and culturally conditioned features of experience and understanding.

This view, founded by historicism, reached widest acceptance through the anthropology and ethnology of the twentieth century. People from different cultures are said to be bound to their various cultural a priori assumptions and for that reason to inhabit different worlds.[9] Contemporary contextualism, relativism, and culturalism all result from this modernist way of thinking.

The Place of Hermeneutics in This Constellation. Hermeneutics in its recent form is the child of historicism. Its belief that every culture is characterized by its own peculiar set of historically conditioned apriorities leads to the demand that in understanding, we enter this specific set of apriorities. Already Herder had developed this new hermeneutic maxim of internalism: we should not attempt to construct an understanding of a culture on the basis of external and abstract notions but seek rather to do so by entering (by way of "empathy") its own logic.[10]

But this demand suffers from a paradox. If every culture is characterized by its own apriorities, then it would seem that, as much as another culture's apriorities are truly different, it is not possible to genuinely understand the other culture but only to misrepresent it according to the features of one's own culture (within which one is supposedly strictly bound). Thus the historical concept results conceptually, in spite of all good intentions, in the impossibility of understanding a foreign culture. The problem is a serious one that hermeneutic approaches have heretofore been unable to solve.[11]

Nor has Gadamer's hermeneutics – to which, as we shall see, Vattimo subscribes – been able to escape this dilemma. The expansion of one's own horizon through "fusions of horizons" leads only to the broader horizon of the "history of effect" of one's own cultural tradition. This horizon, however, is supposed to represent an impassable boundary. "The history of effect determines in advance both what seems to us worth inquiring about and what will appear as an object of investigation."[12] Thus, it is not possible to exceed the limits of our own cultural tradition by proceeding along this path. Other cultures and their histories of effect remain foreign. We cannot get beyond a figure remaining at best in unrecognized sameness in the midst of a self-created otherness. The understanding of the foreign remains constrained by self-imposed shackles. Thus the prison-like nature of the anthropic principle makes itself felt even in this superficially more flexible hermeneutic version of the historistic approach.

Nietzsche: Our Truth Is "Anthropomorphic Through and Through."
But does not everything change by the time Nietzsche comes on the scene? Does he not free us from all constraints? Does he not do that, for example, with his critique of historicism? Not at all, for Nietzsche's objection suggests a further narrowing of one's own horizon.[13]

If one takes into account that Nietzsche used Kant's concept as his point of departure and then radicalized it,[14] it can hardly be expected that he should have moved beyond the modern mindset. Thus, one of his basic theses states that our truth is "thoroughly anthropomorphic" and "contains not a single point which would be "true in itself" or really and universally valid apart from man."[15] "We see all things by means of our human head, and cannot chop it off."[16] For that reason

Nietzsche confronts philosophy with the prognosis that in the future it will be able only "to emphasize the *relativity* and *anthropomorphic* character of all knowledge as well as the all pervasive ruling power of *illusion.*"[17] Nietzsche develops an artistic version of anthropomorphism, he accentuates the element of free invention and fiction. In his conception of the human as an *animal fingens* he acts out the productionism of the modernist view. By advocating a fundamental anthropomorphism, he stands completely within the tradition of modernist thought.

One might perhaps think that Nietzsche's idea of the "overman" would stand in opposition to this and see it as aiming beyond the human and thus beyond the anthropic principle. But that would be wrong. True, in his overman Nietzsche is thinking of someone who "shoots the arrow of his longing beyond man"[18] – but in fact only beyond the *present* human, whose self-satisfied nature Nietzsche scorns in the figure of the "last man."[19] In contrast, the overman is expected wholly to realize the full potential of humanity. Nietzsche's overman is that individual who has shed every thought of an under or over world and – as Gianni Vattimo has repeatedly and brilliantly shown – lives out the *conditio humana* creatively and, free from any transcendental authority, has only himself as the single and highest point of orientation. Overman's world will finally be a completely anthropic world. Nietzsche is – particularly in his view of the future – an anthropic thinker par excellence.

But Nietzsche would not be Nietzsche if the antithesis to his principle idea were not also to be found in his own writing.[20] On one occasion he formulates an imperative completely different from the anthropic one. It reads, "feel cosmically!"[21] This is surprising. What does Nietzsche mean exactly?

Usually, Nietzsche's references to the cosmos remain within the anthropic paradigm. For him, the cosmos is as much a human product as the newspaper[22] and long since bereft of magic.[23] A different view appears only in scattered references: the notion that the universe does not, perhaps, conform to anthropic logic after all[24] and that – contrary to the prevailing humanization of nature and the universe – a naturalization might be in store for us,[25] or that we are ultimately co-agents of the cosmos[26] and that a hard look at the universe could teach us humility.[27] In the passage cited above, Nietzsche considers the idea that even "what goes on inside us" could have a dimension completely different from the human, since it is "in itself *something different* which we do not know" and which we systematically fail to grasp because of our habitual, decidedly anthropic perspective.[28] Nietzsche suggests an opposing view that steps beyond the human perspective ("beyond 'you' and 'me'"). "Feel cosmically" articulates a guideline that breaks through anthropism, leaves it behind. And *here* Nietzsche does not voice his usual objection that, like everything else, such cosmic feeling could be nothing more than a humanistically made-up goal. Here Nietzsche thinks rather determinedly beyond the anthropic trope. (Why do Nietzsche's fans only ever recognize the anthropic Nietzsche and not this other Nietzsche as their model?)

The determining function of the anthropic principle for the contemporary human and cultural sciences. Contemporary scholars of the human and cultural sciences follow completely in the wake of the anthropic principle. Programmatically they state that their concept rests on the notion "that only one a priori exists, the historical a priori of culture."[29] This is nothing other than a reprise of the historical credo in an updated outfit. If anthropic transcendentalism had become concrete and varied with historicism, under culturalism it becomes totally empirical and micrologically differentiated.

In this microanalytic turn, the anthropic principle constitutes the prosperity-driving axiom of the human and cultural sciences. For if cultural specifications are constitutive for all our experiences, views, and deeds, then it is necessary to pursue the detailed analysis of just these cultural specifications in all their multiplicity and diversity in "a nearly infinite internal differentiation and particularization."[30] And exactly that is what contemporary human and cultural sciences have done in the extreme. Full of pathos, they wave the standard of liberty: such microanalytic revelations should provide individuals with the chance to become aware of the manifold constraints and thereafter enable them to make their own choices and decisions. It is overlooked that the terms of their very own axioms mean that these choices amount to no more than picking one cell over another in the same prison; in no way can they result in freedom.

Analytic philosophy. Analytic philosophy is a further example of the contemporary and largely unconscious dominance of the anthropic mindset. Outstanding representatives of this movement referred early on to the *homo mensura* phrase by Protagoras (a classical preformulation of the modern anthropic principle). For example, Neurath declared in 1930/31 that "the scientific world view" promotes "the proud but at the same time self-limiting conviction ... that man is the measure of all things."[31] In 1963 Sellars, too, referred to Protagoras's phrase to characterize his own position in the philosophy of science: "in the dimension of describing and explaining the world, science is the measure of all things, of what is that it is, and of what is not that it is not."[32]

Behind all this stands the decided orientation of analytic philosophy toward Kant, the true founder of the modern anthropic principle. The specific twist, however, that the principle is given is defined by the "linguistic turn." All references to things are said to be determined within the framework of language (rather than within the framework of mental a priori forms, as Kant would have it). Lingualism is the analytic version of the anthropic principle.

Language (which of course is looked upon as a purely human business: *we* speak, the world is mute[33] – remember Diderot) still imposes, according to contemporary analytic philosophy, anthropic boundaries upon our understanding similar to those previously recognized by the "philosophy of consciousness." Truth exists only "relative to language," and, we are assured, "that is as objective as can be."[34] Thus the world to which we finally come is also for analytic philosophy fundamentally a world determined by humans, a world where man is the measure.[35]

Thus analytic philosophy, too, still follows the anthropic mindset of modernity. Beneath all the newfangled terminology and posturing (the turn toward language and the pathos of a new beginning), it continues to act out the anthropic principle of modernity. One could comment critically on this permanence of the anthropic worldview by citing Wittgenstein: "A *picture* held us captive. And we could not get outside it, for it lay in our language and language seemed to repeat it to us inexorably."[36] Yes, a picture holds us moderns captive.

Vain Critiques of the Anthropic Mindset

To be sure, various philosophers have proposed energetic critiques of the anthropic mindset. But their objections have all disappeared like water into sand.

The Logical Critique of the Anthropic Mindset (Frege, Husserl). Frege initiated the topic toward the end of the nineteenth century. He wanted to show that the validity of logical and mathematical truths is independent of anthropic conditions. In this sense he objected to the psychological infection of logic.[37] He supported the "unconditional and eternal validity" of the logical laws – in opposition to their typically modernist limitation "to our thought as it is now."[38] But Frege was never able to make his absolute conception of logic really plausible.

Following in Frege's footsteps, Husserl also advanced an energetic critique of psychologism. He regarded it as a variation of "anthropologism," the view that all human understanding is relative to the human constitution, to the "human species."[39] Husserl saw "the modern and recent philosophy" to its detriment stubbornly veined with anthropologism.[40] He considered it "quite rare to encounter a thinker free from the taint of such erroneous doctrines."[41] Husserl's objections, too, focused on the concept of truth: truth should have the status of ideal, not simply empirical, validity and could not therefore be relative to an empirical given like the human condition. If something is true, it must be true for any creature – "for men or non-men, angels or gods"[42] – in the same way.[43]

But as impressive as Husserl's critique was, even he himself was not able to sustain it but, rather, converted in later years to a transcendental anthropological relativism: "every existent is ultimately ... *relative to transcendental subjectivity.*"[44] The whole situation seems full of irony. Husserl, who had set out to banish anthropologism from modernist thought once and for all, came in the end to espouse the view that human consciousness is the ultimate horizon. The prominent critic of the anthropic mindset finally rejoined the ranks of its proponents. He simply located the centrality of the human at a deeper – namely, transcendental – level.

Heidegger: Ontological Deepening of Anthropology, but No Overstepping the Boundaries of the Modernist Mindset. And how about Heidegger? I maintain that hardly anything is different. True, Heidegger is known as a great critic of modernism who was most definitely aware if its anthropocentric thrust – the tendency to relate "all reality first and finally to the human"[45] – and who objected to the elevation of anthropology to the "fundamental discipline of philosophy"[46] on the grounds that in this whole enterprise the human remains essentially underdefined. What is lacking in this approach, according to Heidegger, is the realization that the human cannot be understood on the basis of itself alone, for the reason that the human is "more than merely human":[47] "there is no such thing as a man who exists singly and solely on his own."[48] The human must rather – against the modernist tendency to "*humanify* the human"[49] – be conceived in terms of its relationship to being, and in this relationship not the human but being has the lead. Reflecting on "the relation of Being to the essence of man"[50] was Heidegger's principal concern throughout his life.

But what is really altered if one does not determine the human simply on its own grounds but rather from its relationship to being? Certainly this does go beyond ordinary anthropology. But in its place enters another anthropology, only this time a deeper, being-accentuated anthropology, an onto-anthropology.

In order to realize that Heidegger is effecting just a deepening reformation (and not a fundamental transgression) of the anthropological mindset, it helps to consider Heidegger's explicit relationship to humanism. At first Heidegger states that humanism designates "that philosophical interpretation of man which explains and evaluates beings as a whole from the standpoint of, and in relation to, man" (which recalls even in its choice of words Diderot's formulation of modernism's anthropic axiom).[51] But Heidegger's subsequent critique of traditional forms of humanism results finally only in the establishment of a new type of humanism – a humanism that now "thinks the humanity of man from nearness to Being."[52]

Heidegger's efforts are bent all in one direction: to develop in place of the deficient traditional one, finally, a complete and genuine understanding of the human – but not to transcend the anthropic horizon as such. The *framework* within which the full understanding of the human would apply remains unchanged. Now as before it remains valid that the – henceforth authentic – understanding of the human is to be the foundation for everything.

That things are thus – that Heidegger's turning of previous anthropology to a being-accentuated anthropology does not leave the anthropic worldview behind but only roots it more deeply – derives from a very significant aspect of Heidegger's understanding of being: being has, according to Heidegger, only humans for partners. Only the human is "the neighbor of Being"[53] and "the shepherd of Being."[54] He is the unique addressee of being – rocks are not, animals are not, neither is a work of art or a machine, an angel or God.[55] Humans are the exclusive partners of being.

In this sense Heidegger has remained an *exclusivist with respect to the human*. He has transformed anthropology into onto-anthropology, but he has not moved beyond the anthropic way of thinking. All he has done has been to replace within it the old distinction of the human as the *animal rationale* with a new one, the "neighbour" of being. In this Heidegger's thinking remains within the anthropic configuration of modernity. He only opened a deeper dimension for it. But he has not gone beyond it.[56]

What may we anticipate with regard to Vattimo's thought? In Nietzsche and Heidegger I have discussed two of Vattimo's principal inspirations. I have shown that Nietzsche developed the anthropic figure as fully as it is possible to do and that Heidegger remains, even with all his changes to the interpretation of the human, within the modernist way of thinking. For that reason we may expect that Vattimo will continue as well on this same modernist track.[57]

Reasons for Questioning the Modernist Way of Thinking

We have seen that the task of supplying an efficient critique of the anthropic mindset is still unfulfilled. Yet it remains necessary. For apparently the modernist mindset paralyzes our thought.

Paralysis, Satiety, Self-satisfaction. We long have known the answer to every question. It reads, "it is the human." This self-fulfilling certainty suffocates thought instead of allowing it to breathe.

In fact, the entire contemporary philosophical and intellectual scene is peculiarly lame. Oh yes, the activity is immense and the differentiation is impressive in its detail. But all our pathways bend around in the same tiresome circle. For everything that we do not yet understand in detail and set out to investigate, we are certain in advance that all our discoveries, present and future, will result in nothing more than insights on the human plane – *huis clos*. We have settled into the cocoon of anthropic thinking, with all its restrictions, and we feel comfortable there. It provides us with security – the epistemological equivalent of the "steel cage" of modernity. It is hardly possible to exaggerate the degree to which we are trapped in this mindset. Even ordinary everyman is convinced that our entire understanding is bound (contextually, socially, culturally) to the human. This is the most profound *communis opinio* of modern humanity.

By citing the popular usage of two terms I would like to demonstrate the arrogance connected with this reflex. What does it mean today to say that someone is "cosmopolitan"? And what do we have in mind when we attempt to claim "universal validity" for an idea?

When the Stoics spoke of a "cosmopolitan" (a "citizen of the world") or said that one should live one's life according to the cosmos, they really meant the entire world, the universe. A "citizen of the world" was someone who took the *cosmos* (or its underlying reason) as his measure. When people speak of a "citizen of the world" today, they mean only a competent citizen of the Earth, an international Earthling. This person may then pick up a magazine such as *Cosmopolitan* and while reading it, be assured he has left unchallenged his shrinking of the cosmic measure to the concerns of a life-style society.

And whoever says "universal" today accepts automatically a similar limitation of the universe to just the earth and even to a single species on the earth, homo sapiens. "Universal" no longer means "universally valid" but just "generally valid for people" – but the latter is supposed to represent the former. What arrogance, yes even impudence! Just not bottomless impudence – I have shown where its bottom lies.

The Inconsistency of the Modernist Mindset. But why, as many would like to ask, should one try to move beyond modernist thinking? Is it not actually quite wonderful and just fine in every way? Are we not really well off with it? At this point I do not wish to venture any criticism from the outside but only to point to a grave internal inconsistency in modernist thinking.

Modernist thinking is quite evidently self-contradictory. It maintains that all our understanding is determined by our physical, cultural, social, etc., parameters and contains nothing capable of reaching beyond them. But a determination and limitation of this kind could in any case be stated only from a position outside these parameters, from the perspective of a God's-eye view. Otherwise the assertion would be itself subject to the same restrictions and thus could itself be at best only relatively valid and hence unable to serve as a binding principle. But according to the modernist position, precisely such an overview is unavailable to us. Thus, according to the assumptions of this mindset itself, we have no way of knowing that our understanding is in fact strictly limited. Yet this very claim is made over and over again. In this the modernist position is fundamentally inconsistent, self-contradictory.[58]

The really amazing thing, however, is that pointing out this inconsistency has absolutely no effect. The counterargument remains unchallenged – but also fruitless. The modernist axiom is accepted as a self-evident truth. Its supporters counter any challenge by continuing, unmoved, to reiterate the axiom being tested, as though it were beyond question, and then maintain that such questioning is after all doubtlessly a human formulation and is therefore (as everything is, according to the axiom) simply a "humanly valid" argument, one that is not only unable to shake the axiom but helps, rather, to sustain it. To be sure, such immunity to questioning and testing of its own assumptions is, according to modernism, not precisely a sign of rationality but rather a sign of ideology. But in this case, no one is worried. When our own assumptions come under scrutiny, we ignore our self-proclaimed standards. With self-indulgent satiety, we cling fast to the untenable position. Good feelings outrank argument. But for how much longer?

VATTIMO'S THOUGHT IN THE ANTHROPOLOGICAL CONTEXT OF MODERNISM

Now let us ask how Vattimo's thought fits into the context of the anthropic thinking of modernism. I have already hinted at my answer: his decided links to Nietzsche and Heidegger suggest, on one hand, that he, too, will imagine humanity and its situation in a nonconventional way but, on the other hand, that he will not question the anthropic framework of modernity.

Philosophy for Humans

Vattimo's thought always relates to and affects the life we live. His interventions cause us to understand ourselves differently and gain a new perspective on our situation and our social and political relationships.[59] If you read Vattimo and follow his reasoning for part of the way, you will begin to act, judge, and live differently in a number of situations. In that respect, this new-style philosopher is an old-fashioned intellectual: his thought has an influence both in the annals of philosophy and in everyday public affairs. His personal involvement, which reaches from the cultural scene in Turin to the European Parliament and from sexual politics to religion, reflects the practical bent of his thought. Vattimo is convinced that the effort of thinking should result in an improvement of the human condition. He is ever ready to remind others of this omission when they overlook the political situatedness of their thought. Vattimo sees thinking as grounded in the concrete human realm and seeks to help achieve clarity and orientation within it.

Vattimo's Hermeneutics – "We Are a Conversation"

Vattimo's idea that "we are a conversation" is not just a personal option; it has a philosophical basis that lies in the realization that all our thinking is rooted in the stream of our heritage and tradition. This applies to philosophical thinking as well as the everyday variety. Our mores and institutions, too, are products and manifestations of the tradition from which we come.

That is the fundamental insight of Vattimo's hermeneutics. For him hermeneutics is not a superficial art of interpretation but rather a description of our way of being. In this Vattimo remains true to Heidegger. For the latter, we humans are not beings who exist and then engage in, among other things, the business of understanding; rather, we fundamentally comprehending beings whose very *way of being* is characterized by understanding. In our constitution we are creatures of tradition and understanding. Hölderlin's phrase "since we are a conversation" expresses this paradigmatically. Doubtless the human is a *zoon logon echon*; however, his *logos* has the character not of pure reason (Kant) but rather of social communication (Aristotle) with a historical lining (Vattimo). A thought is not just the deed of an autonomous subject but an overlay in the braid of tradition and today. This insight has performative authority for Vattimo. When he refuses to argue directly (which systematic philosophers find objectionable) but always in conversation with other voices (Nietzsche, Heidegger, Gadamer, Rorty, Derrida, Ricoeur, etc.), he does so because he knows (and wants us to realize) that our voice can emerge and be heard only in a chorus of other voices. This seems to me the essence of Vattimo's original and deeply considered version of hermeneutics.

This hermeneutic position results neither in an apologia for the status quo (as some believe) nor in a historical conservatism.[60] And this is true, if for no other reason, because the present is both more multifaceted and the tradition richer than contemporary conventional wisdom or a historical orthodoxy would have it be. There are always other voices.[61] The history of philosophy bears various potentialities; in our present discourse the task can be precisely to help repressed voices express themselves;[62] each and every voice is open to differing interpretations. Thus there are always alternative possibilities that can be used critically. The full compass of the conversation leads (in contrast to the reductionism of the established "idle talk") not to conservatism but to diverging options.

Problems with Justification

Nevertheless, can such a hermeneutics, which is not conservative but seeks the energizing force of criticism, lead to anything more than a multiplicity of contrary interpretations and options? Is it able, in fact, to justify the preference for one particular option over another? Vattimo would like it to be. He wants to avoid the relativism of "anything goes."[63] He would like to privilege some values over others. *Caritas*, for example, he considers to be an "absolute value."[64]

But how can such a distinction be possible? Is it not unavoidably the case, that – once the possibility of ultimate justification has faded away[65] – one thing can be preferred only on the basis of individual interests and prejudices, by one person, this, and by another, that? Decisions are made on the basis of predisposition, taste, or power – not on the basis of the right. After the abandonment of any "fundamentalism," it does not seem possible to do more than express a plausible recommendation and try to promote it.[66]

According to Vattimo, history should help us out of the difficulty. History should make a trend apparent. Vattimo points to Hegel. He had determined history to be "progress in the awareness of freedom." Vattimo believes himself to recognize a process of "weakening."[67] With that he establishes what postmodern theoreticians otherwise eschew: a metanarrative. Of course he admits his view is an "interpretation" rather than an objective determination. Fine. But such an interpretation stands in opposition to others. How should we decide among them, particularly when it is said that there exist "always only interpretations of other interpretations"?[68] For this problem – the multiplicity of competing interpretations and the absence of a noninterpretative metacriterion – Vattimo has no solution. True, he assures us that we have criteria "which we are called upon to distill from the messages which reach us."[69] But once again, we receive various messages; as messages, they have not objective but rather interpretative status; we can respond to them only with an interpretation; and in doing so different interpreters will give even the same message a different interpretation and thus derive from the historical tradition (for Vattimo the single hoard of truth[70]) divergent criteria. Vattimo wrestles incessantly (he deserves credit for this) but never fully successfully (and he is aware of it) with the problem of criteria, which should be able to be derived from the historical tradition but which never emerge with complete clarity because of the variety of the historical messages and the logic of interpretation. This is the unsolved dilemma of his hermeneutic concept.[71]

The Limits of the Hermeneutic Approach
– and How They Might Be Overcome

In the discussion of such problems, Vattimo regularly runs into a barrier. He likes then to speak of paradoxes and unavoidable contradictions. He does not even believe it possible to say why he would defend himself if his life was in danger.[72] Of course it is not possible to know such things when one only listens to the voices of the historical record, because some among these justify self-defense, while others call for unconditional nonviolence.

It seems to me that it is the obstinate reliance on history that finally produces all these problems (the variety and contradictory nature of the message, preference without sufficient justification, the running into ultimate contradictions, the alleged undecidability). History is the shibboleth of hermeneutics: "there is nothing outside history."[73] But thus it is also that history is its limit in every sense. And therefore hermeneutics comes up short. It swears allegiance to origins but equates these origines only with "history" (and even with a history understood to consist exclusively of linguistic messages, of texts)[74] and thus overlooks and ignores the by far greater part of our origin: prehistory and the entire evolutionary trajectory of humankind.[75] As though humanity had dropped from the sky into history or had created itself exclusively through historical processes. As though our history did not itself rest on an evolutionary past and on prehistoric ages. As though our existence did not, as science currently demonstrates in great detail, draw on evolutionary and prehistoric conditioning. As though these were not the criteria, which the hermeneutist senses but cannot explain on the basis of his exclusively historical hermeneutics.

Vattimo once said: "When we argue, we always argue inside a horizon which our interests have opened for us ... What matters here, are points of reference for which we cannot give theoretical reasons but which do delimit the horizon in which we already find ourselves."[76] This may well be true. The interests involved, however, did not come about for the most part historically but rather within a prehistoric and evolutionary timeframe. If anything, they have been historically modified but not historically grounded. And just because they are in this sense pregiven, they do, in fact, constitute a body of interests that precede any communication and provide manifest criteria (cf. the reflex

of self-defense). These interests indeed provide what history and interpretation alone cannot guarantee: orientation and common patterns
that we involuntarily follow. Compared to this, our prehistoric *koiné*,
the *koiné* of hermeneutical history is secondary (and in many aspects
parasitic).

My suggestion is therefore that, when speaking of the origins of
humankind, we should include the *entirety* of human origins in our
scope – not only their historic, but also their prehistoric and evolutionary stock. When speaking of "history of effect," we should also take
into account our prehistoric elements, without which we would not
exist and which continue being alive and active within us. And when
speaking of the "history of being," we should not limit ourselves to the
literary tradition beginning with the pre-Socratics but include the entire
history of being since the evolution of life, indeed of the cosmos itself.[77]
If we were to do this, we would find answers to the questions for which
those hermeneutists who reduce humanity to a textual tradition hit an
impasse and can find refuge only in the rhetoric of an "unfathomable
origin" (Pareyson) or of unavoidable contradictions (Vattimo).[78]

I spoke finally about the limits of hermeneutics and earlier about the
limits of modernist thinking. Both limits are related. The practices of
following the anthropic principle of modernity and of explaining
human existence solely on the basis of history have belonged together
since historicism originated. A look at history should tell us everything
we need to interpret the world from the human point of view. In doing
so, the surrounding framework of anthropic thinking is not transcended; its inner sphere is only restructured over and over again.

On the other hand, breaking out of the cocoon of history would also
take us beyond the anthropic mindset. A look at prehistory and evolution can show that the situation concerning the possible objectivity of
our knowledge and understanding is different from what the (in this
matter) nihilistic modernists believe it to be. Our understanding and
perception is not a free creation without objectivity but at base a reflex
of the world through which and in which we have become what we are.
The development of this notion in detail (the suggestions made here will
necessarily be left open to misunderstanding) must wait for another
opportunity.[79]

NOTES

1 Denis Diderot, "Encyclopédie," in: Diderot, *Œuvres complètes*, vol. 7, Encyclopédie 3 (Paris: Hermann 1976), 174–262, here 213.

2 Ibid., 212.

3 Immanuel Kant, *Critique of Pure Reason*, trans. Norman Kemp Smith (New York: St Martin's 1965), 22 [B 16].

4 Ibid., 239 [A 220].

5 "We cannot proceed in any other way; we have to anthropomorphize." Immanuel Kant, *Anthropology from a Pragmatic Point of View*, translated by Victor Lyle Dowdell, revised and edited by Hans H. Rudnick (Carbondale: Southern Illinois University Press 1978), 62fn. [AB 76, par. 30].

6 Thus we arrive, two hundred fifty years after the *cosmic decentralization* effected by Copernicus, at an *epistemological recentering* of the human by Kant. Of course the position of humans in the cosmos remains decentralized. But this now meets up with an *epistemological recentring*. Bertrand Russell lucidly noted this in saying that Kant, instead of speaking "of himself as having effected a 'Copernican revolution' ... would have been more accurate if he had spoken of a 'Ptolemaic counter-revolution,' since he put Man back at the centre from which Copernicus had dethroned him" (Bertrand Russell, *Human Knowledge*, New York: Simon and Schuster, 1948, xi).

7 Finally, in his *Opus postumum* Kant even stated: "We make everything ourselves." Immanuel Kant, *Opus postumum*, ed. Eckart Förster (Cambridge: Cambridge University Press 1993), 189 [2:82; 7th fascicle, sheet 7, page 2].

8 Significantly, Kant explained that the classical questions of metaphysics ("What can I know?"), of ethics ("What ought I to do?"), and of faith ("What may I hope?") all come together in the question "What is man?" and should be answered in this regard. Immanuel Kant, cited from Gottlob Benjamin Jäsche, "Immanuel Kant's Logic: A Manual for Lectures" [1800], in *Immanuel Kant: Lectures on Logic*, ed. and trans. J. Michael Young (Cambridge: Cambridge University Press 1992), 538.

9 "The worlds in which different societies live are distinct worlds, not merely the same world with different labels attached." Edward Sapir, "The Status of Linguistics as a Science," in Sapir, *Culture, Language and Personality* (Berkeley: University of California Press 1958), 65–77, here 69.

10 "*The whole nature* of the soul, which *rules through everything*, which *models* all other inclinations and forces *in accordance with itself*, and in addition *colors* even the most indifferent actions – in order to share in feeling this, do not answer on the basis of the word but go into the age, into the clime, the

whole history, feel yourself into everything." Johann Gottfried Herder, "This Too a Philosophy of History for the Formation of Humanity" [1774], in *Philosophical Writings*, ed. and trans. Michael N. Forster (Cambridge: Cambridge University Press 2002), 292.

11 It could be solved only in terms of a universalist view – for instance the thesis that the diversity of cultures rests on or includes a foundation of commonalities. But this thesis runs counter to the inveterate faith in specificity, and both the paradoxical consequences of unrestrained cultural relativism and the bitter debates between cultural relativists and universalists are telling examples of this dilemma. Cf. for the first of these, the declaration written principally by Melville Herskovits, in which in 1949 American ethnologists went to bat for tolerance and nonintervention in foreign cultures: If every culture is strictly bound within the framework of its own cultural axioms, then the consequence for research is clear: all ethnological efforts should cease, because researchers themselves are bound within the framework of their own cultures and therefore constitutionally unable to do justice to other cultures. They can note things down only according to the patterns familiar to them; i.e., they can only engage in cultural imperialism. Cf. as a case study for the second point (the relativistic rejection of universalist claims); Paul Ekman, "Afterword," in Charles Darwin, *The Expression of the Emotions in Man and Animals* (Oxford: Oxford University Press 1998), 363–93.

12 Hans-Georg Gadamer (1960), *Truth and Method* (New York: Continuum 1989), 306, 300.

13 "[T]his is a general law: every living thing can become healthy, strong and fruitful only within a horizon." Friedrich Nietzsche, *On the Advantage and Disadvantage of History for Life*, trans. Peter Preuss (Indianapolis: Hackett 1980), 10.

14 "It has to be *proven* that all constructions of the world are anthropomorphic, indeed, if Kant is right, all sciences." Friedrich Nietzsche, "The Philosopher: Reflections on the Struggle between Art and Knowledge" [1872], in *Philosophy and Truth: Selections from Nietzsche's Notebooks of the Early 1870s*, ed. and trans. Daniel Breazeale (Humanities Press, 1979), 32.

15 Friedrich Nietzsche, "On Truth and Lies in a Nonmoral Sense," in *Philosophy and Truth*, 85.

16 Friedrich Nietzsche, *Human, All-Too-Human: A Book for Free Spirits*, trans. Marion Faber (Lincoln: University of Nebraska Press 1984), 17 [9].

17 Friedrich Nietzsche, "The Philosopher," 13.

18 Friedrich Nietzsche, *Thus Spoke Zarathustra*, trans. Walter Kaufmann (New York: Modern Library 1995), 17.

19 Cf. ibid., 7 f.

20 Cf. his motto of honesty: "Never keep back or bury in silence that which can be thought against your thoughts! Give it praise! It is among the foremost requirements of honesty of thought. Every day you must conduct your campaign also against yourself." Friedrich Nietzsche, *Daybreak: Thoughts on the Prejudices of Morality*, trans. R.J. Hollingdale (Cambridge: Cambridge University Press 1997), 169 [370].

21 "To learn step by step to *cast off the supposed individual*. To discover the errors of the ego! To comprehend *egoism as a mistake*! Not to view altruism as its opposite! That would be love for the *other supposed* individual! No. Beyond *'me'* and *'you'*! *Feel cosmically!*" Friedrich Nietzsche, *Nachgelassene Fragmente: Anfang 1880 bis Sommer 1882*, in Nietzsche, *Sämtliche Werke*, vol. 9, 443.

22 "We take not only God, but every other thing we recognize, even if nameless, into ourselves: we are the cosmos, *as far as we have comprehended or dreamed it*. The olives and the storms have become a part of us: the stock market and the newspaper as well." Ibid., 216.

23 "This carefree profundity! What once was called a star became a smudge." Nietzsche, *Nachgelassene Fragmente. November 1887 bis Anfang Januar 1889*, in Nietzsche, *Sämtliche Werke*, vol. 13, 571. One is reminded of Hegel's remark to Heine: "the stars are only a gleaming leprosy in the sky." Heinrich Heine, "Geständnisse," in Heine, *Sämtliche Werke*, vol. 13. (Munich: Kindler 1964), 89–144, here 118.

24 "[H]ow could we reproach or praise the universe? Let us beware of attributing to it heartlessness and unreason or their opposites: it is neither perfect nor beautiful, nor noble, nor does it wish to become any of these things; it does not by any means strive to imitate man." Friedrich Nietzsche, *The Gay Science*, trans. Walter Kaufmann (New York: Vintage Books 1974), 168 [109].

25 "When may we begin to *'naturalize'* humanity in terms of a pure, newly discovered, newly redeemed nature?" Ibid., 169 [109].

26 "[E]very individual helps create the whole cosmic entity – whether we know it or not – whether we want to or not!" Nietzsche, *Nachgelassene Fragmente: Juli 1882 bis Herbst 1885*, in Nietzsche, *Sämtliche Werke*, vol. 10, 494.

27 "[T]oday the true cosmic ideas have significance for the mind, they point people toward modesty." Nietzsche, *Nachgelassene Fragmente: Anfang 1875 bis Ende 1879*, in Nietzsche, *Sämtliche Werke*, vol. 8, 171.

28 Nietzsche, *Nachgelassene Fragmente: Anfang 1880 bis Sommer 1882*, *Sämtliche Werke*, vol. 8, 443. "We are buds on One tree – what do we know of what we may become in the interest of the tree!" Ibid.

29 Hartmut Böhme, Peter Matussek, and Lothar Müller, *Orientierung Kulturwissenschaft* (Reinbek: Rowohlt 2000), 106.

30 Ibid., 13.

31 Otto Neurath, "Wege der wissenschaftlichen Weltauffassung," *Erkenntnis* 1 (1930/31): 106–25, here 125.

32 Wilfrid Sellars, *Empiricism and the Philosophy of Mind* (Cambridge, MA: Harvard University Press 1997), 173. Recently Rorty has also joined the Protagoras camp. According to Rorty we have "no responsibilities ... except those, which we have toward other people." Richard Rorty, "Die moderne analytische Philosophie aus pragmatischer Sicht," in *Die Renaissance des Pragmatismus – Aktuelle Verflechtungen zwischen analytischer und kontinentaler Philosophie*, ed. Mike Sandbothe (Weilerswist: Velbrück Wissenschaft 2000), 78–95, here 95.

33 Cf. Rorty: "The World Does Not Speak. Only we do." Richard Rorty, *Contingency, irony, and solidarity* (Cambridge: Cambridge University Press 1989), 6.

34 Donald Davidson, "On the Very Idea of a Conceptual Scheme," in Davidson, *Inquiries into Truth and Interpretation* (Oxford: Oxford University Press 1984), 183–98, here 198.

35 "Our conceptions ... define a kind of objectivity, *objectivity for us* ... Objectivity and rationality humanly speaking are what we have." Hilary Putnam, *Reason, Truth and History* (Cambridge, MA: Cambridge University Press 1982), 55. Significantly, Putnam refers this view back to Kant, who, he thinks, first developed "the 'internalist' or "internalist realist" view." Ibid., 60.

36 Ludwig Wittgenstein, *Philosophical Investigations*, trans. G.E.M. Anscombe (New York: Macmillan 1968), 48e [115].

37 He saw "the prevailing logic" as "infected through and through with psychology." Gottlob Frege, *The Basic Laws of Arithmetic* [1893], ed. and trans. Montgomery Furth (Berkeley: University of California Press 1964), 12. Already in 1884, in *The Foundations of Arithmetic*, he had stated as his first axiom, "always to separate sharply the psychological from the logical." (Gottlob Frege, *The Foundations of Arithmetic: A Logico-mathematical Enquiry into the Concept of Number*, trans. J.L. Austin (Evanston, IL: Northwestern University Press), 2d ed., 1980, 10.

38 Frege, *The Basic Laws of Arithmetic*, 14.

39 Edmund Husserl, *Logical Investigations*, vol. 1 [1900], trans. John N. Findlay (London, Routledge and Kegan Paul 1970), 138 [par. 34].

40 Ibid., 139 [par. 36].

41 Ibid., 139f.

42 Ibid., 140.

43 Husserl was aware that the waywardness of anthropology had begun with Kant, who had fallen victim to a "fickle anthropologism." Edmund Husserl,

Erste Philosophie, Erster Teil: Kritische Ideengeschichte, ed. Rudolf Boehm, Husserliana vol. 7 (Haag: Nijhoff 1956), 228.

44 Edmund Husserl, *Formal and Transcendental Logic* [1929], trans Dorion Cairns (The Hague: Nijhoff 1969), 273 [par. 103].

45 Martin Heidegger, *Der Deutsche Idealismus (Fichte, Schelling, Hegel) und die philosophische Problemlage der Gegenwart* (Vorlesung Sommersemester 1929; *Gesamtausgabe*, II. Abteilung: Vorlesungen 1919–44) (Frankfurt/Main: Klostermann 1997), 18.

46 Ibid.

47 Martin Heidegger, "Letter on Humanism," in Heidegger, *Basic Writings*, ed. David Farrell Krell (San Francisco: Harper 1993), 217–65, here 245.

48 Martin Heidegger, "The Question concerning Technology," in Heidegger, *Basic Writings*, ed. David Farrell Krell (San Francisco: Harper 1993), 307–41, here 337.

49 Martin Heidegger, *Besinnung*, in Heidegger, *Gesamtausgabe*, vol. 66 (Frankfurt/Main: Klostermann 1997), 161 [61].

50 Heidegger, "Letter on Humanism," 217.

51 Martin Heidegger, "Die Zeit des Weltbildes" [1950], in *Off the Beaten Track*, ed. and trans. Julian Young and Kenneth Haynes (Cambridge: Cambridge University Press 2002), 70.

52 Heidegger, "Letter on Humanism," 245.

53 Ibid., 245.

54 Ibid., 234, 245.

55 "Being is ... nearer to man than every being, be it a rock, a beast, a work of art, a machine, be it an angel or God." Ibid., 234.

56 For reasons of space, it is not possible here to go into the critique that Foucault offered of the modernist anthropic mindset. He presented a brilliant settling of accounts with this manner of thinking in *The Order of Things* (1966). But soon thereafter – with the analysis of the human sciences in *Discipline and Punish* (1975) and completely with his search for forms of ameliorated individual life in *The Use of Pleasure* and *The Care of the Self* (both 1984) – he returned as well to the games of anthropic thinking.

57 To avoid any misunderstanding, I should say that there is no doubt that Vattimo interprets both Nietzsche and Heidegger in a very original and fruitful manner. As a young German student who grew up in a climate influenced by Heidegger, I was extremely happy to get to know Nietzsche und Heidegger as Vattimo understood them. It liberated me in an important way (as did the French Nietzsche-interpretation of Deleuze and the Heidegger-interpretation of Derrida). But here our task is not to discuss Nietzsche and Heidegger interpretations but to debate the question of whether a thinker has reached

beyond the anthropic trope of modernity – or at least sees and problematizes its limits and deficiencies.

58 in addition, its axiom is logically inconsistent in that it is based on an unjustified equation of *access* conditions with *validity* conditions. Of course certain access conditions must be met before we will be able to recognize anything. But in no way does that mean that the matter thus recognized would have to be *determined* by the means through which it was accessed – that it could not have an existence and validity apart from that. Access conditions have, it is true, an *initiating* function for the *discovery* of a matter – but they do not because of that have an eo ipso *constitutive* function for the *essence* of these matters *as such*; they do not simply *make* them. The equation of access conditions with validity conditions is, from the point of view of logic, an elementary error. Yet the anthropic axiom is founded on this very mistake: it concludes on the basis of human *access* to matters directly the human *constitution* of these very same matters.

59 Herein lies his proximity to Rorty.

60 This is the source of Vattimo's reservations vis-à-vis Gadamer and of his insistence on Heidegger's critical thrust. Cf., for example, "Truth and Rhetoric in Hermeneutic Ontology," in Gianni Vattimo, *The End of Modernity*, trans. J.R. Snyder (Baltimore: Johns Hopkins University Press 1988), 130–44, here 140–3.

61 "[I]t seems to me that tradition is polyphonic ... it has to do with a multiplicity of voices." "Die Stärken des schwachen Denkens. Ein Gespräch mit Gianni Vattimo," in Martin G. Weiß, *Gianni Vattimo. Eine Einführung* (Vienna: Passagen 2003), 171–82, here 174.

62 This was a great theme of Lyotard.

63 Cf. Gianni Vattimo, *Etica dell'interpretazione* (Turin: Rosenberg & Sellier 1989), 147.

64 "Die Stärken des schwachen Denkens," 175.

65 Here Vattimo joins the older Wittgenstein.

66 Rorty sees it this way.

67 In fact, Vattimo says his "weak thinking" is a sort of "watered down Hegelianism." "Die Stärken des schwachen Denkens," 173.

68 Ibid.

69 Ibid., 174.

70 "The only truth comes from history." Ibid.

71 I mentioned these problems already in 1995 in *Vernunft. Die zeitgenössische Vernunftkritik und das Konzept der transversalen Vernunft* (Frankfurt/Main: Suhrkamp, 1995), 206–10.

72 "I do not claim that this is a reasonable course of action, I don't even claim that I would have the right to kill in order to defend myself – it just happens." "Die Stärken des schwachen Denkens," 175). This recalls Wittgenstein's "This is simply what I do." Wittgenstein, *Philosophical Investigations*, 85e [217]. But the question is *why* it is then so, that we act in such a way (that "it happens").

73 "Die Stärken des schwachen Denkens," 173.

74 "History is a sum of books." Ibid., 178.

75 For this aspect, Vattimo has only the defensive label of "naturalism" in readiness. Ibid., 180. But "naturalism" is a buzzword that offers no food for thought but simply calls for a reaction.

76 Ibid., 176.

77 Again, I would recall Nietzsche's maxim "feel cosmically!" (in which he transcends his otherwise radicalized anthropomorphism).

78 Cf. Welsch, "Über Besitz und Erwerb von Gemeinsamkeiten," in *Tradition und Traditionsbruch zwischen Skepsis und Dogmatik: Interkulturelle philosophische Perspektiven*, eds. Claudia Bickmann, Hermann-Josef Scheidgen, Markus Wirtz, and Tobias Vosshenrich (Amsterdam: Rodopi 2006), 113–47.

79 I hope to have ready a book dealing with this notion, *Homo mundanus: Jenseits des Anthropismus der Moderne*, in 2008.

6

Can the Globalized World Be in-the-World?

HUGH J. SILVERMAN

Si può parlare del mondo al singolare?

Gianni Vattimo

"A shot heard 'round the world'" – a phrase linked with the American Revolution and Bunker Hill – was often repeated after the American president John F. Kennedy was assassinated in 1963. Here was an event that marked the world, marked it with "shock and awe." How could death come to such a young leader – very much in his prime, whose promise as president held a great sense of pride and hope for a new world? Cut off at this crucial moment, that hope for a new world came to an end. Around the world people would remember where they were and what they were doing on that ominous day. On that day I was in my first year of university and I had just returned to the residence halls when I was told of this horrendous event!

In August 1998, Lady Diana was riding with Dodi El-Fayed in a chauffeured car in the centre of Paris through a tunnel along the Seine; the car crashed into a support structure in the tunnel, killing everyone in the car except Lady Diana's bodyguard. It was reported that the French driver was intoxicated at the time and that the paparazzi who were mercilessly following the car did not cause the accident. The world was shocked, and the world mourned.

On September 11, 2001, two planes crashed into the Twin Towers in New York City and a third was reputed to have crashed into the wall of the Pentagon. A fourth plane went down in a field in Pennsylvania as a result of brave acts of heroic passengers, or so we were told. Viewers everywhere in the world shared the horror and fear that US airplanes could be forced to crash into the very symbols of American economic and military prowess. Many saw the event on TV as the second plane flew into the towering buildings, and the US president achieved notoriety for an event that took place during his presidency. The world changed that day, and we – around the world – all remember where we were when we learned that it had happened. The world changed and our lives changed. From this event on, living and travelling in the world could not be the same ever again.

One assumption is common to each of these cases – that there is "one" world and that this one world was marked or changed by an event of grand proportions. These three events changed how people in different places in the world view or experience the world, this single world. So we have one world and multiple events. But Gianni Vattimo asks the question: "Si può parlare del mondo al singolare?" In effect, he motivates us to ask whether there are not, effectively, multiple worlds. If Richard Rorty can speak of "the world well-lost," does it make sense to ask whether there is a singularity to the world or whether the world is a multiplicity? On the one hand, it is deemed futile to talk about "the world"; on the other hand, the question is raised as to whether there is not just "one" world but "many." But in any case, whether there is no longer a world, whether there is just one world, or whether there are many worlds, there are surely multiple events that happen ... multiple events like the assassination of JFK, the death of Lady Diana, and the plane crashes of 9/11.

In hermeneutics from the time of Dilthey, it has made sense to speak of a Weltanschauung. But whose Weltanschauung? When JFK died, the Weltanschauung, or worldview, of the USSR was not one of sadness or displeasure, no more than it would have been one of sadness or displeasure at the injury of a player on an opposing baseball or football team. When Lady Diana died, the royal family expressed remorse, but the event was clearly convenient and accorded well with their Weltanschauung. When the events of 9/11 happened, some people rejoiced that the apparently invincible United States was not invincible after all.

And what of what Gadamer calls Uberlieferung? The assassination of JFK was not the first assassination of an American president, and it was not the last attempted assassination – whether with a gun, as in the case of President Reagan, or with devious strategies of character assassination, as in the case of President Clinton. The "accidental" death of Lady Diana will not have been the last in a long line (or tradition) of making British queens or princesses "disappear into a tower" or into a "dungeon" or at the hand of a "beheading executioner." And 9/11 was almost immediately juxtaposed along with Pearl Harbor as a significant event, one in which the United States was attacked from the outside – as opposed to "from the inside," as in the Oklahoma bombing. But then, precisely these "events" and the "tradition" (Uberlieferung) of these kinds of events make one wonder whether they are indeed effected "from the outside," "from beyond the borders," "from an external enemy" – an "external enemy of the State." It is assumed that only an external enemy would want to do such a thing. But what if these very Weltanschauungen also permit these kinds of events to be executed "from the inside" of a determinate world, and what if they understand that such things could happen in "this" world as opposed to that ...

But already now has come the suggestion that these are multiple events that happen perhaps not just in "the" world but also in "a" particular world. What kind of world do "we" live in that "we" are expected to live in fear of the enemy. Such a world was created in the Eisenhower era, when Khrushchev was shown again and again on TV at the United Nations with shoe in hand, beating the table and announcing to the United States, "We will bury you!" Many Americans ran around building "bomb shelters" as places of refuge in the event of a nuclear attack from the Soviet Union.

And now we hear again about "the enemy." We notice that as recently as during the first debate between US presidential candidates George Bush and John Kerry, Bush continued to speak of "the" enemy and promised to defeat this singular enemy. "Fear" and the preservation of "fear" would make it possible for "the world" to believe in all the counterterrorist measures that would be invoked and employed to preserve American "national" security. "Fear" in the post-9/11 era would permit people to be terrorized in order to be preserved from "the terrorists." But which terrorists? Saddam Hussein? Certainly not any more. And yet "the" enemy is still "out there." It helps if the enemy has a face: the face of bin Laden will be useful here. So "the" enemy is bin Laden at the moment, someone else tomorrow. For years bin Laden has been sought after as the face of the enemy, as the ultimate face of the other, as the face of exteriority (with all the weight of these Levinasian ideas). If the enemy can be constituted as "the other," then Afghanistan can be bombed and Iraq can be invaded. Even if there is no connection between Iraq and bin Laden, it doesn't matter – the enemy is everywhere and anywhere that it is convenient to pre-emptively attack – just as long as the enemy is dealt with strongly and with religious conviction.

So now "we" (Americans) have one world, multiple events, particular worldviews, particular traditions, but just "one" enemy and lots of "fear" and one *Heimatsversicherung* known as "homeland security." On the horizon is one central intelligence bureau – a kind of single-minded Stasi that will "protect" everyone because it will be in "control" of "all intelligence." Imagine controlling all "intelligence" in a single bureau of investigation. This will surely make "the world" safer ... We must be careful, as well, about all this "nuclear proliferation." The "nuclear" has to do with the "centre" and when it proliferates, there is danger. So the best way to control this kind of nuclear proliferation is to keep all "intelligence" close to the nuclear centre. Keep it close to the centre, control it from the centre, and "the" world will be a safer place – less nuclear proliferation, more of a nuclear centre ...

As Gianni Vattimo reminds us, in Heidegger's *Being and Time* of 1927, Being-in-the-World (*in der Welt sein*) suggests that when one speaks of the relation to Being, the relation of beings to Being, it is because *Dasein* is "in *the* world." But is *the* world ontic or ontological? In Heidegger, *the* world is not *my* world or *your* world. It is *the* world. *my* world can be ontic. *My* world has to do with beings, with *Seiendes*, with the particularities of being here in *this* world. *My* world can be safe and sound, *your* world can be full of fear; or vice versa, depending on one's point of view. But *the* world happens in the relation to Being. *The* world can be invoked at the level of the ontico-ontological. But *the* world is not any particular world. And yet it is a differential world, since it happens in the Being of beings. *Dasein*, the being that is here, is *here* in *the* world. *Dasein*, being here, is not in *my* world or *your* world. It is not even in *our* world or *their* world. *Dasein* is just "*in der Welt*" and *Being-in-the-World* is differential since it happens in the "ontico-ontological difference." This differential space is where truth happens, but in this *Being-in-the-World*, the truth is not the truth that George Bush is able to so steadfastly offer. Many will say that *his* world is not *my* world. But in Heidegger's sense, it is not as a *his* or *my* world that we are *in-the-World*. The *Dasein* that is *in-the-World* is differential, a differential space.

In this differential space of *Being-in-the-World*, event-ing (*Er-eignis*) happens. In Heidegger – the Heidegger of the late 1930s, as in the *Beitrage*, – *Er-eignis* is not multiple. And *Ereignis* is not singular either.[1] And yet, in Gianni Vattimo's sense, one might indeed ask whether one can "get over" *Ereignis* – "get over" *Ereignis* as the *Eventing* that is singular. *Verwindung* can be understood as a convalescence from *Being-in-the-World* as a unitary event, from the singularity of *Ereignis*.

As Gianni likes to point out, in *Der Ursprung des Kunstwerkes* of 1935–36,[2] Heidegger shows that the *Origin* of the Work of Art is in a decentred centre – one in which truth happens, but also one where the Open happens, where there is a worlding of the world as in "the world of the Peasant Woman." Van Gogh's painting of the shoes opens up a space, a world that is not the same world as Van Gogh's own world or my world as viewer of the painting or even the world of art commerce and preservation. So in this aesthetic sense, there are many worlds, many worlds in which an *Ereignis* happens. The *eventing* of the Peasant Woman and her shoes is a particular eventing, one that happens, that is authentic, that is *in-the-World*. So there is a World – the world of the peasant woman's shoes – and such a world is *in-the-World*.

The peasant woman in all of her trials and tribulations is in her world, trying to make ends meet. But in her world, the work of art discloses a truth, and this truth happens in the Open, in the differential space, in the place where the peasant woman's world takes place. But *the* world of this Being *in-the-World* is not anywhere. And yet a *Verwindung* is called for here. And so, it could be said that in the "postmodern" world, the task is to "get over" *Being-in-the-World* and to face the fact (as one might say) that *eventing* is not singular, that *the* world is not singular, that my cellphone company is not singular ... The peasant woman has her trials and tribulations and she lives in a world – her world – because her world is a world of events. She does not have access to *Ereignis*. Her experience is an experience of multiple events. She will not have heard of the assassination of JFK, of the death of Lady Diana, of 9/11, because they all happened "after" her time. Or is it possible for there to be an *after* her time? Doesn't Heidegger mean to say that the "world" of the peasant woman is timeless? Is it not that her life and her experiences and her trials and tribulations belong to her but that since this world is disclosed by a work of art, this world is not *in* the world but rather (as Merleau-Ponty would say) her world is *of* the world (*au monde*)? Her world is a cultural world, a lived world, a world that cannot be discriminated by and in a certain clock time. But her world is also not *timeless*. Peasant life in the twenty-first century is not the same as peasant life in the nineteenth century. Peasant life in China is not the same as peasant life in Heidegger's Germany or in Van Gogh's Holland or France. So the peasant woman's world that is disclosed in Van Gogh's painting is a world that is not the world but that is also not any particular peasant woman's world.

The world is not a world that is not any particular world ...

This is precisely the postmodern question confronting a strict Heideggerian interpretation: how do we get over the idea that the world is not a world that is not any particular world? The e-venting of this world, the world of the peasant woman, that discloses Being-in-the-World as truth, happens in many different places and at many different times. The e-venting (*Ereignis*) can be understood as multiple events, but when understood as multiple events, something different happens. When 9/11 happens in the postmodern world, it happens not only as an event but as an *Ereignis*. The assassination of JFK was an *Ereignis*. These postmodern *Ereignisse*, if they happen at all, happen in multiple places. And they mean much more than the events themselves mean. Not all events are the same. Not all events happen in the same way. Not all events are *Ereignisse*. *Ereignisse* are not events that can be chronicled in history books. Ereignisse happen when they happen in the interstices of lived spaces, in the gaps where everyday life goes on, in the breaks in the continuity of human experience. Postmodern *Ereignisse* happen in the here and now, but they don't have spaces of their own. They are not outside the world, but they are also not in the world. They are at best "of" the world. They are interruptions in a particular world.

There are many worlds: George Bush's world is not my world. He sees the world differently than I do. George Bush's world is not John Kerry's world. Kerry sees the world differently from the way Bush sees it. Does this mean that each of these worlds is a different world? Or does it mean that between the worlds, in the places of difference between the worlds, something happens and that this "something that happens," if it happens, is an *Ereignis* that makes these worlds different. But then, is there a world that is independent of these worlds? One could say that there will always be another world to face, another challenge to confront, another world to be viewed, lived, experienced, differenced. What kind of world this world would be depends on the circumstances. But it does not mean that there is one and only one world to face, to shape, to change, to improve, to rule over, to control, to fear. The world is always other, always differential, always displaced in relation to any particular world.

So what does this say of a politics of "the" world? Globalization is a politics of "the" world rather than a politics of differential worlds. Jean-Luc Nancy makes the distinction between "globalisation" and "mondialisation." While in French "globalization" is typically translated as "mondialisation," Nancy wants to distinguish between the two accounts. Globalization is the attempt to impose a single worldview on the whole world. It assumes that "the whole world" is "the world." It takes "the world" for "the whole world" and seeks to impose "my" world on it. Nancy wants to suggest that to understand "mondialisa-tion" is to understand that "worlding" (to follow Heidegger) happens, that different worlds can exist, can hold sway, can have meaning, can occupy space without having to compromise a single worldview – political, cultural, technological. Mondialization can recognize that differences will happen and yet that there can be a concern for "the" world. The world must not be transformed into a world in which one world is superimposed on another. The world is comprised of the events of difference between worlds. The world is in fact many different worlds, many different events. And each event that marks the world as an *Ereignis* will have changed the world. How to live with these *Ereignisse*, how to live in the world and to be of the world is the post-modern task, a task that does not have univocal answers – for instance answers that presume that preemption is better than good judgment and just action. Nor does it presume that imposing my world because of one event on other worlds is a worthy strategy or that an event that marks a significant difference should be taken as a license to create other events so that one world will replace another. Globalization has its virtues – it can make trade between countries possible; it can lead to the sharing of technological advances; it can provide means of access to and interaction with others; and it can improve communication and systems of communication. But when it means imposing one world upon another in-the-World, it ignores the strength of weak thought (*pensiero debole*) and seeks to impose its codes upon others with bombs, with soldiers, with fear (and precious little trembling), with a claim to be right and a claim that the right is right and that it is its right to make "the" world not "its own" but "his" or "theirs" ...

NOTES

1 *Beitrage* (1989) is the German title of Martin Heidegger's *Contributions to Philosophy: (From Enowning)*, trans. Parvis Emad and Kenneth Maly (Indiana University Press 1999) [editor's note].

2 *Der Ursprung des Kunstwerkes* (1935) is the German title of Martin Heidegger's essay "The Origin of the Work of Art," included in *Off the Beaten Track*, ed. and trans. Julian Young and Kenneth Haynes (Cambridge: Cambridge University Press 2002) [editor's note].

7

Deconstruction Is Not Enough: On Gianni Vattimo's Call for "Weak Thinking"

REINER SCHÜRMANN

Vattimo's paper on weak thinking is strongly argued, at least in its general strategy.[1] He first describes the dialectical mode of philosophizing, then opposes it to the differential mode that "combats" dialectics while remaining "deeply complicitous" with it, and finally sublates both: weak ontology is "constructed not only by developing the discourse of difference, but also by recalling dialectics." This is strong thinking indeed, perhaps unintendedly so. The Hegelian as well as the Heideggerian positions are to be *aufgehoben*, since ours is the time in which both modes of reappropriating the past have proved asthenic. They are elevated and at the same time cancelled as they turn into interpretation. Such is the strength of weak thought.

Methodologically, all that we can and should make our own is the softness with which hermeneutics has corroded hard thinking since the late nineteenth century. What is at issue in the advocacy of *il pensiero debole* is the conviction, not exactly unheard of the twentieth century, that systematic thinking – the thinking that seeks "deductive cogency" – has reached a closure. Philosophers, once the least dispensable civil servants who, for everyone's benefit, ascertained supreme points of conceptual moorage from which to deduce norms for all our cognitive, moral, and political endeavours, have forfeited that mission. They have become incapable of providing the community with foundations on which our lives could find security, stability, and rest. How have they achieved their own professional demise? The respective careers of dialectics, difference, and interpretation each offer their own narration of that story. Soft sublation leaves us in a landscape of hard constructs in decay, among which we move like cats through the coliseum in Rome – with, in addition, pious recollections. Such has become the weakness of strong thought.

There is also a weakness in weak thought that in Vattimo's paper is perhaps equally unintended. It could be put in geographical terms: is Italy closer to its Latin sister to the northwest or to the Germanic tribes to the north? Jacques Derrida distinguishes between two ways of practising deconstruction: one consists in "deciding to change terrain, in a discontinuous and irruptive fashion, by brutally placing oneself outside [metaphysics] and by affirming an absolute break"; the other, in "attempting an exit without changing terrain, by repeating what is implicit in the foundational concepts." The first, he adds, "dominates France today"; the second "style of deconstruction is mostly that of the Heideggerian questions."[2] Vattimo likewise distinguishes between "overcoming" metaphysics and, with a pun on the German word *Verwindung*, "distorting" it from within. The former program would aim at leaving metaphysics behind. The latter, in the quasi-Freudian connotation *Verwindung* has in Heidegger, would remain content with working through it, which is similar, Heidegger writes, "to what happens when, in the human realm, one works through grief or pain."[3] It is with some relief that I see Vattimo attempting to work through metaphysics rather than to overcome it, and thereby siding with the ways of Freud and Heidegger – or with Paul Klee, whose angel contemplates with compassion the ruins, accumulated by history, at its feet. Nevertheless, since Vattimo is interested in a *postmetaphysical* "'layout' for the relation between philosophy and society," deconstruction, whether French, German or Italian, cannot be enough.

Having gone through the strength of weak thinking, the weakness of strong thinking, and the weakness of weak thinking, I need not rehearse the fourth permutation, since one wonders who on either side of the Atlantic is still interested in the strength of strong thinking.

Deconstruction (a word that has turned into a slogan only after having been translated into French fifty years after Heidegger coined it as *Abbau*) is not enough, and for Heidegger himself neither *Abbau* nor *Verwindung* could be, nor has been, the last word. Nor is Derrida, on the other side of the Rhine, content with brutally placing himself outside metaphysics and affirming an absolute break. In this entire debate, what is needed are some skirmishes outside the orderly battle of dialectics, difference, and interpretation. Although I will sketch these advances in three steps, I trust that they will not lend themselves to one more radical dialectical cooptation. Theirs is a modest strength. It comes from what metaphysicians would call distinctions; analytical philosophers, concept definitions; and postmodernists, displacements.

THE ENDS OF PHILOSOPHY

The end of philosophy – a certain end, at least – has been proclaimed for a little over two hundred years now, ever since the publication of Kant's *Critique of Pure Reason*. Current variations on that endgame share the conviction that the necessary distinctions, concept definitions, and displacements set apart two modes of thinking: theories focusing on "systems" (such as functionalism and structuralism) stand in irreconcilable oppositions to the theories focusing on "man" (humanist Marxism, initial trends in phenomenology, and hermeneutics). Both participants in this polemic, systems theorist and humanist, link the fate of philosophy to "man" as the standard or measure for thought.

On the antihumanist side, the best example for such coupling may be found in Michel Foucault. His effort to lay bare what in his early work he called *epistemai* – "systems of positivities" or "systems of simultaneity" – made it necessary for him to treat man as only one variable in cultural networks and to proclaim that if our own cultural arrangement, perhaps no older than a century and a half, were to undergo a shift, "then one can certainly wager that man would be erased, like a face drawn in sand at the edge of the sea."[4] Such an erasure of man as the measure entails the erasure of philosophy: "What I am doing cannot, in any way, be regarded as philosophy."[5] The coupling of philosophy and anthropocentrism is as obvious in this twofold rejection as it remains unquestioned. It remains equally unquestioned in the attempts made to save philosophy from its deadly fate at the hands of the systems theorist. To illustrate these attempts, I mention only the "return to the subject" urged by the transcendental phenomenologist as philosophy's one and only hope for staying alive.

Such linkage between philosophy and man as its measure is what stands in need of distinctions, concept definitions, and displacements. Heidegger has taken more than one step in that direction. He has charged that "what is peculiar to all metaphysics is that it is humanistic." He has invited "an open resistance to 'humanism.'" In the title of his last public lecture, "The End of Philosophy and the Task of Thinking,"[6] the word "thinking" stands in polemical opposition to the word "philosophy" and thereby to "man." "Thinking" is thus distinguished from an entire cluster of concepts: metaphysics, philosophy, humanism, man. Thinking is displaced, placed outside the arena where these concepts serve to define one another. Why should it resist them? Why should that cluster be denied a function? Because of a quite different endgame, which has preceded and overdetermined the modern verdict on speculation, the endgame played by philosophy itself, whose native preoccupation has been *man: its end*, its measure understood as its ultimate referent. The cluster of concepts just mentioned only instantiates teleology as the basic law of the tradition on whose extreme edge Vattimo locates *il pensiero debole*. The end, or *eschaton*, of philosophy requires, then, an open resistance to "man" as the end, or *telos*, of philosophy.

If deconstruction is not enough, if skirmishes are to be attempted outside the battlefield where "theses" confront one another, and if "thinking" is the stalker that may lead us beyond the closed field mined by inherited vocabularies, then the distinction between two ends of philosophy is helpful. The *eschaton* of philosophy is only the historical moment at which the systematic closure that its *telos* has been producing all along is recognized. The distinction between the two ends of philosophy does not yet break that closure. It remains a deconstructionist distinction. It suggests, however, a question that may eventually lead us beyond the metaphysics: Is there a "measure" for thinking that would not be its *telos*? My second set of distinctions, concept definitions, and displacements addresses, then, the question, Can there be a nonteleological *metron, mensura, Mass*?

THE MEASURES FOR THINKING

Vattimo calls metaphysics that kind of thinking that argues for "strong" characteristics of being. The strongest among such arguments would claim that there is one being that meters out being and nonbeing. That is what Protagoras is said to have taught: "Man is the *metron* of all things: of those that are, that they are; and of those that are not, that they are not."[7] In a different context, Augustine, too, claims that there is one such mensurating being. God is "the *mensura* which pre-

figures for everything its way of being."[8] The modern, transcendental-
ist revolution in no way gives up the idea of ultimate mensuration. In
the *Critique of Judgment* this function is assigned to the "principle of
ideality." By virtue of it, "in our general estimate of beauty, we seek its
Richtmass a priori in ourselves."[9] The strong sense of measure is "standard." Inasmuch as man, God, and the principle of ideality assign ends
to whatever is or is to be done or known, they are standards for being,
acting, and knowing. This metaphysics of teleological measures, of
standards, has perhaps constituted the very strength of what is called
Western civilization.

That the recognition of measures need not stand or fall with strong,
i.e., teleological, thinking – that all measures need not be standards – is
what I should like to suggest now. If it is possible to distinguish between
teleological and nonteleological measures, the old *topos* of mensuration
will find itself displaced, placed outside of metaphysics.

In Aeschylus the defeat that the Persian army suffered at Salamis is
described as incurred by its hubris. This word *hybris* stems from *hyper*,
"beyond": hubris is what makes us overstep a norm or measure. In
several of his inventions for crossing the Hellespont, Xerxes trans-
gressed the measure set by nature. First he had two boat bridges placed
across the strait. Then, after a storm had destroyed them, he had the sea
whipped as punishment and the pontoons rebuilt. Lastly, he undertook
a massive engineering work, having a channel dug so as to avoid round-
ing a dangerous promontory. Aeschylus comments:

> In youth's rash mood he sought
> To curb sacred Hellespont with fetters,
> As though it were its slave, and sought to alter
> The stream of God, full-flowing Bosporos,
> And with his hammered chains around it cast,
> Prevailed to make his mighty host a highway.
> Nay, was not my poor son oppressed with madness?[10]

The bounds Xerxes overstepped with his stratagems were indeed
"strong" in Vattimo's sense. They suggest some traits pertaining to
every metaphysical concept of measure. Nature is man's Other: were it
not, Xerxes could not have whipped, shackled, and humiliated it.
Nature is furthermore an Other that transcends human action: were it
not, Xerxes could not stand accused of disrespect. It is also a well-
ordered Other, resembling a society in which there are superiors and

inferiors: were it not, his war ruses could not appear as an attempt to turn the strait into his slave. The natural order is, in addition, rational: were it not, it would not be madness that Aeschylus sees in Xerxes' expedition. As a standard, nature is unchangeable: building the second bridge constituted no less a transgression than building the first. Otherness, transcendence, order, rationality, permanence: such are a few essential characteristics of every measure that sets ends, *tele*, for our projects.

In a remarkable conflict of interest, philosophers have been both the legislators establishing such bounds and the judges passing sentence on their legitimacy. This accumulation of charges, although in conflict with the enlightened principle of the separation of powers, has not been recognized, let alone raised, even in Kant's criticism. In modernity, too, philosophers have been called upon to secure end-setting, tele-thetic measures. That function has made them the prime civil servants of their societies and has given Western civilization its global reach.

Nonmetaphysical thinking would do more than reallocate the legislative and judicial functions of reasons: it would, Vattimo suggests, "enfeeble" all inherited characteristics of thought and presumably cancel their titles of strength so conspicuously displayed in contemporary technology. In a nonmetaphysical ontology, he writes, being "gives itself to thought in a radically different way." By restoring, or instoring, being's "temporal essence," such an ontology would put out of use the machinery of legitimation that has produced the world in which we live.

This delegitimation through the temporalization of being requires some further analysis. The issue can be phrased straightforwardly: What measures are left for thinking and acting once ontology's strong claims have been challenged from within through an understanding of "being as time"?[11] The so-called crisis of legitimation proves to be a crisis affecting the representations of measure as they undergo a displacement. Can the very issue of legitimation survive the break by which standards shift from a conceptual economy marked by otherness, transcendence, order, rationality, and permanence to an economy marked by figures of time? It is with some reservation that I follow Vattimo's diagnosis of the "enfeeblement of the idea of being" if this diagnosis is to imply the impossibility of ascertaining measures for thinking beyond the hypothetical closure of metaphysics. It is true, however, that after the reduction of entitative standards into temporal measures, the professionals of legitimation may hardly recognize their subject matter.

Since the context in which Vattimo develops his diagnosis is a discussion of Heidegger, I will suggest what might be described as a nonmetaphysical understanding of measure in Heidegger – nonmetaphysical understandings, rather, since Heidegger enumerates three. Each of them corresponds to one period in his writing: "After *Being and Time* [my] thinking replaced the expression 'meaning of being' with 'truth of being.' And so as to avoid any misapprehension about truth, so as to exclude that it be understood as conformity, 'truth of being' has been elucidated as 'locality of being'... Hence the expression 'topology of being.'"[12] From "meaning" to "truth" to "locus," the measure of thinking in Heidegger becomes more and more explicitly temporal.

The question of the meaning of being guided Heidegger's analysis in *Being and Time.* The word translated as "meaning" hints at the solution of the problem as he attempted it in that first period: *Sinn* (just like the French *sens* and, a least in some expressions, the English sense) indicates the direction a given movement is taking. One may speak of the sense in which a pendulum swings, of a *rue à sens unique* (a one-way street), or the *sens* of a river (the course it flows). What, then is the *Sinn* according to Heidegger's existential analytic? It is the three-fold time-dimension by which *Dasein* stands out of itself. That ecstatic temporality was his first attempt at a nonmetaphysical measure. It remained perhaps no more than an attempt, since despite the novelty of the question of being, Heidegger's early treatment of time retained much of the neo-Kantian preoccupation with meaning, as well as the Husserlian notions of protention and retention. Still, *Dasein's* temporality is its measure, inasmuch as everything we can experience must occur within the finite framework of "the 'towards-oneself,' the 'back-to,' and the 'letting-oneself-be-encountered-by.'"[13] Ecstatic temporality is a measure that excludes from possible experience any in-itself, and that encloses all possible experience within the horizon drawn by death. As Vattimo states it with all desirable clarity: "The analysis of *Dasein* leads Heidegger to radically temporalize the a priori." What is measuring all our projects a priori is being-towards-death.

Heidegger's second attempt at a nonmetaphysical measure, inasmuch as it articulates the "truth," *aletheia*, of being, should be called aletheiological. Each epoch in Western history is one such network of concealment-unconcealment in which everything that can be thought or done remains inscribed. The epochal beginnings from the Greek to the atomic age are measure-giving, *massgebend*, now.[14] Heidegger does not hesitate to equate measure, being, and the history of being: "the history of being alone is being itself,"[15] and "being itself is the sole measure for entities."[16] Here Professor Vattimo's explanations are most pertinent: it is the "series of 'positions,' of occurrences, or – as Heidegger calls them – historical-cultural disclosures which constitute the meaning of being" ... or better, the successive modes of its truth.

A historical-cultural epoch, the network of phenomenal interconnectedness that always situates us anew diachronically, is a measure for acting and thinking, but it is not a standard. Although it determines every possible occurrence, it does not set any ideal to which whatever occurs is to be referred. It is not man's other. It transcends him, but more like a system of transcendental conditions than like a transcendent model. That transcendentality likens the measure to a structural a priori, but one that allows for a posteriori objectification. We so objectify past epochal measures whenever we speak of Rome, the Middle Ages, the Renaissance, or the seventeenth or the eighteenth centuries. Also, if it indeed yields an order – in Vattimo's words, a "set of canons historically constituted" – these canons are in constant transition, set apart by breaks and ruptures. Nor is the *epoché* a measure that is rational or even intelligible to the individuals and communities it posits.

The temporality of epochal measures results from Heidegger's key discovery after *Being and Time*, namely, that everydayness has a history. We know our epochal order through having always practised it already, just as according to the existential analytic we know utensils through using them. Aletheiological measures thus are nothing permanent, and they come in the plural. They instantiate Heidegger's concept of time after what he called the turn in his thinking: epochal temporality. With Vattimo, one may wish to say that Heidegger radically temporalized the a priori only at the second stage of his thinking. From ecstatic to epochal temporality, the measure for acting and thinking becomes empirically finite as it "turns," unsteady, contingent upon historical context.

This concept of time, worked out in the late thirties and early forties, has proved fruitful in Michel Foucault's archeology of knowledge. But the structuralist consequences also point to a possible misapprehension concerning their phenomenological antecedent: in tracing the history of *aletheia*, Heidegger ran the risk that epochal time might turn "being" into a sequence of positivities for representation. In his last concept of time, "event," Heidegger therefore reclaims from epochal measures their diachronic contingency, but he moves beyond what Vattimo describes as his historicism. Now it is the simple synchronic movement of coming to presence, of "presencing" – that is, a phenomenon's *phainesthai* – that functions as measure for our acting and thinking. This, his last word on the temporality of being, was also the first word in the history of philosophy: *physis*. This truly nonmetaphysical measure, irreducible to any existential or historicist notion, had served in Heraclitus precisely as a measure for acting: *poieîn kata physin*, acting according to presencing.[17] *Physis* here – such is at least Heidegger's interpretative violence – is comparable to the representation of nature in the lines from Aeschylus, as *Ereignis* is to ontic representations or as *rheuma* (the flux) is to standards. Heidegger's understanding of "event" as presencing is topological inasmuch as the *topoi* where presencing occurs are many: not only diachronically but also synchronically. *Ereignis* designates the originary phenomenon, which is the condition for historical, as well as ecstatic, time.

Of this move beyond *Dasein* as well as of history in Heidegger, I see no trace in Vattimo's paper. It may not have been his topic, since it would have been impossible to say that the concept of that originary time phenomenon "assimilates and pursues the dialectical heritage, binding it to difference." *Physis* as an event-like measure is irreducible to dialectics, since it implies no reappropriation of past historical effects. Its time-dimension is, rather, the simple appearance of a phenomenon, any phenomenon, here and now. To be sure, its concept addresses a difference, but one whose terms are in no way comparable to the earlier "ontological difference."

Vattimo's paper was perhaps not intended as a contribution to the question, What remains, and what perishes, in the break between metaphysical and nonmetaphysical thinking? – although his discussion of *überwinden* and *verwinden* hints at precisely that question. At any rate, from the viewpoint of normative thinking, which has been the backbone of metaphysics, Heidegger allows one to answer: measures remain, although radically temporalized, but the standards perish. Had Vattimo chosen to follow Heidegger's itinerary to its last and decisive stage, he could not have concluded that the ethics resulting from weak thought would be an ethics "in which the supreme values – those which are good in themselves and not because they are means to an end – are symbolical formations, monuments, traces of the living (everything that gives itself to and stimulates interpretation; hence an ethics of 'values' rather than of 'imperatives')." If weak thought is meant to thematize simultaneously the event of presencing, which escapes representation, and values, which are the representational contents par excellence, then it aims at squaring the circle, at amalgamating the nonmetaphysical and the arch-metaphysical.

THE GENDERS OF STRENGTH

The interest at work behind Vattimo's deliberately panoramic text may be gathered from his remark about Klee's angel and the ruins accumulated at its feet by history: "Compassion for these ruins is the only real instigator of revolution – not some project legitimized in the name of a natural right or an inevitable course of history." Compassion is considered a *forte* of the so-called weak sex; reaching for higher principles such as natural right, a foible of the so-called strong sex. I worry about the revolution Vattimo foments: will it come from the bad weakness of the strong sex in need of standards and finding only scattered but hardened pieces of them, or will it come from the good weakness of the weak sex, which consists, Nietzsche writes, in "*trying very hard* to appear superficial and thoughtless"? Bad weakness would be the virilization of the feminine. It would be bad because it would produce more of the same in the West: more standards, more universals, more metaphysics. Good weakness would be the feminization of the masculine. It would be good because it would transmute timeless standards into thoroughly temporalized, Heraclitean measures – at least if Nietzsche is right that the strength of women consists in "seeming utterly changeable and unfathomable." That is also why "truth is a woman who has reasons for not letting her reasons be seen." In other words, I worry about the sex of Paul Klee's angel. Is it feminine like a feminist's angel, a woman turned masculine as she holds fast to the principle of eternal femininity – to what Nietzsche calls "das Weib an sich" – or is it feminine as the Greeks were, namely, "superficial out of profundity"? If the angel is compassionate because it cannot be other, one must worry indeed. To Nietzsche, weakness is an invention: women "invent weaknesses, thus they defend themselves against the strong and their 'fist-right.'"[18] Vattimo does not tell us how he views "post-metaphysical humanity," that is, post-revolutionary humanity. I worry whether it will draw its strength from the invention of weaknesses or from enfeebled – because disarticulated – versions of the old fistright.

In his call for a revolution, one strategy tends to demarcations between weak and strong, soft and hard, feminine and masculine. But a counterstrategy toward intrametaphysical interpretation so paralyzes the attempted denaturation that the good weakness of women trying hard to appear unprincipled out of profundity ends up being co-opted for the bad weakness of men trying hard to appear principled out of what Nietzsche also calls stupidity: "What is unfeminine in women is their stupidity."[19] It would be asking a lot from interpretation to expect it to loosen the world-wide grip of principled fistright. But even Kant's "revolution in the way of thinking" (Revolution der Denkungstart), which was to lead mankind to universal enlightenment, was less defeatist. Kant defined enlightenment as "man's release from his self-incurred tutelage." Which tutelage is more blatantly self-incurred than the one under normative phantasms such as natural right, the course of history, femininitude? I doubt that literary and art criticism can serve as a model for a *Denkungsart* capable of denaturing these hegemonic referents, of releasing us from them.

The various forms of time in Heidegger have at least one trait in common: they yield measures that are neither referents, (i.e., representable) nor hegemonic (i.e., commanding). In that sense, a postmetaphysical ethics could indeed not be one of imperatives. The sought-for turn in the way of thinking can only lead us *from* representational thinking, whose allies are transcendent norms and global violence, *to* a thinking more *sotto voce*, in an undertone, whose allies would presumably be less overpowering. In Nietzsche's vocabulary: a masculine undertone would ring through the sought-for feminine voice in philosophy. "A deep and powerful alto voice of the kind one sometimes hears in the theater can suddenly raise the curtain upon possibilities in which we usually do not believe."[20] In a Heideggerian vocabulary: the turn would be a transition from obeying standards held to be timeless to complying with pliant measures – pliant as they come and go with the mutations in presencing.

Does Vattimo perhaps expect too much from compassion? Is a revolution in the way of thinking not more likely to spring from the scepticism that Nietzsche praised (particularly in older women), from an analytic shrewdness that sees right through the highly principled devastations, both past and in preparation, rather than from piety for their effects? Has "constructivity," which he calls for and of which he finds elements in Heidegger's *Verwindung*, as well as in Derrida's deconstruction, not been the very craze of strong thinking, that is, its ever new fad and its mania? How can weak thinking end up as a companion to the oldest *déformation professionnelle* among philosophers, the rage to build ever new edifices of obligation under some ultimate representation? Does this call for constructivity not prove beyond doubt that the weakness in *il pensiero debole* is bad weakness? Concretely, how can Vattimo wish to distort metaphysics with, of all metaphysical fantasms, an ethic of values? Is it because strong thinking exerted on strong thinking results in a double negation? Neither pious compassion for the ruins nor constructivity in another key can set the pace for transgressing our self-incurred tutelage. They can only engulf us further in the worst effects of metaphysics – its most ruinous effects, to be precise.

To give one further turn of the screw to my suspicion that "weak thinking" puts to work bad, masculine weakness, recall the weakness of Robespierre who, in the name of the principles of the revolution, forgot the revolution. Likewise, in line with the examples mentioned by Vattimo, for the sake of the principles of right and of history metaphysicians have tended to forget right and history. They have done so not occasionally but professionally. The substitution of principles for life is inscribed in the regularity of the metaphysical discourse itself. Both dialectical and differential thinking had set out to undo precisely that substitution – with only partial success, as Vattimo has shown. It has remained partial from Marx to critical theory, inasmuch as both Marxism and critical theory have had to rely on new instances of ultimacy. It remains perhaps partial still in Heidegger, inasmuch as the issue of time, even if it is certainly not a referential fantasm, is worked out in opposition to the old quest for immutables. Therefore, it may be tempting to turn against Heidegger's negation of timelessness what he said about contemporary forms of negating technology: "they all are mere re-actions against it, which means, the same thing."[21]

Robespierre's dilemma, the unswerving substitution of hard standards for soft measurement, has been exacerbated today as those standards have lost much of their credibility. It would be all the more awkward for us to seek refuge in inherited edifices of legitimation whose every window of vulnerability we know. Intellectuals today would like to freeze and, if possible, dismantle the guillotine and its successor machines stockpiled East and West. Piety and compassion for their victims are generous feelings. But weakness of thought, if it means no more than ruminating monuments, comes close to abdication. Could such awkwardness and abdication be at work in Vattimo's invitation "to follow Being along its evening decline and *thereby* prepare for a post-metaphysical humanity"?

NOTES

1 This paper was written in response to Vattimo's essay "Dialectics, Difference, and Weak Thought," *Graduate Faculty Philosophy Journal* 10, no. 1 (spring 1984): 151–64.

2 Jacques Derrida, *Margins of Philosophy,* trans. A. Bass (Chicago: The University of Chicago Press 1982) 135. Note: although all references to books translated from another language cite the English edition, translations in the text, except for that from Aeschylus, are mine.

3 Martin Heidegger, *The Question concerning Technology,* trans. W. Lovitt (New York: Harper and Row 1977): 39.

4 Michel Foucault, *The Order of Things,* trans. from the French, (New York: Vintage 1973): xxiif., 387.

5 Michel Foucault, *The Archeology of Knowledge,* trans. A.M. Sheridan Smith (New York: Harper and Row 1972), 206.

6 Martin Heidegger, *Basic Writings,* trans. F.A. Capuzzi and D.F. Krell (New York: Harper and Row 1972), 202, 225.

7 *Die Fragmente der Vorsokratiker,* ed. H. Diels (Berlin 1903), frgn B1, 518.

8 Augustine, *De Genesi ad Litteram,* book 4, 3, 7 (99); 2 vols., ed. P. Agaësse and A. Solignac (Brugge: Desclée de Brouwer 1972), 1:288.

9 Immanuel Kant, *The Critique of Judgment,* B252; trans. J.C. Meredith, 9th ed. (Oxford: Clarendon Press 1980), 220.

10 Aeschylus, *Tragedies,* trans. E.H. Plumptre, 2 vols. (London 1868), 2:40.

11 M. Heidegger, *Nietzsche,* vol. 1: *The Will to Power as Art,* trans. D.F. Krell (New York: Harper and Row 1979), 20.

12 M. Heidegger, *Vier Seminare* (V. Klostermann: Frankfurt 1977), 73.

13 M. Heidegger, *Being and Time,* trans. J. Macquarrie and E. Robinson (New York: Harper and Row 1962), 377.

14 M. Heidegger, *Poetry, Language, Thought,* trans. A. Hofstadter (New York: Harper and Row 1971), 77.

15 M. Heidegger, *The End of Philosophy,* trans. J. Stambaugh (New York: Harper and Row 1971), 77.

16 M. Heidegger, *Gesamtausgabe*, vol. 55: *Heraklit* (Frankfurt: V. Klostermann 1979), 326.

17 Ibid., 367.

18 All quotations from Friedrich Nietzsche, *The Gay Science*, translated by
W. Kaufmann (New York: Vintage 1974), 38, 125, 128.

19 Friedrich Nietzsche, *Human All Too Human*, book 2, no. 273.

20 Friedrich Nietzsche, *The Gay Science*, 127.

21 Heidegger, *Heraklit*, 203.

8

Weak Thought 2004:
A Tribute to Gianni Vattimo

PIER ALDO ROVATTI

Translated by Robert T. Valgenti

A DECISIVE ENCOUNTER AND AN AGREEMENT
FOREVER POSTPONED

I think that the most sincere tribute to a friend and thinker – one to whom I feel profoundly tied and with whom I have publicly shared a philosophical adventure in which I continue to believe – should return to the very grounds of our encounter, beginning with the so-called differences between us. Gianni Vattimo is one of the most original and significant Italian philosophers of our time (I write "one of" out of modesty and *bon ton*; in reality, I consider him the most important). This is already a great difference between us, one that I will assume is taken for granted in the following pages. I beg the reader not to forget it, while allowing me to offer an immodest comparison.

I would like to discuss the differences in our philosophical attitude and in our distinct personal histories that, at a certain point, become interwoven. A student of Luigi Pareyson and the product of a distinct environment in Turin where even religious themes were rather prevalent, Vattimo crossed the philosophies of Heidegger and Nietzsche with a very original *clinamen* and with a gesture that I would define (borrowing the term from Gilles Deleuze) as *agencement*, a gesture that allowed him to effectively read each of the two great philosophers through the other, in a sort of *après coup* that unhinges their chronological linearity, producing a fruitful play of anticipations and delays.

One need only read Vattimo's texts dedicated to Heidegger and Nietzsche in the 1960s and 1970s to understand that fact. And while this
course is certainly accompanied by Gadamerian hermeneutics (which, in
a novel way, pointed to a declension of the ideas of "truth" and "interpretation"), it is in the world of Nietzschean pluralism and the Heideggerian weakening of Being that Vattimo finds his own philosophical
identity, hypothesizing a subjectivity beyond the subject and instilling a
politics of philosophy and a commitment to the surrounding reality that
are irreducible either to academic intellectualism or to disciplinary spe-
cialism. This identity corresponds to a kind of anti-authoritarian thinking that is, precisely, a way to do philosophy that radically criticizes the
effects of the power produced by thought in the course of its own
history. Therefore, it is a way of thinking that is, so to say, ultra-Kantian
as to the inquiry into its own conditions but also decidedly Nietzschean
in its nihilistic rejection of any reassuring ground provided by an ultimate foundation or a presumed one.

Quite literally, I am indebted to Vattimo for the discovery of Heidegger and the rethinking of Nietzsche's work, which was already a part of
my philosophical repertoire, due to the influence, in a critical and
emancipatory key, of the so-called Nietzsche Rénaissance. When I first
encountered Vattimo and his work (here, with Vattimo, a clear example
of the coincidence between biography and theory), I was a student of
Enzo Paci's concrete phenomenology, which was strongly influenced by
the horizon of postexistentialist thought where Merleau-Ponty and
Sartre were being read in a predominantly humanistic key. In the seventies, Paci attempted a crossing of Marx and of Marxisms by using
notions of Husserlian origin (subject, intentionality, *Lebenswelt*, but
above all *epoché*), in order to "lighten" any scientistic guarantee by
means of critical thinking similar to that of the Frankfurt School. I was
thus an intellectual formed through phenomenology and postphenom-
enology, interested in the critique of capitalistic society and its presuppositions but also and not secondarily in the critique of every dogmati-
zation of Marxism and of Marx himself. And while Vattimo and I
found common ground in our projects and shared interests, we
nonetheless confronted a tradition of thinking with very diverse presuppositions.

Our felicitous encounter opened up pathways that had previously
been blocked in my apprenticeship (the example of Heidegger is the
most obvious), but nonetheless I had to pay – at least so I was warned

– the price of an unrealizable agreement. I was warned that Vattimo was not open to any alliance with phenomenology. In fact, he appeared to be deaf to this – namely, to the use of phenomenological tools and certainly to the possibility that someone, like me, could have arrived at the philosophical requirements of the "weak" sort, very close to his, through a means that in his eyes seemed decidedly inappropriate. At that time Vattimo believed that the thought of Husserl had been mortally wounded by metaphysics and therefore belonged to the great contingent of authoritarian and foundationalist philosophy. I doubt that he would have changed his mind even if he had continued to claim himself to be, with that tone of witty tolerance that has always been his, an agnostic in matters of phenomenology, to the point of saying that he did not know enough and that some day he would think about it seriously.

I remember that just before the publication of *Pensiero debole* (1983) he said more than once, "One day you will explain to me how it is possible to use Husserl in the way that you do." Naturally, it was not a real request, and that day has yet to arrive. But there was an episode that was a reaction, if only marginally, to the pleasant provocation of Vattimo. This occurred during the internal vicissitudes of the management – to call it that – of "listening" that, for better or for worse, led up to the publication of the aforementioned anthology. It now seems useful for me to remember this episode because it calls attention to the three pages that I had planned to add to my essay in *Pensiero debole*. For the better, as one says, these pages were never printed, since they were destined for an American edition of the anthology that was never published. They deal with a brief phenomenological excursus. For me (and maybe for the Italian reader of *Pensiero debole*), this excursus was implied, but I had taken the opportunity to imagine, so to speak, an external reader. This game of modesty is curious, given that my second move in the territory of weak thought, one that I initiated myself, was made with Alessandro Dal Lago in a small volume entitled *Elogio del pudore*[1] (Praise of modesty). But it is even more curious because my initial reservation, which resulted in the final pages being cut from the essay, was in truth directed at Vattimo himself. In our co-authored pages of *Pensiero debole* there is an un-said that refers specifically to Husserl, and it seems useful at this time to deliver it in detail, since I doubt that Vattimo himself had ever come to recognize it (which was probably the very thing I wanted).

HUSSERL, A CROSSING

At stake is the subject. It is a matter of crossing over a place without deleting it, of rediscovering an orientation rather than speculating about somewhere else. Furthermore, and at the same time, it is a matter of restoring philosophy's characteristic attitude and practice.

It is said that Husserl was the last to feel nostalgia for the *strenge Wissenschaft*: with him the claim to an "absolute" knowledge of the subject would push itself to a point of tension and extreme contraction as the failure of a project that coincides with modern philosophy, already inscribed in his Cartesianism. This was the swansong of strong thought in philosophy, and Heidegger would have the honour of making us grasp this fragmentation, this point of no return. The hermeneutic opening would be a thinking against the philosophy of the subject. Phenomenology would be the giving/revealing of the phenomenon: the self-manifesting always partial and one-sided, a faint glimmer from out of obscurity.

But Lévinas and Merleau-Ponty, and in Italy Enzo Paci, have pointed out a different reading. As Derrida also pointed out, Husserl enacts a weakening of the subject when he tries desperately to cross over to a new figure of scientificity. The result is the "paradox of subjectivity," the *Krisis*' true philosophical centre of gravity. The territory he discovers – as Lévinas has insisted – is that of passivity. Time and passivity, in their enigmatic intertwining, result in the not-so-secure place to which phenomenology necessarily brings us by means of an insistent and insatiable descriptive spiral. There is a doubling that is very symptomatic in Husserl: it is certain that he was following a rational phantasm by contrasting his work to solid and already materialized rationalisms. But it is equally certain that for him "scientificity" corresponds to this insatiable excavation of the subject – that is, a real rolling towards *x* that remains in his notion of *Lebenswelt*. The passive synthesis is a paradox, just as the "internal consciousness of time" is paradoxical. The part of the ego that does not know itself obscures clear reflection; the more one applies phenomenological rigour, the more the subject becomes opaque. But at the same time – Husserl continually expresses this dramatic certainty in his boring and pathos-less style – the subject becomes more "true."

In Husserl, strength and weakness destroy each other in the attempt to describe experience beyond the already constructed systems of reference; rather than constrict itself, the cone enlarges more and more, and the territory ends up unknown and boundless, but also ends up – and this is the most important point – more and more strangely familiar. The discovery of the intricate world of precategorical passivity does not produce a loss of self but the mark of an acquisition: not simple homelessness but the emotive sign of finding oneself at home again in homelessness. This is the strange optimism of a neo-Kantian philosopher who looks to crumble, one after the other, all of his "eidetic" claims. In the end the *eidos* will have to reject every position that is not that of the "typicality" of a style, of a way of proceeding, of a special voyage in subjectivity.

The emptiness of contents, several times blamed on Husserl, is in reality the index of a crucial problem: the question of baggage. In this crossing, the equipment will in fact have to undergo a continual lightening. Here the rigorous traveller is the one who will know how to refrain from topographical maps and who will listen with suspicion to the accounts of previous journeys. He will literally have to strip himself of all the *Ideenkleiden*, also knowing that he will never be able to make it to the end. What else is the much discussed *epoché*, the legacy of Cartesian solitude and skeptical disbelief, if not this attempt at lightening? The *I-pole*, which remains to hold subjective acts together as a species of optical fire without any recognizable substance, conserves the force of its extreme poverty. The more it impoverishes itself, the more the voyage will be profitable.

Heidegger exposed the rationalistic phantasm that accompanies Husserl from the *Logical Investigations* to the *Krisis*; yet he concealed the other, radically antimetaphysical face of phenomenology, considering it a corollary to the fleeting idea of the subject. There is no doubt that Heidegger has transmitted some decisive metaphors to today's philosophical sensibility. Exemplary among all the metaphors is that of "oscillation," the image of the unstable equilibrium between Being and nothing. The efficacy of Heideggerian philosophical language rests in the very constellation of figures that are in no way demonstrative but that manage to enter into resonance, into a sort of *Einfühlung*, with the demands of our condition of thought. This linguistic constellation, essentially metaphorical, subtends an idea of subject and of relation between the I and the world that Heidegger refuses to render explicit; yet, it nonetheless runs through his thought and places him in harmony with our own.

In order to bring into view the metaphysical phantasm that accompanies Heidegger from *Sein und Zeit* through his final lectures, that is, in order to read a modality of weak thought in Heidegger, it is necessary to go beyond the objective features of his description. Thus, it is necessary that his philosophy does not arrive – as it can seem – from a different, remote, and solemn location; rather, it should arise in the uncertain place of the interrogation, here and now, that belongs to the subject who has an experience, feels exposed, apprehends the impossibility of maintaining itself as centre and comes to recognize the Nietzschean element of illusion in every true language.

While it is always an elsewhere that speaks in Heidegger by pointing out things that we have in common, in Husserl the invitation is that of colliding with our obstinate repetition, of standing up to the claim of scientificity installed in our identity, of trying to loosen our grip. Both are projected beyond truth-as-correspondence, and the territory they cross is made of metaphors, even if they shun them. One can say that the philosophical intention is freer in Heidegger, more artistic and more intense; but the material of images that we have been able to collect from him will have to cross over the narrow passage of phenomenological subjectivity. It will have to be weakened – in respect to its claim of message – by reliving the prose of first person experience.

This caution, which comes to us from a phenomenology brought to its point of maximum tension and internal self-contradiction, cannot translate itself into a cognitive technique. The subject broken up by phenomenology no longer maintains a clear definition but only a style of thought. One can hold on to the ethical investment of the Husserlian *epoché*: the attitude through which we try, without ever having success, to place ourselves in our own experience. Certainly, Husserl had only indicated this legibility of ours without managing to follow it completely. In doing so, he would in fact have recognized the fragility of his own philosophical language. He would have thematized the fundamental element or even the necessary metaphorical nature of every philosophy of the subject. He would have thus defeated his phantasm.

Husserl can therefore be crossed by following the thread of a thought-attitude no longer containable within the limits of gnoseology. One cannot, however, erase the rational shadow of subjectivity by making the one coincide with the other, as Heidegger seems to do.

PARADOX, SILENCE, PLAY, AND EVEN A BIT OF HUMOUR

In this "crossing," which is but a hasty outline, I have condensed many themes that I tried to articulate in the twenty years that followed after

1983, from *La Posta in gioco*,[2] where I once again asked the question of the subject by reading Heidegger with Husserl (and vice versa, almost with a repetition of the gesture that Vattimo had made with Heidegger and Nietzsche), to *La Follia in poche parole*,[3] where I attempted to re-read Husserl's *dreaded* "Fifth Cartesian Meditation" as a place where, neither more nor less, "the folly of the other" is described. But the re-utilization of *epoché* as silence and listening and the commitment to give body and voice to the "paradox of subjectivity," which for me occupies the heart of the *Krisis* and of his entire thought, remained the undeniable zones of density in the philosophical method I espouse. And I do not believe that *Pensiero debole* can avoid it without degenerating into a way of thinking that is too irregular and not radical towards its own operations.

In the encounter with Vattimo, who was advancing his own reading of contemporary society by hypothesizing a "beyond" of hermeneutics, the shared admiration for our ways of thinking remained intact. But the encounter also lacked – for many reasons, some of them banally tied to histories and urgencies of life – an acknowledgment of its differences and its potential for reciprocal exchanges. I have never succeeded in completely affirming the meaning of the expression "weak ontology," on which Vattimo has constructed his most recent thought. This is how I think that Vattimo, on his part, has rendered the self-enquiry about the question of the subject philosophically disconnected and unproductive, an unresolved and unresolvable question that leads to aporia. Surely my phenomenological prejudice against the use of the word "Being," however rewritten and de-metaphysicized in a Heideggerian way, and also further weakened in the intentions of Vattimo, stands alongside his hermeneutic suspicion towards every phenomenology of the subject that is dedicated to solitude and to an abstract consumption of its own tail. This prejudicial element, never really settled between us, verifies itself – if we want to use an excellent example – in our diverse connections to the philosophical work of Jacques Derrida. While I was making my many Derridian arguments (all of them revolving around the aporias of deconstruction and aiming at a "logic" of the paradox), and above all building on his profound dialogue with Lévinas within the horizon of a philosophy of hospitality, literally a phenomenology beyond phenomenology, Vattimo had never effectively crossed this field, suspecting he would find himself facing something like a pseudo-argumentation that was too confined to a form of literary writing and ultimately in danger of becoming detached.

Derrida could actually represent the litmus test of what I am trying to say. The paradox of subjectivity is in fact an aporia that will lose its philosophical importance if we try to destroy it or overcome it. We need, rather, to remain within it, developing its potentialities for thought and possibly recognizing that such a double-linked and "cross-eyed" style, while certainly a risky tool that is difficult to use, is nonetheless the tool best suited for orientation in the present reality. We are thus taken back to the conditions of weak thought: not only to the relation with tradition and its legacy but even to what Michel Foucault would call the "ontology of actuality," intended as the socio-historical picture whose lines of strategic force we successfully grasp or, as Vattimo himself would say, the process of the weakening or of the "decline" of Being.

From this crucial perspective, turned to the present and at the same time to our past, Vattimo was the teacher of many, and he surely taught me how to handle the notion of *pietas* as the nonviolent gathering of traditions and the opening to a more-than-verbal pluralism and how to place myself in the so-called "transparent society" without remorse, a society where the communications of mass society open and close spaces of experience. This has permitted me – as well as many others – to de-ideologize the ideas of "after" and of "future," purifying them of the philosophico-historical or simply idealistic accretions that my Marxist origin was still willing to entertain. For Vattimo, weakening has never meant the rejection of emancipation. On the contrary, the lowering of the tone and the refusal – this is true – of such a concept's purity have made the experience of it accessible. What the myopic detractors love to stigmatize (and not always in good faith) as a resigned description of existing, without any political prospects, results, on the other hand, in a practicability of the experience of emancipation in the factical conditions of present society, where an act of theoretical force (namely, a return to parcels of pre-fixed values or to a defense of "reason" as such, or, worse, the invoked rebirth of foundational philosophies) does not produce emancipatory effects and, indeed, is almost immediately caught up in the backlash of its countereffects.

Nevertheless, the lesson of Vattimo (of which his activist politics of rights are a result) casts its gaze across everything I have just now (rapidly) remembered, and that in itself makes us question. I refer, as is clear, to the subjective conditions of weak thought, to the subject in question, to the working that this "strange" subject has to do with itself, to the representation that it can give and of which it can make use as a tool for understanding and participation. These conditions, which seem to me to occupy a decisive place and to be even the undeniably phenomenological side of weak thought, function naturally in the reflections of Vattimo but remain, so to say, *in nuce*, as if there were in him an excitation that would make them become the explicit philosophical theme. The ethical – but not normative – tone of weak thought introduces an idea of the subject, but certainly also introduces some reasonable cautions concerning a theoretical-thematizing gesture. These cautions notwithstanding, I do not think that it can avoid taking a suitable side or simply choosing a sphere of influence.

Who is the subject of weak thought? Which characteristics can we attribute to it to explain how it functions? These are the phenomenological questions, due either to their provenance or to the terrain that they open, namely the terrain that we can and must locate and investigate, beginning with the very paradox of subjectivity. It is, nevertheless, the place where I have sought to advance over the years. I have redoubled the listening that is inherent as a problem in *pietas* through the silence of a required suspension or by producing and maintaining, for a time, a distance. We can then represent the subject that we are as divided, unstable, oscillating, and certainly even insecure. Resolving the paradox would mean taking up positions either here or there in respect to the line of oscillation, cutting oneself out of reality in a sterile philosophical solipsism, or exposing oneself completely to the side of the object, of being, of external reality. I am simplifying in order to be clear: in any case, weak thought has nothing to do with the first relapse, or even with the second, because its challenge consists in successfully thinking through the oscillation while remaining within that very oscillation. Internal and external, inside and outside – these are no longer contrary and contradictory aspects; one does not exclude the other, nor do they resolve themselves in some higher-level synthesis.

In this unstable condition, or position, of the subject that we are, there is something that corresponds to the experience that we always attribute to "madness" (I have tried to write about it by exploiting many suggestions from Derrida). We are sitting astride a little wall, as has also been observed – in a position that is neither comfortable nor sustainable for a long time and that is thus always provisional. The distance I am discussing, which I believe deals with dwelling but in which, literally, it is *impossible* to take up residence, gives an image of this so-called madness (of which – I say this incidentally – a thinker-writer like Thomas Bernhard is the master), because it is first and foremost a distance from oneself. But is not this silencing the condition for listening? The paradox, as one sees it, rather than freeing itself, redoubles itself in a game whose score, however, is not zero. Placing a break between us and us, an impossible gap if we were to want to fix it in an attitude and one which therefore has the rapidity of a countermovement, we multiply the paradox of the subject, mimicking its instability, but in so doing we keep the game open, weakening the subject itself, practising on it, so to say, weakness.

In contrast to Vattimo, it seems to me to be appropriate in this investigation into the conditions of weak thought to take advantage of the experience of play in philosophy. Even he likes "to play," but I don't believe that he is disposed to load this notion with much importance. He does not see in the literature and in the related applications the advantages that play has for the question of the subject in weak thought, nor has he discovered how this experience permeates many thinkers of the twentieth century – and not exclusively Heidegger. In play (as authors like Gregory Bateson and Irving Goffman teach us, authors who I would add to the already fertile fields of weak thinkers) we encounter a paradox of factical experience: the subject of the play-space is always both active and passive, both player and played. It is not only the idea of oscillation that finds a very useful verification here but a whole battery of theoretical operations tied to the problem of weak thought that present themselves and can thus be utilized: from the suspension required in order to enter into the game and furthermore to remain there, to the transformation that the very idea of "reality" undergoes in the environment of this suspension, to the theoretical knot of reality/fiction that, as a consequence, furnishes a representation and a practice for the unstable equilibrium and oscillation between the two dimensions that are so often held in opposition.

Once again it seems that we must pass through Nietzsche. Among philosophers he has given more theoretical credit to an experience that is almost always held at the margins (with certain important exceptions). But regarding Nietzsche I would also like to summon another philosophical agent of great importance for the subjective style of weak thought: the element of "comedy" or – one could say – the "theatricality" of thought, or more simply, its comic tonality. It is one of the characteristics of the weak subject that I have been sketching out. Many fellow travellers after Nietzsche help us forge ahead on a journey that desecrates theoretical seriousness (Deleuze, to point to one example). This ironic downplaying of truth is, to be certain, also one of the chords of Vattimo's philosophy and his very style of life. Again, it is his reading of Nietzsche that taught us how to manage the masks; and yet he has partially abandoned this path. We cannot leave it interrupted because the impossible distance that the subject needs to maintain from itself in its paradoxical experience and in its weak madness functions only as ironic, auto-ironic, and ultimately, comic distance.

If one takes the subject seriously, there is no longer a place for weak thought. But this would be the lesser problem: there would also no longer be any possibility of dwelling in our world with a critical and emancipatory chance. It is a world, I recall, where every day marks the forceful resumption of oppositions and *aut-aut*, beginning with the choice between good and evil, between truth and error. It is a world that, in this way, presents itself as tragic and that often simplifies the tragedy in the dilemma of life and death. Let us consider Nietzsche's *Gay Science*, and not only the philosophical centre of this book, which is the aphorism about the "madman" and the "death of god." Let us try to understand with him why the comedy must "begin," why it never really begins and is returned to the given by destining itself to those conditions we therefore come to meet when the tragic homelessness of the death of absolute values intermingles with an ironic practice of truth.

Is not this situation of instability and of "convalescence," which Nietzsche is the first to describe, perhaps comparable to the oscillation of the weak subject that we are looking to inhabit today, so as not to remain confined in a condition without exit? The paradox is a mixture of the comic and the tragic, but it seems that only by practising the art of ironic distance, further weakening the irony in a comic nature, only by accepting this game as our own, and thus representing it to ourselves in its fictional component, and in conclusion, only by making reality just a bit less real that we manage to remain in this mixture and to live it as such, never deluding ourselves that we are outside of it.

TWENTY YEARS LATER:
A WEAK THOUGHT TO DESCRIBE OUR REALITY

Perhaps *Il pensiero debole* should have taken into consideration the analyses that François Lyotard had proposed shortly before in *The*

Postmodern Condition. I have come to this conclusion by going back to that period and trying to present it in a nonschematic way to someone who, like weak thought itself, is twenty years old. My understanding of this omission is that Lyotard's analyses of postmodernity – however much I would like to endow the so-called postmodern with a unitary philosophical trait, recognizable in the pluralization of "narratives" and perhaps in the very idea of narration – were re-using a word already used in architecture and elsewhere. These analyses were only a timid beginning and would still require a more significant articulation in order to stand on their own. It was as if Gianni Vattimo and I were taking this beginning for granted by overestimating the risk that the slogan, due to its popularity, might oversimplify and thus end the discourse. In our view, the focus of the analysis needed to be pushed back and thus to come to terms with Nietzsche and Heidegger in this order of philosophical implication. The question of truth also needed to be linked closely to the question of power (and for this it was much more important to refer to Foucault). But the questioning of the subject also needed to be re-opened, joining it with the other and with alterity. And one needed, in the end, to show that weak thought veered towards the practical, overflowing beyond every theoretically blocked objective truth. As is apparent, many other articulations still needed to be spelled out, especially the connection with language intended as "writing."

I would say, however, that at the age of twenty, not only does weak thought enjoy good health (one still reads the book of the same name, and above all the theme is widely accepted and even rooted in a number of human sciences and practices) but the analytic task that I wanted to promote is also clear to many: a task of re-reading present society and the tradition of thought whence we arise, the task that becomes ever more urgent and complex in the multicultural – and consequently conflicted – situation in which we all live. I would therefore rather speak of weak thought and of this task than of postmodernity. And I would ask myself, Do we have the theoretical tools that are up to the task of problematizing this situation at the highest level?

When I ask myself this question I have the precise feeling that the stigma of relativism and the subsequent eulogy for foundational thought, with their related polemics, spin aimlessly and push themselves backwards. This occurs all too often today, as if nothing had transpired in philosophy or in thought in general during the last two decades. To believe today that there is a war over the pure state – a war between foundations and therefore between forces – clearly prohibits the possibility of understanding reality. The battles for realism or for objective ontologies clearly indicate a great difficulty, and maybe even that we have lost our way. A minimum of weak critique is enough to notice that these are merely reactive battles, unable to defend their acquired positions, which are now menaced by a society marked by uncertainty (as Robert Castel would say). A glance at the world of the university is enough to point out a microcosm rather congenial to the same workings of thought, or a glimpse at the world of work, the macrocosm that everyone navigates on demand.

Weak thought asks, first of all, for a description of reality in terms of power and the authoritarian effects of reason (beyond Marx, in order to come to terms with him, but not *against* Marx). Precisely because it chooses this terrain and tries not to leave it behind – as a decisive and unavoidable component of its argumentation – weak thought seems to be able to construct philosophical alliances (with the thought of Foucault, as I noted, but also with that of Derrida) and to single out with a certain precision the face of so-called adversaries, namely, all those positions that tend towards authoritarian niches and often legitimize themselves with leftist declarations. There are authoritarian implications for everyone, including weak thinkers, implications that require continual supplements of self-critique or further weakening, that is, an always greater surveillance of the tools in use, of their unceasing "unfounding."

For example, there is the "ticklishness" (to use one of Slavoj Zizek's terms) of the very notion of subject, which we can neither abandon nor even utilize (no matter what analysis of society we undertake) without loading it with paradoxical elements and without submitting it to a continual critical reexamination; or, precisely, there is the "ticklishness" of the very notion of play that I find very productive as an analytical tool and that can be usefully referred to the very idea of subject but that risks becoming rigid every time that we attempt to make use of it without the awareness of always being, in some way, played by it.

This scenario, to which we can also give the name "globalization," demands tools for observation and adequate description that, in large measure, are more akin to constructing. The metaphysical clashes that promise to cut globalization short are of little or no use here. The "construction" of thought I have in mind, necessary today more than ever, is slowed down only by so-called conclusions of principle that would rapidly impose order through a simple formula. While trying to deal with a description of "reality" itself, we risk remaining bogged down in philosophical ideologies. This construction can take hold only if it moves closer to practices while actively eliciting new theoretical questions from them.

Did something in philosophy change after September 11? Without needing the label of "weak thought," many commentators have perceived that after this "event," those who were asking questions about knowledge could and ought to have adjusted the notions of "inside" and "outside," or even, if one prefers, of inclusion and exclusion, in respect to the eruption of an apparently irreducible alterity in the globalized world. Can we successfully face this "other" and "welcome" it into our way of thinking? And at what price? These are some of the general questions that we receive from analyses of the facts and that put the logic of friend versus enemy in check, along with every inclusive logic of the sort that says "we are all in this together." These questions necessarily set thought in motion, even against itself. This thinking, our thinking, can no longer seek refuge in an isolated academic space. We need this thinking to be nothing other than "political," if for no other reason than the necessity of facing the questions of life and death that now intersect all of our activities.

In the recent past, one said "commitment," "situation," or "taking a side"; but what matters now is "responsibility," namely, to respond to, or simply to correspond to the complexity of the scenario, divesting oneself of every metaphysical presupposition and attempting to listen without prejudice to the things that happen and in which we ourselves happen. The "rigour" of this listening is unknown to our habitual modes of thinking, and it in fact does not overlap with what we normally call rigour.

While writing these lines I heard the sad news of Jacques Derrida's death. In recent years I have found myself in agreement with his work and above all with his most recent reflections on hospitality and the gift. Derrida has given us a large number of tools for orienting ourselves in our ticklish situation. In my view, his insensitivity towards hermeneutics and his lack of interest in weak thought are not important. What really matters and what makes him an important ally in the task I first identified is that he has presented – in a way that is always more recognizable and efficacious – political thinking that revolves around responsibility and that uses tools whose experimentality corresponds to an original and productive antimetaphysical practice. By allying itself with Derrida, any practice of weak thought gains a precious deconstructive tool, one that can bore into metaphysics and discover the internal paradoxes that we face and that we have the task of removing.

Allow me to point out but one of the utensils that we can take from his drawer: the close relationship, and, I will even say, the near identification between "event" and "alterity." Not only is there no event without alterity, but every event, every time that it arrives or that something arrives here, resists becoming our "own" – neither is it able to be assimilated nor can it become our property. I believe that the capacity to deconstruct "one's own" (*il proprio*) in our description of the event, and thus the paradoxical capacity to "stand" in the event, accepting the risk and the uncertainty of it, is precisely the weakening we need in order to prepare a new idea of responsibility and in order to access a horizon "yet to come."

Although the description we seek is aimed towards the future, in a situation in which the normal idea of the future (always guided by some philosophy of history) seems to implode in on itself, the task of weak thought, which perhaps includes all of them, is to produce conditions of thinkability for a movement forward in which the word "future" can reacquire a legibility and a meaning. This meaning is not added to the things that happen but functions in the events through which we in fact live. In 1983 Vattimo was already speaking of an emancipatory potential for weak thought: it is not one point among the others but rather the place where the analyses of reality prove both their political and their philosophical capacities. It is a place – I must admit – where we still act blindly, more so than we ever recognize. It is a question that demands the maximum philosophical commitment, if for no other reason than to free itself from nihilisms and mythologies by now equally dispensable.

NOTES

1 P.A. Rovatti and A. Dal Lago, *Elogio del pudore: Per un pensiero debole* (Milan: Feltrinelli 1990).
2 P.A. Rovatti, *La posta in gioco* (Milan: Bompiani 1987).
3 P.A. Rovatti, *La Follia in poche parole* (Milan: Bompiani 2000).

PART TWO
Weakening Metaphysical Methods

9

Heideggerianism and Leftist Politics

RICHARD RORTY

Gianni Vattimo's writings are among the most imaginative contributions to the tradition of philosophical thought that flows from Nietzsche and Heidegger. They are well suited to the needs of those who
would like to gain an understanding of the intellectual outlook he calls
"nihilism."

That outlook might also be called "common sense Heideggerianism."
It is widespread among European intellectuals. Many people who, like
Vattimo and Derrida, were students in the 1950s were deeply impressed
by Heidegger essays such as "Letter on Humanism," "The Question
concerning Technology," "The Origin of the Work of Art," and "Nietzsche's Word: God is Dead."[1] Many of them presuppose, in their own
writings, their readers' familiarity with Heidegger's story about the
history of Western thought – his account of how the Platonic dream of
escaping from Becoming to Being has been dreamt out and of how Nietzsche brought metaphysics to its destined end by inverting Plato, giving
Becoming primacy over Being.

Common sense Heideggerianism has little to do either with Husserlian phenomenology or with existentialism. It drops (as Heidegger
himself did) the notions of "authenticity" and "resoluteness," which
were prominent in *Being and Time* and which Sartre reworked in *Being
and Nothingness*.[2] Nor does it take either Heidegger's idiosyncratic
retranslations of pre-Socratic texts or his peculiar interpretations of

figures such as Leibniz and Kant with any great seriousness. But it does accept the main outlines of the story that Heidegger called, portentously enough, "the history of Being."

According to this story, Nietzsche marks the point at which it became impossible for Western intellectuals to believe what Plato had taught: that there is something stable for human beings to rely on, a fixed point in the changing world around which to rally. Simultaneously, it became impossible to believe that there is some privileged vocabulary – even Nietzsche's own talk of the will to power or the jargon of the early Heidegger's "ontology of Dasein" – in which to state the final truth about the human situation. For, as Hegel had already realized, we are historical creatures, continually remaking ourselves by redescribing ourselves. The hope for finality is futile. Philosophers should stop looking for necessary and universal "conceptual" truths and should realize that concepts are as malleable as any other social institutions.

Vattimo calls this Heideggerian outlook nihilism because it is not a positive doctrine but rather a series of negations – denials that any proposed principle or jargon or insight enjoys a privileged reality concerning the nature of man or of the universe. For the idea that either of these *has* a nature is no longer credible. Vattimo wants to show how leftist political and social initiatives can not only survive but profit from jettisoning traditional philosophical attempts to reveal such things as The Ultimate Nature of Reality or the Ultimate Meaning of Human Life.

Heidegger was a passionately committed Nazi and a thoroughly dishonest man. His life provides further evidence that genius among philosophers as well as among artists and scientists has no particular connection with ordinary human decency. Many find it hard to imagine that any good could come from reading such a writer. Such readers may find it ludicrous that Vattimo should treat Heidegger's account of modernity as the best theoretical background for leftist social and political initiatives. The very idea of a Heideggerian social democrat may strike them as absurd. But reading Vattimo may help to persuade them that leftist politics would indeed benefit from giving up on Enlightenment rationalism. They may come to agree with Vattimo that nihilism and emancipation do, in fact, go hand in hand.

Heidegger is often described as an irrationalist, and his putative irrationalism is often linked to his Nazism. But it is easy to forget that John Dewey – America's most influential social democratic thinker – was also repeatedly accused of irrationalism and that Dewey's and Heidegger's criticisms of the Western philosophical tradition have much in common. Both the most important German intellectual to have supported Hitler and the philosopher whose writings helped shape American leftist thought from the Progressive Era to the New Deal urged us to abandon the rationalism common to Plato, Descartes, and Kant. After skimming through Heidegger's *Being and Time*, Dewey said that it sounded like his own *Experience and Nature* "translated into transcendental German." Had Dewey lived to read Heidegger's later writings, he might have seen them as taking up themes from his own *Quest for Certainty*.

Vattimo is, of course, not the only eminent philosophy professor who has in recent decades been active and influential on the political left. But most of the others are suspicious of what he calls nihilism. A leading contemporary American philosopher of law, Ronald Dworkin, has done a great deal for the cause of social justice through his analyses of issues in constitutional jurisprudence in the *New York Review of Books*. Jürgen Habermas' frequent contributions to such publications as *Die Zeit* have done the sort of good for the German left that Dewey's forty years' worth of contributions to magazines like the *Nation* and the *New Republic* did for the American left. But Dworkin and Habermas have little use for Nietzsche. They remain faithful to an intellectual legacy that Vattimo thinks it would be better for the left to renounce.

Dworkin has nothing but contempt for Heideggerian approaches to such notions as objectivity and truth. Habermas concedes more to the "relativist" side of controversies about such topics than does Dworkin; he is willing, for example, to follow Dewey in abandoning the correspondence theory of truth. But Habermas regrets Heidegger's pervasive influence on recent European philosophical thought. Both Dworkin and Habermas insist on retaining various Kantian ideas that Vattimo urges us to reject. So Vattimo is currently the most salient example of a philosopher who argues that the left's political purposes will be better served if we stop talking about unconditional moral obligations, claims about universal validity, and transcendental presuppositions of rational inquiry.

Philosophers such as Vattimo, Derrida, and myself have become convinced – some of us by reading Hegel and Dewey, some by reading Heidegger, some by reading both – that philosophy should no longer aim at revealing the ultimate context of human existence – a context that, while not merely biological, is nevertheless transcultural and ahistorical. Candidates for such a context include, obviously, the Platonic realm of pure Forms and Kant's transcendental conditions of the possibility of experience. But they also include the materialists' Ultimate Nature of Physical Reality, the theists' divine commands, the Kantian moral law, and Marx's inevitable movement of history. Heidegger lumps Lucretius, Augustine, Kant, and Marx together as examples of what he calls, more or less interchangeably, "metaphysics" or "onto-theology."

Vattimo describes those of us who agree that metaphysics in this broad sense is no longer worth pursuing as trying to make philosophy into a hermeneutic discipline. To think of philosophy in that way means accepting Nietzsche's claim that "there are no facts, only interpretations." That claim epitomizes the thought that none of the words human beings have invented to describe themselves and their environment enjoy a special relation to reality. So there is no division to be made between areas of culture in which we seek correspondence to reality and those in which we do not – disciplines in which there is a "matter of fact" to be discovered and other, "softer" disciplines. To give up on the idea that either human beings or nonhuman reality has a nature to which true statements correspond is to put everything up for grabs, to admit that we are at the mercy of the contingencies of history.

This means that the best philosophers (or anybody else) can hope to do is to say how things are with human beings now, as contrasted with how they once were and how they might someday be. So philosophy ceases to be ancillary either to theology or to natural science. Instead, it takes the form of historical narrative and utopian speculation. For leftists like Vattimo and Dewey, it becomes ancillary to sociopolitical initiatives aimed at making the future better than the past.

Vattimo thinks that philosophers should stop trying to rewrite Kant's *Critique of Pure Reason*. They should instead rewrite the narratives offered in Vico's *New Science*, Hegel's *Phenomenology of Spirit*, Comte's and Marx's stories of progress, and Nietzsche's account (in *Twilight of the Idols*) of "How 'the true world' became a fable."[3] Part of this rewriting should consist in removing any suggestion of inevitability, any hint that the story being told is itself more than another possible interpretation.

The other task that remains for philosophy is what Vattimo calls "the ongoing task of secularization … the unmasking of the sacrality of all absolute, ultimate truths." This task will never be completed, he says, because "the springs of metaphysical authoritarianism will never run dry" and so "antifoundationalism itself is at risk of hardening into a

metaphysics." Every narrative written in support of some leftist emancipatory project runs the risk of degenerating into yet another claim to
have gotten beyond interpretation to hard fact, beyond contingency to
necessity, beyond historical specificity to universality.

What I have dubbed "Heideggerian common sense" produces what
Vattimo calls "the general tendency of contemporary philosophy to
think of itself as 'sociology' or as a theory of modernity."[4] By "contemporary philosophy" he of course means philosophy in most European and Latin American countries, as contrasted with the analytic
tradition that is dominant in the philosophy departments of the
English-speaking world. In the latter departments, few people offer (or
would bother to read) a theory of modernity. Most British and American teachers of philosophy regard theirs as a quasiscientific, problem-
solving, discipline – one that has nothing in particular to do with either
history or sociology and that should culminate in theories rather than
narratives. Analytic philosophy is still for the most part "metaphysical"
in the pejorative sense that Heidegger gave to that term. It still hopes to
place human history in an ahistorical context and thus to offer something more than just one more historically determined interpretation,
one more response to the transitory problems of the present.

Although many philosophers in the analytic tradition (for example,
admirers of the later Wittgenstein like Donald Davidson and Robert
Brandom) have provided valuable ammunition for use against the
legacy of Platonic and Kantian rationalism, the mainstream of analytic
philosophy is continuous with what Heidegger called "onto-theology."
For what might be called the common sense of analytic philosophy consists in the belief that natural science enjoys a privileged relation to the
way things really are. Philosophers who take this common sense for
granted in their writings do not share Thomas Kuhn's and Hilary
Putnam's doubts about the idea that inquiry in the natural sciences converges to an accurate representation of the intrinsic nature of things.
They think of such doubts as lending aid and comfort to an insidious
relativism, one that is likely to spread from philosophy of science to
moral philosophy and thereby undermine leftists' attempts to achieve
social justice.

But even analytic philosophers who are receptive to Kuhn's and
Putnam's debunking of the idea that natural science is ontologically or
epistemologically privileged are likely to scoff at Vattimo's suggestion
that Heideggerianism is just what social democracy needs. Ever since
the early 1930s, when Carnap, a good leftist who was forced into exile

by Hitler, squared off against Heidegger, an opportunistic Nazi, it has been part of the self-image of analytic philosophy that it is fighting on the side of social justice. Many analytic philosophers think that Heideggerianism not only rots the mind but corrupts morals.

This suspicion extends back to Hegel, whom Karl Popper, another of the initiators of the analytic tradition in philosophy, interpreted as a precursor of totalitarianism. Bertrand Russell also wrote of Hegel with contempt. Many analytic philosophers still think of Hegel and Heidegger as enemies of human freedom. The idea that reading either might assist us in our thinking about sociopolitical problems strikes them as ludicrous. That is why those two authors are infrequently taught in British and American philosophy departments, while remaining staples of instruction elsewhere in the world.

For Vattimo the shoe is on the other foot. It is analytic moral philosophers concerned to preserve the Platonic and Kantian notion of unconditional obligation who are giving aid and comfort to authoritarianism. Whereas these philosophers believe that appeal to such obligations gives us a defense against the fascists, Vattimo sees Kant's moral philosophy as a poisoned chalice. For the Kantian idea that sufficient rational reflection will lead you to make the right moral choice, and would have led any rational being to make the same choice regardless of the epoch in which they lived, should itself be seen as a relic of authoritarianism. It is an attempt to attribute ultimate authority to a quasi-divinity called Reason and is no better than the attempt to attribute such authority to God. It is one more attempt to say, "What I am saying is not just one more interpretation; it is *true*."

On the view that Vattimo shares with Heidegger, the Platonic-Kantian idea that Reason can cut through prejudice and superstition and lead you toward truth and justice is, just as Nietzsche suggested, merely an etiolated version of the Platonic-Augustinian idea that the immortal part of us can triumph over the animal part. It substitutes the philosophers' contemptuous suggestion that people who act badly are irrational, and therefore less than fully human, for the priests' threat that they will suffer postmortem punishment.

Heideggerians like Derrida and Vattimo (and also revisionist Hegelians such as Terry Pinkard and Robert Pippin) are happy to agree with the scientific materialists that we have no immortal part and no faculty that puts us in touch with the eternal. We are simply animals that can talk and so can praise and blame each other, discuss what should be done, and institute social practices to see that it is done. What lifts us above the other animals is just our ability to participate in such practices. To be rational for these philosophers is not to possess a truth-tracking faculty. It is simply to be conversable.

Heidegger, once he gave up being a Nazi, did not adopt a different political position. He simply despaired of the modern world, which he saw as dominated by a blind faith in technology. He mocked the hope that concrete political initiatives could make any difference to its fate. As Vattimo says, "Heidegger and Adorno never escaped from a vision of technology dominated by the model of the motor and mechanical energy, so for them modern technology could do nothing except bring about a society subordinated to a central power dispatching commands to a pure passive periphery, as gear wheels are driven, whether these commands were mechanical impulses, political propaganda, or commercial advertising."5

In contrast, Vattimo asks us to consider that perhaps "the possibility of overcoming metaphysics ... really opens up only when the technology – at any rate the socially hegemonic technology – ceases to be mechanical and becomes electrical: information and communication technology." One of his most distinctive contributions to philosophical thinking is the suggestion that the Internet provides a model for things in general – that thinking about the Worldwide Web helps us to get away from Platonic essentialism, the quest for underlying natures, by helping us see everything as a constantly changing network of relations. The result of adopting this model is what Vattimo calls "a weak ontology, or better an ontology of the weakening of being." Such an ontology, he argues, "supplies philosophical reasons for preferring a liberal, tolerant, and democratic society rather than an authoritarian and totalitarian one."

Il pensiero debole (Weak thought) was the title of a much-read collection of essays by various Italian philosophers that Vattimo coedited in 1983. The contributors had all been impressed both by the later Heidegger and by the later Wittgenstein. They turned Wittgenstein's criticism of his own Tractatus as juvenile picture-thinking into a supplement to Heidegger's criticism of metaphysics. They turned Heidegger's criticism of Nietzsche as a power-freak against the apocalyptic tone that Heidegger himself adopted. Like Wittgenstein, they hoped philosophers would stop thinking of their discipline as capable of taking charge of the intellectual or moral worlds.

Vattimo continues to use "weak" as a term of praise and to caution against the temptation to erect nihilism into one more metaphysics – one more claim about the one true context in which human lives must be lived. The Internet is a model of weak thinking because everything that appears on it is continually being recontextualized and reinterpreted as new links are added. It is thus a model of human existence as centreless and historically contingent and an example of what Vattimo calls "the dissolution of the principle of reality into the manifold of interpretations."[6]

On a "weak" conception, morality is not a matter of unconditional obligations imposed by a divine or quasi-divine authority but rather is something cobbled together by a group of people trying to adjust to their circumstances and achieve their goals by cooperative efforts. That is how Dewey thought of morality and how Vattimo urges us to think of it. Whereas those concerned to preserve the legacy of Plato and Kant think that adopting this conception of morality will lead to "relativism" and moral flabbiness, Vattimo thinks that it will produce a desirable humility about our own moral intuitions and about the social institutions to which we have become accustomed. This humility will encourage tolerance for other intuitions and a willingness to experiment with ways of refashioning or replacing institutions.

Vattimo sees this humility as an antidote to the pridefulness characteristic of those who claim to be obeying unconditional, ahistorical, transcultural, categorical imperatives. Adopting this "weak" attitude toward our moral obligations is, he thinks, the culmination of a long, drawn-out process of secularization. He interprets Heidegger's "definition of the West, the *Abendland*, as the place of the going down of Being" as "a recognition of the profound vocation of the West (probably contrary to Heidegger's own self-interpretation) as a series of secularizations."[7] He views the history of the West as constituted by "interpretations that one after another have undermined the pretended absoluteness of the 'principles' on which the West was based." An emblematic case of this, he says, is "the ebbing away of the literal mode of understanding the Bible."

This last example is of particular importance for Vattimo, who in his book *Belief* writes that "in Christianity I find the original 'text' of which weak ontology is the transcription" and that "the rediscovery of Christianity is made possible by the dissolution of metaphysics."[8] He is impatient with what he calls "the scandalously superstitious character of much of the official teaching of today's [Catholic] Church." But he interprets the Christian message of *kenosis* – the emptying out of God into man that was the Incarnation – as a prefiguration of nihilism, as a wholesale and complete transfer of authority from the nonhuman to the human.

On his account, the growing refusal by European Christians to accept the authority of ecclesiastical institutions is of a piece with contemporary intellectuals' inability to view philosophical reflection as a way of escaping from historical contingency. So for Vattimo, secularization is Christianity by other means. Both represent the triumph of love over law, of kindness over obedience. He sees the gradual rise of the modern Western social democracies and the gradual decline of onto-theology as signs that human beings are losing the need to feel themselves subject to the eternal and are becoming courageous enough to endure the thought of their own mortality.

Vattimo's way of weaving together Heidegger, Christianity, and social democratic ideals is as audacious as it is original. Different as his outlook is from Habermas', these two philosophers' writings are both good examples of philosophical and historical erudition yoked to the service of leftist political initiatives. Different as his tone is from Dewey's, Vattimo nevertheless stands in the same relation to Heidegger's revulsion against technology and to his debilitating nostalgia as Dewey stood to Carlyle's and Henry Adams' despair over modernity.

NOTES

1 M. Heidegger, "Letter on 'Humanism'" [1967], in M. Heidegger, *Pathmarks*, ed. William McNeill (Cambridge: MIT Press 2002), 239–76; *The Question Concerning Technology*, trans. W. Lovitt (Nerw York: Harper & Row 1977); "The Origin of the Work of Art" [1950], in *Off the Beaten Track*, trans. Julian Young and Kenneth Haynes (Cambridge: Cambridge University Press 2002), 1–56; "Nietzsche's Word: 'God Is Dead'" [1950], in *Off the Beaten Track*, 157–99.

2 M. Heidegger, *Being and Time*, trans. Joan Stambaugh (New York: State University of New York Press 1996); Jean-Paul Sartre, *Being and Nothingness*, trans. Hazel E. Barnes (New York: Citadel Press 1956).

3 Immanuel Kant, *Critique of Pure Reason*, trans. Norman Kemp Smith (New York: Palgrave 2003); Giambattista Vico, *New Science*, trans. David Marsh (London: Penguin); G.W.F. Hegel, *Phenomenology of Spirit*, trans. A.V. Miller (Oxford University Press 1979); Friedrich Nietzsche, *Twilight*

of the Idols, trans. Duncan Large (New York: Oxford University Press 1998).

4 G. Vattimo, *Nihilism and Emancipation: Ethics, Politics, and Law*, ed. Santiago Zabala and trans. William McCuaig (New York: Columbia University Press 2004), 10.

5 Ibid., 14–15.

6 Ibid., 20.

7 Ibid., 57.

8 G. Vattimo, *Belief*, trans. Luca D'Isanto and David Webb (New York: Columbia University Press 2004). The Italian original of this book, *Credere di credere*, was published by Garzanti in 1996.

10

The Universality Claim of Hermeneutics

MANFRED FRANK

Translated by Jim Scott

I send Gianni Vattimo the most heartfelt best wishes on his birthday. The number fully justifies a jubilee; and yet it ill fits the youthful charm, the elegance, the humour, the intellectual and physical presence of the man whose name occurs immediately to one and all when someone calls for the leading Italian philosopher and intellectual.

I met Gianni Vattimo in the early eighties at a colloquium at the Goethe-Institute in Turin. The topic was the tradition of the "new mythology" in German and Italian fascism and the debates were passionate and not very harmonious. Nevertheless, this first meeting resulted in regular exchanges at settings now in Tübingen, now in Turin, often regarding questions on which we differ: do consciousness and thought exist apart from language? Is self-*awareness* (Selbst*bewusstsein*), particularly, completely subsumed under what Gadamer called self-*conception* (Selbst*verständnis*), with the implication that we ourselves have to use the fallible tools of hermeneutics to arrive at a meaning that we can adhere to?

Gianni Vattimo, a generation older than I, studied, as did I, hermeneutics and Greek philosophy with Hans-Georg Gadamer (at that time already elderly) in Heidelberg. Like me, he was subsequently open to the movement that I was the first to call French "neo-structuralism," with Derrida presiding over its centre. But while I accused both Gadamer and also, more decidedly, Derrida of having a blind spot for the collaboration of the self-aware individual in the transformation of language and in the creation of new meaning, Vattimo concentrated on the antifundamentalist character ("weak" validity claim) of thinking and speaking, which had removed the subject from the centre ("de-centred"). Thought, it was said, should be not demonstrative but rather edifying. If that means that our arguments, however finely honed, can never be absolutely crushing or conclusive, then I agree with him: arguments basically always survive their refutation, even if "at a price," as David Lewis wrote in the introduction to his *Philosophical Papers*.[1] For Gianni Vattimo, the price of a relapse into the so-called subject philosophy seems to be too high, as is for me the price of philosophizing without recourse to the completely unfoundationalistically and modestly applied collaboration of a subject-in-the-role-of-an-individual.

All the same, I am not willing, as I said before, to give up the hope, reaching from Descartes through Kant and Fichte to Husserl and Roderick Chisholm, that subjects play some role or other in the justification of our convictions. Accordingly, I will, like Gianni, go with a weak validity claim. But even if we give up on these bold hopes of justification that would link traditional strategies more closely to our topic, it still remains true that self-consciousness enjoys a priority that demonstrates its epistemological importance. And this fact has to do with its essential irreducibility.

Such approaches are understandable, as is the worldwide popularity of reductions arguments. All reductive classes mentioned thus far belong to the world of things and may be investigated using scientific methods. But if there was something like an irreducibile "subjective factor," then we would have to restrict the explanatory monopoly of scientific explanation. I believe there is an irreducible subjective factor, and two fundamental intuitions lead me to this conclusion.

The first is that the practice of philosophy would be impossible if we gave up understanding ourselves as subjects (that is, understanding ourselves in a way essential to veracious self-description.) We would, namely, not be able to distinguish what we mean when relating to ourselves from what we mean when referring to physical entities. But then we would also be driven to the consequence that all explanation of human reality must be left to the sciences based on physics.[2] Further, argumentation would not be acceptable as the proper method of philosophy, since there is a distinct difference between the character of arguments and that of scientific explanation.[3]

My second intuition is ethical. It fears that with the naturalizing of subjectivity a version of the categorical imperative loses its addressee.

According to this version of Kant's categorical imperative, one should never treat a person (only) as a means to an end, but rather (additionally) always as an end in himself or herself. If there is no such thing as irreducible (nonreifiable) subjectivity, then we are left without the *fundamentum in re* needed for the operation of the imperative. Subjectivity must have an internal quality that cannot be reduced to (physical) objects or events. And this quality must also be the reason why the deterministic discourse of physics cannot be applied exhaustively to the facts of our inner life.

This shows what I think of the fashionable thesis of the "death of the subject." Just like all fashions it need only await the next change in taste to lose its appeal. Whereas some philosophers following in the footsteps of structuralism or the "linguistic turn" are determined to reduce subjectivity to language, other younger semanticists and philosophers of consciousness have been speaking for some time now of a "turn away from language."[4] It has taken some time, but analytic philosophy today can no longer be described as the analysis of language. It has rediscovered the reality of certain phenomena that exist independently of language or of consciousness. Included in these phenomena are consciousness and subjectivity themselves.

But one thing at a time. In order to present Gianni with an appropriate birthday gift, I thought to begin at the point from which we both departed: a variety of Gadamer's and especially Schleiermacher's hermeneutics (to which we were both convinced that Gadamer had not done justice). I will so direct my journey, and register my differences with neostructuralists, in such a way that Gianni will – I hope – long be my companion. And in consequence, it will be all the clearer where our paths do separate. (But maybe I am just imagining that and Gianni will disabuse me of the error.)

Hermeneutics – "the art of understanding particularly the written discourse/speech of another person correctly" – is in the history of ideas a relatively young invention, namely that of Romanticism. Granted, problems of interpretation and the discovery of systematic solutions to them were already ancient conundrums, and even the universalization of the hermeneutic scope to include all sign-mediated interaction was fundamentally an achievement of the Enlightenment. Yet in breaking away from the interpretation model of the Enlightenment, Romanticism was concerned less about the universality claim of "artconform" understanding than about views on the essence of language as the object of all interpretation. With great simplification, one may say that interpretation did not play a role of its own as a specific problem in the *language-related disciplines* up to the middle of the eighteenth century. This was due to the belief before that time that the form of language, taken in its truth, is a representation of so-called logical form,[5] which in turn represents facts in the world. Thus a twofold preestablished harmony seemed to reign between reason and grammar, on the one hand, and between grammar and the world, on the other. In addition, it was commonly held that all reasonable (coextensive with informative) speech is essentially general, true, and intelligible. There were thus no problems of how to arrive at a consensus about the specific *meaning of a usage* in well-formed speech or about the ways in which the world is linguistically constructed: grammatically correct speech gave an immediately reliable representation of ideas combined with one another according to reason. Grammar and reason were both general – and every application of their laws reproduced (or rather instantiated) this essential generality *in concreto*, just as a case falling under a law does not modify, but rather manifests the law. To understand something as something on the basis of this epistemological premise means to illuminate the reasonable content of spoken or written expressions, that is, to grasp them as generalities. They do not cease to be general simply by having only one application in history.

According to the validity conditions prescribed by a representation model of universal grammar, hermeneutics – the art of understanding written or spoken discourse correctly[6] – is reduced completely, or at least largely, to the rules of a "reasoned" decoding of the language in which speeches or texts are formulated.

This changes fundamentally with Romanticism in two respects. First, doubts arise as to whether we can at all rely on a transhistorical unified reason, which, besides, is harmonized a priori with reality. But this means that understanding can no longer be considered unproblematic. Understanding is not granted to interlocutors simply on the basis of their equal share of common reason (or of the common alignment of a linguistic community towards a world of identical objects); rather, understanding must in each single case "be desired and sought."[7]

Even more decisive in the development of hermeneutics' universality claim was perhaps a second paradigm shift, namely, the novel conviction that the fundamental dimension of philosophy is not the representation of objects but rather the understanding of meaning. We represent objects, whereas we understand sentences (one used to say "judgements"). Judgements alone can be true or false. And philosophy has to do with knowledge, that is, with expressing what is true. Ancient philosophy was largely concerned with the world as it is. "Ontology" is the name given to the focus on οντα, beings or objects. Here doubts arose in modern times and ontology was replaced by epistemology. One reflected on the fact that objects are mediated to us through subjective ideas: this gave the impetus to the epistemological shift in philosophy from Descartes and British Empiricism to Kant and Reinhold. They were then followed by Schleiermacher: what we represent in veridical ideas are not really objects but facts. And these correspond on the subjective level to propositions or judgments. The primary unit of understanding thus becomes the sentence, because it is also "the smallest intersubjective unit of understanding."[8]

Schleiermacher was the first to show that we seldom diverge from one another in how we fixate objects, but do so regularly when we assign properties to them. And properties are conferred on objects in judgments (*Dial J* 586); individual objects themselves are not facts and don't have meaning. Meaning (i.e., what we understand) is mediated to us through judgments, which do not refer directly to objects but rather interpret them to be this or that – and thus refer to truth. In philosophy we are concerned with understanding meaning, from which we derive facts about the world. Schleiermacher is convinced, to the same extent as Wittgenstein, that the world is not an entirety of objects but of facts and that judgments, through which facts are constituted, form the "semantic minimum."[9] Therefore, if meaning is what is understood, then the fundamental discipline of philosophy is hermeneutics as the theory of understanding interpretations of facts, and not epistemology, as the theory of prelinguistic representations of objects. Hermeneutics thus inherits the universality claim of ancient ontology and modern epistemology but is the first to accomplish their goals. This view was later advocated by Wittgenstein, Heidegger, Strawson, Gadamer, and Tugendhat. The latter, in his contribution to Gadamer's 1970 festschrift, commented on this surprising coincidence of interests among such widely differing philosophical schools:

Hermeneutics is, among philosophical topics, more extensive than both language analysis and phenomenology. Despite its origins in phenomenology, it is methodically closer to language analysis. One can regard language analysis as a reduced hermeneutics, as ground-floor hermeneutics. It still lacks a historical dimension and more extensive concept of understanding. Hermeneutics, on the other hand, dwells dangerously on the highest floor, without concern for the stability and need for repair of the bottom level. It inherits this trait from phenomenology or from earlier philosophy. Hermeneutic criticism, especially Heidegger's, of older metaphysics in general, and thus also of phenomenology, concerns only their limitedness; this heritage in fact remains as a base level, like a historical monument, to be built on top of or into the depths underneath. Language analysis has never reached thus far, yet it does not want to simply demolish the building like positivism, but rather believes that it possesses new means and methods for a more stable reconstruction.[10]

Schleiermacher's lectures in *Hermeneutics and Criticism* initiated the paradigm shift from an orientation towards representations of particular objects to facts or sentence-meanings. In the 1819 version, the hermeneutic course commenced with the renowned claim that "*hermeneutics as* the art of understanding *does not yet exist* in a general manner," but rather "*only* [in] *several forms* of specific hermeneutics."[11] Schleiermacher – guided by traditions of Bible exegesis, familiar to him – has in mind techniques such as cabalistic, dogmatic, or allegorical explication.[12] These techniques concur in that they each perform a proper understanding of texts through preconceived schemes and they each are valid only for specific kinds of texts; i.e., they are not universally valid. Schleiermacher alleges that special hermeneutics in the latter case provides "always and only a collection of observations, for they do not fulfill any scientific demands."[13] Even rationalistic hermeneutics he calls unscientific and therefore misguided as to the actual meaning of texts, for it implies that timeless rationality (and this means understandability) belongs to all well-formed speech and needs only to be uncovered by the interpreter using his own reason.

This, for example, is how Spinoza and Hugo Grotius proceeded. They recommended considering the Scriptures *as* in large part reasonable and leaving to historical explanation only what cannot be understood – the so-called *res impercetibiles*. These may, for instance, be understood as the remains of a naive stage of enlightenment that has shortcomings or is blinded by superstition. The predications in the title of Johann Martin Chladenius' *Introduction to the Correct Understanding of* Reasonable *Oral and Written Speech* (my emphasis) illustrate links in his theory of interpretation to an axiology of reason. Chladenius assumes that there are passages in the Scriptures that "contain something surpassing reason."[14] Such passages are explained historically, i.e., eliminated as senseless. What remains is the "perfect understanding" of all else, such that one "thereby thinks of all that words in accordance with reason and with the rules of the soul can awake in us."[15] Reason is transhistorically one and common to all mankind. But even the problem of reference does not really arise: Georg Friedrich Meier's *General Art of Interpretation* defines hermeneutics in 1757 as "the science of the rules by which, when followed, meaning (and by this he means the things referred to,"[16] can be understood from their signs."[17] *Sub specie rationis*, understanding does not present a problem *sui generis*.

Schleiermacher calls the method devoted to these premises "*the more lax practice.*" It "assumes that understanding results as a matter of course and expresses the aim negatively: 'misunderstanding should be avoided.'"[18] This lax approach to interpretation contravenes "the more strict practice." The latter assumes conversely that "misunderstanding results as a matter of course and that understanding must at every point be desired and sought."[19] The stricter praxis is thus a direct reversal of the rationalistic practice, which takes understandability to be the common rule and misunderstanding to be the only exception requiring explanation. For Schleiermacher, hermeneutics becomes universal not by assuming the understandability of any single assertion but rather by demanding that all understanding result from an artistic effort. This effort is required because neither the interpreter nor the interpreted can depend on semantic agreement based on a pre-established consensus – such as an identical understanding of the world, as Schleiermacher says.

But even if we did assume an identical grammar (as the entirety of common rules in language use), it would still hold that no rules carry the certainty of their application within themselves. This is because every application of a rule is the accomplishment of a judgment "that cannot be mechanized," i.e., "which itself [at the risk of an infinite regression] cannot be brought under rules."[20] For this reason, I cannot assume perfect understanding even where a fusion of the horizons of interpreter and text occurs – I am always confronted with something foreign that "never entirely resolves itself into understanding."[21] Another consequence of the universalization of hermeneutic scepticism is that understanding becomes an "infinite task" instead of a *fait accompli* or that we can only ever attain "an approximate certainty" about the meaning of foreign discourse (*HuK* 80f., 168, 400f.). That not-understanding can never completely disappear is, moreover, exactly the reason that I must deal with others in accordance with their irreducible "otherness," rather than remaining engaged in a speculative monologue with myself.[22] This, again, is related to the fact that, first, the various subdivided spheres of a language – the medium of our understanding – become more specific in steady progression towards increasing individuation and, second, that nothing individual can be conceptualized. Yet only conceptual facts can be linguistically transmitted;[23] thus, there always remains an only conjecturable (as Schleiermacher says, only divinable)[24] and thus principally mistakable remnant of incomprehension in all understanding.[25]

Schleiermacher's hermeneutic universality claim thus breaks away from rationalistic-realistic assumptions in two respects. Language no longer ensures the representation of eternal truths of reason; and reason no longer reliably corresponds to a reality existing in itself (although Schleiermacher does hold onto this reality). In the face of the complexity of epistemological-ontological alternatives in the eighteenth century, I realize that this is a great over-simplification. But I may say *this* much without reservation: after the universality axiom of reason collapsed, the Romantic theory of language believed that it must take on the task of explaining the supra–individual validity of language differently than by referring to language as itself possibly or necessarily reasonable due to its natural transparency for reason. Language can be granted relative generality – namely, a generality limited to a "community of thinkers" – only as an idealistic abstraction from countless (and in each case historically situated) speech acts, which are themselves not completely describable if they are not grasped, first, as acts of individual construction of the world and, second, as answers to other speech acts (thus as continuing or contradicting other speech): that is, if they are grasped as moments of a dialogue (relating to justified beliefs). Put differently, language is sheer virtuality, an idealization, and nothing more than a mere hypothesis, continually contested by the actual or situational discourse of individuals. Far from determining the reality of the linguistic world construction (which, if reduced to its mere legitimacy, would be "reason"), language is never more than the changeable and generalized state of discourse within a speech community, consisting of countless single individuals communicating with one another. Discourse is a single universal; it is general, because without supra-individual fixation of the meaning of expressions, understanding would be impossible on principle; but it is also individual, because the universality of available sign-syntheses and combination rules must always stand the test of a single speaker's construction of the world:

Just as ... untransferable feeling necessarily becomes external again and acquires the character of communality, so also must generally valid thought again acquire the character of belonging to the individual. First, from the perspective of language, this means that language must individualise itself. Otherwise, it could only be thought of as a potentiality, but not actually exist. And it does exist. In the process of individualisation, language, as the supreme product of organisation, first is subject to the larger cosmic conditions of organisation in general. It then descends to greater specification, ending with individualisation in the style and language use of every single person. We acknowledge these as true and necessary with as much certainty as we believe in higher criticism.[26]

"Language" thus exists only in the reality of actual discourse; but again in actual discourse, the meaning of the signs by which we make ourselves understood to one another are not simply reproductions of a transhistorical codex of reason but rather the frozen results of a principally indeterminate process of communal, but ultimately individual, interpretation of the world. Dialogue thus confirms the validity of language as a "fait social," as well as limiting it. It is confirmed because language exists only in communal discourse as a common framework of meaning and understanding. But discourse also contests this framework, because we are justified in describing a transaction of signs as *conversation* (unlike the language of bees) only if an answer is facultative. Individuals who are (within certain limits) free to answer have at their disposal the communality of symbolically coded accords; their ability to interpret these agreements differently results in a breakdown of the social code.

If I am correct, the major trends in contemporary linguistics and philosophy of language are gradually moving away from this Romantic experience. Impressive evidence of this is offered by the famous sentence with which Saussure, in concluding his *Cours de linguistique generale*, recapitulates his "idee fondamentale" (which, as is widely known, did not originate with him but was smuggled in from Bally and Sechehaye): "the true and unique object of linguistics is language considered in and for itself" (la linguistique a pour unique et seul objet la langue envisagée en elle-même et pour elle-même).[27] This formulation, which may already be found in Humboldt or Grimm and which freshens up a sort of topos of classical linguistics, may appear trivial if one does not consider that "language" here is understood in the spirit of structuralism as, the system of *langue*,[28] and that it abstracts from innovative acts, which Saussure (like Schleiermacher) saw to be grounded in individual language usage. It abstracts also from the level of actual symbolic interaction.

In the following, I will venture another oversimplification. I thereby intend to clarify a common premise of theoretical models of language and text. This premise acts as a kind of tacit minimal agreement, unifying in a single paradigm such widely varying schools as (text) linguistic structuralism, generative grammar, classical analytical philosophy of language, epistemological archaeology, and information and speech act theories, as well as areas in the hermeneutics of reception history.

These trends each carry out what is often referred to as the *linguistic turn*. They thus testify to their origin in the crisis of reflection (or representation) philosophy. Yet in contrast to the hermeneutic theory of language in Romanticism, they attempt to replace the loss of a world fully laid out by concepts of reason (as it is represented by universal grammar for the purpose of communication) by a model of linguistic "code" (i.e., of grammar, of a language game, language system, structure, archive, taxonomy of illocutionary acts, or of historically effected consciousness, and so on). Whichever concept is taken, the single events of situational discourse are deduced from it, like particular cases from a general rule. The shared consequences of this quasirational denial of the crisis of classical rationalism are the problems these schools have with plurivocity and semantic innovation, as well as with linguistic change and determining the status of sign identity. The minimal consensus among linguistic theories that flirt with the code model (or with a related operational scheme, such as the model of "traditions" that determine understanding and that – as symbolic entities – themselves require formation rules, just like a Foucaultian "archive") is grounded in an interest that may be characterized as scientific. In order to gain scientific knowledge of the object "language" one must inevitably assume that linguistic events are rule-governed. Whereas these rules do not unconditionally require the status of timelessness, as rationalism in the seventeenth and eighteenth centuries demanded (regardless of whether conventional or traditional systems are meant), they do guarantee that various occurrences of such linguistic events can be recognized as realizations of one and the same linguistic (or archaeological or pragmatic, etc.) *type*. In Searle's words,

Any linguistic element written or spoken, indeed any rule-governed element in any system of representation at all must be repeatable, otherwise the rules would have no scope of application. To say this is just to say that the logician's type-token distinction must apply generally to all the rule-governed elements of language in order that the rules can be rules. Without this feature of iterability there could not be the possibility of producing an infinite number of sentences with a finite list of elements; and this, as philosophers since Frege have recognized, is one of the crucial features of any language[29]

This quotation is a precise formulation of the basic assumption of the code model. And at the same time, it makes clear that the theoretical decision to grasp language by means of systematization defines what the object of linguistics has to be from scratch. Assuming (but only hypothetically) that languages are systematically constructed and that they determine their utterances, it is analytically true that every repetition of a linguistic type (or of a typified linguistic act) "involves the notion of the repetition of the same."[30]

Of course, choosing a conventionalist view of language can itself be justified only by an epistemological decision; nothing can prove that this choice must be made. The experience that the unity of meaning can shift during dialogue and the awareness that assigning a token to a certain type is indeterminate make the code model appear especially unsuited as a foundation for a theory of discourse. If dialogue falls under the scientistic premise that the self-sameness of the linguistic type must be left untouched in the back and forth of conversation, then all speech reduces to the practice of *parole vide*, which is what it is most commonly viewed as when subjected to those social techniques that refer to themselves as "conversational analysis." What entitles one to speak here of "empty speech"?

Jacques Lacan introduced this expression in 1953 in his extensive congress report *Fonction et champ de la parole et du langage en psychanalyse*, and thereby intended to call attention to the fundamental, yet in contemporary linguistics often disregarded, fact that all speech demands a response and without this aim remains "empty" ("toute parole appelle reponse," "il n'est pas de parole sans reponse".)[31] Remaining empty does not mean that speech does not, in fact, receive a response. On the contrary, the silence of one of the discourse partners can be construed as a sign of "resistance," and an all too ready response can make the voice itself into an impenetrable wall, returning to the ear of the addressee not a response but an echo. Empty speech incorporates the response of the other person not in an actual dialectic but in a specular monologue (Feuerbach accused Hegel of this) in which both roles are played by one and the same subject.

Initially Lacan's critique of empty speech seems to converge with the deepest impulse of Gadamer's hermeneutics, or at least with that impulse that most affected hermeneutic discussions in the German-speaking world of the sixties and seventies. Both abandon the naivety of believing that participation in dialogue could be controlled by a discourse-independent, and thus transhistorical, code. They also reject the view that individuals entering discourse are the sovereign producers of signs, with the aid of which they address each other. In fact, the conversation that we rather *are*, rather than that we conduct,[32] cannot be deceived: it is not the representation of a "truth" beyond discourse, but rather it first constitutes truth in the process of fusing two horizons: namely, the horizon of tradition (whether it be spoken or written discourse) and the horizon of that which appropriates this tradition (text or spoken discourse). In this sense the narcissism of a subject understanding itself self-reflectively is already averted by the theoretical approach: understanding oneself is always preceded by a reference to the speech of the other, which in its turn does not leave the conversation unchanged, because it was fused with the horizon of its partner. Meaning emerges from the reciprocity of an understanding that cannot be anticipated in advance and that Gadamer has characterized as "historically effected consciousness" (*wirkungsgeschichtliches Bewusstsein*). This well-known term means that the self-understanding of each historical subject arises from reference to a tradition with which it converses and through which it achieves knowledge of itself.

One recognizes in Gadamer's approach the traces of an idea to which the whole of post-Hegelianism, and especially Heidegger was obligated: namely, that our self-consciousness arises from a foundation of which it itself is not the author. Gadamer shares this premise with the philosophy of neostructuralism, for example with Lacan (but also Derrida); being situated in a symbolically articulated world is a condition for self-consciousness. This world provides me with the signs by means of which I can identify myself (it doesn't matter here whether I speak of "tradition" or "symbolic order"). The world, language, the context of "involvement" (*Bewandtniszusammenhang*) define the place where subjects can gain understanding of themselves – and of being in general.

It now remains to observe that although the priority, or, as Gadamer prefers to say, the "unsupercedability" (*Unüberholbarkeit*) of tradition over the self-understanding of the subject interrupts the reflexivity of such subjective self-reference and obscures its transparency, it does not prevent it: "it still remains true that all such understanding is ultimately self-understanding."[33] The circularity of "prior-having" (of always having existed in the disclosedness of a symbolic tradition) and "foresight" (of progressively transgressing tradition in the direction of its future meaning-for-me) determines that the "projected projection," as Gadamer and Heidegger understand existence, will exist in a speculative relationship. This relationship converts being that is at first not accessible to the subject into forms of self- or self-present-being. Thus, at its outset Gadamer's hermeneutics encounters Hegelian dialectics, whose reflexive and integrative power emerged in its critique of Schleiermacher and distinguished it from the concept of being an impotent reconstruction of what was originally meant:[34] understanding is sublation (*Aufhebung*), i.e., an overstepping self-appropriation (*Sich-zueigen-machen*) of the apparently other.

Gadamerian hermeneutics can thus far be considered a modification (with emphasis on the finiteness of "existence") of the model of "dialectic"[35] or "speculative" self-relation. This explains the consistent ambiguity of its argumentative style: on the one hand (emphasizing the finiteness of consciousness, namely its inability to become fully transparent to itself), the narcissism of specular and unhistorically conceived self-presentation (*Selbstvergegenwärtigung*, as in Lacan) is humbled and the subject is placed under the "event of tradition" (*Überlieferungsgeschehen*) as its historical a priori. On the other hand, in order to salvage the possibility of reflexivity in "self-understanding," either the history of reception (*Wirkungsgeschichte*) itself must be thought of as subjectivity, or one must concede that tradition realizes itself first in the act of an understanding self-relation, which would then be attributable to a single subject. In the first case, what Gadamer appropriately characterizes as a "continuum of meaning"[36] (there is no continuum without previous unity) would become indiscernible from that supra-individual subject conceived by Hegel as absolute spirit; in the second case, the single subject would become the last authority on the coinage of meaning, since only in the single subject can tradition relate to itself in a way that grants meaning, truth, or consciousness. In both cases, however, a "fusion of horizons" does not really occur, but rather one of the relata is subjected to its counterpart: either the "event of tradition" (*Überlieferungsgeschehen*) is usurped by the appropriating subject, or the subject of interpretation is usurped by the event of tradition. The speculative dialogue of the history of reception (*Wirkungsgeschichte*) thus becomes a variation on the speculative monologue of dialectics, that is, of empty speech.

Gadamer underlines this tendency of his hermeneutics not only by explicitly referring to Hegel but also in considering the "speculative structure" of language.[37] Language, which reflects tradition and the interpretation of tradition reciprocally in a "unity of effect" (*Wirkungs-einheit*),[38] is the "actual subject of the playing."[39] The way language as a subject subsumes its relata is analogous to how "spirit" in Hegel subsumes being-in-itself and being-for-itself. As Gadamer himself notes, one may say that it is "a duplication that is still only the one thing."[40] It can be called speculative (in a literal sense), for its subject has "no tangible being of its own and yet [reflects] the image that is presented to it":[41] it can thus be referred to as a *reflective relation*, and not an overcoming of this relation. After all, Gadamer wants what he calls "language as medium" no longer to be understood as the superiority of one of the relata over the other (such as the superiority of the "event of tradition" over the interpretative act or vice versa): self-understanding, as he says, is grounded in a self-less relation that has "primacy" over both relative parts comprehended by it, namely what understands and what is understood.[42]

In this third attempt to grasp speculatively the nature of a hermeneutic fusion of horizons, it admittedly remains obscure how the claim can be justified that all understanding adds something to the being that is understood, a claim that is indicated by Gadamer's reference to an "increase in being" (*Seinszuwachs*)[43] or by his assertion that each time we understand at all, we understand in a principally different way ("einem prinzipiellen Anders-Verstehen in jedem neuen Verständnis").[44] Individuals cannot here be used to explain semantic innovation, as in Schleiermacher and Saussure, for they are not allotted any independence from the "event of tradition" in which they "participate,"[45] as Gadamer's telling words put it. If the event of tradition reproduces itself in all instances when something is understood, it could confront something different or foreign and thereby broaden its horizons only *if* it pays the price of breaching its self-enclosed reflexivity. But this possibility is itself blocked if the event of tradition is explicitly interpreted as speculative, that is, as the gesture of one thing self-reflecting itself in itself ("It is a duplication that is still only the one thing"). In this case there would be no criteria for identifying the foreignness of the other. One can ascertain this foreignness only if it either vanishes into the horizon of the interpreter (this would then demand some minimal autonomy [*Selb-ständigkeit*] of the subject of interpretation, which Gadamer rejects) or if the horizon of the interpreter "enters into" (*einrückt*) the horizon of the event of tradition or if the fusing horizons are identified specularly (in the "medium of language") by means of a higher-order dyadic reflecting reflex. But in the latter case a judgment concerning the difference between the two would come too late. The independence of meaning in the text (*Sinneigenständigkeit des Textes*) that is to be interpreted is in a similar situation to the self-consciousnesses fighting for reciprocal recognition (*Anerkennung*) in Hegel: the moment that on both sides generates insight into the selfness of the other sublates 1 the difference between them, without which knowledge would be impossible, and abolishes 2 their individuality (their difference in being [*ihr Anderssein gegen einanander*]), because it converts (*überführt*) them into that uniform "essential self" or "general self-consciousness" that always already lies beyond the apparent alternatives between the I and you, or what is ours and what is foreign.[46]

Therefore, doubts are likely to arise concerning the hermeneutics of historically effected consciousness, regardless of whether one adopts the perspective either of Schleiermacher or of Lacan. Doesn't the "fusion of horizons" – contrary to its deepest intention, simply because of the speculative model it employs – remain in the final analysis chained to the paradigm of reflexive philosophy that it so impressively challenges? Does it establish a positive model that can ward off suspicions of self-affective, i.e., "empty" speech? In any case, if the horizon of the interpreter enters into the meaning-horizon of the interpreted (e.g., of the text) or if both interlocutors merge in the tradition event's autonomous continuum of meaning, which would at that point be wearing two hats and would conduct a speculative monolog with itself (all understanding would be in fact only self-understanding)[47] – if that were true, the manifest differences between Gadamer's model of understanding and that of the code-theorists would diminish in several respects. Both approaches would at one level at least share an enduring, if minimal, consensus.

I admit that it requires some malice to point out the structural convergence between the "fusion of horizons" and what Lacan calls "empty speech." More distinctive formulations of empty speech are psychological (or psychoanalytical) empathy – "cette tarte à la crème de la psychologie intuitionniste, voire phénoménologique, a pris dans l'usage contemporain une extension bien symptômatique de la raréfaction des effets de la parole dans le contexte social présent"[48] – and the cybernetic model of conversational information transfer, according to which an encoded content is decoded by another subject following the same rules and with the same constant and ensured meaning.

No one has rejected the methodology of the code-model more passionately than Gadamer. He has further shown very emphatically that the agenda of "empathy" does not present a tenable alternative. But he has not shown how individuals can escape the pressure of tradition to the extent that they can demonstrate that their understanding is an "understanding-differently."

Initially, there seems to be no greater contrast than that between empathy (which Gadamer insinuates Schleiermacher instrumentalized for his hermeneutics) and decoding: whereas the discursive, understanding subject in empathy gets in his own way and can confront only himself instead of the other (granted, this is his narcissistic strategy), the subject according to the theoretical information model actually goes outside of itself by handing over its message to the supraindividual rules of "discourse" (Lacan refers to "discourse" as the "ordre symbolique"). In somewhat derisive passages, Lacan has often emphasized the affinity between theoretical information code-models and the model according to which the language of bees was decoded. He intends in this way to demonstrate that both models – "pour les résultats les plus contus" (for the most striking results) – want to bind factual understanding to rules of playing, the unremitting rigidity of which can alone be trusted to guarantee the unambiguity of the messages.[49] A code would then consist of a system of pairs, signifier/signified, in such a way that every expression would be allotted one and only one meaning according to certain conventions: the en-closure of meaning by the addressee would accord with the dis-closure by the receiver; and the identity of the messages would be guaranteed by the trans-subjectivity of the rules of enclosure. According to Lacan, this is not a scientifically tenable alternative to the irrationality of empathy. Both models uphold a discursive ideal guided by a reflexive model (of speculative monologue). The relativity of discursive reason is based on "accepting the principle of a rule of debate which does not function without an explicit or implicit accordance with what one refers to as its base" (une acception de principe d'une régle du débat qui ne va pas sans un accord explicite ou implicite sur ce qu'on appelle son fonds). It is this dependence on a historically instituted "corpus of rules" (corps de regles) (law [droit], and even logic [logique] are referred to by Lacan under the same paradigms) that dismiss discursive reason as narcissistic prejudgments (that one can speculate about and nearly always anticipate) of the initiation of the discourse it purports to conduct ("ce qui équivaut presque toujours à un accord anticipé sur son enjeu").[50]

Lacan differentiates between these forms of empty speech and "symbolic interpretation," with which "parole pleine" commences.[51] Like what Schleiermacher termed the "more strict practice,"[52] "symbolic interpretation" tests its actual understanding by first subjecting it to "resistance," thereby preventing a mistaken belief that one had understood from the start: "C'est qu'elle nous présente la naissance de la vérité dans la parole." (It is this that provides us with the birth of truth in speech.)[53]

The reference to a possible "truth" of discourse foreshadows a misunderstanding: as though it were conceivable that an authentic understanding, abstracting from the prejudices of the subject, could be demanded. Lacan's argument, however, points in a different direction. He means, rather, that understanding (in which a foreign horizon is brought into one's own) does not alone provide the guarantee that the others have been appreciated for their otherness. In this sense, "symbolic interpretation" – which seems less concerned with providing resistance than with making the interpreter conscious – intends not to interrupt, but rather to first establish communication. It does so by clearly differentiating between actual communication (address and reply) and the practice of conversation-with-myself-in-the-presence-of-another (text/discourse), whereby the former is referred to as "imaginary," and the latter as true. There is one unmistakable test of the success or failure of "full speech": namely, the criterion of semantic novation.[54] A semantic "horizon" (in Gadamer's sense) remains closed upon itself as long as it does not cause the speaker interpreter, following the shock of disappointed expectations, to devine a new and previously inaccessible meaning (this does not mean just new vocabulary or information). This kind of innovative appropriation of meaning, which does not confirm but, rather, disrupts semantic expectations, can succeed only when there is actual contact with the other, which Lacan writes with a capital O. Understanding in the emphatic sense of the word can occur only when the interpreter's existing prejudices are not virtualized through some gesture of "goodwill" but are disarmed or disorganized as the real effect of the other's discourse.

In order to release this effect, however, one must abandon not only the model of empathy – as Gadamer believed in his attack on Schleiermacher – but also the model of a fusion of horizons, which is only apparently more favourable to communication, as well as the code-model, which, although it takes into consideration the autarkic "speculative structure" of language and the idea that "language must be studied in and for itself," does not account for the fact that encoded or inherited messages are constantly subverted by the replies of the other. For discourse is not intersubjective simply if – due to the uniformity of all linguistic schemata – an arbitrary number of subjects participate in it according to identical *démarchess* (pratices) but rather only if the discourse of one subject cannot, not even in principle, be anticipated by the horizon of the other, and thus indeed remains "unconscious."[55]

The impossibility of ascertaining (or anticipating) the meaning of discourse is thus grounded in its symbolic nature and in its intersubjectivity, the very factors used by system theories of language to affirm that meaning *is* ascertainable and foreseeable.[56] Only an interpersonal domain in which one person confronts another person as the other can be called "true." These persons must be capable of semantic innovation and at all times take advantage of this opportunity, as long as the communication is conducted seriously and is not simply "talking about the weather."[57] This is also why every description of the effects of discourse that localizes the establishment of continuity in the single subject (in the sense of a motivated life context) is bound to prove inadequate. Meaning is created, rather, by the intersubjectivity of discourse as such; i.e., it is created neither by individual reserves ("trésor") of signs at the disposal of the subject nor by the grammar of a "language studied in and for itself," one that guarantees the meaning of discourse, nor even by an "event of tradition." Rather, it is the response and comprehension of the other that determine the meaning, and in a way that is always provisional and subject to change – for discourse is open and can come to an end only through fate or violence.[58]

Before concluding, I would like to ask the following question: how does the universality claim of hermeneutics, first advanced by Schleiermacher, relate to the conclusions I have just reached? Gadamer distinguished his project of a universal hermeneutics essentially in contrast to Schleiermacher's hermeneutics of empathy, which supposedly neglects tradition. Now we have seen that Schleiermacher means something very different by "divination" from the transposition of the interpreter's soul into the intent of another subject. "Divination," rather, characterizes the leap that the interpreter dares to take, with no assurance of success, in order to register the change that occurs within an established context when it is disturbed by the intervention of an individual. That this change does occur is positively maintained also by Gadamer: "All understanding is understanding differently." Schleiermacher could have posed the question, how do you know that? According to which criterion is change to be measured? And how can tradition change, if not through the collaboration of individuals within the event being handed down?[59] An alternative answer would be fetishism à la Heidegger: "language speaks." Does language thus change itself? (Wittgenstein had the same problem.) Schleiermacher would have answered, no, on the contrary: it is the product of individuals communicating with one another and creating predictable meaning. One misses the real motive behind the universalization of the hermeneutic task if one does not take these individuals into account. For only the individual "collaboration (Mitwirkung)" of subjects in the meaning of tradition prevents me from simply reading meaning into a "tradition," "language," or "code," or even deducing it from them.

Schleiermacher can also explain a distinction that Habermas, at the beginning of the seventies, assumed Gadamer would need to level. I mean the distinction between the "event of tradition," on the one hand, in which we "participate" (einrücken),[60] which presents "prejudices" without questioning them, but indeed must be seen as "a positive and productive opportunity for understanding,"[61] and truth, on the other hand. The title of Gadamer's major work emphasizes precisely that truth does not have a place outside the "continuum of meaning" in a tradition. The question of the truth of tradition is suspended in favour of the question of whether or not factually practised understanding is able to understand itself as a self-explanatory possibility of what is understood: the "continuum of meaning" alone can guarantee here that the interpreter understands himself in interpreting the text. His individuality is not only completely absorbed by the event of language, through which meaning is autonomously validated; it also does not even have the opportunity to raise an objection.

The situation is different with Schleiermacher. He could easily grant Gadamer that we have no reason to assume that we could ever step out of relations of factual, and thus fallible, forms of conviction. Yet his *Dialectics* sets its sights on "knowledge" (*Wissen*) as a goal and therefore uses the ideal of approaching truth antisceptically as a point of orientation. Truth is conceived realistically, as correspondence with reality,[62] but the *criterion* for truth is (in addition to the coherence of our system of beliefs) a correspondence in the manner that the "community of thinkers" "constructs" (or "schematizes") the common world. Thus it is possible to distinguish between convictions that are based only on "linguistic traditions," i.e., on factual consensus, and "certainty itself." At this point a "critical ... procedure" becomes a factor in the business of understanding,[63] precisely what Habermas saw to be suspended in Gadamer. But in contrast to Habermas – and this time on Gadamer's side – Schleiermacher does not believe that even profound efforts at enlightenment would be able to break the natural power of tradition once and for all. Otherwise we would end up sublating the possibility of intersubjective understanding, and truth is not simply reality (existing for itself) but rather a well-founded, shared conviction at a certain time and within a certain "world view" – as Wittgenstein says in continuing the Schleiermacher-Humboldt tradition.[64] Schleiermacher connects the external and internal aspects of knowledge in the idea of an "infinite approximation." Gadamer, in contrast, must almost identify truth with (factual) disclosedness or understandability, and he thus exposes himself to Tugendhat's criticism of the Heideggerian theory of truth,[65] which Heidegger himself finally acknowledged.[66]

But none of this hindered, in the years I studied under Gadamer in Heidelberg, his hermeneutics from providing a powerful and critical impetus to the student protest generation of which I was a part and which took as its motto "challenge assumptions" (*Hinterfragen*). "Challenging assumptions" meant making interpretations, symbolic systems, and institutions conscious of their roots in tradition and thus also of their changeability, as well as of the hypothetical status of their existence. Their native and perhaps illegitimate permanence would thereby be shaken. Thus Gadamer's influence itself pointed to the need for a critical justification, the very thing I have just noted as a deficiency in his own work. Perhaps it was Gadamer who first drew my attention to the great importance of language and tradition in Schleiermacher's works. Whatever the case may be, even Gadamer's most important ideas have long since been swept into the current of "after-historical consciousness" (*wirkungsgeschichtlcibes Bewusstsein*) and separated from the intentions of their author. It is thus valid to say even of his words that they are to be understood "'first just as well and then better than [their] author.'[67] For because we have no immediate knowledge of what is in him, we must seek to bring much to consciousness that can remain unconscious for him."[68] I believe that Gadamer means something similar when he reminds us that in all understanding "there is more being than consciousness, and in a way that cannot be sublated."[69] And so at the end we should reach out to each other as we engage in an unavoidable dispute that finally seeks nothing more than mutual understanding. In this field, Hans-Georg Gadamer has always gotten the better of his opponents.

CITED WORKS

Chladen [Chladenius], Johann Martin. *Einleitung zur richtigen Auslegung vernünfftiger Reden und Schriften.* Leipzig 1742.

Dummett, Michael. *Ursprünge der analytischen Philosophie.* Frankfurt a.M.: Suhrkamp 1988.

Foucault, Michel. *Les mots et les choses: Une archéologie des sciences humaines.* Paris 1966.

– *Préface à la Grammaire générale et raisonnée ... de Arnauld et Lancelot.* Paris 1969, iii–xxvii.

Frank, Manfred. *Der unendliche Mangel an Sein: Schellings Hegel-Kritik und die Anfänge der Marxschen Dialektik.* Frankfurt a.M., 1974 (second, revised edition Münich: Suhrkamp 1992).

– *Das individuelle Allgemeine: Textstrukturierung und –interpretation nach Schleiermacher.* Frankfurt a. M.: Suhrkamp, 1977 (paperback edition 1985).

Gadamer, Hans-Georg. *Zur Problematik des Selbstverständnisses.* In *Einsichten: Festschrift für G. Krüger.* Frankfurt a.M.: Vittorio Klostermann 1962, 71–85.

– *Kleine Schriften.* 3 vols. Tübingen: 1967, 1972.

– *Truth and Method.* 2d, revised edition. Trans. Joel Weinsheimer and Donald Marshall. New York: Crossroad Publishing 1989. Original version, *Wahrheit und Methode.* Tübingen: Mohr 1969 (cited as *WuM*).

Heidegger, Martin. *Zur Sache des Denkens.* Tübingen: M. Niemeyer 1969.

– *On Time and Being.* Trans. J. Stambaugh. Chicago and London: University of Chicago Press 1972.

Lacan, Jacques. *Écrits.* Paris: Le Seuil 1966.

Lewis, David. *Philosophical Papers.* Vol. 1. Oxford: Oxford University Press 1983.

Meier, Georg Friedrich. *Versuch einer Allgemeinen Auslegungskunst.* Halle 1757. Photomechanical reprint edited by Lutz Geldsetzer. Düsseldorf: Stern-Verlag, Janssen & Co. 1965.

Quine, Willard Van Orman. "Epistemology Naturalized." In: *Ontological Relativity and Other Essays.* New York and London: Columbia University Press 1969 (2nd ed. 1971).

Sartre, Jean-Paul. *Que peut la littérature? (Intervention à un débat).* Ed. Yves Buin. Paris: Editions de l'Herne 1965, 107–27.

– *L'idiot de la famille Gustave Flaubert de 1821 à 1857.* 3 vols., Paris: Editions de l'Herne 1971, 1972. (cited as IF).

De Saussure, Ferdinand. Introduction to *Cours de linguistique générale (1908/9).* Ed. R. Godel. In *Cahiers Ferdinand de Saussure* 15 (1957) (cited as CFS 15).

– *Course in General Linguistics.* Trans. Wade Baskin. New York: Fontana/Collins: 1959. Original version: *Cours de linguistique générale.* Critical edition prepared by Tullio de Mauro. Paris 1972, 1980.

Schlegel, Friedrich. *Kritische Ausgabe seiner Schriften.* Ed. Ernst Behler. München, Paderborn, and Wien: Schöningh.

Schleiermacher, Friedrich, *Dialektik* [1814/15], 1828 (text according to Ludwig Jonas' edition, Berlin 1839) and 1822 (manuscript notes together with Rudolf Odebrecht's [Leipzig 1942] lecture notes prepared on the order of the Prussian Academy of Sciences on the basis of previously unpublished materials. Ed. with an introduction by Manfred Frank. 2 vols. Frankfurt/Main (stw 1529), 2001 (editor's preface and introduction, vol. 1, 7–135) (Vol. I cited as *Dial J*).

– *Hermeneutics and Criticism.* Ed. and trans. Andrew Bowie. Cambridge: Cambridge University Press 1998 (cited as HaC). Original version: *Hermeneutik und Kritik: Mit einem Anhang sprachphilosophischer Texte Schleiermachers* Ed. with an introduction by Manfred Frank. Frankfurt: Suhrkamp 1977 (cited as: HuK).

Searle, John R. "Reiterating the Differences: A Reply to Derrida." *Glyph: Johns Hopkins Textual Studies* 1, 1977: 198–208.

Tugendhat, Ernst. *Der Wahrheitsbegriff bei Husserl und Heidegger.* Berlin 1967.

– "Phänomenologie und Sprachanalyse." In *Hermeneutik und Dialektik (Festschrift für H.-G. Gadamer),* ed. R. Bubner, K. Cramer and R. Wiehl. Vol. 2. Tübingen: Mohr Siebeck 1970, 3–23.

– "Heideggers Idee von Wahrheit." In *Wahrheitstheorien: Eine Auswahl aus den Diskussionen über Wahrheit im 20. Jahrhundert.* Edited by Gunnar Skirbekk. Frankfurt a. M.: Suhrkamp 1977, 431–48.

Vattimo, Gianni. "Dialectics, Difference, and Weak Thought." *Graduate Faculty Philosophical Journal* 10, no. 1 (1984): 151–63.

– *The End of Modernity: Nihilism and Hermeneutics in Postmodern Culture.* Baltimore: Johns Hopkins University Press 1988 (original 1985).

– *Beyond Interpretation: The Meaning of Hermeneutics for Philosophy.* Cambridge: Polity Press 1989 (2d ed. 1992).

– *The Adventure of Difference: Philosophy after Nietzsche and Heidegger.* Baltimore: Johns Hopkins University Press 1993 (original 1980).

- "The Age of Interpretation." In R. Rorty and G. Vattimo, *The Future of Religion,* ed. Santiago Zabala. New York: Columbia University Press 2004, 43–54.

Wittgenstein, Ludwig. *Über Gewißheit.* In *Werkausgabe.* Vol. 8. Frankfurt a.M.: Suhrkamp 1984 (cited as *ÜG*).

Zabala, Santiago. "'Weak Thought' and the Reduction of Violence: A Dialogue with Gianni Vattimo." *Common Knowledge* 8, no. 3 (autumn 2002): 425–63.

NOTES

1 Lewis, *Philosophical Papers*, x.
2 Cf. Quine, "Epistemology Naturalized."
3 Frank, *Das individuelle Allgemeine.*
4 *Common Knowledge* (1995): 24ff.; Dummett protests against this in *Ursprünge der analytischen Philosophie*, 11f., 284ff.
5 Cf. Foucault, *Préface*, ixff.
6 *HuK* 75.
7 *HuK* 92.
8 Tugendhat, *Phänomenologie und Sprachanalyse*, 23.
9 *HuK* 88 (17, 18; cf. 98: "The proposition as a unit is also the smallest thing that can be understood or misunderstood" (28).
10 E. Tugendhat, "Phänomenologie und Sprachanalyse, vol. 2, 3–23.
11 F. Schleiermacher, *Hermeneutics and Criticism*, 5.
12 Ibid., 17f.; German, 87ff.
13 Ibid., 16f.; German, 75ff.
14 Chladen, *Einleitung zur richtigen Auslegung*, preface, 64–5.
15 Ibid., §155, 86.
16 Cf. Meier, *Versuch einer Allgemeinen Auslegungsjunst*, §57, 30.
17 Ibid., §1.
18 *HaC*, p. 21; German, 92.
19 Ibid.
20 *HuK* 81, 360.
21 *HuK* 328.
22 The avoidance of this danger is a main motive of Gadamer's hermeneutics, with its strong intersubjective approach. This is already demonstrated by the motto from Rilke at the very start of his most important work: "Catch only what you've thrown yourself, all is mere skill and little gain."
23 Schleiermacher, *Hermeneutics and Criticism*, 80 and 172, 5.

24 Schleiermacher himself occasionally translates "divination" as "conjecture" (*Erraten*) (e.g., German *HuK* 318).

25 Ibid., *HuK* 169f., §6; 176f.

26 Schleiermacher, *HuK* 364.

27 De Saussure, *Course in General Linguistics*, 232.

28 That is, of "code"; cf. 423, editor's note 66 of De Saussure, *Cours de linguistique générale*, critical edition by Tullio Mauro, Paris: Payot 1972.

29 Searle, *Reiterating the Differences*, 199.

30 Ibid., 207.

31 Lacan, *Écrits*, 247.

32 *TaM* 383; *WuM* 361.

33 *TaM* 260; *WuM* 246.

34 *TaM* 165; *WuM* 158 f.

35 *TaM* 1, 388; cf. 345, 6; *HuK* 366, 328.

36 *TaM* 369; *WuM* 351.

37 *TaM* 456f.; *WuM* 432ff.

38 *TaM* 282; *WuM* 267.

39 *TaM* 490; cf. 101f.; *WuM* 464, cf. 97ff.

40 *TaM* 466; *WuM* 441.

41 *TaM* 474; *WuM* 449.

42 Gadamer, *Zur Problematik des Selbstverständnisses*, 77.

43 *TaM* 140, 147f.; *WuM* 133, 140 f.

44 *TaM* 297; *WuM* 280.

45 *TaM* 290f.; *WuM* 274.

46 I have given detailed reasons for this conclusion in *Der unendliche Mangel au Sein*, 94ff. (esp. 99) 155ff. (in the 1992 edition, 178ff., 240ff.

47 *WuM* 246.

48 *E* 252. Translation: "this pie in the face of intuitional, even phenomenological, psychology, has acquired in contemporary usage an extended meaning quite symptomatic of the dilution of the effects of speech in the present social context." An English translation exists for selected articles in Lacan's *Écrits*. Frank has quoted, however, from an article not included in this selection. The translator, Jim Scott, has therefore rendered Frank's quotations into English himself, in consultation with his colleague Dr Jean-Marc Braem.

49 *E* 18f., 297.

50 *E* 430f.

51 *E* 254.

52 *HaC* 22; German 92.

53 *E* 255f.

54 "La *novation* analogique (mieux qu'innovation)." (De Saussure, *CFS* 15, 88.

55 "Unconscious" according to Lacan does not mean that nothing is thought or imagined in actual discourse but rather that none of the partners can know for certain what the other is thinking or imagining by the signs that he expresses: "L'inconscient est cette partie du discours concret en tant que transindividuel, qui fait défaut à la disposition du sujet pour rétablir la continuité de son discours inconscient." Lacan, *Écrits*, 258f.

56 Ibid.

57 Schleiermacher, *HaC* 13; *HuK* 83.

58 "L'omniprésence du discours humain pourra peut-être un jour être embrassée au ciel ouvert d'une omnicommunication de son texte. Ce n'est pas dire qu'il en sera plus accordé. Mais c'est la le champ que notre expérience polarise dans une relation qui n'est à deux qu'en apparence, car toute position de sa structure en termes seulement duels, lui est aussi inadéquate en théorie que ruineuse pour sa technique." Lacan, *Écrits*, 265.

59 Schleiermacher, *HaC* 90; *HuK* 167, 3.

60 *TaM* 290; *WuM* 275.

61 *TaM* 278, 281.

62 *Dial J* 48f., 54.

63 Ibid., 550, §11.

64 Wittgenstein, *Über Gewissheit*, 139ff., esp. §§94, 102, 105, 140ff.

65 Tugendhat, *Der Wahrheitsbegriff* and *Heideggers Idee*.

66 Heidegger writes: "the question of *aletheia*, of unconcealment as such, is not the same as raising the question of truth. For this reason, it was inadequate and misleading to call *aletheia* in the sense of opening, truth." *On Time and Being*, 70.

67 This phrase is put in quotes by Schleiermacher. He seems to be referring to Friedrich Schlegel's renowned Athenäum-fragment number 401: Kitische Ausgabe 2, 241; cf. 18, 63, no. 434.

68 Schleiermacher, *HaC* 23; German 94; cf. 324f.

69 Gadamer, *Kleine Schriften*, 1, 127; cf. the preface to the second edition of *TaM*: "The consciousness of being affected by history is finite in such a radical sense that the affected being in our entire destiny essentially outstands its knowledge of itself" (xx). Cf. Frank, *Das individuelle Allgemeine*, 358ff.

11

On the Continuation of Philosophy: Hermeneutics as Convalescence

JAMES RISSER

Gianni Vattimo wants philosophy to continue. This obvious statement appears at first sight to be vacuous, almost nonsensical, when employed to begin writing about a philosopher. After all, does not every philosopher by the act of philosophizing engage de facto in the continuation of philosophy? The apparent emptiness of this statement quickly disappears, though, when, as in the case of Vattimo's philosophical project, there is an announcement of the end of philosophy such that there is indeed a question not actually of whether philosophy is to continue but of the way in which it is able to continue. The announcement of the end of philosophy is for Vattimo a borrowed idea, for it was first made by two of the principal thinkers who stand behind Vattimo and are the source for much of Vattimo's own work. Those thinkers are, of course, Nietzsche and Heidegger. Supported by them, Vattimo announces the end of philosophy that is signalled with the end of modernity and its ensuing nihilism. In relation to this nihilism, which follows Nietzsche in the proclamation that the highest values (including the value of truth) are devalued, philosophy can no longer be understood as a discipline concerned with the advancement of truth. Naturally so, this nonadvancement includes a retreat from metaphysics that operates according to a particular use of reason. But for Vattimo the advent of nihilism is not to be taken as a negative state.[1] Insofar as it entails the dissolution of foundations and the restraints imposed by the logic of demonstration, it has something of the character of emancipation, where constraints are shed and we gain opportunities to choose.

How, though, is this emancipation and with it the task of philosophy to be understood? It would appear that without a logic of demonstration and a connection to a history of truth, philosophy has been eviscerated and is no longer capable of lending a hand in any emancipation that would be of real substance. Vattimo himself lends credence to this view, for he maintains that philosophy can continue only in relation to "weak thought" (*pensiero debole*). This idea, which is the central philosophical idea in Vattimo's work, can easily be misunderstood, and Vattimo on more than one occasion has been asked to clarify precisely what he means by it. In response, he tells us most emphatically that it is not a weakness of thinking in which philosophy is no longer able to give directions to the *concerns of life*; rather, it is simply the way in which philosophy takes into account the transformation of its role whereby it takes up a thought of the weakening of the weight of objective structures and, ultimately, the weakening of being itself. "After [Marx, Nietzsche and] Freud," Vattimo says, "we can no longer believe that 'being,' as a type of incontrovertible evidence, can be apprehended by us."[2] But this is not to say that we can at the same time escape from the meaning of being. Vattimo, following Heidegger, does not abandon ontology. In fact, he wants to link philosophy's new-found emancipation to an ontological happening that does not involve an actual return to being but is simply caught up in a story of a "long goodbye."[3]

If such is the task of philosophy, it is also at once the task of hermeneutics, for hermeneutics is, according to Vattimo, the *koiné* of contemporary thinking. In this context we must identify a third thinker who stands behind Vattimo and is yet another source for his work. Taking up the thought of the "weakening of being" is nothing less than Vattimo's way of developing hermeneutics, as he tells us, beyond Gadamer's own intentions.[4] Here, then, we come to the heart of the matter for the way in which philosophy is to continue for Vattimo. What *kind* of hermeneutics is it that enables philosophy to continue without real progression and advancement? Certainly it is not simply Nietzschean, since a Nietzschean hermeneutics of suspicion would not in fact be compatible with a hermeneutics that follows at least in some basic sense the hermeneutics of Gadamer.[5] But then neither is it, strictly speaking, a Heideggerian hermeneutics, for, again, it is not without a relation to the hermeneutics of Gadamer. To then simply call this position a postmodern hermeneutics is also not sufficient, since we are not yet clear on what precisely this now means. If indeed such a hermeneutics cannot be understood as an advancement in truth because nihilism shatters the old order in such a way that it cannot inaugurate itself as a new order, i.e., in such a way that it cannot define itself as an advance and progression beyond the old, then certainly we are faced with the prospect of a hermeneutics that will not be a solution to the crises of metaphysics and humanism that appear in the wake of nihilism.[6]

Our question then remains. In the following remarks I want to answer this question as a way of paying tribute to Gianni Vattimo. What follows, though, is not so much an attempt to present the position of Vattimo as it is an analysis that remains in close proximity to it, such that the Gadamerian effort to have the word speak again is carried out.

Let me begin to take up this question of hermeneutics from a perspective broader than the one we find in Vattimo's own work. It is the perspective found in the story at the end of Plato's *Republic*, in which Er tells of the journey of souls in the afterworld. At the point where each soul chooses a new life for itself, Socrates reminds Glaucon of the importance of being able to learn to distinguish the good and the bad life so as to be able to choose with care the better life from among those that are possible. In the story, after each soul chooses a life, the souls are led to the plain of *Lethe* and camp by the river *Ameleta*, the river of neglect and carelessness. Here all the souls have to drink a certain measure, and those not saved by *phronesis* drink more than the measure. With this drink everything is forgotten, but Er is not allowed to drink, and thus the story is saved and not lost.

This story is interesting for several reasons. As the counterpart to the story of the turn to philosophy in the middle books of the *Republic*, in it we see that for Plato the theoretical enactment of philosophy does not stand by itself but is taken up in relation to a practical demand. The enactment of philosophy is dramatically joined to accomplishment in life, to living well, for which one cannot be without care. Equally important, the story reminds us that for Plato the acquiring of insight transpires within the dynamics of memory. The enactment of philosophy, tied as it is to the accomplishing of life, takes shape as a recovery from forgetting. And here we should immediately add that Plato is not alone in determining the shape of philosophy as a process of recollection and recovery. We see it also in Augustine and Hegel and, of course, in the philosophical hermeneutics of Heidegger and Gadamer.

Heidegger in fact makes use of this very story by Plato to tell one version of his own story of sorts of *aletheia* and its counteressence *lethe*, which is at once for Heidegger the story of the being of beings. But even before Heidegger was telling this story, he had already ascribed to philosophy the task of recovery and saving relative to life's falling away from itself. For the Heidegger of the early 1920s, philosophy was a matter of a hermeneutics of facticity: the interpretation of life from out of the way I am already in the hold of life. More to the point, philosophy is here an interpretive encounter with ruinant life in which the interpretation of life must proceed by way of a "tracing back and repeating."[7] When the later Heidegger then abandons the idea of a hermeneutics of facticity, he does not at the same time abandon the recovery and saving character of thinking with respect to the issue of being. That issue becomes one of overcoming metaphysics, in terms of which thinking is a thinking back to a site of origination in relation to an essential forgetting. Heidegger uses many words for this thinking: *Erinnerung, Andenken, Gedächtnis*. Its essential character, though, remains the same: to remember in the manner of an attentive keeping in mind in which there occurs something like the saving of the phenomenon – in this case, the being of beings. And for Gadamer, who also begins from the perspective of a hermeneutics of facticity, philosophy is likewise a matter of recovery, perhaps preeminently so. Whether it is a matter of understanding the historical object, the meaning of a text, the word spoken by another, or one's own enterprise of freedom in a technological age, these endeavours of understanding all take place for Gadamer in relation to an anterior life from which we are removed by virtue of distance and forgetting, such that everywhere philosophizing is attempted a recollection of being takes place.[8] A philosophical hermeneutics is Gadamer's attempt at telling us how we are to recover and save the words that tell us about the enterprise of our human living.

If we let this perspective serve to answer the question of hermeneutics, we see that we are actually not so far from the position of Vattimo. Here hermeneutics, which remains tied to the basic experience of philosophy in Plato – an experience that will keep in play the relation between philosophy and life – is a matter of a kind of recovery with respect to life that can be characterized only as a matter of convalescence. The general meaning of this word is clear enough. Convalescence is a gradual return to health after an illness. More precisely, convalescence concerns a time in which one does not, in the manner of accomplishment, enter a state of health; rather, it concerns a time of getting over in which the source of the illness never really withdraws completely. Of course, it cannot go unnoticed that Plato himself speaks of convalescence at the end of the *Phaedo*. Socrates' last words, spoken after his covered face is uncovered, were to remind Crito not to forget that a cock is owed to Asclepius, the son of Apollo who is the god of medicine. The practice of philosophy has been for Socrates a matter of convalescence, and now at that point where the convalescing is brought to an end by forces outside itself, Socrates wants to pay what is owed to Asclepius. This word, then, already has much to say about the nature of the recovery that operates in hermeneutics and certain philosophies of recollection. At the outset, it indicates that the recovery is a matter of a recovering in which the recovery itself remains outstanding. And insofar as hermeneutic recovery is such that it can't get over its own operation of recovery, we will want to distance this hermeneutic recovery from the idea that hermeneutic recovery is simply a matter of a memory that opposes itself to forgetting and concealing by fetching the lost object back to presence and unconcealedness. When thought of in terms of a convalescence, hermeneutic recovery could only be, to say the least, something like "the time of memory," i.e., the living out of one's own history in loss and regeneration. Hermeneutic recovery is a recovery tied to a source from which it can't recover, and yet everything depends on there being a recovery.[9]

At the outset of this attempt to describe hermeneutics as convalescence, it becomes immediately apparent that any such description is not without its difficulty. Any description would seem to depend on whose version of hermeneutics one takes as a starting point. One could in fact say that there are at least three possible versions of hermeneutics as convalescence: a direct version given by Nietzsche, an analogical version given by Gadamer, and an indirect version given by Heidegger. In mentioning only these three, we are forgetting for a moment that Vattimo's hermeneutics could in fact constitute a fourth version. We should not forget, however, that the authors of these three versions coincide with the three principal thinkers for Vattimo's own work.

Nietzsche gives us a direct version insofar as he takes as his main problem the sickness of spirit that, as he tells us, has lasted for over two thousand years. This sickness, which is aided by philosophers, theologians, and moralists through their explanations of the life of spirit, is the sickness of weakness and decay that issues in nihilism. The overcoming of this sickness of the degeneration of organic activity – an overcoming that is in principle available only to the free spirit – will consist of a return to a condition of enhanced strength, as the condition of living well. The hermeneutics of recovery with respect to this health – the hermeneutics that issues in suspicion and perspectivism but is ultimately directed at an accomplishing of life – is a long road of recovery that he explicitly identifies as a convalescence. The road is long in part because, befitting convalescence, the sickness remains as a resistance within the organism.[10] Accordingly, great health – "that mature freedom of spirit, which is equally self-mastery and discipline of the heart and permits access to many and contradictory modes of thought"[11] – is not absolutely measured but always measured against the way in which the organism confronts its inevitable threat of destruction. And because the will to health often disguises itself as health already achieved, the measure of health must constantly be taken within the organism by way of a certain measured thoughtfulness. And let us not forget that Nietzschean convalescence also includes a recovery with respect to history. This convalescence will require an active forgetting that entails a certain kind of measure-taking with respect to itself: one must be able to forget and to remember at the right time; one must possess "a powerful instinct for sensing when it is necessary to feel historically and when unhistorically."[12] But even here Nietzsche knows that the sickness remains as a resistance within the organism, and the will to health often disguises itself as health already achieved, thus requiring a constant measure-taking of health. Great health – that condition of overcoming a certain loss in relation to becoming who you are – is accomplished through a kind of practical wisdom that would prescribe health for oneself only in small doses.[13]

With respect to Gadamer's hermeneutics, we have an analogical version insofar as interpretation stands in relation to the wholeness of language that is comparable to what he calls in *The Enigma of Health* the self-maintaining and self-restoring totality that is the hidden mystery of health. Hermeneutics for Gadamer enacts, in effect, a convalescing not unlike a return from the interruption of illness in which one returns to one's accomplished form of life. For Gadamer, the living whole of language has its wholeness interrupted by the foreign word – that word of the other in voice or text that interrupts communication in language and that testifies to an experience of loss. Hermeneutics is here the recovering of that loss – a convalescence directed at overcoming the resistance to our familiarity and being at home in the world. The resistance to meaning occurring in foreign words is like a broken wound that is to be healed by bringing the resistance into its relation to a living whole. And here too, not unlike what we find in Nietzsche, such healing depends on a peculiar measure-taking of health. For Gadamer this is the measure-taking of dialogical conversation, which by its very nature of performative enactment, does not produce a measure from a fixed standard, in which case language would have available to it a mechanism for determining "correct" interpretation. And here too hermeneutics remains a convalescing, for the broken wounds remain as the permanent condition of living language and historical life. They remain in a way that will set philosophical hermeneutics against the progressive "ontological self-domestication belonging to [Hegelian] dialectic,"[14] where the wounds of spirit leave no scars. Philosophical hermeneutics cannot ultimately make the return home, because the resistance to what we share together remains. Hermeneutic convalescing becomes, in effect, the vigilance against the infectious night of self-forgetting and loss that empties words into lifelessness.[15]

And then, thirdly, we can see in Heidegger an indirect version of convalescence, one that is merely inferred, in the idea of getting over, i.e., of overcoming, metaphysics. For Heidegger we have not in fact accomplished the getting over, for we do not come to the end of metaphysics in the manner of a Hegelian *Aufheben*. It is with respect to this possible misconstrual that Heidegger will identify his work as a "step back" out of metaphysics, and in connection with this step back, which retains its association with a recovery, Heidegger makes a subtle shift in his wording. It is a matter not of an *Überwindung* of metaphysics but of a *Verwindung* of metaphysics.[16] In ordinary German the word *verwinden* is used in connection with getting over a sickness. The word is also linked to *winden*, meaning "to twist," and with respect to convalescence the word implies the idea of resignation. By using this word Heidegger recognizes that metaphysics is not something that can be left behind or put aside but remains that from which we are recovering. Thus, at the end of metaphysics is the convalescing from metaphysics.

But what then constitutes the convalescing? If the forgetting of being defines metaphysics, the convalescing will recover from this forgetting, but in such a way that it cannot get over the forgetting as such. Accordingly, the recovery from metaphysics appears limited to tracing out the multiple paths of errancy – the history of metaphysics – and to identifying the source of this errancy. This gesture of re-reading the history of metaphysics in search of the source of its errancy constitutes at the same time for Heidegger the continuation of hermeneutics after *Being and Time*. Here hermeneutics is no longer a matter of *Auslegung*; rather, it is a matter of *Andenken*, a remembrance as thoughtful response to what is always earlier. This recollection and response of Heideggerian convalescence is actually a very complicated form of recovery. It is not in fact a simple recollection of being, as if the recollection consisted in recalling the difference between being as presence, which constitutes metaphysics, and being as making-present, i.e., as event. If thought of in this way, *Andenken* would be nothing other than a making present – the making present of being as making present. As Heidegger attempts to make clear in various texts throughout his later writings, the thoughtful response of *Andenken* also stands in relation to a loss that cannot be recovered. *Andenken* is a response to a giving or granting (*Es gibt sein*) that, in the act of giving, the source of the giving withdraws.[17] Although the result of this nonrecovery turns hermeneutics into an infinity of interpretation, this infinity is not *consumptive*. There is in fact *convalescence*, a recovering relative to a constant abiding and attentive keeping in mind,[18] which will require, as we saw in both Nietzsche and Gadamer, a certain measure-taking. In the dark night of global calculation and planning, Heidegger finds the measure-taking of health in poetic dwelling, and the thinking that mirrors this poetizing knows that this measuring is beyond the measure of calculation and planning. As a standard for thinking, it is the measure that lets us see what conceals itself without taking away the self-concealment. This is the appearance against which human life must measure itself. This kind of measuring, which preserves "the silence of what is alien" in its appearing, becomes for Heidegger the responsibility of thinking.

Certainly these three versions of hermeneutics have much in common. I would like at this point to proceed further towards a more thematic analysis of hermeneutics as convalescence by considering some of these common aspects, especially in relation to the hermeneutics of Heidegger and Gadamer, who hold in common a distinct hermeneutics of historicity. But let us see exactly what some of these common aspects are. In all three versions of convalescence the recovery is oriented, as we see it in Plato, to a saving relative to the dynamics of forgetting that directly bears on human living. Moreover, all three versions configure the act of recovering, again as we see it in Plato, in relation to a measure-taking. For hermeneutics in general this measure-taking becomes, in effect, the operation of transformation in the recovering such that the recovery cannot be equated with the simple act of recovering loss, even for Gadamer. Such measure-taking, in other words, will constitute the condition of transcendence with respect to what is to be hermeneutically gotten over. This measure-taking, then, will determine the mode of being of the recovery and saving in convalescence. In more familiar language, this measure-taking is what Gadamer has in mind when he says that the task of hermeneutics is to find the word that can reach the other. As we know, this sought-after word is neither a mere repeated word nor a canonical word, as if it were the same word lost and now found. The sought-after word is, relative to the measure-taking, the right word that appears as the new word. This new word, by definition, is a different word, and hermeneutic recovery thereby becomes inseparable from an experience of difference.

This suggestion that hermeneutics in its character of convalescence is concerned with the opening of a certain kind of difference is not without its own difficulty. Hermeneutics has been taken to be nothing more than a convalescence with respect to the sickness for home, i.e., nostalgia. Even Nietzsche has not escaped the charge that hermeneutic getting over wants to recover an origin that has been lost, in his case that of heroic culture. In the case of Heidegger and Gadamer, notwithstanding an internal consideration of Heidegger's radicality in relation to Gadamer's project, this implied nostalgia has carried with it the further charge of conservatism. Gadamer's hermeneutics of history is taken to be a preserving of cultural tradition, and Heidegger's new beginning is taken to be something like being's first beginning – not a new era but the old Greekified world uncorrupted by *Gestell* and *Machenschaft*. But this charge, I would argue, is misplaced; for hermeneutics the recovery and saving is not conservatism. To make this distinction between saving and conserving, and at the same time to bring forward the more explicit thematic analysis of hermeneutic convalescence, I want to pose and respond appropriately to three interrelated questions.

First and most basically, against the charge of nostalgia, let us attempt to see what constitutes the actual *character* of convalescence, this basic operation of recovery, in hermeneutics. If we follow mainly the direction of Heidegger and Gadamer here, the answer to this question would appear to be simple enough. The character of convalescence conforms to the character of the repetition in the concept of historicity. Historicity is the condition of a historical life that cannot get over its time, and with respect to this condition we as historical beings move forward in life only through a recovering-retrieval of our having-been (*Gewesenheit*). As we see from Heidegger's analysis of this concept in *Being and Time*, this retrieval takes the form of a rejoinder (*Erwiderung*) and a disavowal (*Widerruf*) such that the retrieving is not only a critical reply to the continuity of the past but also a countering of that past. The disavowal counters the past in the present such that the retrieval is not an actualization in which what was once known now becomes explicitly known again; it is not, in other words, a remembering as the retrieval of the forgotten but, by virtue of the disavowal, a kind of dialogue with the past. Thus, one can say that the retrieval in historicity is the interrogative opening of life from our time. When Heidegger then explicitly shifts his emphasis after *Being and Time* to take up the question of the truth of the history of being, he does not yet abandon the concept of historicity, since it is the very historicity of truth, i.e., the truth of the movement of being in its differentiated modes of openings, that is to be experienced. And Gadamer, for his part, will root this same concept of historicity in the understanding of life: understanding the words of the past, as well as the words of the other before me now, is caught up in time, such that it too proceeds by way of a questioning encounter with what has come before.

But if we let convalescence be defined by simply pointing to this basic feature of Heidegger's and Gadamer's hermeneutics, we will have not done enough to sufficiently combat the charge that convalescence remains nothing but the recovery of a loss. To sufficiently combat this charge we have only to point once again to what distinguishes convalescence as an operation of recovery. It is a recovery that is also at once a loss of recovery. It is a recovery in which there is no pretense about a full recovery and getting over its condition. There is, in other words, a restraint on the very idea of overcoming as it is ordinarily understood as progress and advance. One can state this position even more strongly: in hermeneutic convalescence there is, paradoxically, the overcoming of the very idea of overcoming, and in this "overcoming" hermeneutic convalescence opposes the specifically *modern* idea of progress as the idea of a true and permanent advance. This means, accordingly, that in its mode of convalescence hermeneutics cannot produce a new age; it cannot turn over to a new beginning.[19] And, more importantly, if hermeneutic convalescence opposes the *modern* idea of progress, which is in fact rooted in a linear concept of history, it must also oppose the counterconcept of progress within modernity, namely, the nonadvance from the old to the new that attempts to conserve from loss – what we ordinarily call conservatism. Hermeneutic convalescence is actually constitutionally incapable of conserving, even for Gadamer. What constitutes the ongoing acquisition of tradition for Gadamer should not be confused with the dynamics of linear history, or a history that remains self-same in its transmission – a philosophy of history attributable more to Hegel than to anyone else. To say that hermeneutic convalescence is neither a permanent advance nor a conserving in relation to tradition and its transmission is to say that hermeneutics operates on a plane *beyond* a logic of development. Here we cannot fail to notice that this character of hermeneutics describes precisely the basic character of hermeneutics for Vattimo. As such, it is a hermeneutics that is properly postmodern – a hermeneutics situated between critical overcoming and acceptance.[20]

But if hermeneutics can neither simply accept nor progress through, in the manner of overcoming, the messages in terms of which one situates oneself in life, what is it that hermeneutic convalescence can do? In this situation of "weakness," it appears that all it can do is to respond to the very operation of recovering. But this response is no insignificant matter. For Vattimo the response cannot escape the "twisting," i.e., the deviant alteration, that occurs in the recovering. Following closely the implications of Heidegger's notion of the *Verwindung* of metaphysics, Vattimo maintains that "metaphysics and the *Gestell* may be lived as an opportunity or as the possibility of a change by virtue of which both metaphysics and the *Gestell* are twisted in a direction that is not foreseen by their own essence, and yet is connected to it."[21] To speak more broadly, if not in a more Gadamerian way, about this matter, responding to the very operation of recovering constitutes the very accomplishing of tradition, *Überlieferung*. This term is to be understood in its literal sense as carrying over, i.e., as the transmission of meaning, and is accordingly to be distinguished from a specific tradition or heritage for which we can use the Latinate term *Tradition*.

The importance of this distinction cannot be underestimated. *Überlieferung* is what every specific tradition (*Tradition*) presupposes. Every specific tradition presupposes – and here I am following Giorgio Agamben – "that there is language and opening to sense ... in every determinate event of signification."[22] The very possibility of having a tradition depends on the fact that we can transmit language to ourselves. Now, the transmission of language – transmissibility itself – is unlike an ordinary presupposition that, as antecedent condition, can be further exposed to a basis. The transmission of language is like a first one that cannot bring itself before itself. This is, in effect, what Gadamer maintains when he says that *Überlieferung* is language and then insists that the limits of language can be exposed only by language itself, rather than by something outside it.[23] And insofar as transmissibility, openness itself, is this first that is not identical to its content, i.e., to remembered things, it must be regarded as immemorial in memory.[24] Hermeneutic convalescence, then, is engaged in this operation of transmission, an operation that in the end is inseparable from a specific content, and this transmission of meaning constitutes the basic operation of recovery. *Überlieferung* as transmission is accordingly the very setting of things out in the open – a liberating by way of tradition, but not a liberating from tradition.

In understanding the operation of recovery in this simple way, we are in a position to add a more specific determination to it. It would appear that by virtue of its condition of liberating by way of tradition, what is proper to hermeneutic convalescence is a passing through propriety, i.e., possession and ownership. We see something of this in Heidegger's use of the word *Ereignis*, but it would apply equally to Gadamer as well. The word *Ereignis* literally means to make own's own, *eigen*, in a continuing fashion, *er-eigen*. What is continually made one's own for Heidegger is, of course, being itself, such that being is always in relation to a self-possession. Within the history of philosophy, this self-possession has been named *ousia*, as being's enduring presence. But as Heidegger insists, in coming to presence in the manner of either *physis* or *poiesis*, being undergoes at the same time a dispossession by virtue of its condition of finitude.

And Gadamer, too, is attentive to this dispossession. Gadamer knows full well that *Überlieferung* is not a simple transmission of exchange into self-possession, just as dialogue is not a simple conversation of exchange into self-possession. *Überlieferung* is the becoming different of what it transmits because its time changes everything. When in our time a war appears, we immediately and inescapably place it in its transmission so as to ask questions of it and of us. And of course every hermeneutic conversation carries out a back and forth kind of exchange that perhaps resembles ownership, but in fact this exchange is productive only when it enters its freedom, when it becomes that play that, as Gadamer insists, calls the interlocutor into question. As an interlocutor in dialogue, one's own words suffer from the resistance of every word to becoming one's own. Being attentive to this poverty of dispossession – the condition that in hermeneutics is called, quite simply, the experience of strangeness – hermeneutics is always taking the "second-best course" with respect to self-possession in transmission. It proceeds in a manner not unlike what we find in Plato, who realized that all speaking suffers the weakness of the *logos*. That weakness pertains to the fact that every speaking subjects what it speaks about to determination, to an "as-what," which is never identical to the thing itself spoken about,[25] and this means that speaking takes up its objects of concern through an already constituted division within interpretation. In passing through ownership, hermeneutic interpretation cannot come into self-possession and thus continues in the mode of recovering.

Second, let us ask, then, what constitutes the specific character of *recovering* in convalescence? With this question, we return to the issue of repetition: the recovering, as a recovering from forgetting, is, again quite simply, the repetitive act of remembrance. Of course, for hermeneutics this remembrance must not be understood psychologically, and yet it does designate something like a keeping in mind. We can begin to see precisely what this means by first noting that there is a repetition demanded by all memory. Even the act of memory that wants to be mere preservation, i.e., a memory that wants to retain a lost object in constancy through time, requires renewal and thus repetition. In hermeneutics the renewal is of a different order, since what is opposed to forgetting is not memory as the capacity for retention, as if there is to be a return of a lost memory. And yet there is a repetition. To say the least, then, no matter what form remembrance takes, it will require, in its act of repetition, a certain exercise, a practice in memory.

Here we should recall that in the ancient classical tradition memory exercises were schooled, and, befitting an oral tradition, were undertaken as an aid to learning poetry. This link between learning and memory appears in Plato in the concept of *anamnesis*. For Plato this practice in memory that goes under the name *anamnesis* is not an exercise that would correspond to a memory of constancy, since what is to be remembered is not given in advance in the way that the poem is given in advance to the rhapsode. Thus, as a training (not in poetic recitation but in philosophy, where the object is in some sense immemorial in memory)[26] *anamnesis* will have the character of a *constant attention*. The exercising of philosophical memory, in other words, does not preserve a specific truth, but, as the concluding myth of the *Republic* would seem to indicate, it is the becoming vigilant with respect to the soul's capacity for openness. In drinking a certain measure of the water from the river *Ameleta*, the soul is gaining the measure of its careful attention with respect to its life. It is taking the measure of its neglect and indifference with respect to itself. And this indifference, configured in relation to the field of *Lethe* cannot be dialectically overcome, since *lethe* is itself *indifferent* to memory. And yet, a measure is taken that is saving for life.

Now it would appear that the recovering specific to hermeneutic convalescence is not unlike this Platonic *anamnesis*. Hermeneutic recovering is a matter of a memory exercise that can be understood only as a constant attention. This constant attention will in turn enact the measure-taking required of convalescence. For hermeneutics generally, the idea of a measure-taking within life that avails itself to the opening of life and that would also be in accord with a constant attention is precisely what we find in questioning. Of course Gadamer has much to say about questioning, which he identifies with the logical structure of openness. For Gadamer the question is the referent point for the determination of meaning insofar as the understanding of texts is related to the question that is at stake in it. And he is not alone in this regard for the question.

Already in 1921, Heidegger saw that the potentiality for the nonrecurrence of life that resides in life's own resistance to itself in ruinant life is "overcome" through questionability (*Fraglichkeit*). In questioning, "factical life attains its genuinely developed self-givenness," and "genuine questioning consists in living in the answer itself in a searching way, such that the answering maintains a constant relation to the questioning."[27] But what does it mean for questioning to live in the answer itself in a searching way? It would appear that questioning is more than the activity of placing into the open. The question operates on the plane of discourse by starting from a divided determination (divided because it is impossible for discourse to begin outside of what the Greeks called *dihairesis*) that the question then sets in movement. But this means that the questioning word has the function of displacement. This displacing and dividing by the question, which is not identical to *dihairesis* proper and with it the self-movement of truth, will accordingly bring about a transmutation of memory. The recovering in hermeneutic convalescence, then, is that constant attention that will take hold of life in transformation.

Third, let us ask, what is it that convalescing actually accomplishes? With this question we return to the issue of the saving. Let us recall the

principal aspect of the double saving that occurs in Plato's story.[28] For
the souls entering life a certain saving is enacted by drinking a fitting
measure. This saving does not conserve but keeps the souls from completely losing their unease over life whereby they would no longer be
attentive to their having-to-be of life. In this context, what is accomplished in the recovery in life is the lasting or preserving – what Heidegger calls *wahren* – of the recovering itself. In a preliminary way we
have already inscribed this operation and accomplishment into hermeneutic recovery: hermeneutic recovery is a going back over *Überlieferung* in such a way that it accomplishes *Überlieferung*. But what then
does it mean to accomplish transmission? The answer to this question
is no small matter, for I think that it stakes out the place of hermeneutics in contemporary philosophy. We know already this much: in transmission there is a "passing on" of meaning in the form of determinations. These determinations are in effect partial aspects of a missing
whole that constitute our history. Not unlike the weakness of the *logos*
that Plato speaks of, the event of tradition decomposes meaning into
partiality. Tradition, not as a stockpile of events, but as the event of
transmission, lives from this condition in which its very existence
effaces the whole and subjects every matter of concern to partiality and
ongoing decision.[29]

In this configuration, hermeneutics undoubtedly stands in relation to
other currents in contemporary philosophy. Derrida, for example, sees
that undecidability, as itself an act of division, depends on reactivating
the moment of decision that underlies our involvement in the world.
And Deleuze sees that in being without origins, philosophy cannot
extricate itself from the repetition of simulacra. If it is the case, then,
that the transmission of tradition is not accumulation but, in its own
way, that repetitive retracing of division, we return to our question and
ask, what does it mean to accomplish tradition? Bearing in mind that
accomplishing tradition entails the hermeneutically distinctive property
of passing through ownership, we have here a decisive clue for our
answer. Since the passing through ownership does not keep ownership
in place, can we not say that such passing through is actually an originating turning out of ownership, which is the literal meaning of emancipation? Obviously, this emancipation will have a distinctive character.
It is not enough to say, in other words, that this emancipation is coextensive with the movement of history. History itself and politics tell us
that too often this movement is simply a camouflage for possession.
History is replete with scenes of exchange where possession is simply

transferred from one to another, where one foundation is replaced by another. But hermeneutics is not in the business of exchange or of keeping the goods for itself.

One can see something of this in Gadamer's notion of the fusion of horizons in which one cannot escape having a horizon and yet there is at the same time an expropriating – in the sense of depriving of possession – of own's own horizon. This movement of history in which the past rises from its ashes in dispossession, is what hermeneutic recovery recovers and is perhaps freedom in its deepest sense. Freedom here is neither a regulative idea nor self-legislation relative to what ought to be done. It is, rather, the opening of life in the loss of recovery. It is the opening of life that takes place in relation to bearing the weight of life that wants to drift into forgetfulness. Hermeneutic convalescence cannot escape from the very suffering of freedom it wants to achieve. In this peculiar enactment of freedom one feels the distress of life at every step and gesture of recovery, turning the recovery into a memory of care.

This care is not to be understood so much from the perspective of Heidegger's existential analytic, in which the structure of care pervades *Dasein*'s basic structure of being-in-the-world. The care at issue here wants to harken back to the care that Plato ascribes to the project of philosophy in the guise of Socrates, a care directly related to the ethics and politics of community. And all this is to say that Plato was right: convalescence is not simply a recovery from forgetting but a recovery wedded to a certain enactment of life, an enactment that unfolds in a relation of responsibility to itself. And with respect to the postmodern hermeneutics of Vattimo, who praises the virtue of nihilism at the end of philosophy and shares in this thought of convalescence, would we not also want to place him here?

NOTES

1 In an interview Vattimo refers to his basic position as "optimistic nihilism." See Gianni Vattimo and Santiago Zabala, "'Weak Thought' and the Reduction of Violence: A Dialogue with Gianni Vattimo," *Common Knowledge* 8, no. 3 (fall 2002): 463.

2 Vattimo and Zabala, "'Weak Thought' and the Reduction of Violence," 453.

3 Gianni Vattimo, *Beyond Interpretation: The Meaning of Hermeneutics for*

Philosophy, trans. David Webb (Stanford: Stanford University Press 1997), 13.

4 See Vattimo's interview with David Webb and David Wood in *Warwick Journal of Philosophy*, 2, no. 2 (autumn 1989): 18–26. Vattimo wants to claim, despite the title of the third part of *Truth and Method*, that Gadamer would not accept that hermeneutics is strongly connected with ontology.

5 For a discussion of the relation between a Nietzschean hermeneutics and that of Gadamer, see James Risser "Die Metaphorik des Sprechen," in *Hermeneutische Wege: Hans-Georg Gadamer zum Hundertsten*, ed. Günter Figal, Jean Grondin, and Dennis J. Schmidt (Tübingen: Mohr/Siebeck 2000), 177–90.

6 Rodolphe Gasché explores this aspect of Vattimo's hermeneutics in his essay "In the Separation of the Crisis: A Post-Modern Hermeneutics?" *Philosophy Today* 44, no. 1 (spring 2000): 3–15.

7 See Martin Heidegger, *Phänomenologische Interpretationen zu Aristoteles*, Gesamtausgabe 61 (Frankfurt: Klostermann 1985), 133; English translation by Richard Rojcewicz, *Phenomenological Interpretations of Aristotle* (Bloomington: Indiana University Press 2001), 99.

8 See Hans-Georg Gadamer, "Reflections on My Philosophical Journey," in *The Philosophy of Hans-Georg Gadamer*, ed. Lewis Hahn (Chicago: Open Court 1997), 35.

9 See Charles E. Scott, *The Time of Memory* (Albany: SUNY Press 1999).

10 For Nietzsche the sickness is not only instructive for life (see *On the Genealogy of Morals*, Third Essay, section 9), it is also necessary to life, for it is in relation to sickness that the physician is able to judge the strength of the organism. Here one is reminded of Nietzsche's often quoted remark, "what does not kill you makes you stronger."

11 Friedrich Nietzsche, *Human, All Too Human*, trans. R.J. Hollingdale (Cambridge: Cambridge University Press 1986), preface, section 4.

12 Nietzsche, *Untimely Meditations*, trans. R.J. Hollingdale (Cambridge: Cambridge University Press 1983), 63.

13 *Human, All Too Human*, preface, section 4.

14 Gadamer, "Destruktion und Dekonstruktion," in *Gesammelte Werke*, vol. 2 (Tübingen: Mohr/Siebeck 1993), 367; English translation by Geoff Waite and Richard Palmer, "Destruktion and Deconstruction," in *Dialogue and Deconstruction: The Gadamer-Derrida Encounter*, ed. Diane Michelfelder and Richard Palmer (Albany: SUNY Press 1989), 109.

15 I would maintain that the lifeless word is a better description for what Gadamer calls in *Truth and Method* the idealized word. The argument is simple: if the word of language has its interpretation in living language, the

word that does not yet speak is not ideal but (temporarily) robbed of its vitality.

16 See Heidegger, "Overcoming Metaphysics," in *The End of Philosophy*, trans. Joan Stambaugh (New York: Harper & Row 1973), 84. The analysis of the word *Verwindung* and its use by Heidegger is taken up in detail by Vattimo in *The End of Modernity*, trans. Jon R. Snyder (Baltimore: The Johns Hopkins University Press 1988), 164–81. With the idea of *Verwindung* we are required at this point to no longer forget the position of Vattimo. For Vattimo *Verwindung* is the word that hermeneutics takes over, such that by virtue of it contemporary thought can no longer return to origins or progress to new beginnings.

17 Vattimo discusses Heidegger's notion of *Andenken* in detail in "An-Denken: Thinking and the Foundation," in *The Adventure of Difference*, trans. Cyprian Blamires (Baltimore: The Johns Hopkins University Press 1993), 110–36.

18 Here one should recall Heidegger's analysis of thinking in relation to memory in *Was Heisst Denken?* See Heidegger, *Was Heisst Denken?* (Tübingen: Max Niemeyer Verlag 1954), 157–9; English translation by J. Glenn Gray and F. Wieck, *What Is Called Thinking?* (New York: Harper & Row 1968), 143–7.

19 But this is not to say that the convalescent does not believe in the coming of the event, which, as Derrida says, is another name for the future itself.

20 "For Heidegger, as for Nietzsche, thought has no other 'object' (if we may even still use this term) than the errancy of metaphysics, recollected in an attitude which is either a critical overcoming nor an acceptance that recovers and prolongs it." *The End of Modernity*, 173.

21 Ibid., 173.

22 Giorgio Agamben, "Tradition of the Immemorial," in *Potentialities*, trans. Daniel Heller-Roazen (Stanford: Stanford University Press 1999), 104.

23 In "Towards a Phenomenology of Ritual and Language," Gadamer writes: "Language intends the other person and the other thing, not itself. That means that the covering over of language as language has its basis in language itself and accords with the human experience of language." Gadamer, "Zur Phänomenologie von Ritual und Sprache," in *Gesammelte Werke*, vol. 8 (Tübingen: Mohr/Siebeck 1993), 432.

24 See "Tradition of the Immemorial," 105.

25 See Gadamer, "Platos ungeschriebene Dialekit," in *Gesammelte Werke*, vol. 6 (Tübingen: Mohr/Siebeck 1983), 129–53; English translation by P. Christopher Smith, "Plato's Unwritten Dialectic," in *Dialogue and Dialectic* (New Haven: Yale University Press 1980), 124–55.

26 The object here is the *eidos*, and it is immemorial in memory precisely

because the *eidos* is never given in advance such that it can be recollected; and yet, the *eidos* is recollected. See Gadamer "Dialekit und Sophistik im siebenten Platonischen Brief," in *Gesammelte Werke*, vol. 6; English translation by P. Christopher Smith, "Dialectic and Sophism in Plato's Seventh Letter," in *Dialogue and Dialectic*, 93–123.

27 *Phänomenologische Interpretationen zu Aristoteles*, 153; *Phenomenological Interpretations of Aristotle*, 114.

28 The myth of Er recounts a double saving. There is the saving relative to indifference and carelessness in the soul's journey in life and the saving of the story itself by Er.

29 The general frame of this argument is made by Agamben in *Potentialities*, 27–38.

12

Vattimo's Latinization of Hermeneutics: Why Did Gadamer Resist Postmodernism?

JEAN GRONDIN

We have many reasons to be grateful to Gianni Vattimo for his continuing contribution to philosophy and public life. Undoubtedly, his most decisive philosophical impulses have come from the German philosophical tradition, and mostly from the Holy Trinity of Nietzsche, Heidegger, and Gadamer, who was his teacher. Yet he was not German but a proud Italian and for some reason more able than others to carry this tradition further. The German philosophical tradition has to a large extent dominated philosophy since Leibniz and Kant, but its dominion ebbed considerably after Husserl, Heidegger, and Gadamer. One could attribute this decline to the catastrophic impact of the Second World War. As if their philosophical tradition had anything to do with it, German-speaking philosophers have shied away from their traditions, readily espousing, for instance, the analytic tradition, which is perfectly well suited to the American psyche and its technical mind-set but which somehow rings a little bizarre when translated into German.

This is also true in the field of the history of German philosophy, which the Germans traditionally dominated, obviously enough. If a student asked his North American teachers where to go if he or she wants to pursue graduate studies in Germany on Kant or Hegel (the Plato and Aristotle of the Germans), they would be hard-pressed to give any recommendations. Indeed, most major specialists of Kant or Hegel will take their cue, for better or for worse, from the work of their American counterparts. The same could be said about figures like Husserl,

Nietzsche, Heidegger, and Gadamer: they have often found more productive interpreters outside Germany than in their home country. A major case in point is Jürgen Habermas, Germany's most prominent intellectual figure after Gadamer and Heidegger. Despite the decisive influences of Schelling, Heidegger, and the Frankfurt School on him, he too turned away from the allegedly "bad" philosophical tradition of Nietzsche and Heidegger. Gadamer was the last major intellectual figure to be relatively untouched by a feeling of guilt about his own philosophical tradition, but it could be argued that this was the case because he received his major philosophical upbringing before the calamity of National Socialism. So it came to be that this philosophical tradition was carried further by foreigners and more often than not, by the French, as is confirmed by the work of world-renowned thinkers such as Sartre, Merleau-Ponty, Lévinas, Foucault, Derrida, Ricoeur, and so many others.

But these authors were rather foreign to the hermeneutical tradition of Schleiermacher, Dilthey, and Gadamer. It is in this tradition that Gianni Vattimo stands: he had the good fortune to work on Schleiermacher under the supervision of Gadamer in the glorious sixties, while at the same time preparing the first translation of Gadamer's *Truth and Method* (which appeared in 1970), thus contributing to the international fame of that work. In no other country is Gadamer as celebrated as a major philosopher as he is in Italy today. For this also, we owe gratitude to Gianni Vattimo.

More importantly, it is a way of thinking that Gianni Vattimo transformed and urbanized, I would say "latinized," since he translated it into a new and Mediterranean language. He was the first to defend the idea that hermeneutics was the *koiné* of our age, and he coined such famous expressions as "weak thought" and "optimistic nihilism."[1] A German philosopher who had spoken of an optimistic nihilism (an oxymoron by any other standards than those set by Gianni Vattimo) or who had attempted to draw democratic consequences out of Nietzsche and Heidegger would have been burned at the stake. In his most recent texts, Vattimo indeed unearthed unsuspected parallels between Popper's critique of Platonism and Heidegger's destruction of metaphysics, claiming that Popper's notion of an "open society" had affinities with Heidegger notion of *Ereignis*. The politician that Gianni Vattimo has since become thus praised Heidegger as a "philosopher of democracy"![2] This time, it would perhaps have been Popper who would have burned him at the stake, if not Heidegger ...

It was by no means Vattimo's only momentous contribution to redrawing the map of contemporary philosophy, of which he is now one of the most preeminent figures. Since his very personal *Credo di credere*,[3] he has also established a convincing (and for some quite surprising) link between the stream of "nihilistic hermeneutics" and the Christian tradition, or to be more specific (since one needs to be), with the Christian tradition of charity, humility, and *kenosis*. In this too, he could rely on his latin roots. Guided in this regard by the groundbreaking work of René Girard, he believed that hermeneutical perspectivism – and the strong acknowledgment of human finitude it entails – could be reconciled with the Christian imperative of turning the other cheek, with forgiveness and generosity. Both traditions, the hermeneutical tradition and the Christian tradition he heralds, relinquish strong validity claims in the name of the strength of weakness, as it were. The major impact of this insight was not only that it shed new light on the Christian tradition itself, one, lest we forget, that had been a major target of attack and disdain in the footsteps of Marx, Nietzsche, Freud, and Heidegger. More importantly, it underscored the fact that hermeneutical nihilism (in spite of its name) was not without ethical and even political resources. Thus his notion of an optimistic nihilism: instead of fighting religious wars in the name of strong claims ("I am right, you are wrong, so you must perish"), he argued, it is perhaps wiser, especially in the age of assured nuclear annihilation, to learn to get along in the name of the idea of peaceful coexistence, which is tolerant of everything except violence. Hermeneutics and nihilism thus became ethical options instead of enemies of morals. Quite an achievement and quite a turnaround!

For many, these ethical ideas are now commonplace, as one could say with Richard Rorty,[4] but no one would have thought about distilling them from the hermeneutical tradition of Nietzsche and Heidegger and from the Christian worldview (which most would more readily associate with a form of authoritarianism). But it is a feat Gianni Vattimo accomplished.

The only issue I would like to discuss here is whether hermeneutics, and thus philosophy itself, must be seen as a form of nihilism. If "nihilism" means only a tolerance for the view of others to the extent that they do not violently limit the liberty of others, one can agree with Gianni Vattimo. But if one understands under "nihilism" the notion that there are no truths in the sense of *adaequatio*, one can challenge this view.

The question must be raised not only because of the apparent self-contradiction of a negation of truth that itself lays claim to truth (a point that has repeatedly been made). I raise it also because Gianni Vattimo sees this forsaking of the notion of *adaequatio* as the only plausible consequence of Gadamer's thesis according to which "Being that can be understood is language," which is for him another way of saying that human understanding cannot relate to the things themselves but only to the way we talk about them. And the way we talk about them is always framed by a historical perspective. Vattimo often faults Gadamer for not acknowledging fully the consequences of his own thought, i.e., the nihilistic consequences of his hermeneutic ontology.

Yet one must ask, Why has Gadamer failed to proclaim a nihilistic hermeneutics? In other words, why did Gadamer resist the postmodernism of some of his followers? To be sure, there are many relativism-friendly pronouncements in his work. For example: there is no understanding without prejudices; history does not belong to us, we belong to it; consciousness is carried by a *Wirkungsgeschichte*; understanding is linguistic in nature, and so *Truth and Method* can indeed be read as a manifesto of nihilism. But the fact is that Gadamer recoiled from the nihilistic consequences of the postmodernists.[5] One has to ask why and whether he was right in doing so.

In order to answer this question, it is important to bear in mind that an author such as Nietzsche played a far different role for Gadamer than he did for Vattimo. There is no chapter, indeed no real place, for Nietzsche in the scope of *Truth and Method*. This is to a certain extent comprehensible for a hermeneutics that stands in the tradition of Schleiermacher, Dilthey, and even Heidegger, for whom the primary task of hermeneutics is uncovering truth, whereas Nietzsche aim is arguably to undermine it ("truth as an illusion"). In his book, Gadamer jumped from Schleiermacher and Dilthey to Husserl and Heidegger as if Nietzsche did not exist. This was an understandable omission insofar as the purpose of Gadamer's hermeneutics was to justify (*rechtfertigen, auf ihre Legitimation hin befragen*, etc.) a truth claim in the realm of the humanities and in the experience of art and language.

But this exclusion appeared less defensible for astute interpreters like Gianni Vattimo, for whom Nietzsche marked the decisive turning point of hermeneutics. For him, the universality of hermeneutics could be understood only in light of the Nietzsche who declared that there are no facts, only interpretations (*The Will to Power*, 481), or of the Heidegger who claimed that our understanding was framed by anticipations and the history of Being. In this regard, it can be argued that Vattimo was even more Heideggerian than Gadamer himself. The genius of Vattimo, who was followed by many others, was to associate this Nietzschean-Heideggerian outlook with Gadamer's seeming critique of scientific objectivity, his stress on the prejudices of interpretation, and his insistence on the linguistic nature of understanding. Stressing these elements, hermeneutics, they believed, jettisoned the idea of an objective truth. There is no such thing, given the interpretative and linguistic nature of our experience. This conclusion drove Gianni Vattimo to "nihilistic" consequences and Richard Rorty to a renewed form of pragmatism: some interpretations are more useful or amenable than others, but none can per se be claimed to be "closer" to the Truth. In the name of tolerance and mutual understanding, one has to accept the plurality of interpretations. Only the notion that there is only one valid one is harmful.

There are at least two ways of explaning why Gadamer resisted nihilistic hermeneutics. I pointedly say "resisted" and not "rejected." A conciliatory thinker to the core, Gadamer never really rejected any theory out of hand. On occasion, he even welcomed hermeneutic relativism as a welcome antidote to too positivistic conceptions of understanding. Yet, in the face of radical relativists, he stressed that it was a "*Sache*," a truth, that one seeks to comprehend. The first way is to explain why he went such a distance towards Nietzsche, and the second lies in the manner in which his most famous thesis, according to which "Being that can be understood is language," must be read, an issue on which Gianni Vattimo has written extensively.

THE DISTANCE TOWARD NIETZSCHE AND THE MEANING OF INTERPRETATION FOR GADAMER : THERE ARE ONLY FACTS "THROUGH" INTERPRETATION

"There are no facts, only interpretations" is a thesis with which Gadamer could have sympathized to a certain degree, but with a specific emphasis that is often overlooked. The postmodernists often tend to use this sentence of Nietzsche to thwart or "weaken" the truth claim of interpretation: every interpretation is only *one* way of seeing the world; there are and should be others. While he recognizes the virtues of pluralism, this is perhaps not the point on which Gadamer would insist. I believe he would rather reformulate Nietzsche's famous dictum by saying, "There are only facts *through* interpretation(s)." For him, this means that there are no facts without a certain language that expresses them. But he is adamant that it is the *Sache*, the thing itself (or the "facts"), that comes to light through this linguistic unfolding. His model of interpretation is taken from the performative arts and the role *interpretation* plays in them. In a dance, a play, an opera, and all the performing arts (which we call in French les arts d'interprétation), to interpret is not to bestow a meaning on something from an outside perspective; it is to play out the work itself, since the work requires such a playing out: music that isn't played isn't music. The very important point here is that interpretation is not a meaning-giving activity that is applied to an otherwise meaningless reality; instead it is the enacting of a meaning that strives to be expressed. The rendering can be more or less adequate, but it is obviously bound by what has to be transmitted.

Gadamer's conviction is clearly that there is no art without interpretation, but this interpretation is less the meaning that is bestowed upon a work from the observer who sees things differently from how another bystander sees them, than it is an interpretation that productively brings forth the meaning of what is presented and that even brings forth, Gadamer would insist, its very essence. That is the case, for example, with a painting of a king or an event (say, a cruxifixion). It is always an interpretation by the artist, one could say. But for Gadamer, the artist and his intention are not really important in this process: the work of art is successful and "true" only if it brings forth the essence or true reality of what is presented. To be sure, this is impossible without the virtuosity of the painter, sculptor, writer, or musician, but it is a secondary matter for the "truth event" that Gadamer heralds in the art experience. In his famous painting, *The Second of May*, where Goya depicts helpless peasants raising their arms in the air while being fired upon by French soldiers, what is brought to the fore is the essence of the occupation of Spain by Napoleon's army, and of any human occupation for that matter. It is not an interpretation in a subjectivistic sense. The interpretation brings out the reality that was and a truth that teaches us something

And what strikes Gadamer here is that this truth transcends in a way its historical context. In his later works, he pointedly spoke here of the "transcendence of art."[6] Surely, an artist is rooted in a context and a tradition, without which his creation would be impossible, but he is only a great artist to the extent that his work rises above this historicity and brings about a truth of lasting value. What is this truth, asks

Gadamer? To the postmodernists who insist on the relativity of inter-pretations, Gadamer answers: But what about the superior truth of a work of art that transcends its time? What about the strident eloquence of a poem or the binding rigor of a philosophical thought? This, he holds, is not a truth that can be ascertained by method, nor is it a truth that can be relativized by pointing out its contextual nature.

In other words, to insist on the "merely subjective" nature of inter-pretation or its "relativity" is for Gadamer to miss what interpretation is all about. It is always subsidiary to the work and the *Sache* that it interprets, even if it comes out only *through interpretation*. Gadamer likes to say that the best interpretation is the one that is not noticed as such, that disappears in the work itself, so that its *Sache* and truth matter comes to the fore. This is also true of a good translation : the better the translation (which is obviously an interpretation), the less one has the feeling of reading a translated text.

Thus, for Gadamer, Nietzsche assertion according to which (in slight modification) "there are no truths, only interpretations" is itself some-what one-sided. There are only truths *through* interpretation, to be sure, but there are no interpretations without truth to bring out. An interpretation that is not oriented toward truth is but a vain exercise that cannot be distinguished from another interpretation.

According to Gadamer, the Nietzschean and postmodernist destruc-tion of truth secretly rests on the *nominalism* of modernity, according to which there is no meaning in the "world itself," which is nothing but senseless matter. In this perspective, sense comes out only through the act of the understanding subject, who "injects" meaning into the world "out there." The often overlooked subtlety of Gadamer's distinction of "truth *and* method" lies in the suggestion that the more or less pro-nounced relativism of postmodernism is the contemporary form of nominalism, which corresponds to the prevailing scientific view of the world: Being per se has nothing to say, meaning comes about only through our interpretations and language. In this predicament, the postmodernists conclude, it is pointless to ascertain if an interpretation is closer to the Truth or to Being, given that there is no language-free access to reality. On this perspective (!), one can never overcome the realm of historical and linguistic interpretations, and from this per-spective arise the "nihilistic" consquences of modernity's insistence on subjectivity (or human language) as the only origin of meaning: what is of value is what is posited for subjectivity, but there is no other value above and beyond subjectivity itself.

Thus, for Gadamer, Nietzschean postmodernism would not be the consequence of hermeneutics but only of an understanding of Being according to which everything depends on the view of subjectivity (or the outlook on things). According to Heidegger, this was the result of the metaphysical understanding of Being as *eidos* or *idea*, which tacitly subjected it to a human perspective (Gadamer disagreed here with Heidegger's reading of Plato, but he mostly agreed with his interpretation of modernity). For Heidegger and Gadamer, Nietzsche was the last metaphysician, in that he maintained this equation between Being and what a particular perspective makes of it. He was only more consequential than earlier metaphysics by proclaiming a universal perspectivism and by equating it with a cultural nihilism.

In other words, for Gadamer, hermeneutic relativism is a closet Cartesianism (in spite of what it claims, of course!): it is only because there is no Cartesian truth to be had, i.e., a truth that rests on a *fundamentum inconcussum*, that one can claim that all is relative. Compared to such a "strong truth," our modest attempts at understanding can appear only as mere perspectives that have no legitimacy outside themselves. For Gadamer, it is Nietzsche's tragic *non sequitur* to derive from this a nihilism, i.e., the idea that there is no truth in the sense of *adaequatio*. This idea holds, Gadamer claims, only if one presupposes the Cartesian-methodical notion of truth.

Hence Gadamer distance from Nietzsche professed nihilism, according to which there are no binding truths or values anymore. This also holds, he argues, only if one expects an absolute truth or value in the quasi-mathematical sense of Descartes. Only the gods have such certainties, he reminds us, after Plato. But that does not mean that we are deprived of any foundation and any truth. In his eyes, it is intellectual arrogance to equate the absence of a truth that would satisfy the Cartesian's thirst for ultimate foundations with the absence of truth and of an experience of Being.[7] Truly, Being can be understood only through language, but it is then a Being that is understood, not a perspective. We can now turn to the meaning of Gadamer's well-known thesis, which in some respects is the epitome of his philosophy.

BEING THAT CAN BE UNDERSTOOD IS LANGUAGE: GADAMER'S EMPHASIS ON BEING

Gianni Vattimo brilliantly seized upon this declaration to defend his nihilistic, or historicist, appropriation of Gadamer.[8] For him, Gadamer's thesis would amount to saying that every understanding, every access to Being, depends on our language, just as it depends on its time and its history. Gadamer is thus seen as the advocate of a radical historicism. To be sure, he had been criticized for that reason often before. Betti and Habermas, to name only two of his most important critics, had already voiced their fears about what they perceived as Gadamer's relativism. For his part, Gianni Vattimo faults Gadamer for not being historicist enough, i.e., for not acknowledging the nihilistic consequences of his thought, expressed in the sentence "Being that can be understood is language." But one must ask, is the meaning of this thesis really nihilistic?

In the impressive interpretation he gave of Gadamer's thought at a conference honouring his one hundredth anniversary in February 2000, Gianni Vattimo indeed interpreted Gadamer's thesis as a form of linguistic relativism, and was followed in this regard by Richard Rorty, who spoke on the same occasion.[9] He did so with convincing arguments, which correspond to the atmosphere of the time, as the striking agreement with Rorty's pragmatism only underscored. To say that there is no access to Being except through language *can* indeed be read as a linguistic relativism, a thesis Gadamer seems to defend when he claims that language determines not only the process (*Vollzug*), but also the object (*Gegenstand*) of understanding.

But it is not the only way one can understand Gadamer's famous dictum. In his reading, Vattimo puts the emphasis on language, which ends up absorbing Being in what can be called a linguistic ontology. Its major tenet is that one cannot talk about Being itself but only about an "understood Being" that is, as it were, created, if not "invented" by language.

But what if in Gadamer's statement, one puts the emphasis on Being itself? Or to put it differently: what if it would be Being itself that would unravel *its* understandability in or through language? Needless to say, this sounds rather odd to our nominalistic ears. Nevertheless, it is a thought Gadamer defends in the last pages of *Truth and Method* if one reads him carefully. It is a difficult section, to be sure. It deals with the medieval doctrine of transcendentals, but it gives further depth to the thesis that "Being that can be understood is language."

The point is that language for Gadamer is not only the language of our understanding, or "our" language but also the language of things. Gadamer argues not only in favour of a fusion of horizons between understanding and language but also for a perhaps more discrete, but no less important, fusion between language and Being itself. There is such a thing, as strange as it may sound, as a language of Being, or a "language of the things," what he often calls the "*Sprache der Dinge.*"[10] This could seem to be a simple metaphor or *façon de parler.*

Yes and no. Yes, because we are the ones who speak in such and such a way. But we speak in such a way because there is a bond between Being and language. And it is in order to understand this enigmatic tie that Gadamer alludes, surprisingly enough, to the medieval doctrine of the transcendentals in the final section of *Truth and Method*, where one finds the discussion of the much quoted dictum "*Sein, das verstanden werden kann, ist Sprache.*" And Gadamer does so because this doctrine succeeded in providing an understanding of a link between Being and language that is not one of opposition (on this side Being, on the other language) but one of kinship or direct filiation.

What fascinates Gadamer is the fact that the light (*lumen*) in which language stands, and which it spreads, is something like the light of Being itself. One can see what he means when one speaks of the "essence" of something. (By the way, Gadamer appeals very often in his work to this notion of essence, and it is never to destroy this notion, quite on the contrary.) A work of art, for instance, brings out the essence of someone or something, he always says, that which persists. If I say, to take the most classical of examples, that the essence of man lies in the fact that he is a "rational animal," it is obvious enough at first sight that one is dealing with a view of understanding, of language or of our mind. Yet, what is envisioned by the notion of essence, is always more than that. It is Being itself. In the case just mentioned, it is the human reality as it is encountered, that I wish to understand in its essence. It is also this human reality that allows me to say, for instance, that the notion of a "rational animal" is perhaps not the best, the most felicitious or adequate to the human essence. There are other components that make up that essence: humans are also beings who can laugh, become crazy, write papers, etc. But, one has to ask, what is it that allows us to say that the essence of a thing is this or that? Gadamer answers: the things themselves and their language.

Allow me to invoke one last example of this language of things, an example based on more recent insights. It is well known that research in genetics has mapped what is called the "humane genome," the genetic code of humankind. It is obvious that we are dealing here with a scientific explanation, which is thus a falsifiable view of human intelligence about our genes. Nevertheless, we are not only dealing with an invention of our intelligence or our language. It is the code of the genes themselves, of the things themselves, that the scientist aims to sort out, not the code of our language. I am not interested here in the genetic theory for its own sake. My only point is that science aims, as does every human understanding, to discover a language that is already the language of the things themselves, the one that enables us to revise our constructions and linguistic framings of this language. There is thus a language of the things themselves, of Being, that we hope to bring out when we try to understand and open our ears.

This echoes what was said earlier about interpretation in the world of art. An interpretation of a play, an opera, a piece of music, or a dance is not merely a subjective enactment with no bearing on Being: it is an enactment that is called for by the work of art itself. The presentation (*Darstellung*) is not foreign to the work, or to Being, but its true unfoldment.

It is in the same spirit that Gadamer, in his famous discussion of the hermeneutical circle in the second section of *Truth and Method*, insisted far less on the insuperable determination of our understanding by prejudices than on the constant process of revision of our prejudgments when confronted with the thing itself (*Sache*) and what it has to say.[11] In more ways than one, Gadamer keeps insisting that our prejudices have to be corroborated, to be confirmed and verified by the things themselves. These passages were never to the liking of the more postmodern readers of Gadamer, who thought that their mentor contradicted himself: how on Earth could one speak of the things themselves in a panhermeneutical philosophy that otherwise appears to defend a universal perspectivism according to which it is nonsensical to speak of the things themselves?

They thus felt obliged to radicalize Gadamer's hermeneutics, to rid it of its Platonic or essentialist elements, thus claiming to be more coherent than Gadamer in espousing a nihilistic ontology. Yet Gadamer resisted this consequence because the things themselves resisted this appropriation. It is not true that Being and its language can be reduced to our language. If this were the case, one could not explain why one is able to rectify a too one-sided view of Being. It is Being itself that is understood in language.

Now, I do not expect Gianni Vattimo to agree with me. But if he disagrees, it is only because he does not believe that my interpretation corresponds to what Gadamer *has to say*. There is thus, for him, a language of Gadamer that is not reducible to my interpretation, or that I misconstruct, and to which his reading corresponds better. The same holds for our interpretation of the world: he would certainly claim that his reading of reality (of language, of Being, etc.) is more accurate than mine. He thereby only confirms that there is a language of things that our interpretations can touch, or miss, to varying degrees.

The Gadamer who insisted on the language of Being was not very well received by his postmodern inheritors. Yet it is also part of his legacy. To be sure, Gianni Vattimo stressed the perspectival and nihilist elements of Gadamer's hermeneutics. But he was right in acknowledging that it was a hermeneutic *ontology* that Gadamer was after. For this also, one has to be grateful, beyond the differences, for his latinization of hermeneutics.

NOTES

1 G. Vattimo, "Optimistic Nihilism," *Common Knowledge* 1, no. 3 (1992): 37–44, and his interview with Santiago Zabala, "Weak Thought and The Reduction of Violence," *Common Knowledge* 8, no. 3 (2002): 452–63.

2 G. Vattimo, "Heidegger filosofo della democrazia," *Filosofia e politica* 55, no. 135 (2003): 55–61.

3 *Credere di credere* (Milano: Garzanti 1996). The original title means something like "I believe I believe," but it was rendered into English simply by *Belief*, translated by L.D'Isanto and D. Webb (Cambridge: Polity Press 1998). Following Karl Barth, Rudolf Bultmann reminds us of the Lutheran origins of this idea in the famous essay "Die liberale Theologie und die jüngste theologische Bewegung" (Liberal theology and the more recent theological movement), which opens his essay collection *Glauben und Verstehen* (Faith and understanding), vol. 1, 1933 (9th ed., Tübingen: Mohr Siebeck 1993), 24 (my translation from the German): "The new man is always the other-wordly (*der jenseitige*), whose identity with the man of this world can only be believed. This is why Barth can even renew Luther's paradoxical sentence according to which we only *believe* that we believe."

4 R. Rorty, foreword to G. Vattimo, *Nihilism and Emancipation: Ethics, Politics and Law*, edited by Santiago Zabala, translated by William McCuaig (New York: Columbia University Press 2004).

5 In the first part of *Truth and Method*, Gadamer resisted the "hermeneutical relativism" of Paul Valéry, according to which the meaning of his verses is

the one they have for the reader ("mes vers ont le sens qu'ont leur prête"). This Gadamer pointedly dismissed as an "untenable nihilism." (Das scheint mir ein unhaltbarer hermeneutischer Nihilismus) (*Gesammelte Werke*, vol. 1, Tübingen: Mohr Siebeck 1986, 100). On Gadamer's distance from Nietzsche, see my piece "Hans-Georg Gadamer and the French-speaking world," in my collection *Von Heidegger zu Gadamer* (Darmstadt: Wissenschaftliche Buchgesellschaft 2003), 136–43.

6 The phrase forms the title of an entire section ("Zur Transzendenz der Kunst"), of his last book, *Hermeneutische Entwürfe* (Tübingen : Mohr Siebeck 2000), 145–91.

7 See Gadamer's letter of 1982 to Richard J. Bernstein, published in R.J. Bernstein, *Beyond Objectivism and Relativism: Science, Hermeneutics, and Praxis* (Philadelphia: University of Pennsylvania Press 1988), 263: "Don't we all succumb to a horrifying intellectual arrogance when we equate Nietzsche's anticipation and the ideological confusion of the present with the life that is really lived and with its solidarities. In this regard, my distance from Heidegger is fundamental » (Verfallen wir nicht alle einem schrecklichen intellektuellen Hochmut, wenn wir die Antizipationen Nietzsches und die ideologische Verwirrung der Gegenwart mit dem wirklich gelebten Leben und seinen Solidaritäten gleichsetzen? Hier ist in der Tat meine Abweichung von Heidegger fundamental.) See Gadamer's essay of 1983 under the eloquent title "Nietzsche – the Antipode: The Drama of Zarathustra," in his *Gesammelte Werke*, vol. 4, 448–62.

8 See G. Vattimo, "Histoire d'une virgule: Gadamer et le sens de l'être," *Revue internationale de philosophie* 54 (2000): 499–513.

9 See G. Vattimo, "Gadamer and the Problem of Ontology," in *Gadamer's Century: Essays in Honor of Hans-Georg Gadamer*, edited by J. Malpas, U. Arnswald, and J. Kertscher (London: The MIT Press 2002), 301–6, and R. Rorty, "Being That Can Be Understood Is Language," *Gadamer's Repercussions: Reconsidering Philosophical Hermeneutics*, edited by Bruce Krajewski (University of California Press 2004), 21–9. All these contributions can be found in *Sein, das verstanden werden kann, ist Sprache: Hommage an Hans-Georg Gadamer* (Frankfurt: Suhrkamp 2001).

10 See, for example, his work of 1960, contemporaneous with *Truth and Method*, "The Nature of Things and the Language of Things," in *Philosophical Hermeneutics*, translated by David E. Linge (Berkeley: University of California Press 1976), 69–81 ("Die Natur der Sache und die Sprache der Dinge," *Gesammelte Werke*, vol. 2, 66–75).

11 See the decisive passage in *Truth and Method*, WM, GW 1, 272: "A person

who is trying to understand is exposed to distraction from fore-meanings that are not borne out by the things themselves. Working out appropriate projections, anticipatory in nature, to be confirmed 'by the things' themselves, is the constant task of understanding." Hans-Georg Gadamer, *Truth and Method* (1960), trans. Joel Weinsheimer and Donald G. Marshall (London: Continuum 2004), 270. It is obvious to me not only that Gadamer maintains here the notion of truth as *adaequatio* but that his notion of a fusion of horizons can be read as a form of *adequatio rei et intellectus*, as I have suggested in my essays "La fusion des horizons: La version gadamérienne de l'adaequatio rei et intellectus?" *Archives de Philosophie* 68 (2005): 401–18, and "La thèse herméneutique sur l'être," *Revue de métaphysique et de morale* 111 (2006).

13

Looking Back on Gadamer's Hermeneutics

RÜDIGER BUBNER

Translated by Jim Scott

Jürgen Habermas occasionally characterized Hans-Georg Gadamer's work with gentle irony as the "urbanization of Heideggerian parochialism." As a student, I myself took a lively interest in this kind of controversy. The so-called Frankfurt School retreated from neo-Marxism to a Kantianizing theory of speech acts. On the other hand, the Heideggerian efforts on behalf of ontology merged into the universe of hermeneutic interpretation. I heard a lot of tales from inside the Heidegger School and met and fully admired the master himself on his sporadic visits to seminars that he held for his disciples in Heidelberg. Habermas participated in my PHD exam in 1964. All that has now long since become history, and for that reason I need to reminisce a bit to help smooth the path for newcomers and the curious.

Hegel's glorious appearance at the newly founded University of Berlin was the apogee of German idealism, which had its origin in Kant's critical shift toward transcendental philosophy. The scornful critics of this idealism were legion, however, in the nineteenth century: Feuerbach and Marx, Kierkegaard and Nietzsche, and all philosophizing scientists like Helmholtz, du Bois-Reymond, and Haeckel. In addition to these, the next generation of academics began to make itself heard. After the midcentury they followed Otto Liebmann's claim that it was necessary to go back beyond idealistic speculation to Kant himself. According to Liebmann, Kant had taken a clear position with regard to the rapidly progressing natural sciences. This position had shown itself to be the only way left open for philosophy in the face of the fresh successes registered by the natural sciences day by day. Philosophy should recognize the "fact of scientific accomplishment" and could hope at best to provide it retroactively with a methodology, or a "logic of scientific discovery," as Popper called it later.

Next we note a complex of themes in competition with the natural sciences that, according to Wilhelm Dilthey, had constituted already in early modern times an – admittedly unrecognized – system: namely, the entire theoretical discussion of the *human world*, which included natural law, faith-based social structures, and the humanistic literary canon from the classical texts through rhetoric and poetics, but also the need, evident since the eighteenth century, for a universal history without divine planning and intervention.

Labelled the *human,* or *cultural*, sciences, this inheritance from the early modern period took its place beside the natural sciences. However, a methodological competition ensued. The human sciences, responding to the pressure of the epistemological example of the natural sciences, called for their own scientific base. In the mature neo-Kantianism of Windelband and Rickert, as well as of Dilthey, their task is to describe and understand significant details, in contrast to the natural sciences, which explain facts in terms of general laws. To reduce this to a formula: the idiographic took its place as an equal beside the nomothetic.

In the realm of history it is not possible to subsume a particular case under a general rule. On the contrary, the individual case represents the realization of such a generality. Here we find the outstanding epoch, the unique work of art, the great statesman or conqueror, the intellectual elite of a society, the character of a nation, the splitting off of a sect, the dissidents – nothing of any of these is adequately described if stylized into an example of some rule within a unified theory of knowing. Rather, the individual events that draw our attention are unmistakably embedded in their particular contexts. One epoch displays a characteristic break in comparison with another, the great individual grows up under a unique set of circumstances, the artistic masterpiece is the product of an extraordinary genius and supplies itself and all who follow with its own standards.

Individuals and events claiming *general interest* of this order can be described only by approximation, are to be made part of a narrative context, require empathetic understanding. Now an art of understanding has existed for ages under the name of hermeneutics. Dilthey responds to the open methodology problem of the human and cultural sciences by referring them to the authentic process of hermeneutics.

Traditional hermeneutics provided an artificial battery of techniques that were able to go beyond common sense and its necessarily trivial accomplishments. Such efforts were made chiefly on behalf of three things, each of which posed special difficulties that needed to be understood and each of which was also exceptionally meaningful and therefore worthy of understanding. First among these was the Bible, the book of books, which speaks to us of essential matters, although it is written in two foreign languages, namely, Hebrew and Greek. It reflects a view of the world no longer current and hence requires interpretation to make it relevant. The preacher in the pulpit is the prototype of the translator offering orientation, especially after Luther's reformation rejected the Catholic Church's claim to authority.

Beside the Bible stands Roman law, which accompanied Western legal culture into the age of revolutions and recodification. The partly archaic and systematically brief precepts of the Codex Justinianus continually required new translation appropriate to the decisions at hand. Then, finally, the Renaissance salvaged an entire literary culture in danger of being forgotten by investing its greatest effort in restoring the Greek and Roman classics to their role as exemplary works and making them accessible again to modern readers. It was this trio of Bible, Roman law, and classics that the hermeneutists first regarded as their proper subjects.

Dilthey expands the reach of hermeneutics beyond issues of theology, jurisprudence, and aesthetics. He vitalizes it, one could say, by analogy with Hegel's concept of the spirit (*Geist*), into an all-embracing *life context*, which bears both consciously apprehended intense experiences and their expression. The subsequent interpretation of the remaining documents of such intensified moments makes it possible to overcome historical distance by reintegrating the former event as an understood happening into life as it is lived. The original experience, whose petrifaction exists in such forms as works, documents, traces, or legacies, as well as the renewed integration of the objectified relics of past subjectivity into the subjectivity of the contemporary interpreter, completes a span of self-actualization of the surrounding life context. That effort extends beyond the pure methodology of the human sciences. True, Dilthey explicitly warned against the implicit metaphysics of Hegel's theory of the spirit, all the while valuing most highly and imitating

Hegel the historical thinker. He was no dry preceptor of correct how-to procedures in the historical and literary disciplines. His essays on German literature, which have since become famous, demonstrated the capacity for empathy and the emotional range of this scholar's mind.

If this were not so, then Heidegger, taking up where Dilthey had left off, could not have radicalized understanding to mean the continuous productivity of our practical life. Heidegger leaves the scientific model in its entirety behind him. Understanding, in the fundamental ontological enquiry of the early Heidegger, is no longer the isolated act of the interpreter giving a controlled response to a historical source, a persisting sign of the past, or a standard-setting work of art.

Understanding is the *basis of our general conduct of life* in the world of things, which have always so surrounded us that we have needed to interpret them to serve our ends and enable us to live. For that reason we actually never confront strange objects and set about to discover their properties empirically as though in the normal course of events we were all in the position of the scientist. Rather, we create for ourselves within the framework of our existence, i.e., within the daily and hourly necessity of being, an entire world in which we feel at home and in which we accept the need to act and do so in accordance with a project of life that, as a whole, makes sense to us.

Understanding is without question the most fundamental operation of all human existence. Understanding is relating to the world for the sake of life and its continuation. Science, on the other hand, is derived from this and is therefore a secondary specialization. To be sure, the cost of a horizon narrowed by experts is made up for by efficiency in the sense of exactness and the technical application of tested results. But the sum of scientific discoveries, because of their inherent progressive nature, never comes together to constitute a unified worldview. We heirs of a scientistically renovated civilization know a thing or two about that.

Heidegger followed his path from the concept of hermeneutics as an elevated art of understanding he inherited to an analysis of the constituent conditions of existence itself. From this position, the old problem of ontology, which is supposed to supply a general concept of being, was open to a completely new solution. The subtle and insightful arguments that Heidegger presented in light of this goal from early on I will ignore completely at this point. I will hang on to just one idea – that understanding is essentially bound to language. If, as the consequence of the critique of science, the limitation to a scientific track was abandoned in favour of an expansion into the full spectrum of life experience, then only language could unveil the totality of our relationship to the world. In connection with this, a prephilosophical understanding of being arises out of the existential disposition to deal with the world on a daily basis. That fundamental insight was described phenomenologically in *Being and Time* (1927). An important early sketch surfaced just a while ago in the form of Heidegger's *Phenomenological Interpretations of Aristotle*.[1]

This is more or less the situation that Gadamer found himself in. He spent his life thinking himself into it, and finally, at the end of his academic life, as an old man he summed everything up in *Wahrheit und Methode* (*Truth and Method*) (1960). Since its appearance more than forty years ago, it has resonated powerfully within philosophic circles, but also in other disciplines as well, and then beyond the limits imposed by language, especially in exchanges with French, Italian, and American philosophy. In the second half of the century, one can claim a comparable effect at most for the late Wittgenstein.

The success of *Truth and Method* shows that an existing need had been addressed. Naturally, the latent expectations from which a successful book then profited can later only be roughly described. So what was Gadamer's principal work responding to when it appeared in 1960, and why does it continue to exert an unbroken influence down to the present day?

In general terms, it was the widespread *need for mediation* that the book fulfilled, and that thanks to its sense of tact and in any case because it did not intend to engage in mediation. Those who would woo others with their offer to act as a mediator regularly fall victim to the effect, intentionally or unintentionally, of calling attention to themselves instead of aiding the cause. In need of mediation were, first, those interested in science, whom neo-Kantian epistemology had split into two camps. That is to say, the business of separating knowledge about nature from knowledge about mind had remained, finally, a puzzle; for both sides oriented themselves clearly to a theory of the world. What is, after all, structurally so different about the scientization of human affairs, on the one hand, and the objectification of things in nature on the other? Here the broadly conceived concept of understanding supplied a key word and a perspective for mediation.

To cite just one example, the marriage of positivism and pragmatism had returned the independent investigation of nature to the realm of human interests. In his later works John Dewey had shown how attempts to gain knowledge and pursue interests could be related. Thomas Kuhn's convincing model of "paradigms" was a plea for the historization and humanization of the knowledge of the natural world, and so it came close to hermeneutics. An understanding without difficulty then arose that reached across disciplines and was also able to make connections with the practical aspects of natural research, which can never be separated cleanly from theoretical considerations. By reaching back to Gadamer's hermeneutics, Richard Rorty was finally able to develop this line of thought to the point that the view of the entire modern project of science as an exact and objective "mirror of nature" has begun to fade, in order to make room for a cultural enrichment of the "conversation of mankind."

A further problem needing mediation had arisen from the creeping estrangement of history. In the course of the forward march of science, the notion that history is but one scientific discipline among others had silently become dogma. But no justice had been done in this way to the real historicity of human existence. History is always our history and remains the history of us all and as such may not be definitively handed over to a faculty of experts. The intricate relationship emerges in phases when the political battle for public attention refers to the supposed lessons of history.

An outstanding example of this is the embattled notion of progress. During the Enlightenment, rationalism was associated directly with progress. Following Rousseau's critique of culture, however, this progress stood revealed as a category offering very little orientation. If, during the breathless forward march of progress, we are unable to say where it is headed, the underlying teleology must dissolve, and we must find ourselves caught in the restlessness of constant motion without being able to say for sure that we are not in fact just running in one place. This image of progress seems unattached to actual historical situations, with their breaks and tendencies, their effects and contingencies, in which we find ourselves enmeshed. However, since we do not pursue historical research in some special methodological preserve, but rather within the framework of specific historical situations, we need to create a convincing link.

Incidentally, the artistic avantgarde has provided a parallel scenario for more than a century now. The regular replacement of yesterday's fashion in art undoubtedly keeps everything going. But innovation in aesthetic experience is not necessarily the same as aesthetic gain. Cultural climate change apparently possesses its own charm, while the truly great achievements emerge only over time. The comparison may appear risky, but scientific methods, which appear in all disciplines, seem to obey a similar principle. Sizable numbers of graduate students follow them, but true discoveries remain rare.

On this front, too, the hermeneutic recollection of the origin of concepts and schools, as well as the relativization of the triumphant here and now associated with such recollection, can help us achieve a more balanced judgment. All the things we used to know, all the abandoned worldviews going back to mythology, which had provided the necessary coherence for an archaic society, should no longer be seen as happily outgrown evolutionary nursery toys and subjects for mockery. Romanticism had already presented an alternative to our fixed concentration on rationality that was both worthy of consideration and capable of revival. Nietzsche had forged courageously ahead with his radical criticism of progress. The French succession to hermeneutics from Foucault to Derrida also picked up from Heidegger and Nietzsche and successfully differentiated our concept of modernity. In Italy, Gianni Vattimo in particular has long been an unfailingly insightful dialogue partner.

We stand on the shoulders of giants. This old metaphor provides a lot to think about. How much accumulated and, indeed, unconscious preparation for the work of understanding is contained in all the traditions? This is true above all for history, if one is not inclined simply to turn away from it in moral indignation as a permanent "shambles," as Hegel once described it. Benjamin, for example, seized on this motive, which Hegel had rejected, with negative and eschatological pathos and succeeded in making its echo ring down to the present day.

No less important, surely, is the permanent process of sedimentation in all scholarly disciplines, where innovation builds upon a school or sets itself apart from another school. In any case, the popular stories of the great innovators can scarcely be written without such embedding. The latter generalization is even true for language itself, since it carries the wisdom of the past onward and places it at our disposal anew. For that reason, one of the principal branches of hermeneutic mediation is called simply "the history of concepts."

In the case of language, which we use and take as much for granted as the air we breathe, it seems more difficult to keep the account book of the past as efficiently as in a well-run bank. All of us hang from threads our forbears have spun and trade their coinages in our particular national idiom, except that we have allowed the imagination of our predecessors to sink to the level of a routine. We really do not know the riches that we constantly have at our disposal when we direct even the simplest utterance to someone else, who understands us effortlessly. Nietzsche spoke in this regard of the army of dead metaphors whose roots in past lives we have forgotten, so that we deal in words worn down like old coins. Hans Blumenberg's contributions to the history of ideas sought to use this observation to create "metaphorology" as a new philosophical project. With metaphor as the main concept he ended up, naturally enough, in systematic proximity to rhetoric.

At this point we may make the comparison with Wittgenstein, although the Wittgensteinians – and their number is legion – unanimously maintain that they stand apart from the insights of hermeneutics. In fact, with his concept of language game, Wittgenstein attempted a return, similar to that of hermeneutics, to the ordinary use of language that we all take for granted, wherever it may function. Of course, Wittgenstein was interested in language therapy and had no historical perspective in mind. This explains why, following a deemphasis on the real intention to focus on therapy, the concept of a language game figured so prominently in the categorical thinking of the social sciences. Ethnologists, as well, are beginning to apply its precepts to their contact with foreign cultures. As reference points, the names of Peter Winch and Clifford Geertz may suffice.

Finally, let us remember one additional front where the need for mediation has now arisen. The global spread of Western civilization, the channelling by sophisticated media with their ever more perfect information systems and an ever present technology, together with the politics of internationalism, dangle before us the vision of a world where all things conform to a degree previously unknown. Without question the ecumenism of contemporary civilization represents an astonishing fact never seen before. But along with it goes the deep ambivalence of all those stereotypes under whose smooth surfaces the differences and tensions slumber. To be sure, making each and every thing conform to a universal standard has great advantages. Think only of the financial events resulting from the unification of the currency of expanding European markets with the Euro. Even more ambitious is the hope of realizing the cosmopolitan dreams of political philosophy through the United Nations, for which the European Union is explicitly intended to be an intermediary step.

On the other hand, we find everywhere, bit by bit, an inestimable loss of authentic cultural values through wear and tear, accommodation and retreat. The negative hermeneutics of Derrida's Paris School, for example, reacted to this phenomenon by privileging the "other." In the meantime, the history of the world appears to provide its real-life dramatization in the competitions, indeed the battles, of the "culture wars." Without leaping to conclusions in these complex matters, which would be entirely out of place, we should note in any case that hermeneutics returns to our perceptions their ability to resonate, which our vaunted modernization had systematically flattened.

Understanding means precisely not just learning the signposts on the roundabout of economic mobility and its playful mirror image in mass tourism. Phrases in Pidgin English, iconic images of the film industry, canned statements of consensus, and the lingua franca of television culture are with us day and night. And yet we are not everywhere and at all times the same; indeed, the same is, contrary to appearances, not everywhere itself. In opposition to the instrumentally perfected appearance of understanding, hermeneutic reflection keeps spaces free where unexpected forms of interaction are possible, without making it necessary for us to join the bandwagons on well-worn paths. In short, hermeneutics helps us to avoid the wholesale integration of what is foreign and different and to value it in its particularity.

Some observers have suspected a double meaning in the title of Gadamer's main work, on which his later studies were variations. *Truth and Method* sounded like a misnomer, since there was hardly any mention of methodology. Some said the title should actually have been *Truth and Non-method*. In fact, Gadamer had not provided a methodology for the human sciences or, more broadly, for the social and cultural sciences. He consciously refused to continue arguing in the same direction as Dilthey, the high priest of humanistic methodology. The complex of disciplines that, thanks to his broad educational background, provided Gadamer with his orientation would in the Anglo-Saxon scheme of things be called "the humanities." In this we hear the echo of the *humaniora*, the term used in the Renaissance to refer to all the knowledge that sets us free as human beings, which comes to us from our classical heritage and which set the Renaissance apart from the narrow dogmatism of medieval scholasticism.

At this point finer distinctions are necessary. As much as Gadamer fit the image of the great scholars of old, an image today threatened with extinction by the massed forces of specialization, he radiated just as little of scholasticism and loyalty to any one school of thought. He never abandoned his teacher, Heidegger, even when the latter came under ideological attack. But in Heidegger's school there are examples of real and slavish imitation that evince an entirely different sort of fealty. Gadamer used the power of his intellectual perspicacity to continue to develop Heidegger's ideas and elevate them to that level of urbanity of which I spoke at the outset.

All his life Heidegger enjoyed a genially arbitrary relationship to the history of philosophy. He was able to look into the abyss but was not bothered in the least by the pedantry and prejudices of the philologists. Thus he was confronted as long as he lived with the criticism that he systematically rode roughshod over the existing textual evidence. Indeed, Heidegger pressed traditional metaphysics radically into the service of his own questions. In contrast with him, Gadamer proves the more flexible and skilled hermeneut. He cares about understanding what has already been said because, for one thing, he suspects it might contain buried treasure that could get a thoughtful mind going before proceeding to the radicalized deep drilling for the repressed or unexpressed. Gadamer thinks in dialogue with the past; Heidegger in protest against its silence. Both, however, and each in his own way, manage the trick of giving history a voice.

If the diagnosis is correct that Gadamer was not just belatedly supplying a class of sciences with a methodology, then it remains to decipher a polemical implication in the title *Truth and Method*. Truth should not be invoked, in the absence of a method, as the vague intuition of a gifted mind. But truth must most definitely be defended against a methodical cutting off of access to the world and, by overcoming the barriers on all sides put up by those views, barriers for which we have none other than the sciences to thank. Truth must be declared an unfinished human project. Truth is not what scientists discover and articulate, as though the oldest and still principal concern of philosophy could be handed over to a plurality of experts whose confused voices we cannot finally disentangle. Truth is not the sum of all that the cohorts of professionals have discovered for us and that they promise to discover in the future. If it was, truth would slip away from ordinary people to become the preserve of an anonymous apparatus of scientific industriousness with proven efficacy in technical applications, an apparatus where careers are made with funds allocated and prizes awarded from outside academe.

It was Aristotle who founded the "still to be sought after" episteme of ontology with the insight that we all possess many sciences, each of which "carves out" its bit of reality (*Metaphysics* 4.1). Thus, being as such and as a whole must be sought by thoughtfully superseding the scientific particularization of mere aspects of reality. Aristotle adds a systematic analysis of the phenomenon-revealing potential of language. Gadamer takes up the suggestion of such a "linguistic analysis" in the sense of the Aristotelian formula πολαχως λεγεται in his own way, namely by joining linguistic analysis as Aristotle understood it with the effect of a work of art. In doing so, he follows explicitly a hint of the older Heidegger in his essay on art and ends up in a surprising parallel to Adorno. The common denominator in all of these is the critique of rationality in view of the administered world.

For neither Gadamer nor Adorno trusts the organized, scientific explanation of the world – in the name of strict objectivity and the exclusion of the human dimension – to tell truth seekers what they are searching for, because for Gadamer and Adorno truth has an existential, life-affirming meaning. Whether the danger lies in the hyper-differentiated, myopic perspective of the specialist (Gadamer) or in an all-inclusive "systemic blindness" (Adorno) does not really matter. For both science skeptics there is in any case one thing whose appearance does not deceive us, and that is *art*. The appearance that does not deceive does not allow firm conceptual statements about the world with which we are concerned. But in the realm of aesthetics stand unveiled those things that we as truth seekers are all concerned with. This insight offers an escape from the directionlessness of our overscientized modernity.

At this point, the classical term *mimesis* makes itself felt. Mimesis shows us a practice that we know in such a way that we do not know it, i.e., in the light of the significant, the general, and the probable. This is the source of the cathartic effect of mimesis on the audience, which, thanks to the lens of art and its works, is able to see the conditions of and the threats to their lives more clearly than through the plain glass of their individual everyday concerns. Along with this, reconciliation is a utopian accent that Adorno emphasizes. Gadamer contents himself with the essential expansion of the horizon of our assumed worldview that we owe to art and that trumps our delegation of truth to science through a division-of-labour.

In this context it becomes clear what is perhaps the last and most fundamental reason for the continuing influence of Gadamer's work across a broad front. In the age of science and technology, under the sign of a humanly conceived estrangement of humanity from itself, Gadamer insists, thanks to the highly developed reflectivity of our epoch, as well as a familiarity with the tradition that would be hard to surpass, that *the world belongs to humans, because humans belong in the world.* Heidegger, like Adorno, had brought subsurface theological motives into play. Gadamer supports a humanism free of pathos, which in dialogic exchange across disciplines argues socially and historically across epochs and in this way elevates the cause of truth seeking to the unfinished task of humanity. Certainly, in the back and forth of argument, criticism also finds a place. But the primary interest is not in the rejection and dismissal of existing circumstances, instead of synthesis. And this then constitutes a roughly drawn line of demarcation for the postmodern orientation. That this synthesis, however, could be a chimera is a frequently expressed concern and one that continues to be heard; thus no one needs to be seriously worried that skeptical voices are being muffled.

A further, and for some unexpected, alliance has been developing for some time now with the pragmatically shaded linguistic holism of Donald Davidson, whose predecessor in the holistic approach to the philosophy of language was Quine. Already Quine had introduced the "principle of charity." His successor Davidson expanded the idea to a quasi-hermeneutic maxim. The basic idea holds that it is possible to understand an utterance only within the totality of a natural language, which speakers must know completely before they can appropriately interpret even one sentence. This so-called "holism" is thus the heir of Wittgenstein's language-game concept, although it departs from family resemblances, where therapeutic concerns are involved, to focus instead on the totality of all true utterances.

It is a cultural fact that we not only know many languages, but can even learn them: translation and interpretation provide the bridge. Exemplary is the fictitious figure of the ethnologist, who meets a strange tribe speaking an unknown language and following idiosyncratic practices. That person must feel his way to the sense of the initially incomprehensible utterances under field conditions. And in this process there is no such thing as a dictionary-like word-for-word correspondence. Rather, he must transfer his inferences from the global context of the language, which is embedded in a way of life, to his own language, which is itself connected to a way of life. Practical considerations create pressures to make the business of translation, which is a business of interpretation, as uncomplicated as possible.

At this point the principle of charity comes into play, a principle we should not confuse with sloppiness born of love for our fellow humans.

The principle is absolutely required for anyone who wants to get on with the business of translation, or indeed with any cross-cultural exchange. The principle assumes that the initially uncomprehended partner possesses, in the main, correct notions about the world and accordingly will tend to make correct, rather than false, statements. For without this assumption, it would not be possible to explain how a tribe of natives, or indeed any interacting group of people dominated by mistaken views, could have dealt successfully with day-to-day issues on a continuing basis. The foreign language is by definition always different from ours; but it permits foreigners, these culturally different individuals, these irritating others, to find their way in the world with results that, finally, compare favourably with our own.

Gadamer speaks analogously of the *anticipation of completeness* (Vorgriff der Vollkommenheit), but there is no evidence to indicate that the two formulations could have influenced each other. Davidson used an opportune moment to mention his dissertation on Plato's *Philebos* in connection with Gadamer's qualifying thesis *Platos dialektische Ethik*. The two works are objectively separated by the Second World War and subjectively by utterly different approaches to philosophical conceptualization.

Nevertheless, we do have to deal here with a real theoretical convergence between continental hermeneutics and advanced American linguistic analysis. The "anticipation of completeness" yields, like the "principle of charity," an a priori bonus to help accomplish the job of translation. Those things that one has not understood completely or exactly enough are rendered on the basis of familiar understanding to create a meaningful whole. For when we would understand something, we do not want a handful of fragments, which resist coming together and never fit with one another. Rather, we desire when we understand something – whatever it may be that we are trying to understand – to understand it thoroughly and as a whole. This assumption directly explains, by the way, the background for objections and the criticism of mistakes. We will discover falseness only if a broad consensus supports the point of greatest disagreement.

I will close by referring to one of the last texts written by Hans-Georg Gadamer. He provided an up-to-date preface for the critically revised new edition of *Überweg*, a well-regarded history of philosophy based on the self-assured erudition of the nineteenth century. The preface reminds us that, in contrast with specialized disciplines, its own history represents for philosophy a source of inspiration and astonishment, a source of instruction, of training in critical thinking, and of doubt and a place of affirmation. I quote: "One notion of Hegel's is true: it is in the nature of the spirit that it unfolds over time. And so it is, that philosophical thinking hardly ever has more to do with itself, than when it turns to its own history" (1999). This is the credo and testament of a hermeneutics as the deceased Gadamer explicated it throughout his Methuselahlian life span.

NOTES

1 Martin Heidegger, *Phenomenological Interpretations of Aristotle: Initiation into Phenomenological Research*, translated by Richard Rojcewicz (Bloomington: Indiana University Press 2001).

14

Pharmakons of Onto-theology

SANTIAGO ZABALA

What I mean, expressed more concisely, is that one cannot talk with impunity of interpretation; interpretation is like a virus or even a pharmakon that affects everything it comes into contact with. On the one hand, it reduces all reality to message – erasing the distinction between Natur and Geisteswissenschaften, since even the so-called "hard" sciences verify and falsify their statements only within paradigms or pre-understandings. If "facts" thus appear to be nothing but interpretations, interpretation, on the other hand, presents itself as (the) fact: hermeneutics is not a philosophy but the enunciation of historical existence itself in the age of the end of metaphysics

Gianni Vattimo[1]

It is worth noticing that while never suggesting a new philosophy or philosophical method meant to correct past positions, Martin Heidegger became the most original and important philosopher of twentieth century. George Steiner presented him not only as "the most eminent philosopher or critic of metaphysics since Immanuel Kant but also as one of that small number of decisive Western thinkers that would include Plato, Aristotle, Descartes, Leibniz, and Hegel"; Hannah Arendt described him as "the secret king of thought throughout twentieth-century philosophic sensitivity"; and when he died on 26 May 1976, a number of European philosophers affirmed that "in the domain of the spirit our century would be that of Heidegger as the seventeenth century could be that of Descartes." His thought not only contributed to the philosophical fields of phenomenology (Maurice Merleau-Ponty, Emmanuelle Lévinas), existentialism (Jean-Paul Sartre, José Ortega y Gasset, Karl Jaspers), analytical philosophy (Ernst Tugendhat, Stanley Cavell, Robert Brandom), critical theory (Jürgen Habermas, Karl-Otto

Apel, Richard J. Bernstein), deconstructionism (Reiner Schürmann, Jacques Derrida, William Spanos, Paul A. Bové, Julia Kristeva), and diverse cultural sciences such as political theory (Herbert Marcuse, Hannah Arendt), psychology (Ludwig Binswanger, Medard Boss), theology (Bernhard Welte, Rudolf Bultmann, Karl Rahner, Paul Tillich), and science (Thomas Kuhn, Bas van Fraassen), but most of all he elevated, for the first time, hermeneutics "to the center of philosophical concern."[2] Although Heidegger never wanted to have his own school of thought or students in the classical sense, three philosophers remained, in very different ways, strictly Heideggerian, and we should consider them his direct students and continuators. The first is Jacques Derrida (1930–2004), who continued his philosophy through *deconstruction* (deconstructionism); the second is Ernst Tugendhat (b. 1931), through *semanticizing* (analytical philosophy); and finally, the third is Hans-Georg Gadamer (1900–2002), through philosophical hermeneutics. They all represent different appropriations and developments[3] of Heidegger's question regarding the Being of beings and of his emphasis on language as the main dimension of *Dasein*.

The title of this chapter cannot but recall Derrida's long essay entitled "Plato's Pharmacy," published for the first time in two issues of the distinguished French journal *Tel Quel* in 1968 and then reprinted as a significant part of one of his major books, *La Dissémination*,[4] which today is considered a classic in contemporary philosophy. My intention here is not to comment on Heidegger's enormous philosophical and sociological influence just thirty years after his death or on Derrida's great investigations of the word *pharmakon* (which in Greek can mean both remedy and poison, a baneful drug or a medicinal restorative, as he discussed) just one year after his death, but to use the concept of *pharmakon* in order to put forward three theses that I have developed from my master, Gianni Vattimo, three teachings and indications:

1 The virus of onto-theology consists in understanding Being as presence.
2 Deconstruction, semanticizing, and interpretation are philosophical *pharmakons*.
3 Interpretation is the most appropriate *pharmakon* of onto-theology.

Since Plato, philosophers have been incapable of answering the "question of Being" (*Seinsfrange*), because they have thought of Being as an essence, an "optical model" in accordance with an ideal or empirical image or representation of objective experience. If the task of philosophy has always been to answer the question of Being and if Heidegger recognized that we have all fallen into the so-called metaphysics of presence, or logo-centrism, because we think of Being as an objective presence, then since *Being and Time* philosophy has become a constant search that assumes that the Being of beings is outside this same metaphysical structure of Western objectivist culture. I believe that finding a *pharmakon* can be functionally understood as the goal that many postmetaphysical philosophers have given themselves since Heidegger, after whom philosophy has become a matter of therapy rather than discovery, a historico-practical meditation on the search for a *pharmakon* for Being. Postmetaphysical philosophy's major concern has been to find a position capable of adjusting this objectivism, which leads to violence and fundamentalism: this *pharmakon* is the cure for metaphysics through postmetaphysical philosophies. Although, as mentioned, the word *pharmakon* reveals that in ancient Greece the very same treatment could serve as either remedy or poison, to act as a remedy, the treatment has to be given in the right amount and at the right time for a correctly diagnosed disease. The nature of our disease today is objectivism created by metaphysics, and the best remedy would be a philosophy capable of overcoming this mentality so that we may live without the violence and oppression that arise from it, such as the violence and oppression of political, cultural, and religious fundamentalism.[5] It is important to understand from the start that we cannot neglect metaphysics (Being as presence, or objectivism) once and for all, because we cannot completely overcome it, *überwinden,* but only surpass it through acceptance, or *verwinden.*[6] Heidegger's deconstruction of objectivistic metaphysics cannot be carried forward by replacing it with a more adequate conception of Being, because one would still have to identify Being with the presence characteristic of the object.[7] This is why in *Nietzsche,* Heidegger wrote "that within metaphysics there is nothing to Being as such."[8] So, if the same treatment can serve as either medicine or poison, the best postmetaphysical philosophy will be one capable not only of overcoming this metaphysical mentality but also of producing it on some occasions, since, as with any sickness, it is impossible to completely recover from it.[9]

Derrida, Tugendhat, and Gadamer understood not only that onto-theology contains a harmful virus (Being as presence, objectivism) but *also* that its baneful drug could be counteracted by a postmetaphysical practice capable of overcoming this objectivism. Each of them put forward one practice to achieve this end: deconstruction, semanticizing, and interpretation. These three philosophies are neither "methods" nor "new" positions but rather ways to overcome objective metaphysical polarities such as presence vs absence, Being vs nothingness, truth vs error, mind vs matter, soul vs body, and man vs woman; cultures that favour polarities such as religion vs science and literature vs philosophy; and authoritarian institutions such as the church, the state, and universities, because they privilege cultures based in these dual polarities.[10] After confronting the *pharmakons* (philosophical solutions) of Derrida, Tugendhat, and Gadamer, I will conclude this chapter by explaining why we should consider Gadamer's solution best adapted to Heidegger's own requirements for overcoming metaphysics. Readers might find it alarming that I am entering into the heart of the problem with a solution right from the beginning, but to "assign the naming word is, after all, what constitutes finding,"[11] as Heidegger used to say.

Derrida, Heidegger's French disciple, has taken very seriously paragraph 6 of the introduction to *Being and Time*, entitled "The Task of a Destructuring of the History of Ontology," as well as the last paragraph, where Heidegger states that "the distinction between the being of existing Dasein and the beings of beings unlike Dasein (for example, reality) may seem to be illuminating, but it is only the *point of departure* for the ontological problematic; it is not something with which philosophy can rest and be satisfied."[12] This difference is at the centre of his *pharmakon* for overcoming metaphysics. Derrida's goal was to move beyond modernism by revealing its inconsistencies – such as the ones I have already outlined between Being and nothingness and presence and absence within the Western European tradition from Descartes to the present – in order to move away from grounding truth in ideologies or divinities. Deconstruction does not deconstruct the meaning of a text but the unequivocal domination of one of the two signifiers over the other because the second term was always considered as the negative, undesirable version of the first, a corruption of it: woman from man, body from soul, error from truth. Since there are no reasonable arguments to privilege identity, man, and mind over difference, woman, and matter, deconstruction is specifically democratic, because it tries to emphasize how the two terms are not simply opposed in their meanings but organized in a metaphysical hierarchical order that always gives priority to the first term, therefore to the interpretation of Being as *presence* instead of difference. Derrida, in a famous interview entitled "Implications," said that "what I have attempted to do would not have been possible without the opening of Heidegger's questions. [It] would not have been possible without the attention to what Heidegger calls the difference between Being and beings, the ontico-ontological difference such as, in a way, it remains unthought by philosophy."[13]

The other two disciples of Heidegger, Tugendhat and Gadamer, did not take the ontological difference, or even the historical destruction of metaphysics, so seriously; they were more focused on *Being and Time*, paragraphs 33 ("Statement as a Derivate Mode of Interpretation") and 44 ("Da-sein, Disclosedness, and Truth"). These paragraphs are extremely important because here Heidegger formulates his ontological understanding of the concept of truth, which he never abandoned. Tugendhat and Gadamer interpret these paragraphs in different ways, the first favouring the idea of truth as linguistic propositions and the second as a unique ontological event. Both Tugendhat and Gadamer have emphasized the two main linguistic particularities of Heidegger's philosophy: the *propositional* and *dialogical* nature of language. Although Heidegger did not take either of the two very seriously (considering hermeneutical philosophy "Gadamer's business"[14] and not even mentioning Tugendhat's studies of his concept of truth as *aletheia*[15] or his *Traditional and Analytical Philosophy: Lectures on the Philosophy of Language*,[16] which was not only dedicated to Heidegger but also the first Heideggerian justification of analytical philosophy), it is through them that the linguistic turn has become the paradigm and the guiding concept for overcoming metaphysics. Although most analytical philosophers find it difficult to consider Tugendhat an "analytical" philosopher, he has used linguistic analysis to overcome the analytical/continental divisions of contemporary philosophy, becoming not only the first philosopher to introduce analytical philosophy to Europe but the first to answer Heideggerian questions with analytical methods. Tugendhat believes that the principal false presupposition of classical modern philosophy was that "the field of givenness reflected upon was conceived as consciousness, a dimension of representation in ideas," whereas it should be conceived as the "sphere of the understating of our linguistic propositions." Gadamer, on the other hand, constructing a "hermeneutization" of onto-theology, rejected Tugendhat's construction of logic on the basis of propositions, because he considered a reliance on logic "the most fateful decision of Western culture"; instead, he suggests understanding language on the basis of dialogue. "Language is most itself not in propositions," explains Gadamer, "but in dialogue," because propositions can never be excluded from the historical context of motivation (tradition) in which they are embedded and which is the only place they have any meaning.

According to Gadamer's philosophy, we are "historical effected conscious beings" finally aware of the limits placed by this same hermeneutic enlightenment. This enlightenment of our own finitude (specifically, in Gadamerian terms, "prejudices") does not paralyze reflection or limit understanding, but on the contrary, it is precisely our constituted limitedness that enables us to learn from one another and remain always open to other experiences. If knowing does not always mean certifying and controlling, since understating cannot be grounded once and for all, then it must itself be the ground floor on which we are always already situated. Gadamer pointed out in *Truth and Method* the ungrounded nature of understanding and knowledge without allowing a mere relativization of reality; instead, he insisted on a hermeneutical relativization of relativism.[17] This was one of the main goals of Gadamer's magnum opus: to recall that there has never been such a thing as "absolute relativism." We may speak of relativism if, and only if, someone presupposes an absolute point of view (or view from nowhere),[18] because there can be relativism only in relation to an absolute truth. Gadamer, operating with this "hermeneutical relativization of relativism," was also preparing hermeneutics to become a *prima philosophia* without metaphysics.[19]

Of the three philosophers, Gadamer is certainly the one who has remained most faithful to Heidegger's linguistic dimension of *Dasein*, Derrida to his "task" of destructuring the history of ontology, and Tugendhat in searching for a correct solution to *die Grundfrage der Metaphysik*. Although they all contributed to overcoming metaphysics (objectivism) through the so-called "linguistic turn," it is hermeneutical philosophy that has succeeded in remaining faithful not only to its own onto-theological tradition but, most of all, to the main concept that has led to an overcoming of philosophy's metaphysical nature: interpretation. Although a dialogue was never established between the three philosophers, there were encounters between Gadamer and Derrida in 1981 and 1993 that clearly showed how engaging in a conversation was still a problem for deconstructionism, while for hermeneutics it is a philosophical necessity, as we will see. During this encounter, Gadamer, in Derrida's eyes, seemed like a relativist who believed that dialogue was more significant than experiencing the inevitable limit to understanding the "other." For Derrida there is no meaning beyond the linguistic signifiers of a text, only a ceaseless deferring of meaning that is never accessible outside its own signs; therefore we are always imprisoned within an already given sign system that we never entirely understand. If truth and meaning are never given independently of a sign system, then the fundamental task of philosophy is to deconstruct the predeterminations of the linguistic framework in order not to be misled by them. Derrida was also very suspicious of Gadamer's hermeneutic concept of *horizon*, since he understood it as a metaphysical necessity to retain all the possible horizon of meaning, but in 1993 Gadamer explained not only that the *horizon* is never reached but also that for hermeneutics there is no final, fixed metaphysical meaning, only a meaning brought along with the unpredictable effective history (*Wirkungsgeschichte*) in which we stand.

Contemporary hermeneutical philosophy has become a consequence of and a consequence from deconstructionism: a consequence of deconstructionism because we have learned we cannot overcome (*überwinden*) metaphysics, leaving it completely aside, and a consequence from deconstructionism, because we may only surpass (*verwinden*) it, as Gianni Vattimo's philosophy has shown.[20] We finally have come to understand today that deconstructing the presence of Being was certainly an inevitable task for philosophy, but now it is time to inherit the consequences of this contest, and the most suitable philosophy capable of enabling us to do this is hermeneutics, which focuses on understanding through a philosophy of conversation.

Although Gadamer and Tugendhat taught during the same years in Heidelberg[21] and knew each other very well, they never established a real discussion or debate; the only record of a confrontation can be found in a review Tugendhat wrote for the *Times Literary Supplement* in 1978, where he proposes to interpret the title of *Truth and Method* to mean "truth *versus* Method."[22] Only in 1993 did Gadamer respond (indirectly) to Tugendhat, in an interview with Carsten Dutt, by saying:

This interpretation conveys the one-sided impression that I think there are no methods in the humanities and social sciences. Of course there are methods, and certainly one must learn them and apply them. But I would say that the fact that we are able to apply certain methods to certain objects does not establish *why* we are pursuing knowledge in the humanities and social sciences. To me it seems self-evident that in the natural sciences one pursues knowledge ultimately because through them one can stand on one's own feet: one can orient oneself and through measurement, reckoning, and construction eventually gain control of the surrounding world. By doing this we can – at least this is their intention – live better and survive better than if we just confronted a nature that is indifferent to us. But in the humanities and social sciences [*Geisteswissenschaften*] there can be nothing like such ruling over the historical world. The humanities and social sciences bring something different into our lives through their form of participation in what has been handed down to us, something that is not knowledge for the sake of control [*Herrschaftswissen*], yet it is no less important. We customarily call it "culture."[23]

The effects of Derrida's and Tugendhat's philosophies were felt more quickly in the English-speaking world than those of Gadamer's, but in examining which line of thought philosophers are pursuing today, we would have to recognize that Gadamer's influence on contemporary philosophy is still inestimable. This is because Gadamer has taken to the farthest reach Heidegger's elevation of hermeneutics "to the center of philosophical concern," reconstructing not only the history of interpretation philosophically but the history of philosophy interpretatively. Gadamer's philosophical hermeneutics has become a reference not only for European philosophers (Paul Ricoeur, Luigi Pareyson, Walter Schulz, Gianni Vattimo, Manfred Frank, Michael Theunissen, Werner Hamacher) but also for North Americans (Richard Rorty, Richard J. Bernstein, James Risser, John Sallis, Barry Allen, Jean Grondin, Robert J. Dostal, Brice Wachterhauser, Dennis J. Schmidt, Kathleen Wright, Stanley Rosen, Hugh Silverman, Gerald Bruns) who not only represent today the so called "continental" branch of contemporary philosophy but most of all a Gadamerian culture that Rorty individuated in his conference in Heidelberg. Recent publishers have picked up on this and created series such as Studies in Hermeneutics,[24] Hermeneutics: Studies in the History of Religions,[25] Judaica: Hermeneutics, Mysticism, and Religion,[26] Studies in American Biblical Hermeneutics,[27] and The Interpretations.[28]

A great deal of attention was focused on hermeneutical philosophy from around the world when the University of Heidelberg invited Micheal Theunissen, Richard Rorty, and Gianni Vattimo to celebrate Gadamer's one-hundredth birthday on 12 February 2000, with a conference.[29] (This event was broadcast by all German television networks and covered by most of the newspapers around the world, situating hermeneutics at the forefront of our globalized planet). Theunissen[30] stated in his lecture that "the reception of philosophical Hermeneutics has for several decades shown two dominant tendencies: one is expansive, opening it up to other currents of thought (Rorty), while the other is reflexive, orienting it toward the tradition (Vattimo)."[31] For Rorty, Gadamer is the architect not only of hermeneutical philosophy but also of a brand new culture capable of overcoming what C.P. Snow called the twentieth century's "two cultures": the positivistic phase of philosophy and the humanist phase. In order to abandon definitively the scientific problem-solving model that arose from this distinction, emphasized by Gottlob Frege and Bertrand Russell, Gadamer has proposed a conversational model, "in which philosophical success is measured by horizons fused rather than problems solved, or even by problems dissolved."[32] Rorty concluded his magnum opus, *Philosophy and the Mirror of Nature* (1979), by recognizing not only that descriptions should be replaced by conversations but also that "epistemology should be replaced by hermeneutics." Recently, Rorty has defined conversational philosophy[33] as the opposite of analytic philosophy not only because conversationalists are sufficiently "historicist as to think of themselves as taking part in a conversation rather than as practicing a quasi-scientific discipline" but also because analytic philosophy "looks like the last gasp of the onto-theological tradition."[34] Having surpassed this, we no longer need to build a new tradition but must simply recognize the old one in order to understand that we are always conditioned by some description from the past. Although Rorty was not a direct disciple of Gadamer, as Theunissen and Vattimo were, he considered Gadamer "a representative of the old school of German philosophy that centred around Plato, Aristotle, Kant, and Hegel. He had enough cosmopolitanism, charm, breadth, and sympathy to speak for that tradition to the rest of the world and make it intelligible. He deliberately assumed the role of ambassador between German and American philosophers. In his 60s, he sat in on my seminars to learn philosophical English so that he could lecture in English. In his 80s, he did the same thing in Italian. This was characteristic of his philosophical cosmopolitanism, which he employed in the service of cultural diplomacy."[35]

Most philosophical investigations begin by showing what a certain philosopher has done to philosophy in order to illuminate his work, but according to Heidegger, every philosopher always works within a certain pre-comprehension that conditions his understanding, and this pre-comprehension is experienced by the author only through a process of concretization and creation. This is why, as Heidegger explained in *Being and Time*, we need "a[n explicit] *Wiederholung* of the question of being," a repetition of it because "knowledge [*Wissen*] in the widest sense" includes "not only theory, but approaching something, knowing one's way around it, mastering it, penetrating its substantial content e.g. in a trade." Heidegger's *Ontology: The Hermeneutics of Facticity* shows how the term "hermeneutics" derives from a Greek word connected with the name of the god Hermes, the reputed messenger and interpreter of the gods, and why it was originally concerned more narrowly with interpreting sacred texts. As I've explained in the introduction to this volume, although hermeneutical philosophy originated in problems of biblical exegesis, it was in the eighteenth and early nineteenth centuries that theologians and philosophers developed it into a more encompassing theory of textual interpretation in general, preparing the way for Dilthey and Heidegger to make of it a recognized position in twentieth-century German philosophy. It is important to remember that in his classic of 1927, Heidegger used the term "hermeneutics" not in the sense of a theory of the art of interpretation nor of interpretation itself but rather to attempt a first definition of the nature of interpretation on hermeneutic grounds.

The consequences of hermeneutic philosophy or just of the concept of interpretation are too vast to receive a complete analysis in this essay and would probably require a few volumes at this point. But although my goal was just to justify a thesis (*interpretation as the pharmakon of onto-theology*), it is interesting to notice these historical justifications before entering into the heart of the argument, because they constitute the same thesis. The reason for such justifications can be found only in this same concept of interpretation, because today, after two thousand years of submission to unquestioned metaphysical paradigms, we have "achieved a discourse on discourse, an interpretation of interpretation," as Julia Kristeva explains, which will finally make the "word become flesh."[36] This is emphasized by the French philosopher as a success, because it is a way out from what Hegel called "the desire for absolute knowledge": interpretation stood secretly side by side for all this time with this desire (until Heidegger elevated it to the centre of philosophy), providing a practice that finally could begin to free this entire encompassing framework.

Having studied a tradition of philosophers who centred their work on the concept of interpretation, Heidegger did not regard it as an operation of construction but as an announcement of what had already been constituted; namely, bringing into speech the meaning of Being. In the famous dialogue with Professor Tezuka of the Imperial University of Tokyo in 1953, he gives a clear account of the meaning of hermeneutics for philosophy:

HEIDEGGER: The expression "hermeneutic" derives from the Greek verb hermeneuein. That verb is related to the noun hermeneus, which is referable to the name of the god Hermes by a playful thinking that is more compelling than the rigor of science. Hermes is the divine messenger. He brings the message of destiny; *hermeneuein* is that exposition which brings tidings because it can listen to a message. Such exposition becomes an interpretation of what has been said earlier by the poets who, according to Socrates in Plato's *Ion* (534e), *hermenes eisin ton theon* – "are interpreters of the gods."

TEZUKA: In the passage you have in mind, Socrates carries the affinities even further by surmising that the rhapsodes are those who bear the tidings of the poets' word.

HEIDEGGER: All this makes it clear that hermeneutics means not just the interpretation but, even before it, the bearing of message and tidings.

TEZUKA: Why do you stress this original sense of *hermeneuein*?

HEIDEGGER: Because it was this original sense which prompted me to use it in defining the phenomenological thinking that opened the way to *Being and Time* for me. What mattered then, and still does, is to bring out the Being of beings – though no longer in the manner of metaphysics, but such that Being itself will shine out, Being itself – that is to say: the presence of present beings, the two-fold of the two-fold in virtue of their simple oneness. This is what makes its claim on man, calling him to its essential being ... accordingly, what prevails in and bears up the relation of human nature to the two-fold is language. Language defines the hermeneutic relation ... If man is in a hermeneutical relation, however, that means that he is precisely *not* a commodity. But the word "relation" does not want to say that man, in his very being, is in demand, is needed, that he, as the being he is, belongs within a needfulness which claims him.

TEZUKA: In what sense?

HEIDEGGER: Hermeneutically – that is to say, with respect to bringing tidings, with respect to preserving a message ... It is on purpose that the first page of *Being and Time* speaks of "raising again" a question. What is meant is not the monotonous trotting out something that is always the same: but to fetch, to gather in, to bring together what is concealed within the old.[37]

If this is true, then the *pharmakon* of Being must be *interpretation* itself, because it is not only what allows Being to come through (the remedy) but also what rejects it (the poison). Interpreting is the only act, practice, or way capable of reaching the Being of beings and allowing the Being of beings to reach us. Although Heidegger used hermeneutics to characterize the interpretative access, beyond the metaphysical, to the fundamental question of Being, it is essential to understand that this question gives itself and is given only in a *hermeneia*: the most primordial, primitive, authentic meaning of which will have to be elucidated. Further, the meaning of Being cannot be reached by hermeneutic means, but *hermeneia* is the meaning of this being that we are – humans, interpreters of logos.

As Vattimo explained in the epigraph to this chapter, the practice of *interpreting* affects (infects) everything it comes into contact with (eliminating the distinction between objectivity and subjectivity, human and scientific sciences, continental and analytical philosophy), and most of all it restores (cures) Being from the oblivion that has taken it over. Interpretation helps us to recognize how beings, the things of our experience, become "visible" to us only within a horizon that is historically determined by the language of Being, and also to recognize that this same horizon cannot be understood as a stable, eternal structure given to us once and for all, because the encounter with the truth of Being is the fact of being informed not on a given state of affairs or situation but on the edification the encounter itself provides. The hermeneutical nature of our relation to the world by no means relinquishes truth; rather, it accommodates truth in its historical context in order to organize the spectre of nihilist relativism in which philosophy finds itself today.[38] In this way, not only has hermeneutics replaced epistemology, but also analytical philosophy has recognized, through interpretation, how it stands for "no precisely formulated program." "In the very pursuit of its own tradition, explains Jean Grondin, analytical philosophy came to the recognition that it is faced with the same challenges as is transcendental hermeneutics on the Continent. Both are impelled toward a pragmatic philosophy of finitude that must take its chances and weigh its risks. That is one way of describing the dissolution of philosophical analysis, or at least its convergences with hermeneutic philosophy."[39]

Derrida's deconstruction was instrumental in finding the unnecessary "objective" polarities that constitute metaphysics, just as Tugendhat's semantical dissolution was for understanding the linguistic nature of our comprehension of the world, but neither offered a suitable answer to the question of Being. Neither offered a way to let Being itself shine out. The main reason that hermeneutics is the best *pharmakon* of ontotheology inheres in its capacity to allow us to bring out the Being of beings in "linguistically comprehensible tidings" without the illusion of overcoming metaphysics once and for all.[40] These tidings have been described as the realm of language. *Being that can be understood is language*, says Gadamer in *Truth and Method*, because only within the realm of language can we "raise again" the fundamental question of philosophy without the idea of an objectified, external Being. If forgetting the question concerning Being defines metaphysics today, a genuine hermeneutic conversation will determine an exchange that calls the interlocutor into question. This questioning will not preserve a specific understanding of Being, but rather the capacity to remain vigilant and attentive to a loss that cannot be recovered. Gadamer's hermeneutics is the philosophical position that includes the possibility of not finding Being, of failing in this search, because when investigation uncovers Being, it can also accidentally cover it. In one of his last books, *The Enigma of Health*, Gadamer showed how hermeneutics itself should be also understood as an art of healing, of recovery, where both the doctor and the patient must base the cure in a dialogue. This relationship was intended by Heidegger as the relationship between mankind and Being in order to recover Being from man's obliviousness. Philosophy becomes a process of recollection and recovery, therefore of convalescence.[41] If convalescence is the gradual return to health after an illness, then we should recognize that philosophy was, for Socrates, a matter of convalescence, a matter of finding the best pharmakon.

Rorty declared in Heidelberg that in "a future Gadamerian culture, human beings would wish only to live up to one another, in the sense in which Galileo lived up to Aristotle, Blake to Milton, Dalton to Lucretius and Nietzsche to Socrates. The relationship between predecessor and successor would be conceived, as Gianni Vattimo has emphasized, not as the power-laden relation of 'overcoming' (*Überwindung*) but as the gentler relation of turning to new 'purposes' (*Verwindung*)." With these words, he was alluding to Gadamer's and Vattimo's intentions when they said that the task of hermeneutics is to find "the word that can reach the other" and "to continue to speak of Being." Books such as Bas van Fraassen's *Empirical Stance*, Robert Brandom's *Tales of the Mighty Death*, Hilary Putnam's *Ethics without Ontology*, and Barry Allen's *Knowledge and Civilization* are examples and consequences of the Gadamerian culture of dialogue. All these books belong to our postmetaphysical culture, in which we philosophize not because we posses the absolute truth but, as Plato emphasized in the *Symposium*, because we will never posses it. Gadamer's and Vattimo's hermeneutical philosophy has not only weakened the idea of philosophy as the search of truth but also used this same weakness in order to_repudiate the claim of a universal validity: the interpretative nature of truth has dissolved the claim to truth as objectivity.

NOTES

1 G. Vattimo, "The Age of Interpretation," in Richard Rorty and Gianni Vattimo, *The Future of Religion*, edited by Santiago Zabala (New York: Columbia University Press 2005), 45.

2 Jean Grondin, *Introduction to Philosophical Hermeneutics* (New Haven, CT: Yale University Press 1994), 91. Heidegger himself remembered that "the term 'hermeneutics' was familiar to [him] from [his] theological studies. At that time, [he] was particularly agitated over the question of the relation between the word of the Holy Scripture and theological-speculative thinking. This relation, between language and Being, was the same one, if you will, only it was veiled and inaccessible to [him], so that through many deviations and false starts [he] sought in vain for a guiding thread" (M. Heidegger, *On the Way to Language* (1959), trans. Peter D. Hertz (New York: Harper & Row 1982), 9–10). On Heidegger's hermeneutics, see Richard Palmer, *Hermeneutics: Interpretation Theory in Schleiermacher, Dilthey, Heidegger, and Gadamer* (Evanston, IL: Northwestern University Press 1969); Rod Coltman, *The Language of Hermeneutics: Gadamer and Heidegger in Dialogue* (New York: State University of New York Press 1998); and Gail Stenstad, *Transformations: Thinking after Heidegger* (Madison: University of Wisconsin Press 2005).

3 For an accurate study of different ways of talking about and using Heidegger, see *Appropriating Heidegger*, ed. James E. Faulconer and Mark A. Wrathall (Cambridge: Cambridge University Press 2000); and also Michael Esfeld, "What Heidegger's *Being and Time* Tells Today's Analytic Philosophy," *Philosophical Explorations* 4 (2001): 46–62.

4 Jacques Derrida, *Dissemination* (1972), trans. B. Johnson (Chicago: University of Chicago Press 1981), 63–171.

5 On the connection between metaphysics and violence, see J. Derrida, "Violence and Metaphysics," in *Writing and Difference*, trans. Alan Bass (Chicago: Chicago University Press 1978), 79–153; and on the cultural-religious consequences of objectivism, see the great study by Abdelwahab Meddeb, *The Malady of Islam* (2002), trans. P. Joris and A. Reid (New York: Basic Books 2003).

6 I have explained the difference between *überwinden* and *verwinden* in the introduction to this book and also in my introduction to *The Future of*

Religion, by R. Rorty and G. Vattimo, ed. S. Zabala (New York: Columbia University Press, 2005).

7 On the history of Being, see Reiner Schürmann, *On Being and Acting: From Principles to Anarchy*, trans. C.-M. Gros (Bloomington: Indiana University Press 1990), and *Broken Hegemonies*, trans. R. Lilly (Bloomington: Indiana University Press 2003).

8 M. Heidegger, *Nietzsche*, vol. 3 (1961) trans. David Farrell Krell (San Francisco: Harper & Row 1991), 202.

9 Nietzsche was one of the first philosophers to discuss the problem of health in philosophy as the "sickness of spirit" that lasted two thousand years. Although he did not intend it as part of Being's oblivion but as the spirit of an age decaying in nihilism, he did understand it as something necessary and instructive for life, because, as he used to say, "what does not kill you makes you stronger." See Nietzsche, *On the Genealogy of Morals*, third essay, section 9. See also Robert D'Amico, "Spreading Disease: A Controversy concerning the Metaphysics of Disease," *History and Philosophy of the Life Sciences* 20 (1998): 143–62.

10 Meddeb, *The Malady of Islam*, shows how objective interpretations of the sacred text are always inadequate to understand the spiritual and hidden meaning of God's words. He shows that if modern Islamic fundamentalism is supposed to help us to return to a "pure Islam," then contemporary philosophical hermeneutics helps us to return to the richness and diversity of its own religious tradition. "According to the hermeneutic system of the Ismailians," explains Meddeb, "the letter of the Qur'an that is revealed to the Prophet remains a dead letter if the imam does not give it life by illuminating the secret it conceals, one that is in his authority to disclose. The fundamentalist Wahhabites' approach to Qur'anic literature is the complete opposite of the esoteric Ismailians: The former are maniacs of the apparent meaning, the latter devote a cult to the hidden meaning. Within the Islamic landscape, Wahhabism and Ismailism constitute two irreconcilable positions."

11 M. Heidegger, *On the Way to Language* (1959), trans. Peter D. Hertz (New York: Harper & Row 1982), 20.

12 M. Heidegger, *Being and Time* (1927), trans. Joan Stambaugh (New York: State University of New York Press 1996), 397.

13 J. Derrida, *Positions* (1972), trans. A. Bass (London: Continuum 2002), 9.

14 Martin Heidegger, letter to O. Pöggeler, 5 January 1973, in O. Pöggeler, *Heidegger und die Hermeneutische Philosophie* (Freiburg: Alber 1983), 395.

15 Although Heidegger never mentioned Tugendhat in his writings, it is now certain that in his essay "The End of Philosophy and the Task of Thinking," included in *On Time and Being* (1969), trans. Joan Stambaugh (Chicago: The

University of Chicago Press 2002) 70, he is referring to Tugendhat's analysis when he writes that: "to raise the question of *aletheia*, of unconcealment as such, is not the same as raising the question of truth. For this reason it was inadequate and misleading to call *aletheia* in the sense of opening, truth ... How the attempt to think a matter can at times stray from that which a decisive insight has already shown, is demonstrated by a passage from *Being and Time* (1927). To translate this word (*aletheia*) as 'truth,' and, above all, to define this expression conceptually in theoretical ways, is to cover up the meaning of what the Greeks made 'self-evidently' basic for the terminological use of aletheia as a prephilosophical way of understating it."

16 Ernst Tugendhat, *Traditional and Analytical Philosophy: Lectures on the Philosophy of Language*, trans. P.A. Gorner (Cambridge: Cambridge University Press 1982). On Tugendhat's philosophy see S. Zabala, *Tugendhat: The Hermeneutical Nature of Analytic Philosophy*, trans. Michael Haskell and S. Zabala (forthcoming).

17 Jean Grondin explains that in its defense against the charge of relativism, hermeneutics begins by recalling that, in fact, there has never been such a thing as absolute relativism. Relativism, understood ordinarily as the doctrine that all opinions on a subject are equally good, has never been advocated by anyone. For there are always *reasons*, be they contextual or pragmatic, that urge us to choose in favor of one opinion rather than another ... There is relativism only with respect to an absolute truth. But how is one to reconcile the claim to an absolute truth with the experience of human finitude, which is the point of departure for philosophical hermeneutics? According to hermeneutics, particularly that inspired by Heidegger, absolutism is left behind, linked as it is to metaphysics." J. Grondin, "Hermeneutics and Relativism," in *Festivals of Interpretation: Essays on Hans-Georg Gadamer's Work*, ed. Kathleen Wright (New York: State University of New York Press 1990), 46–7.

18 The "view from nowhere" alludes to Thomas Nagel's classic text *The View from Nowhere* (New York: Oxford University Press 1986).

19 For a Gadamerian answer to the question of whether truth exists after interpretation, see Brice R. Wachterhauser, "Introduction: Is There Truth after Interpretation?" in *Hermeneutics and Truth*, ed. Brice R. Wachterhauser (Evanston, IL: Northwestern University Press 1994), 1–24. This marvelous edited volume contains texts not only by Hans-Georg Gadamer and Ernst Tugendhat but also by R.J. Dostal, Rüdiger Bubner, David Carpenter, James Risser, Jean Grondin, Brice R. Wachterhauser, Karsten R. Stueber, Josef Simon, and Georgia Warnke.

20 Richard Rorty explained this idea in his conference at Heidelberg, the pro-

ceedings of which can now be found in a book edited by Bruce Krajewski: *Gadamer's Repercussions: Reconsidering Philosophical Hermeneutics* (University of California Press 2004), 21–9.

21 Habermas remembers that Gadamer, by becoming the "successor to Jaspers's chair, gained in public stature in West Germany and [had] an outstanding influence in his discipline. Gadamer, together with Helmuth Kuhn, made the *Philosophische Rundschau* the leading journal in the field. And Heidelberg would not have become the philosophical centre of West Germany for two or three decades had he not brought Löwith back from emigration and, with such colleagues as Henrich, Spaemann, Theunissen, and Tugendhat, gathered round himself the best of the succeeding generation as well. J. Habermas, "After Historicism Is Metaphysics Still Possible?" in *Gadamer's Repercussions: Reconsidering Philosophical Hermeneutics*, ed. Bruce Krajewski, 15–20. Berkeley: University of California Press 2004, 18.

22 Ernst Tugendhat, "The Fusion of Horizons," review in *Times Literary Supplement*, 19 May 1978, 565; also in *Philosophische Aufsätze* (Frankfurt a.M.: Suhrkamp 1992), 426–32.

23 Hans-Georg Gadamer, *Gadamer in Conversation* (New Haven, CT: Yale University Press 2001), 41.

24 Edited by Joel Weinsheimer for Yale University Press

25 Published by the University of California Press.

26 Published by SUNY Press.

27 Published by Mercer University Press.

28 Published by Melbourne University Publishing.

29 Jürgen Habermas anticipated the event in a German newspaper by saying that "this weekend when guests from all over the world rush to the celebration of lectures of Richard Rorty and Michael Theunissen, in Heidelberg, when almost the entirety of German philosophy gathers there around the master, the reasons for this are not exclusively to be found in their respect for his work, nor in the anticipated affability of a doyen in his dotage. He is, in fact, still quite capable of passing judgments with a sharp tongue. Their respect is also devoted to the person, and to his role as mediator between two generations of philosophy." Habermas, "After Historicism Is Metaphysics Still Possible?" 18–19. Since this event, a number of outstanding reviews and books have been published on Gadamer (I will list only the English ones):*Gadamer: Contemporary Philosophers*, a whole issue of *Revue Internationale de Philosophie*, no. 3 (2000) dedicated to Gadamer; A. Harrington, *Hermeneutical Dialogue and Social Science: A Critique of Gadamer and Habermas* (London: Routledge 2001); J. Malpas, U. Arnswald, and J. Kertscher, eds., *Gadamer's Century* (Cambridge, MA: MIT Press 2002); J.

Grondin, *The Philosophy of Gadamer* (Montreal: McGill-Queen's University Press 2003); L. Code, ed., *Feminist Interpretations of Hans-Georg Gadamer* (State College: Pennsylvania State University Press 2003); R.J. Dostal, ed., *The Cambridge Companion to Gadamer* (Cambridge: Cambridge University Press 2002); and recently Bruce Krajewski, ed., *Gadamer's Repercussions: Reconsidering Philosophical Hermeneutics* (Berkeley and Los Angeles: University of California Press 2004); C. Lawn, *Wittgenstein and Gadamer: Towards a Post-Analytic Philosophy of Language* (London: Continuum 2005), and P.R. Horn, *Gadamer and Wittgenstein on the Unity of Language: Reality and Discourse without Metaphysics* (London: Ashgate 2005).

30 M. Theunissen, one of the major living German philosophers, contributed to the theme of intersubjectivity from a hermeneutical point of view in various studies. Only two are available in English: *The Other: Studies in the Social Ontology of Husserl, Heidegger, Sartre, and Bubner* (Cambridge, MA: MIT Press 1986), and recently, *Kierkegaard's Concept of Despair* (Princeton, NJ: Princeton University Press 2005.)

31 M. Theunissen, "Philosophische Hermeneutik als Phänomenologie der Traditionsaneignung," in *Sein, das verstanden werden kann, ist Sprache: Hommage an Hans-Georg Gadamer* (Frankfurt: Suhrkamp 2001), 61; translation mine.

32 R. Rorty, "Being That Can Be Understood Is Language," in *Gadamer's Repercussions: Reconsidering Philosophical Hermeneutic*, ed. Bruce Krajewski (Berkeley: University of California Press 2004), 28.

33 Rorty has used this term for the first time in his essay "Analytic and Conversational Philosophy," in *A House Divided: Comparing Analytic and Continental Philosophers*, ed. Carlos Prado (Amherst, MA: Humanities Press 2003), and discusses it with Vattimo and myself in R. Rorty and G. Vattimo, *The Future of Religion*, 68.

34 Rorty, in Rorty and Vattimo, *The Future of Religion*, 68.

35 R. Rorty, interview by Danny Postel, in "The Legacy of Hans-Georg Gadamer: A 'Philosopher's Philosopher,'" *Chronicle of Higher Education*, 5 April 2002.

36 J. Kristeva, "Psychoanalysis and the Polis," in *Transforming the Hermeneutic Context: From Nietzsche to Nancy*, ed. Gayle L. Ormiston and Alan D. Schrift (New York: State University of New York Press 1990), 99. The recent publication of M. Foucault, *The Hermeneutics of the Subject: Lectures at the College de France, 1981–1982* (London: Palgrave Macmillan 2005) will be very useful for understanding the significance of hermeneutics in France, which till now has been attributed only to Paul Ricouer (1913–2005). A very interesting dialogue between Ricouer and Gadamer can be found in *The Con-*

flict of Interpretations, in R. Bruzina and B. Wilshire, eds., *Phenomenology: Dialogues and Bridges* (Albany: State University of New York Press 1982), 299–320.

37 M. Heidegger, *On the Way to Language* (1959), trans. Peter D. Hertz (New York: Harper & Row 1982), 29–36.

38 Vattimo has explained the nihilism in which philosophy finds itself in relation to ethics, politics, and law in G. Vattimo, *Nihilism and Emancipation*, ed. Santiago Zabala and trans. W. McCuaig (New York: Columbia University Press 2004).

39 J. Grondin, *Introduction to Philosophical Hermeneutics* (New Haven, CT: Yale University Press 1994), 10.

40 I agree with John D. Caputo when he says that "hermeneutics has always seemed to me a more moderate and ... even a more conservative version of deconstruction, where hermeneutics does what deconstruction likewise sets out to do but in a more radical way ... Gadamer says that hermeneutics is a way of putting one's standpoint into play (*ins Spiel*) and hence of putting it at risk (*aufs Spiel*). That brilliant formula I do not know how to improve upon. Hermeneutics is a way of escaping the circle of the selfsame, a way of breaking the forces by which we are riveted to ourselves. It is the way the different comes along and saves the same from itself" (J.D. Caputo, "In Praise of Devilish Hermeneutics," in *Thinking Difference: Critics in Conversation*, edited by Julian Wolfreys (New York: Fordham University Press 2004) 119–20).

41 James Risser has given a very accurate account of the nature of "convalesce" in philosophical hermeneutics in his contribution to this volume.

15

Gianni Vattimo; or rather, Hermeneutics as the Primacy of Politics

PAOLO FLORES D'ARCAIS
Translated by Robert T. Valgenti

In a decisive way, Gianni Vattimo has helped to make hermeneutics the hegemonic philosophy of our time, bending the Heideggerian legacy towards "the left," where the theme of the forgetting of Being and the nostalgic commitment of philosophy to its "recollection" transforms itself into Being's weakening/exhausting, into Being's dissolutive destiny; that is, into modernity equated with the "long goodbye" to Being.

But it is hardly ever pointed out how this way of thematizing Being makes the philosophy of Vattimo an *essentially* moral philosophy, or more precisely, an ethico-*political* philosophy. In fact, it is an antimeta-physical, antidogmatic and antiauthoritarian philosophy, where the theoretical purpose (antimetaphysical and antidogmatic) is nonetheless explicitly commanded by a political purpose (antiauthoritarian). The task that Vattimo assigns to philosophy is, in fact, radically political – to contribute to the emancipation of humanity. Philosophy *as* philosophy must be the instrument of *liberation*. Such a liberating and eman-cipatory vocation constitutes – also and above all – the *responsibility* of the philosopher. It constitutes a "duty," but in the sense of a *profes-sional* duty that is inherent in the *Beruf* itself – a tool of the trade that can't be given up, like the surgeon's ability to use a scalpel.

This summary description of Vattimo's philosophy (and of what philos-ophy must be, according to Vattimo) might seem a bit "forced" (it ought to be tolerable to hermeneutic philosophy, however). Actually, it is neither forced nor exaggerated; on the contrary, the declarations of Gianni[1] on this issue sound unmistakable, often decisive, even final or ultimate.

In his own words, "Philosophy, project, historicity, theorists, emancipation, for me signify the same thing."[2] His is philosophical vocation oriented towards politics,[3] nourished by "projects of radical transformation."[4] "I began my study of philosophy because I felt involved in a project of human transformation, in a program of emancipation."[5] More than a merely personal inclination, this is understood as an orientation/destiny of a whole historical epoch: "the idea of universality ... as task or project or regulative idea ... which clearly motivates all philosophical culture after Kant, I believe ought to be *rigorously* tied to a political project, and ought even to be recognized as a *political construction* in every case. This idea is not Eurocentric, even if it is the product of Europe: it bears an *objective* meaning."[6] I emphasize "objective," an unusual term in his work, and indeed a somewhat disconcerting one, since Gianni, the good hermeneutician, uses it with a parsimony greater than that of Shylock.

Conclusion: Vattimo believes that "there is *always* a political good at stake in philosophy, a question of political community,"[7] to the point of having confirmed that for him "the only philosophy, the only way to do philosophy is that which I have described," namely, "beginning ... with the political,"[8] he will end up asking himself "if Husserl's project, the origin of which was in mathematics, were really 'philosophy.'"[9]

Politics and philosophy are therefore only two articulations of the same *acting* oriented towards liberation and emancipation; but then, politics and philosophy are both *political* and constitute only two modalities of it. Of course, there is "some difference" between "politics by a philosopher" and politics "by a professional and specialized politician,"[10] but these are differences in the arms of politics, and in fact, since "the democratic intention leads rather to this [politics by a philosopher] and not to politics immediately and directly" (as "if to support democracy one must first of all produce that which we call theory, or at least ideas, cultural attitudes")[11] it follows that the philosopher-turned-politician is the *most political* choice today, because it is necessary from a democratic point of view, whereas becoming a career politician is only, politically speaking, "second best."

For the moment let us withhold judgment whether this theoretical-educative commitment is really the most necessary and efficacious form of engaging in democratic politics (and whether it really was such in 1968: for example, "when Pareyson in '68 was saying 'I am much more revolutionary than the students who are demonstrating,' I shared and understood perfectly his point of view")[12] or if privileging politics as a theoretical-educative commitment (in essays and newspapers, but also in the university and in academia) becomes inevitable only when the occupation of public life by the political "apparatus" assumes the distorted character of a pervasive monopoly. The essential fact remains that for the philosophy of Vattimo, doing philosophy is always one of the ways to do politics: "I do not think that there is a difference between what I do while teaching at the university and what I do while writing a newspaper article,"[13] or when, we can add, in coherence with such philosophical presuppositions, Gianni carries out his activity as a European deputy for five years in Strassburg.

Philosophy, therefore, is not only not a science (it can not be a science, and less than ever must it set itself to the task of becoming a science), but it is not even one of the "forms of knowledge" whose scientific status is still – following the standards of science – a disputed one (the "human sciences" *latu sensu*). "Philosophy is more of an edificatory discourse than a demonstrative discourse, it is more oriented to the edification of humanity than to the development of knowledge and to the progress of the sciences."[14] "To edify" stands both for constructing a free and equal humanity and also for inviting others and persuading them to share in such a project ("I exhort you to").[15]

But if this is the *Being* of philosophy, its vocation and responsibility, it must be able to reveal itself potentially to everyone, without ever withdrawing, through a language of initiation, into an esoteric and self-referential exercise. Also for this reason, Vattimo views every logicistic philosophy with incurable suspicion and openly declares that when faced with a page of formulas, "I jump past all of [them] and look to see the conclusion in order to know what it means to me,"[16] because philosophy must be "a discourse in everyday language,"[17] and it cannot be otherwise without betraying itself. Not by chance hermeneutics, like any other theoretical "offering," is judged according to the "consequences for the traditional problems of philosophy,"[18] that is, morality, religion, science, and art.

Gianni emphasizes, to the point of challenge, the directly political character of philosophy, nearly claiming that it "loses its soul,"[19] that is, it can never escape from "talk" about daily events and must dedicate itself to them. His, therefore, is a philosophy that does not fear, but rather demands, "deserting its post in favor of praxis" (despite the "taste of scorn" with which "such a philosopher, as morally mediocre as he is speculatively grandiose" had placed one of his students "on guard" almost eighty years ago).[20] "In every way, I did exactly this," Vattimo could respond with Günther Anders. Gianni in fact says much more: this "getting lost in praxis" is already doing philosophy, and every philosophy is always a "getting lost in praxis," because it is not yet a matter of "desertion," but rather of conforming to the most authentic vocation/responsibility of philosophy.

We have seen that this philosophy-for-emancipation is always already "a political construction in every case";[21] but, it is not for that reason arbitrary. Philosophy, according to Vattimo, must flee from every subjectivistic tendency, the "risks of irrationalism, relativism, and traditionalism,"[22] since Gianni joins the chain of rigorous argumentation with the awareness of the unavoidably personal character of all philosophizing (existence can not be repeated). Philosophical discourse must, in the end, "render explicit the arbitrary *and at the same time necessary* nature of what one says and of the ways one says it,"[23] demonstrating that the antinomy between the two demands is merely superficial.

This signifies an attitude that does not privilege the human "sciences" over the experimental sciences. In fact, by confirming that "even the 'hard' sciences ... are not pure descriptive knowledge," Vattimo underlines how "that does not in fact mean that physicists lack reason, or that science lacks an *indisputable objectivity.*"[24] Furthermore, philosophy must not only protect the "performances" of the idea of truth characteristic of modern science but also "acknowledge the experience of truth that we all have, whether it be in openly defending the validity of an affirmation or in putting forward a rational critique of the existing order (a mythical tradition, an *idolum fori*, an unjust social structure), or, above all, in correcting a false opinion and so passing from appearance to truth."[25] Philosophy, in the end, can discount and frustrate neither science nor the "objectivity" of language and of common sense.

According to Gianni, today only the hermeneutic *koiné* can meet such demanding and even reckless conditions and requirements. In fact, with more precision, it is "that philosophy developed along the Heidegger-Gadamer axis"[26] whose programmatic essence (and noble legacy, which returns to Nietzsche) is crystallized in the principle according to which there are no *true* descriptions of *facts* (or, they can't be given) but only interpretations.

After all, the hypothesis of truth as correspondence with the facts would constitute a chimera, given that "the idea of an objective description of the situation is improposable because the situation is always built upon the effects of reflection"[27] and given that anyone who says, "'I am only interested in the truth' is, in reality, making choices, and chooses this or that truth."[28] In this critique of truth not even axiomatic-deductive, tautological, a priori, or logical truth remains. "If there are eternal logical laws, I must subject myself to them, and, if I am subjected to them, I lose all that is determinant for me, and in particular the difference between me and someone who lived 2,000 years ago, or the difference between my actions from yesterday and those of tomorrow, my individual historicity and historicity in general."[29] Therefore, Gianni's "objection to the conception of truth as correspondence is not based on its inadequacy as a faithful description of the experience of truth"[30] but rather, as we know, on the moral handicap of suffocating the critical question in the "silencing authority of objective evidence,"[31] that is, of frustrating the vocation/responsibility of philosophy as antidogmatic, and thus antiauthoritarian, activity: "one cannot hold on to a conception of truth as correspondence, since this implies a conception of Being as *Grund*, as an insuperable first principle that reduces all questioning to silence."[32]

We are left, therefore, with philosophy as hermeneutics. There are no facts, only interpretations. And nevertheless, adds Vattimo, if one stops here, hermeneutics does not in fact satisfy what is required of it, and indeed constantly risks falling into the "vices" of metaphysics, into truth as the definitive and authoritative *Grund* of obedience. Hermeneutics, in fact, is "the philosophical theory of the interpretative character of every experience of truth,"[33] but "if hermeneutics were only the discovery of the *fact* that there are different perspectives on the 'world,' or on Being, the conception of truth as the objective mirroring of how things are (in this case, of the *fact* that there are multiple perspectives) would be confirmed."[34] This "evil" hermeneutics would end in the antinomy of affirming the very thing that it wants to contest and would thereby institute a new compulsory obedience. Further, such truth/cogency would then be that of a definitive relativism. And authoritarianism and relativism are two of the very shoals that Gianni calls upon philosophical navigation to avoid.

One can no longer adopt hermeneutics in its "respectful" version, corrupted by authoritarianism and relativism, but rather only in the radical and nihilistic version of Nietzsche: there are no facts, only interpretations, *and even that is only an interpretation.* "Hermeneutics is not only a theory of the historicity (horizons) of truth: it is itself a radically historical truth. It cannot think of itself metaphysically as a description of one objective structure of existence among others."[35]

Gianni is nonetheless perfectly aware of the difficulty that such a hermeneutics takes on due to its nihilistic coherence. This difficulty is summed up as follows: how is it possible to find *rigorous* arguments (arguments that do not reduce themselves to a matter of merely personal taste) that allow one to prefer this version of hermeneutics over the "respectful" hermeneutics, considering that radical/coherent hermeneutics, presenting itself as an interpretation, puts every other interpretation into play, whether it arises from incoherent hermeneutic theories or from the most diverse and rival "metaphysical" ones? And how can one close the hermeneutic circle in a virtuous way, (de)monstrating (with rigorous arguments) that for reasons of rational preferability, philosophy today must be the political theory of liberation (and not, for example, the preserving sanctification of the existing order)?

The hermeneutic line of reasoning often appears labyrinthine, but at least in the case of Vattimo, Ariadne's thread is easy to follow: truth as correspondence or as description is unattainable in reality, since it is always conditioned by a "prior opening" where such a truth is given. The truths of common sense and above all of science are objective truths, but only as *secondary* truths – only relative to an "opening." Such openings cannot, however, be intended as a merely casual and contingent juxtaposition of "culture" or of "linguistic universes" unrelated to each other. In such a case, the comparison between such "openings" would reduce itself to the brute facticity of force, to the priority of a will to power. They must, instead, belong to a "history of Being." Without it, one renounces Being and reduces it to mere being, advancing an "unintentional metaphysical presupposition"[36] and falling back into its silent authority. Such "openings" must thereby constitute the truth of Being, a truth that does not give itself as a stable *Grund* resistant to further questioning but rather a truth in the form of *event.* Hermeneutics opposes the metaphor of truth as "dwelling" to metaphysical truth as the *"possession* of truth." In this "communal dwelling" it can only offer – in order to persuade rationally, to make one prefer – the very history or in fact "fable" of modernity as the dissipation of Being and the death of truth (which is the version synonymous to the "death of God"). It is the only "fable" that successfully takes into account a world that has become a fable.

Can *this* Ariadne's thread really lead us out of the labyrinth? Can it really avoid drifting back into metaphysics, that is, can it avoid both the Scylla of authoritarian *Grund* and also the Charybdis of the mere "matter of taste ... a state of mind that remained as wholly unexplainable to oneself as to others (precisely because [it was] intractable to argument),"[37] and can it thus avoid facticity and the clash of mere power?

Let us place these questions in order. In the first place, why would it be so dramatic to renounce Being (apart from the fact that one would have to renounce *every* version of Heideggerianism, including that "of the left")? This is an *obligatory* question, since silencing the questioning means remaining ensnared by the metaphysical *Grund*. Gianni's response is that one would nevertheless have to identify the opening "with the brute factuality of a certain form of life not open to discussion, and which shows itself only in its holding as the horizon of every possible judgment."[38] In this way we would be authorized to "identify the paradigm or cultural universe into which we are thrown with the real world *tout court*"[39] and, as a result, to colonize or globalize in our image and likeness through force – according to a totalitarian logic and inclination – every diverse "cultural universe." And finally, to renounce Being means assuming the opening as a mere contingency and therefore as "a brute fact" that reduces it "inevitably to an effect of force (truth as 'will to power')."[40]

Everything falls into place: we cannot renounce Being (recognizing it, for example, as mere shorthand for the totality of beings) in the name of a moral urgency, of an ethical need to escape from the abyss of "anything goes." This is the same moral "necessity," one notes, that Dostoevsky (using the name of "God," rather than "Being") valued, in anticipation, *against* Nietzsche and nihilism.

Since we cannot renounce Being, the openings cannot be mere conditions or paradigms or horizons within which "each confirmation or falsification of a proposition can occur,"[41] but each must in its turn be the "truth." Inescapably if one is not to be overwhelmed by the brute facticity of the will to power, "the truth of the opening – Gianni quickly specifies – can, it seems, only be thought on the basis of the metaphor of dwelling,"[42] since it must not in any way replicate or substitute truth as *Grund*.

Gianni means three things primarily: the "voices" of this dwelling together ((*co*)*abitazione*) "speak with an irreducible multiplicity,"[43] their dwelling together occurs "in a landscape bearing the marks of a tradition,"[44] and the condition of each one finding itself "always already thrown into a project, into a language, a culture, that it *inherits*"[45] implies not just the mere belonging to a tradition, but rather an "active inheritance of the past."[46] In conclusion,"Thrownness in a historical opening is always inseparable from an active participation in its constitution, its creative interpretation and transformation,"[47] of the sort that "dwelling implies, rather, an interpretative belonging which involves both consensus and the possibility of critical activity."[48]

Vattimo points out that "as a metaphor for speaking of hermeneutic truth, dwelling might best be understood as though one were dwelling in a library,"[49] but that is an idyllic presupposition, hardly compatible with any interpretation of the human condition. The human, or too human or inhuman, dwelling together among an "irreducible multiplicity of voices" does not unfold, or if ever extremely rarely, in the form of a civil conversation between readers of good books, in the welcoming atmosphere of an English club. The truth of "openings," that is, of the "irreducible multiplicity of cultural universes,"[50] constitutes itself – primarily and especially! – in a dwelling together that is conflict, hostility, war, *mors tua vita mea*. The "irreducible multiplicity," which Gianni rightly assumes to be strictly lacking in presuppositions, then happens to be surreptitiously exchanged by Gianni for a "harmonious" and eventually reconcilable multiplicity within the scope of a well-working democratic coexistence. But without this petition of principle, a *wishful thinking* analogous to that of Habermas (one that "deduces" democracy from communicative action, even though this communicative action occurs and gives itself only in democratic conditions), we slip once more into the brute facticity where the arbitrator of the relations of force takes the place of truth – the very abyss from which the coherent-nihilistic hermeneutics of Vattimo promised to save us.

Gianni shows that he is well aware, however indirectly, of this *impasse*. He recognizes, in fact, that hermeneutics "is unable to describe 'original' truth in terms of dwelling without recourse to a further metaphor rooted deeply in the metaphysical tradition; namely that of 'community,' or even, in Hegel's terms, the 'beautiful ethical life,'"[51] a "passage" that "in the hermeneutic conception of truth ... is comprehensively liquidated"[52] and could not be otherwise. How can he get out of this? Is the recourse to the *common tradition* that constitutes the "landscape" in which existence is thrown enough?

"The reasons for preferring a hermeneutic conception of truth to a

metaphysical one," Vattimo maintains, "lie in the historical inheritance[53] of which we venture an interpretation and to which we give a
response."[54] But can this inheritance really *bring a community together*
in a way that makes a "guiding thread for interpretations, choices, and
even moral options"[55] "possible," one that makes the irrational hypothesis of the fight to the death among ugly wills to power a thing of the
past? Hitler, Göhring, Göbbels, and the other giants of "radical evil"
shared a similar "landscape" with pastor Dietrich Bönhoffer, one
marked by Luther, Goethe, Beethoven ... ; yet, this did not give rise to
any "integration"[56] in a common "interpretative belonging."[57] "Dwelling," for the giants of the swastika and all their followers, signifies
above all *destroying* (through the "dialogue" of the cremation ovens)
every "diverse thing" in itself: for "race," political conviction, moral
resistance, or mere survival of "humanity." And further, isn't it historically true that the most divisive and ferocious conflicts are the civil wars
born from the interpretative controversy over a shared tradition of
faith?

The recourse to "inheritance" does not resolve the problem of
Vattimo (and of hermeneutics), because no inheritance exists that isn't
in its crucial aspects a *choice*. Tradition (*tra-dizione*: literally, to pronounce the origins) is always and essentially a choice among options
(*tra-scegliere*: literally, to choose the origins) within that chaotic and
contradictory *accumulation* constituted by the past, by the totality of
past events – that one *decides* to consider essential for one's own identity. And further, even if in such an accumulation everyone were to
decide to "reconfigure" an inheritance comprised of the same events, of
the same "classics" and cultural messages, of the same word-values, the
diverse interpretations of it (the translation (*tra-durre*) and the betrayal
(*tra-dire*) that would unavoidably constitute such a legacy) would never
guarantee an integration in a peaceful "interpretative belonging" in
respect to the threat of an irreconcilable struggle to the death.

In conclusion, as René Char (one of the poets most loved by Heidegger) wrote, "notre heritage n'est precede d'aucun testament":[58] for
something essential, we are the ones to write it down. For something
crucial (even if it were infinitesimal, but *crucial*, since it makes our existence an *unrepeatable* event), such an inheritance is not something
received but, rather, something *decided upon*. As Europeans, are we
really *brought together* by an inheritance that understands the Old Testament and the Greeks and the "good word" of Jesus and two thousand

years of "authentic" interpretation according to the apostolic tradition of the Holy Roman Church and the arrows of Voltaire against the "disgrace" and the spur from Königsberg who summons us to *sapere aude*"? Furthermore (and what is more alarming), are we brought together by the past events that have "produced" Europe and the Europeans? Do they not include the democracy that sentenced the philosopher to death by hemlock, and the holocaust of the Albigenses, and the "auto da fè" of the Inquisition (immediately duplicated by the "heretics" who came to power: Lutherans, Calvinists ...) and the night of Saint Bartholomew (the horror of the Twin Towers pales in comparison), right up to the millions of unrepeatable existences *annihilated* at Auschwitz? And which Jesus do we inherit, the Christ of the Crusades or the evangelical healer who "turns the other cheek"? And why not Odin, or Gilgamesh rather than Abraham?

It is not enough to recognize that thrownness "is always inseparable from an active participation in its constitution, its creative interpretation and transformation,"[59] unless one recognizes that this "*active inheritance of the past*"[60] is a *decision for it* that can give rise not only to the co-existence of hermeneutic antinomies in the inexhaustible dialogue of dialogical argumentation but (much more often, above all) to the *throat-slitting* within the mortally violent struggles of historical-existential conflicts. And so the hermeneutic logic hypothesized by Gianni as "proposals to interpret our common situation according to a certain line and originating from shared presuppositions"[61] is only an irenic limit of the situation ("do you want to pay attention to the experience I had while reading Nietzsche, Marx, Freud, etc. as if you could still ask this.")[62] because in the name of Marx, like that of Jesus and of almost all the traditions and legacies that articulate the "epochs" of history, one slaughtered (and still slaughters) at will.

To Vattimo, the problem of *arbitrariness* tied to thrownness does not in fact go away. He believes, however, that he can take leave of it, affirming that "this gathering," that is, thrownness, does not become a "background" by its "purely confusing and yet arbitrary nature," because it constitutes a "response ... to a call that comes from the *Über-lieferung*."[63] But we have seen that this very provenance, namely inheritance, is not handed down but rather *decided upon* (in a way that is perhaps infinitesimal but *decisive*), so that this coming cannot come-to-us but is assigned to the past *by us*. Our response therefore is a response only to our decision about our provenance. We respond to ourselves.

On the other hand, what we really and in *strictu sensu* inherit as a mere *assignment* without any "active" element, our being-thrown in the most brute and "unexplainable" (and therefore irrational) contingency, is even more pervasive than Vattimo says: we "passively" inherit DNA, the time and place in which we live, health or illness, our parents' language, economic conditions, our childhood friends, and, in the end, everything that was our infancy. However, the meaning, the depth and the surface of the Heideggerian discovery of "thrownness" would become something less if it were not – once and for all – a mere contingency, that is, a "brute fact." On the contrary, thrownness would in fact disappear in the constellation of the providentiality/necessity, in either Christian or Spinozian or Hegelian variations.

The "truth" of every "prior opening, not transcendental but inherited" that, alone, accompanies "every confirmation or falsification,"[64] namely, the occurrence of "secondary truths," does not therefore escape contingency. Nor does it escape the crucial (residue of an) ugly collision between wills to power, armoured against every critical urgency. At this point, in order to avoid collapse and "to prove" instead the very ability to avoid both a metaphysical *Grund* and also an irrationalistic, relativistic, traditionalistic demise, hermeneutics follows the path of the consummate poker player: it raises the stakes. It declares that even the thrownnesses/openings of the diverse cultural universes constitute *events in the history of Being.* The truth of Being presents itself only historically, but history is always and reciprocally the history of the truth of Being: not, however, a mere succession and stringing together of events, radically contingent events (every thing would be able to occur or not occur differently). This unity or continuity that *is* history (otherwise it would not be the history of *Being*) "is not the history of a necessity," Vattimo is careful to remember; in fact, "it is the event that teaches how to defend against dogmatism, and against that which is presented as necessity."[65] But hermeneutics does not consider the diachronic stage on which *Homo sapiens sapiens* has been performing to be "a tale told by an idiot, full of sound and fury, signifying nothing."[66] On the contrary, history is equal to the "acknowledgement of a course of events in which we are implicated and that we do not describe objectively, but interpret speculatively."[67] A meaning and a telos should be decipherable (interpretable) in the intricacies of the mere chaos of the *succession of events*, given that "to recognize this giving as an event ... means to find in the multiplicity of voices in which the a priori is dissolved not only an anarchic confusion, but the call of a *Ge-schick*, of a destiny."[68] "Destiny" is the telling term that is repeated and confirmed: "The unfounding horizon within which ... particular truths ... acquire their authentic truth, that is come to be 'founded,' would be neither the historically determined paradigm ... nor merely the disordered multiplicity of paradigms ... nor a harmonious integration into a canon ... nor the pure relativist-historicist detachment" but rather "one gets back to truth as opening by taking the unfoundation as destiny."[69]

That this decipherable telos is not an "objective description" but a "risky interpretation" implies that *everyone* is entitled to "take a risk" as to what the history of Being *means* (or "where it will go"). There will be, accordingly, multiple and conflicting histories of Being (all of them equally dangerous). No single history will be "preferable" to the other (and less than ever, *rigorously* so) without returning to *a* shared criterion that is able to judge them all. Such a criterion would construct, inevitably, a metaphysical truth. Hermeneutically, for that reason, multiple criteria will exist (meta-interpretations) that all have equal authority. How is it possible, then, to escape this "anarchic confusion," since not only are the a priori dissolved in a multiplicity of voices, but so is the famous call/provenance/destiny. A multiplicity of calls/destinies will exist, even of opposed meanings (to the point of a self-exclusion that implicates the "fight to the death") that include the rejection – as mere illusion or wishful thinking – of any call/destiny.

One cannot escape this dilemma: either there exists a criterion by which to choose one interpretation over another, one that avoids the anarchic confusion but supplies a criterion that is (metaphysical) truth and not interpretation, or this criterion does not exist, and consequently everything is really interpretation (including this affirmation) but unavoidably (in its turn a truth, above all!) there is anarchic confusion (which closes the discussion on preference, and entrusts it to the contingent facticity of the battle among wills to power).

If, on the other hand, there is "destiny," any escape from a Hegelian sort of necessity seems impossible, no matter how one adjusts it. This is surely not the necessity of Marx, that is, of an end to history in the communist future of the definite reconciliation between the individual and the human race. Rather, it is that of the "authenticity" of an interpretation, that is, of *a* "listening to Being" against the other "inauthentic" and debased ones. Without this authenticity, it is impossible for it to differentiate itself with any certainty from "history" as labyrinthine and insensate entanglings of an "aggregate" and of the contingent display of "that which happens" and could not have happened or could have happened in another way.

For hermeneutics, the situation presents itself as a Siberian dilemma.[70] In one way or another, it is forced to bring about its own dissolution. If all the "openings" were hermeneutically coherent, in fact, a coherent hermeneutics would not be an interpretation but *the* truth. It must therefore recognize the alternation of metaphysical "openings" and of hermeneutical "openings" (incoherent and coherent). But even this alternation, then, would no longer be an interpretation but rather a corresponding description (if it were not a corresponding description it would weaken the metaphysical "openings" and fall again to the first hypothesis: even it would be self-dissolving, as we have seen).

At this point Gianni reveals his final and decisive card: "the 'proof' that hermeneutics offers of its own theory" is only and exclusively "a history ... perhaps also in the sense of 'fable' or myth, in that it presents itself as an interpretation (whose claim to validity is such as will even present itself as a competing interpretation that belies it),"[71] the hermeneutic-nihilistic interpretation of modernity. "Hermeneutics ... is legitimated as a narrative of modernity, that is, of its own provenance; and moreover it is also, indeed above all, a narrative of the meaning of Being."[72] It must deal, therefore, not just with any interpretation but with the "most pervasive philosophical interpretation of a situation or 'epoch,' and thereby, necessarily, of a provenance"[73] able to single out much more than just "chance points of convergence."[74] Beginning from the "beautiful fable" of modernity, "hermeneutics presents itself as a philosophy of modernity (in both subjective and objective senses of the genitive) and even professes to be *the* philosophy of modernity; its truth may be wholly summed up in the claim to be the most pervasive philosophical interpretation of that course of events of which it feels itself to be the outcome."[75]

But is all of that really *more persuasive*? There are competing interpretations galore, ones that will even "belie" Vattimo's, depending on what hermeneutics means and allows by "belie." Can a "fable," in fact, prove another fable wrong? There are innumerable "fables" of modernity; this is certain. But no fable can prove another one wrong: they all co-exist in the limbo of a common undecidability, unless there is a criterion given from a higher level, from all of these "fables" recognized as binding and cogent, on the basis of which to decide when one "belies" the other and when it does not. This is something similar in function to the abhorred metaphysical criterion of "truth," in the absence of which, only the naked decision remains, the "matter of taste ... a state of mind that remained as wholly inexplicable to oneself as to others (precisely because intractable to argument)."[76]

Vattimo presents hermeneutics as *the* philosophy of modernity, as the only one able to view "logically" the nihilistic outcome of the history of Being. But such a modernity is already only that one *presupposed* by hermeneutics (against all the other possible alternative interpretations): modernity as the occurrence of nihilism. And nevertheless, before ever having prejudged the preferability of Vattimo's "fable" about modernity over that of Max Weber or of Karol Wojtyla or of Gyorgi Lukacs,[77] only a succession of events appears before our interpretation. Some of these will become a part of our own interpretations, obviously. But only by presupposing modernity as the occurrence of nihilism does this interpretation become more persuasive than that of modernity as an unbridgeable gap or as the totalitarian aberration of the Enlightenment. In the end, the "truth" or greater persuasiveness of hermeneutic interpretation reduces itself to the claim: "I will tell the fable in this way!"

Not by chance, Gianni plays it safe: "The *Ge-schick* retains something of metaphysical *Grund* and its capacity for legitimization."[78] Not something, but rather many things. And at second glance, everything. For only the interpretation of modernity that gives rise to the *Ge-schick* supports the possibility of escaping from the anarchic confusion: thus, such an interpretation is a *foundation*. Nor is it enough to say that such a *Grund* gives itself "only in the paradoxical, nihilistic form of a vocation for dissipation that cannot, precisely for this reason, present itself as compelling in the metaphysical sense."[79] It cannot, but it pretends to perform the *identical* function. Such a *Grund*, then, constitutes not only "a possible rationality for thought, a possible 'truth of the opening,'"[80] but also the only one allowed. Every other alternative interpretation, by lessening the *Ge-schick*, would kill the reasons behind it.

It should be emphasized that this Being, which not only constitutes a *destiny* but even possesses a *vocation*,[81] exhibits more and more the characteristics of a *Person*. It is therefore a hypostasis, technically speaking, a functional surrogate for God. But it is "more" functional and more dangerous than those religious ones and traditional philosophical surrogates, metaphysical or dialectical. Throwness is in fact mere contingency. If one, however, were to hypothesize that the "opening," namely, every historical-cultural condition, every contingency and every thrownness (including the unrepeatable thrownness that each one of us is), were a question of truth, it would be able to represent its own finite existence – and relative "point of view" – with the venerable term of "truth" (of Being). It would be a nonreligious and nonmetaphysical *Gott mit Uns*, but from the most efficacious *hybris*, because it would be immune to all the critics who have "destroyed" those ancient traditions. The only really radical solution to preventing the will to power from becoming authorized to cover itself in the truth of Being is not to *weaken* the truth (or Being) but to refuse to accept that the "openings of truth" can in turn be considered "truth": there are only contingent circumstances, historical-cultural horizons, to which one cannot apply a standard of true or false.

Furthermore, why not renounce Being definitively, avoiding all the unavoidable "complications"[82] that bind us, rather than reaffirming it as necessary in order to then weaken it (precisely in order to flee away from those "complications," seeing that "at the end of this history Being is given as that which *is not*")?[83] Gianni has even hypothesized: "Is speaking about the history of Being merely ornamental, is it something superfluous? Perhaps it is not enough and sufficient to talk about history, about the history of science, and about the transformation of knowledges?"[84] Why not omit the first question mark and render the second question rhetorical?

Therefore, one can leave this impasse behind only with a radical and ascetic *renunciation of Being*, leading the term truth (whose common use one will not renounce, however) back to its sober and limited use as an indicator for the grade-one verification (ac-*certo*-amento) characteristic of an epoch (an "opening"): the affirmations of experimental science and the testimonies of common sense (but only those "beyond every reasonable doubt" of historical philology – in the end, only the *humble factual truths* in the Arendtian sense of the term).

We know, however, that hermeneutics insisted on *Being* in the fear that all reality would otherwise be reduced to beings, that is, to the modality of "mere presence." But experimental science does not in fact make claim to "the appropriation of a certain content via an adequate representation,"[85] if by *content* one means the totality of what an "object" is; it claims only to describe some constants as verifiable (true). Newton's apple does not in fact claim to exhaust the "totality" or the "reality" of the apple. $F = G \, Mm/r^2$ does not in fact negate the reality of Adam's apple, the apple of Cezanne, the apple of Snow White, the apple of Escoffier (or of the recipes of the grandmother), the apple of the Macintosh I am using to write this essay, and all the other (inexhaustible) interpretations and other meanings that constitute (and will constitute) the Being of the apple (or of the famous "pitcher" of Heidegger). Simply, the verifiability of $F=G \ Mm/r^2$ is intersubjectively cogent in radically diverse ways with respect to the interpretative conflicts that may arise concerning the apple of Adam or of Snow White (or concerning the choice of the first value of ethics: the *thou* of the individual-in-solidarity or the *we* of the group-destined-by-god-or-by-Being). $F=G \ Mm/r^2$ constitutes the first degree, and the choice of the first and un-groundable ethical value constitutes the zero degree of intersubjectively cogent verifiability. I will call the first "truth" and the second "decision."

That does not mean that Adam's apple (and the others) is not a reality (a reality of religion, in fact); it is just not verifiable according to the intersubjectively cogent categories of true/false. Nor does it mean even that it is a reality of "inferior rank"; this is not the logic of science or even of some metaphysics (perhaps scientistic but always metaphysical, namely, unrelated to science). However, for the *scientist* Pascal, the *wager* on salvation was infinitely more important than the verified truth about "Le vide, l'équilibre des liquers et la pensateur de l'air." In the end and simply, the physico-chemico-biologically verifiable characteristics of objects are not "thrown" – they have always been (in that relative *always* that covers, however, many billions and billions and billions of times the temporality of the human species), even though they constitute but one side of such objects, never exhausting the "Being" of them.

And so precisely in order to have "enhanced the critical function of truth,"[86] hermeneutics must proceed beyond and outside hermeneutics, definitively renouncing Being and the truth of its openings. The critical conception of the idea of truth as inexhaustible integration, which Gianni wants to save, must push hermeneutics to overcome the antinomies that have ensnared the notion of Being (however weakened), in a direction that we will be able to identify as "empirical-existential (or existential empirical) disenchantment."

Such antinomies hold on to the very omni-interpretative character of the real. Vattimo has brought that to light perfectly for nonradical-nihilistic hermeneutics, but, we have seen, it does not save his "Nietzschean" version of hermeneutics ("there are no facts, only interpretations, and even that is an interpretation"). In order to make it really preferable, in fact, Gianni must admit that "hermeneutics can defend its theoretical validity only to the precise degree that the interpretative reconstruction of history is a rational activity."[87] It must, that is, return to Hegelianism (even in a rectified version), namely to some version (even if it is masked or surreptitious) of necessity. Or if he really does hold on to the rejection of every metaphysics (and of that totalizing hybris of metaphysics that is Hegelian dialectic – and its variants), then he ought to support a beyond (outside)-hermeneutics in the form of a philosophy of finitude, where the word truth is valuable for the practices of validation-one that is experimental science and historical philology – and the openings are recognized no longer as universes of truth (of Being) but rather as normative universes (of must-being) brought about according to contingency.

If Gianni refuses this final step (in my view implied by his logic and in the presuppositions chosen by him – and discussed at the beginning), it is perhaps because he does not want to reject a *strong* hope (of salvation). He has nonetheless claimed that "the only emancipation I can think about is an eternal life in charity,"[88] that is, not of this world. He wants to hold on to co-existence as "an act of interpretation that is confirmed in dialogue with other possible interpretations,"[89] instead of accepting an absolutely ir-rational prime element (even if it is infinitesimal) because it is absolutely protected against the possible dia-logue of argumentation: the aut-aut between the *thou* of the individual-in-solidarity and the *we* of the group-destined-by-god (and the fight-to-death always waiting in ambush). He wants the hope of salvation to be something more than our wager/commitment, if not inscribed dialectically in history, at least standing as the *rigorously preferable* response to the sending (even if it is not cogent) of Being.

But the arbitrariness of this first choice is, on the contrary, unavoidable. That is because hermeneutics, if it doesn't go beyond and outside itself, risks becoming the last temptation of metaphysics.

NOTES

1 I realized at the end of this piece that I often referred to Vattimo using his baptismal name (Gianni) instead of his last name. While this occurred without any deliberate intention, it is possible that the choice of his first name, which is more confidential and intimate, reveals the moment when I decided, rather than reconstruct (or de-construct) his thought, I would like to "persuade" him.

2 Gianni Vattimo, *Vocazione e responsabilità del filosofo* (Genoa: Il Melangolo 2000), 116. Other works by Gianni are perhaps more important, but these are the only ones where his philosophy is set forth in a complete and an organic way. Furthermore, analogous or even identical citations can be found in all his works.

3 *Vocazione e responsabilità*, 117.

4 Ibid., 118.

5 Ibid., 114.

6 Ibid., 124 (my italics).

7 Ibid., 113 (my italics).

8 Ibid., 121.

9 Ibid.

10 Ibid., 117.

11 Ibid.

12 Ibid., 118.

13 Ibid., 109.

14 Ibid., 64.

15 Ibid., 74.

16 Ibid., 87.

17 Ibid., 88.

18 Gianni Vattimo, *Beyond Interpretation*, translated by David Webb (Stanford: Stanford University Press 1997), 11.

19 *Vocazione e responsabilità*, 119.

20 Cf. Günther Anders, *L'uomo è antiquato*, vol. 2, 6.

21 *Vocazione e responsabilità*, 124.

22 *Beyond Interpretation*, 78.

23 *Vocazione e responsabilità*, 112 (my italics).

24 Ibid., 82 (my italics).

25 *Beyond Interpretation*, 75.

26 Ibid., 2.

27 *Vocazione e responsabilità*, 101.

28 Ibid., 105.

29 Ibid., 90–91.

30 *Beyond Interpretation*, 76.

31 Ibid., 89.

32 Ibid., 76.

33 Ibid., 7.

34 Ibid., 8.

35 Ibid., 6.

36 Ibid., 12.

37 Ibid., 8.

38 Ibid., 87.
39 Ibid., 84.
40 Ibid., 85.
41 Ibid., 14.
42 Ibid., 81–2.
43 Ibid., 90.
44 Ibid.
45 Ibid., 91.
46 Ibid., 90.
47 Ibid., 83.
48 Ibid., 82.
49 Ibid.
50 Ibid., 91.
51 Ibid., 83 (with an explicit appeal to Habermas!).
52 Ibid., 84.
53 Translator's note: I have, for the sake of consistency, replaced the word "legacy" with "inheritance," which is how David Webb translates "eredità" in the remainder of *Beyond Interpretation*.
54 *Beyond Interpretation*, 6.
55 Ibid., 94.
56 Ibid., 84.
57 Ibid., 82.
58 *Oeuvres completes* (Parigi: Gallimard-Pléiade 1983) 190: "Fueillets d'Hypnos," n62.
59 *Beyond Interpretation*, 83.
60 Ibid., 113 (my italics).
61 *Vocazione e responsabilità*, 71.
62 Ibid., 72.
63 *Beyond Interpretation*, 92.
64 Ibid., 14.
65 *Vocazione e responsabilità*, 96.
66 Shakespeare, *Macbeth*, 5, 5, 26–8.
67 *Beyond Interpretation*, 6–7.
68 Ibid., 92.
69 Ibid., 93–94.
70 Russian soldiers call the following situation a Siberian dilemma: in the event that the ice breaks and you fall into the icy waters, you die if you are not pulled out within four minutes; but, if they do pull you out in time, the freezing air will kill you in two minutes.
71 Ibid., 9.

72 Ibid., 12.

73 Ibid., 10.

74 Ibid.

75 Ibid., 10–11.

76 Ibid., 8.

77 Or of Marcel Gauchet ("Il Disincanto del Mondo" [Turin: Einaudi 1992]). I have sketched out an interpretation of modernity as ejection in my l disincanto tradito, *MicroMega* 2 (1986) and also in the volume, Bollati Boringhieri, (Turin 1994).

78 *Beyond Interpretation*, 92.

79 Ibid.

80 Ibid.

81 Ibid., 93.

82 Ibid., 82.

83 Ibid., 93.

84 *Vocazione e responsabilità*, 95–6.

85 *Beyond Interpretation*, 85.

86 Ibid., 94.

87 Ibid., 107.

88 *Vocazione e responsabilità*, 103.

89 *Beyond Interpretation*, 137.

PART THREE
Weakening Metaphysical Beliefs

16

Weakening Religious Belief:
Vattimo, Rorty, and
the Holism of the Mental

NANCY K. FRANKENBERRY

I believe that I believe.
>   Gianni Vattimo

We believe without belief, beyond belief.
>   Wallace Stevens

Notwithstanding Lyotard's characterization of postmodernity's incredulity toward grand metanarratives, the most interesting and provocative philosophy in our time is that being painted with meta broad brushes. When distinguished philosophers fashion overarching narratives, they help us hold things together in a synoptic vision; by painting forests for us, they make those of us who read too many books able at least to see more than just the trees. Gianni Vattimo and Richard Rorty, metanarrators both, and two of the most original philosophers writing today, invite comparison of their overlapping but distinct narratives on religion and secularization, which I will undertake in the first parts of this essay. In the last part, I will consider how to adapt certain tenets of semantic holism – particularly as developed by Donald Davidson – to fill the lacunae that exist in both Vattimo's and Rorty's treatments of "the return of religion."

Vattimo's narrative pivots on Philippians 2:6–8, the New Testament text that announces the *kenosis*, or self-emptying, of the preexistent divine Christ into a human being in the form of a servant.[1] Becoming incarnate, the divine gave up sovereign dominion and embraced weakness, humility, and vulnerability. The story of the incarnation of the Son of God represented the thorough and complete emptying of God the Father. In this radical account of the Christian God's self-weakening and self-exhaustion, Vattimo sees a parallel and a template for the "weakening of Being" that was to occur throughout the modern history of philosophy. By now the ontotheological tradition has yielded to the loss of all absolutes, first causes, and metaphysical foundations. Metaphysics has been dissolved and replaced by hermeneutics, already prepared for in the Reformation and the religious wars of sixteenth- and seventeenth-century Europe. These events broke the controlled interpretation of scriptures by ecclesiastical authorities and made possible a plurality of conflicting readings of one and the same texts. Self-emptying is at work in hermeneutics, Vattimo says, as its "nihilistic vocation."[2]

Ours is a time oddly marked both by a worldwide resurgence of religion and a philosophical postmodernism that abolishes all fundamentalisms. The latter condition much more than the former inspires Vattimo's reimagining of Christianity. His story casts together Nietzsche's "death of God," Heidegger's "end of metaphysics," postcolonialism, and the relativization of Christianity. *Pensiero debole*, the illuminating trope for Vattimo's narrative, signals the progressive weakening of philosophy's absolutist claims and foundationalist ambitions. The story of philosophy's weakening is at the same time a story of Christianity's coming to fulfillment in the very process of secularization. Vattimo's narrative is distinctive for asserting a causal relationship between the Christian message of kenosis, on the one hand, and philosophical antifoundationalism, antiessentialism, and the collapse of capital-T Truth, on the other hand. By reading the history of philosophy from a religious perspective, rather than reading the history of Christianity through a philosophical lens, Vattimo is able to see love – charity, *caritas* – as the point of convergence between philosophy's downward path and the historical transmission of Christianity. As the message of the Christian gospel empties into philosophical nihilism, it finds its precise fulfillment and destiny.

Vattimo's narrative is a story that begins with a presentation of secularization as the fulfillment of the central Christian message, thus preparing for a reappropriation of Christianity. Following Nietzsche, it is a story of the death of God as the death of the "moral God," leaving room for the emergence of new gods. It encompasses such postmodern conditions as fragmentation, anti-Eurocentrism, and postcolonialism and argues that these can be understood in light of Joachim of Fiore's thesis of the Spiritual Age of history. Now that "all is interpretation," there are no absolute or hard and fast objectivist truths. We can recognize "weak thought" in our time as opposed to the "strong" foundationalist claims of metaphysics in previous times. Yet weak thought is not to be understood as a truth somehow objectively real apart from its own hermeneutical transmission, or it would become a kind of metaphysics.

As the main elements of Vattimo's account unfold from his *Beyond Interpretation* and *The End of Modernity* to his recent works *Belief* and *After Christianity*, a striking thesis becomes clear. We are to read Heidegger's own narrative about the history of being as a history of weakening in which being itself gives itself as event in much the same way Christianity describes the kenosis of God's incarnation in history – a total dissolution of transcendence into the world. The history of being is portrayed as the history of nihilism, and reality becomes the history of the dissolution of the real as sheer objectivity. In short, it is the history of secularization understood as an essential part of the history of salvation. This is a story of loss but also of gain, just as the weakening of the strong structures that attempted to establish absolute truth or incorrigible foundations is a profound breakthrough in what amounts to *Heilgeschichte*. Being is an event, and the God who is being itself is the event of self-abandonment.

Our postmodern condition, therefore, enacts an exact replication of the dissolution that is at the heart of the Christian message: claims to objective truth or metaphysical grounds or natural law have all alike been dissolved, eroded, ended. Christianity's historical importance was to have supplied the starting point of this dissolution, which ends in secularization processes that form the point of departure for contemporary thought. Rather than adopt any of the contested meanings of "secularism" in the current debates, Vattimo creates a new meaning for the term, one that posits self-abandonment and self-emptying as the very direction of Western thought. "Weak thought" can now be seen as the philosophical fulfillment of 2 Corinthians 12:9: "for power is made perfect in weakness." Philippians 2:6–8 finds its issue in 1 Corinthians 13: "And now these three remain: faith, hope and love. But the greatest of these is love."

The central figures who propel Vattimo's narrative are Nietzsche and Heidegger. When Nietzsche announced the Death of God, it was with reference to the death of Christ on the cross in the biblical narrative.[3]

The joyful nihilism that follows from this good news constitutes all the truth there is of Christianity.[4] When Heidegger announced the End of Metaphysics, he heralded the culmination of "the ontology of weakening" that is first revealed in the Incarnation. If the history of Western civilization can be told as a history of the progressive "weakening of Being," it is because both the End of Metaphysics and the Death of God are in fact philosophical expressions of "the development and maturation of the Christian message" itself.[5] In its most radical core, according to Vattimo, Christianity is a catalyst of secularization, and nihilism a product of it. This nihilism that fulfills the Christian tradition is a positive and optimistic one, not the loss of all meaning but its redistribution pluralistically across many perspectives. Intensely rethinking the relationship of Christianity and nihilism, Vattimo distances himself from the Hegelian scheme of *Überwindung*, or dialectical overcoming, in which a new absolute overcomes and replaces an old absolute. He opts instead for the Heideggerian *Verwindung*, or a patient coming to grips with. This is the style best suited for comprehending our times. Vattimo's cheerful nihilism thus joins with Rorty's genial pragmatism, both denying things few philosophers any longer want to assert, thanks, in large part, to their work in eroding essentialism about human nature, foundationalism about knowledge, and simple entities that serve as the source or guarantors of thought and capital-T Truth.

Now that philosophy is properly weakened, Vattimo continues, the main rationalist bases for atheism have been swept away. Positivism and Marxist historicism have crumbled under the weight of their own too-strong claims, and, with them, the belief in science as the exclusive citadel of truth or history as the path of progress toward emancipation.[6] Anti-foundationalism has won the day in epistemology, ontology, and ethics. The end of metaphysics is the end of the ontotheological tradition's staging ground for the thought of divinity. Saturated with the joyful nihilism of Nietzsche and stirred by the end of metaphysics heralded by Heidegger, Vattimo can renounce doctrinal authority, papal encyclicals, and church discipline as thoroughly as he disposes of philosophical foundationalism and ontotheology. They are of a piece. Paradoxically, in such a time a space is opened for a new experience of the Christian religion as love and gift. The climax of Vattimo's narrative, encapsulated in his essay "The Age of Interpretation," can be expressed by saying "postmodern nihilism constitutes the actual truth of Christianity."[7]

More radically than those who trace the origins of modern historical consciousness to the influence of Christian eschatology, Vattimo sees the *terminus ad quem* of modernity and of Western philosophy itself in Christian love. The meaning of this love is nothing less than "the reduction of violence, the weakening of strong identities, the acceptance of the other, to the point of charity."[8] The "return of religion" at the end of metaphysics can now be greeted as a creative event (*Ereignis*) of being. If secularization is a continuation of Christianity, rather than its overcoming, then "the main philosophical outcome of the death of the metaphysical God and of the almost general discreditation of philosophical foundationalism is the renewed possibility of religious experience."[9] We may think of ourselves as living in Joachim of Fiore's third age of the Spirit, which has superceded that of the Father and the Son.[10] The fragility of life in the Spirit comes to expression in the postmodern condition of fragmentation, postcolonialism, and anti-Eurocentrism.

What one easily appreciates about Vattimo's version of Christianity, "after Christianity," is its expansive and affirmative quality. No nostalgia for old myths mars Vattimo's narrative, as it haunts Heidegger's. He does not weep for lost absolutes. He resists the seductions of the mystical turn and recognizes the authoritarian snares inherent in Levinas's *tout autre*. Divested of metaphysics, the God of Power morphs more pleasantly into the law of Love. De-hellenized, Vattimo's Christianity looks almost attractive, a gentler, kinder practice, a matter of love and friendship rather than of metaphysical beliefs or violence. Gone are the powers and the principalities, the angels and the demons, virgin birth, creation, fall, heaven and hell. Gone are the mythical originating causes and final ends. All causes and all ends are now found within the many mansions of this world. This is rightly, as Santiago Zabala says, "a faith without precepts."[11]

Theologically, Vattimo's cultural narrative represents a serious and thorough working out of the logic of liberalism, historicism, and demythologization, developed in successive cycles throughout the nineteenth and twentieth centuries. As historians of religion point out, however, the eventual outcome of liberal theology was Religion Lite, a series of halfway houses on the road to unbelief.[12] In America, it was famously parodied in H. Richard Niebuhr's words: "A god without wrath brought men without sin into a kingdom without judgment through the ministrations of a Christ without a cross."[13]

Is there some point at which Christian "belief" is so weakened that it ceases to be recognizably Christian? Or to constitute "belief"? Can it be indistinguishable from humanism? I am reminded of Malcolm

Diamond's way of expressing his ambivalence some years ago about Paul Tillich's redescription of Christian faith in the language of philosophy. Diamond recalled the dialogue in E.M. Forster's *A Passage to India* between two missionaries, Mr Graysford, who was older and conservative, and Mr Sorley, younger and open-minded. They are discussing the subject of heaven and concurring that the exclusivism prevalent on earth should never be mirrored in heaven. All human beings should be allowed in. Forster gives their dialogue on the subject of heaven an ironical turn:

In our Father's house are many mansions, they taught, and there alone will the incompatible multitudes of mankind be welcomed and soothed. Not one shall be turned away by the servants on that verandah, be he black or white, not one shall be kept standing who approaches with a loving heart. And why should the divine hospitality cease there? Consider, with all reverence, the monkeys. May there not be a mansion for the monkeys also? Old Mr Graysford said No, but young Mr Sorley, who was advanced, said Yes; he saw no reason why monkeys should not have their collateral share of bliss, and he had sympathetic discussions among them with his Hindu friends. And the jackals? Jackals were indeed less to Mr Sorley's mind, but he admitted that the mercy of God, being infinite, might well embrace all mammals. And the wasps? He became uneasy during the descent to wasps, and was apt to change the conversation. And oranges, cactuses, crystals, and mud? And the bacteria inside Mr Sorley? No, this was going too far. We must exclude something from our gathering, or we shall be left with nothing.[14]

The point is that Tillich's world seems indistinguishable from the secular world, just as Mr Sorley's heaven would be indistinguishable from earth. This leads Diamond to raise the question, Why talk Tillichese? Vattimo, like Tillich, manages to redescribe religious belief in a way that finesses the major challenges of the modern critique of religion. Removing religion from the metaphysical and epistemic arena neatly eliminates the dogmatism and exclusivism of religious fundamentalisms. No doubt Vattimo is right that in exchange we get pluralism, tolerance, and a lot more *caritas* to go around. At the same time, one can question whether there is any longer any reason to talk about Christianity if we can more simply talk about love. If everything said in terms of the Christian belief system could equally well be communicated in the vocabulary of existentialist humanism, one language or the other would seem to be superfluous.

In their joint consideration of *The Future of Religion*, Richard Rorty wonders whether "belief" is the right description for Vattimo's return to Christianity.[15] The category of belief does not figure very prominently in the declension story that Rorty himself tells about the fate of religion and secularization. His narrative could be called a History of How the West was Weaned – first from God, and then from other quasi-divine authorities such as Science, or Nature, or History.[16] Once upon a time, the story goes, humans felt a need to worship something that lay beyond the visible world. By the seventeenth century, however, we were able to substitute a love of truth for the love of God. Then the world described by science was treated as a quasi-divinity. By the end of the eighteenth century, we were able to substitute a love of ourselves for a love of scientific truth. The quasi-divinity consisted of our own deep spiritual or poetic nature. The successive de-divinization of monotheism, metaphysics, and science (all attempts to say what the world *really* is) ended with the substitution of poetry for religion. Monotheism yielded to polytheism, as now philosophical realism yields to pragmatism. Realism is like monotheism in giving a sense of importance to "something out there with which to get in touch" – either capital-R Reality or the Divine. Both urge us to humble ourselves. An opponent of authoritarianism in any form, Rorty ties his narrative to a description of various changes in self-image on the part of Western humans as we have come out from under the authority of any Supreme Narrator, whether God or Science or Reason or Nature. The will of God, like its philosophical analogue, the Intrinsic Nature of Reality, is the idea of something outside human beings that has authority over human beliefs and actions. We have outgrown religious self-abasement, Rorty argues, and now it is time to root out its philosophical analogue as well and stop casting the world in the role of the nonhuman Other before which we are to humble ourselves. Summing up his story line, Rorty writes, "Once again, I am telling the old Nietzschean story about how 'Truth' took the place of 'God' in a secular culture, and why we should get rid of this God-surrogate in order to become more self-reliant."[17] As John McDowell sees it, Rorty's missionary zeal is devoted to "persuading people to renounce the vocabulary of objectivity [which] should facilitate the achievement of full human maturity. This would be a contribution to world history that is, perhaps surprisingly, within the power of mere intellectuals."[18]

The history of philosophy triumphs with the creation of a "literary culture," the third of three stages through which Western intellectuals have passed. Rorty's three stages hardly resemble Joachim of Fiore's transitions from Father to Son to Spirit, but they do correspond to successive ways of hoping to find "redemptive truth." The revival of Platonism in the Renaissance marked the period in which humanists could ask "the same questions about Christian monotheism that Socrates had asked about Hesiod's pantheon." In the period after Kant and Hegel, Kierkegaard and Marx helped us to see philosophy as a transitional genre rather than as a set of beliefs that represent things in the "one true way they really are." During the last two hundred years, as a literary culture has replaced philosophy, Western intellectuals, according to Rorty, have been less interested in questions about Being, the Really Real, and the Nature of Man and more apt to ask forms of the question, "Does anybody have any new ideas about what we human beings might manage to make of ourselves?"[19]

Literary culture, or what we might think of as Rorty's version of Joachim de Fiore's "Age of the Spirit," has substituted literature for both religion and philosophy. It "finds redemption neither in a noncognitive relation to a nonhuman person nor in a cognitive relation to propositions, but in noncognitive relations to other human beings, relations mediated by human artifacts such as books and buildings, paintings and songs. These artifacts provide a sense of alternative ways of being human."[20] Literary intellectuals in this ideal high culture are interested less in the Socratic idea of self-knowledge and self-examination than in the idea of "enlarging the self by becoming acquainted with still more ways of being human."[21]

The long transition from Platonism to pragmatism succeeded in de-transcendentalizing all absolutes and began the work of democratizing the forms of human community. Philosophy no longer seeks the redemptive power of Truth "out there" and religion is better off seeking the romance of diverse, even conflicting, ideals and forms of private self-perfecting. Polytheism, in the twist given it by Rorty, stands for the idea that "there are diverse, conflicting, but equally valuable forms of human life," but that "there is no actual or possible object of knowledge that would permit you to commensurate and rank all human needs."[22] As a species of romantic utilitarianism, polytheism shares with the Romantic movement a hope that religion, having died as dogma, might be reborn as art, especially the art of literature. In this stage, religion can be viewed as one literary genre among others.

True belief semantically considered is of no more importance to Rorty's story than to Vattimo's. Rorty apparently thinks of religion in

Kierkegaardian terms as a "noncognitive relation to a nonhuman person." In religion's "uncontaminated form," he says, "argument is no more in point than is belief." Only as it is diluted by philosophy does religion lose its pure form and begin to be mediated by a creed, and "only when the God of the philosophers has begun to replace the god of Abraham, Isaac, and Jacob is correct belief thought to be essential to salvation." To take seriously the idea that redemption can come in the form of true beliefs, whether religious or philosophical, Rorty thinks one must hold two convictions: "one must believe both that the life that cannot be successfully argued for is not worth living, and that persistent argument will lead all inquirers to the same set of beliefs." The glory of "uncontaminated religion" and of literature is that both are indifferent to these convictions.[23]

However, it is not clear to me that many religious folk could make sense of Rorty's indifference to true beliefs. On the same page that he cites the irrelevance of beliefs to religious intellectuals like Saint Paul, Kierkegaard, and Karl Barth, Rorty goes so far as to assert that "beliefs are irrelevant to the special devotion of the illiterate believer to Demeter, or to the Virgin of Guadalupe, or to the little fat god on the third altar from the left at the temple down the street."[24] Having been careful enough to specify "western intellectuals" as the focus of his previous narratives of cultural history, now he seems to run together two different cases that call for different kinds of study – the case of sophisticated theological apologists who go noncognitive rather than cope with the exactions of providing plausibility conditions, and, on the other hand, the devotion of "illiterate believers" for whom the element of belief is not only highly relevant but also very literal and nonmetaphorical. To miss this is to miss a central feature of the global phenomenon of religion in our time. Just as seriously, without the element of belief it is impossible for interpreters to go about identifying anything *as* religious.

Turning to the lacunae in the ways Vattimo and Rorty would "weaken" religion, I want to draw attention to the most notable omission in the recent philosophical rethinking of religion, namely, its failure to theorize the resurgence of *unweakened* traditional religious belief manifested "on the ground," rather than in postmodern philosophical texts. The prevalence of literal, nonhermeneutical, and nonprivatized forms of religion constitutes an obvious and overwhelming exception to any secularization thesis. Vattimo and Rorty have given us powerful stories applicable to and sustained by Western intellectual elites, but they have largely ignored the wider and harder to explain phenomenon of the postmodern "return to religion" going on throughout the world, except, apparently, in Western Europe and certain metropolitan areas of North America. That return is twofold or double, as Vattimo recognizes. At the famous conference he organized with Derrida in 1994, Vattimo could refer to "the return of religion in popular consciousness" as he pointed to two concurrent developments in the return of religion – one in philosophy and one in "popular consciousness."[25] Ten years later, as I write, religious belief continues on a roll in popular consciousness. The data pours in with every poll taken by Gallup, Pew, or Newsweek. The United States offers perhaps the most glaring example of the easy compatibility of modernity and religiosity. If surveys are to be trusted, 84 percent of American adults call themselves Christian, 82 percent see Jesus as the son of God, and 79 percent believe in the Virgin Birth.[26] Almost half of all Americans believe human life was created about ten thousand years ago, one-third are biblical literalists; and 81 percent profess a belief in God.[27] Superhuman beings abound. More than a quarter of Americans believe in witches, almost half believe in ghosts, half believe in the devil, and 87 percent believe that Jesus was raised from the dead. A recent Pew survey reports that religion is much more important to Americans than to people living in other wealthy nations. Six in ten people (59 percent) in the United States say religion plays a very large role in their lives. This is roughly twice the percentage of self-avowed religious people in Canada (30 percent) and an even higher percentage when compared with Japan and Western Europe. Americans' views are closer to people in developing nations than to the publics of developed nations.[28]

Of course a high incidence of belief in superhuman beings is hardly limited to American culture, and historically it is nothing new. In culture after culture, people report beliefs that the soul lives on after death, that rituals can change the physical world and divine the truth, and that illness and misfortune are caused and alleviated by spirits, ghosts, saints, fairies, angels, demons, devils, gods, and *nats*. My point is not that Vattimo and Rorty are out of touch with real religious folk but that the secularization thesis that undergirds both their narratives has been in trouble for as long as it has been around. Peter Berger, earlier one of the key proponents of secularization theory in modern social science, now recants: "The key idea of secularisation theory is simple and can be traced to the Enlightenment: modernisation necessarily leads to a decline of religion, both in society and in the minds of individuals. It is precisely this key idea that has turned out to be wrong."[29] Contemporary society is, according to sociologist Jose Casanova, "witnessing the 'deprivatization' of religion," as "religious traditions throughout the world are refusing to accept the marginal and privatized role which theories of modernity as well as theories of secularization had reserved for them."[30] From Falum Gong to Pentecostalism, the surprising vitality and extreme pluralism of fundamentalist and supernaturalist forms of religion constitute a "return of religion" in terms that are directly antithetical to postmodern philosophy. It has nothing to do with Derrida's "impossible possibility" or with the continued apparition of Nietzschean "shadows of God." It is armed with all the certainties and absolutes and literalisms that Vattimo's weak thought would dissolve.

What have these two "returns of religion" to do with each other, one wonders? And why is it that at the very moment religion is operating with impressive and even alarming strength worldwide, postmodern continental philosophy is fascinated with a very different "religion without religion"? I suggest that at least two things are at work. First, philosophers have generally preferred to valorize discourse about the Other as a bare, abstract category rather than grapple with what concrete religious others actually have to say. What believers invariably say, as scholars of religion know, indicates that they hold as true sentences what most Western intellectual elites cannot and do not assert as true. In short, they believe that, to consider a Christian example, "Jesus rose from the dead." Second, philosophy's attention to religion typically focuses on the category of belief and omits any study of *practice*, sometimes even treating it as a category independent of belief. As a result philosophy has little to say about *practice as embodied belief*, an omission that scarcely enables it to theorize the resurgence of religion on the ground and also goes far toward explaining postmodern continental philosophy's ignorance of the concrete forms of "the return of religion."[31]

Vattimo thinks that each of these developments – one in philosophy and the other in popular consciousness – has involved a particular response to modernity and its social changes. Popular consciousness has given rise to a "new vitality of churches and sects" and to the "search for different doctrines and practices, the 'fashion' for Eastern religions, and so forth" because of "the sense of impending global threats that appear quite new and without precedent in the history of humanity."[32] According to Vattimo, the widespread fear evoked by the threat of nuclear war that began after World War II has been intensified by anxiety about environmental conditions, by the emergence of an array of risks attendant upon new technologies, and by the experience of threat as specifically apocalyptic, an experience that is intensified against a background of the "true and profound boredom which seems inevitably to accompany consumerism."[33] The "return of religion," then, has arisen out of a popular consciousness that is looking for a kind of "God-as-foundation."[34] Religious fundamentalism flourishes as popular consciousness rejects aspects of modernization that it feels are destructive of "authentic roots of existence."[35] At the same time, the destruction of metanarratives by late-twentieth-century critical theories has produced two somewhat contradictory events. First, through its onslaught on Enlightenment philosophy, postmodern critical theory has accomplished a "breakdown of the philosophical prohibition of religion" in a way that permits the western religious tradition to be encountered anew.[36] Second, however, because "philosophy and critical thought in general [have] abandoned the very idea of foundation, [they] are not (or no longer) able to give existence that meaning which it therefore seeks in religion."[37]

The first point has important implications, but the second explanation is less satisfactory, in my opinion. Vattimo is certainly right that the main philosophical bases for atheism have been swept away with the demise of positivism, Marxist historicism, and rationalism's faith in science as the exclusive zone of truth and history as the march toward emancipation. Without a doubt, most rationalist ideologies are in crisis today, and "there are no good philosophical reasons to be an atheist, or in any case to dismiss religion."[38] In that case, none of them prove very useful for explaining the resurgence of supernaturalist religious beliefs. Forsaking Enlightenment rationalist assumptions means that we cannot brand religion as "irrational," as "superstition," or as "false consciousness" *simpliciter*. Only a very naïve grasp of religion would put it in opposition to reason, science, enlightenment, or critical thought. To the extent that Marxian criticism, Nietzschean geneology, or Freudian psychoanalysis have been presented and defended as alternatives to religion, they have failed strikingly.

Unfortunately, the second type of explanation – in terms of fears, threats, and the search for meaning – does not fare any better. Among current theories of religion none is more pervasive than the claim that religion is a response to the anxieties that are produced by the human experience of cognitive, physical, and moral uncertainty. This assertion is based on the theoretical hypothesis that religion is a function of needs – for example, the need to reduce uncertainty or the need for existential meaning. The attempt to explain religion and other cultural elements as responses to certain needs by means of causal analysis is known as functionalism. I have yet to discover any response that salvages functional accounts of religion from the devastating critique of the logic of that theory by Carl Hempel in the social sciences and by Hans Penner in the study of religion.[39] In the invalid form, functionalism commits the fallacy of affirming the consequent (if y, then z; z; therefore y), and in a valid form it reaches only a trivial conclusion. Nor do we have any successful account of semantics based upon functionalism. Needs – even the deep human need for meaning – do not explain anything. *Needs are what need to be explained.* The way in which religious institutions themselves have been powerful in *producing* the very needs that are said to be satisfied by religion makes the appeal to the satisfaction of needs even more circular. In explaining religion as a function of certain enduring human needs (for meaning, for foundational certainty, and so forth) I doubt we understand religion or human beings any better. What exactly is shown? Are the purported needs any less obscure than the religious phenomena they are supposed to explain?

Students of theory and method in the study of religion today know to repudiate theories of religion defined as symbolic expressions of the sacred or of a person's ultimate concern, or of something Wholly Other. Most of them agree that religious beliefs are not to be understood simply as premodern hangovers or as sutures for disintegrative forces that divide societies or psyches or as emotional emollients. These were the standard explanations of religion that characterized modern critiques of religion and all of them harbour major fault lines that have been traced often enough. Rather than reading this, however, as an occasion for a return to religion (Vattimo) or for embracing the romance of literary culture (Rorty), we might regard it instead as an indication that we should *develop a better theory*. Where do we turn to explain the astonishing fact that hundreds of millions of people on the planet believe they have commerce with superhuman beings? My modest suggestion for beginning to think about this question draws on the interpretive resources of semantic holism, which provides an important way of understanding certain constraints on the interpretation of religious beliefs, as well as understanding the way religious beliefs about superhuman beings fit with the picture of the mind we are accustomed to think of holistically.

To clarify my argument, I will simply summarize five elements of what philosophers have come to call "the holism of the mental" and try to indicate how these elements bear upon the interpretation of religious beliefs. The first, perceptively summarized by Terry Godlove, is that "while students of religion need not believe in God, we do need to believe in belief."[40] That is not only because belief is integral to thought, meaning, and action but also because we face a peculiar circumstance in the interpretation of any beliefs and practices *as religious*. In the majority of ordinary cases, it is guaranteed that the intentional objects of beliefs will be among their causes. But we cannot say this in the case of religious beliefs having to do with superhuman beings. To identify anything *as* specifically religious, the interpreter has to be in a position either to traffic with gods, goddesses, ancestors, ghosts, water spirits, and other superhuman powers or else, failing that, to find that the people one is trying to interpret hold beliefs and attitudes concerning superhuman beings. The first position is simply unavailable. Unlike other contexts in which we study people's economic status or political actions, frequently dispensing with their own intentions, desires, beliefs, hopes, and fears, there is no distinguishable religious context that can be discerned apart from people's propositional attitudes. Superhuman beings, in other words, cannot be identified by an interpreter apart from people's beliefs about them, and so in that case it is *statements and assertions* about superhuman beings that are crucial to the interpretation of any given practice or belief *as* religious.

Second, the concept of belief requires two other concepts: truth and meaning. Only if a person shares a concept of truth with others can she be said to have beliefs. And to know the conditions under which a belief held to be true would be true is to know what it means. Belief, meaning, and the concept of truth are so interdependent that neither can be said to come first. Their interconnection is precisely what helps us understand other people's behaviour and beliefs and desires. The liturgical actions performed in St Peter's Basilica or the ritual pilgrimage to the Ka'baa in Mecca can be understood only by ascribing to the performers certain beliefs, that is to say, by interpreting them as holding as true certain propositional attitudes. This is one reason why the effort of various scholars of religion to eliminate beliefs in favour of ritual and noncognitive dispositions will always be hopeless. The holism of the

mental means that even those religious traditions that differ over stem
cell research must first agree in many respects about what the biological composition of the human body is; identification of creationism as
a creed depends on prior agreement about the visible world; disagreement about the ordination of women in the Catholic Church makes
sense only among people who share many other notions and are able to
identify "male" and "female."

   Third, beliefs and desires are the most basic and irreducible of the
propositional attitudes. Neither one can be analyzed in terms of the
other.[41] Belief is the spring of action, desire the spring of intention. The
attitude of belief is that of holding-true, while the attitude of desire is
of wanting to arrange the world so that the proposition that is the
object of the desire will be true. Mingling both belief and desire, intention is born. The most general thing we can say of intention is that it is
always the making of a judgment to do x because of a belief that x will
lead to y, which is desired. The belief-desire structure, then, comprises
everything that we call upon for reason-explanations. Reasons can be
causes that not only explain actions but also sometimes justify them. In
this they differ from the causal explanations given in physics and
biology.

   Fourth, by understanding the holism of the mental as a field on which
belief-desire-meaning-truth-world-minds-action-language all hang
together, we see that rationality comes with this field. Rationality comes
with having a mind, as Davidson has argued. It is the necessary background of interpretation. For holist reasons, we have to assume that
rationality is more pervasive than irrationality. Furthermore, any one
propositional attitude means what it does only in a web of other propositional attitudes that can be mapped onto the interpreter's own norms
of rationality. Words and concepts – such as "God" or "karma" – are
meaningful only as defined by their place in sentences and by their relations to other concepts and sentences. Belief may be but one particular
kind of attitude toward a proposition – an attitude of holding-true –
but it is constitutively interwoven with the other major kinds of propositional attitudes, which include wish, desire, intention, regret, remembrance, delight, and hope. When challenges to the truth of particular
religious beliefs arise, they are not a challenge to the overall rationality
of human persons who hold religious beliefs, for two reasons. First, in
truth-conditional semantics, judging specific religious beliefs to be false
is not the same as calling them irrational. The history of science is
replete with examples of beliefs once thought to be true and later

declared false, but no one is tempted to regard this as evidence of irrationality on the part of individual scientists or science as a whole. Second, specific religious beliefs *can* be evaluated as irrational as well as false without jeopardizing the rationality of the individuals who hold those beliefs. In the totality of a person's beliefs, the overall proportionality of religious beliefs held irrationally will always be dwarfed by the preponderance of rational beliefs held about all other, nonreligious matters. I conclude that the modern preoccupation of philosophers of religion with questions about "the rationality of religious beliefs" has been a red herring.

Fifth, the preponderance of rationality calls attention to the need to understand exceptions. The issues that seem to me both hard and urgent for the study of religion currently have to do with what I will call, with some misgivings, "bizarre, controversial, and anomalous beliefs." The question how best to explain these cases is no doubt too complex and labyrinthine to address at the level of particular examples. And of course there is no magic bullet, no single explanatory scheme that fully theorizes the overdetermined phenomenon of religion. Nevertheless, it seems important to acknowledge, if only formally, that bizarre, controversial, and anomalous beliefs do occur in religion, as elsewhere in human life, and to attempt to provide a schematic model of how the rationality of propositional attitudes and the holism of the mental can be maintained in the face of the obvious exceptions. My claim is that if we are to understand these sorts of religious beliefs, the interpretive task in philosophy of religion will require notions of wishful thinking, self-deception, and psychic division or partitioning within the mind along the lines laid out in several papers by Donald Davidson.[42] At least some forms of religious belief should be understood as cases in which mental causes that do not count as reasons are assigned to acts. Adequate explanations of traditional religious behaviour and beliefs, I am claiming, need to incorporate attention to causes that are *not* reasons, as much as to reasons that are causes.

Rorty offers a related way of preserving the holism that is crucial to pragmatism while allowing for the interpretation of anomalous religious beliefs, but his account is incomplete and pulls in a different direction than Davidson's. In reviewing Jamesian "will to believe" arguments, Rorty proposes that we think of religious beliefs as disengaged from the usual web of inferential links by which beliefs are justified by other beliefs. It would be like the mother who loves her psychopathic child or Kierkegaard's belief in the Incarnation. These are unjustifiable beliefs, according to Rorty, that can be given content only by correlating their utterances with patterns of behaviour rather than with patterns linked inferentially to other beliefs. Traditional religious beliefs could in this way be explained, as well as recognized as anomalous. There is neither evidence for them nor any good fit with other beliefs held true, but people are entitled to hold them as a matter of personal preference.[43]

Rorty's recommendation for interpreting apparently anomalous religious beliefs not only forfeits the literal meaning asserted by many religious folks but also amounts to an unfortunate prescription for compartmentalization. If religious beliefs, like all beliefs, have content only by virtue of inferential relations to other beliefs, it is hard to see how they can be disengaged from that interlocking web of beliefs without plunging into vacuity. The question is how far they can be fuzzed up (Rorty) or weakened (Vattimo) without losing all content and ceasing to be propositional attitudes. The charitable interpreter trying to translate the propositional attitudes of Kierkegaard and of the psychopath's mother divides up and delineates different zones: those beliefs one has to justify to others versus those that need no such justification and can be entertained privately. From this angle it seems that Rorty is mainly interested in examining the *interpreter's* best options. But what of Kierkegaard's own propositional attitudes? Or the state of mind of the mother? Don't we also want to understand them and to make sense of their adhering to patently false beliefs? How can we explain why people would hold as true beliefs that are not only anomalous but also patently false?

In *The Future of Religion* Rorty defends the strategy of compartmentalization by claiming that religious believers are entitled "for certain purposes, to opt out of" giving reasons and asking for reasons. "They are entitled," he says, "to disconnect their assertions from the network of socially acceptable inferences that provide justifications for making these assertions and draw practical consequences from having made them."[44] At the same time, he considers it a good thing for both religion and science that science can claim cultural supremacy over religion and religion can be taken out of the epistemic arena in the way that Vattimo recommends. In fact, it does seem that most religious believers know that their beliefs cannot be supported by scientific reason and most do not reflect on their beliefs much at all. As Steven Pinker notes, they "don't pause to wonder why a God who knows our intentions has to listen to our prayers, or how a God can both see into the future and care about how we choose to act."[45] At the same time, however, this scarcely strikes us as healthy-mindedness. Science and religion cannot, after all, be assigned the separate and nonoverlapping magisteria that Stephen Jay Gould assumed would end their conflict. They can and do conflict, not the least because religion makes factual claims, and science involves evaluative judgments.

Rather than *recommend* Rorty's way of unhealthy compartmental-ization, which would promote the loss of an important kind of integrity, I want to redeploy it as a *description* of a certain kind of irra-tionality that Davidson has diagnosed as "partitioning of the mind." Davidson's dissection of this Freudian idea is meant to account for the possibility of irrationality in cases where mental causes that do not count as reasons are assigned to beliefs and actions. Although highly formal and not meant to be a detailed psychology, this account of psychic division should be useful in theorizing a certain range of reli-gious beliefs about superhuman beings under the rubrics of wishful thinking, self-deception, and akrasia.

We can think of the mind as a network of interlocking desires, beliefs, memories, and so on, in which there may be subdivisions or partitions that largely, but not entirely, overlap with the whole. A necessary but not sufficient condition for irrationality is the presence of causes that are not reasons. Most of the time in human action the fabric of reasons and causes, and beliefs and desires, is so interwoven that we do not discern their different textures. When they come apart, however, the cause is like a compelling force, drawing a boundary between two or more conflicting beliefs. We can postulate such a boundary, Davidson thinks, even if it is not something available to introspection and not exactly a line between conscious and unconscious states either. It is best thought of as "a conceptual aid to the coherent description of genuine irrationalities."[46]

In the continua of cases involving irrationality, wishful thinking is the simplest case and perhaps also the most commonplace feature of reli-gious belief and practice. A wish may cause a belief, nonrationally and not necessarily with partitioning occurring. Wishful thinking involves a desire that something be true causing the belief that it *is* true, but in no case can the desire be a *reason* for believing something to be true. Simple wishful thinking does not constitute a paradox of irrationality of the kind that poses serious problems in the interpretation of religious beliefs. A large number of religious beliefs, particularly those whose content is future-oriented, may well be classified as wishes or as elaborated forms of wishful thinking without generating any paradoxes. Beliefs such as "Jesus raises the dead" or "my sins will be washed away," for example, do not involve acceptance of any contradictory propositions. People can genuinely believe what they *want* to believe, as the force of their desire to live beyond death or to be forgiven for their transgressions comes to construct their belief that they *will* indeed live and *are* in fact forgiven.

Paradox beckons, however, once wishful thinking leads a person to act in such a way as to promote the belief. Self-deception, a more complicated case of irrationality, can thus emerge out of wishful thinking. On Davidson's account, this consists in accepting each of two contradictory beliefs at the same time, rather than accepting a single contradictory proposition. Kierkegaard's faith, for example, that "Jesus is fully human" and "Jesus is fully divine," conforms to the logical structure of self-deception. Not that he was of two minds, but neither was he a single mind wholly integrated. By way of a partitioning or compartmentalizing of the mind, two obviously opposed beliefs can coexist by being kept separate and not allowed to mingle in a single sweep. Here too we must allow a form of explanation that is causal but that does not rationalize what it explains. States of self-deception are primarily caused by desires rather than by reasons. When a person acts in such a way as to provide herself with reasons for altering an unpleasant belief (or adopting a more pleasant one), the desire to change a belief causes the change but is not a reason for holding the new belief true or the old one false. However much self-deception functions like a belief, its *content* is always a desire.

We can imagine a continuum running from wishful thinking, fuelled by desire and fantasy, at one end, to self-deception, fed by desire and inner division, at the other end. In some cases, the phantasizing that frequently accompanies repression takes place unchecked by a distinction the person is otherwise normally capable of making between belief and make-belief. Triggered by a wish, this kind of phantasizing serves a defensive purpose. If it ignores available evidence, it becomes a form of self-deception and calls for the model of a divided mind. If it ignores what is in the agent's own best interests, it becomes a case of akrasia, yet another kind of divided mind.

Although desires can never make a proposition true or false, taking into account the systematic effects of desires on the formation of beliefs will mean that reflection on religious belief, its reasonableness or truth, cannot be severed from the study of human desires.[47] If philosophers of religion were to explore the belief-desire nexus more deeply in connection with the holism of the mental, they would raise in a new way the issue of irrational beliefs about superhuman beings and the possibility of wishful thinking or self-deception in the lives of those who practise religion – and those who reject it.

At present, philosophy of religion vacillates between conceptions of religious belief as having to do necessarily and problematically with superhuman beings and far more nuanced and weakened conceptions like Vattimo's ("I believe that I believe") or Wallace Stevens' ("We believe without belief, beyond belief"). It was Stevens who, moving beyond a struggle with the idea of the Christian God, attempted like Rorty to give art the place of religion. In "Sunday Morning," very probably the finest expression of religious naturalism in American poetry, Stevens managed to encompass the spirit of both Vattimo's self-emptying and Rorty's self-assertion in the evocative closing lines in which pigeons display the inevitable direction that reality exerts:

> We live in an old chaos of the sun,
> Or old dependency of day and night,
> Or island solitude, unsponsored, free,
> Of that wide water, inescapable.
> Deer walk upon our mountains, and the quail
> Whistle about us their spontaneous cries;
> Sweet berries ripen in the wilderness;
> And, in the isolation of the sky,
> At evening, casual flocks of pigeons make
> Ambiguous undulations as they sink,
> Downward to darkness, on extended wings.[48]

NOTES

1 Curiously, Vattimo does not explicitly cite Philippians 2:6–8 in connection with his emphasis on kenosis. More often, he refers to John 15:15: "No longer do I call you servants ... But I have called you friends." See Gianni Vattimo, *Belief*, translated by Luca D'Isanto and David Webb (Cambridge: Polity Press 1999), 26, 44, 53, 55, 78. For the most thorough theological radicalization of the kenotic theme, see the works of Thomas J.J. Altizer over the last thirty-five years, especially *Godhead and the Nothing* (Albany: State University of New York Press 2003). In contrast to Altizer, an element of super-

sessionism hovers over Vattimo's view of the relationship of the New Testament to the Hebrew Bible but is never made explicit.

2 Gianni Vattimo, *Beyond Interpretation* (Stanford: Stanford University Press 1997), ix.

3 Gianni Vattimo and Richard Rorty, *The Future of Religion*, ed. S. Zabala (New York: Columbia University Press 2005), 46.

4 Ibid. 47.

5 Ibid.

6 Gianni Vattimo, "After Onto-theology: Philosophy between Science and Religion," in Mark Wrathall, ed., *Religion after Metaphysics* (Cambridge: Cambridge University Press), 34.

7 Vattimo, *The Future of Religion*, 47.

8 Vattimo, *Beyond Interpretation*, 73.

9 Gianni Vattimo, *After Christianity* (New York: Columbia University Press 2002), 16.

10 Vattimo, *Beyond Interpretation*, 48, 50.

11 Santiago Zabala, "A Religion without Theists or Atheists," in Santiago Zabala, ed., *The Future of Religion* (New York: Columbia University Press 2005), 16.

12 James Turner makes this argument in connection with nineteenth-century American religious thought in his *Without God, without Creed: The Origins of Unbelief in America* (Baltimore: The Johns Hopkins University Press 1985), and Gary Dorrien has brilliantly chronicled the liberal movement and its failure in twentieth-century American religious thought in *The Making of American Liberal Theology: Idealism, Realism, and Modernity: 1900 – 1950* (Louisville: Westminster/John Knox Press 2003).

13 H. Richard Niebuhr, *The Kingdom of God in America* (Harper & Row Torchbook 1937, 2d ed., 1959), 193.

14 Malcolm Diamond quoting E.M. Forster, *A Passage to India* (New York: Random House, 1924, 38) in *Contemporary Philosophy and Religious Thought* (McGraw-Hill 1974), 388.

15 Rorty says that "Vattimo might have done better to say: I am becoming more and more religious, and so coming to have what many people would call a belief in God, but I am not sure that the term 'belief' is the right description of what I have." *The Future of Religion*, 34. If the propositional attitude "believing" entails holding as true, and if the truth conditions of a belief obtain, then "everybody ought to share it," but Vattimo's strategy is to remove religion from the epistemic realm altogether.

16 The next few paragraphs appear in my essay "'Sleepwalking through History': Reflections on Democracy, Religion, and Pragmatism," *American*

Journal of Theology and Philosophy 26, nos. 1&2 (January–May): 45–59. For the most recent elaboration of Rorty's metanarrative, see Richard Rorty, "Philosophy as a Transitional Genre," in *Pragmatism, Critique, Judgment: Essays for Richard J. Bernstein*, edited by Seyla Benhabib and Nancy Fraser (Cambridge: MIT Press 2004), 3–28. See also Rorty, "Afterward: Pragmatism, Pluralism, and Postmodernism," *Philosophy and Social Hope* (New York: Penguin 1999).

17 Rorty, "Philosophy as a Transitional Genre," 4. Rorty has rightly left behind certain positions. He now says for instance that his response to Stephen Carter that religion is a conversation-stopper was insufficiently reflective and that Nicholas Wolterstorff and Jeff Stout have convinced him that religion's place in the public sphere can be allowed slightly more accommodation than he previously expressed. See the exchange with Wolterstorff in *Journal of Religious Ethics* (2003) 31, no. 1, 141–9. For an important study of the relation of religion and democracy and the role of truth claims, pluralism, and public debate, see Jeffrey Stout, *Democracy and Tradition* (Princeton University Press 2004).

18 John McDowell, "Toward Rehabilitating Objectivity," in Robert B. Brandom, ed., *Rorty and His Critics* (Blackwell Publishers 2000), 110.

19 Rorty, "Philosophy as a Transitional Genre," 9.

20 Ibid., 10. Although I cannot develop the point here, it is puzzling that Rorty resorts now to the very distinction ("noncognitive" versus "cognitive") that was so basic to logical positivist critiques of religion and that he has shrewdly avoided in other essays dealing with philosophy of religion. See especially "Religious Faith, Intellectual Responsibility and Romance," *The Cambridge Companion to William James*, Ruth Anna Putnam, ed. (Cambridge: Cambridge University Press 1997), 84–102. In "Anticlericalism and Atheism," he draws the distinction not between the epistemic arena and what lies outside it, but between "topics on which we are entitled to ask for universal agreement and other topics" (in *The Future of Belief*, ed. S. Zabala, 41).

21 Ibid., 13.

22 Richard Rorty, "Pragmatism as Romantic Polytheism," *The Revival of Pragmatism: New Essays on Social Thought, Law, and Culture*, ed. Morris Dickstein (Duke University Press 1998), 23.

23 Rorty, "Philosophy as a Transitional Genre," 10. Again, the association of "uncontaminated religion" with "noncognitive" suggests that Rorty is drawing his understanding of "religion" largely from Kierkegaard's eccentric *oeuvre*.

24 Ibid.

25 Gianni Vattimo, "The Trace of the Trace," in *Religion*, eds. Jacques Derrida and Gianni Vattimo (Stanford: Stanford University Press 1998), 82.

26 Reported by Nicholas D. Kristof, "Believe It, or Not," *New York Times*, 15 August 2003.

27 Gallup Poll, November 2004.

28 *U.S. Stands Alone in Its Embrace of Religion* (Washington, DC: The Pew Global Attitudes Project 2002).

29 Peter Berger, *The Desecularization of the World* (Grand Rapids, MI: Wm. B. Eerdmans 1999). There are, of course, earlier critiques of the modernization/secularization paradigm. See, for example, D. Martin, *The Religious and the Secular: Studies in Secularization* (London: Routledge and Kegan Paul, 1969) and P.E. Glasner, *The Sociology of Secularization: a Critique of a Concept* (London and Boston: Routledge and Kegan Paul 1977).

30 J. Casanova, *Public Religions in the Modern World* (Chicago: University of Chicago Press 1994), 5. See also J. Casanova, "Religion, the New Millenium and Globalization," *Sociology of Religion* 62, no. 4 (2001) 415–41; and J. Casanova, "Civil Society and Religion: Retrospective Reflections on Catholicism and Prospective Reflections on Islam," *Social Research* (New York) 68, no. 4 (Winter 2001): 1041–80.

31 I am grateful to Amy Hollywood for suggesting this linkage. See her exceptional study "Practice, Belief and Feminist Philosophy of Religion," in *Feminist Philosophy of Religion: Critical Readings*, ed. Pamela Anderson and Beverley Clack (Oxford: Blackwell Publishers 2003).

32 Vattimo, "The Trace of the Trace," 82.

33 Ibid., 79, 80.

34 Ibid., 83.

35 Ibid., 81.

36 Ibid.

37 Ibid.

38 Vattimo makes a good case for this in "After Onto-theology: Philosophy between Science and Religion," in *Religion after Metaphysics*, ed. Mark A. Wrathall (Cambridge: Cambridge University Press 2003).

39 See Carl Hempel, "The Logic of Functional Analysis," in *Aspects of Scientific Explanation* (New York: Free Press 1965), and Hans H. Penner, *Impasse and Resolution: A Critique of the Study of Religion* (New York: Peter Lang 1989), 143–57. I suspect, but am unable to show here, that functionalism is the implicit theory of religion both Vattimo and Rorty espouse.

40 Terry F. Godlove Jr, "Saving Belief: On the New Materialism in Religious Studies," in *Radical Interpretation in Religion*, ed. Nancy K. Frankenberry (Cambridge: Cambridge University Press 2002), 24.

41 Emotions comprise a different but related story. They have a logical relation to beliefs and desires, and they can be rational or irrational. Like intentions, emotions are constituted by belief and desire and get attributed in all

processes of understanding or interpretation. However, there seem to be no general laws or rules we can use to describe emotions, and no precise or single type of propositional attitude they yield.

42 Davidson considers such cases in "Paradoxes of Irrationality" (1982), "Incoherence and Irrationality" (1985), "Deception and Division" (1985), and "Who is Fooled?" (1997), all reprinted in Donald Davidson, *Problems of Rationality* (Oxford: Clarendon Press 2004). See also "How Is Weakness of the Will Possible?" in Donald Davidson, *Essays on Actions and Events* (Oxford: Clarendon Press 1980), 21–42. The issues here are widely debated and no consensus exists among philosophers as to how to characterize self-deception. For criticisms of Davidson's approach, see Mele, Anspach, Beyer, and Bach in J.P. Dupuy, ed., *Self-Deception and Paradoxes of Rationality* (Stanford: CSLI Publications 1998).

43 See Rorty, "Religious Faith, Intellectual Responsibility, and Romance," 95.

44 Rorty, in *The Future of Religion*, 37–8. If the question is one of coherence and integrity, rather than of rights and entitlement, more needs to be said than Rorty allows.

45 Steven Pinker, *How the Mind Works* (New York: Norton 1997), 557.

46 Davidson, *Problems of Rationality*, 211.

47 Needs differ from both beliefs and desires in not being governed by any fundamental norms in the way they get attributed in processes of understanding. That is why I ruled them out earlier as not genuinely explanatory. Moreover, needs are not intentional. They lack the belief that one might fulfill a desire by doing or believing what one does. Desires may very well use fantasy and make-believe as the causal paths through which they are gratified, but needs cannot, since in themselves they have no causal properties. Not only do I reject the idea that we can explain religion by grounding irrational beliefs in pre-rational needs, but I also reject any equivalence between need-fulfillment and wish-fulfillment. A theory of religion as involving (in part) wish-fulfillment differs from functionalist theories involving need-fulfillment as fantasy's reference to merely possible events differs from biology's to actual events.

48 *The Collected Poems of Wallace Stevens* (New York: Alfred A. Knopf 1976), 70.

17

Christianity as Religion and the Irreligion of the Future

FERNANDO SAVATER

Translated by Ileana Szymanski

Surely some revelation is at hand;
Surely the Second Coming is at hand.

W.B. Yeats

A few years ago, a dialogue of more or less theological character between Umberto Eco and Cardinal Martini was published; as an annex, it included interventions by other important Italian thinkers. The title of the book surprised me: *Belief or Nonbelief?*[1] Since the question in the title referred to the beliefs of those who do not believe in God or in religious dogmas, the answer was a fairly obvious one: they believe in the demonstrations of the natural phenomena established by science, in what is endorsed by historical or social studies, in the pertinence of moral values, and so on. And they believe in each and every one of these cultural constructs according to the level of belief that is consistent with their epistemology: since Aristotle we have known that "exactness" is not the same as "rigour" and that one cannot demand the same degree of certainty from history or from the principles of ethics as we can from the results of physics. On the whole, those of us who are called – from an exclusively religious point of view – "incredulous" can give a very competent account of what we believe in and, above all, of the reasons why we believe in such things, rather than in others.

Thus I was surprised to find that something sthat is hardly mysterious would become a transcendental question in the title of the little book mentioned above, especially since it is obvious that once we are ready to ascend to a misty theological plane, there is a much more urgent question that is also much harder to answer.

I mean, of course, the following question: In what do those who do believe, believe? And also, its logical corollary: Why do they believe in that if they are clear about what they believe? Obviously, we take it as given that these "believers" *are* believers in religious and theological matters. However, it does not seem to me especially difficult, at least in the first instance, to clarify the rational and reasonable *content* of each one of the beliefs of those considered theologically "incredulous," while, conversely, establishing the content of the belief in God (as the principal example) or in the Holy Trinity or in the Incarnation of the Divine Word seems to be a more difficult task. This is not about asking someone who believes in "God" to clarify the content of her belief and the reasons that led her to adopt such a belief and to do so with the same clarity with which some one else might respond to similar questions concerning her belief, say, in the phanerogamic function of plants or in the existence of the Yeti. But could she at least enlighten us on this topic with as much precision as can be exhibited by one who believes in the economic causes of the French Revolution or in the virtuous character of veracity? I quite doubt it. And that is why it seems to me that it would be much more intriguing to understand what those who do believe, believe in than to understand what those who do not believe believe in.

To believe, not to believe ... and to provide reasons to support the belief or the incredulity: and what if the whole enterprise was the residue of a heavy metaphysics that gives the notion of "truth" (that is to say, of what we ought to believe in, whether we like it or not) itself an excessive heaviness (*gravidez*), and what if it was already hermeneutically unjustifiable? For postmetaphysical thought (i.e., post-Heideggerian thought), the operational concept of truth is excess baggage to be declared in the philosophical customs office. Both believers and nonbelievers are, in theological questions, entangled in a spider's web spun by the most dangerous and already fortunately endangered tarantula, the metaphysical tarantula. "Today there are no longer strong, plausible philosophical reasons to be atheist, or at any rate to dismiss religion,"[2] announces Gianni Vattimo, freeing us from restraint. It is understood that this theoretical emancipation originates in the that neither the belief in God nor the acceptance of religion can count on its being favoured with better reasons. As Richard Rorty summarizes this position, "Vattimo wants to dissolve the problem of the coexistence of natural science with the legacy of Christianity by identifying Christ neither with truth nor with power, but with love alone."[3] The secularization of modernity first saves scientific verification from the fetters of religious dogma but then immediately proceeds to release religion from the traps of a science that is determined to verify what is in its reach. Christianity, more than a way of thinking, becomes a way of speaking and interpreting the discourse that expresses us, as well as a way of acting based on the commandment of love. The French poet Pierre Revérdy said, "There is no love, only tokens of love." If I am not misinterpreting him, Gianni Vattimo declares that Christianity as dogma or belief in a capital-T Truth exists no more: there are only tokens of Christian love.

However, this interpretation of Christianity is not universally shared, especially if one refers to the origins of that religious doctrine (not to mention the interpretation of Pope John Paul II in, for instance, his encyclical *Fides et Ratio*). In an especially combative page of his polemical book *Straw Dogs*, whose subtitle is, significantly, *Atheism, the Last Consequence of Christianity*, John Gray maintains a radically opposed theory, which we could read *a rébours* as a complement to that of Vattimo. According to Gray, through secularization modern atheism has wanted to achieve a world from which the Christian God would be absent. However, if it reached its goal, atheism would put an end to itself as well: "secularism is like chastity, a condition defined by what it denies. If atheism has a future, it can only be in a Christian revival; but in fact Christianity and atheism are declining together." However, Gray's reasoning follows a line opposite to Vattimo's. For Gray, it is the pagan polytheists who did not give decisive weight to truth considered in – let us say – "metaphysical" terms, while it was the first Christians who absolutized the cult to truth as a primordial correlate of their creed: "Atheism is a late bloom of a Christian passion for truth. No pagan is ready to sacrifice the pleasure of life for the sake of mere truth. It is artful illusion, and not unadorned reality that they prize. Among the Greeks, the general goal of philosophy was happiness or salvation, not truth. The worship of truth is a Christian cult." And this radical cult ended up turning against Christian dogma itself. For Polytheists, for whom the acceptance of some gods before others had to do with choosing a lifestyle, and not with processes of verification, total incredulity was unheard of. But in reclaiming faith as the only true one and, therefore, the only acceptable one, Christians created an expeditious path that led directly to the progressive abolition of any and all faiths. At first faith monopolizes the truth, evicting *ad inferos* all the other gods that seemed only to be *significant*, but not true. Then subsequently truth monopolizes faith, putting an end to all unverifiable beliefs – however significant they may be – and opening the way for science and modernity. In this way, John Gray concludes, "Christianity struck at the root of pagan tolerance of illusion. In claiming that there is only one true faith, it gave truth a supreme value it had not had before. It also made disbelief in the divine possible for the first time. The long-delayed consequence of Christian faith was an idolatry of truth that found its most complete expression in atheism. If we live in a world without gods, we have Christianity to thank for it."[4]

Following a similar line of thought, Marcel Gauchet has spoken on several occasions (notably, in *The Disenchantment of the World*)[5] about Christianity as "the religion to quit religion," that is to say, as the religion that has displaced social identity from the theocentric heteronomy that had to be accepted without any examination or without being put into question with regard to its verification. In doing so Christianity has led to the human autonomy that decides what is to be accepted or rejected in the name of a rational search for truth and of an agreement between joint partners:

To quit religion must be understood in the sense of quitting a way of being of humanity by which it was itself conceived and it stood on the sign of the Other ... To quit religion, then, is this phenomenon in every way prodigious, when one dreams of stepping back a little, which consists in distancing alterity from the definition of humanity. The human community thus defines itself departing from itself. It gives itself its reasons from itself: the kingdom of heteronomy makes [way for] the world of autonomy. Man, [who] was separated from himself, now rejoins himself. He was subjected, now he becomes subject.[6]

From religion as myth, for which questions of verification did not arise but which was useful for promoting societal integration that was safe from human criticism, we move to Christianity and its emphasis on the unveiling of absolute truth, and then onto humanity's inherent sense of membership in a community.

The concept of truth is not only the distinguishing characteristic of rationality but also the key to the autonomous constitution of modern man as social subject. If we remember this, we will be aware of what we renounce by relieving ourselves of its gravity. As I understand it, the intellectual position of Gianni Vattimo aspires to concede to Christianity the standing of *myth*, a myth like the polytheistic religions before the advent – precisely! – of Christianity itself. That is to say, he wishes to find for it some sort of middle road between the complete secularization of modern society and a single nonsecularized – but also completely nonverifiable – standpoint, which is the commandment of love. This desideratum is formal in the same way as the Kantian categorical imperative, "which does not command something specific once and for all, but rather [seeks] applications that must be 'invented' in dialogue with specific situations and in light of what the holy Scriptures have revealed."[7] Myth is what anybody can tell again, but also what nobody can completely contradict. It is an instrument that can be used to search "in private," but without completely renouncing the collective tradition of the sense of social connection with those similar to oneself. It is therefore something, of course, that the church – any church, I suppose – as a hierarchical institution peopled by a team specialized in establishing the acceptable narratives in the face of the unacceptable ones, will reject merely out of an instinct for self-preservation. But it is also something that allows the liberal individual of our times to assume what is fundamental in Christian belief (as a belief in which she thinks she believes and not merely as a "belief that creates that which is believed," as Miguel de Unamuno would say) without paying the coercive toll of submitting oneself to dogmatic restrictions in matters of sex, and so on.

What is the advantage of a Christianity that is transformed into a myth that upholds the commandment of charity in the face of, say, mere modern reason – of, let us say, a Spinozist tint – and one that also recommends "philia," and not merely strategic harmonious agreements as a way to social reconciliation? Probably the advantage lies in the suppression of cosmic *arbitrariness*, as Blumenberg established in his monumental *Work on Myth*: "Myth is a way to express the fact that the world and the forces that govern it have not been left to the mercy of pure arbitrariness. In whatever fashion one presents it, be it as a partition of powers, be it through a codification of competencies or a legal regulation of relationships, it is a system for the suppression of arbitrariness."[8] The reason that searches for the truth and needs it as a sign of the success of its efforts cannot discard or reject what is arbitrary: it only pretends to moderate its intensity to a level we can live with, searching for convenient transactions that will provisionally rescue us from it. Myth, conversely, promises something more: it aspires to reward our efforts with a "supplement of soul" that grants something like a destiny favourable to our freedom, but does not settle for freedom as a sole and cheerless destiny.

At the end of the nineteenth century, Jean-Marie Guyau (an author unjustly little remembered in our days, who was a sort of affable predecessor of Nietzsche, less truculent in his position but, in the end, no less audacious) wrote a work entitled *L'irreligion de l'avenir*, which he published shortly before his death, when he was in his very early thirties. Although, as is to be expected, the book suffers from what we nowadays consider some of the limitations and scientistic narrowness of his time, I believe it still constitutes one of the best and most complete philosophical characterizations of the religious phenomenon. Its thesis is that religion (any religion whatsoever) "is a physical, metaphysical, and moral explanation of all things by analogy with human society, under an imaginative and symbolic form. It is, in short, a universal sociological explanation in a mythical fashion."[9] In the case of Christianity, Guyau signals love as the doctrinal axis of that "sociological" reading of the world that, thanks to this social character, makes us feel better received into the oddity of the cosmos. For this French author the "irreligion of the future" will consist in an assumption – not mythical but scientific – of such a postulate, one that will transform social harmony into the significant centre of human life. Nietzsche certainly knew this work, and he probably studied it with as much attention as he paid to the previous work of Guyau (*Esquisse d'une morale sans obligation ni sanction*), which he filled with abundant notes. I will allow myself the whim of supposing that the current position of Gianni Vattimo might be something like a reading, itself annotated, of the reading that Nietzsche did of Guyau's work.

NOTES

1   Umberto Eco and Cardinal Martini, *Belief or Nonbelief?* (Arcadia 2000.)
    Note from the translator: the title of this work in Spanish is *¿En qué creen los que no creen?* [Literally translated, the title is rendered as *In what believe those that do not believe?* Savater's remarks are better understood on the basis of this literal translation of the title; however, for bibliographical purposes I have kept the title in English as it is found in the available translation by Arcadia Publishing (2000).]

2 Gianni Vattimo, *Belief*, trans. L. D'Isanto and D. Webb (Stanford: Stanford University Press 1999), 28.

3 Richard Rorty, *The Future of Religion*, edited by S. Zabala (New York: Columbia University Press 2005), 36.

4 J. Gray, *Straw Dogs* (London: Granta Books 2002), 126–7.

5 M. Gauchet, *The Disenchantment of the World* (1985), trans. Oscar Burge (Princeton: Princeton University Press 1997).

6 Translated from the French edition: M. Gauchet, *La condition historique* (Paris: Stock 2003), 199.

7 Vattimo, *Belief*, 66.

8 Translated from the Spanish edition: *Trabajo sobre el mito*, (Barcelona: Paidós 2003) 51. The latest English edition is H. Blumenberg, *Work on Myth*, Studies in Contemporary German Thought, trans. Robert M. Wallace (Cambridge: MIT Press 1998).

9 Translated from the French edition: J-M. Guyau, *L'irreligion de l'avenir*, (Paris: Felix Alcan 1925), 3. The latest English edition is *The Non-religion of the Future* (New York: Schoken Books 1962).

18

Israel as Foundling, Jesus as Bachelor: Abandonment, Adoption, and the Fatherhood of God

JACK MILES

As the author of books explicitly about the Jewish and Christian scriptures – books, however, in which by design I reveal nothing about my personal stance with regard to religion, I am often asked whether or not I am, after all, a believer. My extemporaneous answers never satisfy me but only, perhaps, reveal why I have so studiously avoided the question. But since the publication of Gianni Vattimo's *Credo di credere,* I have developed a better answer. Read Vattimo, I say, and you will acquaint yourself with my predicament better than I could acquaint you with it myself.

My only regret is that Vattimo's charming and perfectly targeted Italian title cannot be put in a single, comparably colloquial English sentence. "I Think I Believe" comes close in meaning but loses the playful echo of the Italian. "I Believe I Believe" sounds in English like insistence by repetition, though someone might just conceivably speak that sentence in the course of a conversation and mean by it something close to *Credo di credere.* "I Believe That I Believe" has a laborious epistemological pomposity in English that *Credo di credere* quite lacks.

Languages – not language *in se* but, as I might put it here, *le lingue fra di loro* – do matter in philosophy, though I am resigned that those whose intellect is equal to the philosophical forest will rarely trouble with mere linguistic trees. Meanwhile, I retain on my long list of reasons to visit Italy the following: only in Italy can I answer the question, "Are you a believer?" by saying, "As Gianni Vattimo might put it (but didn't), *Non credo di non credere.*"

"Who do you say that I am?" Jesus asks his disciples (Matthew 16:15; Mark 8:29; Luke 9:20); unless otherwise noted, biblical quotations are from the Jewish Publication Society Tanakh. His question, on the one hand, and, on the other, his emotional response when Peter answers, "You are the Messiah," suggest an ancient awareness of what we think of as the postmodern insight that even personal identity is not a simple given but is rather the product of an ongoing transaction. Through two millennia of Christian, anti-Christian, and post-Christian thought, an extraordinary array of answers has been given to Jesus' question. Bible scholarship over the past two centuries has sought most often to shift the terms of the debate from theology to history. It has sought to situate the four canonical Gospels in their first-century historical context and to proceed from there to a reconstruction of the historical Jesus of Nazareth. Some critics have always doubted that such a reconstruction was possible. Others, as far back as Albert Schweitzer, have doubted whether, even if it was possible, it could be religiously decisive. In our own day, these attempts to fix the identity of Jesus firmly in the historically knowable have finally come to seem as doomed as earlier attempts to fix it in the philosophically inevitable. Richly interesting and inherently rewarding as historical research remains, it has finally come to seem as inconclusive as the reports circulating about Jesus in his own day. The ancient question has returned in a new, more subjective way: Who do *you* say that I am?

Postmodern literary criticism, while more at ease than traditional philosophy, theology, or historical criticism with the notion, so to put it, of allowing "you" a role in the creation of literary meaning, is true to its belletristic origins in that it continues a marked preference for the concrete particularity of the text. The venerable dictum that the Bible is its own best commentary has taken on new vitality in a form of Bible criticism that otherwise seems to license subjectivity. Rather than spring from a pregnant verse to a philosophical speculation, rather than link a geographical or temporal reference to an archaeological excavation, contemporary literary criticism of the Bible often prefers to link one verse to an unexpected verse within the text itself. Interpretation then becomes, rather in the manner of ancient Jewish midrash, a virtuoso juxtaposition of texts that, once in position, do most of the interpreter's work for him.

The verse "Who do you say that I am?" is particularly apt for this kind of interpretation. The question, asked not in the Gospel of John but only in the three synoptic Gospels, nonetheless invites juxtaposition with John 1:19, where John the Baptist is asked, "Who are you?" Recall that in the "Who do you say that I am?" passage in Matthew, Mark, and Luke, Jesus' disciples, speaking shortly after the judicial murder of John the Baptist, report that some of their contemporaries think Jesus may be John risen from the dead, while others think that he is Elijah or another prophet come to announce the Messiah. Peter knows better, and he bears witness that Jesus himself is the messiah, but one might well ask, Who did John the Baptist think that Jesus was?

Famously, the Gospel of John opens with a prologue in which Jesus is identified as the Word of God – that is, as God himself – become flesh. But the first sentence after that prologue reads *Kai hautē estin hē martyria tou Iōannou"*: "And this is the testimony *of John.*" It is as if the Fourth Gospel intends to tell us that, yes, Peter knew that Jesus was the Messiah but John knew more: he knew that Jesus was God Incarnate. In its entirety the key passage reads:

This is the testimony of John when the Jews sent to him priests and Levites from Jerusalem to ask him, "Who are you?" He declared – he did not deny but declared – "I am not the Messiah." So they asked, "Then are you Elijah?" He replied, "I am not." "Are you the Prophet [presumably Moses]?" He answered, "No." So they said to him, "Who are you? We must take back an answer to those who sent us. What have you to say about yourself?" So he said, "I am a voice of one that cries in the desert: 'Prepare a way for the Lord. Make straight his paths,' just as Isaiah prophesied."

Elijah, it was understood, would return to prepare the way for the Messiah. John announces that his is a higher assignment than Elijah's: he is to prepare the way for the Lord himself.

So many key literary elements occur both in the "Who do you say" passage from the Synoptics and in this passage from the Gospel of John that it is plausible enough to imagine that John was written as a conscious advance beyond the Synoptic tradition. Yet, leaving that essentially historical question aside, the literary fact remains that these passages invite association by any attentive reader. To put it more strongly, they defy separation, particularly once the four have been bound into a single composite work. Once the socioliterary habit of hearing all four

Gospels as a kind of chorus has been established and sanctioned – and this habit was established by the end of the second Christian century – the divinity of John's Jesus cannot easily be denied to the Synoptic Jesus.

But once the divinity of Jesus permeates the Gospel narrative (not just by this juxtaposition but by many others as well), the question of Jesus' identity becomes the question of God's identity. And if the answer to the question, "Who is God?" is to be sought in Jesus' story, then that story must begin not with his birth in Bethlehem but with his creation of the world. A literary approach to the identity of Jesus in the Gospels leads us, in short, to read the Gospel narrative as an utterly surprising epilogue to the story of the self-creation of God as it has unfolded in the earlier Jewish scriptures.

Who is God? For Jews, Christians, and Muslims alike, God is the creator. But how far does his creativity extend? Does it extend to himself? That is, must we say simply and statically that God is uncreated, or may we say instead and more dynamically that God creates himself? If we may employ the latter formulation, then we approach the metaphor that for Jews and Christians has been the supreme descriptive metaphor for divinity – namely, fatherhood. As creator of himself, God is metaphorically his own father. Yet as created by himself, he is metaphorically his own son as well. When speaking either of or to himself, he may employ either half of this two-sided metaphor with equal reason.

The identity of Jesus as both a continuation and a revision of the identity of God as Father is of exceptional interest not just because of the salience of this metaphor in later Jewish and Christian religious rhetoric but also, and more to the literary point, because of its salience in the usage of Jesus himself on the Gospel page. At issue, ultimately, is the understood relationship both of divinity to humanity (as father to children) and of individual human beings to one another (as children to their fellow children within a single family).

If I may offer a brief American digression, Senator John Kerry, asked during a public debate whether homosexuals are as they are by nature or by choice, saw fit to answer the question by saying, "We are all God's children." He expressed a commendably liberal sentiment in a religiously legitimate way; but within the Bible, it is ultimately inadequate to say simply, "We are all God's children." What the Bible offers, on close reading, is not a simple statement that we are all God's children but rather a complex story of how we *became* God's children once God decided to become our father.

God *became* a father, I shall argue, only by somewhat hesitant steps. Moreover, even after he became a father to some, he was not a father to all, and, accordingly, his fatherhood was not initially such as to create a basis for universal human brotherhood. This point is reached in the end, at least when the Christian scriptures are read as the continuation of the Jewish, but it is not reached by early and effortless declaration. God was, it seems, almost as reluctant to embrace his human creatures as children as they themselves are slow, even now, to embrace one another as brothers and sisters.

To justify this claim about the evolution of God's fatherhood in the Bible, let us begin with the Book of Genesis, for if we are all God's children, is it not because we are all descended from his first children, Adam and Eve? But were Adam and Eve really God's children? Was that their relationship to him? If so, how would we expect to know this? We would expect to know it, would we not, from the fact of their addressing him as father or from his addressing them as son or daughter.

But read Genesis 1–3. Nothing of the sort ever happens. God never addresses Adam as "My son" or Eve as "My daughter." Neither of them ever addresses him in a sentence beginning, "O Father." By what terms do the three address one another? As it happens, terms of address simply do not occur in these chapters. Eve does refer to God, using the word *'elohim,* but neither she nor her husband ever addresses him in any form of that name. In referring to them, God uses the common nouns *man* and *woman,* but he too employs no terms of direct address: neither those words nor the names *Adam* and *Eve.*

Granting, then, that terms of direct address do not reveal to us any familial relationship between God and the first human couple, does something else in the text suggest such a relationship? The most basic relationship between him and them is that of creator to creatures, but we who read the story know this in a way that the humans who appear in it do not, for unlike us they do not witness their own creation. We know, moreover, that God has made them in his image and likeness, and perhaps we may infer that looking upon God as they apparently do, they may recognize something of a resemblance. But on what textual grounds, if any, could we claim that this resemblance in itself constitutes a familial relationship between him and them?

I confess that I see none. God conducts himself with solicitude – the word *love* may not be too strong – toward his human creatures, at least until he grows angry with them, but solicitude need not imply paternity. No, as the myth unfolds, God reveals himself to his first human creatures rather as their master than as their father. Adam and Eve, whether or not they fully appreciate that God is their creator, do acknowledge his mastery over them in some preliminary way. Though they will disobey him, they do not challenge his right to command their obedience. A bit later, when he sentences them and all their offspring to death, when he blights the Earth that Adam will cultivate, when he turns childbirth into torture for Eve, they are given a grim demonstration of his mastery, although God seems, if anything, less determined to punish our first parents by this demonstration of his power than he is to rebuke the clever serpent who tempted them and has thereby so thoroughly disrupted God's arrangements for them. In any case, we must conclude that it is mastery rather than paternity that defines God's relationship to his first human creatures in the opening chapters of Genesis.

And it is mastery, is it not, rather than paternity, that would seem proper to a celibate god like this one? If there is no mother goddess, and there evidently is none, then how can there be a father god? Athena may have sprung full-grown from the brow of Zeus, but paternity normally requires maternity, and indeed most ancient gods were sexual beings who created by some kind of sexual generation. The God of the Book of Genesis, by sharpest contrast, is celibate. He has no spouse, and he does not create by sexual generation but rather by serene and lordly speech. He creates by commanding.

If we were disposed to speak of God's form of creativity as analogous to parturition, and some later Jewish and Christian thinkers were indeed so disposed, we could say that his firstborn offspring, born from his mouth, was the sentence *yehi 'or,* "Let there be light." Before light appeared, that sentence emerged. God begot the word in his mind and bore it from no other womb than his mouth, and thereupon the word begot the light.

But having forced even this much of an opening for a paternal or paternal/maternal understanding of divine creativity, we must immediately note that if God fathers humankind by speaking it into existence, he fathers everything else in just the same way: the heavens and the earth, the "seed-bearing plants of every kind, and trees of every kind bearing fruit with the seed in it," and so forth. Even granting that everything fathered forth in this way reflects its divine parentage in some way, parentage so understood bears little resemblance to the tender and dignifying relationship that we ordinarily understand by the sentence

"We are all God's children." But the author of the creation myth that we find in the Book of Genesis had a clear reason for his refusal to suggest any genealogical relationship between God and his first human creatures.

When monotheism was a new and strange idea, an idea in acute danger of being normalized back toward the culturally dominant poly- theism, to claim a filial relationship with a father god was dangerously close to claiming divinity for oneself. *Like father, like son* is a rule that applies, after all, right down to our own day. In Semitic antiquity, more- over, much suggests that rather than mere physical resemblance, we must understand in the father-son relationship something much stronger, something, in fact, approaching true identity transference. It was because of identity transference that the sins of the fathers could justifiably be visited upon the sons. But what would become of monotheism if the one God, the *monos theos,* had children to whom his divine identity could be similarly passed down?

Later in the development of ancient Israelite thought, as monotheism hardened gradually into a stable belief, it became possible to employ paternity as a metaphor without compromising this belief. But, as I hope to demonstrate in discussing the image of the foundling, it would be necessary even then to put certain reminders in place that the pater- nal metaphor was indeed only a metaphor. As a true historical hypoth- esis, my contention that fatherhood is a late-arising metaphor rather than a part of Israel's earliest monotheistic belief about God cannot really be proven. It can be offered only as an interpretive invitation, as if to say, "Taste and see. Read the text expecting, as a mere working hypothesis, that fatherhood-language will emerge gradually rather than being omnipresent from the start, and then see how things work out."

Gradual development, I must now hasten to add, does not mean step- by-step logical development. What we see, in fact, is a process by which true sexual parenthood for God is apparently rejected, then quite boldly and explicitly entertained as a possibility for him, then rejected again with greater clarity, then readmitted but in an adoptive or metaphori- cal form, and finally embraced with growing emotion and yet with a crucial correction of the metaphor.

As background for this entire evolution, there stands the universal human observation that it is sexual intercourse that enables men and women to make other men and women and that the boys and girls who are made in this way frequently resemble their mothers and fathers. But does this observable fact about humankind mean that human beings have a power like the one that God exercises at Genesis 1:27 when he creates a man and a woman in his own image? The answer is evidently yes. Sexuality is indeed a godlike power. But then is God's version of this power necessarily sexual? The answer is no, eventually, but clarity on this point does not come without a struggle, and, dramatically enough, the struggle seems at times to take place within God himself, for at times he seems to regard the free exercise of human sexual fertility as if it were the key power of a rival divinity and therefore to be combatted rather than fostered.

The core transaction of all great literary art is the transformation of thought into story. Changes of thought en route to clarity become in the hands of a literary artist stages in a story en route to its resolution. If this is easily said, it is not at all easily done, particularly when it is through the story that the thought first takes shape.

With regard to the story of God's fatherhood, I invite you to put yourself in the condition of someone who does not yet know whether or not divine and human generativity are both sexual in character. Maybe God is a truly sexual being, maybe he isn't. If he is, then the possibility of divine breeding exists, bringing with it a potential multiplication of divinities, of whom none would ever disappear, because all would be immortal. Moreover, this multiplication of sexual immortals will open the further possibility of divine-human hybridization and perhaps the sexual transmission of immortality from gods to men. How exciting! This idea does have its appeal. But now imagine that having entertained seductive ideas like these, you have in the last analysis decided to reject them but are allowed to do so only in the form of a story. What sort of story do you tell?

The story you tell might conceivably come out a little like a strange but crucial episode in Genesis that comes as a transition between the creation myth and the flood myth. In Genesis 6:1–8, we read:

When men began to increase on earth and daughters were born to them, the sons of God saw how beautiful were the daughters of men and took wives from among those that pleased them. The Lord said, "My breath shall not abide in man forever, since he too is flesh; let the days allowed him be one hundred and twenty years." It was then, and later too, that the Nephilim appeared on earth – when the sons of God cohabited with the daughters of men, who bore them offspring. They were the heroes of old, the men of renown.

The Lord saw how great was man's wickedness on earth, and how every plan devised by his mind was nothing but evil all the time. And the Lord regretted that He had made man on earth, and His heart was saddened. The Lord said, "I will blot out from the earth the men whom I created – men together with beasts, creeping things, and birds of the sky; for I regret that I made them. But Noah found favor with the Lord.

In the Book of Genesis, the destruction of the world by water is a stage in the plot corresponding to a movement of thought from an understanding of divine and human generativity as equally sexual to an understanding of them as different in that regard. The correction of a mistaken idea becomes, when turned into myth, the story of one world being destroyed and another replacing it. Earlier leads to later in the story as mistake leads to correction in the argument. Before the flood, God is capable of breeding and in fact does breed in a very literal sense of the word; the Nephilim – sexual immortals like the gods of so many other ancient cultures – are his offspring. But after the flood, the Nephilim are gone, and God no longer engages in the kind of activity that could produce a new generation of Nephilim. The flood thus constitutes a narrative rejection of the idea that God could ever be sexually generative of fully divine children.

But what of the human beings created in God's image? Just how large a share in the divine life do they have? They have his breath in them. Does that mean that, like him, they will breathe forever? The answer, initially, is yes, but then God changes his mind. In Genesis 3, he angrily sentences the first humans to death. In Genesis 6, he assigns humanity a finite lifespan as a revision or correction of his initial plan. And because God is a single character, equally himself wherever he appears in his story, the story itself gains in power as he makes these changes. We see him doing one thing, then regretting it and doing something else. We see him evolving in and through his own words and actions.

God seems utterly celibate in the magisterial, world-creating recital of the first chapter of Genesis. But by strong implication God seems to have been anything but celibate when he brought the Nephilim into existence. Yet because in that very passage he ends up destroying the world in which his own celibacy seemed so negotiable, his celibacy thereafter seems quite beyond negotiation, a fixed feature of his character. God does not begin celibate, in short, but, rather, *adopts* celibacy. The surprise is that, having resolved with such violent finality to have no divine offspring of his own, God immediately develops an intense interest in the generativity of his human creatures. Having forsworn actual fatherhood, he develops an apparent hunger for vicarious fatherhood.

After the floodwaters recede, God makes a covenant with Noah and his descendants – in effect, a covenant with what remains of the entire human race. Why did God make no such covenant with Adam and his descendants? An Adamic covenant may be implicit in the physical arrangements God put in place, arrangements that make obedience to his commands feasible, but there is no explicit covenant in the creation story, and on the human side there is no act of ratification. If we read Genesis 1–3 in light of the opening of Genesis 6, then perhaps we may infer that it was not entirely clear at the start whether God's relationship to his human creatures would be familial or contractual. Were Adam and Eve to acknowledge God as their father or as their lord? The opening chapters of Genesis suggest that he regards himself as their lord rather than their father; but if some uncertainty on this point remains, the Noachic covenant removes it. God's covenant with Noah has thus a double meaning or a double effect. First, under the sign of the rainbow, it ends the estrangement between God and his now renewed creation. Second, it establishes beyond doubt that the relationship between God and his human creatures is now truly and only a contractual rather than a physical relationship. The fertility command given to Adam and Eve is repeated to Noah and his descendants: "Be fertile and increase, and fill the earth" (Gen. 9:1); but though they will multiply, it is now clear that God himself will not. There will not be a second generation of Nephilim.

As in the creation myth, so also in this destruction myth, God never addresses his human interlocutor as "My son," and he himself is never addressed as "My father." Noah never speaks to God at all, but he does silently ratify the contractual nature of his relationship to God by offering a sacrifice, as we read: "Then Noah built an altar to the Lord and, taking of every clean animal and of every clean bird, he offered burnt offerings on the altar. The Lord smelled the pleasing odor, and the Lord said to Himself: 'Never again will I doom the earth because of man, ... nor will I ever again destroy every living being, as I have done'" (Gen. 8:20–1).

Israel has not yet been mentioned in the biblical epic, and yet Israel is here by anticipation. If Israel's later relationship with God is to be essentially covenantal rather than familial, then it is of considerable importance that no *other* nation be capable of claiming that its relationship with him is familial. The Noachic covenant will make it possible for Israel in a future generation to assert, by implication at least, "We are not God's biological children – and neither are you." Nobody has a familial relationship with God because God is simply not that kind of god. What everyone does have is a covenantal relationship, but there can be special covenants within that generic covenant.

I said a moment ago that once God definitively renounces conventional, genital paternity for himself and establishes his first-ever covenant with humankind, his interest in human reproduction seems to grow more intense. Let me now add that it is because of this interest that God's involvement in human history grows as tangled as it does. It need not have been so. If God was going to be a god who himself did not perform any act of sexual generation, he might have expressed no interest in those that humans perform. But the opposite turns out to be the case. He promises Abraham miraculous fertility, offspring as numerous as the stars, and human history is broken open when he keeps his promise. The Israelites in Egypt grow astoundingly numerous, their women giving birth essentially without labour, and the Egyptians strike back. To save his people, God is forced to go to war for the first time in his career; and at that point like a ship slipping anchor, he and Israel are fairly launched on their long historical voyage. Had God not elevated Israelite fertility so far above the human norm, he himself would never have had to go to war. But had God not become celibate, perhaps he would not have needed to make this unexplained and otherwise unmotivated promise of miraculous fertility to Abraham.

There is an undeniable grandeur about major human events: war and peace, the exile and homecoming of entire nations, retribution and vindication, and so forth. Yet we all know that family formation and family life have their own emotional intensity: finding a spouse, trying to conceive, conceiving, making it through the pregnancy, bringing the newborn through the perilous first year, and so forth. The birth of a single child over all the obstacles that can and so often do arise may seem no less momentous than victory in a great war. The call of Abraham begins the story of a great nation, the nation of Israel. The story will eventually include war and peace, exile and homecoming, punishment and vindication, and all that makes for grandeur in a national epic, yet the story will never lose the special intensity of an intimate family drama in which the birth of every Jewish child seems a victory over obstacles as large as those that faced Abraham and Sarah. This is the special quality, as it has always seemed to me, of the Jewish vision of Jewish history. And yet we must wonder, What motivated God to begin it?

God's involvement in the drama of Abraham's fatherhood, not to speak of Sarah's motherhood, is both intense and intensely ambivalent. Let me note, to begin with, that "the God of my Father," a phrase that we begin to hear at this point in the Bible, is not "God my Father." Like Adam and Noah, Abraham never addresses God as his father, and God never addresses Abraham as his son. God's attention to Abraham's reproduction is as intense as that of any grandfather expecting a grandson, yet God's involvement, to repeat, is intensely ambivalent: Does he want his own promise kept, or does he want it frustrated? We see this ambivalence when, having promised Abraham fertility beyond all natural limits, God postpones his first conception deep into old age and arranges a narrow brush with death in childhood for Ishmael, as well as Isaac. It is as if God has renounced paternity for himself, chosen in its stead a vicarious and divinely enlarged paternity in Abraham, and then struggled to accept his own compromise.

Circumcision, the sign of the covenant by which God promises Abraham miraculous fertility, entails Abraham's giving a share of his fertility – symbolized by his foreskin, the excised part of his sexual organ – back to God. God paid no such attention to Adam's or Noah's genitalia, though God commanded both of them to increase and fill the earth. God takes the interest that he does take in Abraham's genitalia as a way of assigning himself a share of Abraham's fatherhood perhaps – though his motive is never stated – because at this point in his story he can hope for nothing more. And yet his share remains contractual rather than truly familial, and neither Ishmael nor Isaac will ever address God as father. God can bestow fertility, and does, but there is a poignant difference between doing that and being an actual father.

Let me now turn to the Book of Exodus and particularly to a pair of verses that might seem to reverse everything I have claimed to this point. At Exodus 4:22–23, God gives Moses the language in which he will warn Pharaoh to release Israel or prepare to pay a terrible price: "Then you shall say to Pharaoh, 'Thus says the Lord: Israel is My first-born son.' I have said to you, 'Let My son go, that he may worship Me,' yet you refuse to let him go. Now I will slay your first-born son." God's way of characterizing his relationship with Israel certainly sounds paternal here, but note well: God is not explaining this relationship for the benefit of Moses or the Israelites. He is putting it in alien language for an alien ruler and an alien god. Pharaoh, according to Egyptian religion, was not just the king but also the divine fertility guarantor of the Egyptian people – in effect, the all but literal father of his country. God is, so to speak, translating his relationship to Israel into Egyptian theological terms for the benefit of the rival god whose claim to be a god is about to be destroyed in the destruction of Egypt itself.

Were this God's own understanding of his relationship to Israel, were this the understanding that he wanted to implant in the nation he is about to bind to himself by the covenant at Sinai, then at some point he might well say to them, "You are Israel, my first-born son." He might well instruct them to pray to him, "You are our father, and we are your first-born son." But during the lifetime of Moses, no such words are ever spoken; no such instruction ever imparted. On the contrary, it is at Sinai that the contractual seems most overwhelmingly to eclipse any remaining trace of the familial. As if to stress that God's liberty to form new covenants is not inhibited by any fatherly feeling he may have toward Israel, God goes so far as to propose after the incident of the golden calf (Exodus 32) that he exterminate Israel on the spot and create a new people for himself using Moses as the new Abraham. Moses, in a famous bit of biblical bargaining, talks him out of it. But once again God had shown an astonishing ambivalence, a truly lethal volatility, with regard to his own undertakings.

Within Torah, to be sure, the paternal image remains available as a general metaphor for care. In the Book of Deuteronomy, Moses says, looking back on Israel's forty years in the desert, "The Lord your God carried you, as a man carries his son, all the way you traveled until you came to this place" (1:31), and again, "The Lord your God disciplines you just as a man disciplines his son" (8:5). But the more poetic the language, the more easily things may be said that no one is expected to take literally. Thus, elsewhere in Deuteronomy 32, the poet sings of God as "The Rock! – His deeds are perfect, / Yea, all His ways are just (32:4)," and a bit later, mixing metaphors, sings of him again as a paternal rock: "You [Israel] neglected the Rock that begot you, / Forgot the God who brought you forth" (32:27).

At Deuteronomy 14:1, we even encounter the flat statement, "You are children of the Lord your God," but the context somewhat dilutes the assertion. The fuller passage reads: "You are children of the Lord your God. You shall not gash yourselves or shave the front of your heads because of the dead. For you are a people consecrated to the Lord your God: the Lord your God chose you from among all other peoples on earth to be His treasured people" (14:1–2). In context, the phrase "children of the Lord" seems synonymous with the milder "consecrated to the Lord." Clearly, however, the relationship rests on the free and therefore revocable choice of God, while true parenthood is irrevocable: once the child is born, the relationship ceases to be a matter of choice. By the end of the Book of Deuteronomy, there is an undeniable emotional ardour burning within God's contractual relationship to Israel, but to love someone, even to love him like a son, is not to be his father.

Granting that paternal language, even if not entirely absent, is strikingly rare in Torah, whence comes the paternal language that now seems so central to our imaginings of God and was so for Jesus as well? It comes at the time and really in the person of King David. It comes in particular in words that God speaks to David through the prophet Nathan. God's story can be read, in a way, as the story of fatherhood lost and found. Imagine, if you will, a childless man who yearns to be a father. Imagine a man with an immense capacity to do good yet one whose path to normal human paternity is blocked. What can he do? Well, he can adopt a child, can't he? But will he? First he must *decide* to adopt; he must adopt for *himself* the role of father to another's child before he can invite the child to adopt the corresponding role of child to himself.

I describe the process as if the initiative must lie entirely with the prospective parent; but in the real world of adoptions, as you may know, the initiative sometimes begins with the child. My wife, Jacqueline, and I have had the experience of having a teen-age boy invite us to adopt him. I know a couple with several children of their own who were asked to care temporarily for a foster child, intended initially to do no more, but fell in love with him and ended up adopting him. In the Books of Samuel, as Harold Bloom has taught us to see, God falls in love with David, but David is far from a passive partner in the transaction. David in some sense seduces God. In 1 Samuel 7, David does something so spontaneous and winning that God is moved to enter a paternal relationship with the entire House of David. And if this is a boon for Solomon, it represents a momentous change in God himself.

As the story opens, David is embarrassed to be living in a cedar-paneled palace, while the Ark of the Lord – in effect, the Lord himself – is housed in a mere tent. The prophet Nathan guesses what David is about to do – namely, build God a temple – and endorses the idea, but God then intercepts David and outdoes him.

While the king was settled in his palace and the Lord had granted him safety from all the enemies around him, the king said to the prophet Nathan: "Here am I dwelling in a house of cedar, while the Ark of the Lord abides in a tent!" Nathan said to the king, "Go and do whatever you have in mind, for the Lord is with you."

But that same night the word of the Lord came to Nathan: "Go and say to My servant David: Thus said the Lord: Are you the one to build a house for Me to dwell in? From the day that I brought the people of Israel out of Egypt to this day I have not dwelt in a house, but have moved about in Tent and Tabernacle. As I moved about wherever the Israelites went, did I ever reproach any of the tribal leaders whom I appointed to care for My people Israel: Why have you not built Me a house of cedar? ...

The Lord declares to you that He, the Lord, will establish a house for you. When your days are done and you lie with your fathers, I will raise up your offspring after you, one of your own issue, and I will establish his kingship. He shall build a house for My name, and I will establish his royal throne forever. I will be a father to him, and he shall be a son to Me. When he does wrong, I will chastise him with the rod of men and the affliction of mortals; but I will never withdraw My favor from him as I withdrew it from Saul, whom I removed to make room for you. Your house and your kingship shall be secure before you; your throne shall be established forever. (1 Samuel 7:1–7, 11b-16)

I said earlier that election is a revocable relationship, while parenthood is an irrevocable one. In promising to adopt David's son, God speaks of chastising him "with the rod *of men* and the affliction *of mortals.*" Chastisement of this sort – a mild, merely human sort – is to be contrasted with the wrath of God, which takes the form of outright revocation of the relationship, extending even to the extermination of the offender, as in the flood or, very nearly, after the episode of the golden calf. By renouncing his right ever to revoke the relationship, God becomes a true, if adoptive, father to Solomon and so promises David a house, a dynasty, that will last for all time.

As a moment in the life of God, 1 Samuel 7 is a moment of poignancy and beauty. And yet it is a moment that brings trouble in its wake, for though God intends only adoptive fatherhood, Israel is surrounded by nations that believe in literal divine-human fatherhood. Historically, the establishment of kingship in Israel does seem to have opened a cultural path to the reintroduction of a Canaanite idea that might be put in the form of this syllogism:

The king is identified with the god.
The people are identified with the king.
Therefore, the people are identified with the god.

Using paternal language, this syllogism can be restated:

The king is the son of the god.
The people are the children of the king.
Therefore, the people are children of the god.

I said earlier that Torah avoids father-language for a reason. This is the reason. Father-language is a standing invitation to the multiplication of divinities and to the blurring of the distinction between the one true God and his human creatures. This blurring can be avoided if care is taken to distinguish biological from adoptive fatherhood, but pride and ambition are all too likely to get in the way. From within this world of belief, the impulse is overwhelming to say, in effect, "All humankind are God's subjects, and he rules them with a firm hand. We alone are God's children, flesh of his flesh and bone of his bone, and he cares for us alone with true paternal love."

Against this impulse, the prophets of Israel developed a small but scathing set of counternarratives, symbolic retellings or corrective images of the entire history of Israel. The intent of these narratives was, on the one hand, to preserve and defend the new and rightly cherished understanding of God as Israel's adoptive father while, on the other, reviving and underscoring the older view that Israel had no physical relationship with God and that therefore Israelites must not regard themselves as inherently – much less as physically – closer to God than other peoples.

If pure Israelite ancestry conferred some kind of physical nearness to God, then it would indeed be something to be cherished and preserved, but in these prophecies Israelite ancestry is denied to Israel itrself. What might seem a genealogical contradiction has a rhetorical point: Israel becomes Israel in one way and one way alone – namely, by the free, unprompted action of God. Thus, we read in Ezekiel 16:1–7:

The word of the Lord came to me: O mortal, proclaim Jerusalem's abomina-tions to her, and say: Thus said the Lord God to Jerusalem: By origin and birth you are from the land of the Canaanites – your father was an Amorite and your mother a Hittite. As for your birth, when you were born your navel cord was not cut, and you were not bathed in water to smooth you; and you were not rubbed with salt, nor were you swaddled. No one pitied you enough to do any one of these things for you out of compassion for you; on the day you were born, you were left lying, rejected, in the open field. When I passed by you and saw you wallowing in your blood, I said to you, "Live in spite of your blood. Yea, I said to you: Live in spite of your blood. I let you grow like the plants of the field: and you continued to grow up until you to attained to womanhood, until your breasts became firm and your pubic hair sprouted.

We may well imagine that in the Israel of Ezekiel's day, "Your father was an Amorite" was an insult, and "Your mother was a Hittite" another. In Judaea after the Babylonian exile, a disparaging distinction was drawn between the true Israelites – namely, those who had been carried into exile or who had been born in exile of Israelite parents – and those who had remained in the land but now seemed to the returnees more Canaanite than Israelite. "Born in the land of the Canaanites" would then have been yet another ethnic slur.

In this shocking passage, however, God himself delivers just these insults to his people as a whole. Amorite, Hittite, Canaanite – who knows the genealogy of a foundling? A foundling is an orphan, a castoff, nobody's baby, abandoned, unknown, and forever unknowable. Ezekiel describes this infant in a deliberately revolting way as lying in the slime of the afterbirth, flailing about helplessly in that mess of blood and amniotic fluid. Her umbilical cord has not been tied or cut. Without God's immediate intervention, she will die within hours. But God says to her, "Live," and takes her in. This is the image of a kind of fatherhood that can only be adoptive fatherhood.

The story of this foundling continues as she comes of age and marries her loving father-protector, then deserts him and debauches herself with a series of lovers, and finally repents and is taken back by him. These two images – Israel as God's child and Israel as God's spouse – would together be an image of incest if we were not in the realm of adoptive, analogous, or metaphorical relationships. In Torah, marital imagery is avoided even more scrupulously than parental imagery, presumably out of fear that it would be taken literally. In the prophets, not only do we find both images, we sometimes find them mingled in the same incident to make a strong point even stronger. Clearly, the prophets write with some confidence that metaphorical language will be recognized as such. The challenge has become one of finding the metaphors that say what needs to be said.

If the image of Israel as a discarded orphan whom God has rescued from a hideous and pathetic death is powerful, more powerful still, perhaps, is the image of Israel as *hijodeputa,* a whoreson or a whore's daughter, and of God himself as a man married to the whore. This is the image that we encounter in the Book of Hosea (1:2–5, 8–9):

When the Lord first spoke to Hosea, the Lord said to Hosea, "Go, get yourself a wife of whoredom and children of whoredom; for the land will stray from following the Lord." So he went and married Gomer daughter of Diblaim. She conceived and bore him a son, and the Lord instructed him, "Name him Jezreel; for, I will soon punish the House of Jehu for the bloody deeds at Jezreel and put an end to the monarchy of the House of Israel. In that day, I will break the bow of Israel in the Valley of Jezreel."

She conceived again and bore a daughter; and He said to him, "Name her Lo-ruhamah ["No Pity"]; for henceforth I will have no pity on the House of Israel nor will I pardon them." ...

After weaning Lo-ruhamah, she conceived and bore a son. Then He said, "Name him Lo-ammi ["Not My People"]; for you are not My people, and I will not be your God."

Are Gomer's three children Hosea's children? Since she makes a living by sleeping with many men, he cannot know whose these children of hers are, and that is just the point of the story. If Hosea stands for God, and these children stand for Israel, then Israel has no automatic or inherent or quasi-physical relationship with God. Hosea would be fully within his rights to reject Gomer's children as presumptively no children of his, and God, by unmistakable implication, would be fully within his rights to reject Israel as no child of his either.

In Hosea, as in Ezekiel, the marital image functions alongside the parental image. Though Gomer's three bastards represent Israel, so does Gomer, the whore herself. But what if Hosea actually loves her? What if he is willing to accept her children, no matter whose they are, as his own? If so, and if Hosea represents God, what does this tell us about God? In an ecstatic passage, God says that he loves Israel despite all debaucheries and will somehow seduce her back into fidelity to himself. Having accomplished this miracle, he promises that he will take pity on the girl named No Pity and say to the boy named Not-My-People, "You are my people."

I have been quoting so far from the Jewish Publication Society

Tanakh, but let me quote this climactic passage in Hosea from the King James Version (2:19–23), which does have its moments:

I will betroth thee unto me for ever; yea, I will betroth thee unto me in right-eousness, and in judgment, And in lovingkindness, and in mercies:

I will even betroth thee unto me in faithfulness; and thou shalt know the Lord.

And it shall come to pass in that day, I will hear, saith the Lord, I will hear the heavens, and they shall hear the earth;

And the earth shall hear the corn, and the wine, and the oil; And they shall hear Jezreel.

And I will sow her unto me in the earth; and I will have mercy upon her that had not obtained mercy; And I will say to them which were not my people, Thou art my people; And they shall say, Thou art my God.

As I tried to indicate earlier, Ezekiel and Hosea want to humble Israel, and yet theyexalt Israel. They want in the bluntest, rudest way possible to deny Israel any automatic intimacy with God, as if the mere accident of birth could ever be enough, and yet they want to promise Israel that because of God's great love, Israel can be God's baby anyway, in both the nursery and the honeymoon sense of the word – God's little kid and God's sweetheart, both at the same time.

If it is to this point that the Old Testament brings the story of the fatherhood of God, how may the New Testament be seen to continue the story? With regard to fatherhood, as in many other respects, the New Testament seizes upon a tension or contradiction within the Old Testament and carries it to a rhetorical, narrative, and logical extreme. When the celibate God becomes incarnate, he becomes, as we would expect, a celibate man. Jesus of Nazareth is a bachelor. He has no wife. He has no children. Moreover, when the God of the Jews becomes a Jew himself, he delivers, again just as we would expect in view of his oracles to Ezekiel and Hosea, a blunt rebuke of genetic filiation, on the one hand, and a warm embrace of adoptive filiation, on the other.

The rebuke comes at various points and in various ways. Perhaps the sharpest is Mark 3:31–35:

Now his mother and his brothers arrived and, standing outside, sent in a message asking for him. A crowd was sitting round him at the time the message was passed to him, "Look, your mother and brothers and sisters are outside asking for you." He replied, "Who are my mother and my brothers?" And looking at those sitting in a circle round him, he said, "Here are my mother and my brothers. Anyone who does the will of God, that person is my brother and sister and mother."

Earlier, I asserted that if God is both his own creator and his own creature, then he is, metaphorically, both his own father and his own son, but this relationship is unique and beyond literal duplication. It is to the uniqueness of this relationship that the Christian creed refers when it calls Jesus God's "only begotten son," the *huios monogenēs* or *filius unigenitus*. Human beings enter this unique relationship only by adoption. As father, God may adopt them as children. As son, God may adopt them as brothers and sisters or even, at the extreme, as human fathers and mothers.

The more God insisted, through his prophets, that his relationship with Israel was that of adoptive fatherhood, the more the stage was set for the extension of this adoptive fatherhood to the rest of mankind. The tenderness of an adoptive father, like that which we heard in Hosea, is matched at John 13:33–5. Jesus, having washed his disciples' feet just hours before his arrest, addresses them as his beloved children: "Little children, I shall not be with you much longer. You will look for me, but as I told the Jews, where I am going, you cannot come. I have given you a new commandment: Love one another. You must love one another just as I have loved you. It is by your love for one another that all will know that you are my disciples."

A bit later, he prays in a similar vein: "May they all be one, Just as, Father, you are in me and I am in you, So that they also may be in us, So that the world may believe it was you who sent me" (John 17:21–3). He has adopted them as his children; he has also adopted them as his brethren. For their part, by loving others as he has loved them, they are to expand his adoptive family to include the entire world.

Paul, speaking as a Jew to his fellow Jews, sees this initiation through Christ into a filial relationship with God as a step beyond the relationship that Israel has previously enjoyed with God. Thus, Israel gains even though the new relationship ceases to be exclusive. Thus, we read (Galatians 3:23–4:8):

But before faith came, we were kept under guard by the Law, locked up to wait for the faith which would eventually be revealed to us. So the Law was serving as a slave to look after us, to lead us to Christ, so that we could be justified by faith. But now that faith has come we are no longer under a slave looking after us; for all of you are the children of God, through faith, in Christ Jesus, since every one of you that has been baptized has been clothed in Christ. There can be neither Jew nor Greek, there can be neither slave nor freeman, there can be neither male nor female – for you are all one in Christ Jesus. And simply by being Christ's, you are the progeny of Abraham, the heirs named in the promise.

What I am saying is this: an heir, during the time while he is still under age, is no different from a slave, even though he is the owner of all the property; he is under the control of guardians and administrators until the time fixed by his father. So too with us, as long as we were still under age, we were enslaved to the elemental principles of this world; but when the completion of the time came, God sent his Son, born of a woman, born a subject of the Law, to redeem the subjects of the Law, so that we could receive adoption as sons. As you are sons, God has sent into our hearts the Spirit of his Son crying, "Abba, Father"; and so you are no longer a slave, but a son; and if a son, then an heir, by God's own act. (New Jerusalem Bible translation.)

As always, Paul piles metaphor upon metaphor. For the purposes of this discussion, I wish to note only two features of his argument: first, his background awareness that if Israel's experience as God's child has undergone a long evolution, then so has God's experience as Israel's father. God's Son has existed from all eternity, but he has not been crying "Abba" in all human hearts from all eternity. This may be the end of the evolution, an end that lies some time in the future, even for Paul, but it was not the beginning.

The beginning was a covenantal relationship between lord and liege, master and servant, and this relationship lives on. The earlier, covenantal relationship, in which paternal language played little or no part, lives on alongside the later quasi-familial relationship, in which paternal language virtually eclipses all other language. In Torah, as we said earlier, all God's interactions with human beings bespoke mastery rather than paternity, but this more austere, more august relationship is repudiated neither in Rabbinic Judaism nor in any form of Christianity.

Islam sees all the legendary figures of Torah as proto-Muslims because they acknowledged God as their master. They put themselves in a relationship of submission to God, which, for Islam, is the only proper relationship for a human being ever to claim. Thus, the Qur'an at sura 5, verse 18 admonishes: "The Jews and Christians say, 'We are sons of God and his loved ones.' Say: Why then does he punish you for your sins? No, you are mere mortal men whom he has created. He forgives whom he will and punishes whom he will. God is the ruler of the heavens and the earth and all that is between them, and unto him is the journeying." The Qur'an is right: Jews and Christians do indeed speak of God as their father and of themselves as his children. And there is perhaps something salutary about the Qur'an's rebuke. However, if Jews and Christians acknowledge the full complexity of their respective traditions, they will know God is, first and last, as in Islam, the Lord of the World, the Master of the Universe. He is *avinu,* but he is also, and immediately, *malkenu.* Christians may pray to him as "Our Father," but their prayer must immediately continue in humility, "Thy kingdom come, Thy will be done." In and of ourselves, we are all orphans and foundlings, whoresons and bastards. If we are in any sense God's children, it is only because he has taken us in and made us his own. This is what makes our story his, and in the very last reckoning, this is what makes it a divine comedy.

19

Postmodern Disarmament

JEFFREY M. PERL

... the reign of the man of violence is at an end.

Gianni Vattimo[1]

A disclaimer, to begin with: I was trained not as a philosopher but as a scholar of comparative literature, and Italian is not among the languages I read. Neither Gadamer, Gianni Vattimo's teacher – nor Heidegger, Gadamer's – is a thinker who means much to my own work or had any place in my education. I find aspects of the hermeneutic enterprise counterproductive. My relationship to Vattimo, therefore, is unobvious, yet definable precisely. Our relation is editorial.

Gianni Vattimo is a member of the *Common Knowledge* editorial board. He and other writers whose relation to one another was unobvious joined me in founding that journal around 1989. The intellectual disorder that the media named "the culture wars" was under way and ruining lives (among them, my own). Tests were devised to place academics on Left or Right, Old Left or New – and to place them among modernists or post-modernists. In Cambridge, England, a career might end abruptly if a young scholar cited Derrida too often. At Columbia, the ax might fall if Foucault or Woolf was discounted in a seminar or a preface. This sorting process was fast, the thought process casual but vehement, and the results for intellectual life were deadening.

The most intelligent people were committing, or so it seemed to me, elementary errors of association and dissociation. I remember the unease I felt when the National Association of Scholars – a group raised up in the United States to combat postmodernism – included W.V. Quine among the signatories of its manifesto. Why should the author of *Ontological Relativity and Other Essays* feel affronted by postmodern skepticism? A decade before Derrida's *Grammatology* saw print, Quine had written:

It makes no real difference that the linguist will turn bilingual and come to think as the natives do – whatever that means. For the arbitrariness of reading our objectifications into the heathen speech reflects not so much the inscrutability of the heathen mind, as that there is nothing to scrute. Even we who grew up together and learned English at the same knee, or adjacent ones, talk alike for no other reason than that society coached us alike in a pattern of verbal response to externally observable cues ... For the obstacle to correlating conceptual schemes is not that there is anything ineffable about language or culture, near or remote ...The obstacle is only that any one intercultural correlation of words and phrases, and hence of theories, will be just one among various empirically admissible correlations, whether it is suggested by historical gradations or by unaided analogy; there is nothing for such a correlation to be uniquely right or wrong about.[2]

"We persist," Quine protested, "in breaking reality down somehow into a multiplicity of identifiable and discriminable objects," though there are no "fixed ideas beneath the flux of language."[3] Even "water," he argued, is a "provincial adult bulk term" that infants apprehend – in the way they apprehend "mama" and "red" – as "a scattered portion of what goes on."[4] Infants come to accept "water" and "mama" as coherent objects (and "red" as a quality that some objects evince) only once they have been "beaten into an outward conformity to an outward standard."[5] In later years, Quine would try to explain away his imputation of arbitrariness to translation, interpretation, and objectification. Still, what else but arbitrary could even objectification be in a world where, as Quine put it, "there is nothing to scrute" – where there is nothing "to be uniquely right or wrong about"?

And so, I would have thought that Quine and Derrida, Foucault and Quine, would have had much to say to each other, that the French would have acknowledged Quine as a precursor, and that Quine would by no means have signed his name to a document censuring anyone's thinking as radical. But Quine was an "analytic philosopher" in the "Anglo-American tradition." Foucault and Derrida were "continental" philosophers (and were suspected, by Anglo positivists, of indiscipline). Those labels, and many others of the kind, seemed to matter at the time. Still, as Jerry Fodor has pointed out recently, it was Quine's article

"Two Dogmas of Empiricism," that – as early as 1953 – blew analytic philosophy out of the water:

Quine's target was mainly the empiricist tradition in epistemology, but his conclusions were patently germane to the agenda of analytical philosophy. If there are no conceptual truths, there are no conceptual analyses either. If there are no conceptual analyses, analytic philosophers are in jeopardy of methodological unemployment.[6]

A case parallel to Quine's is Kuhn's. Thomas Kuhn, like Quine, had as much or more in common with the Young Turks he resisted than with the colleagues – often scientific realists – with whom he chose to publish and confer. Kuhn's case was the more resonant of the two because, unlike Quine, Kuhn was fancied by the adventurers he feared. Rhetorical flourishes in *The Structure of Scientific Revolutions* (a book published in the *International Encyclopedia of Unified Science*, whose editors and advisory board included great positivist barons: Rudolf Carnap, Alfred Tarski, Bertrand Russell) were cited regularly by postmodernists as authoritative support of frankly irrealist views. Kuhn laboured to explain away his bolder remarks ("What were ducks in the scientist's world before the revolution are rabbits afterwards") – but *there they are* in his text, posing for quotation.[7] Further, it was not that quotable remarks of Kuhn's were misconstrued or read out of context: the problem was, again, one of association and dissociation. The duck/rabbit shibboleth, if whispered at the back gate, admitted guests to his party that Kuhn would have preferred to exclude. I suppose that Donald Davidson's resistance to the use that Richard Rorty has made of his work may be another example of reluctance to have influenced the wrong colleagues.[8]

A contrasting case of labelling and mislabelling, from roughly the same era, is represented by Harold Bloom. When Rorty was holding off detractors with epithets like "metaphysical prig," Bloom was on the offensive against what he called "mouldy figs" and "antiquarians" in literary studies. Bloom assaulted modernism and its canonizers on behalf of movements that came before and after it: Romantic and postmodern literature and theory.[9] Yet anyone who read Bloom carefully in those years could have prophesied he would ultimately defend both canonicity and the standard canon. (His book *The Western Canon* has been an academic best-seller.)[10]

Bloom disclaimed affinity with deconstruction even as he contributed to *Deconstruction and Criticism* – the program or charter of the "Yale school" – alongside Paul de Man, Geoffrey Hartman, J. Hillis Miller, and Derrida.[11] Bloom's aim had never been to undermine canonicity as an idea or a project but only, much more simply, to invert the standard list enshrined by New Critics in the Yale literature curriculum. Bloom was not opposed to axiology per se but only to the specific rankings of writers that, as he saw it, T.S. Eliot had intimidated the New Critics into accepting.[12] If Eliot regarded *Hamlet* as "an artistic failure," then Bloom pronounced the play supreme; if Eliot demeaned Wordsworth and Shelley, Bloom called them "demigods"; if Eliot valorized Ezra Pound, Bloom compared Pound and Eliot in significance to Cowley and Cleveland.[13] The result of Bloom's involvement with postmodern theory was not a revolution in thinking but a coup d'etat in the curriculum – an assertion of the will to power. His most original contribution to literary theory has been to name the quality of poets that qualifies them for canonization as *strength*. Bloom the "strong critic" promotes the reputations of "strong poets."

The point I am trying to make is that the content – the tendency or meaning – of postmodern thought was not substantially at issue in the culture wars. Postmodern arguments and terms were used as an excuse for obdurate resistance by some, like Quine and Kuhn, who ought to have found them useful or at least interesting. On the other hand, postmodern arguments and terms comprised simply an arsenal for those, like Bloom, who had no commitment to their meaning or tendency. That tendency became explicit, I would say, around the time that *Common Knowledge* was formed. The Berlin Wall disappeared as if its existence had been provisional all along, or even imaginary; it came apart so readily and its stones dispersed so rapidly across the globe that dispatches from Berlin said that the wall had "deconstructed." At which point it was revealed that important dissidents involved in the velvet revolutions of 1989 were not mere readers but actual pupils of important postmodernist thinkers.[14] Derrida was "imprisoned on fabricated charges" in Prague for his underground teaching there.[15] Rorty taught in the "underground university" as well and signalled support for peaceful revolution by featuring, as the Polish pope did, the word *solidarność* in speeches and encyclicals. Rorty's encyclical – published in 1989, as Wałesa rose and Jaruzelski fell – was called *Contingency, Irony, and Solidarity*.[16]

Yet still, in the West connections were not commonly drawn between postmodernism and the "antipolitics" of György Konrád, Václav

Havel, and Adam Michnik.[17] Nor were distinctions drawn between intellectuals (for example, dissidents in communist states) who were influenced by a "flower child" mentality and those (such as Derrida and Foucault) more influenced by the confrontational politics of the sixties. Konrád, Havel, and Michnik urged graciously that their own former jailers not be penalized. They opposed the exclusion of communist apparatchiks from future governments of Hungary, Czechoslovakia, and Poland. Asked why he had opened a dialogue with General Jaruzelski after the fall of the martial-law regime, Michnik replied:

For my generation, the road to freedom began in 1968. While students in Paris and Berkeley were rejecting bourgeois democracy, we in Prague and Warsaw were fighting for a freedom that only the bourgeois order could guarantee ... I wanted to behave like a normal human being in a free country: I had been [Jaruzelski's] unrelenting opponent, his prisoner, but I was interested in what he had to say. He's an intelligent man and Poland's roads to freedom sometimes took very different courses. Some went through prison, others through the corridors of power. Deep down, I'm convinced that Jaruzelski is a Polish patriot and a partisan of democracy. He's not a cynic ... We must reject one camp's domination over another, with endless settling of scores. Our country must make room for everybody.[18]

Michnik's thinking was and remains authentically postmodern. Intellectual humility and its concomitants – forgiveness, gentleness, empathy, compassion, magnanimity – were, logically, conclusions of premises to be found in works of Lévi-Strauss, Derrida, and Foucault. Yet west of Prague, those conclusions played little part in postmodernist *strategy*. In the West, postmodernism was used, as I have implied, chiefly as an armory: it offered tools for the defenestration of "antiquarians" from our academies.

The idea behind *Common Knowledge* was to experiment with realigning these misalignments. Here is not the place to specify why any one philosopher or literary critic or historian or social theorist or political dissident was invited to participate; nor is it the place to set out what I believe that, over more than a decade, we may as a group have accomplished. Here is the place to observe that in the West, Gianni Vattimo recognized, before anyone else did, what postmodern thought most profoundly concerned. His coinage "weak thought" reminded postmodern warriors in the early 1980s that the initiating and crucial texts of their milieu spoke against cruelty, violence, the will to power, competition, axiology, zeal, assertiveness, vindictiveness, and metaphors of strength.[19] That understanding is only now, some two decades later, beginning to bear fruit; and even now, not all the fruit is edible. By the time of his death, Jacques Derrida, who in 1998 coedited a book on religion with Vattimo, had trod but half the distance to his colleague's epiphany.[20] Derrida was torn between two claims on his attention – one that Rorty termed "sentimental" and one that Michnik might call "cynical." These two opposing claims were, more or less, the same ones that fueled the student movement of the sixties. Derrida's waffle between the two is unsettling, though edifying:

First, I would like to say, even if this shocks certain amongst you and even if I myself took my head in my hands when Richard Rorty said that I was sentimental and that I believed in happiness, that I think he's right ... I am very grateful to Richard Rorty for having dared to say something very close to my heart and which is essential to what I am trying to do ... [However,] I am completely in agreement with everything that Ernesto Laclau has said on the question of hegemony and power, and I also agree that in the most reassuring and disarming discussion and persuasion, force and violence are present. None the less, I think that there is, in the opening of a context of argumentation and discussion, a reference – unknown, indeterminate, but none the less thinkable – to disarmament. I agree that such disarmament is never simply present, even in the most pacific moment of persuasion, and therefore that a certain force and violence is irreducible, but none the less this violence can only be practised and can only appear as such on the basis of a non-violence, a vulnerability, an exposition. I do not believe in non-violence as a descriptive and determinable experience, but rather as an irreducible promise and of the relation to the other as essentially non-instrumental. This is not the dream of a beatifically pacific relation, but of a certain experience of friendship perhaps unthinkable today and unthought within the historical determination of friendship in the West. This is a friendship, what I sometimes call an *aimance,* that excludes violence; a non-appropriative relation to the other that occurs without violence and on the basis of which all violence detaches itself and is determined.[21]

Given his personal history, Derrida had good reason to waffle about "disarmament." He was not always so interested in scholarly *aimance.* Postmodernism of the academic kind is often said to commence with Derrida's attack – in the essay "Sign, Structure, and Play in the Discourse of the Human Sciences" – upon Lévi-Strauss, though as cogent a history of postmodernism could begin with Lévi-Strauss's attack, some years earlier, upon Sartre.[22] In each case, a grab for intellectual power was made in the name of an ethics that should have precluded it, and at least some poststructuralists took note of the irony and pathos. Geoffrey Hartman, for one, understood that the structuralists whose work he was questioning were devoted, like Hartman himself, to the application of a levelling morality to cultural hierarchies.[23] (Structuralist method, after all, applies as well to comic strips as it does to *Phèdre*.) As for Derrida, he condemned structuralism because it failed, in his view, to live up to the ethics – or more precisely, the counter-axiological sentiments – that he shared with Roman Jakobson and Lévi-Strauss. Derrida found their fascination with binary oppositions too serenely scientific because the oppositional patterns uncovered by the structuralists were invitations to violence. Derrida portrayed Lévi-Strauss as complicit in those violent hierarchies, just as Lévi-Strauss had portrayed Sartre as complicit in the racism that Sartre had done so much to oppose. There are thus reasons to regard structuralism and poststructuralism as continuous – Manfred Frank is exhaustively persuasive on the subject – and James Wilkinson has shown that the joint lineage goes back to the French intellectual Resistance of the forties.[24]

On the one hand, then, *postmodern* and *postwar* mean much the same thing; while on the other hand, *postmodern* means something like *antifascist*. The problem with antifascism, in the absence of rampant fascist movements or governments, is that it can fast become self-contradictory. Antifascism, when it is not a matter of self-preservation or of lending aid to threatened individuals or groups is, like fascism itself, an assertion of the will to power. And in the case of Derrida's critique of structuralism, the fascist elements that he perceived in structuralist theory and practice – the aggression and the binary hierarchies – were basically metaphorical. Structuralism, for all its imperious quantification, began with beliefs even more sentimental than those of Derrida. Structuralist method was a means to unite humanity by demonstrating that "savages" have a developed logic and cultural system that, structurally speaking, are not inferior to those of Western science. But Derrida found structuralism still implicated in metaphysics, and he argued that metaphysics is at the root of all violence: a doctrine that by now virtually defines postmodernism. Each successive generation since the war has discovered that the preceding generation had not rid itself adequately of metaphysics – and the discovery has been in each case accompanied by rhetorical violence in the service of establishing a purist new regime of thought.

There is no sense pretending that Vattimo does not belong to the postmodern consensus about metaphysics. In his latest book, *Nihilism and Emancipation*, he reiterates the doctrine: "the true meaning of metaphysics [is] will to power, violence, the destruction of liberty."[25] Still, Vattimo may be the first participant in this consensus to observe the self-contradictory character of the process – the process of intellectual denazification – that follows from it. He has questioned, time and again, the postmodern yearning to start over clean. He has reminded us that purification can itself be violent, that purity (or perfection) is a metaphysician's dream, that starting over is the very definition of modernity.[26] But how to give up starting over without starting over again? How, in other words, do we become at last *post*modern? It is characteristic of Vattimo's courage that his choice of exit from our postmodern Nuremberg is a term of Heidegger's. Vattimo has written consistently in the discourse initiated by an actual (as opposed to a notional) fascist – and unlike many Heideggerians he has made no excuses for Heidegger's political commitment and has not tried to pretend it away. The term of Heidegger's of which Vattimo has made the most significant use is *Verwindung*, though he has had to redefine the term to make it salutary:

Heidegger's thought is generally taken to be an expression of the apocalyptic *Kulturkritik* of the first part of [the twentieth] century, a critique that was very negative about the modern epoch and especially about its science and technology. But the importance of Heidegger in the philosophy of our epoch consists precisely in that he summarizes the capital themes of philosophical pessimism and antimodernism yet transforms them into a different attitude, an attitude whose name is *Verwindung* ... [Heidegger] concludes that a complete overcoming of metaphysics ... is impossible. Overcoming metaphysics would require a capacity for leaping out of the tradition into which our very existence is "thrown." But if *Überwindung*, an overcoming, is impossible, what we can have instead is *Verwindung*: a resigned acceptance that continues the metaphysical tradition in a distorted form. In the term *Verwindung* resound not only the meanings of "resignation" and "acceptance," but also of "convalescence." (*Verwinden* is the act of carrying the traces of an illness that has been overcome but not totally cancelled from the body.) The term *Verwindung* also means "distortion" ... a meaning that Heidegger does not emphasize but which in my interpretation of the term is crucial. That my emphasis differs from Heidegger's is, in its turn, a *Verwindung*, a distorted acceptance, of Heidegger's doctrine.[27]

Verwindung names an attitude or perhaps a practice that Vattimo recommends. His choice of the term, moreover, serves to exemplify that attitude or practice. To valorize a term of Heidegger's in some degree rehabilitates the philosophy of a Nazi for beneficial application in our own time. Rehabilitation (or, as Vattimo says, "convalescence") may result from distorting our memory of Heidegger. That distortion comes neither through bad faith – Vattimo performs it in broad daylight – nor through faulty scholarship. It is simply that Heidegger, like the rest of us, had his limits. Heidegger had his limits *even as a Heideggerian*: "We must affirm, then," Vattimo concludes,

the necessity of explaining why Heidegger's thought can appear so important even from a point of view utterly unsympathetic to Nazism. The *Verwindung* I propose is a way – the sole way, as far as I can see – of solving the problem: Heidegger himself, when he supported Hitler, misunderstood the authentic meaning of his own philosophical premises. Such a reading of Heidegger authorizes the effort to interpret him beyond the letter of his own self-under-standing.[28]

Vattimo's distortion of *Verwindung* (his redefinition of *Verwindung* as distortion) is meant as charity both to the living and to the dead. Charity can temper the severity of justice – this every judge and juror knows. But charity can also temper the severity of truth. This latter principle is not yet so clearly established for academics, because their investment in justice as a concept is more shallow than their investment in truth.

As for justice, it is historians in particular who, among academics, have done the most to banish the concept from their professional lives. Historians routinely express contempt for colleagues who judge the behaviour of men and women now dead, or who judge the mores of bygone cultures. Herbert Butterfield's famous critique of judgmental historiography is judgmental, to the say the least, but meant to encourage acts of historical charity. We must imagine history, Butterfield writes,

as working not to accentuate antagonisms or to ratify old party-cries but to find the unities that underlie the differences and to see all lives as part of the one web of life. The historian trying to feel his way towards this may be striving to be like a god but perhaps he is less foolish than the one who poses as god the avenger. Studying the quarrels of an ancient day he can at least seek to understand both parties to the struggle and he must want to understand them better than they understood themselves; watching them entangled in the net of time and circumstance he can take pity on them – these men who perhaps had no pity for one another; and, though he can never be perfect, it is difficult to see why he should aspire to anything less than taking these men and their quarrels into a world where everything is understood and all sins are forgiven.[29]

The fading of Butterfield's book from the syllabi of history proseminars signals only that its viewpoint – its preference for charity over justice – has by now been absorbed fully into the historians' culture. Whereas the preference for charity over truth is only beginning its pilgrimage toward respectability.[30] Vattimo's argument, that Heidegger "misunderstood the meaning of his own philosophical premises," is a version of Butterfield's injunction to understand people of the past "better than they understood themselves." But Vattimo seems pleased to go further than any professional historian has done in pursuit of *caritas*.

Postwar skepticism, in both its continental and Anglo analytic forms, has so worn away at terms like *true* and *real* and *factual* that it has become, over the past few decades, possible – if still problematic – to acknowledge distorting another writer in the service of charitable understanding or contemporary benefit, or both.[31] Bloom has written extensively about the distortions of dead poets by living ones, though none of the distortions that he charts is charitable, and most, since they are oedipally motivated, are both agonistic and unconscious.[32] Vattimo – who has devoted much energy to removing both will and power from the concept "will to power" – does not approach the idea or practice of distortion in Bloom's spirit.[33] For Vattimo, distortion is akin to filial mourning, in a sense that is not Freudian. He suffers (at least in print) no love/hate ambivalence in relation to Heidegger or Nietzsche; he expresses no brute rivalry with, and hence no guilt regarding, them. He transforms them much as Ariel, in *The Tempest*, says that fathers are distorted naturally after death: "Nothing of him that doth fade / But doth suffer a sea-change / Into something rich and strange." Vattimo's fathers are conjured up in his work as philosophers strange to us, but also as richer than we had supposed them to be.

When the philosophers' "principle of charity" was formulated, at the time Vattimo began his publishing career, the formulators – Neil Wilson and Quine – meant only that we should assume that a partner in conversation is using a comprehensible language rather than speaking nonsense.[34] Davidson and others then proposed applying the principle of charity "quite generally to prefer theories of interpretation that minimize disagreement." "My point," Davidson emphasized, "has always been that understanding can be secured only by interpreting in a way that makes for the right sort of agreement."[35] Even Davidson, however, felt (and gave much of his career to specifying) the "subtle pressures on the Principle of Charity" – he was as much concerned with the limits as with the blessings of *caritas*.[36] But Vattimo has extended the principle toward its outmost Catholic frontier: we must help to save our neighbor's soul, even after he or she is dead. We must become, he says, resigned to Heidegger's thinking, as to other disquieting features of the European inheritance, and deprive our relation to them of neurotic drama.[37] In other words, we must learn to mourn, modify, and thus recover the entire cultural past.

Verwindung, in Vattimo's use of the term, has been widely misconstrued; or rather, it has been construed uncharitably. I once overheard Vattimo's philosophy described as "watered-down Heidegger." It is worth examining the presuppositions that make that metaphor work as an insult (though I imagine Vattimo himself might take it as a compliment). One waters down a brew that is too strong "for the ladies." Or one waters down a soup so that, in impoverished households, it will last longer or nourish more children. Both of these are acts of *caritas*, though in a domestic, rather than a heroic, mode. Moreover, water is of course the basic constituent of living bodies and has an array of associations with cleansing, salvation, rebirth; it is odd to think of water in that context negatively. But the insult to Vattimo ("watered-down") concerns the specific context of an intellectual controversy, the culture wars, on which I have been commenting here. The culture warriors, like controversialists of any kind, have been ranged on "sides," which is to say that controversies are imagined as games, played on square or oblong fields (or boards or courts). Such games have rules that participating players or teams – though arrayed geometrically in opposition – share equally on both sides. One metarule, to which boyish folklore is attached, is that players must feel no ambivalence as they prepare to face and best their adversaries. The requisite commitment is apparently so difficult to maintain in a species so busy and self-conscious as *Homo sapiens* that teams and individual players require coaches to rev them up in advance. When Stanley Fish argues that, for instance, one cannot be both a literary critic and a theorist simultaneously – when he argues that professionals can wear, as he puts it, only one hat at a time – he is playing the role of coach. In particular, his book *Professional Correct-*

ness reads like a pep talk for ambivalent scholars with faded uniforms and too much on their minds before the game.[38] What Fish fears is that team spirit will be diluted – watered down – and the game exposed as pointless.

"Watered-down," in sum, is meant to insult its object as below our social standing, effeminate or lily-livered, and incapable of single-mindedness or revving up (even with the help of a coach). I will not bother saying from which side of the culture wars the insult at issue came – it could have come equally from either side, and that is my basic point. The supposedly adversarial teams (in this instance, the continental and the analytic) share more with each other than either shares with Vattimo. I am not suggesting that between these two, or any two, opposed milieus there is a middle to which the wise ascribe – and in the case of Vattimo, it would be absurd to regard a soi-disant nihilist as "a moderate." What I do want to suggest is that with respect to any game – and I mean *game* as meant by Wittgenstein but also R.D. Laing – there are usually to be found spoilsports nearby. Intelligent spoilsports toy with self-denigration – with metaphors of dilution, effeminacy, impotence, spinelessness – as a means to obviate abuse and also as goads to chuckling. When in spoilsport mode, Rorty refers to anyone who shares his views as "she," and this ploy is meant to disarm the macho reader by amusing and nearly flattering him. Vattimo's version comes articulated in metaphors of invertebracy. His call for "destructuration" (as opposed to deconstruction) is usually understood in architectural terms, where it makes limited sense. A building without structure will collapse, and Vattimo means for his destructurated structures to remain standing. After hearing the insult "watered-down," though, it occurred to me that the figure Vattimo uses is perhaps culinary. We might think of destructuration in terms of fish-boning: the expert removal of a skeleton in the service of genteel and prudent dining. We like to think of ourselves, most of us, as having backbone – as having principles for which we would "stand up" and kill – but Vattimo consistently prefers spinelessness as an intellectual trait. And in this preference, he is not alone.

"*Surtout pas de zèle,*" Clifford Geertz quoted Talleyrand to a literary (rather than diplomatic) audience recently, then went on to define the intellectual's responsibility in a way consonant with Vattimo's.[39] Geertz advised his listeners to undertake scholarship and teach courses that "wound our complacency," that "make us a little less confident in and satisfied with the immediate deliverances of our here-and-now imperious world." He confessed that this approach makes of intellectual life "a sub-versive business" but then added that "what it subverts is not morality. What it subverts is bluster, obduracy, and a closure to experience. Pride, one could say, and prejudice."[40] Compiling lists of those who share this approach to life and thought with Geertz, Vattimo, and Rorty would serve no righteous end. Doing so would form another team, kick off another game – and "spoilsport" should be a metagame for one non-player at a time. In any case, teams and spoilsports have been converging on points of agreement for some years. Old deconstructionists address morality now with far less indirection than they once did, and the most embattled of the science warriors has published an inspiring treatise on making peace.[41] Given this emerging concord – to which he has con-tributed extensively – Vattimo has characteristically taken steps to have himself evicted from it. He has embraced the Roman Catholic Church and has redescribed "weak thought" in explicitly Christian terms. This development in itself is not so astonishing – what were Jesus and St Paul if not spoilsports? But that Vattimo has emerged from this conversion with his credentials as a nihilist intact and burnished is a bonafide post-modern miracle.

I have long been suspicious of periodization, but clearly we are no longer in the epoch when, fallen to his knees before the *Pietà* of Michelangelo, T.S. Eliot could mortify a group of secular companions. Eliot's conversion, not quite eighty years ago, lost him the respect of more or less the entire avant-garde simultaneously. Whereas Rorty, in a recently coauthored book with Vattimo, accepts every argument that his colleague makes in support of Christianity – though Rorty remains an atheist or, as he now puts it, religiously tone-deaf.[42] And it is Rorty who makes their book's central claim: that hermeneutics, with whose "attitude" he identifies himself, "is in the intellectual world what democracy is in the political world. The two can be viewed as alterna-tive appropriations of the Christian message that love is the only law."[43] Or put in Vattimo's more continental language: "It is not so very absurd to assert that the death of God announced by Nietzsche is … the death of Christ on the cross … it is the advent of Christianity that makes possible the progressive dissolution of metaphysics … postmod-ern nihilism constitutes the actual truth of Christianity."[44] Hence Vattimo proposes – "without in the least wishing to convert" his col-league – that Rorty's antifoundationalism is thinkable "only because we are living in a civilization shaped by the biblical, and specifically Chris-tian, message."[45] Which was exactly Eliot's argument about his teacher

Bertrand Russell's humanitarianism ("Why Mr. Russell Is a Christian" was the argument's title).[46] Unfortunately for Eliot, in 1927 the actor playing Mr Russell was Russell. In the present revival, however, Rorty plays Russell's role, Vattimo gives Eliot's lines a more genial accent, and the scenario seems (but is not) altogether different.

A part of the difference is that Christianity has changed since the 1920s. A tradition is subject to interpretation, and the loner or pariah of one generation – Simone Weil, notably – may seem magisterial, a regenerative mutation, to orthodox theologians of a later time. As the present archbishop of Canterbury, an admirer of Weil's, writes: "the church is always renewed from the edges rather than the centre."[47] "A healthy church," Rowan Williams adds, is one "with plenty of bizarre characters" – "difficult" and "awkward" people (he calls them "holy") who "are not easily *reduced* to a formula, not easily conscripted into being reliable supporters of a cause, not good party members."[48] Weil herself never joined the church, indeed. For the good Christian, as Williams writes, is "in flight from conformity – not to secure a freedom of individual expression" but to be free "from the little games of control and evasion that take up so much room in the talking of most of us."[49] Thus the Primate of All England – *primus inter pares* of Eliot's own church – depicts ecclesiastical health. And its opposite? "An unhealthy" church, Williams says, "is a group in which ... virtue becomes identified with uncontroversial ordinariness and there is a nervous cultural 'sameness' in the way people talk, dress and so on. Beware of thinking this is a problem just of the right or of the left or, in general, of 'them' rather than us."[50] He proposes as a therapeutic model the outsider, like Weil, who refuses a role in the church: "We live in a society that is at once deeply individualist and deeply conformist; the desert fathers and mothers manage to be neither, and they suggest to us that the church's calling likewise is to avoid both these pitfalls."[51]

The "desert literature" urges us to "flee from human company" for proleptically Freudian reasons: "we are being encouraged to flee from 'projection' – from other people's projections onto us, ours onto them, and our own inflated expectations of ourselves."[52] We possess, the archbishop counsels, a "deep-rooted propensity to be drawn in to ... games," and he reminds us of "Macarius's blunt summary, that the world is a place where they make you do stupid things."[53] Still, to flee the social world is not the same as to abandon it selfishly. The archbishop, following Weil, defines *flight* as hesitation, silence, pause, attention: "Without a basic education in attention, no deeply ethical behaviour is really going to be possible; we may only keep the rules."[54] For what Christian ethics requires, he maintains, is "making sure that my development of my own vocation isn't squeezing out someone else's" – and *that* requirement means "running from what makes us feel smug and in control, what gratifies our longing for approval and respect."[55] I should mention, before quoting this next passage, that Archbishop Williams was originally an academic: "The times when we can be absolutely sure that we are wasting words are when we are reinforcing our reputation, or defending our position at someone else's expense – looking for a standard of comparison, a currency in the market of virtue."[56] That last sentence could be a death's-head on the desk of every theorist urging respect for otherness and difference ...

I have quoted an archbishop at such length on the subject of Christian withdrawal as a reminder that *caritas* – the law of love, to which Rorty and Vattimo refer as the basis of liberalism, democracy, and hermeneutics – is not a demand that can be met by any social or intellectual system. The law of love was not met in the thirteenth century by feudalism, scholasticism, or even monasticism and will not be met today or tomorrow by social democracy, sexual revolution, and radical hermeneutics. Williams makes plain how nearly impossible it is for the Christian soul to exist at all in society, where it is beleaguered by "stupid things": inattentiveness, projection, presures to conform, noise, self-promotion at others' expense, smugness, longing for approval, games of evasion and control (to say nothing of the Seven Deadly Sins). Vattimo draws a sharp distinction between Christianity and Christendom, explaining that he rejects the ersatz faith and morals of the latter – but I would like to learn how far he is prepared to follow the severities of the former. Which is another way of inquiring how far postmodernism may yet take us, before backing off, toward all that respect for otherness and difference would finally entail. Even Weil, who recoiled from the knowledge that "one loves only what one can eat" and eventually starved – even she, as death approached, asked for potatoes "done in the French way" or "a little butter roll."[57]

Historically, Christendom has kept Christianity at bay by emphasizing ethical regulation, and thus limitations on self-denial. Lately, Vattimo has been arguing – along with other philosophers and, for that matter, theologians – in favour of ethics without transcendence, a morality with no grounding in metaphysics.[58] Whereas, if I have not misread the Sermon on the Mount wholesale, Jesus appears to stipulate the opposite. Devotion to divine splendour, he teaches, can be so mindless of self that ethics becomes unproblematically obvious. If your neighbor wants your coat, give him your cloak also; if he strikes your right cheek, offer your left as well:

Love your enemies, bless them that curse you, do good to them that hate you, and pray for them which despitefully use you, and persecute you; That ye may be children of your Father which is in heaven; for he maketh his sun to rise on the evil and on the good, and sendeth rain on the just and on the unjust ... Take no thought for your life, what ye shall eat or what ye shall drink; nor yet for your body, what ye shall put on ... Consider the lilies of the field, how they grow; they toil not, neither do they spin: and yet I say unto you, That even Solomon in his all his glory was not arrayed like one of these.[59]

I am not at all sure that what the Gospels teach in passages such as these is ethics. The regulation of behaviour seems beneath a faith that commands, in Weil's summary, to "love what is intolerable."[60] The archetype of an *ethical* religion is what the Gospels refer to as pharisaism. Like canon law and, later, casuistry – which typify what Vattimo means by Christendom – pharisaic ethics concerns itself with limits.[61] Pharisaism and casuistry measure, on the basis of what is generally bearable, the limits on how much one human being may be told to sacrifice his or her own self-interest – told to humble his or her own vanity, silence his or her own wants – on behalf of another creature's. But Jesus rejects pharisaism, the ethics of limitation, explicitly: "except your righteousness shall exceed the righteousness of the scribes and Pharisees, ye shall in no case enter into the kingdom of heaven."[62]

The price of admission there is absolute: "A condition of complete simplicity," as Eliot defined it, "(Costing not less than everything)."[63] I take it that "everything" includes the comforts of ethics as much as the solace of metaphysics and that "not less than everything" means that nothing, not even "sense and notion," persist beyond the final conversion – the refusal of that last butter roll.[64] When Eliot, another admirer of Weil's, knelt before the *Pietà* in St Peter's, his ethics and ontology were still traceably nihilist. The Buddhist and especially Mādhyamika texts that he read in Sanskrit and Pali grant no reality to perceived states or objects and dismiss beliefs about them as superstition.[65] "No one," Eliot had learned from Irving Babbitt, "was ever more unfriendly than Buddha to persons who had 'views.'"[66] Views – "sense and notion," objectifications, perceptions, perspectives – are not just mistaken; by definition, they can intrude cruelly on the views of others.

This last sentence of mine is a liberal interpretation of what the Buddha and Babbitt and Eliot meant, so it can hardly be accurate (and it is, moreover, in itself a view). *Caritas* is not a matter of entitlement, a room of one's own, a view from one's room, a committee to set zoning laws that ensure no one's view is of brick. "Love is the only law" is a hard saying and cannot be equated, as Rorty would prefer, with "insouciance."[67] "It takes time," Archbishop Williams writes in explication, "to discover that the apparently generous horizon of a world in which my surface desires have free play is in fact a tighter prison than the constrained space chosen by the desert ascetics."[68] Then he quotes Abba Moses, a desert father: "Sit in your cell and your cell will teach you everything."[69] But the archbishop himself frames it best for postmodern eyes: charity is "a room with no view."[70]

NOTES

1 Gianni Vattimo, *The Adventure of Difference: Philosophy after Nietzsche and Heidegger,* trans. Cyprian Blamires (1980; Baltimore: Johns Hopkins University Press 1993), 107.

2 W.V. Quine, "Speaking of Objects" (1957), in *Ontological Relativity and Other Essays* (New York: Columbia University Press 1969), 5, 25.

3 Ibid., 1, 25.

4 Ibid., 7.

5 Ibid., 5.

6 Jerry Fodor, "Water's Water Everywhere," *London Review of Books* 26, no. 20 (21 October 2004): 17.

7 Thomas S. Kuhn, *The Structure of Scientific Revolutions* (1962; Chicago: University of Chicago Press 1970), 111. Kuhn's responses are collected in *The Road since Structure: Philosophical Essays, 1970–1993,* ed. James Conant and John Haugeland (Chicago: University of Chicago Press 2000).

8 For Rorty on Davidson, see Richard Rorty, "Pragmatism, Davidson, and Truth," in Ernest Lepore, ed., *Truth and Interpretation: Perspectives on the Philosophy of Donald Davidson* (Oxford: Blackwell 1984). For Davidson's response, see "After-thoughts" to "A Coherence Theory of Truth and Knowledge," in Alan Malachowski, *Reading Rorty: Critical Responses to "Philosophy and the Mirror of Nature" (and Beyond)* (Oxford: Blackwell 1990).

9 See Jeffrey M. Perl, "Hugh Kenner (1923–2003)," *Common Knowledge* 10, no. 3 (fall 2004): 371–6.

10 Harold Bloom, *The Western Canon: The Books and School of the Ages* (New York: Riverhead 1995). Moreover, Bloom's Literary Criticism Collection, published by Chelsea House, has by now published more than four hundred volumes. As a recent advertisement for the series has it, "Professor Bloom has set out to chronicle and illuminate the major achievements of the Western literary tradition."

11 Harold Bloom et al., *Deconstruction and Criticism* (New York: Seabury 1979).

12 See Jeffrey M. Perl, *Skepticism and Modern Enmity: Before and after Eliot* (Baltimore: Johns Hopkins University Press 1989), 27–33.

13 T.S. Eliot, "Hamlet and His Problems" (1919), in *Selected Essays* (1932; New York: Harcourt Brace Jovanovich 1978), 123. Harold Bloom, *A Map of Misreading* (New York: Oxford University Press 1975), 28.

14 I believe that the first public disclosure of the "underground university" operating in Czechoslovakia during the 1980s was Roger Scruton's article "A Catacomb Culture," *Times Literary Supplement*, 16–22 February 1990, 170, 176. I should add that visiting professors from the West were not biased in favour of postmodernism; scholarly distinction and courage appear to have been the criteria for the selection and self-selection of this extraordinary group.

15 Ibid., 170.

16 Rorty, *Contingency, Irony, and Solidarity* (Cambridge: Cambridge University Press 1989).

17 See György Konrád, *Antipolitics*, trans. Richard E. Allen (1983; New York: Harcourt Brace Jovanovich 1984).

18 Philippe Demenet, "Adam Michnik: The Sisyphus of Democracy" (interview), UNESCO *Courier*, September 2001: 2–4.

19 Gianni Vattimo and P.A. Rovatti, eds., *Il pensiero debole* (Milan: Feltrinelli 1983); see also Vattimo, "Dialectics, Difference, and Weak Thought," trans. T. Harrison, *Graduate Faculty Philosophy Journal* 10 (1984): 151–63. And of course the title of this present volume is *Weakening Philosophy*.

20 Jacques Derrida and Gianni Vattimo, eds., *Religion* (Cambridge: Polity 1998).

21 Jacques Derrida, "Remarks on Deconstruction and Pragmatism," in *Deconstruction and Pragmatism*, edited by Chantal Mouffe (London: Routledge 1996), 77, 83.

22 Jacques Derrida, "Structure, signe et jeu dans le discours des sciences humaines," presented in 1966 as a paper at a conference in Baltimore attended by Lacan, Barthes, and Todorov, among others. The critique of Sartre appears in Claude Lévi-Strauss, *La Pensée Sauvage* (Paris: Plon 1962);

but see also Lévi-Strauss's *Le Totémisme aujourd'hui* (Paris: Presses Universitaires de France 1962) for its evaluation of Sartre's position as Hobbesian.

23 Geoffrey H. Hartman, *Beyond Formalism: Literary Essays, 1958–1970* (New Haven: Yale University Press 1970), 3–41.

24 Manfred Frank, *What Is Neostructuralism?* trans. Sabine Wilke and Richard Gray (1984; Minneapolis: University of Minnesota Press 1989); James D. Wilkinson, *The Intellectual Resistance in Europe* (Cambridge: Harvard University Press 1981).

25 Gianni Vattimo, *Nihilism and Emancipation: Ethics, Politics, and Law*, edited by Santiago Zabala, trans. William McCuaig (New York: Columbia University Press 2004). I read this book before its publication: the passage quoted is on page 27 of the final TS.

26 In conversation with Vattimo, Rorty discusses the problem of purity in their coauthored book, *The Future of Religion*, edited by Santiago Zabala (2004; New York: Columbia University Press 2005), 79. For more on modernity as a process of successive new beginnings, see Perl, *Skepticism and Modern Enmity*, 40. For another, quite opposed definition of *modernity*, see Jeffrey M. Perl, *The Tradition of Return: The Implicit History of Modern Literature* (Princeton: Princeton University Press 1984), 17–33.

27 Gianni Vattimo, "Optimistic Nihilism," *Common Knowledge* 1, no. 3 (winter 1992), 37–8. The symposium in which this article appears is titled "Beyond Post-: A Revaluation of the Revaluation of All Values." Obviously, the symposium was planned *sous le signe de* Vattimo.

28 Ibid., 39.

29 Herbert Butterfield, *The Whig Interpretation of History* (1931; New York: Norton 1965), 3.

30 See "Benefits of the Doubt," part 5 of "Peace and Mind: Seriatim Symposium on Dispute, Conflict, and Enmity," *Common Knowledge* 9, no. 1 (spring 2003): 199–310. My introduction, "A Brighter Past," briefly surveys both the possibilities of such historical writing and the obstacles to it: 199–203.

31 I want to emphasize again that the Anglo analytic philosophers, or at any rate the more severe among them, have done as much as any continental philosopher to undermine the concept of truth. Quine went so far, in his *éminence grise* retirement, as to indicate that we are fortunte that *truth* is almost, but not quite, definable, because "its genuine definability" would be both trivial and "lethal": *Quiddities: An Intermittently Philosophical Dictionary* (Cambridge: Harvard University Press 1987), 215. As for the charitable distortion of another writer's work, Rorty's *Verwindung* of Davidson is an example as sweeping as Vattimo's of Heidegger – and has had equally influential results. Until Rorty reinterpreted Davidson's work (see note 8), the

latter was regarded outside the community of analytic philosophers as a technician merely, whereas afterward Davidson began to publish in journals such as *Critical Inquiry*, and his essays are now required reading even among literary theorists.

32 Harold Bloom, *The Anxiety of Influence: A Theory of Poetry* (Oxford: Oxford University Press 1973); *A Map of Misreading* (Oxford: Oxford University Press 1975); *Agon: Towards a Theory of Revisionism* (Oxford: Oxford University Press 1982).

33 Rorty has commented on Vattimo's unusual stance toward predecessors in the essay "Being That Can Be Understood Is Language," *London Review of Books*, 22, no. 6 (16 March 2000): 25: "The relationship between predecessor and successor would be conceived, as Gianni Vattimo has emphasized, not as the power-laden relation of 'overcoming' (*Überwindung*) but as the gentler relation of turning to new 'purposes' (*Verwindung*)." The closest that Vattimo comes to Bloom's position is in "The Will to Power as Art," in *The Adventure of Difference*, 85–109. Vattimo's most extensive reinterpretation of the will to power occurs in *Il Soggetto e la maschera: Nietzsche e il problema della liberazione*, 2d ed. (1974; Milan: Bompiani 1994), the most relevant sections of which were revised and translated for serial publication in "Common Knowledge": "Beyond Despair and Conflict: A Reading of Nietzsche's Positive Nihilism," trans. Dannah Edwards. Part one appeared in 7, no. 1 (spring 1998): 15–59; and part two, in 7, no. 2 (fall 1998): 27–56.

34 W.V. Quine, *Word and Object* (Cambridge: MIT 1960), 58–9. In that text and elsewhere, Quine acknowledges Wilson as the principle's inventor.

35 Donald Davidson, *Inquiries into Truth and Interpretation* (Oxford: Clarendon 1984), xvii. And see, for instance, also Moshe Halbertal, "Canon and the Principle of Charity," in *People of the Book: Canon, Meaning, and Authority* (Cambridge: Harvard University Press 1997), 27–32. The principle of charity, *avant la lettre*, informed the interpretive style of many twentieth-century formalist critics, their presumption being that a canonical author never makes mistakes and that therefore critics should look for coherence and meaning even where these are not immediately apparent.

36 Davidson, *Inquiries*, xvii; see also essays 10 ("Belief and the Basis of Meaning") and 11 ("Thought and Talk") in the same volume.

37 "Neurotic" and "drama" are both Vattimo's terms: "Optimistic Nihilism," 43.

38 Stanley Fish, *Professional Correctness: Literary Studies and Political Change* (Oxford: Clarendon 1995).

39 Clifford Geertz, "A Strange Romance: Anthropology and Literature," Modern Language Association *Profession* 2003: 33.

40 Ibid., 29.

41 For deconstructionists on ethics, see, for example, Hartman, *The Fateful Question of Culture* (New York: Columbia University Press 1997); J. Hillis Miller, *The Ethics of Reading* (New York: Columbia University Press 1987); and, among Derrida's late essays about religion and morality, *On Cosmopolitanism and Forgiveness* (1997; London: Routledge 2001) and *Philosophy in a Time of Terror: Dialogues with Jürgen Habermas and Jacques Derrida*, ed. Giovanna Borradori (Chicago: University of Chicago Press 2003). The "science warrior" to whom I refer is Bruno Latour, and the treatise is *War of the Worlds: What about Peace?* trans. Charlotte Bigg and ed. John Tresch (Chicago: Prickly Paradigm Press 2002).

42 Rorty and Vattimo, *The Future of Religion*, 30: Rorty used to describe himself as an atheist but now prefers to be thought "religiously unmusical" (30).

43 Ibid., 74.

44 Ibid., 46–7.

45 Ibid., 51–2.

46 T.S. Eliot, "Why Mr. Russell Is a Christian," *Criterion* 6 (August 1927): 177–9.

47 Rowan Williams, *Silence and Honey Cakes: The Wisdom of the Desert* (Oxford: Lion 2003), 109.

48 Ibid., 58.

49 Ibid., 69.

50 Ibid., 59.

51 Ibid., 51.

52 Ibid., 62, 63.

53 Ibid., 70.

54 Ibid., 73–4. *Attention* is a key term in Weil's writing. See Sharon Cameron, "The Practice of Attention: Simone Weil's Performance of Impersonality," *Critical Inquiry* 29, no. 2 (winter 2003): 216–52. Cameron defines *attention* in Weil's sense as "regard without motive" (224).

55 Williams, *Silence and Honey Cakes*, 79, 75.

56 Ibid., 76. Cf. Weil: "To consent to being anonymous ... to renounce prestige, public esteeem – that is to bear witness to the truth, namely, that one is composed of human material, that one has no rights. It is to cast aside all ornament, to put up with one's nakedness. But how is this compatible with social life and its labels?" *The Notebooks of Simone Weil*, trans. Arthur Wills, 2 vols. (1953; New York: Putnam 1956), 1:59.

57 Cameron, "The Practice of Attention," 239.

58 See, e.g., Vattimo, "Ethics without Transcendence?" translated by Santiago Zabala, *Common Knowledge* 9, no. 3 (fall 2003): 399–405.

59 Matthew 5:44–5; 6:25, 28–9.

60 Simone Weil, *First and Last Notebooks*, trans. Richard Rees (London: Oxford University Press 1970), 260.

61 The articles on pharisaism (by Shira Wolosky) and casuistry (by Albert R. Jonsen) in the *Common Knowledge* symposium titled "Platonic Insults" define better than I can here what I mean by "limitation," and they show that ethical limitation is by no means negative. The symposium appeared in 2, no. 2 (fall 1993): 19–80. Stephen Toulmin's introductory essay is especially clarifying.

62 Matthew 5:20.

63 Eliot, "Little Gidding," 5.253–4, *Four Quartets*.

64 Ibid., 1.43.

65 For details on Eliot's study of Buddhist philosophy, see Perl, "Foreign Metaphysics," *Skepticism and Modern Enmity*, 43–65.

66 Irving Babbitt, "Buddha and the Occident" (1927), *Representative Writings*, ed. George A. Panichas (Lincoln: University of Nebraska Press 1981), 242.

67 Rorty and Vattimo, *The Future of Religion*, 30.

68 Williams, *Silence*, 80.

69 Ibid., 82.

70 Ibid., 87.

20

The Hermeneutics of Christianity and Philosophical Responsibility

CARMELO DOTOLO

Translated by Robert T. Valgenti

In the history of Being presented by postmodernity, does Christianity represent a *chance* for rethinking Being and rewriting the meaning of the philosophical vocation? This seems to be one of the most meaningful demands put forth in the reflections of Gianni Vattimo, especially in the wake of his philosophical proposal that finds an *ouverture* under debate in the metaphor of weak thought, in the sense that it radicalizes a form of reflection that is (seemingly) closer to deconstruction. The issue appears even more intriguing if it is limited to the relation between philosophy and religion. There is a well-known irreconcilability between these two forms of knowledge. This may be due to the Hegelian legacy, which treats religion as philosophy, attempting to rescue it rather than agree with it, and which in any case, does not relegate religion to an aesthetic *Erlebnis*. Or it may be due to the considerable burden carried by the theoretical limitations of religion, which could only give rise to thought in the form of myth and an insensitivity to the real. Certainly, that is the claim. At stake in Vattimo's philosophy is a paradoxical rediscovery and return to origins that, as narrated in *Belief*,[1] recovers Christianity through a journey that finds in the philosophical axis of Nietzsche and Heidegger "the acute awareness that they have of their own time as *dürftige Zeit*, as a time of privation and of waiting,"[2] with the risk of entering into Christianity with interpretative keys alien to the revelation of Christianity itself. And yet, even if we are dealing with an unsuspected encounter, it alludes to the possibility of an opening-return to somewhat hermeneutical religious experience in order to reformulate the question *what does thinking mean?*, along with its conditions of possibility beyond the protected spaces of certain evidences and ultimate ends.

PATHWAYS FOR A REDISCOVERY

In Vattimo's reading of the course of Western philosophy, it is important to bring a theoretical feature, or even a fracture, into relief, one that interprets a transition, and maybe even an overcoming, that is also a new beginning: the difference between the metaphysical identity of modernity and the postmetaphysical style of late modernity – or, in more theoretical terms, between metaphysics as the ontology of presence and objectivity and hermeneutic ontology intended as the process that arises in the historicized creases of Being's messages and transmissions. The postmetaphysical option that derives from it coalesces in that *Denkweg* that is the ontology of actuality[3] tied to the contingency and the epochal nature of the question:

Defined as the ontology of actuality, philosophy is practiced as an interpretation of the epoch, a giving-form to widely felt sentiments about the meaning of being alive in a certain society and in a certain historical world. I am well aware that defining philosophy as the Hegelian spirit of the age is like reinventing the wheel. The difference, though, lies in the "interpretation": philosophy is not the expression of the age, it is interpretation, and although it does strive to be persuasive, it also acknowledges its own contingency, liberty, perilousness.[4]

Thus, from within a tradition interpretation brings to light those differences and oscillations of meaning that tradition slowly sends forth as the game of historico-destinal calls and responses, on the condition that hermeneutics knows how to place in crisis the grammatical and categorical roots of our elementary experience of the world, which is ordered according to the cognitive registers of the relation between subject and object, subject and predicates, substance and accident, and so on. Philosophy that is equal to the times therefore assumes the task of preparing to correspond to the event of Being that arises in the finitude of existence, in fallenness, that is, where Being itself arises in impressions, traces, and signs that are different each time. Just such an event demonstrates that the Same (*das Selbe*) of Being is not the repetition of the Equal (*das Gleiche*), but the hint of an un-said and an unthought that demands an untiring return to the discovery of Being.

And yet, only the nihilistic vocation of hermeneutics can liberate man from the cogency of the contests into which historical existence is thrown, allowing him to venture onto the pathways of difference that are the condition of *Dasein*. For *Dasein*, the interpretative risk shakes up an identity that has grown accustomed to, and has even taken for granted, the certainty of foundation and the tranquility of conceptual representation. From such a perspective one understands why "interpretation is an *in(de)finite* process in which every response changes and modifies the character of the call to the extent that it affects the very being of that which calls as the 'other' in the dialogue; far from closing the discourse, it actually stimulates further questions."[5] Therefore, if it finds its essential identity only in hermeneutic nihilism, it is because it agrees with a different exercise of thought, one that is less neurotic with regard to the possibility of grasping the experience of the postmodern world's oscillation and with regard to the unsettling of every definitive and conclusive claim.

LISTENING TO NIHILISM

The appearance of nihilism in the contemporary world describes a new modality of the experience of thought, creating the premises for a movement towards Being that provides the conditions for its radical interrogation. If nihilism proposes some other beginning for thought, it does so by agreeing to journey through and remove what has already occurred in the history of metaphysics as the history of the forgetting of Being.[6] Thus, metaphysics and nihilism belong to each other in the history of Being as the destiny of Being, by virtue of which the same nihilism constitutes an originary memory of Being in its withdrawal as foundation. But is nihilism thinkable as the foundation of Being that announces itself in its anti-foundationality and inexhaustible transcendence? If the interpretative conflict endures, the hermeneutic direction of nihilism stands forth as a possible route, namely, as the passion of disenchantment willing to risk the move beyond the historical forms of metaphysics (for example, Christian Platonism) by reproposing the question of salvation. It is here that the Nietzschean[7] and Heideggerian[8] readings of nihilism simultaneously come together and separate themselves, the event that began the current age as the crisis and transformation of a radical meaning for life. With a little bit of simplification, one can claim that the statement about the death of God impresses an important orientation upon the logic of nihilism, because it exposes the inconsistency of a Christianity twisted into moralistic spiritualism, especially where faith adopts a cunning disguise by justifying reality through the illusion of eternal salvation. The event of the death of God liberates the divine through the critique of a religiosity intended as the decadent and inadequate form of life, but also in the encounter with a thought that, against a skeptical-idealistic imposition, limits the perspective on reality to an anticreative knowing. According to the Heideggerian reading, the consequence involves embracing the most important event of our time, the death of God. One does not read this step simply as a sort of atheism of negation but rather as the dissolution of the metaphysical notion of God intended as Foundation, Reason, and *Causa Sui*. Therefore, if the coincidence of Being and God overturned itself in the reciprocal annulment (forgetting of Being and the death of God) brought about by the history of metaphysics, this tragic destiny is blamed on the reflexive modality of Western philosophy that has forgotten its true origin, where the destiny of the truth of Being occurs in its event that conceals while it reveals. The only possible itinerary is that of a *gott-los* thought capable of thinking God *without-God*, that is to say, capable of moving itself closer to God-divine without the burden of the traditional metaphysical conception of God. This could be the invitation that the section "Der Letze Gott" of the *Beiträge*[9] leaves open: the ultimate god is not Being but the need for Being, in the way that Being needs the divine. Here is the salvation of the truth that the ultimate god can ensure in his passing that escapes any capture, because it invites man to enter into the question of Being as a researcher, the caretaker ready for the listening and abandonment in the opening of the sacred.

The theoretical lesson of nihilism seems to trace out the modality of thought and of life that can liberate the search for meaning from the pretense of stable and incontrovertible substances, since they do not take into account the historicity and the undeniable alterity that resides in the real. When Vattimo emphasizes that postmodern thought can be nothing other than the thought of fruition, of contamination, and of a return to a more originary event, or when he points out that "weak thought"[10] appeals to the impossibility of a consciousness seduced by the logic of presence and by the affirmation of the given – in order to invent provisory and contractual cognitive forms respectful of the

common language of existence – he does nothing other than point out
the meaning of a direction that is free to listen to the current times and
that is attentive to the demand for overcoming what encases thought
within stable and rigidly preordained constructions of meaning. It is no
wonder that within such a horizon the theoretical symbolism of religion, and in particular of Christianity, reemerges. This reemergence
seems to outline an unsuspected weaving of philosophy and theology;
or better, the weaving of the intentionality of weak thought and the perspective of secularization, a hermeneutics of that *Verwindung* of metaphysics within which, paradoxically, weakness and nihilism encounter
each other "somehow in the arms of theology."[11]

PERSPECTIVES ON A RETURN

I do not believe that one can remain indifferent to or inauthentically
distant from the return of religion, given the limitations of meaning and
of the multiple sources of cultural and value-oriented forms. A hasty
response oriented towards solutions that ascribe such a return to pathol-
ogy or to a necessary adjustment to the need for the differentiation of
the social would be equivalent to reproposing interpretative forms characteristic of the world's rationalization, ones indebted to the myth of
man's self-emancipation. In my view, the awkwardness of certain sociological readings that are called upon to reinsert the analyses of religious
phenomenon into the agenda of their own work are rather telling.
Moreover, they need to reexamine the models and categories of their
own approach, as is brought to our attention in the symptomatic case of
the use of the term "de-secularization."[12]

However it may be, the return of religion invokes a different interpretation of the given and seems never to get beyond its potentialities
because it places a certain conceptual habit in crisis, carrying it from a
situation of apparent *familiarity* to a displacing *alienation* in the face of
the given. The effect is that the understanding, in the self-appropriation
of the religious system, finds itself expropriated, that is, led to the verge
of a complex figure, just as the mistaken morphology of the religious
shows that it demands a more articulate and less simplistic reading of
the meanings concealed within. The turning point is just this: the question of meaning, of which religion is a determinate trace, belongs to and
expresses the constitutive opening of man and of history onto an alterity that cannot be deduced and that, by transcending finitude and the
limit, prepares it for listening, but also for the test of reliability or even

of provenance.[13] And yet, as evidenced above, it does not eliminate the suspicion that the religious, precisely in the form of its return, loses itself in an emotive and mystical haze. What jumps into view is a form from the most disparate intentionalities, extended more from the desire for the rediscovery of the I than from the opportunity to enter into the spaces of an alterity that appeals to a real decentring, or at least to a hermeneutic listening that leads to the thing itself.

The roots of the return of the religious ground themselves in various motivations: some are geopolitical, such as the fall of colonialism, "which has *de facto* liberated 'other' cultures, thereby making Eurocentric historicism itself impossible;"[14] some develop in relation to some cultural problems brought forth by certain recent developments of science and technology; and others develop as the erosion of the sense that the endeavours of contemporary man take place under conditions from which there seems to be no escape and require a particular conception of transcendence.[15] What remains decisive, however, is, first and foremost, the elimination of the philosophical bases for atheism as a consequence of the end of metaphysics, in the sense that "the return of religion ... seems to depend on the dissolution of metaphysics, that is, on the dismissal of all doctrines, which claimed absolute and definitive values as the true description of Being's structures."[16] If one then includes the need for identity, a need that appeals to the religious life as the basis for valuative cohesion, cohesion that can mitigate the discrepancy of social anomy and anonymity, it is clear that any prejudicial attitude that insists on interpreting religion as a point of escape in the search for a reason for living is nothing more than a rationalistic pretense, and one that is myopic even from the point of view of the dialectic of the Enlightenment.

Thus it is not a matter of attempting to avoid the losses of a philosophical past that has happily accepted the disenchantment of the world and whose even greater effect seems to be the demythification of the very idea of disenchantment. In effect, Vattimo's critical warning about the possible deviations of and limits to the rebirth of religion in common consciousness does not compel us to abandon the proper exercise of critical thought, not even with the end of the great metanarratives. The irrationalistic demands of fundamentalisms, the isolated legitimization of the return to myth, and the insistence on forms of communitarianism that are not far from attitudes of cultural apartheid must still be the focus of philosophical reflection, lest it run the risk of distancing itself in an esotericism unable to cope with the everyday dealings of life.[17] Without doubt, the return of religion cannot be assumed as the simple bringing into view of a given, following the example of an automatism that presents itself again periodically, without regard for the signs and reasons for its appearance. If there is a return, it is because postmodernity has made it possible. This return is simultaneously the hermeneutic condition for the thinkability of such a return. Here the antecedent understandings that allow for interpretative access to this return might differ and even come into conflict; but the difference inscribed in the forms of return cannot be downplayed, otherwise the exceedingly arbitrary outcome would be fundamentalism or irrationalism.

In other words, it is not enough to remain on the level of questions of fact. Rather, it is important to retrace a "why" in the return of religion, which in Vattimo's reading is represented by secularization as the expression of the change in direction that postmodernity impresses upon religious experience.[18] The process of secularization reveals the impasse confronting metaphysics and exchanges it in favour of a procedural philosophical discursivity, giving form to a dialogical disposition that characterizes the hermeneutic reflection on postmodernity. Interpreting secularization means, therefore, to intuit and follow the intentionality of that very *Verwindung* of metaphysics[19] beyond its dialectical overcoming, in the recognition of the very weakness of Being emergent in the process of the secularization of modernity in its link with religion.

It is not surprising that the dynamic of secularization damages the immobile structure of the origin so that it can no longer be the guarantor of truth and its evidence; nor is it uncommon to claim that modernity is the first to have reached a historical awareness that the meaning of Being resides in its veiledness, in the mystery of its weakening more than in the ideal of the transparency of its principles. In this view, the coming of nihilism and the event of the death of God accompany the process of secularization through a progressive *weakening-decline* of the strong structures of Western thought: from the monotheistic faith in God, guarantor of the *ordo rerum*, to the ethical transmutation of values in their functionality of exchange; from the passage from the *uni-verse* of meaning to a plural conception of the true, all the way to the decodifying of alternative paradigms to the religious-metaphysical establishment, such as ideological atheism and the so-called lay morality. Clearly, the process of secularization has disempowered the metaphysical violence of *identity*, symbolized by the centrality of the subject, allowing *difference* to emerge as the interpretative criterion for history. The intuitions of Adorno's utopian-dialectic perspective and of Levinas' *ontology as ethics* of the *Autrui*[20] bring this out, as does, to an even greater degree, Max Weber's *theory of modernization.*[21]

The Weberian thesis represents, according to the Torinese philosopher, one of the more distinct formulations of the correlation between modernity and secularization by virtue of the originary, Judeo-Christian religious matrix. He knew to single out the differential element of such a process in the *rationalization* of the existent as the inheritance and distortion of the ethical and theoretical dynamism of Christianity. Whether it is the disenchantment of the world made possible by monotheism – by excluding every possible interpretative form of the real based on the magical-polytheistic reading of nature – or whether it is ethics as the progressive reduction of the eschatological emphasis in favour of an assumption of duty for the present, each opens the space of history to the increase of a formal rationality that can orient the organization of society. In Weber's theory more than in other possible interpretations, the antimetaphysical presupposition of secularization emerges as neither loss nor decadence but as the continuation of a religious inheritance-provenance.

PRESUPPOSITIONS OF SECULARIZATION

The appearance-provenance of the Christian inheritance entrusts secularization, in its link with modernization,[22] with a new and particular constructive function. Specifically, it stands in relation to an interpretation of history and of religious experience unburdened by dogmatic weights and metaphysical glitter. It develops that *de-Hellenifying* tension introduced by Christianity on at least two levels: on the first is the eschatological revolution of ontology, where the meaning of transcendence pushes towards a conception of the future as difference; on the second is the weakening of the onto-theological substance of religious contents in view of a re-proposing of Christianity in nonreligious terms for the majority of humans in late modernity.

In such a way one understands why desacralization,[23] more than being the specific contribution of the interpretative impact of Christianity, constitutes an unavoidable presupposition of secularization. It carries with it the demand for a demystification on behalf of Christianity, one that is opposed to the metaphysical sublimation of the sacred.

But still more it liberates the hermeneutic potential of mythological, religious, and poetical discourses from the grasp of the rationalistic ideal of truth, offering the possibility of entering into the linguistic plurality of religious experience. This is confirmed by the recovery of the "link between the development of hermeneutics and the emancipation from dogma"[24] as the site of an interpretative freedom of the plurivocity of Being, whose many ways of appearing are already witnessed by the narrative fabric of the Bible. It is not surprising that modern philosophical hermeneutics arises in Europe, since a religion of the book concentrated attention on the phenomenon of interpretation, sending that hermeneutic culture, which created the idea of a productive and interpretative act, on its way.

This element, if joined with the nihilistic vocation of hermeneutics, accounts for a "thinking that is well-disposed towards religion,"[25] capable of recovering, even if partially, the *value of the Christian inheritance*, of which hermeneutics constitutes a return, and maybe the only possible return. It is not surprising, therefore, that the widespread need for religion,[26] which attempts to stitch together the tear between existence and meaning and to rediscover the problem of God, is closely tied to the *aporias* of modernity. This occurs not simply as an external fact tied to sociopolitical reasons but as the reality implicit in the dissolution of metanarratives. Let us begin with the main philosophical theories and their reassuring myths about the liquidation of religion: "positivist scientism, Hegelian and then Marxist historicism. Today there are no longer strong, plausible philosophical reasons to be atheist, or at any rate to dismiss religion. Atheistic rationalism had taken two forms in modernity: belief in the exclusive truth of the experimental natural sciences, and faith in history's progress towards the full emancipation of humanity from any transcendent authority."[27]

While postmodernity has demonstrated the opposite of such a claim by considering atheistic rationalism to be a belief that has been overcome, weak thought, on the other hand, has assumed the risk of coexisting with nothingness and preparing history, in the apparent unsustainable lightness of Being, for the investigation of the sources of a positivity not yet experienced. If weak thought, as the motivational link between the *Verwindung* of metaphysics and nihilism, points to weakening as the structural characteristic of Being in postmodernity, if such thought has rediscovered its nihilistic vocation in the ontological decline of the strong structures and of the incontrovertibility of the real, and in the end, if the meaning of weak thought inscribes itself in the process of the secularization of philosophy in order to become the *philosophy of secularization*,[28] it is no wonder that weak thought is the exponent of the secularizing process of Christianity and that "maybe secularization (the end of the strong, objective notion of reality as verifiable presence of objects – *Gegenstände* – in space and time) is that which reopens the way to the transcendent."[29]

And, more expressly, "the meaning of this relation between philosophy (weak thought) and the Christian message [is the one] that I am able to think of only in terms of secularization, that is, weakening, incarnation."[30]

For this reason, secularization is able to re-propose the question of God as the question of the meaning of contemporary reality, but on the condition that one does not substitute another God for the metaphysical one, even if freed from the sacred arrangements of natural religion. It is necessary to push the *relationship of secularization and hermeneutics* to its completion, all the way to the recognition that the ontology of weakness discloses itself in the kenosis of God to such a point that the very same weak thought can consider itself to be the transcription of the Christian message.[31] "Nihilism is too much 'like' *kenosis* for one to see this likeness as simply a coincidence, an association of ideas. We are led to the hypothesis that hermeneutics itself, as a philosophy with certain ontological commitments, is the fruit of secularization as the renewal, pursuit, 'application' and interpretation of the substance of the Christian revelation, and preeminently the dogma of the incarnation of God."[32]

KENOSIS AND THE HERMENEUTICS OF SALVATION

Weak thought, in its commitment to overcoming metaphysics – its commitment to the distortion-weakening of the objectifying categories of metaphysics in a postmetaphysical way – not only amplifies the dissolving program of Nietzschean-Heideggerian reflection but rediscovers in its most profound intention, which is far from a dogmatic-disciplinary vision, one of the constitutive traits of the Christian message: Christianity, in comparison to any other religion, is bound to the fact that the heart of its novelty rests in the *fact-principle of incarnation*.[33] Jesus Christ is that expression of the weakening of the onto-theological notion of God, the principle that revolutionizes the very idea of God, no longer revealing him as the *Ipsum esse subsistens* but, according to an interpretation present in the hymn of the Letter to the Philipians

(2,7), as He who emptied himself of his absoluteness and of his "form of God." In conformity with such a premise, for Vattimo the rethinking of Christianity constitutes the occasion for reflecting on the implications that the thought of incarnation can have for the hermeneutic question and for the very possibility of thinking a postmetaphysical religious experience.

The event of the incarnation demonstrates the necessity of thinking differently about a conception of divine transcendence that is confined to a kind of metahistorical eschatology. This necessity is brought to the attention of reason by the paradox of a God who has taken on the human condition and its worldly reality, making them his own: thus, not a God who is totally Other or Infinitely distant, one who in his transcending ontological quality would stand counter to a dialectic of antitheses between the infinite and the finite and thereby reiterate a tragic paradigm of finiteness that led to a finitude crushed against its own unfathomable closing; but rather, a God appearing in history who manifests his involvement in the events of time by indicating, through immanence, an interpretative key directed towards a comprehension of transcendence.

From such an angle, the theoretical and ethical re-reading of kenosis is upsetting in light of the valuative paradigms of lived religion, since, paradoxically, it does not demand the sacrifice of philosophical reason when confronting the incomprehensible and the mysterious but calls it the amazement that appeals to the very thing of incarnation. Translated into Christological terms, it signifies affirming that the symbolic character of the encounter with transcendence and with the divine happens by virtue of the Event of the divine itself that arises in the forms of the human and the visible as the space for its own recognition.[34] Outside this exercise, which could be called interpretative phenomenology, the event of kenosis would provide an unreliable basis for a reflection that does not intend to follow faithfully the prejudicial forms of the approach to the traces of history.

In the final analysis, the philosophical appropriation of the truth of religion still takes place in accordance with a law of philosophy, of the reason that reconciles itself to itself. But the *kenosis* that occurs as the incarnation of God and most recently as secularization and the weakening of Being and its strong structures (to the point of the dissolution of the ideal of truth as objectivity) takes place in accordance with a "law" of religion, at least in the sense that it is not by its own decision that the subject is committed to a process of ruin, for one finds oneself called to such a commitment by the "thing itself."[35]

In this frame of reference, the very Vattiminian affirmation that "salvation passes through interpretation"[36] not only implies recognizing that hermeneutics belongs to the tradition of Western religion but also intuits the *theoretical reciprocity* of such a belonging. It unfolds, on the one side, in the centrality of interpretation as the condition of thinking countermarked by the principle of incarnation,[37] and on the other, in the reinterpretation of the meaning of Christianity in postmodern culture that, beyond a critical rethinking of its disciplinarian nature, places the *question of salvation* and its meaning today on the agenda. From this perspective, one understands how the interpretative approach of the Bible involves the re-reading of the very philosophical experience of religion: if the viewpoint of secularization on the scriptural text frees the Bible from a different approach of truth, the same novelty of the biblical message is the carrier of a *Wirkungsgeschichte* that contributes to a listening that is more attuned to the signs of the times. The result of this rethinking of hermeneutics is traced within the horizon of meaning of the Joachimian prophecy in which emerges ever more the "spiritual" meaning of Scripture, whose scenario is the logic of charity that takes the place of a literal and strict reading. The process of secularization, as a result, not only demythifies dogma and morality, which so often worried about shutting reality within the limits of the intellect, but announces a salvation that incarnates itself in history and, through interpretation directed to understanding the present meaning of scriptural texts, agrees to "read the signs of the times with no other provision than the commandment of love."[38]

Here one finds the meaning (by philosophical rediscovery) of the inheritance of the Christian tradition:[39] the principle of incarnation, intended as desacralization and as kenotic manifestation that speaks the being of God, marks the return of the possibility for hermeneutic philosophy to gather the meaning of the evangelical value of *love* and the *friendly dynamic* of interpretation. In other words, this indicates the urgency of following through on the stand taken against every instance of metaphysical violence and against those attempts to return to it that are not friendly to the idea of a weakened truth in the movement of Christ's incarnation, an idea that "continues to realize itself more and more clearly by furthering the education of mankind concerning the overcoming of originary violence essential to the sacred and to social life itself."[40] It appears rather clear that the specificity of Christianity for thought grounds a continual invention of history in the inspiring model of the incarnate God's self-weakening and in the principle of *caritas*, a critical principle that is clear enough for orienting itself on the traces of the divine. Is Christianity not, perhaps, *the trace of the trace* that reopens the possibility of a relation to the divine when it is thought of not as stable and full Being but as the Event not dominated by the imperative of self-preservation, and that is thus able to point out a logic different from one of mortal struggle? The discovery of the evangelical "I no longer call you servants but friends" (John 15:15) constitutes, then, the interpretative translation of the principle of love. Its characteristic is that of an ecumenical opening that is able to bring value to the truth-bearing substance present both in other religions and in the plurality of cultures, as well as through recognizing the positivity of those dissolutive experiences that, emptying out the certainties of metaphysics, prepare for the event of salvation as the history of interpretation.

This line of thinking embodies the critique of the Dostoevskian-Pareysonian brand of tragic thought that seems to represent "the last great metaphysical misunderstanding of Christian thought."[41] Such an emphasis on the loving dimension of Christianity does not, in the unsuccessful recognition of the role of the negative, isolate the arbitrariness of a thought and of a faith that is simplistically friendly in the face of man; rather, it points to the consequence of the principle of incarnation whose *Weltanschauung* avoids a natural-metaphysical guarantee hardened by the violence of dogmatism and punishment. Would it be possible to stand before Being and the divine in wonder without the discovery of the love that allows me to live the religious experience as the feeling of dependence and awareness of the initiative begun by the continual self-revelation of God? The temptation to mask religious experience in a sort of *divertissement* in regard to an impossible reality, because of the unbearableness of evil and the tragic nature of the finite, seems again to follow the idea of a Christianity either of the "leap" or of *deus ex machina*; that is, it seems to follow yet again a stop-gap Christianity (recalling Bonhöffer) that, facing the impediments of reality, cannot avoid returning to God in order to bring an end to the trials of failure and defeat. Beyond a possible consolatory effect, one such resolution would remain within an interpretative error, one that is surely possible, but one that is insufficient because of a neutralization

of the principle of incarnation that returns to the communal and eschatological logic of charity, within which "perhaps I can endure and sec-
ularize evil insofar as it concerns me, but I have to take it seriously
when it has to do with the neighbor who calls for my help, or at least
for my understanding of his suffering."[42] Whether or not we are
dealing with an overly optimistic, if not even anarchical, conception of
kenosis is the question that immediately strikes Vattimo himself, a question that, nonetheless, confirms his preference for a friendly conception
of God and of the meaning of religion. He states with self-awareness
that

the salvation I seek through a radical acceptance of the meaning of kenosis
does not depend exclusively on me, and is not indifferent to the need for grace
as the gift that comes from the other ... The fact that the philosophical kernel
of the argument developed here is hermeneutics, that is, the philosophy of
interpretation, shows the fidelity of the latter to the idea of grace, understood
in its double sense: as a gift that comes from an other, and as a response that
inseparably expresses the most intimate truth of the one who receives it in its
acceptance of the gift.[43]

The conclusion of such a journey rests in the questioning whose theoretical and ethical gains can be recognized in the close ties between
philosophy and Christian religious thought. If the Biblical heritage
requires philosophy to recognize the eventuality of Being and the violence of metaphysical essentialism, then the reciprocal belonging of secularization, incarnation and the ontology of actuality is something
more than a simple historical recovery of the history of Being. It is the
indication of another thought, of a trace that is perceived in the *link
between the history of salvation and the history of interpretation*, since
the fact of incarnation in its revolutionary, revelatory nature says that
redemption rests in the rediscovery/return to origin of a history of calls
and responses. Thus the *other* of interpretation resides in the *surfeit*
that must accompany the interpreting, in that productivity of the interpretative act[44] whose path is sketched out in the principle of incarnation and in its perspective of a truth for living – neither for seizing, nor
for possessing. In this way, hermeneutics recognizes more and more its
prophetic vocation and its dimension as an ethic of provenance that, in
the critique of Western thought's attempt to conceptualize Being,
compels philosophical-religious experience to dwell in the opening
where man is always thrown in the call towards that very opening.

It is, definitively, the meaning of incarnation as the theory of the historicity of reality and of radically historical truth, for which neither the leap of faith nor the leap of reason is required; rather, it requires recognition of the interpretative reciprocity that it inhabits. But this, as Vattimo shows, is only the perception of a task:

The overcoming of metaphysics, in other words, can only take place as nihilism. The meaning of nihilism, however, if it is not in its turn to take the form of a metaphysics of the nothing ... can only think of itself as an indefinite process of reduction, diminution, weakening. Could such a thinking be thought outside the horizon of the Incarnation? If hermeneutics really wishes to continue along the path opened by Heidegger's call to recollect Being (and thus *Ereignis*), this is perhaps the decisive question to which it must seek a response today.[45]

INCONCLUSIVE POSTSCRIPT

We find ourselves faced with an unforeseen task. It has been made possible by the postmodernity[46] that favoured a return of religion by subduing anachronistic objections and resistant prejudices. And yet the future of Christianity seems to define itself with more difficulty when interpreted within the common sense notion of religion. In other words, the meaning of the return of Christianity is not to be discounted, particularly if it inscribes itself within a different vision of history brought forth by a hermeneutics of the process of secularization. The emancipative centrality of the subject, the progressive linearity of history, the capacity of reason to reach the foundation of the real through a protocol of constant adaptation: these characteristics express a cognitive modality of modernity that the events have placed in crisis, maybe because of excessive confidence in the autonomy of the logic of the I. The hermeneutic circle of weak thought (philosophy) and Christian faith (theology), whose figure casts an interesting reflection on the philosophy of religion, demonstrates how Christianity represents a possibility for thinking and dwelling in the contemporary world. Now, if religion returns in the form of Christianity, it does so not only because of historical causes inherent in a social-cultural place of origin. There is something else to consider: this Christianity is open to the interpretation of history and to the lighting up of truth with a modality that is attentive to the questions of meaning, promoting a critical reading of what damages research into the salvation of man. The relation between the world and the God revealed in Jesus Christ extends far beyond the canons of a natural or reassuring religiosity, or even beyond an anonymous theism signalled by the neutrality of Being. With the event of the kenosis, the Being of God has meaning and decisiveness for us only in relation to the Being of Jesus Christ, *being-for-the-other*, which ends in his total gift of life. Is not this absolute dedication to the other the expression of the radicality of transcendence, the condition for rereading omnipotence and the other attributes traditionally ascribed to God? If the Being of Christ reassumes the meaning of the presence of God in the world, one understands how Christianity opens pathways of exploration for the postmetaphysical task of philosophy that Vattimo reads in the wake of Christian heritage. In other words, Christianity welcomes into the realm of investigation a call that beckons philosophical reflection to take responsibility in the wake of the paradigm of *charity*,[47] even as the critical capacity of the existent. One will get used to the idea that the belief in God as the first foundation of the world has become useless; it will also be possible to think of the elaboration of an ethical discourse in the face of the dissolution of metaphysical absolutes. It will become difficult, however, to attribute a universal task to Christianity in the intercultural and interreligious dialogue without recognizing its revelatory novelty as the location of dialogue, as well as of interpretative conflict. Could not the nature of the Christian message rest in the fact that it is able to take you, in thought, beyond even the perspective of a religious individualism?[48] "I hold firm that Jesus came from God because the things he says are really of divine origin, that is, they really are the most divine that I have found in my life ... I believe in the divinity of Jesus Christ above all because of what he has said to me."[49]

NOTES

1 Gianni Vattimo, *Belief*, trans. Luca d'Isanto and David Webb (Stanford: Stanford University Press 1999).

2 Gianni Vattimo, *Essere, storia e linguaggio in Heidegger*, 2d ed. (Genoa: Marietti 1989), 48.

3 Translator's note: The reference here is to Vattimo's notion of the "ontologia dell'attualità," which might be translated less literally as "ontology of the present" or "ontology of the current times."

4 Gianni Vattimo, *Nihilism and Emancipation: Ethics, Politics, and Law,*

ed. Santiago Zabala and trans. William McCuaig (New York: Columbia University Press 2004), 87–8.

5 Gianni Vattimo, *The Adventure of Difference*, trans. Cyprian Blamires (Baltimore: Johns Hopkins Press, 1993), 25.

6 Cf. Gianni Vattimo, *The End of Modernity*, trans. Jon R. Snyder (Baltimore: Johns Hopkins University Press 1991), 164–81.

7 Friedrich Nietzsche, *The Gay Science*, n125, in *The Complete Works of Friedrich Nietzsche*, vol. 10, ed. Oscar Levy (New York: Russell and Russell 1964), 167; *Daybreak*, n547, in *The Complete Works of Friedrich Nietzsche*, vol. 9, ed. Oscar Levy (New York: Russell and Russell 1964), 377–9; *Thus Spoke Zarathustra*, in *The Complete Works of Friedrich Nietzsche*, vol. 11, ed. Oscar Levy (New York: Russell and Russell 1964), 6–7.

8 Cf. M. Heidegger, "Nietzsche's Word: 'God is Dead'" in *Off The Beaten Track*, trans. Julian Young and Kenneth Haynes (Cambridge: University of Cambridge Press 2002), 157–99; and *Nietzsche*, trans. David Farrell Krell (New York: Harper Collins 1991), 187–253; E. Jünger and M. Heidegger, *Spuren, Ernst Jünger u. Martin Heidegger: Das Walten des Nihilismus und die Rückkunft der Zukunftigen*, in *Gesamtausgabe*, vol. 90 (Frankfurt a.M.: Klostermann).

9 Cf. M. Heidegger, *Contributions to Philosophy (From Enowning)*, trans. Parvis Emad and Kenneth Maly (Bloomington: Indiana University Press 1999), 285–96. Cf. the reading by I. Mancini, *Frammento su Dio* (Brescia: Morcelliana 2000), 191–276 (on Vattimo's reading, 192–5).

10 One remembers the programmatic essay *Dialettica, differenza, pensiero debole*, in G. Vattimo and P.A. Rovatti, eds., *Il pensiero debole* (Milano: Feltrinelli 1983), 12–28; in English, "Dialectics, Difference, and Weak Thought," trans. T. Harrison, *Graduate Faculty Philosophy Journal* 10 (1984): 151–63).

11 Gianni Vattimo, *Beyond Interpretation*, trans. David Webb (Stanford: Stanford University Press 1997), x.

12 Cf. J. Casanova, *Public Religion in the Modern World* (Chicago and London: University of Chicago Press 1994); P.L. Berger, ed., *The Desecularization of the World: Resurgent Religion and World Politics*, Washington, DC: Ethics and Public Policy Center 1999.

13 Gianni Vattimo, "The Trace of a Trace," in Jacques Derrida and Gianni Vattimo, *Religion*, trans. various (Oxford: Polity Press 1998), 87. "However, this does not remove the fact that the experience of finitude, above all in the inadequacy of our responses to the 'demand' that comes to us from others (or from the Other in Levinas' sense) takes the form of a need for a 'supplement' that we cannot picture for ourselves otherwise than transcendent."

14 Gianni Vattimo, *After Christianity*, trans. Luca D'Isanto (New York: Columbia University Press 2002), 18.

15 Cf. Vattimo, *Belief*, 20–8.

16 Vattimo, *After Christianity*, 18–19.

17 One reads in *After Christianity* (87–8): "can a philosophy that is aware of the absence of strong reasons for atheism ally itself with the new popular religious consciousness – imbued as it is with fundamentalism, communitarianism, anxiety over ethnic identity, and paternalistic reassurances at the cost of sacrificing freedom? ... Philosophy can no longer see the social vitality of religion as a phenomenon of cultural backwardness promoted by cunning priests, or as the expression of ideological alienation to be overcome through revolution and through the abolition of the division of labor. Rather, it must grasp within the historical process the principles for critically appraising its outcome, recognizing that philosophy itself belongs to the same process that promotes the return to religion."

18 The centrality of the category of secularization in the development of Vattimo's thought constitutes a topical moment both in terms of the connotation of philosophy and also in the interpretation of religious experience. It is a discriminating theoretical leit-motiv. Cf., for example *The End of Modernity*, 1–15; "Metaphysics, Violence, and Secularization," in *Recoding Metaphysics: The New Italian Philosophy*, ed. Giovanna Borradori, trans. B. Sprachman (Evanston: Northwestern University Press 1988), 45–61; *Etica dell'interpretazione* (Turin: Rosenberg & Sellier 1989), 27–37; *The Transparent Society* (Baltimore: Johns Hopkins University Press 1992), 39–40; *Filosofia al presente* (Milan: Garzanti 1990), 68–79; *Beyond Interpretation*, 42–57; *Belief*, 38–43, 46–8, 62–5, 80–4. What Vattimo writes in the introduction to *Filosofia '86* on page ix is indicative: "The choice of the theme of secularization indicates first of all the proposal to interpret the experience of the end of metaphysics ... as the delineation of a positive task for philosophy, a task different from that of negating or reducing it to the simple archaeological care of our own lineage." But what seems particularly meaningful is the link that Vattimo establishes between secularization and Christianity, in a reading that, beyond any results, seems to grasp decisive aspects of the liberating importance of Christianity in history. What he writes in *After Christianity* brings it all together: "This is the sense in which I employ the term *secularization*: it is an interpretative application of the biblical message that situates it beyond the strictly sacramental, sacral, or ecclesiastical realm. Whoever argues that this gesture betrays the biblical message obviously defends the literal interpretation of Christian doctrine, which, therefore, can be legitimately opposed by the idea of secularization as 'spiritual' interpretation" (45).

19 Vattimo writes in "Metaphysics, Violence, and Secularization" (in *Recoding Metaphysics: The New Italian Philosophy*, ed. Giovanna Borradori, trans. B. Sprachman (Evanston: Northwestern University Press 1988), 61: "In its 'theoretical' and, inseparably, its 'epochal' aspects (*GeStell*), the *Verwindung* of metaphysics is nothing other than secularization.

20 See "Metaphysics, Violence, and Secularization," 48–59.

21 Cf. "Ontologia dell'attualità," in *Filosofia '87* (Laterza, Roma-Bari 1988), 212–20; *After Christianity*, 78–82.

22 This is one of the more noticeable theses in *Belief*. He writes: "I am deliberately putting forth this idea in scandalous and provocative terms. In my view, this is necessary in order to shake the religious and the philosophical habit of taking for granted the threat of modernization to values, authenticity, freedom and so on" (52).

23 In Vattimo's reading one finds the reference to Rene Girard's exegetical work on the question of the sacred and the link with violence. R. Girard, *Origine della cultura e fine della storia: Dialoghi con Pierpaolo Antonello e João Cezar de Castro Rocha* (Milan: Raffello Cortina Editore 2002), 201–11.

24 *Beyond Interpretation*, 43.

25 Ibid., 44.

26 One reads in *The Trace of the Trace*: "If critical reflection wishes to present itself as the authentic interpretation of the religious need of common consciousness, it must show that this need is not adequately satisfied by a straightforward recovery of 'metaphysical' religiousness, that is, by fleeing the confusions of modernization and the Babel of secularized society towards a renewed foundationalism. Is such a 'demonstration' possible?" (82).

27 Vattimo, *Belief*, 28.

28 Cf. *Etica dell'interpretazione*, 36–7.

29 G. Vattimo, "Scienza, ontologia, etica," in *Valori, scienza e transcendenza, 2; Un dibattito sulla dimensione etica e religiosa nella comunità scientifica internazionale* (Turin: Edizioni della Fondazione Giovanni Agnelli 1990), 88.

30 Vattimo, *Belief*, 36.

31 Ibid., 47, 82–3.

32 Vattimo, *Beyond Interpretation*, 52.

33 Cf. G. Vattimo, "The Trace of the Trace," in Derrida and Vattimo, *Religion*, 92–3.

34 Cf. C. Dotolo, *Kenosi e secolarizzazione nella riflessione teologica del Novecento*, in A. Ales Bello, L. Messinese, and A. Molinaro, eds., *Fondamento e fondamentalismo* (Rome: Città Nuova 2004), 323–49.

35 Vattimo, *Beyond Interpretation*, 53.

36 Ibid., 43. Cf. More extensively, Vattimo, *After Christianity*, 57–68.

37 In *Beyond Interpretation*, Vattimo says: "the nihilistic 'drift' that hermeneutics reads in the 'myth' of incarnation and crucifixion does not cease with the conclusion of Jesus's time on earth, but continues with the descent of the Holy Spirit and with the interpretation of this revelation by the community of believers. According to the line that, with no pretence to philological accuracy, I propose to call here Joachimist, the meaning of scripture in the age opened by the descent of the Holy Spirit becomes increasingly 'spiritual' and thereby less bound to the rigour of dogmatic definitions and strict disciplinarian observance" (49–50).

38 Vattimo, *Belief*, 77.

39 One reads in *Belief* that: "another reason to recover Christianity, apart from the (interpretative) recognition of our belonging to this tradition, is that Christian doctrine 'fore-sees' interpretation and fore-sees the history of Being in its interpretative (kenotic) universal character" (68).

40 Vattimo, *Belief*, 48.

41 Ibid., 80.

42 Ibid., 96.

43 Ibid., 97.

44 Cf. Vattimo, *After Christianity*, 60–1.

45 Derrida and Vattimo, *Religion*, 93.

46 See P. Heelas, ed., *Religion, Modernity and Postmodernity* (Oxford: Blackwell 1998); C. Taylor, *Varieties of Religion Today* (Cambridge: Harvard University Press 2002); M.A. Wrathall, ed., *Religion after Metaphysics* (Cambridge: Cambridge University Press 2003); R. Rorty and G. Vattimo, *The Future of Religion*, ed. S. Zabala (New York: Columbia University Press 2005).

47 One reads this in G. Vattimo, *Vero e Falso Universalismo cristiano* (Rio de Janeiro: Editora Universitaria Candido Mendes 2002) 15: "That which seems to me to be an effect of 'Christianization,' even if it occurs without awareness of today's philosophy, in which one can speak of a transformation of the very idea of truth towards that of charity, of respect and attentiveness to the other" (15) [my translation].

48 This is clear, for example, in U. Regina, *La soglia della fede: L'attuale domanda su Dio* (Rome: Edizioni Stadium 2001), 89–98; D. Hervieu-Léger, *Il Pellegrino e il convertito: La religione in movimento* (Bologna: Il Mulino 2003), 138–9.

49 G. Vattimo, in G. Vattimo, P. Sequeri, and G. Ruggeri, *Interrogazioni sul cristianesimo. Cosa possiamo ancora attenderci dal Vangelo?* Edizioni Lavoro/Editrice Esperienze (Rome: Fossano 2000), 48–9. Useful developments of this theme can also be found in J.M. Mardones, *Síntomas de un ritorno: La religión en el pensamento actual* (Maliaño: Editorial Sal Terrae 1999),

17–34; A. Matteo, *Della fede dei laici: Il cristianesimo di fronte alla mentalità postmoderna* (Rubbettino: Soveria Mannelli 2001), 88–96; S. Zabala, "La Religión de Gianni Vattimo: El cristianismo después de la muerte de Dios," *Claves de Razón Práctica* 132 (2003): 57–62; R. Ottone, "Ontologia debole e caritas nel pensiero di Gianni Vattimo," in *La Scuola Cattolica* 132 (2004): 171–203.

21

The Rights of God in Hermeneutical Postmodernity

TERESA OÑATE

Translated by Ileana Szymanski

HERMENEUTICS AND POSTMODERNITY: ACTIVE NIHILISM

Let us recall that in the mid-1980s, with the echoes of the year 1968 still audible and following the example of the literary and architectonic aesthetics that were saying their good-byes to modernity – J.-F. Lyotard announced the advent of the *postmodern condition*.[1] However, the most disquieting thing was, without a doubt, the tempestuous news that, in a fashion similar to the announcement of the death of God by Nietzsche, was contained in his report on the societies of telematic capitalism: the news of the end of the Western metaphysical metanarratives, demythologized as tall tales written by – and, moreover, mimicking W. Benjamin – those who had been vanquished. Consequently, the problematic of the philosophy of history was also placed in the foreground, with the aim of putting in question – and asking for a response from Hegel-Marx – the metaphysical violence of universal history and the perverse progress of historical-dialectical rationality. Logically, the exigencies of "altering the times that run" (W. Benjamin) was also experimented with from the post-Marxian context of French post-structuralism, all in search of an alternative rationality-epochality. Postmodernity as a postmetaphysics and a posthistory had just been born, and I investigated first Lyotard's philosophy and then Vattimo's thought, but only thanks to Vattimo was

I able to understand the real reach of Gadamer's hermeneutical ontology, and I could reread with amazement the deep lucidity of Heidegger and Nietzsche, so that, taking them as a starting point and going backwards, I could take on the study of the documentary traditions and texts of European philosophy, starting with a reinterpretation of the Greeks.

Since then – and forced by the philosophical texts of our hermeneutical traditions – I have never abandoned that double mode of reading: from the Greeks to contemporary thought (starting with Hegel) and from the contemporary thinkers to the Greeks. I have not abandoned this mode because in the light of my rational experience from the enclave of that disjunctive synthesis, the temporal space of a transverse critical expropriation of the present can be opened today (for the intra-Western hermeneutics of the postmodern transhistoric rationality) up to its documentable borderlines. Such critical expropriation is what the two intensive limits of our vital memory operate amongst themselves: our Greeks and our (post)moderns, intertwined with difference.

Let us return, nevertheless, to the mid-1980s. Then it was only Vattimo, the most communicative of H.-G. Gadamer's disciples, who allowed us to understand the bonds and the density of the problematic transmissions set in motion through hermeneutics by Nietzsche and Heidegger until we reached postmodernity. We had to take to heart the *active nihilism* of the ontology of Nietzsche and Heidegger if we were not to do violence to or colonize but rather to read their postmetaphysical philosophies in a hermeneutical fashion: as postidealists, postmaterialists, and posthumanists. Let it be placed on the record, then, how the philosophical works of Vattimo, particularly those written at the end of the 1980s and the beginning of the 1990s, operated in the hermeneutics of the end of the twentieth century, providing a substantial place, in short, for four phenomena of singular importance: On the one hand, it is understood that hermeneutics presents itself, may be transformed, and is indeed transformed in the new *koiné* of Western thought as a critical alternative to the dialectic of metaphysical rationality continually superseding itself. On the other hand, it is understood that this same philosophical hermeneutics is constituted in an ontology of being-language-history-transmission-interpretation, as a postmetaphysical ontology of postmodernity, in the era of telematic capitalism and in a communication society. Third, one can also point to the fact that Vattimo, in a very significant way, has configured the context of the new Western (post-Marxist) democratic left. Indeed, he has retraced the lineage of Gadamerian hermeneutics, which goes back from Heidegger to Nietzsche, which is why it converges, going backwards, with the Nietzscheans of French poststructuralism, notably Michel Foucault and Gilles Deleuze, and converges with the deconstruction of Jacques Derrida, which takes the same origin, but in a very different fashion. It is not strange, then, that the pragmatism of Richard Rorty or the critical hermeneutics of Jürgen Habermas and K.O. Apel (to give only three examples) can be added, among others, to the dialogue that Vattimo allows them – and forces them – to maintain with each other and with today's philosophy.

Finally, the fourth aspect I wish to highlight is the question of the divine, which is situated in the realm that refers us to Vattimo's essential contribution to today's hermeneutics, his contribution with regard to the opening and the constitution of the ontological space of such rationality. Since already in Vattimo's reference to Nietzsche and Heidegger (and also, though in a different manner, to Gadamer), in whose texts the question of the divine constantly recurs, as well as that of symbolic-poetic thought, a *Kehre* is traced that lets itself be felt as a conversion and a return inscribed in the very movement of thought that interprets and produces the sense of the transmission of Western rationality after the death of God, and the dogmatic atheism of the Enlightenment.

THE LIMIT OF INTERPRETATION: THE QUESTION OF A CRITERION

If *active nihilism,* as a debolist[2] critical-hermeneutical principle, was to find a *limit of interpretation* of fundamental principles, as well as of the indifferentist relativisms and their thesis that *all is valid* – equally violent because of being indisputable – it was to have not only a methodological status but also an ontological-hermeneutical status. That is to say, it was to translate and understand the fundamental message of the metaphysics transmitted by history to us, to understand it precisely as the weakening/dissolution of the being-fundament and its strong structures. That is why pursuing the hermeneutics of the history that is sent to us as dissolution determines or delimits, according to Vattimo, the task of critical hermeneutics as active nihilism and signals the common vector of modern secularization, as well as of postmodern debolism. Thus, the greatest risk of debolism hinged, in my opinion, as was to be expected, upon the most arduous of the questions that the

Nietzschean legacy makes us place in the very centre of postmetaphysical philosophy, namely, the question of nihilism. And the risk was on
the side of Vattimo, above all, because he pursued nihilism *until the last
man* of Nietzsche's Zarathustra. He did so because of a dislocation
(*Verwindung*) of the diachronic-dialectic historicism of Hegel, which
would end up in a mere emancipatory inversion-repetition of the
rational dialectic of history: it would end up in an inverted Hegel,
almost fractured by Adorno, giving way to a minimalist historicism or
to the *subtraction* that would progressively undo, dissolve, and weaken
towards nothingness: as a result it would be transformed in a counter-
fundamentalist regulatory ideal. The most important risk factors were,
then, on the side of Vattimo and, to put it briefly, lay in the following
items:

1 In a diachronical or kinetic-temporal reading, be it of the *death of
   God* of Nietzsche, be it of the *end of metaphysics* of Heidegger.
2 In the (very disputably) consequent application of the Vattiminian
   idea of time, radically contingentist and eventualist, to the *eternal
   recurrence* of Nietzsche and the *Andenken* and the *Ereignis*, or even
   the *alétheia* of Heidegger (as if, for instance, the *léthe* were tempo-
   rally before and the *a-létheia* of the un-veiling came afterward, or as
   if the *Happening-Ereignis* were an event, deprived of necessity). This
   is why the full measure of the thought and coherence of Vattimo was
   reduced, essentially, to justify item 3.
3 A risk also lay in the right invoked by debolist nihilism to allow it to
   inherit the hermeneutic ontologies of Nietzsche and Heidegger as
   sources of rational legitimacy, in the capacity of origin or in the
   capacity of future.
4 The problem resides, especially, in item 3 because, indeed, if the
   target of the critique of Nietzsche and Heidegger was nihilism (in the
   history of Western metaphysics), how could one try, seemingly
   according to Vattimo, to proceed to intensify the active nihilism of
   that backward dialectic, in which the ontology of dissolution – an
   ontology that is proper to weak thought – seemed to be resolved?
5 Was Vattimo not plainly working in favour of the nihilistic *Metaphysics as History* of the oblivion of being, and doing so precisely
   because he proposed to dissolve metaphysics? Had not the vertiginous circle of this repetitive infinite shown already its power to
   absorb (on the side of the capital) all the dialectical movements that
   were opposed to it as antitheses into a great black hole? In this way,

was the recurrent stability of the crisis that perpetuated the indifferent *illness of history* and the *violence of metaphysics* denounced by Nietzsche and Heidegger not achieved?

6 But, besides, there were the Greeks, so to speak, and it was impossible to ignore the constant references – in diverse ways, but always of central importance – to the Greek philosophers in the hermeneutics of Nietzsche, Heidegger, and Gadamer. (They all shared, especially, the very significant reference to *Philosophy in the Tragic Age of the Greeks*: to pre-Socratic philosophy, established, as we know today (thanks precisely to Heidegger and Gadamer) by Aristotle – the founder of Greek hermeneutics – as a critique against the dialectic of Pythagoreanism-Platonism and in defense of the primacy of the languages of life over the ideal of mathematical scientism designed for the salvation of the soul of man in the realm beyond death ... and that was already even in Plato! It was also present in the Orphic-eschatological myths that were progressively taking over the Academy of Athens, as the teacher Plato was becoming Pythagorean despite the critical reinterpretation with which Aristotle's hermeneutics delimited and dislocated Platonism, transforming it in an immanent and pluralist ontology of the reinterpretation of the linguistic senses of being-communication-action that is given/said in different ways.

And how could this not have anything to do with hermeneutics and its genealogies? Was it not the case that ever since Nietzsche Platonism was to be inverted?[3] How could all of this have nothing to do with the contemporary hermeneutics of postmetaphysical and posthistoric thought, with Nietzsche, with Heidegger, with the Greeks, and with the history of the traditions of the possible pasts, traditions that were not consumed but rediscovered by hermeneutics as a radical denial of the historicism of the superseding-salvation proper of the reason of the dialectic of the Enlightenment? How to forget now the power-willing backwards of the eternal recurrence of Nietzsche, seen as able to want the open possible of the pasts or the *Ungedachte-Ungesachte* (the unthought and unsaid in what *is* thought and said) that is remembered and renowned in Heidegger's *Andenken*, as in Gadamer's hermeneutics? And is that turn, the transhistoric turn, precisely the one that is central to the hermeneutical praxis that has become intralinguistic ontology? Or is it that all pasts are not texts? How could the status of the future anterior of the hermeneutical, historical, and textual possible-pasts not be affected by the question of the rationality of history, which had become the metaphysics of the history of the only and universal salvation, simply because of the weight of the Platonic-Christian monotheism-nihilism since Paul of Tarsus and Augustine of Hippo? But perhaps things are more complex, since this is about Vattimo.

VATTIMO'S *VERWINDUNG* AND THE HISTORY OF SENSE/MEANING

For the time being one has to admit, in Vattimo's favour, that a hermeneutical ontology of the present that does not flee to any transcendence is forced to trace the nexus between the philosophy of the present and the philosophy of history in order to notice immediately that the latter is, also, awaiting an interpretation. This is why it offers a surface for contextual inscription that is as problematic as it is indispensable – in respect to the situation of nonmetaphysical philosophy in its own context of hermeneutical belonging. As we shall see, the knot that paralyzes rationality in this aporia has two ends, and double too is the diachronic and synchronic articulation that puts into play Vattimo's proposal *in* the language-history of being. For what is our concrete situation in this history? Which philosophy of history decides on the concrete history of philosophy where one will situate internally a current ontology if – as Vattimo rightly demands – one is to be faithful to the condition of strict immanence that is essential for hermeneutics, to the extent that it is a critique of the metaphysical violence of the absolute transcendentals?

In the meantime, does not the reach of this topic – which is none other than the topic of a criterion – affect, also, all contemporary hermeneutical rationality from the "there are no facts but only interpretations" of Nietzsche to the latest American postmodernism? Does it not put into question everything from the *Andenken* of Heidegger to the *Monumenta* of Gadamer and the ideal speech community or the aprioris of language defended by the critical hermeneutics of Habermas and Apel, not to mention, in the poststructuralist tradition, the *incommensurable Epistemai* of Foucault, the unassigned *Diferend* of Lyotard, or the virtual noetic of Deleuze? And with regard to the pragmatic hermeneutics of Rorty, what can one think of the principle of continuity (of the conversational game, etc.) as a preferential criterion for interpretation? And what about Jacques Derrida? Although deconstruction is not a method or even a postmetaphysical intervention, is it not, however, the case that ruin, trace/print, the undone, spectrum, margins, etc., are the names of an apophatic metaphysics of absence and the *léthe* (or the *chóra*, or the *chaos*) with which Derrida might be continuing the negative theology of the absolute alterity defended by Lévinas?

Vattimo, too, wagers everything on this question, since it is equated, from the ethical and epistemological point of view, with being able to ask which preferential criterion is to be used with respect to the interpretations of justice, of what is convenient, of what is correct, of what is true, etc. That is to say, it is equated with being able to interpret and choose currently and, moreover, legitimately according to such a criterion, while departing from the rational hermeneutical point of view. And Vattimo needs to be able to demand that one should prefer debolism and interpret according to it, or, what is the same, according to the democratic criterion of the critique and efficacious diminution of the violence of the imposing absolutes (the arrogant god, the arrogant subject, the dogmas, the authoritarianisms ...) and all that does not allow us to engage in hermeneutical conversation, etc. To what other theoretical motives could he appeal that are not also the ethical motives that reject the violence of metaphysics precisely in the name of the debolist hermeneutical principle applied to the denunciation of the arrogance of all things that do not allow themselves to be interpreted or discussed? And, does it not seem that the hermeneutical circle is thereby vertiginously closed?

However, the contrary is the case, since it is precisely because the question about a criterion refers us back to the question about the context of the interpretation, and because the latter sends us, also, intra-hermeneutically, to a history of being-language-transmission that Vattimo can positively find the sought-after limit-criterion of interpretation. This is because if we are to know where we are and to be able to orient ourselves in the matter of choices, the only intrahistorical road is that given by the interpretation of the sense of the message that transmits the actuality of hermeneutics as communal *koiné*, or common language, of contemporary democratic thought after the death of God and the end of metaphysics.

The wise Heraclitus of Ephesus had already said it: the road – *méthodos* – we must follow to travel somewhere and to return from there is one and the same. Perhaps it is there, then, in the apparent assimilation of the philosophy of history and the history of philosophy, that we find Vattimo's most original and surprising thought with respect to the interpretation of the Hermeneutic circle. It might seem from a purely formal point of view that we could be falling into the closing of ontological difference that is characteristic of metaphysical positivisms. However, it is precisely there, in that crossing of ontological planes, that Vattimo positions himself, following with a rare profundity the lessons on philosophy of the Berlin mythology of the last Schelling and some precise indications of the signalling of Heidegger.[4]

And if one stops there, in that crossroads of Hermes, it is because since the inscription of that crossing-limit one can perceive an abyss *downward*, towards the infinite plane that extends between the two directions of the past and the future, crisscrossing again in the present, while *upward* one sees the opening of a darkness.

The most difficult, deep, dangerous and amazingly coherent aspect of Vattimo's thought is in that crisscrossing, in that historical-hermeneutical crossroads where is situated the mystery of the death and resurrection of the god that was the son of God and son of man, the Jesus Christ who, according to the Scriptures and the hermeneutics of the beliefs proper to the Christian faith and religion, had become incarnate as a *kenosis*, or weakening, of God the Father, sending himself to human beings by making himself immanent history and scripture, as a live and saving message of good news. Was the good news of the Gospel itself something other than the resurrected Christ himself? That is to say, was it something other than the history transmitted by the incarnation itself, inasmuch as it was the history of the dissolution of the absolute that was sending itself in the *kenosis* (diminution) of the God made man, made history, or live Scripture? Vattimo understood, then, departing from the religious turn of his thought, that debolism was nothing but the evangelic *kénosis* of hermeneutical Christianity as the history/message of incarnation and the history of redemption that was being transmitted/realized in the ontological hermeneutics of nihilism as the dissolution of the strong, or metaphysical, structures: the Foundation, the subject ... and their logic of imposition, projection, production.

The exigency of turning, or reorienting, oneself towards the sense of the law, which traversed bit by bit the reposing of a hermeneutical post-Enlightenment rationality in Nietzsche, as well as in Heidegger, seemed to translate, then, the same position. Indeed, its deep cry for a reorienting of modernity as a change in the course of modern (metaphysical) violence towards the sense of legislative rationality could coherently be interpreted as the debolist continuity of active nihilism, responding profoundly to the same motives that intertwined Nietzsche's and Heidegger's critique of metaphysics with the history of modern emancipation – the same history that continued, all the way to us, in postmodern interpretation as debolist interpretation of the sense of modernity, in the era of a telematic hermeneutical rationality that is proper to the societies of communication.

A POST-CHRISTIAN TIME

It is not surprising at all that the most daring pronouncements of Vattimo were progressively making explicit the rational-religious nucleus of his hermeneutics. On the contrary, it was onto the long and rational road, for whose problems and achievements I am trying to account in these few pages, that this rational-religious nucleus came out, through crossing after crossing, all the way from the volume *Filosofía '86* (in whose introduction and the contribution "Metaphysics, Violence, Secularization" Vattimo already identified the absolute central proposition that it had to positively assume secularization for postmodern hermeneutics) to the 1992 essay *History of Salvation, History of Interpretation*, and the exceptionally brave *Belief* from 1996. These works are rigorously coherent landmarks of the search for profundity and of philosophical exploration that end up pointing toward a nondogmatic Christianity lived as a personal religion but lived also in consonance with historical-hermeneutical debolist rationality – a rationality that opens itself to postmodernity exactly in the departure of Christianity as secularized from power and at some time, in that sense, in the departure of post-Christian Christianity. It is a time that comes – in the words of one of the paradoxical titles of one of Vattimo's most recent works – *After Christianity*. Christianity after Christendom. This is the point of inflection where the dissolving hermeneutics of Vattimo ended up, *backward*, in the past decade, in the last years of the twentieth century and in the first years of the twenty-first century, in the last days of the second Christian millennium, until it came close to point zero of the return of the philosophical-religious divine of the philosophy of history of the East and the Christian West, namely, the moment of the birth of its god: the birth of baby Jesus in Bethlehem.

Subsequently, one will try to retrace – always following Vattimo – the death and resurrection of the god-incarnated and to reinterpret the sense-message of these sacred-scriptural events, those of the Gospel or the hermeneutical good news according to the only principle-criterion of the (holy) spirit: that of charity, friendship, love, and the lightening of all judgment, be it epistemic or moral, through a subordination of its pretensions and its literary, dogmatic and coercive, violent and excluding sanctions on the spiritual sense of love.

None other than this was the hermeneutical teaching of the life and preaching of Jesus of Galilee:[5] the teaching of a spiritual or superior rationality that is less violent, that does not judge because it interprets. And it does not condemn but dissolves or dislocates what does not enter into dialogue but imposes itself in a unilateral fashion. It is a rationality of the *charis* or grace (of charity) of the gift (*lo gratuito*) that is given without any calculation or commerce, because it belongs to the affirmation of the nonliteral sense and surpasses the justice that will be subordinated to it, as every law is to the spirit – but not to the spirit of the law (because one would be saying the same thing twice) but to the spirit of love, charity, and forgiveness. In short, it is a rationality that is spiritual-free and communitarian (in friendship and love), as an unearned donation of the divine in man and as a superior criterion of orientation and over-determination for the interpretations-actions of the nonmetaphysical hermeneutics, which still *must* (even to think) always dissolve the positions of the violent metaphysics: human, all too human. Those that link the reactive nihilism and the spirit of resentment do so because they tend to compensate for the fear of death in the double way of a stable slave-like oscillation: in the dogmatic adherence to the absolute authoritarian-universal judgments and the transcendent fugue in any *beyond* where it can be delivered of the heavy law, or evade itself, even if only momentarily, of its supposed imperative (violent) rationality. Fundamentalism and relativism are the two faces of the same *will to power* that the active debolist nihilism, following the hermeneutical principle-criterion of the diminution of violence as a critique of the metaphysical cultures of customs, which are dogmas, according to the nondogmatic affirmation of the spiritual *will to truth* – love, charity, grace, forgiveness – as principle-limit and criterion of interpretation.

This seems to be, then, the essential message of Vattimo, following the radically coherent interpretation with which the *Verwindung* of the debolist hermeneutics reads Nietzsche's death of God and Heidegger's end of metaphysics; the *Übermensch* or the ultra-man of good temperament and the spirit of the free gay-knowing beyond the subject-fundament. These are the motives of the active, dissolving nihilism that are now intertwined with the Heideggerian *Andenken* as a rethinking, remembering, and renaming of the tradition of the history of Western metaphysics, seen from the perspective of the Christian metaphysics of history. In the meantime, these are linked with the eternal recurrence of Nietzsche, understood, on the one hand, as the synchronic spiritual-unity of the three persons-ages of the Trinitarian divinity folded in on themselves; on the other hand, as a prosecution of the backward genealogical view of dialectics, which demythologizes progressive rationality, unmasking it as the secularized forgetfulness of the estate that derives it from the history of salvation. To continue on the way of recurrence up to its limit and from there to jump to the affirmation of the spiritual sense of interpretation requires, in this way, going back to the mythological message of the hermeneutical Gospel as sacred history inspired by the spirit of the Scriptures. This is because it is only in the interpretation of the message that transmits the text of this sacred or symbolic history that we find that the traces of the sense signalling the events or the landmarks of the different epochs of that history are given, according to Vattimo's current reading of the ontology of the Heideg-gerian *Ereignis* – a reading done once more in a kenotic and debolist key, retracing the hermeneutical philosophy of history, which folds in the differential synchrony of the age of the spirit. Thus are distinguished and intertwined the three ecstasies of the space-time of the *Ereignis*: the age of the father-law-fundament and the age of the son and the dialec-tic of the cross, which *lasts* from the death of the god-man and the freeing of man, until the death of the man-subject-god and the libera-tion of god. And, lastly, the age of the Paraclete: the time-place of the resurrection or coming of the spirit as the sense of the rational hermeneutics of the pluralistic and pluri-lingual community, oriented to and made possible by the only criterion of love and friendship, in the task of understanding-communicating-transmitting (the sense of) the messages after secularization.

This is, then, the coherent message of Vattimo: that of the religious turn of hermeneutics as a preparation for the advent of the Age of the Spirit that other millenarians had announced before: from one of the first Church Fathers, Gregory Nazianzus, to the inspired Calabrian Gioacchino di Fiore, on whom Vattimo places so much hermeneuti-cal importance – probably because the Christian hermeneutics of Novalis or Schleiermacher also placed such importance on him so as to elaborate the idea of a Europe linked by the Spirit of Pentecost,[6] which made it possible for the different *tongues of fire* to understand each other, because they communicated with the spirit of love and because they were willing to receive it, translate it, interpret it, and transmit it.

THE RETURN OF THE DIVINE PLURAL IN HERMENEUTICAL POSTMODERN RATIONALITY: THE PRIMACY OF SPIRIT

What can we conclude from all this? Is it not true that the spiritual turn of kenotism radically transforms the sense of active nihilism by way of orienting the dissolving critique towards the nondogmatic affirmation of the being-sense of the spirit, as alterity and limit not only of interpretation, but also of the dialectical process of history as emancipation-secularization? From there, and thanks to the radical postmodern coherence of the spiritual turn of kenotism, "Vattimo and I" could now be in agreement on an ample meeting ground. The question acquires, indeed, the utmost theological-political importance because if it were not for the spiritual limit reached by the religious turn to the recurrence of the divine, the history of the emancipation-secularization of man would tend to prolong itself to the infinite – at least tendentiously, or by way of inertia – thus perpetuating the metaphysical utopianism of enlightened modernity as an always unfinished project.

This problem lurks agonizingly and with stability in the *in between* of the nihilist dialectic. That is to say, it oscillates in a stable way between the reactive nihilism of fundamentalisms and the active-dissolving nihilism of its critic without end.[7] Thanks to the religious-spiritual turn of kenotism, Vattimo was faced – just as Gadamer was – with an unusual prudence in our contemporaries, with the biggest temptation and perversion of our age: that of the potential for dialectic rationality (process-like, methodological, critical), when put in the place of the absolute, to become the last absolute-fundament of history, because it believes it can extend endlessly or limitlessly as the dialectic of an infinite process, an infinite dialectic that has forgotten its origin and that undertakes (se *libra a*) an endless quest. Blind movement put in place of limit. A vertiginous trunk circling without feet or head. A Christ incarnated that would have forgotten the meaning and would refuse to live and to die, positioning himself forever in the agony of the nihilistic cross, rooted in the middle of the progressive and endless war of forces. A swastika cross, or a "suicidal war machine" – as Deleuze would say – for imagining the Capital.

No, not Vattimo. Vattimo was with the hermeneutical *ontology* of differences, and therefore he was with the affirmation of the transversal limit and the assumption of the limit – not only in respect to the radical finitude of man, but, after the *Kehre* of Heidegger and the *Kehre* of Vattimo, also in respect to the decisive affirmative assumption of the limit as constituting difference, as alterity of the other of man in man: namely, the spiritual divine, to which Vattimo had access through the way of the principle-criterion of love, as the limit of interpretation demanded from inside historical rationality that was ethically committed with the hermeneutical imperative of nonviolence.

Ever since the interview entitled *Ontología y Nihilismo*, which I prepared throughout several days of work at Strassburg in July 1999, "Vattimo and I" knew that we were in agreement about the essential things. The centre of our discussion continued to be, of course, the interpretation of the different senses one can give to the *eternal recurrence* and – because of this – the understanding of the ontology of post-historical time and its link with the philosophy of history and with Greece, in all its senses. However, it is true that I have often reflected about the complex coherence of his position in respect, above all, to the particular care he devoted to and the profoundness of the rational motives that made him think (and how he came to think this) that a hermeneutical-Christian interpretation of Nietzsche and Heidegger is commonsensical, an interpretation oriented in a way that it would free Christian spirituality from its territoriality (as Deleuze would say) on the side of the dogmatic-metaphysical Christianity of Western history.

Indeed, we were effectively in agreement about the essential things: the return of the divine to postmodernity and the religious or theological or spiritual turn of postmodern hermeneutics. Nevertheless, that we were in agreement about that does not cease to be amazing when one takes into account that I was reaching the affirmation of the hermeneutical spiritual limit of judicative rationality (the same limit that in Greek is called *noesis-understanding*), through a series of assumptions and phenomena similar to the following:

1 Aristotle's critique of Plato and the pre-Socratics' critique of the doctrine of the Pythagoreans, which are, in fact, the same critique, since it was none other than Aristotle who instituted the pre-Socratic tradition of the birth of philosophy and situated it in Miletus, before the

Pythagoreans of Samos, in order to isolate what he calls the abstract materialism of the Platonists. That is to say, after his unknown and exhaustive critique of the monological, scientism-like, and mytho-logical-technocratic metaphysics of the Pythagorean Platonism of the dualist Academy, Aristotle consequently elaborated a philosophical rationality as delimitation, alteration, and reorientation of the poten-tial dialectic towards the active accomplishment of a strictly pluralis-tic and spiritual hermeneutical rationality: a rationality of spiritual action (*praxis-enérgeia kaì entelécheia*) as limit that provides pos-sibilities for, and is over-determining of, the dialectical kinetic-potential rationality of a limitless violent tendency.

2 The tradition of the history of the Platonic-Christian-reformed-modern metaphysics (stated schematically and without bringing in the multiple overtones that this requires) had never received the Aris-totelian text and would have hidden it or continuously obscured it (transforming it, redescribing it, dislocating it, and over-writing it) in favour of the metaphysics-dialectic and its history; this approach demanded the patient philological-hermeneutical labour of analyzing the archeology of each and every one of the strata and the texts that were transmitted. But such an investigation had an extraordinary interest for contemporary hermeneutics, simply because it was com-mitted to the critique of the metaphysical tradition and its history. And, besides, those were the combined results that academic criticism was producing, working on its own not only in the case of Aristotle but also in the revision of Greek philosophy in its entirety.

3 It was discovered, in parallel, how Nietzsche, Heidegger, and Gadamer had set in motion the device of an actual rewriting of the rational hermeneutics of the Greek pre-Socratic Aristotle – if I may be allowed that expression – in order to repropose the high cultural, aesthetic, and spiritual piety of his *paideía* and the device of the debate on the conflict of rationalities that was working in the same direction. Indeed, it was very important for us – we Western transmoderns – to find in the archaic Greek philosophy and in the classical critical Greek philosophy (above all, in metaphysics), a plurality of reasons inde-pendent of science and superior to it in relation to the interests of life.

4 It allowed us to understand how the hermeneutics of Nietzsche and Heidegger and, of course, Vattimo (and also of Gadamer), operated and also that of French structuralism, and that of Spanish tragic thought, and that of so many other voices ... in the critical interven-tion and the alteration of lineal disputatious history, the single

thought (*pensamiento único*) and the dialectical-metaphysical rationality in global expansion.

Vattimo, for his part, philosopher and former member of the European Parliament for the democratic left, arrived at the same spiritual limit of hermeneutics through the no less complex road of the debolist *Verwindung*, to whose study I have devoted the preceding analyses. Now, in a superficial (*somero*) fashion, this road can be retraced as a convalescing dialectical remembering (Heidegger called it *Destruktion*) that, penetrating inside the displacements (*desplazamientos*), or dislocations, of the metaphysics of the history of liberation – of Christian origin – worked genealogically in dissolving its absolutes, weakening the strong structures of rationalist metaphysics, until it freed the spiritual message of evangelical-hermeneutical Christianity from the imposed burden of power, dogmatic violence, and theological-juridical imposition with which the advance of historic Christian civilization had to be realized, until it ended in modern secularization-emancipation.

Postmodernity, continuing with the emancipation of violence, has to be currently situated in another ontological-rational place: one that goes back to the evangelical (and, consequently, hermeneutical) origins of the Christian spiritual message, assuming them now, transfigured, not as primitive origins at the start of a process, but as symbolic origins that are at the end of the process of liberation, because they are its spiritual sense: that of love, friendship, charity, grace, and forgiveness, as principle-criterion-limit of hermeneutical rationality put in motion. That is to say, the last thing for us is what is first in itself: because the *arché* is the limit, and the limit is indivisible. This is what the teacher Aristotle said, following the sameness and difference of the Heraclitean *logos* and the Parmenidean *noein*.

It is a limit as a selective principle that gives preferential criteria – be it for the interpretation of scientific, ethical, or political practices, or a combination of them. It is also the unitary limit-principle of the non-concurrent differences, viz., the other nondogmatic cultural spiritualities, the supra-juridical or supra-doxatical limit of a hermeneutic and spiritual affirmation. It is the principle of the primacy of love, charity, and friendship that can indeed provide a place for the plural linkage of differences as such in the cosmopolitan hermeneutical *koine* that is opened with postmodernity as the age of the spirit. To put it in other, more historical and perhaps more eloquent words: postmodernity in the era of the technologies of planetary communication consists in continuing modernity (metaphysics, will of potency (*voluntad de potencia*), science, and technique) but reorienting it toward its other, or its limit and sense: toward the essential spiritual provenance of its past *possibles-now*, when we can, for the first time, be a planetary world.

What is essential, therefore, in this agreement between "Vattimo and me," might not reside anymore in how one interprets the provenance of the spiritual turn experimented with by postmetaphysical hermeneutical rationality: whether as the provenance of the counter-mythological or counter-anthropocentric (pre-Platonic and post-Platonic and, in both cases pre-Socratic-Aristotelian) Greek philosophical spirituality through Nietzsche, Heidegger, and Gadamer, or whether as the provenance of premetaphysical and postmetaphysical Christian spirituality, also through Nietzsche, Heidegger, and Gadamer, and through the critical mode of a hermeneutics that dissolves the dialectic of secularization. What is essential and what provides, at least, much food for thought is that the two great hermeneutical traditions of the West, that of the biblical-evangelist historical exegeses and that of the interpretation of the Pagan Bible, which is comprised of fourteen books (always historically transformed and continued) of Aristotle's *First Philosophy*, end in the same rational principle-limit: that of the noetic spirituality of the love for the divine, wherever this divine is given and, above all, in mankind, even if it is not as a self-affirmation of mankind's will to power but as affirmation of mankind's will to action-truth, hermeneutical and plural, because it always cuts across boundaries: it is desire for the other and for the differences that exceed survival and assurance.

And this is what is essential: that from both points of view one currently ends up in the rights of the Spirit. One ends up there from the consequently Christian itinerary that opens itself to the age of the spirit, departing from the rational exigencies of the sense of history, which are established on the basis of the kenotic hermeneutics of the criterion of nonviolence (and the imperative of the diminution of violence) as has been manifested by the exceptional philosophy of Vattimo. And one ends up there from the Hellenic itinerary (which is not at all alien to the very constitution of contemporary hermeneutical philosophy that rewrites it) an itinerary that ends up in the primacy of the noetic-spiritual realm of *philía* (friendship) that is proper to the excellent mode of virtuous-communicative actions, which are demanded as the limit-sense of judgments. And this is the result of departing from the Aristotelian critique of Platonic metaphysics: of the elementary and abstract violence (against the differences of the languages of life) that dominates the potential Platonic dialectic – but not to supersede it or to exclude it but to subordinate it and reorient it toward the realm of spiritual actions. This is exactly the way in which I defend it. Let us stay on this threshold for the moment. Let us remain there, recording that the religious-spiritual turn of current hermeneutics is situated already in full not in the transition from modernity to postmodernity, but in the leap; a leap (*Schritt züruck*) to the past-future made possible in the sense of language that is open for the not-spoken and the not-thought, a leap that finds the place-time of postmodernity as a hermeneutical ontology of limit, be it as a critical delimitation of the inexcludible modernity or as a pluralistic (and nonrelativistic) ontology of differences.

NOTES

1 Note from the translator: I have endeavoured to be as faithful as possible to the style of the original text of Oñate and have therefore respected her syntax, choice of words, and emphases. Wherever a particular term may be problematic, I offer the original Spanish in square brackets. My greatest thanks go to Jeff Mitscherling, who so graciously helped me in this translation.

2 Note from the translator: the term "debolist" and its derivatives come from the Italian *debole*, meaning "weak." Obviously, in the context of this work, Oñate uses the term with the special significance that links it to Vattimo's *Weak Thought*. Thus, Oñate carries the Italian term into Spanish and, in keeping with her practise, I have chosen to use it in English, so that it keeps its significance.

3 Such is the burning issue that the Nietzschean Gilles Deleuze proposes in order to immerse himself in the thousand plateaus of his own thought. At the permanently displaced centre of the *inversion of Platonism* is "the selective eternal recurrence of difference," the only *méthodos* that allows itself to be guided through the Deleuzian-Dionysiac maze from his *Nietzsche and Philosophy* until the latest posthumous writings.

4 Here, Vattimo follows the line of K. Löwith and, above all, of L. Pareyson, both of whom he recognizes as teachers with respect to the philosophy of mythology, or the *positivistic* philosophy of the last Schelling.

5 See Matthew 4: the mystery of the kingdom of Heaven.

6 G. Vattimo, *Schleiermacher, filosofo dell'interpretazione*, (Milan: Mursia 1986). See also Vattimo, *Beyond Interpretation*, chapter 4, on religion.

7 This is perfectly compatible with and capable of integration on the side of
relativistic and unrestricted liberal capitalism, for which the critique and dissolution of fundamentals is equated with the dissolution of reason into multiple opinions and, departing from there, with giving free range to the "force"
of whoever is most able to impose himself on others, without any need for
reason or legitimacy in the conflict of interests that are struggling or at war.
And if by "fascism" one understands the elementary suppression of the differences between "truths of fact" and "truths of right" or, what is the same,
the scorning by the powerful of the limits that are imposed by the rational
and juridical legitimacy, which are taken as superfluous obstacles for the
pursuit of material interests, one also understands that ever since the *invasion
of Iraq* by the United States and its allied forces, there has been talk of a *new
fascism*: the fascism of globalization. In Spain, peace won democratically in
the votes of 2004, and the government of José Luis R. Zapatero seems to be
opening Spanish socialism precisely through the *prudent* road of the postmodern left, in all the senses of its recognizable differences.

22

Atheism and Monotheism

JEAN-LUC NANCY

Translated by Antonio Calcagno

To Gianni Vattimo, I offer the tribute of this text, which is amicably close yet far from the faith that dwells in him.

Not only is atheism a specific invention of the West, but it must also be considered as the element with which the West invented itself. What we call "Greece" can be easily crossed and mixed with many religious paths, not least of which includes, above all things, what distinguishes or even constitutes "the Greek." It is a space of life and thought that neither forms nor marks out the divine presence (except that of the gods of the polis or the gods of speculation, who are, precisely, no longer *presences*). This invention is a response to a change in the general paradigm. A world order that is given and received based on fate (and this word can be understood in terms of an assigned destiny or orientation) is replaced by a regime of constructing the world through the questioning of its principle or principles. When one begins to speak of "nature" within the framework of a system of elements, principles, and consequences, this means that the world no longer includes quality presences and diverse statutes (mortal, immortal, low, high, impure, pure). Rather, it includes the totality of what is given and the order of conditions of what simply can no longer be received, which must, from what is given, give reason in return. This reason can be said to be "divine"; its divinity does indeed take hold of the excellence of its axiological position, but it does not hold onto an intrinsic lack in its nature: Rightfully, on the contrary, this nature shows itself accessible to the mortal, even if it is beyond its death (or, on the contrary, and, preferably, even if its death has to become the royal way to this accessibility). When Plato writes *ho theos*, as is often the case, this designation of God in the singular and without a proper name makes the translation of such a term nearly impossible, because we have to choose between leaving the substantive form behind and speaking of the "divine" or keeping the substantive form and thereby speaking of a unique "god"-person about whom Plato has no idea – "idea" being understood in all its senses.

In Plato's *theos*, it is permissible to say that the gods disappear (even if Plato can refer to them in the plural in the few lines of his text that follow *theos* in the singular). That is to say, the paradigm of the given, ordered, and animated universe – what we call *mythology* in order to replace it with a physiology and cosmology – has ceased to function, and its representations and founding histories are no longer recognised as adaptable modellings of the world but only as fictions.

But if these fictions do not make themselves valued except by means of their forms, characters, and scenarios, that is, by means of the spectacular troupe of divine personages richly endowed with their respective properties, genealogies, avatars, rages and desires, then it is permissible to say that the unique *theos*, deprived of form and name, represents in reality an invention and even the invention of "god" in general. There is no "god," no "divine," perhaps not even "the gods": none of these exist or, more precisely, none of these exist precisely as long as there are people or these types of immortal forms. There are the immortal partners of the mortals but there is not the ontological distance that the word "god" will henceforth measure. We must consider, then, the invention of atheism as contemporaneous with and correlative to the invention of theism. In fact, the two terms are unified in the paradigm of the principle. Never did a god – whether it was named Uranus, Isis, or Baal – possess in principle a position or a nature.

The gods used to act, speak, or observe from beyond the other bank of death; they never allowed mortals to pass through this bank. And if they did, it was never without ensuring that the river that flowed between the two banks was simultaneously wide open and menacing, as was the case for Diana and Acteon. Also, the gods ensured, for example, that the river would continue to flow between human beings and their mortal shades.

The principle, on the contrary – we may even speak of principles, but the singular here is necessary and exigent *in principle* – has no function other than to build a bridge between the two banks. Such is the logical function that substitutes for the mythic function: the double position of a radical alterity (god and humans are no longer together in the world) and a relation between the same and the other (humans are called to the god).

It is indispensable to equip oneself with these initial givens if one does not want to be mistaken about the face-to-face encounter that is always supposed to exist more or less between theism and atheism. Surely, this face-to-face encounter exists insofar as one term is the negation of the other. But we cannot ignore the extent to which this negation retains the essence of what it negates: atheism declares the principle of the negation of a divine principle, that is, of the principle represented in the configuration of an existent that is distinct from the entire world of existents, of which it is held to be the first cause and its final end. Therefore, it postulates in principle that either the cause and the end belong to another immanent order or that these concepts must not be brought into play.

In the first hypothesis, immanence (whether we call it matter or life, history, society, or art) does not strictly displace anything with regard to the ideal statutes of the cause and the end – furthermore, it does not change anything with regard to its practical statutes, because there is no reason why its principles should not become as constraining, even coercive, as that of a "divine will" or even an "economy of salvation." Nineteenth- and twentieth-century Western society raised the experience of these possibilities of coercion to such a degree that it is not difficult to qualify them as crucial. Henceforth, we will know that atheism in this sense is a disaster. (If it is necessary to be very precise, I would point out that all thought about "immanence" does not order itself around the atheistic paradigm that I have just been discussing. There is thought about "immanence" that plays off the opposition between it and "transcendence," but this is not the place to discuss this matter).

With regard to the second hypothesis, it is evident that a certain state of thought, very common today, could not ask for anything better than to be received. We fear that cause and end must not be or must no longer be acceptable concepts outside the limited technological spheres within which evidence of their axioms is to be found. We have no greater indication of this than to consider not technological systems but rather the world-regime called technology (or capital). It is evident that this regime does not cease to dissolve in its own deployment all the possibilities for finding, ascribing, or inventing causes or ends least of all, for identifying it, little by little, with *phusis* itself, inasmuch as technology, after all, stems from *phusis* before redeploying it for its own use. And so, this will lead to a tautological teleology of the world, which would include the launching of a new mythology that is demanded by this new tautology.

We ought, therefore, to be capable of thinking strictly anaetiologically and aetiologically. It would be easy to demonstrate how much this exigency has already preoccupied philosophy since the beginnings of the contemporary world. On the whole, Hegel, who passes for the model of thinkers about the process of achievement, demands also to be understood (or perhaps so does Schelling before and with him) as the first to think beyond all teleology. Being capable of discerning this requirement of interpretation – which testifies to our own attempts and experiences since the suspension of what is called Hegelian history – does not render us the least capable of thinking about teleology anaetiologically or aetiologically. The same can be said of atheistic thought, which we know ourselves to desire. This has been the case for us until now, because such an orientation of thought remains privative, subtractive and, in sum, defective – obstinately and with deafness, it represents in its core the major tone of all kinds of atheism. (Without a doubt, one must hasten to say, this does not authorise one to legitimise positive assertions of theism: it is only a question of placing back to back the two faces of the same Western Janus.)

A day will come perhaps, and maybe it is not even too far away, when we will be able to characterise all contemporary thought as a slow and heavy gravitational movement around the black sun of atheism. Concerning the collapse of the fundamental principle – as witnessed by classical ontotheology from its Kantian deposition to its Nietzschean funeral – has not a new, novel insight (revolutionary? creative? liberating? salvific? how would we like to designate it?) succeeded this collapse and the emptiness that results from it? A new insight – that is to say, that which would produce itself across other prisms of thought that words like "collapse" and "emptiness" express in a banal way.

I do not wish to say that contemporary thought, in its vivaciousness, is not occupied with disorganising and delegitimising these prisms. Contemporary thought does not even do otherwise. Atheism always continues – in a very paradoxical way in the end – to close the horizon. Or maybe it is more precise to say that it continues to form a horizon, exactly where it should be about other things, for horizons and principles are linked.

The horizon of a subtraction, of a retreat, of an absence, even the horizon of what I myself sometimes called "absentheism" – in order to distinguish it from atheism – continues to make a horizon, that is to say, a limit, an impasse, and an end of the world. It encircles more of our thought than the world, and, in effect, touches its limits from everywhere, both in a physical and in a metaphysical manner. It can no longer be a question of exiting the world. But this is not a reason to consider it as a horizon. In other words, finitude does not limit infinity. On the contrary, it must give to infinity its expansion and its truth. Here are the stakes, and there are no others today.

This has definitely to do with nothing other than what Nietzsche understood as nihilism. Atheism *is* nihilism, and if nihilism indicates at the same time that it is through itself, from itself, and almost in itself that it is a matter of "exiting" (if this term is appropriate), it has never gone beyond, until now anyway, its own direction towards other things, other than through a repetition of its own *nihil*. Certainly it is a repetition that is often more powerful, courageous, efficacious, and inventive than those that play on taking refuge in "emptiness," "absence," "disaster," "without end," or "aporia" or even those that ascetically revolve around renunciation of things other than combinations of "forms of life" and differentiated regimes of truth (sometimes with perspectives drawing on the Kantian notion of "regulation.")

In some way it is always about "introducing a new sense knowing that this introduction itself is deprived of sense," as Nietzsche wrote of a paradox in which logic conceals all the force of the injunction and all the difficulty, even the anguish, of our situation. But how does one remove the aporia if the forcing of the sense is something through which sense (nonsensical sense? absent sense? hyperbolic sense, or hypertrophied sense?) has given us nothing other than an exterminating horror in so many forms, a horror that is joined to humanist impotence?

This last word throws us once again towards the black centre of our vertigo: humanism was an atheism, it was the truth, the import, the proposition, and the operation. Because it returned the essence of God to the essence of man, it did nothing other than stamp onto the principle a rotation around itself (a revolution?). Also, on the one hand, it is not the case that it modified nothing in onto-(a)-theological construction. On the other hand, it did not situate its own notion of principle in a place worthy of its stature. Heidegger wrote, "Humanism does not think highly enough the *humanitas* of man."

What does "highly" and "height" mean when spoken of in such a fashion? What does it mean, especially if we reflect upon the fact that Heidegger wrote this sentence after having passed through the blinding of the "grandeur" that today stigmatises National Socialism? Must one even speak in terms of elevation, altitude, or size? This is not certain. In which terms, then, can one speak? Pascal wrote that "man infinitely passes man." What could this "passing" be? Surpassing? Overcoming? Exceeding? Transporting? Transfiguring? Divinising? Naturalising? Technologising? Exposing one to the abyss? Annihilating? And even more: Dehumanising? Inhumanising? Overhumanising? As we see it, we have run through, in a Hegelian spirit, the gallery of all these figures over the last two hundred years, and we are exhausted, discouraged by this our absolute knowing, which does not throw back, in deference to that of the Spirit, any "infinity" other than that of an infamy in which the "surpassing" of man takes the form of an inexorable domination of human beings by a gathering process that is no longer their history but a machinery indifferent to their fate and concerned only with its own proper exponential and exponentially tautological development.

This sadness sums up atheism. Even the tragic possibility, which could have been that of the Greeks discovering themselves deprived, abandoned, or cursed by the gods, is refused to us. Sadness does not admit any of the tragic joy that Nietzsche or the young Benjamin witnessed. This also means, more clearly than ever, that the emergence of capitalism – *here* even if we can speak of "emergence,"[1] or even in whatever sense we can speak of emergence – cannot envision itself other than in terms of nihilism. And, this can only be done in two related ways. On one hand, the formal structure of the "emergence" will be the same (it will be an emergence from within, as Marx and Nietzsche well knew). On the other hand, the stakes will be the same, that is, they are not what I designate here, provisionally, as the necessity of an effective alteration of the tautology (or even of a heterology).

If I begin presently to consider problems related to monotheism, I do this not to take issue with it, not to find a solution or salvation. On the contrary, "salvation" represents to the confirmation of the world of nihilism the necessity that it affirms of redemption. In this sense, monotheism will represent nothing other than the theological confirmation of atheism: the reduction of the divine to the principle found in the logic of the dependence of the world. In a corollary fashion, the tautology of the world simply displaces itself into the tautology of God: the unique god is in effect nothing other than the repetition of its immutable being. This god has neither history nor shape, and it is not by chance that in a decisive moment of its redefinitions god was designated and thought as *logos* present *èn arché*.

In reality, this moment responds to the conjunction of Greek atheism and Jewish monotheism in the elaboration of what, under the name of Christianity, would have constituted the major configuration of onto-a-theology (otherwise replayed under the title of Islam, which would demand for proof, to be precise, a supplementary consideration).

Through the religions of the Book (Judaism, Christianity, Manicheism, Islam) a singularly complex history has actualised itself, even a wily history, in which the driving element or the organising-kernel holds itself at the point of conjunction of the greekjew/jewgreek of Joyce – but only at the same time that this point is also one of disjunction, insofar as this intimate disjunction that lies at the heart of atheism itself demands once again to be truly proven.

On one hand, in effect, the conjunction does not conjoin anything other than two formations of atheism itself. Jewish monotheism as it developed and expanded in the Greek world, such that it opened up Christian thought (which one could rightfully call Stoic-Christian thought), is simultaneously disposed to nothing other than the disappearance of all the divine presences and powers and the designation of a principle that has nothing "divine" about it other than its name – a name empty, to be precise, of all personality or even of its own ability to be pronounced.

Considered from this angle, all history of "God" – of the "God" of the West – deploys nothing other than the process of atheism itself in its most rigorous progression. For example, looking at certain key moments, consider the idea of the "proof" of "God's" existence, which presupposes that *an* existence from which all existence will follow can at least be deduced a priori; the supposed proof collapses into an ontological tautology. There is also Spinoza's *deus sive natura*, which leaves open the question of what this god's unity consists of – a god that exists only in the infinity of its modes. Finally, one can even examine Feueurbach's God, in which man has but to reappropriate predicates by neglecting the imaginary substance. One could continue to add a considerable number of predicates, including Descartes' idea of perfection or the necessary liberty by which the god of Leibniz creates the best of all possible worlds. In all cases, one arrives at the same conclusion that "God" names the principle of a presupposed totality that is founded in unity and necessity.

In this regard, "God" names only the tautology of the unitotality presupposed thus far. In Heideggerian terms, "God" names the consistency of being conceived as principle, foundational, and essential. God most evidently represents being to the principle of a being (l'étant): ens summum, verum, bonum, the ultimate being, a true and good being. This is not surprising, since Heidegger views in Christianity (and saying very little about the link between the two) nothing but an epiphenomenon without any remarkable specificity regarding an epochal history of being that is also marked by destiny – being understood in this instance not as a principle but, on the contrary, as a "principle of anarchy," (if one permits oneself to be satisfied by the paradox developed Reiner Schürmann) or even as the deconstruction of the principality in general.

It is also well confirmed that monotheism would have constituted in sum the second condition of the possibility of (a)theism. The oneness of its god is not to be placed in a numerical relationship with the plurality of gods called "polytheism." Even more, oneness displaces or converts divinity. Either by power or by persons, oneness changes divinity in principle, in its foundation and/or in law, always through the definition that is absent or re-extracted in the depths of being. Deus absconditus: a "god" who pulls out from the "one" the wholeness of its numen insofar as it tendentially dissolves this name "god," which never was a divine name!

If this had been the case, one would have had inevitably to ask why the root of atheism could have had – or ought to have had – a double constitution. The discrediting of Christianity as an epiphenomenon of metaphysics, as well as its reduction by Kant or by Hegel to the status of a representative transcription of the logic of reason or the spirit, does not account for its doubling or its standing-in as a double for something else.

It ought to be said that reason does not reasonably account for its representations of itself. The idea of reason's operations of transcription, of disguising itself or its religious turn, this very idea that definitively commands (even with variations on the themes of "representation," "sentiment," "illusion," and "ideology") the essential in philosophical denouncing, if it can account in many respects for the moral, political, and spiritual infamy indisputably shared by religions (especially monotheistm, which must be examined elsewhere), cannot however account for this singular dehiscence, or rupture, of *logos* and principle, except, of course, in order to designate an inferior degree of reason, an absence that is to be elevated to the heights of thought, so as to deplore more directly once again a veritable perversion or illness of thought, culture, society.

It is strange to think that our whole civilisation poses in principle as the weak, corrupted, or estranged (that is, non-Greek) essence of what has not ceased to constitute it for the past twenty centuries as the internal stand-in or double (*doublure*). All passes as if atheism refuses to consider the possibility that this doubling could be understood in another way as infirmity, illness, or even the perversity of priests.

Without a doubt, infirmity, even debility, illness, and meanness are at play – either alternately or conjointly – as soon as it is a matter of assuring oneself of a mastering and presentation of the principle. The emblematic weakness of the logic of the principles (or, rather, should one say of all logic?) declares itself at the crucial point where theism and atheism come to belong to one another. When the principle is affirmed or even likewise denied, it cannot but decline in its proper position or deposition, for it is incumbent upon the principle, insofar as it is a principle as we have sketched it above, to exceed principality itself. Even more, the principle ought to divest itself of it, withdraw or subtract itself from it. A principle itself ought to destroy principality. A principle or a principate, if I can use this word here, can only be an exception to itself. At least here it is one of the alternative branches before which the principate is ineluctably placed. It even conforms itself, and infinitely so, or even makes an exception of itself and no less infinitely. (The politics of sovereignty, insofar as it is has the power to make exceptions, exactly reproduces this logic; it does so with the extreme delicacy of its unstable equilibrium, always balanced between the legitimacy of an illegitimate (prince) and the illegitimacy of a legitimate (prince). To employ the terms mentioned above, it confirms its aetiological and teleological tautology, or it finds itself exposed as heterogeneous to all tautology, hiding itself in heterology.

Wouldn't it be desirable, then, to examine whether this standing-in as a double (*doublure*) and the dehiscence between monotheism and atheism do not communicate with this heterogenesis? In other words, can we be easily assured, without any further questioning, that monotheism is nothing other than the feeble or grimacing face of atheism – one and the other always residing together in the contraction of the principle (or of the One), which also occurs in the dereliction of nihilism?

Time came to understand our own history otherwise such that it did not want to understand itself until now under the domination of its own principle.

Greek atheism and Jewish monotheism met at a point where the unity of the principle and the unicity of god mutually comforted and contradicted one another, at the same time and by the same contraction – mutual attraction and repulsion – by a double and violent movement in which the effects have not ceased to enervate and irritate our history. On one hand, the unicity of god, in effect, has evidently let itself be subsumed or absorbed by the unity of the principle. Hence, Christianity became, through its own interventions, a humanism, atheism, and nihilism. The always difficult maintenance of its proper religious forms (of its Church, its cult, and its myth) ended by becoming an object of struggle or an inner tearing. (How this works or not, or how this is reversed or not, in Judaism and in Islam and in the relation or nonrelation of the three monotheisms must be examined elsewhere.)

On the other hand, the unicity of god refuses to enter the order of the principle. It is not by chance that Pascal, at the height of modern rationality, proves violently the necessity of disjoining without any reservation the "God of the philosophers and the savants" from the "god of Abraham, Isaac and Jacob, the god of Jesus Christ." This disjunction and the contrariety and contradiction that result from it are lodged at the very heart of atheism, precisely at the place where the principle of the principle itself, as I have discussed above, collapses by itself. In this collapse the possibility and even the demand and call of a completely other anarchic configuration is signalled.

Let us call to mind some of the major traits through which monotheism opposes the "principate," while at the same time comforting it.

To the relation that forms between a principle and its consequences or between a condition and what it conditions is opposed the relation between the creator and the creature in which one must first of all affirm that it separates radically from the preceding relation, because this last one is a relation of identity, of inherence or of consequence (if A, then B; if alpha, then omega) insofar as creation is a relation of alterity and contingency (if "God," then there is no reason for God to create.) The idea of *creatio ex nihilo*, insofar as it is to be distinguished from other forms of production or fabrication, essentially recovers the double motif of an absence of necessity and the existence of a given without reason, without foundation or a principle of its donation (a "donation" through which no concept of "donation" can undoubtedly be understood as convenient.) *Ex nihilo*, that is, nothing to the principle, a nothing of the principle, nothing other than what it is, nothing other than that which grows *(creo, cresco)* with the principle of growth, and even not (above all not) the autonomous principle of a "Nature" (except to reevaluate this concept through Spinoza).

One could say straightaway that the *nihil* is posited. Perhaps this is the only way to exit nihilism seriously. "Nihilism," in effect, means to make principle from the nothing. But *ex nihilo* means to undo all principle, including that of the nothing.

Without examining further the implications and obligations of a similar "undoing," let us add two additional traits.

First and above all, let us add this one here: the relation of creation doubles itself from the relation between the saint and the sinner. Once more it is not identity but alterity that is at play. The saint is other from the sinner in the sense that the sinner is constituted in his/her being by the relation to this alterity. S/he is a sinner by virtue of her/him not being a saint, but this is due to sanctity, because sanctity is not a principle. Sanctity is neither determinable nor representable nor prescribable. Sanctity opens to humans or in humans (at least one ought not to say, it opens to the world and in the world and not for humans alone) the dimension and the movement or the gesture of "(sur)passing oneself infinitely." One could understand this by examining the meanings of the French *se passer*. For example, l'homme passe infiniment l'homme, (man infinitely surpasses man). Also, l'homme se passe infiniment de l'homme" (man manages infinitely without man). (Does "God" or the saint, manage without human beings? As we know, this question has not ceased to circulate in Christianity.)

The last trait I would like to discuss here is faith. If the principle is to be known or well known, as ought also to be the gods, and if, as an outgrowth, religion is a form of knowledge, namely, that of observance and scrupulosity, it is to faith, on the other hand, that the saint turns. Faith is not feeble knowledge. It is not hypothetical or unverifiable, and it is not receivable by means of submission. It is not receivable by reason. Faith is not a belief in the ordinary sense of the word. On the contrary, it is the act of reason relating itself to what it has nothing to do with infinitely. Faith holds itself precisely at the point of an entirely consequential atheism, that is, of a parting with the belief in a principle and a principate in general. It is the point that Kant formally recognises when he speaks, for example, of the "incapacity where reason finds itself, with regard to its needs to give itself satisfaction from itself."[2] Reason is not sufficient to itself; for itself *(pour soi)* it is not sufficient reason. But it is in the recognition of its own insufficiency that reason makes itself right, for it recognises not a lack or a defect for which it must make reparation but, more so, it recognises this: the logic of sufficiency and/or lack is not the logic that belongs to it.

This is why the same Kant described "moral faith" (and not metaphysical, speculative, or even doctrinal faith) as deriving its essence not from any fault of reason but, on the contrary, from the weakness with which reason confronts its own incapacity to be satisfied. And not seeing there an insufficiency, a failure, or a lack that condemns it to a nihilism, faith finds there a "non-sufficiency" in this very precise sense that from now on it is no longer about sufficing or satisfying, for there is neither possible sufficiency nor satisfaction if there is no longer there the principle to which satisfaction must be given. Faith, then, is the firm fidelity of reason geared to its proper atheology.

What the name "god" or even the name "holy" begins to designate in this *atheological* regime – if one accepts to use this word of Bataille to designate an atheism that is clearly detached from the schema of inverse theism – not only leads to a ruin of the principle but in a way more contrary to the principle logic, it leads back to "something," to "someone" or even to a "nothing" (maybe even to the *nihil ex quo* – the nothing from which) in which faith itself is the birthplace or even the creator-event. That "God" itself be the fruit of faith, which at the same time holds to God's grace (that is, it exempts itself from necessity and obligation), is, then, a strange thought and perhaps the strangest to the couple of theism and atheism. It is the thought of alterity opened by and exposed out of sameness, just as that which infinitely exceeds without being that which is principal in it. And, this thought has not been strange to Christian meditation. One could easily cite Macarius of Magnesia: "He who does the will of my Father renders me a child in participating in this action and he is made a child with me. He who believes that I am really the one and only Son of God engenders me in some way through faith."[3]

In conclusion, I would like to make the following observation. The Platonic precept was to "assimilate oneself to the divine," whereas the monotheistic precept was to observe in ourselves the divine similitude.

Omoiosis, *mimesis*, and *methexis*, all together, for there are two possible modes of assimilation: the appropriation of the attributes of a subject supposed to be other and principle or even the alteration of the same into an alterity that is properly infinite and therefore incapable of being appropriated, prescribed; it is anarchic. The question still remains concerning the point of knowing if "god" or even "the saint"/"the holy" can or must still, form names for this alterity of reason, and under which names. Even if "atheism" remains an equivocal term for reason, a term without a future, until this point, no response has been given in this way to the question posed.

NOTES

1 Here, Nancy plays on the word "sortie," which means exit as well as emergence/issuing forth [translator's note].
2 Letter to Fichte dated 2 February 1792 (*Briefwechsel*, Hamburg: Meiner 1972), 553.
3 *Les Monogénès*, French translation and edition by Richard Goulet (Paris: Vrin 2003) 5.2, 23.

Conclusion:
Metaphysics and Violence

GIANNI VATTIMO

Translated by Robert T. Valgenti

I am not going to respond to all of these outstanding essays, not only because doing so would take too much space but most of all because I do not think I could provide a balanced summary of the acute philosophical interpretations, comments, and criticism that have emerged from all these colleagues and friends of mine. The three parts of this book, "Weakening Power," "Weakening Methods," and "Weakening Beliefs," seem to indicate that I have not only gone beyond Nietzsche's and Heidegger's intentions but also pushed hermeneutics to a place that none of its founders (Schleiermacher, Dilthey, Pareyson, Ricouer, or Gadamer) ever thought it could reach: to the standpoint of weak thought. I not only agree but also believe it has reached weak thought because of a question of method, namely, the criticism of metaphysical violence. Since this problem of metaphysics and violence still seems to me to be one of the central problems of contemporary philosophy, in this final essay I would like to show my gratitude to all the contributors by further developing this problem from the two authors on whom I have based all my philosophical research: Nietzsche and Heidegger.

If contemporary philosophy wants to continue its work as philosophy, that is, if it wants to be something more than merely essay writing or the historiography of the thought that has come before it and to avoid being reduced to a purely auxiliary discipline of the positive sciences (as epistemology, methodology, or logic), it must recognize a preliminary problem that is posed by the radical critique of metaphysics. The adjective "radical" is emphasized because only this sort of critique of metaphysics truly constitutes an unavoidable preliminary problem for every philosophical discourse that is aware of its responsibility. Those forms of the critique of metaphysics that, more or less explicitly, restrict themselves to considering it just one philosophical point of view among others – a school or current in thinking that for some philosophically argued reason one ought to abandon today – should not be considered radical. For example, the widespread scientism of twentieth-century thought takes it as more or less evident that one must no longer do metaphysics but rather epistemology, methodology, or logic, or even just the analysis of language. This total "transfer of duties" from traditional philosophy to a scientistic philosophy that can no longer distinguish itself from science (whether as purely auxiliary thought or as the positive scientific approach to everything belonging to a particular domain of philosophy, namely, the human sciences) can be contrasted with a vindication of metaphysics as the "science of spirit," as the place where one elaborates those self-descriptions in which the conscience may achieve the elaborations of its own fundamental conflicts (Dieter Henrich), in which it may achieve what is ultimately a renewed theory of self-knowledge, such as the one clearly defined by Kant as particular to modern metaphysics. This "transfer of duties" not only brings with it the reconsideration of the metaphysics of self-knowledge as its unavoidable shadow and correlate but also carries an obvious metaphysical residue that remains unconsumed to the degree either that, as seen in positivism, it simply transfers the locus of truth from traditional metaphysics to the natural or human sciences or that it simply recovers metaphysics as "semantic-linguistic" ontology in the sense exemplified by Donald Davidson. Even in this case, the critique of metaphysics, classically understood, does not become radical, because – as happens in many areas of neoempirical thought, even within a Popperian idea of metaphysics – its detachment from the metaphysics of the past nonetheless occurs through an explicit terminological continuity that may even express a conceptual continuity. In question here is a philosophical theory of the most general and "constitutive" features of the world of experience, even if they are thought linguistically but not objectively. These observations regarding the limited radicality of the critique of positivistic metaphysics can even be extended to the various forms of "reductionist naturalism" (as Dieter Henrich has called it) or, to use a Nietzschean expression, to the various "schools of suspicion." These schools consider metaphysical propositions, all of the "primary self-interpretations" of humanity and of Being (once again Henrich's expression), as fictions that are brought back and dissolve in reference to the explication of the conditions that determined their formation. Even in these reductionist positions, one has to judge to what degree the suspicion has the courage to be truly radical. The most recent developments of one of the most self-revealing and articulated "reductionist naturalisms" of the last century, Marxism, can also be interpreted as the radicalization of suspicion and the liquidation of every metaphysical residue – that is, at least as regards "Western" Marxism, even in its political manifestations, including the recent crisis and dissolution of communist parties.

The critique of metaphysics is radical and presents itself as an unavoidable preliminary problem, a real "question of method," not only where its formation touches on determinate ways of doing philosophy or its determinate subject matter but where it treats the very possibility of philosophy as such, that is, as the discourse characterized by its logical and even, inseparably, its social status.

Nietzsche is the master of this radical critique of metaphysics. According to him, philosophy emerged and developed as the search for a "true world" that would be able to provide a reassuring foundation in place of the uncertain mutability of the visible world. This true world was, over time, identified with the Platonic Ideas, the Christian afterlife, the Kantian a priori, and the positivist's unknowable. The logic that was the force behind all these transformations – the need to seek out a true world that was authentically so, one able to withstand critique and to "provide a foundation" – eventually led it to recognize the very idea of truth as a fable, a useful fiction in specific conditions of experience. Such conditions have disappeared, a fact expressed by the discovery of truth as a fiction. The problem that Nietzsche seems to open at this point, in a world where even the unmasking attitude is unmasked, is one of nihilism. Once its nature is discovered to be produced and "functional" rather than originary, do we really have to think that the destiny of thought and of the very belief in the value of truth or foundation is to install itself without illusions as an "esprit fort" in the world of the war of all against all, where the "weak perish" and only power is affirmed? Or will it rather be the case, as Nietzsche hypothesizes at the end of the long fragment "European Nihilism" (summer 1887), that in this environment those who are destined to triumph are the "most moderate, those who have no *need* of extreme articles of faith, who not only concede but even love a good deal of contingency and nonsense, who can think of man with a considerable moderation of his value and not therefore become small and weak: the richest in health, who are equal to the most misfortunes and therefore less afraid of misfortunes – men who *are sure of their power* and who represent with conscious pride the strength man has achieved."[1]

Nietzsche does not really develop this allusion to the "most moderate," but it is likely that, as his notes from his final years indicate (the same notes that produce this fragment on nihilism), the most moderate man is the artist, he who knows how to experiment with a freedom derived, without doubt, from having overcome even the interest in survival. It is clear that in this sense his critique of metaphysics is radical: if we accept it, we can no longer continue to philosophize in a world where even philosophy is nothing more than a struggle, a play of forces, the conflict of interpretations. And yet, to the degree that it appears unmasked, it cannot truly be a conflict. Nietzsche does not develop an alternative to the supremacy of the most moderate, nor does his critique result in something "nonphilosophical" or, rather problematically, artistic, as Nietzsche senses the unsustainability of yet another "metaphysical" solution. Such would be the case if moderateness were identified with a transcendental description, a sort of historicism à la Dilthey, which would make philosophy coincide with a systematic description of the *Weltanschauungen* in conflict. This would posit a true world once again, that of the sovereign, historical consciousness, an extreme rediscovery of the Socratic wisdom that confidently claims to know that it does not know.

The link between metaphysics and violence is a less aporetic trait, perhaps one more characteristic of the discourse Nietzsche has with metaphysics, one that provides an unavoidable stage for current philosophy. This connection is presented not univocally but rather in a multiform way that is suggestive precisely in its irreducibility to a definite schema. This connection has two features: on the one side, the unmasking of the metaphysics that marks the advent of nihilism reveals its ties to a condition of violence and is an act of violence itself. As the thinking of foundation, the illusion of grasping the heart of reality, the first principle on which "everything" depends, it was "an effort to take possession, by an act of strength, of the most fruitful lands," an effort that, through a sort of magical reassurance, was reacting to an extremely insecure condition of existence, namely the condition of man before the birth of rationalization and domestication made possible by the very discipline put forward in the name of the metaphysical fictions. Today these fictions are no longer required. The individual of rationalized society no longer needs these extreme forms of reassurance; one can live in "proximity," modeling one's own thoughts on science – not because it is true, objective knowledge but because it is a form of thinking less bothered by the problem of salvation and individual destiny. This is the relatively "optimistic" Nietzsche of the "philosophy of morning" that is ultimately put forth in *Human, All Too Human* and that constitutes the fundamental intonation of the works that appear in the Enlightenment period of Nietzsche's work, from *Human, All Too Human* to *Daybreak* to the *Gay Science*. The later writings (following, however, indications that are already present, for example, in the *Gay Science*), such as the fragment on nihilism just mentioned, insist on a second, inseparable aspect of the crisis of metaphysics, a crisis that occurs in relation to a manifesting of violence as such. This could occur in the more evident sense that once metaphysical beliefs are weakened, there is no longer anything that limits the conflictual nature of existence, the struggle between weak and strong for a supremacy no longer legitimated by anything (*Grund*, natural or divine laws, etc.) but by the mere fact of imposing itself; or it could occur in the sense that seems decisive for Nietzsche (and for the problem of metaphysics in general), whereby the weakening of metaphysical beliefs not only uncovers the violence of existence for what it is and makes it no longer possible but is born as the result of an outburst of violence.

It is difficult to say if the philosophical theses of the late Nietzsche – such as the idea of the eternal return, the *Übermensch*, the will to power – do or do not represent a solution to the problem of placing these two aspects of the critique of metaphysics together. Would the unmasking of the violence have any meaning if it led only to further violence, even if it were unmasked? At stake is more than just the repugnance that comes with accepting that the result of Nietzsche's philosophy is an apology for a return to a primitive, wild state; what also matters is the intimate and contradictory nature of the thesis: the Nietzschean conception of the "symbolic forms," that is, of ideological productions, of the metaphysical, moral, religious fictions, seems to exclude the fact that they act only as superfluous maskings. Considering the problem in this way would still mean professing the typically metaphysical belief in the "naked" truth of the thing itself. The unmasked truth would be "better" only insofar as it ends up being "more true." In some way, therefore, the two features of the link between metaphysics and violence must be of value together. The radical critique of metaphysics does its work to the very degree that it seeks, and eventually finds, a "thinkable" conjunction between the two by resolving the question of their relation more clearly than Nietzsche, and yet still on the path that he opens. In fact, it is likely that the Nietzsche renaissance characteristic of European thought since the beginning of the 1960s is motivated by the very clarity of his presentation of the problem of metaphysics' end and its relation to the question of violence, rather than by the rediscovery of the "constructive" theses of Nietzsche, which still remain problematic. With his conception of the end of metaphysics through the unmasking of its violence – a decisive intuition that opens up a multiple development – Nietzsche anticipates the complex meaning of many, if not all, the discourses that have been at the centre of philosophical attention from the end of the nineteenth century to today. With Nietzsche we can consider the impossibility of the continuation of metaphysics in relation to the unmasking of violence; but one should remember that the two features indicated above (the theoretical unmasking of the school of suspicion and the practical-political coming to light of a violence without limits) are meant to summarize – in one point that becomes the undeniable beginning of twentieth century philosophy and the "question of method" from which one must begin – the transformations and crises that philosophy has undergone in the last one hundred years.

This affirmation is very risky, given the "apocalyptic" tone that seems to characterize it, and it can be consummated only through its further elaboration (which leads it to a conclusion opposed to any apocalyptic temptation). Its verisimilitude seems tied to the preliminary decision to privilege a certain line of twentieth-century thought – primarily that which stands between existentialism, phenomenology, and Hegelian-Marxist critical theory – over those more "sober" and even more professional currents that first and foremost developed the critique of knowledge. Two observations must be put forward here: one is "historical," and the other is systematic. From the point of view of the interpretation of the history of twentieth-century philosophy, one can with verisimilitude maintain that to emphasize the connection between metaphysics and violence in the various forms in which it appears in Nietzsche is not to mistake what at first glance seems to be the problem universally considered as central – that of the relation between philosophy and science. Neither the problematic of the distinction between the natural and the human sciences nor the problematic that is developed within the epistemology of the sciences of nature (from the dispute over the foundations of mathematics to neopositivist physicalism to the later developments of analytic philosophy) seems describable as merely a response to the merely theoretical demand to once again ground the relations between these forms of knowledge according to the affirmation of the importance of the experimental science of nature – taken more and more generally as the model for every form of knowledge that wants to be socially central and effective. It is the more or less explicit reference to the rationalization of society as the event that reveals the connection between metaphysics and violence that determines the central meaning of the epistemology of the human sciences in their relation to the natural sciences in today's philosophical debate. These terms were often left unspoken until the Nietzschean renaissance brought them forth. The connection between phenomenology and existentialism, on the one hand, and expressionism and avant-gardism, on the other, was already thoroughly explored and is by now somewhat commonplace. It must be clarified, however, that even Dilthey and the seemingly exclusively epistemological problematic of the foundation of the human sciences belongs to this same climate (within which one could also include Bergson in France, Croce in Italy, and a bit later, Bloch and the first members of the Frankfurt School and, obviously, the existentialists, Heidegger most of all), which finds literary and, more broadly, cultural expression in the avant-garde and which appeals to the irreducibility of the "spiritual" in the face of scientific-technological rationality, which according to the theoretical dream of the positivists, has become a social reality. Neither the theoretical problem of scientific knowledge's re-foundation nor even the demand to make the human sciences more rigorous serves as a motive for the Heidegger of *Being and Time* or even for the Husserl of the *Crisis*. They, in diverse yet profoundly connected forms, reflect philosophically on the distaste for the rationalization of existence guided by the mathematical sciences of nature. Heidegger reproposes the problem of Being in *Being and Time*, because the concept of Being transmitted by European metaphysics merely thinks the Being of the object of the positive sciences: the verified, measured, manipulated object of science and technology that derives from it can exhaustively describe what is completely unfolded as present in front of us, with neither a past nor a future, something other than the not-yet-present and the no-longer-present. This concept of Being "does not work," and requires a revision by Heidegger, not because it is not theoretically adequate: rather, it is in reality an attack on existence (as Kierkegaard already thought of Hegel's metaphysical rationalism). Not only does it make it impossible for man to think conceptually about his own lived experience, so intimately permeated with projection towards the future and with memories of the past; but, above all, it is one with the practical, social undertaking of the rationalization of society and existence in terms of "total organization."

The idea of the impossibility of the continuation of metaphysics, which is based on the unmasking of violence that is proposed by Nietzsche, seems to be harder to accept if one looks at the epistemological, logical, and methodological problematic associated with positivistic philosophy. Yet, even in this landscape, it appears with increasing clarity that their dominant concerns were not exclusively theoretical or epistemological; or at least, that they enter into a picture of culture that is also marked by the themes of the avant-garde. Such an awareness, one that matures through historiographical self-knowledge, beginning with the discovery of "Wittgenstein's Vienna," is surely not theoretically enough to justify our Nietzschean "reduction," even in the face of the "epistemological" line of twentieth-century thought. It seems nevertheless not arbitrary to maintain that even the apparently purely *erkenntnistheoretisch* themes of analytic philosophy reveal their profound connections with the "Nietzschean" theme of the relation between metaphysics, scientific rationality, and violence. This revelation may occur on the basis of the renewed historiographical self-knowledge that came along with "Wittgenstein's Vienna" or on the basis of the centrality assumed in recent years in the philosophical-analytic realm by the debate about themes like Kuhn's paradigms or about the epistemological anarchism of Feyerabend and Lakatos (themes in which one finds an ever-growing awareness of the relation between the verification or falsification of propositions and the historical-social existence of the scientific community, in which, as a matter of fact, every validity "counts"), including all the historical, political, and economic implications that come with them. Or it may occur on the basis of the increasingly fragmented anthropological interpretation or "application" of the Wittgensteinian theory of language-games and of their relations (the relation between diverse language-games, their ultimate incommensurability, the possibility of a meta-game or nevertheless of a procedure of translation are increasingly tied to the question of the relation between diverse cultural universes; for example, different civilizations, colonizers and colonized, etc.). The reasons for the exposure of this connection are more than merely contingent (for example, it is certain that a decisive factor for American thought was the Vietnam War – and as proof one could cite a certain diminished openness to these themes in British thought), but one can appeal to a continuity both in the "anthropological" thread of classical positivism and also in its usefulness for science, in view of the rationalization and humanization of social relations.

These arguments, and other similar ones more historiographically articulated, can be advanced on the historical level in order to legitimate the Nietzschean reduction of the problem of metaphysics to the problem of violence, which is proposed here as the initial point of attack for every philosophical discourse today. But there is also a systematic observation that produces a more coherent outcome. The question that deals with the end of metaphysics and the impossibility of its continuation is an urgent one not just or principally because, as I think, it appears to be the explicit or implicit motive for the main currents of twentieth-century philosophy but, above all, because it engages the very possibility of continuing to philosophize. Now, this possibility is not really threatened by the discovery of other methods, other types of discourse, other sources of truth that, if sought out, would be able to do without philosophizing and metaphysical arguing. The unmasked connection that these procedures of foundation entertain with domination and violence shines the light of suspicion on philosophy as such and on every discourse that wants once again to engage, on different levels and through different methods, in the procedures of "foundation" and the affirmation of originary structures, principles, and coherent evidence. The reference to this connection, even if it seems accidental, is rather one that, taken seriously, makes the critique of metaphysics truly radical. Without it, every metaphysical truth claim is simply replaced with other "truths" that, without a critical and radical dissolution of the very notion of truth, wind up proposing new foundational events. As one might be tempted to do by referring back to Hegel, this "question of method" could be contrasted with the act of jumping into the water in order to learn how to swim. That is, one could construct philosophical arguments by seeing if it is not possible, against every exaggerated suspicion, to identify some certainties that are somehow "ultimate" and generally shared. Nevertheless, the invitation to throw oneself into the water, the invitation to philosophize, does not arrive from nowhere. It necessarily recalls us to the existence of a tradition, of a language, of a method. The inheritances that we receive from this tradition, however, are not all the same. Among them there is the Nietzschean announcement of the death of God, which is an "experience" more than a theory – the end of metaphysics, and with it, the end of philosophy. If one wants to accept the responsibility that the inheritance of past philosophies places upon us, one cannot dismiss the preliminary question of this "experience." This very faith to philosophy compels us first of all not to avoid the question of its radical negation, a question that, as we have seen, is inextricably linked to the question of violence.

Theodor Adorno and Emmanuel Lévinas are two masters of recent thought who pose the problem of metaphysics in these terms. Their lesson may be the only one that really "jumps headlong" into the Nietzschean themes widespread in all of contemporary culture – the unavoidable question that ties the destiny of metaphysics to the destiny of violence. And yet with respect to Nietzsche and above all to Heidegger, the shared goals of their thinking seem to articulate solutions that nonetheless remain within the realm of metaphysical thinking.

Adorno's "negative dialectic," as we know, connects the crisis of metaphysics, the impossibility of its continuation, to the tragic parody of it represented by Auschwitz, but also more broadly, by the world of total administration. The contempt that metaphysics shows for the transient, the body, the individual in its specific and accidental singularity objectively "prepares" for the extermination of great masses of humans in the name of a theory or even for their subservience to the global rationalization of existence, as one finds in the totally administered society of the advanced technological world. This occurs beyond the intentions of any philosophers or their culture. In Adorno, what happens to metaphysics is something that happens more specifically to the truth of the Hegelian system: while Hegel's thesis that truth is the whole was a valid one for him, today when this truth is realized in the administered world as a parody, the whole becomes the false. Through its "realization," in some way metaphysics is revealed as the thinking of violence (according to a thesis that we have already discovered in Nietzsche). But the right that sanctions the revolt of offended transience, individuality, and existence against the violence of extermination and total administration is nonetheless one of transcendental metaphysics, the *promesse de bonheur* that legitimates every critical and ethical distancing from the present state of affairs. Metaphysical violence is not just any return from the transient to the other or just any passage from "here to there," from appearance to truth, from the accidental to the essential. What belies metaphysics is its unfolding in presence as a totalizing realization: a thesis particularly close to Heidegger's, by which metaphysics ends when it culminates in the actual techno-scientific rationalization of the world, which removes every transcendence and transforms it into totally immanent presence. Unlike Heidegger, however, Adorno seems to claim that we can separate metaphysics as the *promesse de bonheur*, as a utopian reference to an authenticity transcending the present state of affairs, from its unfolding in totalizing rationality and in violence. The happiness that constitutes the content of the metaphysical promise, that to which the finite, in its ephemeral and accidental nature rightfully aspires, is the dialectical sublation that is also the telos of Hegel's absolute spirit: a fully unfolded self-knowledge no longer at odds with nature and therefore, in some way, no longer finite. In respect to this ideal of a sublated subject – one that is transferred to a utopian horizon by Adorno and counts as the unique and only "true" norm of emancipation – the "revocation" of the movement of sublation, the return of the Kantian appearance and the revelation of metaphysical transcendence in the *presque rien,* has nothing other than the flavour of a pure and simple relapse. In effect, the "conclusive" position that aesthetic theory takes in Adorno's philosophical itinerary is not a chronological accident. The negative dialectic has an intrinsic vocation to bring aesthetics to its end. Here philosophy allows aesthetic experience to step in as that which halts the sublation in the moment of appearance.

Many of the arguments in Adorno's critique of metaphysics can be found, and in a more radical form, in the work of Lévinas. For Lévinas, as it was for Adorno, the Holocaust is the biographical event that determines (on theoretical bases previously developed) the unmasking of the connection between metaphysics and violence. As with Adorno, the Nazis' extermination of the Jews imposes itself on his theory not only as a qualitatively unprecedented fact (perhaps Lévinas considers the rest less "extraordinary" than does Adorno, since it is just another manifestation of the sinfulness of man) but for the meaning that it assumes as theoretically "grounded" and rationally planned. What in Adorno was the double significance of metaphysics as the thinking of the violent removal of the rights of the transient – but also the only place for the affirmation of these rights, in the reference to a transcendent promise of sublation – is expressed in Lévinas through the terminological distinction between metaphysics (which is rightfully the opening of the finite onto the infinite) and ontology (which is the knowledge of the general structures of Being, in respect to which the individual is nothing more than the example of a type, already in principle ready to be erased, killed, exterminated). In Lévinas there is also, against the violence of ontology, a vindication of the irreducibility of the individual, its "face." Reducing the other to an example of Being through the knowledge of its essence (according to Lévinas, this is also the "violent" sense of the ontological fore-understanding in Heidegger) means more than just violating the rights of our equals. The ethical nature of the relation to the other is given by the fact that this relation is always asymmetrical and thus imposes a responsibility on us beyond every implicit or explicit contractual relation. The other is the face, and it warrants hospitality and respect because it is turned towards the Infinite. Its desire places it in relation with God, whose trace it therefore carries. Here the violent thinking of metaphysics is contrasted not to an appeal to pure brotherhood, to equal respect for the other, but rather to the idea that the experience of Being, which one has originarily in the encounter with the other, is the experience of an infinite that imposes itself as "majesty," as "command and authority."

If Adorno seems to think about an overcoming of metaphysics and philosophy itself in aesthetic experience, Lévinas – regardless of all evidence to the contrary – prefigures an end to metaphysics and to philosophy itself as the transition to religious experience. It is true that his work is, above and beyond Talmudic commentary, philosophical discourse; yet, it is difficult to imagine it as something other than a *preambulum fidei*, a "destruction of the history of ontology" that is much more radical and definitive than what Heidegger proposed as his program in *Being and Time*.

In their symmetry, the outcomes of Adorno and Lévinas can be placed effortlessly within a familiar schema – namely, the forms of the Hegelian absolute spirit. Both endeavour to "revoke" Hegelian sublation by halting the dialectic at a previous stage, be it art or religion. The return to a "previous" moment of the dialectic seems particularly evident in Lévinas: the departure from metaphysics as the reduction of the other to the same is sought through a restoration of the metaphysical *Grund* in its most originary form and ultimately the most peremptory (and, at least in this sense, most violent) form of the Lord, of majesty and command. But is the relation with this majesty really less violent than the metaphysical "foundation"? Might it not be an authentic experience of the sacred (for example, we can think of René Girard's thesis) that metaphysics was the first secularization – i.e., the first step on the way towards the reduction of violence – one that must be carried to its end through a further secularization?

It seems less clear that also in Adorno the overcoming of metaphysics should be sought through the withdrawal to a previous stage in the Hegelian movement of absolute spirit. Nevertheless, there are many indications that it could be. First of all, what appears paradoxical for an avant-garde apologist like Adorno is his fundamentally "classicist" conception of the beautiful and aesthetic experience. In fact, for Adorno the justification of the avant-garde's revolt against the art of the past is pursued not so much out of the need to overcome the traditional experience of the beautiful – such as the "fullness" of the work of art, its structural perfection – as out of the will to revindicate an ideal of sublation, of harmony, and therefore of perfection and completion, if only in a utopian sense. This revolt stands against the phantasmagoric degeneration of art in the epoch when the market reigns supreme. This still profoundly classicist conception of the beautiful and aesthetic experience is but the revelatory symptom of a more general feature in Adorno's thought, namely that regardless of the emphasis on micrology and appearance, the negative dialectic still conceives of the task of thought in relation to a telos that is always defined in terms of presence, of achieved sublation, of a "fullness" of Being. But is not the unfolded presence of Being – as achieved sublation no less than as authority, majesty and command – what constitutes the violence of metaphysics?

Just as the objections to metaphysics are not principally motivated by "reasons of conscience," i.e., by pure and simple theoretical insufficiencies, so too the greater or lesser resoluteness of the overcoming proposed by Adorno or by Lévinas is not measured merely in terms of internal contradictions or the aporetic nature of their theses. What we try to express in pointing, in theoretical terms, to the limits and the aporias in the Adornian and Levinasian positions is the vague feeling that these two thinkers, each in his own way, "leave out" too many elements integral to the problem of overcoming metaphysics as the thinking linked to violence. The religious conversion that undoubtedly represents Lévinas' final word and the recourse to aesthetic experience that seems to conclude the itinerary of Adorno's critical thought evoke Heidegger's words in *What Is Called Thinking?* concerning the uselessness of humanity's "interventions" or "decisions" unless Being itself reveals (gives) itself in ways different from those that marked the destiny of metaphysics. Certainly also, the almost overly emphatic attitude of "anticipation" and "listening" preferred by Heidegger seems to offer too little for dealing with the problems that thought faces. Heidegger, however, in respect not only to Adorno and Lévinas but also to many other perspectives on the renewal of metaphysics, has a problematic advantage in that he explicitly poses the problem regarding the belonging of thought and the subject to a historical horizon, a horizon of destiny from which one cannot escape through an appeal to some originary experience. Religious conversion and the recourse to aesthetic experience are two solutions that still place the subject at the centre of the decision. In the case of Lévinas, the decision is overly dominated by the ideals of force implied in the very idea of the Infinite. And for Adorno, on the opposite side, the decision is too weak, as it ties itself to the mere appearance of the beautiful. In both cases, however, the departure from violence and the overcoming of metaphysics depend on the capability of the subject to gain access to an experience in some sense not compromised, an experience that retains many metaphysical features, enabling it to reach a sort of authenticity.

Heidegger tries to exit this schema by taking his leave from humanism, insisting on anticipation and listening rather than on decision and conversion, and above all in the later writings, through his conception of the *Ge-stell*. This term ought to be translated as "en-framing," in order to respect Heidegger's intention to grant the German word, which literally means "scaffolding," the significance of the gathering (*Ge-*) of the *Stellen* (to place, to arrange, to impose, to compose, etc.). According to Heidegger, this indicates the nature of the techno-scientific world in which we live today. More or less, it deals with the world of total administration of which Adorno speaks and that, again in harmony with Adorno (not recognized, however, by either of them), Heidegger sees as the realization of metaphysics. Metaphysics, in fact, is ideally directed towards enclosing everything within the schema of the principle of sufficient reason, such that it carries everything back to explicit connections of foundation and completely realizes this program through the fundamentally unlimited dissemination of technology guided by modern experimental science. In contrast with Adorno's conclusion, the realization of metaphysics in the *Ge-stell* is not for Heidegger a mere "parody" that should be contrasted with the revoking of false sublation that takes the dialectical movement back to a preceding moment, such as that of aesthetic appearance. If thought has a chance to go beyond metaphysics and the violence connected to it, this chance is tied to the very movement of the *Ge-stell*, within which thought is totally lost, as in its destiny. The *Ge-stell* is the destinal horizon that does not allow an escape through a religious conversion or the contemplation of the appearance of the beautiful. Only if the *Ge-stell* is distorted or transformed in some way will Being reveal itself again (as in *What is Called Thinking?*) and can we hope to be led beyond metaphysics.

With this conception of the *Ge-stell*, we return to the globality, and even the ambiguity, of the Nietzschean conception of the relation between metaphysics and violence. In its self-showing, the relation places thought in a condition that no longer allows it to think in terms of conversion or even in terms of originary experience. Heidegger, in a context that raises this very question of the connection between overcoming metaphysics and the *Ge-stell*, expresses this condition by rejecting the notion that metaphysics can be considered an error that, recognized for what it is, is dropped like a bad habit. This must be understood first of all in the sense that Heidegger grants it in the pages of his essay on humanism where he speaks of the missed follow-up of *Being and Time* as due to the metaphysical "remnants" that are tied to the language of philosophy, survivors that can not be liquidated solely by terminological and linguistic devices; but it is also understood in the sense that denies metaphysics a new beginning, since this would always risk the possibility of accepting another foundation, another truth that would merely replace an old form of metaphysical thinking with a new one that functions in the same way. Thus the transition of intellectual hegemony in advanced societies from "philosophers," or even from humanistic intellectuals, to the scientists (who practise on everything else a hegemony much less illusory, one that perhaps conforms to the fact that in the *Ge-stell* metaphysics is "realized" by conferring a weight of new reality even to the hegemony of knowledge, which in the times of traditional metaphysics was largely ideological) is still a rebirth of metaphysics, even if in a "final" form that conforms to the *Ge-stell*.

One cannot exit the *Ge-stell* through a renewed access to some originary experience, not even disguised in the garb of scientific knowledge and the new hegemony of the scientists. This, however, confers a profound ambiguity on Heidegger's notion of the *Ge-stell* that conceals both the risks of his position and also its positive importance, namely, the ability to speak of the overcoming of metaphysics and the violence connected to it in terms that are not purely aporetic.

The development of the problems in *Being and Time* – which already began from motives irreducible to merely *erkenntnistheoretisch* terms – led Heidegger to an ever more radical recognition that everything that in the "existentialistic" reflection of *Being and Time* still appeared as the constitution of existence (even if already clearly distinct from the "categories" through which entities or things in the world are given) is carried back to the *event* of Being. The existential analytic speaks not of essential human traits but of the ways of happening (of *wesen*) of the Dasein, of humanity, in the epoch into which we are thrown, the epoch of completed metaphysics. Every claim to oppose a *Verfassung* (an originary or natural constitution of existence or even an authentic experience of the pure structures of Being) to fallenness (the inauthentic existence of average everydayness) or to the destiny of humanity in the age of metaphysics or technology and social rationalization does nothing but remain within the epoch where various "first principles" have hierarchically structured the phases of Western history. They deal with the various configurations of Nietzsche's "true world," which in *Twilight of the Idols* is transformed into a "fable."

The growing awareness of all of this – namely, the clearly nihilistic bearing of the critique of the idea of Being as presence and the attempt to think it radically as event – leads Heidegger to see the destiny of Being in the *Ge-stell*. As already noted, metaphysics is also for Heidegger the thinking that ends in the (fundamentally) total rationalization of the world. But, precisely as such, it is also that event in which ultimately "there is nothing to Being as such" (*es mit dem Sein selbst nichts mehr ist*). Being is completely dissolved in the subjugation of all beings by the power available to technology, a power that always ends up turning against the subject as well (conforming to the critical descriptions of alienation), who thus becomes an "available" element of the *Ge-stell*'s universal imposition. Yet here, where both Being and man are involved in the development of the *Ge-stell*, there also resides the possibility that the *Ge-stell* represents not only the final moment of metaphysics but the first step towards its overcoming. The unfolding of metaphysics in the world of total techno-scientific availability makes the thinking of Being as foundation impossible (since the foundation is completely transformed in sufficient reason, whose founding force is inseparable from the will of the subject who discovers, manipulates, calculates, and utilizes it). But this very fact excludes the possibility that thought, once it undertakes this dissolution of the foundation, can appeal to another "foundation" (originary experience, aesthetic appearance, divine majesty) in order to begin from the top. If there is a chance for a new beginning, it cannot rest in the possibility that the subject turns to a new principle by remaining in the schema of the relation between the human as subject and Being as objective principle, as *gegen-stand*, which stands before us as something that can be returned to after the error, the forgetting, the turning away.

But the *Ge-stell* may be distorted, and Being once again may turn itself to us beyond the forgetting and the dissolution of metaphysics. This possibility carries important consequences both on the ontological and on the "historical" level. Being that possibly reveals itself again, leading thought beyond the metaphysical forgetfulness, can no longer bear the features of the principle, of the authority, of the foundation that belonged to the metaphysical tradition, since both the givenness of these characteristics and their dissolution are not "merely" errors of humanity (the subject facing a being-object, "from the outside") but the destiny of Being itself. On the "historical" level, this radical mode of overcoming metaphysics will mean a particular capacity to gather the announcement of a new existence outside the violence that belongs to the age of metaphysics, outside the unfolding of the society of total rationalization. In the *Ge-stell*, even as mass society, one finds the only chances for overcoming the inauthenticities characteristic of our history.

Here we face two of the most problematic and even scandalous features of Heideggerian thought: his insistence on overcoming metaphysics, not through a human initiative, but through Being itself and its destiny; and secondly, the subsequent "acceptance" of modern social rationalization and of massification, which Adorno had perhaps exaggerated in his critique of Heidegger but which is nevertheless undeniable – regardless of the many signs to the contrary (the "archaism" of Heidegger, his disdain for science and technology). A discussion of Adorno's objections, which capture the essential elements of the Heideggerian position even if he misunderstands them, allows us to clarify that the Heideggerian meditation of the *Ge-stell* contains important indications for completing the discourse on overcoming metaphysics as the thinking of violence. Heidegger's antihumanism, his placing of the destiny of humanity within the destiny of Being, in Adorno's eyes seems to be an illusory satisfaction of the "ontological need" that emerges in contemporary humanity as the need to save, in any way, the substantiality of the I in a world where everything is reduced to a relation of functions. In the view of Adorno, Heidegger opposes a philosophy of Being to the system of these functional relations, a philosophy that is much more insightful and efficacious the more it gathers Being beyond every possible endeavour of the subject in a destinal ordering, one that seems to furnish a solid guarantee but that, to the very degree that by definition it removes every human initiative and decision, comes to an end in an implicit apology for the existing order. To Heidegger's apparent falling back in to objectivity (inspired by an antisubjectivism that, we must remember, is motivated by the need to provide a solid ground, which cannot be sought in a subject impoverished by universal functionalism), Adorno opposes a dialectical ideal of freedom that places itself outside the subject-object dichotomy, with which Heidegger's critique also took issue. But as is clear from the arguments in the pages dedicated to the "ontological need" in *Negative Dialectics*, for Adorno the Heideggerian overturning threatens the free subject precisely insofar as it is conceived as the principle of unlimited self-determination that sets itself against the object as a purely antithetical term, as the material of its domination. Only from the point of view rigidly attached to the juxtaposition of subject and object can the Heideggerian effort to overcome metaphysics by appealing to a destiny of Being appear as a pure overturning in objectivity. It is true, as Adorno writes in these pages, that "the history accumulated in subjects" forbids thought a sharp turn towards positions that, believing themselves to be radical, are but a wandering in the emptiness – like certain migrations towards the East, Zen Buddhism, etc. But the history of Western subjectivity entails more experiences than those gathered in Adorno's work. That is why the subject that he sees threatened by the overturning of Heidegger is only the dialectical subject not yet overcome, either through the existential analytic of Heidegger or even through Nietzsche's critique.

Is the violent nature of metaphysics really, as Adorno sees it, the death of freedom and of the rights of the sovereign subject – the modern subject, for which the reconciliation with the other than oneself coincides with a nonalienated praxis, namely an unlimited one like the will to power – or rather, will we be able to suspect that it begins and already has roots where Being unfolds in the contentious juxtaposition between subject and object? While the *Ge-stell* contains a chance for overcoming metaphysics in the act of stripping the human of its qualities as a subject, Adorno has no doubt that this qualification – in the name of a cultural memory that we must not betray, but that even he limits drastically – has to be defended and affirmed. There is nothing to make him doubt its "validity," which is only practically threatened by total organization. If we are aware of this difference, it will also be clear that while Heidegger's attitude in the face of the *Ge-stell* ought to appear to Adorno like an apology for that very form of existence inspired by metaphysics that becomes a real parody, it in fact deals with an overcoming. To a certain degree, Adorno makes sense: Heidegger sees the *Ge-stell* as a destiny, even in the sense that only from it can one expect, beyond the "height of danger," a maturation into "that which saves" (according to Holderlin's verse cited by Heidegger). If we can no longer believe – since precisely this is forbidden by the unveiling of the connection between metaphysics and violence – that we can appeal to an originary or a different foundation in the form of an aesthetics of appearance or in the form of the majesty of the Lord, then the call that signals the overcoming of metaphysics, by revealing the impossibility of its continuation, must come from metaphysics itself and from its world. If we want to give a plausible meaning to the page (almost the only one) where Heidegger speaks of the *Ge-stell* as "the first lighting of the Ereignis" (in *Identity and Difference*, 1957), we can begin only from the Heideggerian observation that the *Ge-stell* strips humanity and Being "of those determinations given to them by metaphysics," namely, the qualities of subject and object. Both Heidegger and Adorno agree that metaphysics, in a profound way, has pushed violence to its extreme in the world of total organization. But Heidegger goes far beyond this recognition. One cannot attribute to Heidegger the various attempts – beyond the most philosophically distinct ones from Adorno and Lévinas that are under discussion here – to imagine an overcoming of metaphysics through the restoration of previous stages in its development by returning to the moments in which it was not yet dissolved or realized in technology. Such is the case with a certain archaism widespread in Italian philosophy over the past few decades (Emanuele Severino) that is often connected to a philosophy of tragedy inspired by Schelling, Nietzsche, and Heidegger (Massimo Cacciari), but also linked to the continuation of the Enlightenment project by Jürgen Habermas. For Heidegger the realization of metaphysics in the *Ge-stell* makes similar returns "impossible."

The "essential word" that Heidegger always sought, even in his unrelenting return to the dawning moments of European philosophy, is perhaps much closer to the daily chatter of the late-modern world than to the arcane silence of the mystic and the sacred experience.

Heidegger did not follow this path, despite having opened it with his vision of the *Ge-stell*. It would therefore be excessive, at least if one sticks to the letter of his texts, to read, for example, the page from *On the Way to Language* regarding the "simple silencing of the silence" as the only "authentic saying" in the sense of an invitation to "let Being go," not only as *Grund* but also as the silent essential word. Yet it is on this path that one must move forward, with Heidegger and beyond him, even beyond the letter of his texts, if one is to remain faithful to his program of preparing for a new coming of Being by responding to the call of the *Ge-stell*. It is difficult that this call – to depart from metaphysics and, primarily, from its basic schema, the opposition between subject and object – points only in the direction of a recognition of the intersubjective constitution of the subject itself, as in Habermas' theory of communicative action. Habermas rightly maintains a distance from Adorno by noting that he remains tied to a metaphysical conception of the subject, but also Habermas himself, in his turn, remains oriented towards the construction of a normative structure of the "socialized subject"; and since intersubjectivity provides it with a supra-historical constitution, it is not contaminated by the idea of "destiny," of sending, of constant belonging to an event. With that, the "advantage" of discarding the self-centred metaphysical subject ends up rather deficient, or even brings with it the risk of a restorative overturning. Despite all claims to the contrary, the path taken by Habermas, and by Karl-Otto Apel with his notion of unlimited communication, is nevertheless an example of how one should not proceed after metaphysics, lest the subject be consumed. It is the *Ge-stell* (seen even in Habermas as a society of "roles," and for which, after Max Weber, the reference to the experience of racialism within American society is decisive) that makes the subject as self-centred I unthinkable; though yet again, even the imposition of communicative action as a transcendental norm thwarts this beginning and tries to exorcise the dissolution whose continuation was at issue.

One departs from metaphysics and the violence connected to it by letting it recall – and not only negatively – the dissolution that the *Ge-stell* places upon the subject and the object of metaphysics. Heidegger has only vaguely foreseen the many aspects of this dissolution. For example, he has not explicitly thematized the dissolution of the objectivity of the subjects determined by the *Ge-stell* to the degree that the technology that characterizes it is no longer a technology of mechanical force (the motor and, at its extreme, atomic energy are the great examples that Heidegger gives when he speaks of technology) but a technology of collecting, organizing, and distributing information.

Does all this, however, not mean remaining precisely within the world of completed metaphysics, abandoning it all to the *Ge-stell*, accepting it and, as Adorno says, making a more or less explicit apology

for it? But, is there (still) a *Ge-stell*? Conceiving of the ontology of Heidegger as a new deterministic metaphysics that confers upon Being (in
the form of the technological destiny of the late-modern world) a pre-
eminence over human endeavours means developing yet again a relation of "foundation" between the "true world" (the laws of the destiny
of Being that Heidegger mentions) and the "apparent world" (history,
society, human existence); yet, it is precisely a question of the dissolution of this distinction. Heidegger's would be a deterministic ontology
if he were to affirm the primacy of the object over the subject. Then it
would be a matter of defending subjectivity against the monstrous domination of the structures of universal objectification, as seen in Adorno.
But the *Ge-stell* that removes the meaning from the juxtaposition of
subject and object no longer lets it be thought as the true world, as the
necessary structure from which one "deduces" the destiny of humanity.
It is the gathering of the *Stellen* – the technological civilization in which
the world is nothing (more) than the web of "images of the world," and
the subject just the geometrical site of a multiplicity of roles that can
never be fully unified, history itself a sort of constellation of the multiple (and not unifiable) reconstructions that historiography and chronicle give to it. It is impossible to configure the *Ge-stell* as the foundation
of an "objective" necessity that imposes itself upon the subject by limiting its freedom. This impossibility is the true end of metaphysics –
which manifests itself, therefore, as the end of philosophical discourse
as "hegemon" – that culminates in the technological organization of the
world. Heidegger invites us to listen for and to await the renewed call
of Being, which no longer speaks in the form of the *arché*, of the
grounding principle, of the essential structure, or even as the intersubjective constitution of existence. The "true world" is now a fable. A
certain "crumbling" or fraying of Heidegger's philosophical discourse
after *Being and Time* can also be said to mark its stylistic expression. If
Being speaks, its discourse takes the form of a general buzzing, a
polyphony of sounds, a murmuring, and perhaps even the form of the
"neuter" whose announcement Maurice Blanchot says we ought to
expect.

"To tolerate a good deal of chance" (Nietzsche); or to leave "behind
Being as foundation" (Heidegger); or even "to encourage a certain
degree of frivolity when dealing with traditional philosophical questions" (Rorty) – these are the ways in which one can describe the philosophical discourse open to the call of the *Ge-stell*. Could it mean,
according to Adorno's condemnation, simply and cynically abandoning

oneself to the alienating course of things? The alternative – which Adorno never explicitly embraces – would be to cut the link between metaphysics, rationalization, and violence through an extreme and "ultimate" act of violence, a recurring dream found in some of the highest moments of twentieth-century philosophy, from Benjamin to Sartre. Nietzsche and Heidegger, on the other hand, propose a path of "moderation" and of listening, one that does not present the schema of foundation again and again but resigns itself to it, accepts it as destiny, distorts it, and secularizes it.

NOTE

1 F. Nietzsche, *Writings from the Late Notebooks*, edited by R. Bittner (Cambridge, MA: Cambridge University Press 2003), 116–21.

Bibliography of Gianni Vattimo

SANTIAGO ZABALA

PRIMARY SOURCES

Books of Vattimo in Italian

Il concetto di fare in Aristotele. Turin: Giappichelli 1961.

Essere, storia e linguaggio in Heidegger. Turin: Edizioni di Filosofia 1963.

Estetica ed ermeneutica in H.-G. Gadamer. Padua: Tip. Poligrafica Moderna 1963.

Arte e verità nel pensiero di M. Heidegger. Turin: Giappichelli 1966.

Introduzione all'ermeneutica di Schleiermacher. Turin: Giappichelli 1967.

Ipotesi su Nietzsche. Turin: Giappichelli 1967.

Poesia e ontologia. Milan: Mursia 1967.

Schleiermacher filosofo dell'interpretazione. Milan: Mursia 1968.

Nietzsche e la filosofia come esercizio ontologico. Torino: Edizioni di Filosofia 1969.

Introduzione all'estetica di Hegel. Turin: Giappichelli 1970.

Corso di estetica. Turin: Litografia Artigiana M. & S. 1971.

Introduzione a Heidegger. Rome-Bari: Laterza 1971.

Arte e utopia. Turin: Litografia Artigiana M. & S. 1972.

Il soggetto e la maschera: Nietzsche e il problema della liberazione. Milan: Fabbri-Bompiani 1974.

Estetica moderna. Edited by Gianni Vattimo. Bologna: Il Mulino 1977.

Le avventure della differenza: Che cosa significa pensare dopo Nietzsche e Heidegger. Milan: Garzanti 1980.

Al di là del soggetto: Nietzsche, Heidegger e l'ermeneutica. Milan: Feltrinelli 1981.

Introduzione a Nietzsche. Rome-Bari: Laterza 1984.

La fine della modernità: Nichilismo ed ermeneutica nella cultura postmoderna. Milan: Garzanti 1985.

Filosofia '86. Edited by Gianni Vattimo. Rome-Bari: Laterza 1987.

Filosofia '87. Edited by Gianni Vattimo. Rome-Bari: Laterza 1988.

Le mezze verità. Turin: La Stampa, Terza Pagina 1988.

La sécularisation de la pensée. Edited by Gianni Vattimo. Paris: Seuil 1988.

Que peut faire la philosophie de son histoire? Edited by Gianni Vattimo. Paris: Seuil 1989.

Etica dell'interpretazione. Turin: Rosenberg & Sellier 1989.

Filosofia '88. Edited by Gianni Vattimo. Rome-Bari: Laterza 1989.

La società trasparente. Edited by Gianni Vattimo. Milano: Garzanti 1989.

Filosofia '89. Edited by Gianni Vattimo. Rome-Bari: Laterza 1990.

Filosofia al presente: Conversazioni con F. Barone, R. Bodei, I. Mancini, V. Mathieu, M. Perniola, P.A. Rovatti, E. Severino, C. Sini. Milan: Garzanti 1990.

Filosofia, Strumenti di studio: Guide bibliografiche. Edited with Luca Bagetto. Milan: Garzanti 1990.

Filosofia '90. Edited by Gianni Vattimo. Rome-Bari: Laterza 1991.

Filosofia '91. Edited by Gianni Vattimo. Rome-Bari: Laterza 1992.

Filosofia '92. Edited by Gianni Vattimo. Rome-Bari: Laterza 1993.

Filosofia '93. Edited by Gianni Vattimo. Rome-Bari: Laterza 1994.

Oltre l'interpretazione: Il significato dell'ermeneutica per la filosofia. Rome-Bari: Laterza 1994.

Filosofia '94. Edited by Gianni Vattimo. Rome-Bari: Laterza 1995.

Psicoanalisi ed ermeneutica. Debate with R.R. Holt and H. Kaechele. Chieti: Métis 1995.

Credere di credere. Milan: Garzanti 1996.

Filosofia '95. Edited by Gianni Vattimo. Rome-Bari: Laterza 1996.

Filosofía, Política, Religiòn: Màs allà del "pensamiento debil." Edited by L. Álvarez. Oviedo: Nobel 1996.

Il consumatore consumato. Jesi: Centro Studi P. Calamandrei 1996.

Tecnica ed esistenza. Una mappa filosofica del Novecento. Edited by L. Bagetto. Turin: Paravia-Scriptorium 1997.

Vocazione e responsabilità del filosofo. Edited by F. D'Agostini. Genova: Il Melangolo 2000.

Dialogo con Nietzsche: Saggi 1961–2000. Milan: Garzanti 2001.

Dopo la cristianità: Per un cristianesimo non religioso. Milan: Garzanti 2002.

Vero e Falso Universalismo Cristiano. Rio de Janerio: EDUCAM – Editora Universitária Candido Mendes and Academia da Latinidade 2002.

Nichilismo ed emancipazione: Etica, politica, diritto. Edited by Santiago Zabala. Milan: Garzanti 2003.

Vattimo, Gianni, and Luigi Pareyson. *Il problema estetico.* Rome: AVE 1966.

Il pensiero debole. Edited by Gianni Vattimo and P.A. Rovatti. Milan: Feltrinelli 1983.

La Religione: Annuario Filosofico Europeo. Edited by Gianni Vattimo and Jacques Derrida. Rome-Bari: Laterza 1995.

With G. Cavaglia, K. Roggero, and P. Sarkozy. *L'Ungheria e l'Europa.* Rome: Bulzoni 1996.

Diritto, Giustizia e Interpretazione: Annuario filosofico europeo. Edited by Gianni Vattimo and Jacques Derrida. Rome-Bari: Laterza 1998.

Medien – Welten – Wirklichkeiten. Edited by Gianni Vattimo and W. Welsch. Munich: Fink 1998.

Parmiggiani. Edited by Gianni Vattimo and V. Castellani. Turin: Umberto Allemandi Editore 1998.

Pensar en el siglo. Edited by Gianni Vattimo and M. Cruz. Madrid: Taurus 1998.

With P. Sequeri and G. Ruggeri. *Interrogazioni sul cristianesimo.* Rome: Ed. Lavoro 1999.

With G. Iannantuono. *Progetti per l'Europa. Riflessioni sull'identità piemontese.* Turin: Consiglio Regionale del Piemonte 2000.

Atlante del Novecento. Edited by Gianni Vattimo, L. Gallino, and M. Salvatori. 3 vols. Turin: UTET 2000.

With E. Dussel and G. Hoyos. *La postmodernidad a debite.* Edited by L. Tovar. Bogotá: Universidad Santo Tomàs 2002.

Ermeneutica. Edited by Gianni Vattimo, G. Bertolotti, S. Natoli, C. Sini, and V. Vitiello. Milan: Raffello Cortina Editore 2003.

With R. Rorty. *Il futuro della religione. Solidarietà, carità, ironia.* Edited by Santiago Zabala. Milan: Garzanti 2004.

With R. Schröder and U. Engel. *Christentum im Zeitalter der Interpretation.* Edited by Thomas Eggensperger. Vienna: Passagen 2004.

With G. Filoramo and E. Gentile. *Che cos'è la religione oggi?* Pisa: ETS 2005.

Books of Vattimo in English Translation

The End of Modernity: Nihilism and Hermeneutics in Postmodern Culture. Trans. J.R. Snyder. Baltimore: Johns Hopkins University Press 1988.

The Transparent Society. Trans. D. Webb. Cambridge: Polity Press, 1992.

The Adventure of Difference: Philosophy after Nietzsche and Heidegger. Trans.
    C.P. Blamires and T. Harrison. Cambridge: Polity Press 1993.
Beyond Interpretation: The Meaning of Hermeneutics for Philosophy. Trans.
    D. Webb. Cambridge: Polity Press 1997.
Belief. Trans. L. D'Isanto and D. Webb. Cambridge: Polity Press 1998.
With J. Derrida. *Religion.* Stanford: Stanford University Press 1998.
With J. Price and A. Ramella. *Italia America, America Italy.* Cavallermaggiore:
    Gribaudo 2001.
Nietzsche: An Introduction. Trans. N. Martin. Stanford: Stanford University
    Press 2002.
After Christianity. Trans. L. D'Isanto. New York: Columbia University Press
    2002.
Nihilism and Emancipation: Ethics, Politics, and Law. Forword by Richard
    Rorty. Edited by Santiago Zabala and translated by William McCuaig. New
    York: Columbia University Press 2004.
Dialogue with Nietzsche. Trans. William McCuaig. New York: Columbia Uni-
    versity Press 2005.
With R. Rorty. *The Future of Religion.* Edited by Santiago Zabala. New York:
    Columbia University Press 2005.
La vita dell'altro: Bioetica senza metafisica. Lungro di Cosenza: Marco Editore
    2006.
With John D. Caputo. *After the Death of God.* Edited by Jeffrey W. Robbins.
    New York: Columbia University Press 2007.
A Philosophy of Aesthetics: Ontology, Hermeneutics, and Beauty. Edited by
    Santiago Zabala and translated by Luca D'Isanto. New York: Columbia Uni-
    versity Press 2007.

Articles of Vattimo in English Translation

"The Crisis of the Notion of Value from Nietzsche until Today." In *The Search
    for Absolute Values: Harmony Among the Sciences*, vol. 1. New York: The
    International Cultural Foundation Press 1978), 115–30.
"Bottle, Net, Truth, Revolution, Terrorism, Philosophy." Trans. T. Harrison.
    Denver Quarterly, 16 (1982): 24–34.
"Difference and Interference: On the Reduction of Hermeneutics to Anthro-
    pology." Trans. T. Harrison. *Res* 4 (1982): 85–91.
"The Shattering of the Poetic Word." In *The Favorite Malice. Ontology and
    Reference in Contemporary Italian Poetry.* New York: Out of London Press
    1983, 223–35.
"Dialectics, Difference, and Weak Thought." Trans. T. Harrison. *Graduate
    Faculty Philosophy Journal* 10 (1984): 151–63.

"Aesthetics and the End of Epistemology." In *The Reasons of Art: Artworks and the Transformation of Philosophy*. Edited by P.J. McCormick. Ottawa: Ottawa University Press 1985, 287–94.

"Myth and the Destiny of Secularization." *Social Research* 2 (1985): 347–62.

"Myth and the Fate of Secularization." Trans. Jon R. Snyder. *Res* 9 (1985): 29–35; and *Social Research* 52 (1985): 347–62.

"The Crisis of Subjectivity from Nietzsche to Heidegger." Trans. P. Carravetta. *Differentia: Review of Italian Thought* 1 (1986): 5–21.

"The End of (Hi)story." *Chicago Review* 35 (1986): 20–30.

"Hermeneutics and Nihilism: An Apology for Aesthetic Consciousness." In *Hermeneutics and Modern Philosophy*, ed. B.R. Wachterhauser. Albany: Suny Press 1986, 446–59.

"Nietzsche and Heidegger." Trans. T. Harrison. *Stanford Italian Review* 6 (1986): 19–29.

"Project and Legitimization." *Lotus International* 48–9 (1986): 118–25.

"Nietzsche and Contemporary Hermeneutics." In *Nietzsche as Affirmative Thinker*. Edited by Y. Yovel. Dordrecht: Martinus Nijhoff 1986, 58–68.

"Verwindung: Nihilism and the Postmodern in Philosophy." Trans. R. Palmer. *SubStance* 53 (1987): 7–17.

"Hermeneutics as Koiné." Trans. P. Carravetta. *Theory, Culture & Society* 5 (1988): 399–408.

"Metaphysics, Violence, Secularization." Trans. B. Spackman. In *Recoding Metaphysics: The New Italian Philosophy*. Edited by G. Borradori. Evanston: Northwestern University Press 1988, 45–61.

"Nietzsche and Heidegger." In *Nietzsche in Italy*, edited by T. Harrison. Saratoga: Anma Libri 1988, 19–29.

"Toward an Ontology of Decline Recoding Metaphysics." Trans. B. Spackman. In *Recoding Metaphysics: The New Italian Philosophy*. Edited by G. Borradori. Evanston: Northwestern University Press 1988.

"Nihilism: Reactive and Active." In *Nietzsche and the Rhetoric of Nihilism: Essays on Interpretation, Language and Politics*. Edited by T. Darby, B. Egyed, and B. Jones. Ottawa: Carleton University Press 1989, 15–21.

"Byars: The Risky Invention and the Destiny of Mortality." In *The Perfect Thought: Works by James Lee Byars*. Edited by J. Elliot. Berkeley: University Art Museum 1990, 59–64.

"Postmodern Criticism: Postmodern Critique." In *Writing the future*. Edited by D. Wood. London: Routledge 1990, 57–66.

"The End of (Hi)story." In *Zeitgeist in Babel: The Postmodernist Controversy*. Edited by I. Hoesterey. Bloomington: Indiana University Press 1991, 132–41.

"The Secularization of Philosophy." In *Writing the Politics of Difference*. Edited by H. J. Silverman. Albany: SUNY Press 1991, 283–90.

"Optimistic Nihilism." *Common Knowledge* 1 (1992): 37–44.

"On the Challenge of Art to Philosophy: Aesthetics at the End of Epistemology." *Journal of Comparative Literature and Aesthetics* 1–2 (1993): 9–16.

"Postmodern, Technology, Ontology." In *Technology in the Western Political Tradition*. Edited by A.M. Melzer, J. Weinberger, and M.R. Zinman. London and Ithaca: Cornell University Press 1993, 214–28.

"The Truth of Hermeneutics." Trans. D. Webb. In *Questioning Foundations: Truth, Subjectivity, and Culture*. Edited by H. Silverman. New York and London: Routledge 1993.

"Postmodernity and New Monumentality." *Res* 28 (1995): 39–46.

"Christianity and Modern Europe." *I Quaderni di Gaia* 11 (1997): 9–14.

"Hermeneutics and Democracy." *Philosophy and Social Criticism* 4 (1997): pp. 1–7.

"Philosophy, Metaphysics, Democracy." Trans. Paul Kottman. *Qui parle* 2 (1997): 1–10.

"Beyond Despair and Conflict: A Reading of Nietzsche's Positive Nihilism, Part One." Trans. Dannah Edwards. *Common Knowledge* 7, no. 1 (1998): 15–59.

"Beyond Despair and Conflict: A Reading of Nietzsche's Positive Nihilism. Part Two: *The Spirit of Revenge*." Trans. Dannah Edwards. *Common Knowledge* 2 (1998), 27–56.

"The Demand for Ethics and Philosophy's Responsibility." In *Philosophie in synthetischer Absicht*. Edited by Marcelo Stamm. Stuttgart: Klett-Cotta 1998, 419–29.

"The Generalized Communication Society." In *Keys to the Twenty-first Century*. Edited by J. Bindé. Paris, New York and Oxford: UNESCO Publishing/Berghahn Books 2001, 230–33.

"Library, liberty." In *The Book: A World Transformed*. Edited by Eduardo Portella. Paris: UNESCO Publishing 2001, 67–71.

"Bel Paese: Between Natural Disaster and Control." In *With an Open Mind: Tolerance and Diversity*, Frankfurt am Main: Franfurter Allgemeine Buch (in FAZ Institut) 2002, 114–15.

"Method, Hermeneutics, Truth." In *Japanese Hermeneutics: Current Debates on Aesthetics and Interpretation*. Edited by M. Marra. Honolulu: University of Hawaii Press 2002, 9–16.

"After Onto-Theology: Philosophy between Science and Religion." In *Religion After Metaphysics*. Edited by M. Wrathall. Cambridge: Cambridge University Press 2003.

"Ethics without Transcendence?" Trans. Santiago Zabala. *Common Knowledge* 9 (2003): 399–405.

With Santiago Zabala. "A Life dedicated to Hermeneutics." Review Jean Grondin's *Hans-Georg Gadamer: A Biography*. *Books in Canada: The Canadian Review of Books* 33, no. 1 (2004): 27, 34.

With Santiago Zabala. "An Old Scourge of Civilization: Deciphering One's Way to Murder." Review of Abdelwahab Meddeb's *The Malady of Islam*. *Books in Canada: The Canadian Review of Books* 33, no. 6 (September 2004): 23–4.

Interviews

"Gianni Vattimo, Nietzsche e i 'nuovi filosofi' del PCI [interview with A. Santacroce]." *Mondoperaio*, no. 10 (1978): 104–7.

"Oltre le ideologie, tra ermeneutica e nichilismo. Intervista a Gianni Vattimo [F. Mastrofini]." *Religione e scuola*, no. 14 (1985): 69–72.

"Gianni Vattimo, filósofo de la secularización [by José M. Herrera y José Lasaga]." *Revista de Occidente*, no. 104: 115–32.

"Entrevista a Gianni Vattimo: ¿Nietzsche después de Heidegger?" by Teresa Oñate, Madrid 1988. *Revista Anthropos*, no. 10, 1988.

"Duas perspectives sobre Heidegger: Entrevista a Felipe Martínez Marzoa y a Gianni Vattimo, by Carlos Fernández." *Grial*, no. 103 (Verano 1989): 392–404.

"Gibt es eine europäische Kultur? Gespräch mit Gianni Vattimo," with H. Janowski. *Evangelische Kommentare* 1990: 467–471.

"Entrevista a Gianni Vattimo: Hermenéutica y pacifismo radical," by Teresa Oñate. Salamanca 2003.

"Inverview de Vattimo du 29 mars à Turin [by Anne Staquet]." In Anne Staquet, *La pensée Faible de Vattimo et Rovatti: Une Pensée-Faible* (Paris: L'Harmattan 1996), 173–85.

"Entrevista a Gianni Vattimo: Ontología y Nihilismo," by Teresa Oñate. Estrasburgo 1999. *Rev. Éndoxa*, series filosóficas, no. 12, vol. 2. Universidad Nacional Educación a Distancia (UNED), Madrid 1999.

"Come fare giustizia del diritto? Per una filosofia del diritto d'impianto nichilistico. Intervista a Gianni Vattimo [by Santiago Zabala]." *Iride*, no. 32 (April 2001): 123–36.

"De la justice du Droit au droit à la Justice: Entretien à Gianni Vattimo [by Santiago Zabala]." *Le Magazine littéraire*, no. 402 (October 2001): 98–102.

"Diálogo con Gianni Vattimo: Cómo hacer justicia del Derecho [by Santiago Zabala]." *Claves de Razón Práctica*, no. 114 (July/August 2001): 44–52.

"Gianni Vattimo, Dossier: analitici e continentali. Intervista a Gianni Vattimo." *Chora*, no. 2 (2001): 16–21.

"Interpretation and Nihilism as the Depletion of Being: A Discussion with Gianni Vattimo about the Consequences of Hermeneutics," by Sebastian Gurciullo. *Theory & Event* 5, no. 2 (2001).

"'Weak Thought' and the Reduction of Violence [by Santiago Zabala]," translated by Y. Mascetti. *Common Knowledge* 3 (2002): 452–63.

"Die Stärken des schwachen Denkens: Ein Gespräch mit Gianni Vattimo." In Martin Weiss, *Gianni Vattimo: Einführung*. Vienna: Passagen Verlag 2003, 171–82.

"Gianni Vattimo, Intervista, december 2002." In *Laicità: Domande e risposte in 38 interviste (1988–2003)*. Edited by the Comitato Torinese per la Laicità della Scuola. Turin: Claudiana 2003, 211–16.

"Die Religion: Erinnerung einer Geschichte [by Martin Thurner]. In *Aufgang: Jahrbuch f Denken, Dichten, Musik* 1 [Ursprung und Gegenwart]. Stuttgart: Verlag Kohlhammer 2004, 85–99.

"Le conseguenze della differenza ontologica [by Santiago Zabala]." *Teoria: Rivista di Filosofia* 2 (2004): 169–77.

SECONDARY WORKS

Books

Abbagnano, N. *Ricordi di un filosofo*. Edited by M. Staglieno. Milan 1990.

Antiseri, Dario. *Weak Thought and Its Strength*. Trans. Gwyneth Weston. Avebury: Ashgate 1996.

Bambach, Charles R. *Heidegger, Dilthey, and the Crisis of Historicism*. Ithaca, NY: Cornell University Press 1995.

Battistrada, F. *Per un umanesimo rivisitato*. Milan: Jaka Book 1999.

Begam, R. *Samuel Beckett and the End of Modernity*. Stanford: Stanford University Press 1996.

Berti, E. *Le vie della ragione*. Bologna: Il Mulino 1987.

Best, Shaun. *A Beginner's Guide to Social Theory*. London: Blackwell 2003.

Bianco, Franco. *Pensare l'interpretazione. Temi e figure dell'ermeneutica* . Rome: Editori riuniti 1992.

Bibeau, Gilles. *Beyond Textuality: Asceticism and Violence in Anthropological Interpretation*. Berlin: Walter de Gruyter 1994.

Bobbio, Norberto. *Che cosa fanno oggi i filosofi?* Edited by the Biblioteca comunale di Cattolica. Milan: Bompiani 1982.

Bontadini, G. *Metafisica e deellenizzazione*. Milan: Vita e Pensiero 1975.

Borradori, Giovanna. *The American Philosopher*. Chicago: University of Chicago Press 1994.

– ed. *The New Italian Philosophy*. Evanston IL: Northwestern University Press 1988.

Brandom, Robert. *Tales of the Mighty Dead: Historical Essays in the Metaphysics of Intentionality*. Cambridge, MA: Harvard University Press 2002.

Cantarano, G. *Immagini del nulla: La filosofia italiana contemporanea*. Milan: Mondadori 1998.

Caputo, John D. *The Weakness of God: A Theology of the Event*. Indianapolis: Indiana University Press 2006.

Carchia, Gianni, and Maurizio Ferraris, eds. *Interpretazione ed emancipazione: Studi in onore di Gianni Vattimo*. Turin: Cortina 1996.

Carravetta, Peter. *Prefaces to the Diaphora: Rhetorics, Allegory and the Interpretation of Postmodernity*. West Lafayette, IN: Purdue University Press 1991.

Carty, Anthony. *Post-Modern Law: Enlightenment, Revolution, and the Death of Man*. Edinburgh: Edinburgh University Press 1990.

Crespi, F. *L'esperienza religiosa nell'età postmoderna*. Rome: Donzelli 1997.

Cruz, Munuel. *Filosofía contemporánea*. Madrid: Taurus 2002.

– ed. *Hacia donde va el pasado*. Barcelona: Paidós 2002.

Curtler, Hugh Mercer. *Rediscovering Values: Coming to Terms with Postmodernism*. M.E. Sharpe 1997.

D'Agostini, Franca. *Analitici e continentali*. Milan: Cortina 1997.

– *Logica del Nichilismo: "Dialettica differenza" ricorsività*. Rome-Bari: Laterza 2000.

Deibert, R.J. *Parchment, Printing, and Hypermedia: Communication in World Order Transformation*. New York: Columbia University Press 1997.

Docherty, Thomas. *Criticism and Modernity: Aesthetics, Literature, and Nations in Europe and Its Academies*. Oxford: Oxford University Press 1999.

Dotolo, Carmelo. *La teologia fondamentale davanti alle sfide del "Pensiero debole" di Gianni Vattimo*. Rome: LAS 1999.

Dussel, Enrique, *La ética de la liberación: Ante el desafío de Apel, Taylor y Vattimo*. Mexico: Universidad Autónoma del Estado de México 1998.

– *Postmodernidad y transmodernidad: Diálogos con la filosofía de Gianni Vattimo*. Puebla: Universidad Iberoamericana, Plantel Laguna 1999.

Eggensperger, T., U. Engel, and U. Perone, eds. *Italienische Philosophie der Gegenwart*. Freiburg and Munich 2004.

Eldred, Michael. *Twisting Heidegger: Drehversuche Parodistischen Denkens*. Junghans Verlag 1993.

Epps, Bradley S. *Significant Violence: Oppression and Resistance in the Narratives of Juan Goytisolo, 1970–1990*. Oxford: Oxford University Press 1996.

Escher, Enrico. *La visibilità 'mediata' del potere: I presupposti teoretici della comunicazione*. Milan: Franco Angeli 2004.

Ferraris, M. *Nietzsche e la filosofia del Novecento*. Milan: 1989.

- *History of Hermeneutics*. Translated by Luca Somigli. Prometheus Books 1996.

Frascati-Lochhead, Marta. *Kenosis and Feminist Theology: The Challenge of Gianni Vattimo*. Albany: State University of New York Press 1998.

Gargani, Pier Aldo, ed. *Crisi della regione: Nuovi modelli nel rapporto tra sapere attività umane*. Turin: Einaudi 1979.

Gasche, Rodolphe. *Inventions of Difference: On Jacques Derrida*. Cambridge, MA: Harvard University Press 1994.

Geyer, Felix. *Alienation, Ethnicity, and Postmodernism*. London: Greenwood Press 1996.

Giorgio, Giovanni. *Il pensiero di Gianni Vattimo: L'empancipazione dalla metafisica tra dialettica ed ermeneutica*. Milan: Franco Angeli 2006.

Girard, René. *Violence and the Sacred*. (1972). Baltimore: Johns Hopkins University Press 1987.

- *Things Hidden since the Foundation of the World*. (1978). Stanford: Stanford University Press 1987.

Hansjürgen, Verweyen. *Theologie im Zeichen der schwachen Vernunft. Pustet:* Regensburg 2000.

Hart, David Bentley. *The Beauty of the Infinite: The Aesthetics of Christian Truth*. Michigan: B. Eerdman 2003.

Lapper, Richard. "Martin Heidegger und die Interpretation seiner Philosophie durch Gianni Vattimo." Innsbruck, University Diploma Thesis, 1996.

Lee, Robert D. *Overcoming Tradition and Modernity: The search for Islamic Authenticity*. Westview Press 1997.

Livi, Antonio. *Filosofia del senso comune: Logica della scienza & della fede*. Milan: Edizioni Ares 1990.

Maieron, Christine. "Gianni Vattimo's Denken der Schwäche." Vienna, University Diploma Thesis, 1992.

Marini, Alfredo. *Amicizia stellare: Studi su Nietzsche di Beerling*. Milano: Ed. Unicopli 1984.

Marra, Michele. *Modern Japanese Aesthetics: A Reader*. Honolulu: University of Hawaii Press 1999.

Marzano, Silvia. *Lévinas, Jaspers e il pensiero della differenza: Confronti con Derrida, Vattimo, Lyotard*. Turin: Silvio Zamorani editore 1999.

Matteo, Armando. *Della fede dei laici: Il cristianesimo di fronte alla mentalità postmoderna*. Rubbettino editore 2001.

Mattia, Daniele. *Gianni Vattimo: L'etica dell'interpretazione*. Florence: Oxenford Universale Atheneum 2002.

Melaney, William D. *After Ontology: Literary Theory and Modernist Poetics.* Albany: State University of New York Press 2001.

Mensch, J.R. *Knowing and Being: A Postmodern Reversal.* University Park: Pennsylvania State University Press 1996.

Morra, G. *Il quarto uomo: Postmodernità o crisi della modernità.* Rome: Armando 1992.

Moser, Walter. *Gianni Vattimo's "Pensiero Debole," or Avoiding the Traps of Modernity.* Minneapolis: Center for Humanistic Studies 1987.

Mura, G. *Ermeneutica e verità: Storia e problemi della filosofia dell'interpretazione.* Roma: 1990.

– *Pensare la parola: Per una filosofia dell'incontro.* Vatican City: Urbaniana University Press 2001.

Nagl, Ludwig, ed. *Essays zu Jacques Derrida and Gianni Vattimo, Religion.* Frankfurt a. M.: Peter Lang 2001.

Oñate, Teresa. *El retorno griego de lo divino en la postmodernidad: Una discusión con la hermenéutica nihilista de Gianni Vattimo.* Madrid: Alderabán 2000.

Oñate, Teresa, and Simón Royo Hernández, eds. *Ética de las verdades Hoy: Homenaje a Gianni Vattimo.* Madrid: UNED 2006.

Ormiston, Gayle L., and Alan D. Schrift. *The Hermeneutic Tradition: From Ast to Ricoeur.* State University of New York Press 1990.

– *Transforming the Hermeneutic Context: From Nietzsche to Nancy.* Albany: State University of New York Press, 1990.

Palumbieri, Sabino. *Postmoderno e persona: Sfide e stimoli* In Mario Toso, Zbigniew Formella, and Attilio Danese, eds., *Emmanuel Mounier, Persona e umanesimo relazionale: Nel Centenario della nascita (1905–2005).* Atti del Convegno di Roma, Università Pontificia Salesiana, 12–14 January 2005, LAS, Rome, 2005, 59–105.

Parati, Graziella. *Migration Italy: The Art of Talking Back in a Destination Culture.* Toronto: University of Toronto Press, 2005.

Peters, Michael. *Poststructuralism, Politics and Education.* Westport, CT: Bergin and Garvey 1996.

Peters, Michael, Henry A. Giroux, and Paulo Freire. *Education and the Postmodern Condition.* Bergin and Garvey, 1995.

Peyser, Thomas. *Utopia and Cosmopolis: Globalization in the Era of American Literary Realism.* Durham: Duke University Press 1998.

Pippin, R.P. *Hegel's Idealism: The Satisfactions of Self-Consciousness.* Cambridge: Cambridge University Press 1989.

Pongs, Armin. *In welcher Gesellschaft leben wir eigentlich? Perspektiven, Diagnosen, Konzepte.* Munich: Dilemma 2000.

Possenti, V. *Il nichilismo teoretico e la "morte della metafisica."* Rome: Armando 1995.

Quintana-Paz, Miguel Á. *Normatividad, interpretación y praxis.* Salamanca: Ediciones Universidad de Salamanca 2004.

Rappa, Antonio L. *Modernity and Consumption: Theory, Politics and the Public in Singapore and Malaysia.* Singapore: World Scientific 2002.

Reckermann A. *Lesarten der Philosophie Nietzsches: Ihre Rezeption und Diskussion in Frankreich, Italien und der angels hsischen Welt, 1960–2000.* Berlin and New York: De Gruyter 2003.

Robbins, Jeffrey W. *In Search of a Non-Dogmatic Theology.* Aurora: The Davies Group 2003.

Roberts, David D. *Nothing but History.* Aurora: The Davies Group 2006.

Rorty, Richard. *Essays on Heidegger and Others: Philosophical Papers.* Vol. 2. Cambridge, MA: Cambridge University Press, 1991.

Rovatti, P.A. *Transformazioni del sogetto: Un itinerario filosofico.* Padua: Il Poligrafo 1992.

Rovatti, P.A., and A. Dal Lago. *Elogio del pudore: Per un pensiero debole.* Milan: Feltrinelli 1990.

Scheibler, Ingrid. *Gadamer between Heidegger and Habermas.* Lanham, MD: Rowman and Littlefield 2000.

Schönherr, Hans-Martin. *Die Technik und die Schwäche: Ökologie nach Nietzsche, Heidegger und dem "schwachen denken."* Vienna: Passagen 1989.

– ed. *Ethik des Denkens: Perspektiven von Ulrich Beck, Paul Ricoeur, Manfred Riedel, Gianni Vattimo, Wolfgang Welsch.* Munich: Fink 2000.

Schreyögg, Georg, ed. *Organisation und Postmoderne Grundfragen: Analysen, Perspektiven.* Wiesbaden: Gabler 1999.

Scilironi, C. *Il volto del prossimo: Alla radice della fondazione etica.* Bologna: Dehoniane 1991.

Segura, Armando. *Heidegger en el contexto del pensamiento "debole" de Vattimo.* Granada: Universidad de Granada 1996.

Smith, Paul Julian. *Vision Machines, Cinema, Literature and Sexuality in Spain and Cuba, 1983–93.* London: Verso.

Staquet, Anne. *La pensée Faible de Vattimo et Rovatti: Une Pensée-Faible.* Paris: L'Harmattan 1996.

Tarizzo, Davide. *Il pensiero libero: La filosofia francese dopo lo strutturalismo.* Milano: Raffaello Cortina 2003.

Tomelleri, S. *La società del risentimento.* Rome: Meltemi 2004.

Tovar, Leonardo. *La postmodernidad a debate: Gianni Vattimo, Enrique Dussel y Guillermo Hoyos.* Santafé de Bogotá: Universidad Santo Tomás, 2001.

Uhl, Florian. *Zwischen Verzückung und Verzweiflung: Dimensionen religiöser Erfahrung.* Parerga 2001.

Viano, Augusto. *Va'pensiero: Il carattere della filosofia italiana contemporanea.* Turin: Einaudi 1985.

Villani, A. *Le "chiavi" del postmoderno: Un dialogo a distanza.* Naples 1988.

Volker, Friedrich. *Ich bin ein Got: Im Gespräch mit Karl Popper, Max Bense, Gianni Vattimo, Richard Rorty, Neil Postman, Stanley Rosen, Carl Mitcham.* Munich: Boer 1995.

Vötsch, Mario. "Postmoderne Kritik der ökonomischen Vernunft unter Rekurs auf Nietzsche." Vienna, University thesis, 2002.

Waite, Geoff. *Nietzsche's Corps/E: Aesthetics, Politics, Prophecy, or, the Spectacular Technoculture of Everyday Life.* Durham: Duke University Press, 1996.

Ward, David. *Antifascismo, Cultural Politics in Italy, 1934–46: Benedetto Croce and the Liberals, Carlo Levi and the "Actionist."* Madison, NJ: Associated University Presses 1996.

Weiss, Martin. "Hermeneutik der Postmoderne. Metaphysikkritik und Interpretation bei Gianni Vattimo." Vienna, University dissertation, 2002.

– *Gianni Vattimo. Einführung.* Vienna: Passagen Verlag 2003.

Welsch, Wolfgang. *Vernunft: Zeitgenössische Vernunftkritik und das Konzept der transversalen Vernunft.* Frankfurt a. M.: Suhrkamp 1996.

– *Unsere postmoderne Moderne.* Berlin: Akademie Verlag 1997.

White, Stephen K. *Sustaining Affirmation: The Strengths of Weak Ontology in Political Theory.* Princeton: Princeton University Press, 2000.

Zijlstra, Onno, ed. *Letting Go: Rethinking Kenosis.* Berne: Lang 2002.

Zima, Peter V. *Moderne/Postmoderne: Gesellschaft, Philosophie, Literatur.* Tübingen and Basel: Franke 1997.

Articles

Aime, O. "Credere di credere." *Archivio teologico Torinese,* no. 4 (1996): 251–2.

Alvarez, L. "Màs allà del 'pensamiento debil.'" In *Filosofía, Politica, Religiòn: Màs allà del "pensamiento debil."* Edited by Gianni Vattimo. Oviedo: Nobel 1996, 7–28.

Bagetto, Luca. "Die Negation sichtbar machen. Gadamer, Vattimo und die Ontologie des Bildes." In *Deutsche Philosophie im Spiegel der italienischen Forschung.* Edited by M. Ensslen and G. Garelli. Heidelberg: L. Seidler 2002.

Basti, G. and A. Perrone. "Le radici forti del pensiero debole: Nichilismo e fondamenti della matematica." Special issue of *Con-tratto* (1992).

Berciano, M. "Heidegger, Vattimo y la deconstrucción." *Anuario Filófico*, no. 26 (1993): 9–45.

Berti, E. "Credere di credere: L'interpretazione del cristianesimo di G. Vattimo." *Studia Patavina*, no. 44 (1997): 377–83.

Berto, C. "Le ultime interpretazioni italiane di Nietzsche." In *Saggi su Nietzsche*. Brescia: Morcelliana 1980.

– "Il problema del nichilismo in alcuni interpreti italiani di Nietzsche." *Humanitas* B, no. 37 (1982): 89–93.

Beuchot, M. "El impero de la hermeneutica en la postmodernidad: Foucault, Derrida y Vattimo." *Revista Venezolana de Filosofia*, no. 30 (1994): 13–31.

Biagi, L. "Il pensiero debole e l'etica della pietas." *Rivista di Teologia Morale*, no. 85, 1990.

Bolgie, Chris. "Between Apocalypse and Narrative: Drieu la Rochelle and the Facist Novel." *The Romanic Review* 84 (1993).

Bottani, L. "Verità, sospetto et 'epoché.'" *Paradigmi* (1990): 647–57.

Brena, G.L. "Un confronto tra pensiero debole e metafisica classica." *Studia Patavina*, no. 44 (1987): 77–83.

Cantillo, G. "Filosofia italiana ed esistenzialismo." *Razón y Fe*, no. 79 (1988): 241–2.

Capurro, Rafael. "Gianni Vattimo: Denker der Moderne." In Gianni Vattimo, *Das Ende der Moderne*. Stuttgart: Reclam 1990.

– "Gianni Vattimo." In *Philosophie der Gegenwart in Einzeldarstellungen*, edited by Julian Nida-Rümelin. Stuttgart: Kröner 1991, 614–17.

Cenacchi, G. "Storia della filosofia dell'esistenza nel pensiero italiano contemporaneo." *Citta del Vaticano* (1990): 254–60.

Cinquetti, M. "Dio tra trascendenza e 'kenosis': Dialogo a distanza tra Karl Barth ed il 'pensiero debole.'" In *Filosofia e Teologia*, edizioni Scientifiche Italiane, Napoli, no.2 (2003): 324–37.

Cooke, Bill. "Heidegger, Nazism, and Postmodernism." *Free Inquiry* 18 (Fall 1998).

Corradi, E. "Linee del 'pensiero debole.'" *Rivista di filosofia neoscolastica*, no. 77 (1985): 476–83.

Cotroneo G. "Chaïm Perelman: La forza del pensiero 'debole,'" *Prospettive settanta*, 8, no. 1, 1986.

Crockett, Clayton. "Post-modernism and Its Secrets: Religion without Religion." *Cross Currents* 52 (winter 2003).

D'Agostini, Franca. "Oltre l'interpretazione: Ermeneutica e nichilismo." *Filosofia* 45, no. 3 (1994) 361–81.

– "Introduzione: Dialettica, differenza, ermeneutica, nichilismo, le ragioni forti del pensiero debole." In G. Vattimo, *Vocazione e responsabilità del filosofo*, ed. F. D'Agostini. Genoa: Il Melangolo 2000, 11–44.

Del Vasto, Valeria. "Scienza e storiografia" in T.S. Kuhn. *Prospettive settanta* 8, no. 1 (1986): 99–115.

D'Isanto, Luca. "Gianni Vattimo's Hermeneutics and the Traces of Divinity." *Modern Theology*, no. 10 (1994).

– Introduction to Gianni Vattimo, *Belief*. Stanford: Stanford University Press 1999, 1–17.

Eggensperger, Thomas. "Die Widerentdeckung der Religion: Zu Gianni Vattimo's Buch *Glauben* – *Philosophieren*. *Orientierung* 62, no. 7 (April 1998): 77–8.

Epps, Brad. "Technoasceticism and Authorial Death in Sade, Barthes, and Foucault." *Differences* 8 (1996).

Escher Di Stefano, A. "L'esistenzialismo tedesco." In *Grande Antologia filosofica*, edited by M.F. Sciacca. Milan: 1966, 765–6.

Ferraris, Maurizio. "Monumento per l'esistenzialismo: Etica, estetica ed ermeneutica nel pensiero di Gianni Vattimo." *aut-aut*, nos. 137–8 (1990): 97–109.

– "Il pensiero debole e i suoi rischi." In *Ill bello relativismo: Quel che resta della filosofia nel XXI secolo*. Edited by Elisabetta Ambrosi. Venice: Marsilio 2005, 49–57.

Fornero, G. "Postmoderno e filosofia." In N. Abbagnano, *Storia della filosofia*. Vol. 4. Turin: Utet 1996, 39–41.

Früchtl, J. "(Post-) Metaphysik und (Post-) Moderne." *Philosophische Rundschau* 37 (1990): 242–50.

Gadamer, Hans-Georg. "Presentazione." In *Interpretazione ed emancipazione: Studi in onore di Gianni Vattimo*, edited by Gianni Carchia and Maurizio Ferraris. Turin: Cortina 1996.

– "Dialogues in Capri." In *Religion*, edited by J. Derrida and Gianni Vattimo. Stanford: Stanford University Press 1998, 200–11.

Galasso, G. "Pensiero debole ed epoca forte." *Prospettive settanta* 8, no. 1 (1986).

Galeazzi, U. "Scientismo, pensiero debole e capacità conoscitiva della filosofia." In *Lo statuto espistemologico della filosofia*. Brescia: Morcelliana 1989.

Gardner, Michel. "A Postmodern Utopia?" *Utopian Studies* 8 (1997): 89–122.

Gasché, Rodolphe. "In the Separation of the Crisis: A Post-Modern Hermeneutics?" *Philosophy Today* 44, no. 1 (spring 2000): 3–15.

Giacobbe, F. "Das 'Schwache Denken' Gianni Vattimos und die Wahrheitsfrage." In *Wahrheit: Recherchen zwischen Hochskolastik und Postmoderne*, edited by T. Eggensperger, and U. Engel. Mainz: 1995, 116–29.

Gilbert, P. "Nihilisme et christianisme chez quelques philosophes italiens contemporains: E. Severino, S. Natoli et G. Vattimo." *Nouvelle Revue Théologique* 121 (1999): 254–73.

Giorgio, Giovanni. "Pensiero debole' e persona. Scontro o incontro?" In Mario Toso, Zbigniew Formella, and Attilio Danese, eds., *Emmanuel Mounier, Persona e umanesimo relazionale: Nel Centenario della nascita (1905–2005)*, Atti del Convegno di Roma, Università Pontificia Salesiana, 12–14 January 2005, LAS, Rome, 2005, 107–19.

Grion, Luca. "Il problema etico nel pensiero di Gianni Vattimo: Considerazioni su forza e debolezza, tolleranza e carità." In Carmelo Vigna, ed., *Etiche e politiche della post-modernità*. Milan: Vita e pensiero 2003, 283–301.

Groot, G. "Gianni Vattimo: De oscillatie van de moderniteit." *Krisis/Krisis 11 (1991): 36–9.*

Gurciullo, S. "The Subject of Weak Thought: There Are Only Interpretations and This Too Is an Interpretation." *Theory and Event* 5, no. 2 (2001).

Haeffner, Gerd. "Morgenröte über Capri: Die Philosophes Derrida und Vattimo zur Rückkehr des Religiösen." *Stimmen der Zeit* 124, 10 (1999): 669–82.

Laurenzi, M.C. "Credere di credere?" *Protestantesimo*, no. 51 (1996): 321–3.

Lehissa, G. "Säkularisierung und Philosophie." In G. Vattimo, *Abschied: Theologie, Metaphysik und die Philosophie heute*, edited by G. Leghissa. Vienna: 2003, 7–20.

Levy, D.A. "After Modernism," *Times Higher Education Supplement* 2, no. 2 (1989).

Lopez, Oscar R. "La narrativa latinoamericana: Entre bordes seculares." *Chasqui* 31 (2002): 647–8.

Lorizio, G. "Cultura laica e sapere credente." *Nuntium*, no. 1 (1997): 47–52.

Magris, A. "I forti impegni del pensiero debole: Un seminario di Gianni Vattimo a Venezia." *aut-aut*, no. 273–4 (1996): 53–68.

Marcolungo, F.L. "Una fede tracertezza e dubbio." *Studia Patavina*, no. 44 (1997): 69–75.

Mardones J.M. *Síntomas de un ritorno. La religión en el pensamento actual.* Santander: Sal Terrae 1999.

Margarito, D. "Vattimo e la restaurazione etico-nichilistica del soggetto." *L'Ombra d'Argo*, no. 3 (1986): 117–28.

Mari, G. "Postmoderno e democrazia: Sulla 'filosofia militante' e Gianni Vattimo." *Iride*, nos. 4–5 (1990): 264–75.

Mattera, A. "Gianni Vattimo e il pensiero debole." *Prospettive settanta* 8, no. 1 (1986): 117–26.

– "L'emeneutica tra logica e arte." *Prospettive settanta* 8, no. 1 (1986): 67–79.

Meister M. "Erlösende Botschaft: Gianni Vattimos Radikalinterpretation des Christentums." *Frankfurter Rundschau*, 21 March 2002, 18.

Meyer, M. "Gott lebt – aber wo? und wie? Gianni Vatttimos Essay Jenseits des Christentums." In "Neue Zürcher Zeitung," no. 51, 2 March 2004, 33.

Missaglia, Giovanni. "Il pensiero debole come filosofia del dialogo." *Bollettino della Società Filosofica Italiana* 185 (2005): 57–64.

Mojtabai, A.G. "A Missed Connection." *The Wilson Quarterly* 19 (spring 1995).

Mucci, P. Giandomenico. "La ragione 'creativa' di Gianni Vattimo." *La civiltà cattolica* 2 (1996).

– "Un articolo di Gianni Vattimo sul relativismo." *La civiltà cattolica* no. 3741 (2006): 230–34.

Müller-Lauter, W. "Heidegger e Nietzsche." *Teoria* 16 (1996).

Musi, A. "Pensiero debole e storia debole." *Prospettive settanta* 8, no. 1 (1986).

Oñate, T. "Al final de la Modernidad." In *Revista Cuadernos del Norte*, no. 43, 1987. Tb. Aparecido en Revista Meta (Universidad Complutense de Madrid), number 1988.

– "Feminismo alternativo y postmodernidad estética." In *Reflexiones sobre estética y literatura*, edited by José Vidal Calatayud. Madrid: FIM (Fundación de Investigaciones Marxistas) 1998.

– "Al Alba se oye la voz de la Tierra."In Gianni Vattimo, *La sociedad transparente*, edited and translated by Teresa Oñate. Barcelona: Ed. Paidós 1990.

– "Postmodernidad y Diferencia." In Revista *Fin de Siglo* (Universidad del Valle). Colombia: Cali 1992.

– "Tu n'as rien vu à Hiroshima: Postmodernidad/Modernidad." In *Revista: La Boca del Otro*. (Universidad Complutense de Madrid), 1996.

– "Los hijos de Nietzsche y la ontología hermenéutica de Gianni Vattimo." Foreword to Gianni Vattimo, *Diálogo con Nietzsche*. Barcelona: Ed. Paidós 2002.

Orzessek, A. "Zu wenig Nichts: Der erste Berliner Disput mit Gianni Vattimo und Richard Schröder," *Süddeutsche Zeitung* (Munich) 21 March 2002, 17.

Ottone, R. "Ontologia debole e caritas nel pensiero di Gianni Vattimo." *La Scuola Cattolica* 132 (2004): 171–203.

Pallasmaa, Juhani. "Hapticity and Time." *The Architectural Review* 207 (May 2000): 78–84.

Paoletti, L. "Dall'esistenzialismo all'ermeneutica." *Archivio di Filosofia*, no. 63 (1995): 553–8.

Paolozzi, Ernesto. "Falsificazioni e antistoricismo in Karl Raimund Popper." *Prospettive settanta* 8, no. 1 (1986): 51–66.

Paul Thiele, Leslie. "Postmodernity and the Routinization of Novelty: Heidegger on Boredom and Technology." *Polity* 4, (1997).

Pellecchia, P. "Sulle tracce del postmoderno." *Aquinas*, no. 35 (1992).

Perniola, Mario. "Lettera a Gianni Vattimo sul 'pensiero debole.'" *aut-aut*, no. 201 (1984): 51–64.

Pireddu, Nicoletta. "Gianni Vattimo." In *Postmodernism*, edited by Johannes Willem Bertene and Joseph P. Natoli. Boston: Blackwell 2002, 302–9.

Polidori, Fabio. "Dubitare di dubitare." *aut-aut*, nos. 277–8 (1997): 20–6.

Possenti, V. "Nichilismo, ontologia debole, cristianesimo." *Per la Filosofia: Filosofia e insegnamento*, no. 38 (1996): 32–5.

Preve, C. "Il presente come fine della Storia: Pensiero 'debole' e nichilismo 'forte' come interpretazione filosofica del presente." *Fenomenologia e società* no. 8 (1985): 81–101.

Prodomoro, Raffaele. "T.W. Adorno: La suggettività che si autotrascende." *Prospettive settanta* 8, no. 1 (1986): 81–98.

Quesada, J. "La crisi post-moderna de nuestra identidad." *Cuadernos del Sur*, 14 December 1989.

Quintana-Paz, Miguel Á. "Alaska, Heidegger y los Pegamoides: En torno a la movida madrileña, en tono a culturalista." In Víctor Del Río, ed., *Cortao*. Salamanca: El Gallo 1998, 100–35.

– "Una tercera vía: El antirrelativismo de Vattimo, Feyerabend y Rorty." *Laguna*, supplement (1999): 193–204.

– "La hermenéutica se pone en acción." *Revista de Occidente*, no. 235 (December 2000): 131–8.

– "Hermenéutica, modernidad y nacionalismo." In Miguel Giusti, ed., *La filosofía del siglo XX: Balance y perspectivas*. Lima: Pontificia Universidad Católica del Perú 2001, 309–23.

– "¿Qué idea de nación cabe defender desde el pensamiento hermenéutico?" *Laguna*, no. 8 (January 2001): 145–58.

– "Dos problemas del universalismo ético, y una solución." In Quintín Racionero and Pablo Perera, eds., *Pensar la comunidad*. Madrid: Dykinson 2002, 223–53.

– "On Hermeneutical Ethics and Education: 'Bach als Erzieher.'" In Jirí Fukac, Alena Mizerová, and Vladimír Strakoš, eds., *Bach: Music between Virgin Forest and Knowledge Society*. Santiago: Compostela Group of Universities, 2002, 49–109.

– "Los dioses han cambiado (de modo que todo lo demás ya podría cambiar): Anotaciones en torno a la contribución de la hermenéutica de Gianni Vattimo a la condición religiosa postmoderna." *Azafea* 5 (2003): 237–59.

– "De las reglas hacia la X. Racionalidad, postmetafísica y retórica entre Wittgenstein y Vattimo." *Thémata*, no. 32 (2004): 135–57.

– "Cómo no ser universalistas ni relativistas." In Ildefonso Murillo, ed., *Filosofía práctica y persona humana*. Salamanca: Publicaciones Universidad Pontificia de Salamanca-Diálogo Filosófico 2004, 149–67.

– "Gianni Vattimo." In Andrés Ortiz-Osés and Patxi Lanceros, eds., *Diccionario de hermenéutica* 4th ed. Bilbao: Universidad de Deusto 2004, 543–5.

Quintana-Paz, Miguel Á., and J. Vergés. "Diálogo sobre tres modelos de defini-ción de la barbarie y lo civilizado en la filosofía política actual." *Estudios filosóficos* 51, no. 147 (May–August 2002): 195–221.

Restaino, F. "L'area italiana: Crisi della ragione, pensiero debole, femminismo della differenza." In N. Abbagnano, *Storia della filosofia.* Vol. 4. Turin: Utet 1996.

Rey, Dominique. "Gianni Vattimo, Au-delà de l'interpretation." *Revue de Théologie et de Philosophie* 130, no. 2 (1998): 228–9.

Rizzi, A. "Le sfide del pensiero debole." *Rassegna di Teologia*, no. 27 (1986): 1–14.

Rovatti, P.A. "Ci Vuole più pensiero, ma non metafisico." In *Il bello rela-tivismo: Quel che resta della filosofia nel XXI secolo,"* edited by Elisabetta Ambrosi. Venice: Marsilio 2005, 85–90.

Santiago Guervos, L.E. "Gianni Vattimo: El fin de la metafisica u la postmod-ernidad." *Estudios filosoficos* 36 (1987): 551–71.

Scheibler, I. "The Case for Weak Thought." *Times Higher Education Supple-ment*, 5 February 1993.

Schlicht, U. "'Die Liebe ist die einzige Wahrheit.' Die Dominikaner er fnen Berliner Chenu-Institut mit einem Disput: Was hei Glaube in der Postmod-erne?" *Der Tagesspiegel* (Berlin) 20 March 2002, s. 28.

Schönherr, H.M. "Radikale Selbstkritik – oder Swäche? Gianni Vattimo's Analyse der Postmoderne." *Neue Zürcher Zeitung*, 1–2 June 1991.

Schürmann, Reiner. "Deconstruction Is Not Enough: On Gianni Vattimo's Call for 'Weak Thinking.'" *Graduate Faculty Philosophy Journal* 10 (1984): 165–77.

Sciacchitano, Antonello. "Credere, supporre, ammettere." *aut-aut* 277–8, (1997): 27–35.

Scilironi, C. "La filosofia laica italiana interprete del cristianesimo." *Studia Patavina*, no. 44 (1997): 51–2.

Selvadagi, P. "Post-modernità e cristianesimo: A proposito di un libro recente." *Lateranum*, no. 62 (1996): 623–30.

Semerari, F. "Vattimo, Gianni." In D. Huisman, *Dictionnaire des Philosophes.* Paris, PUF 1984, 2580–1.

Sgobba, M. "La fondazione debole." *Paradigmi*, no. 19 (1989): 75–93.

Snyder, J. Translator's introduction to G. Vattimo, *The End of Modernity.* Cambridge: Polity Press 1988, vi–lix.

Sossi, F. "Vattimo Gianni." In P.A. Rovatti, *Dizionario Bompiani dei Filosofi Contemporanei.* Milan 1990, 387–8.

Stein, Olga. "Editor's note." *Books in Canada: The Canadian Review of Books.* 32, no. 1 (2003): 2.

Thomä, D. "Il re e gli stregoni." *MicroMega*, no. 3 (1991): 89–91.

Tomelleri S. "Ressentiment et pensée faible." In M.S. Barberi, ed., *La spirale mimétique*. Paris: Desclée de Brouwer 2001.

– "Ressentiment und Dekonstruktionismus." In B. Dieckmann, ed., *Das Opfer – aktuelle Kontroversen: Religions-politischer Diskurs im Kontext der mimetischen Theorie*. Deutsch-Italienische Fachtagung der Guardini-Stiftung in der Villa Vigoni, 18–22 October 1999. Münster, Thaur: LIT, Druck und Verlagshaus Thaur 2001.

Thurner, Martin. "Selbsterniedrigung Gottes und schwache Vernunft: Zu Gianni Vattimos postmoderner Interpretation des Christentums." *Theologie und Philosophie* 79, no. 2 (2004): 174–87.

Vaccarini, I. "La condizione 'postmoderna': Una sfida per la cultura Cristiana." *Aggiornamenti sociali* 2 (1990): 119–35.

Valori, P. "Fede cristiana e pensiero debole." *Rassegan di Teologia*, no. 39 (1998): 276–82.

Verra, V. "L'ermeneutica di Gadamer in Italia." *aut-aut*, no. 242, (1991).

Vertone, Saverio. "La retorica del dissenso." *Prospettive settanta* 8, no. 1 (1986): 147–60.

Villoria, C. "Hermenéutica y recostrucción de la razón." In *Filosofía, Politica, Religiòn: Màs allà del "pensamiento debil,"* ed. Gianni Vattimo (Oviedo 1996): 190–208.

Viteritti, Assunta. "Gianni Vattimo, Umberto Eco and Franco Rella." In *Organization Theory and Postmodern Thought*, edited by Stephen A. Linstead. London: Sage 2003, 149–72.

Volonté, P. "Crisi della ragione e pensiero debole. Uno sguardo sulla filosofia italiana oggi." *Vita e Pensiero*, no. 70 (1987): 221–31.

Volpato, A. "Alcune interpretazioni italiane di Heidegger." *Aquinas*, no. 21 (1978): 149–52.

Volpi, Franco. "Nietzsche in Italien: Der gegenwärtige Stand der Nietzsche-Interpretation in der italienischen Philosophie." *Philosophische Literaturanzeigner* 21 (1978): 176–7.

Weiss, Martin. "Die Religion der Schwäche: Gianni Vattimos Interpretation des Christentums im Kontext des Schwachen." In Ludwig Nagl, ed., *Essays zu Jacques Derrida and Gianni Vattimo, religion*. Frankfurt a. M.: Peter Lang 2001, 145–67.

Wendel, S. "Vernünftig und begründungsfähig. Aktuelle philosophische Beiträge zum Thema Religion." In *Herder Korrespondenz*, no. 57 (10/2003): 528–32.

Wolosky, Shira. "Moral Finitude and the Ethics of Language: A New World Response to Gianni Vattimo." *Common Knowledge* 9 (2003): 406–23.

Zabala, Santiago. "La Religión de Vattimo: El cristianismo después de la muerte de Dios." *Claves de Razón Práctica*, no. 132 (May 2003): 57–62.

- "Ending the Rationality of Faith through Interpretation." *Sensus Communis* 5, no. 4 (September–December 2004): 422–39.
- "Christianity and the Death of God: A Response to Cardinal Lustiger." *Common Knowledge* 11, no. 1 (fall 2005): 33–40.
- "Introduction: A religion without Theist or Atheist." In Richard Rorty and Gianni Vattimo, *The Future of Religion*, edited by Santiago Zabala. New York: Columbia University Press 2005, 1–27.

Contributors

RÜDIGER BUBNER is Professor of Philosophy at the University of Heidelberg and the author of *Modern German Philosophy* (1981), *Essays in Hermeneutics and Critical Theory* (1988), and *The Innovations of Idealism* (2003).

PAOLO FLORES D'ARCAIS, Professor of Philosophy at the University of Rome "La Sapienza," is the author of *Il disincanto tradito* (1994), *L'individuo libertario* (1999), and *Il sovrano e il dissidente ovvero la democrazia presa sul serio* (2004). He is the founder and editor of the journal *MicroMega*.

CARMELO DOTOLO is Professor of Theology at the Pontifical Urbaniana University and of Fundamental Theory at the Pontifical Gregorian University of Rome. Since 2004 he has been the President of the Società Italiana per la Ricerca Teologica (SIRT). He is the author of *Sulle Tracce di Dio* (1992), *Teologia e sacro* (1995), *La teologia fondamentale davanti alle sfide del "pensiero debole" di Gianni Vattimo* (1999), *Il Credo Oggi* (2001), and *The Christian Revelation* (2006).

UMBERTO ECO, Professor of Semiotics at the University of Bologna, is the author of *Semiotics and the Philosophy of Language* (1986), *Interpretation and Overinterpretation* (1992), *Kant and the Platypus* (2000), and several novels, including *The Name of the Rose* (1980) and, most recently, *The Mysterious Flame of Queen Loana* (2005).

MANFRED FRANK is Professor of Philosophy at Eberhard Karls University in Tübingen and the author of *What Is Neostructuralism?* (1989), *The Subject and the Text* (1998), *The Philosophical Foundations of Early German Romanticism* (2004), and, most recently, *The Boundaries of Agreement* (2006).

NANCY K. FRANKENBERRY, John Phillips Professor of Religion at Dartmouth College, Hanover, New Hampshire, is the author of *Religion and Radical Empiricism* (1987), co-editor of *Language, Truth, and Religious Belief* (1999) and *Interpreting Neville* (1999), and editor of *Radical Interpretation in Religion* (2002).

JEAN GRONDIN, Professor of Philosophy at the University of Montreal, is the author of *Le tournant dans la pensée de Martin Heidegger* (1987), *Sources of Hermeneutics* (1995), *Introduction to Philosophical Hermeneutics* (1997), *Hans-Georg Gadamer: A Biography* (2003), and most recently, *Introduction à la métaphysique* (2004).

GIACOMO MARRAMAO is Professor of Political Philosophy at the Philosophy and Social Sciences Department of Roma Tre University and a member of the Collège International de Philosophie of Paris. He is the author of *Potere e secolarizzazione* (1985), *Minima temporalia* (1990), *Cielo e terra* (1994), *Dopo il Leviatano* (1995), and *Westward Passage* (forthcoming).

JACK MILES is the author of *Retroversion and Text Criticism* (1984), *God: A Biography* (1995), and *Christ: A Crisis in the Life of God* (2001) and the general editor of *The Norton Anthology of World Religions* (forthcoming).

JEAN-LUC NANCY, Professor of Philosophy at the Marc Bloch University of Strasbourg, is the author of *The Inoperative Community* (1991), *The Sense of the World* (1998), *Being Singular Plural* (2000), and, recently, *A Finite Thinking* (2003).

TERESA OÑATE is Professor of Philosophy at the Universidad Nacional de Educación a Distancia (UNED) of Madrid. She is the author of *El retorno de lo divino griego en la postmodernidad* (2000), *Para leer "La Metafísica" de Aristóteles en el siglo XXI* (2001; co-authored with

Cristina G. Santos), *El Nacimiento de la Filosofía en Grecia* (2005), and she edited the *doxa-Gadamer* two-volume monographic study of Hans-Georg Gadamer for the *Revista de Filosofía de la* UNED (2005).

JEFFREY M. PERL, Professor of English Literature at Bar-Ilan University, is the author of *The Tradition of Return: The Implicit History of Modern Literature* (1984), and *Skepticism and Modern Enmity: Before and After Eliot* (1989). He is the founder and editor of the journal *Common Knowledge.*

JAMES RISSER is Professor of Philosophy at the Seattle University, Seattle, Washington. He is the author of *Hermeneutics and the Voice of the Other: Re-reading Hans-Georg Gadamer's Philosophical Hermeneutics* (1997), editor of *Heidegger Toward the Turn: The Work of the 1930s* (1999), and co-editor of *American Continental Philosophy: A Reader* (2000).

RICHARD RORTY is Professor of Comparative Literature and Philosophy at Stanford University. His books include *Philosophy and the Mirror of Nature* (1979), *Consequences of Pragmatism* (1982), *Contingency, Irony, and Solidarity* (1989), *Objectivity, Relativism and Truth* (1991), *Essays on Heidegger and Others* (1991), *Achieving Our Country* (1998), and *Philosophy and Social Hope* (2000). He co-authored *The Future of Religion* (2005) with Gianni Vattimo.

PIER ALDO ROVATTI, Professor of Philosophy at the University of Trieste, is the author of *La posta in gioco* (1987), *Abitare la distanza* (1994), *Il paiolo bucato* (1998), and *Guardare ascoltando* (2003). He edits the journal *aut-aut.*

FERNANDO SAVATER, Professor of Philosophy at the Complutense University of Madrid, is the author of *The Questions of Life: Invitation to Philosophy* (1999), *Ethics as Self-Respect* (1988), *Ethics for Amador* (1991), and, most recently, *Los siete pecados capitales* (2006).

REINER SCHÜRMANN (1941–99) was Professor of Philosophy at the Duquesne University and New School for Social Research of New York. He is the author of *Meister Eckhart: Mystic and Philosopher* (1978), *Heidegger on Being and Acting: From Principles to Anarchy* (1987),

The Public Realm: Essays on Discursive Types in Political Philosophy (1989), and *Broken Hegemonies* (2003).

HUGH J. SILVERMAN is Professor of Philosophy and Comparative Literature at the Stony Brook University, Stony Brook, New York. His publications include *Inscriptions: After Phenomenology and Structuralism* (1997) and *Textualities: Between Hermeneutics and Deconstruction* (1994), and he has edited several volumes for the Routledge Continental Philosophy series.

CHARLES TAYLOR is Professor Emeritus at McGill University and Board of Trustee Professor of Law and Philosophy at Northwestern University. His books include *Hegel* (1975), *Sources of the Self* (1989), *Varieties of Religion Today* (2002), and most recently *The Ethics of Authenticity* (2005).

GIANNI VATTIMO is Professor of Philosophy at the University of Turin and the author of *The End of Modernity* (1985), *Beyond Interpretation* (1994), *and Nihilism and Emancipation* (2003).

WOLFGANG WELSCH is Professor of Philosophy at Friedrich-Schiller University Jena (Germany). He is the author of *Aisthesis* (1987), *Unsere postmoderne Moderne* (1987), *Ästhetisches Denken* (1990), *Vernunft* (1995, 3d edition 2000), *Grenzgänge der Ästhetik* (1996), *Undoing Aesthetics* (1997), and, most recently, *Aesthetics and Beyond* (2006).

SANTIAGO ZABALA is a researcher at the Pontifical Lateran University of Rome. Under the supervision of Gianni Vattimo he obtained his MA from the University of Turin and then his PHD from the Pontifical Lateran University of Rome. During the past few years he has been invited to participate in conferences by, among others, the Université de Montréal, Georgetown University, the University of Rome, *La Sapienza*, and the University of Deusto in Bilbao. He is the editor of Gianni Vattimo's *Nihilism and Emancipation* (2004) and Richard Rorty and Gianni Vattimo's *The Future of Religion* (2005) and the author of *Tugendhat: The Hermeneutical Nature of Analytic Philosophy* (forthcoming). With Gianni Vattimo he is series editor of the Davies Group Publishers Series *Contemporary European Cultural Studies* and the Valter Casini series *Interpretazioni: La collana filosofica delle fusioni.*

Index

Index